The Shopaholic's Guide to Buying Online 2008

Patricia Davidson

Free Subscription Offer

www.thesiteguide.com

www.thesiteguide.com, described by Condé Nast's Glamour.com as 'the web's best shopping directory', is the online version of *The Shopaholic's Guide to Buying Online*, where you'll find direct links through to all the website reviews, plus regular online shopping features and updates and news of the latest site launches.

We're delighted to offer you a year's free subscription to www.thesiteguide.com (normally £9.99) to thank you for purchasing this book. To take this up you need to click on to the site and subscribe. When you're prompted for a Media Code just use the password you'll find at the end of the introduction to Chapter 14, Sunglasses, and you'll be able to use the guide online. If you would like to receive up-to-date information on other Shopaholics Guides to buying online, just sign up on the website to receive regular newsletters.

'Thesiteguide.com is the most comprehensive shopping directory I've found on the web, and is also the first to report on fabulous new sites.'
Condé Nast

'A comprehensive guide to all the best shopping destinations on the web.'
Vogue mail

'This is a good shortcut to smart shopping'
The *Evening Standard*

'thesiteguide.com ... provides a discerning and easy to use guide to the best retail sites on the web.'
The *Times*

The Shopaholic's Guide to Buying Online 2008

Patricia Davidson

CAPSTONE

BICENTENNIAL
1807
WILEY
2007
BICENTENNIAL

First published 2007 by
Capstone Publishing Ltd. (a Wiley Company)
The Atrium, Southern Gate, Chichester, PO19 8SQ, UK.
www.wileyeurope.com
Email (for orders and customer service enquires): cs-books@wiley.co.uk

The right of Patricia Davidson to be identified as the author of this book has been asserted in accordance with the Copyright, Designs and Patents Act 1988

Designations used by companies to distinguish their products are often claimed as trademarks. All brand names and product names used in this book are trade names, service marks, trademarks or registered trademarks of their respective owners. The Publisher is not associated with any product or vendor mentioned in this book. This publication is designed to provide accurate and authoritative information in regard to the subject matter covered. It is sold on the understanding that the Publisher is not engaged in rendering professional services. If professional advice or other expert assistance is required, the services of a competent professional should be sought.

Although all information contained in this book was verified at the time of going to press, the publisher and author cannot take responsibility for any changes in the products or services subsequently made by any of the retailers included herein.

Other Wiley Editorial Offices: Hoboken, San Fransisco, Weinheim, Australia, Singapore and Canada
Wiley also publishes its books in a variety of electronic formats. Some content that appears in print may not be available in electronic books.

Library of Congress Cataloging-in-Publication Data
Davidson, Patricia.
 The shopaholics guide to buying online 2008 / by Patricia Davidson.
    p. cm.
 Includes index.
 ISBN 978-1-84112-783-5
1. Teleshopping--Guidebooks. 2. Shopping--Computer network resources--Guidebooks. I. Title.
 TX335.D385 2007
 381'.142--dc22

                                                                                2007030402

ISBN 978-184112-783-5

Anniversary Logo Design: Richard J. Pacifico

Set in Lucida Bright by Sparks (www.sparks.co.uk)
Printed and bound in Great Britain by Bell & Bain, Glasgow

This book is printed on acid-free paper responsibly manufactured from sustainable forestry in which at least two trees are planted for each one used for paper production. Substantial discounts on bulk quantities of Capstone Books are available to corporations, professional associations and other organizations. For details telephone John Wiley & Sons on (+44) 1243-770441, fax (+44) 1243 770571 or email corporatedevelopment@wiley.co.uk

Contents

Acknowledgements   ix
About the Author   x
Introduction   xi

Section 1   **Fashion at a Click**   **1**
Chapter 1   Fashion Online   3
Chapter 2   Luxury Brands   20
Chapter 3   The Knitwear Store   26
Chapter 4   Tall and Plus Sizes   30
Chapter 5   Shop America   33
Chapter 6   Sportswear to Look Great In   39
Chapter 7   Lingerie   45
Chapter 8   Resortwear Store   54
Chapter 9   Leather, Shearling and Faux Fur   58
Chapter 10   Fashion for Bumps   61
Chapter 11   Bump Essentials – Lingerie, Swim and Sportswear   66

Section 2   **The Accessory Place**   **69**
Chapter 12   Handbag Temptation   71
Chapter 13   Kick Your Heels   81
Chapter 14   Sunglasses   89
Chapter 15   Jewellery and Watches   92
Chapter 16   Scarves, Shawls, Gloves, Belts and More   104

Section 3   **Mainly for Men**   **109**
Chapter 17   Shirts, Ties, Cufflinks and Belts   111
Chapter 18   Tailoring and Formalwear   116

Chapter 19	Best of the Casuals	121
Chapter 20	Shoes and Leather Accessories	125
Chapter 21	Men's Toiletries and Nightwear	130
Chapter 22	Gifts, Gadgets and Experience Days	135
Chapter 23	Cigars, Pens and Small Accessories	140
Section 4	**Babies, Kids and Teens**	**145**
Chapter 24	Baby and Toddler Clothes	147
Chapter 25	Baby Accessories and Equipment	151
Chapter 26	Baby and Pre-School Toys	155
Chapter 27	Furniture and Nursery Bedding	158
Chapter 28	Clothing to Age 11	162
Chapter 29	General Toy Shops	167
Chapter 30	Hobbies, Models, Puzzles and Games	171
Chapter 31	Dressing Up, Magic Tricks and Party Accessories	174
Chapter 32	Dance and Craft Supplies	178
Section 5	**Pamper Yourself**	**181**
Chapter 33	Fragrance, Bath and Body	183
Chapter 34	Healthcare and Contact Lenses	190
Chapter 35	Hair, Nails and Beauty Accessories	194
Chapter 36	Scented Candles	200
Chapter 37	Modern Skincare and Cosmetics	203
Chapter 38	Natural and Organic Beauty	209
Chapter 39	The Beauty Specialists	216
Chapter 40	Spas and Pamper Days Out	222
Section 6	**At Home**	**225**
Chapter 41	In the Bedroom	227
Chapter 42	Bath Time	235
Chapter 43	Living Space – Furniture and Accessories	240
Chapter 44	The Kitchen	252
Chapter 45	Office Stationery and General Supplies	260
Chapter 46	Fabrics, Paints and Wallpapers	262
Chapter 47	Lighting	267
Chapter 48	Wall Hangings and Pictures	270
Chapter 49	Carpets and Rugs	273
Chapter 50	Storage Solutions	276
Chapter 51	The Garden: Equipment, Furniture and Barbecues	279
Section 7	**Food and Drink**	**291**
Chapter 52	The Bakery	293
Chapter 53	The Butcher	298
Chapter 54	The Cheese Shop	301
Chapter 55	The Fishmonger	304
Chapter 56	Gourmet Food/Deli	308
Chapter 57	Organics Online	313

Chapter 58	Speciality Foods, Herbs and Spices	317
Chapter 59	Supermarkets	321
Chapter 60	Tea and Coffee	322
Chapter 61	Wine, Champagne and Spirits	325
Section 8	**Sport and Leisure**	**331**
Chapter 62	Fitness Equipment	333
Chapter 63	Outdoor Equipment and Games (including Trampolines, Slides and Swings)	336
Chapter 64	Walking, Climbing and Camping	340
Chapter 65	Snowsports and Watersports	342
Chapter 66	Fishing, Golf and Horseriding	348
Chapter 67	Tennis, Cricket, Rugby and Football	355
Chapter 68	Everything for the Photographer	359
Chapter 69	For the Artist and Musician	363
Chapter 70	Tickets and Subscriptions	367
Chapter 71	Books, Music and Movies	372
Section 9	**The Gift Shop**	**379**
Chapter 72	Cards and Balloons	381
Chapter 73	Ribbon and Wrap	384
Chapter 74	The Chocolate Lover's Paradise	387
Chapter 75	Flowers	392
Chapter 76	Gifts of Food and Drink	396
Chapter 77	Pamper Someone	401
Chapter 78	Home Accessory Gifts	405
Chapter 79	Gifts For New Babies and Christening Gifts	409
Chapter 80	For New Mums	414
Chapter 81	Gifts for Kids	416
Chapter 82	General Gift Stores	418
Chapter 83	Wedding Gifts	421
Chapter 84	The One Stop Christmas Shop	425
Section 10	**Travel Made Easy**	**439**
Chapter 85	Essential Travel Websites	441
Chapter 86	Car Hire, Ferries, Trains and Planes	443
Chapter 87	General Travel Planning	446
Section 11	**Useful Information – The Essential Websites**	**451**
Chapter 88	Essential Services	453
Chapter 89	To Buy or Not to Buy?	457
Index		467

Acknowledgements

My family, as ever, have been extremely patient with the amount of time I've spent sitting at my computer researching this book so a big thank you to Andrew, Sholto, Calum and Kirstie (and no I'm not going to say any more about Kirstie being the family shopaholic – well not this time, anyway – and in any case, if I'm going to be really honest, I'll have to admit that it's me). My thanks also to everyone at John Wiley, to Sally Smith, Jason Dunne, Emma Swaisland, Iain Campbell, Julia Lampam, Grace O'Byrne and Kate Stanley in particular, for their faith in me to write four books within a year and, yes, my eyes are now definitely square.

Thank you to Lee, Richard and Chris of E2E Solutions for their great work on my website and for managing to keep up with all my last minute demands for change 'because my book's coming out next week'. Thanks also to everyone at Mackerel for their wonderful illustrations – you've contributed more than you know. Finally thank you as always to Kate Hordern, my agent, you're almost certainly the reason I'm still sane – let alone still writing.

This book is for Sarah
And also Robert, Jols and Rupert

About the Author

After 12 years in international designer fashion mail-order, Patricia Davidson started www.thesiteguide.com, an online upmarket fashion, beauty and lifestyle website directory. Her first book: *The Shopaholic's Guide to Buying Online* was published by Capstone in October 2006. *The Shopaholic's Guide to Buying Fashion and Beauty Online, The Shopaholic's Guide to Buying for Mother and Child Online*, and *The Shopaholic's Guide to Buying Gorgeous Gifts Online* are all published by Capstone in 2007. She's a regular contributor to Condé Nast's easylivingmagazine.com and has been published on online shopping in other women's titles and the national press. She lives in Buckinghamshire with her husband, three children and two dogs.

x

Introduction

This is a book about shopping. The kind of shopping that makes you feel good – shopping for fashion and fragrance, for gifts for friends and treats for yourself and your significant other; the totally essential 'I must have that new quilted handbag' type of shopping. I'm sure you know the kind I mean.

Think of this book as a sort of virtual Knightsbridge. Not Bond Street (too rarefied), or Oxford Street – far, far too many people, too many shops all crowded together and with not necessarily the kinds of products you're looking for. But Knightsbridge – ah yes; elegant department stores, beautiful small boutiques, individual places to find famous brands and chic fragrances alongside some of the most covetable shoes and accessories on the planet. Well, my planet, at least.

Did I forget to mention that this is all online? I think I did, but yes, this book is about doing all that shopping online, without having to move from your home (or wherever you choose to be with a fast broadband connection). I have to say that nowadays I'm amazed when I come across people who tell me that 'they don't shop online', or 'don't like the internet'. I think that with the growing number of products and services available, which include not just the delectable items I've outlined above but travel (flights, trains, car hire and hotels), mouth-watering food and drink plus your really tedious 'everyday basics' shopping; it's surely pretty well impossible to stay away.

If you are a beginner start with somewhere like www.amazon.co.uk or www.johnlewis.com and you'll be instantly converted. Alternatively do away with that boring food shopping and go to www.tesco.com or www.ocado.com and have it all brought to your door at your convenience. If I tell you that I have a family of five plus two dogs, that I never – as in never – go to a supermarket to shop and that it takes me just five minutes each week to order what I need, maybe you'll give it a try.

So what do I do with all that extra time *not* spent wearing myself out with my trolley? Well, apart from spending hours and hours online researching this book for you, I shop, of course – online for those things that I enjoy buying online and (yes, truly) out in the shops for special clothes for specific events. Other times I just want to go out to shop, not need to, but want to because one of the benefits that the emergence of online shopping has given us all is choice, the choice to shop for what we decide to – online or offline, when and where we choose.

As a true shopaholic (yes, that's me, however much I try to blame my daughter, although she's one too and that's totally my fault) I've grasped the choice and convenience that the web has brought me with both hands, to find products from all over the world that I never would have had access to before.

Now I can book my flights online and see into the rooms of the hotels that I'm planning to visit to avoid that sense of disappointment on my arrival. I can buy Aberdeen Angus beef from Scotland and the freshest fish from Devon, my cheese from France and olive oils from Italy.

As to that quilted handbag - well I've seen it online and been severely tempted but I haven't fallen quite yet - maybe I will have by the time you read this book.

Happy shopping.

Why Shop Online?

There are four main reasons for shopping online: convenience, time saving, choice and price.

Now that most people are comfortable with sitting down at their computers, clicking away and waiting for their orders to arrive, they're starting to explore the amazing range of products that are available - a range that's growing practically by the day.

Unlike a few years ago, there are now very few products that you can't find online, and that you can't have delivered almost ridiculously fast. Not only that, but the best online retailers have realised that hiding behind their websites doesn't work; we want to have someone helpful, friendly and well informed to give us the answers to any questions we may have. If we send an email we want an answer back fast and, if we call, we want the phone picked up even faster. More and more, excellent service is available from people who really know their stuff, and much faster than you could get it in an offline shop.

So, getting back to convenience: you can find just about anything, you can order at any time of day or night, from your home or office and you can have your order delivered (in most cases) to anywhere in the world. Think back just a very few years ago - say about five - and try to remember if you ever imagined that this would be the case. I'll bet you didn't. We even thought that the internet was something that would be here and gone - how daft were we?

The second major reason for buying online is the amount of time you can save. Time to go out to the movies, to sit down with a good book, to paint your nails (ladies only, please) and to buy something gorgeous to wear for that special event. All of the above instead of going out in your car, trying to find somewhere to park, going round the supermarket or department store etc. etc.- I've said it too many times and I'm sure you don't need me to spell it out again.

The third reason for shopping online is choice. It would simply not be possible to go round and find in the shops the huge selection you can see almost instantly online. Even if you had a month, which most of us don't. You can look at as many or as few products as you want and see the full details and specification for each and every one. On some websites you can click to compare several products together to help you make your choice, which is a really excellent facility.

You may well find that in some cases there's too much choice. You'll certainly never be limited in the way that you can be in the shops.

Finally - price. As I've already said, the high street stores can very rarely compete with the internet (although they're now trying very hard), mainly because without an offline retail presence the overheads are so much lower and the cost benefit can be passed on to you.

Having said that, don't expect to buy your new pair of Gucci shoes cheaper on the internet than in the store. You can find lots of bargains for designer goods online but not (or very rarely) for new season's collections. In terms of top quality fashion and accessories, convenience is what you get by buying online - not usually discounts - but when you're talking about cameras, fridges and HD TVs you'll be amazed at what you can save.

Using This Book

The best websites will give you clear and easy categories and customer information (delivery, returns, contact info) right on the home page so you don't have to waste time clicking through long flash intros which slow down your search for that perfect product. After all, you're interested in buying from them, not seeing endless images for products you don't want.

I am, I have to confess, still horrified at the number that hide their delivery details and wait until you're just about to order before telling you that they want you to allow a month for delivery, or that they don't deliver to your country – it is improving, but not fast enough, in my opinion.

Just for some great examples, take a look at www.eluxury.com and www.neimanmarcus.com, two top US websites offering every designer from Marc Jacobs to Manolo Blahnik with Louis Vuitton and Christian Dior in between. There they are on the front page, ready and waiting for you to browse and buy with clear information about delivery, returns and every other question you can think of just one single click away. No 'clever' flash intros, no extra home page; no nonsense, just straight to what you want to buy.

All the websites included in the guide have been looked at carefully not only for the service and products they offer, but also for how easy the retailers make it for you to shop.

For almost every website you'll find something like the following:

Site Usability:	★★★★★	Based:	UK
Product Range:	★★★★★	Express Delivery Option? (UK)	Yes
Price Range:	Medium	Gift Wrapping Option?	Yes
Delivery Area:	Worldwide	Returns Procedure:	Down to you

In all cases the stars range from ★★★★★ to ★★★ and I'll explain as follows:

Site Usability
How quick and easy is it for you to click round the website and get to the products you're looking for? How quickly can you get to information on delivery, returns, whether or not gift wrapping is offered and how to contact the retailer? Are the pictures clear and attractive? Is there adequate information about every product offered?

Product Range
How much choice there is on the website. Fewer stars here do not mean a lower quality product, just a smaller range.

Price Range
This ranges from luxury through medium to very good value and is just a guide so you know what to expect.

Delivery Area
Does the retailer deliver to the UK, EU countries or worldwide?

Based
This tells you where the retailer is based, so you'll know straight away if you're going to be in for duty or extra shipping costs.

Express Delivery Option

Can you have your order tomorrow? Some websites are very quick anyway but this is specifically for where next day or express service is offered, usually within the country where the retailer is based.

Gift Wrapping Option

Do they or don't they?

Returns Procedure

'Down to you' means you pack it up and pay to send it back. 'Free' means just that and they may even collect it from you. 'Complicated' means that they want you to call them and tell them you're sending your order back. This normally only applies where the product you've ordered is particularly valuable.

You'll find more about returns in Chapter 91, Deliveries and Returns.

Some facts and figures

This year we've definitely accepted the fact that online shopping is here to stay, and even the most sceptical has had to admit that the future for online is bright.

We may not have caught up with the US yet in terms of the proportion of retailers who have launched web shopping but we have in terms of the percentage of retail sales taking place online, which is anticipated to be around 12% this year.

Think about this: total UK retail spend online in 2005 was £19.2 billion. In 2007 it is expected to reach £44.7 billion, or a whopping increase of 133% – all in a period when offline retail is showing very little growth at all. In 2006 e-retail grew at it's fastest ever rate, increasing by an average of £50 million per month. During the same period in 2004 the growth rate was just £16 million per month.

Fashion, which has taken a while to really get going, is now one of the strongest areas of online shopping growth, along with gifts which are wrapped for you by the retailer, and electricals – where the availability of price comparison websites makes buying such products even more attractive as you can make sure that you're getting the best deal.

So, two or three years ago, if you were just beginning to buy your books online and maybe having a dabble at getting your groceries delivered, now you'll probably be buying your new camera and fridge without giving a thought to leaving home, having your supermarket shop delivered to you each week and browsing through the new fashion ranges at the start of each season – picking out the must-have pieces as you go. In most cases what you order can be with you tomorrow, or in just a slightly longer time, anywhere in the world.

Web security has improved much in the past year or so with the emergence of Visa Vericode and Mastercard Secure Code, both of which help to make credit card fraud even more difficult. Also, e-retailer accredited schemes such as ISIS (Internet Shopping Is Safe – look out for the registered sign on approved sites) add extra peace of mind Hopefully, we're also becoming more aware about the checks we need to make to ensure our online shopping is secure. Google Checkout has launched (how did we exist before Google) which will automatically fill in your details wherever you want them in just one click (provided you've registered, of course).

So why are there still some offline stores that are not yet online? It really does make me wonder. Surely they must read the newspapers. I'll make you a bet: if they're not here now, they will be very soon. Anyone out there prepared to join me?

Section 1
Fashion at a Click

Fashion at a Click

Fashion at all price levels is now, thank goodness, one of the fastest growing areas of shopping online and though you still won't find all the brands (don't ask me why not, I'm sure they're going to get there eventually), there's still a really good choice.

One change I've noticed over the past year is that whilst some of the brands have yet to come online, other beautifully designed 'designer' boutiques have, and although these carry just a small range from each label they're usually cleverly edited to include some great basics plus some of the more 'of the moment' items for you to browse round. They also, usually (just hedging my bets here), offer an excellent service and if you need some advice you can just give them a call.

Other areas that are exceptionally good to buy online are lingerie (try and find a better collection offline than at figleaves.com), swim and sportswear, small accessories such as scarves, wraps and belts and high quality leather, suede and shearling.

With all of the above it would take you weeks, months maybe to track down the kind of selection you'll find here. I'm sure you'll be amazed. Get ready to shop till you drop and if it's all just too much temptation I apologise – but you have been warned.

Chapter 1

Fashion Online

Boutique Bliss   Modern Fashion Retailers

Mail Order Specialists   The High Street

Here you'll find four totally different types of online fashion retailers. Firstly, in Boutique Bliss, I've included the small online 'boutiques' who tend to offer a varied collection of clothes and accessories, often by a diverse group of designers whom you (and I) may never have heard of. Others include quite sizable selections from labels such as Amanda Wakeley, Maria Grachvogel, Colette Dinnigan, Temperley and Nicole Farhi.

They all have one thing in common; the style of the boutique and the style of the products on offer will be totally in tune with the buyer or owner, who will be choosing her clothes and accessories for a specific customer base that she knows well. Take a look round here and you'll either love or leave each one's particular style. When you do find something you like, don't delay in placing your order as these retailers do not order lots of stock and if you hesitate your 'must-have' skirt or pair of shoes may be gone.

My 'Modern Fashion Retailers' are different from the boutiques in that they are, in the main, specialised brands such as Agnes b, Evisu, Hobbs and Freda, Matches Fashion's own very specific brand. Here there are some quite idiosyncratic websites from retailers who have not previously offered their clothes and accessories by means other than their stores, but there are some excellent collections, modern, chic and in most cases reasonably priced. I say 'most cases' because there are also some expensive pieces here – when you take a look you'll see for yourself.

Thirdly, there are the Mail Order Specialists, fashion retailers who traditionally sell via a paper catalogue and probably transferred to the web quite early on. Here you will probably find you can order the same products throughout each season, where there's much less risk of them running out and where they often have excellent end-of-season discounts. Think Boden, Lands End and Wrap as places for really good, high quality basics and excellent service.

Finally there's The High Street: a shopaholic's paradise where you can find all the latest looks without having to queue in the stores or pay bank-breaking prices. If you're not sure about the latest trends this is a very good place to start as one of their main aims in life is to keep you well informed and they succeed brilliantly. You may not want to buy your complete wardrobe here, but you'll probably invest in a few key pieces and you'll know for sure what you should be aiming for.

I would never suggest that you should buy your complete wardrobe online – *I* certainly wouldn't, but this is certainly a really great place to start.

Sites to Visit

Boutique Bliss

www.anusha.co.uk

Here's a boudoir style online boutique where you can buy pretty and indulgent designer pieces from clothes, luxurious loungewear, vintage-inspired jewellery and unique accessories to pampering gifts. When your order arrives it'll be beautifully wrapped in layers of fuchsia tissue paper and finished off with a feather butterfly and chocolate brown Anusha label. So come here for a treat for yourself or perfect presents. They deliver worldwide and in the UK you need to allow five to seven days.

Site Usability:	★★★★	Based:	UK
Product Range:	★★★★	Express Delivery Option? (UK)	No
Price Range:	Medium	Gift Wrapping Option?	Yes
Delivery Area:	Worldwide	Returns Procedure:	Down to you

www.boxinthepost.com

Box in the Post is a fashion mail order service and website boutique, delivering everything in a stylish yet simple box. Launched in Spring 2005, Box promises 'non High Street', original yet stunning clothes, an extremely friendly and efficient service and a personal touch with its customers. Run as a chic boutique, stock is updated all the time throughout the season so keep coming back to find something new.

Site Usability:	★★★★	Based:	UK
Product Range:	★★★★	Express Delivery Option? (UK)	Yes
Price Range:	Medium	Gift Wrapping Option	No
Delivery Area:	Worldwide	Returns Procedure:	Down to you

www.brittique.com

This is a beautifully designed new online boutique featuring designers such as Amanda Wakeley, Maria Grachvogel and Louise Amstrap and their list is sure to grow. You'll also find accessories and jewellery by Vinnie Day, Lucy J, Deal and Wire and more, some of which would make perfect gifts, particularly with their speedy delivery services and high quality packaging. Their express service covers the UK and Europe. Keep an eye on this website – it's excellent.

Site Usability:	★★★★★	Based:	UK
Product Range:	★★★★★	Express Delivery Option? (UK)	Yes
Price Range:	Luxury/Medium	Gift Wrapping Option?	Yes
Delivery Area:	Worldwide	Returns Procedure:	Down to you

www.cocoribbon.com

Calling itself London's lifestyle boutique, Coco Ribbon offers a selection of contemporary clothing by designers such as Collette Dinnigan, Rebecca Taylor and Cynthia Vincent, pretty, modern lingerie and swimwear, a small but beautiful range of handbags and jewellery plus gorgeous and unusual girly gifts and candles. There's a lot to choose from here and the range is constantly updated so you need to return regularly for another browse.

Site Usability:	★★★★	Based:	UK
Product Range:	★★★★	Express Delivery Option? (UK)	Yes
Price Range:	Luxury/Medium	Gift Wrapping Option	Yes
Delivery Area:	Worldwide	Returns Procedure:	Down to you

www.jeannepetitt.com

This is a really excellent boutique to have a look round. They offer brands such as Nicole Farhi, Edina Ronay, Pink Soda, Temperley and Yves St Laurent, accessories by Emma Hope and J&M Davidson, jewellery by Angie Gooderham and Tataborello and fragrance by Annick Goutal and Rosine. The pictures are clear and simple and you can enlarge them to see the detail. Prices, needless to say, are at the designer end.

Site Usability:	★★★★★	Based:	UK
Product Range:	★★★★	Express Delivery Option? (UK)	Yes
Price Range:	Luxury/Medium	Gift Wrapping Option	Yes
Delivery Area:	Worldwide	Returns Procedure:	Down to you

www.max-oliver.co.uk

If you're in the mood for a visit to a small but beautiful boutique where you'll find unusual, personally chosen clothes, accessories and homewares you probably won't find anywhere else, then stop by here. Max Oliver is quite simply a treasure trove of French and vintage inspired pieces including dresses, skirts, jackets and coats, cushions, crockery and accessories and there are never large quantities of anything, so if you see something you like, snap it up fast.

Site Usability:	★★★	Based:	UK
Product Range:	★★★	Express Delivery Option? (UK)	No
Price Range:	Medium	Gift Wrapping Option?	No
Delivery Area:	Worldwide	Returns Procedure:	Down to you

www.misamu.com

Citizens of Humanity, Gold Hawk, Ella Moss, Pyrus, Rebecca Taylor and Velvet are just some of the modern brands stocked by this Ireland based online boutique that's willing to ship to you anywhere in the world. Prices are, as you'd expect, at the designer level but well photographed on actual models rather than just as stills. Click on the item that takes your fancy and you can see different views and go straight through to the relevant size chart, which is a huge benefit as designer sizing is definitely not standard, and that's putting it mildly. Delivery is free if you spend over £100.

Site Usability:	★★★★★	Based:	UK
Product Range:	★★★★	Express Delivery Option? (UK)	No
Price Range:	Luxury/Medium	Gift Wrapping Option?	No
Delivery Area:	Worldwide	Returns Procedure:	Down to you

www.my-wardrobe.com

This is a really well laid out designer clothing and accessories website (with lots of designers you'll have found it difficult to buy online before) including FrostFrench, Cacharel, Ann Louise Roswald, Sara Berman, Tocca and See by Chloe. For each item there are several different views, including close-ups of details such as embroidery and prints, plus there's excellent description and commentary under 'My-Advice'. When you spot something you like they'll recommend other items to go with.

Site Usability:	★★★★★	Based:	UK
Product Range:	★★★★	Express Delivery Option? (UK)	Yes
Price Range:	Luxury/Medium	Gift Wrapping Option?	Automatic
Delivery Area:	Worldwide	Returns Procedure:	Free of Charge

www.pantalonchameleon.com

You'll discover colourful, dressy, modern and fun clothing from this unusual London boutique offering an individual collection you won't find anywhere else. They're particularly good if you have a special event to go to and you like long, pretty skirts which they match with embroidered tops and knitwear and some stunning shoes. You can finish off your outfit from their selection of beaded jewellery and other small accessories.

Site Usability:	★★★★★	Based:	UK
Product Range:	★★★★	Express Delivery Option? (UK)	Yes
Price Range:	Medium	Gift Wrapping Option?	No
Delivery Area:	Worldwide	Returns Procedure:	Down to you

www.plumo.co.uk

At Plumo you'll always find something different and interesting, from a gold trimmed basket to a floral print tote. They also offer homewares, clothes and accessories including shoes and jewellery. It's not a huge collection but beautifully edited to be feminine and chic at the same time. There are some lovely gift ideas here as well and express delivery and gift wrapping are just two of the services offered.

Site Usability:	★★★★	Based:	UK
Product Range:	★★★	Express Delivery Option? (UK)	Yes
Price Range:	Medium	Gift Wrapping Option?	Yes
Delivery Area:	Worldwide	Returns Procedure:	Down to you

www.pocket-venus.net

Youthful, happy and alluring is the signature style of Pocket Venus, where you'll find bespoke prints, flattering shapes and unusual embellishments combining to create chic separates and dresses with a vintage feel. Think hand embroidered, slim, silk organza dresses, pintucked silk chiffon shirts and cotton voile sundresses and you'll get the idea. You can see immediately which items are in stock in your size and although it's a small collection there are some really attractive clothes so you should definitely take a look.

Site Usability:	★★★★		Based:	UK
Product Range:	★★★		Express Delivery Option? (UK)	Yes, worldwide
Price Range:	Medium		Gift Wrapping Option?	No
Delivery Area:	Worldwide		Returns Procedure:	Down to you within seven days

www.saltwater.net

Although there isn't yet the facility to order directly online and you have to email them with your enquiry (which I hope won't be the situation for very long) this is a British designed collection well worth keeping your eye on. It's modern, fresh and beautifully realised with great attention to detail, and offers fabrics and styles you won't find anywhere else. There's also a range of accessories here such as slubby raw silk printed bags and floor cushions plus pretty printed makeup purses and totes.

Site Usability:	★★★		Based:	UK
Product Range:	★★★★		Express Delivery Option? (UK)	Yes
Price Range:	Medium		Gift Wrapping Option?	No
Delivery Area:	Worldwide		Returns Procedure:	Down to you

www.shopatanna.co.uk

With stores based in London, Norfolk & Suffolk Anna is an innovative boutique offering clothes and accessories by Betty Jackson, Seven, Issa London, Orla Kiely, Gharani Strock and lesser known designers such as Day and Noa Noa. It's an eclectic and modern collection combining elegance and quirkyness and the designers are being added to all the time, so keep checking back. One of the great things here is that there's lots of helpful information about each designer and their new season's collections.

Site Usability:	★★★★★		Based:	UK
Product Range:	★★★★		Express Delivery Option? (UK)	Yes
Price Range:	Luxury/Medium		Gift Wrapping Option?	Yes
Delivery Area:	Worldwide		Returns Procedure:	Down to you

www.stylebop.com

German based Stylebop offers speedy worldwide delivery and a mix of clothing and accessory designers (with just a few listed here) who go under the headings of Great Luxury - Celine, Burberry, Calvin Klein, Valentino; Contemporary - Isabella Fiore, Kenneth Jay Lane, Kors, Juicy Couture, Day Birger et Mikkelsen; and Young and Trendy - C & C California, La ROK, Ella Moss and Coast: So not much to choose from, then. You can, if you're not sure which designer you want to look at, also choose by category, which I think makes life much easier.

Site Usability:	★★★★★		Based:	Germany
Product Range:	★★★★		Express Delivery Option? (UK)	Express within Germany, elsewhere 2–4 days
Price Range:	Luxury/Medium		Gift Wrapping Option?	No
Delivery Area:	Worldwide		Returns Procedure:	Their DHL service if you notify them with 14 days of delivery

www.valentineandfrench.co.uk

At the Valentine and French boutique there's a treasure trove full of accessories, home treats and gift ideas such as glamorous clutch bags, unusual and beautifully fragranced body products, cashmere separates and pretty jewellery. This is a very attractively designed website and you'll discover all the products under headings such as 'Stepping Out', 'Staying In', 'Little Pleasures', and 'Jewellery Box'.

Site Usability:	★★★★	Based:	UK
Product Range:	★★★	Express Delivery Option? (UK)	No
Price Range:	Medium	Gift Wrapping Option?	No
Delivery Area:	Worldwide	Returns Procedure:	Down to you

Modern Fashion Retailers

www.agnesb.com

You may not necessarily like the music they play you on this unusual but cleverly designed website but you can still buy your perfect fitted white shirts, superbly designed t-shirts and chic trousers from this famous French designer offering addictive quality and cut. It isn't the easiest site to use if you want to place a quick order but if you're an Agnes b addict (and there are many of them) then this is the place to be.

Site Usability:	★★★	Based:	France
Product Range:	★★★★	Express Delivery Option? (UK)	Yes
Price Range:	Medium	Gift Wrapping Option?	No
Delivery Area:	Most EU, China, USA and Japan	Returns Procedure:	Down to you

www.apc.fr

You will need quite a fast broadband connection to get the best out of this unusually designed French website offering high quality and well priced chic designer separates. Collections are offered as complete 'looks' from the outerwear to the basics after which you click on the individual items to buy. You'll find each new season's essentials here as well as their jeans and accessories collections for men, women and children.

Site Usability:	★★★	Based:	France
Product Range:	★★★★	Express Delivery Option? (UK)	Yes
Price Range:	Medium/Very Good Value	Gift Wrapping Option?	No
Delivery Area:	Worldwide	Returns Procedure:	Down to you

www.eveningdresses.co.uk

This is a large collection of classic, elegant, full length and cocktail dresses ranging in price from around £150 to £700. The main collection shown is held in stock and provided they have your chosen colour and size they'll rush it to you by express delivery; so the next time you have a special event to go to and no time to shop you don't need to panic. Alongside their own collection they offer dresses by Alfred Sung and Dessy, which can take longer to deliver.

Site Usability:	★★★★	Based:	UK
Product Range:	★★★★	Express Delivery Option? (UK)	Yes – if dress is in stock
Price Range:	Luxury/Medium	Gift Wrapping Option?	No
Delivery Area:	Worldwide	Returns Procedure:	Down to you

www.evisu.com

Evisu is the brainchild of Japanese jean junkie Yamane who came up with the idea in the 1980s to use reconditioned sewing machines and make new 'vintage style' jeans with old Japanese handicraft traditions. Every pair of Evisu jeans is made from 100% Japanese indigo dyed denim and features 23 details which make each pair unique. In the really fun and different online store there are all the Evisu ranges including Heritage, EV Genes, Mens Mainline, Evisu (European Edition), Kizzu and Shoos.

Site Usability:	★★★★	Based:	UK
Product Range:	★★★	Express Delivery Option? (UK)	No
Price Range:	Luxury/Medium	Gift Wrapping Option	No
Delivery Area:	Worldwide	Returns Procedure:	Down to you

www.fredafashion.com

You'll no doubt be delighted to know that top designer store Matches of Wimbledon has now launched its own collection online, with a beautifully finished and wearable selection of each season's essentials, including chic coats, jackets, skirts, trousers, tops and knitwear, all beautifully in line with the latest trends and all of which you'll probably want to buy immediately. Sizes are from 8 to 14.

Site Usability:	★★★★	Based:	UK
Product Range:	★★★★	Express Delivery Option? (UK)	Yes
Price Range:	Luxury/Medium	Gift Wrapping Option	Automatic
Delivery Area:	Worldwide	Returns Procedure:	Down to you

www.hobbs.co.uk

You may well already have shopped at Hobbs, for beautifully cut workwear, chic eveningwear or casual separates (not to mention their wide collection of shoes). You'll no doubt be pleased to learn that they're now offering an ordering facility on their website. All the items are put together as outfits so you can clearly see what works together and wherever you click you'll get the details for that particular piece, whether it's a scarf, dress, cardigan or pair of shoes, together with the size and colour choices. It's an excellent collection and delivery takes about three days.

Site Usability:	★★★★★	Based:	UK
Product Range:	★★★★	Express Delivery Option? (UK)	No
Price Range:	Luxury/Medium	Gift Wrapping Option	No
Delivery Area:	UK	Returns Procedure:	Down to you

www.jaeger.co.uk

If you haven't looked at Jaeger recently you may well get a surprise here. The website is far more modern than the stores so you get a completely different feel to the clothes that they offer. It's very wearable (with sizes going from 6 to 18) and there's a range of styles for just about every-one. Take a look at Jaeger London for their view on the key looks of the season or the excellent basics in the Jaeger Collection. The overall feel is smart and quite dressy with some very good tailored jackets and trousers plus soft printed skirts which they match for you to their tops and accessories.

Site Usability:	★★★★	Based:	UK
Product Range:	★★★★	Express Delivery Option? (UK)	No
Price Range:	Medium	Gift Wrapping Option?	Yes
Delivery Area:	UK	Returns Procedure:	Contact them to arrange

www.ladress.com

This is a novel idea from a Netherlands-based retailer offering you well styled dresses in a variety of lengths and fabrics, from polka dot satin silk to lace and fine wool, so if you've been searching for that perfect dress for a while you may find it here. They're all very much the same button front shape (at present) so you're likely to either love them or leave them. The website is easy to use and they offer a free returns service provided you email them within seven days of receiving delivery.

Site Usability:	★★★★★	Based:	Netherlands
Product Range:	★★★	Express Delivery Option? (UK)	No
Price Range:	Medium	Gift Wrapping Option	No but dresses are beautifully boxed
Delivery Area:	EU	Returns Procedure:	Email them within seven days for free service

www.no-one.co.uk

No-One is a boutique based in Hoxton, East London and on their website you can find on trend (or even beyond trend, if there is such a thing) dresses, separates and accessories for girls and boys from a collection of cool, cutting edge designers such as Mine, Karen Walker, Louise Amstrap and Cheap Monday. There's absolutely nothing classic here but if you like to be ahead, fashion-wise, you should take a look.

Site Usability:	★★★★	Based:	UK
Product Range:	★★★	Express Delivery Option? (UK)	No
Price Range:	Luxury/Medium	Gift Wrapping Option	No
Delivery Area:	Worldwide	Returns Procedure:	Down to you

www.planet.co.uk

I'm sure you've heard of this brand but if it's not one you normally shop for offline you should stop now and take a quick look round. They've made it very easy to see everything that's offered and tell you straight away all the sizes that are available. Styles tend to be classic and there are quite a lot of (high quality) man made fabrics but it's a very good range, particularly for the jackets and outerwear.

Site Usability:	★★★★	Based:	UK
Product Range:	★★★★	Express Delivery Option? (UK)	Yes
Price Range:	Medium	Gift Wrapping Option?	No
Delivery Area:	UK	Returns Procedure:	Down to you

www.precis.co.uk

If you're under 5ft 3in. (1.6m) tall and prefer not to have to make lots of alterations to your new clothes then this is the place for you. Precis offer ranges with names such as 'Left Bank' and 'Coco Boutique' and in each there are separates that work very well together. If you prefer you can also select by type of clothing, coats, jackets or trousers, for example and sizing goes from 8 to 18.

Site Usability:	★★★★		Based:	UK
Product Range:	★★★★		Express Delivery Option? (UK)	Yes
Price Range:	Medium		Gift Wrapping Option?	No
Delivery Area:	UK		Returns Procedure:	Down to you

Mail Order Specialists

www.artigiano.co.uk

At Artigiano you could buy your whole wardrobe without even going to another website. The emphasis is fairly classic with easy rather than very fitted shapes and standard sizing (not small). You'll find lovely fine and chunky knitwear, excellent t-shirts and tops, trousers in a selection of styles and fabrics and unique jackets and outerwear you can't buy anywhere else. There's some very good leather and suede as well. The collection is updated four times a year.

Site Usability:	★★★★★		Based:	UK
Product Range:	★★★★		Express Delivery Option? (UK)	Yes
Price Range:	Medium		Gift Wrapping Option?	Yes on most items
Delivery Area:	Worldwide		Returns Procedure:	Free using Royal Mail

www.boden.co.uk

It would be surprising if you hadn't already seen the Boden catalogue. It's everywhere, with Johnnie Boden's inimitable style (and commentary) all over it. Provided you like his colourful style the clothes have their own relaxed appeal which is popular with a lot of people. If you're into minimalist chic black don't go there. If you like your pinks, blues, greens and reds then certainly have a browse. There's a mini Boden and menswear as well.

Site Usability:	★★★★		Based:	UK
Product Range:	★★★★		Express Delivery Option? (UK)	Yes
Price Range:	Medium		Gift Wrapping Option?	No
Delivery Area:	Worldwide		Returns Procedure:	Down to you

www.landsend.co.uk

This leading catalogue company originates in the US and offers a wide range of high quality, well priced clothing for men and women. Signature collections include stylish co-ordinates, casual wear, linen wear, swimwear, outerwear, cashmere and footwear with lots of essentials for your new season's wardrobe. Many products are available in extended ranges to fit and flatter Plus and Petite sizes. First-class customer service is backed by a no-quibble money-back guarantee and free delivery on your first order.

Site Usability:	★★★★★	Based:	UK (this website)
Product Range:	★★★★★	Express Delivery Option? (UK)	Yes
Price Range:	Very Good Value	Gift Wrapping Option?	Yes
Delivery Area:	Worldwide	Returns Procedure:	Down to you

www.lauraashley.com

Becoming more up to date by the day (although still retaining some of the feminine influences we've come to associate with this long standing retailer), at Laura Ashley there are some really good tops and knitwear, shirts, skirts, trousers and accessories. Alongside this, and possibly the strongest part of the website, is the home accessories and furniture section, where you can choose everything from pretty gift ideas to handcrafted cabinet furniture and lots of decorating advice.

Site Usability:	★★★	Based:	UK
Product Range:	★★★	Express Delivery Option? (UK)	No
Price Range:	Medium/Very Good Value	Gift Wrapping Option	No
Delivery Area:	UK but there are global sites as well	Returns Procedure:	Down to you

www.orvis.co.uk

Originally a company specialising in fishing equipment, Orvis have now developed their brand to offer a full clothing and accessories range for men and women. You'll find a high quality classic range here from Donegal tweed jackets to quilted, microfibre coats plus knitwear, shirts, polos, t-shirts and accessories, all in a wide choice of colours. There's hardwearing footwear here too plus the Barbour Collection.

Site Usability:	★★★★★	Based:	UK (this website)
Product Range:	★★★★★	Express Delivery Option? (UK)	Yes
Price Range:	Medium	Gift Wrapping Option?	Yes
Delivery Area:	Worldwide	Returns Procedure:	Down to you

www.peruvianconnection.co.uk

Each season Peruvian Connection offers a richly photographed collection of ethnic style separates (with some classics) using Peruvian alpaca and jewel coloured pima cotton. The look is very elegant, matching their unusually coloured tops and fine knitwear with gorgeously patterned skirts. They also offer specialist art knit jackets and sweaters, beaded jewellery, scarves and bags. You'll find excellent quality and in some cases quite steep prices.

Site Usability:	★★★★★	Based:	UK
Product Range:	★★★★	Express Delivery Option? (UK)	Yes
Price Range:	Luxury/Medium	Gift Wrapping Option?	Yes
Delivery Area:	Worldwide	Returns Procedure:	Down to you

www.poetrycollection.co.uk

Poetry is a new, fresh collection of clothing online, offering a very good selection of tops, fine knitwear, tailoring, pretty skirts and dresses in a modern range of colours and all using mainly natural fibres. The prices are reasonable and sizes go from 10 to 24 in just about everything. This is a beautifully photographed and easy-to-use website, and you can see several different pictures of everything offered.

Site Usability:	★★★★★	Based:	UK
Product Range:	★★★★	Express Delivery Option? (UK)	Yes
Price Range:	Medium	Gift Wrapping Option?	No
Delivery Area:	EU	Returns Procedure:	Down to you

www.thelinenpress.co.uk

As far as linen clothing goes I think there are two sorts of people; those who love it and those who don't. It is a pain to iron and always creases the minute you put it on but at least you can now find linen that washes beautifully and doesn't shrink as it used to. The Linen Press have a range of men's and women's clothing in soft, wearable twill weave, fine garment washed linen, natural cotton stretch baby cord and fleecy pure cotton.

Site Usability:	★★★	Based:	UK
Product Range:	★★★	Express Delivery Option? (UK)	No
Price Range:	Medium	Gift Wrapping Option?	No
Delivery Area:	Worldwide	Returns Procedure:	Down to you

www.toastbypost.co.uk

Toast has long been well known for simple, beautifully made clothes in natural colours and natural fabrics and the range of separates includes skirts, tops, knitwear and trousers, plus nightwear and gowns, beachwear and a small collection of bed linen. Don't expect lots of bright colours here, you won't find them. This designer is about quiet, easy style. Their photographs are really beautiful and they offer still life pictures as well as model pics which is extremely helpful.

Site Usability:	★★★★	Based:	UK
Product Range:	★★★	Express Delivery Option? (UK)	Yes but you need to call them
Price Range:	Medium	Gift Wrapping Option?	Yes
Delivery Area:	Worldwide	Returns Procedure:	Down to you

www.wallcatalogue.com

If you haven't already heard of Wall but you like beautifully made, easy-to-wear clothing in unusual fabrics then you should take a good look at this well photographed website. It's a very different and attractive range of modern, flattering separates in muted colours such as barley, oyster, pale grey and black, of course, for winter. The clothes aren't inexpensive but you're buying into real quality and the service is excellent.

Site Usability:	★★★★★	Based:	UK
Product Range:	★★★★	Express Delivery Option? (UK)	Yes
Price Range:	Medium	Gift Wrapping Option?	No
Delivery Area:	Worldwide	Returns Procedure:	Down to you

www.wraponline.co.uk

At Wrap you'll find modern separates in each season's colours attractively photographed on real models, so you can not only see the clothes clearly but there's lots of atmosphere too. There's always a very good selection of tops, knitwear, trousers and skirts using mainly natural yarns such as cotton, silk and cashmere, you can see how they all work together and also tell at a glance whether what you want to order is in stock or not. Check out the new accessory range of casual bags and belts. There are separate websites for the UK, USA and Germany.

Site Usability:	★★★★	Based:	UK
Product Range:	★★★★	Express Delivery Option? (UK)	Yes
Price Range:	Medium	Gift Wrapping Option?	No
Delivery Area:	Worldwide	Returns Procedure:	Down to you

The High Street

www.allsaintsshop.co.uk

All Saints offer up-to-the-minute styling totally in line with each season's different looks on their funky urban appeal website. There are lots of well photographed views of every item available including both model shots and basic product close-ups. Sizing goes from 6 to 14 in most items (although expect general sizing to be on the small size). You can shop by collection or by item and see straight away what's available in your size.

Site Usability:	★★★★	Based:	UK
Product Range:	★★★	Express Delivery Option? (UK)	No
Price Range:	Medium	Gift Wrapping Option?	No
Delivery Area:	Worldwide	Returns Procedure:	Down to you

www.debenhams.com

The excellent range from 'Designers for Debenhams' seems to grow each season. Currently it includes Betty Jackson, Jasper Conran, Ben de Lisi, John Rocha, Julian MacDonald, John Richmond and more. Then you can also find lots of other, less expensive brands such as Principles and Red Herring, lingerie, menswear, childrenswear, electricals; and beauty by brands such as Estée Lauder, Lancôme, Benefit and Elemis. Take a look round now and watch the range on offer grow, season by season.

Site Usability:	★★★★★	Based:	UK
Product Range:	★★★★★	Express Delivery Option? (UK)	No
Price Range:	Very Good Value	Gift Wrapping Option?	No
Delivery Area:	UK	Returns Procedure:	Down to you

www.dorothyperkins.co.uk

Dorothy Perkins' clothes and accessories are modern and amazingly well priced. They use some natural and some man-made fabrics and sizing goes from 8 to 22 for most items. You'll find wearable new looks each season plus some colourful knits, tops and accessories. Take a good look at the start of the season if you're likely to want something here as once a product has sold out they probably won't replace it, however they offer new styles online each week.

Site Usability:	★★★★	Based:	UK
Product Range:	★★★	Express Delivery Option? (UK)	Yes
Price Range:	Very Good Value	Gift Wrapping Option?	No
Delivery Area:	UK	Returns Procedure:	Down to you

www.fcukbuymail.co.uk

This is a company where the words young, funky and high street come straight to mind and, alongside the fashion pieces, you can find some very good basics, in particular their knitwear and t-shirts, which are well priced, good quality and available in a range of colours. French Connection is definitely not cheap but delivers up-to-the-minute styling for men and women and is well worth taking a look at for new, modern additions to your wardrobe.

Site Usability:	★★★★	Based:	UK
Product Range:	★★★★	Express Delivery Option? (UK)	Yes
Price Range:	Medium	Gift Wrapping Option?	No
Delivery Area:	Worldwide	Returns Procedure:	Use their free service

www.ilovejeans.co.uk

You'll find five brands here currently – Made in Heaven, Ruby, !IT, Hudson and NYDJ (or Not Your Daughter's Jeans) and there's a good range of styles and washes and lots of information on fit – essential if you're going to splash out on a pair of designer jeans online. Prices range from around £70 to £160. They aim to stock all items offered so they can be shipped out to you within 48 hours. Check back for new designers being added.

Site Usability:	★★★★	Based:	UK
Product Range:	★★★	Express Delivery Option? (UK)	No
Price Range:	Medium	Gift Wrapping Option?	No
Delivery Area:	Worldwide	Returns Procedure:	Down to you

www.jeans-direct.com

If you're a jeans addict you should take a look at this website, where there's a selection by Levi, Ben Sherman, Wrangler and Diesel although by far the greatest choice is by Levi. Personally I think you really have to know your size in each brand to be sure you won't have to send them back but obviously you can try lots of different styles at home which is a great benefit if you, like me, would rather try your jeans on in private than in a public changing room.

Site Usability:	★★★	Based:	UK
Product Range:	★★★★	Express Delivery Option? (UK)	No
Price Range:	Medium	Gift Wrapping Option	No
Delivery Area:	EU	Returns Procedure:	Down to you

www.kew-online.com

From the same family as Jigsaw, Kew offer modern, versatile, well priced separates in a wide choice of colours and styles. There's a very good selection on this website and there are some great tops and fine knitwear plus easy jackets and skirts with most items being available in a selection of colours, which they show you very clearly. They sometimes take quite a while for each new season's collection to be available online but be patient. It'll be worth it.

Site Usability:	★★★★	Based:	UK
Product Range:	★★★★	Express Delivery Option? (UK)	Yes
Price Range:	Medium/Very Good Value	Gift Wrapping Option?	No
Delivery Area:	Worldwide; call for international delivery	Returns Procedure:	Down to you

www.layer-up.co.uk

Here's a new, young, modern, brand-driven retailer offering labels such as Chilli Pepper, Fever, Looking Glass and MbyM. They have an excellent trend section where they've put all the looks together so you can see exactly what you need to buy. This is great teen/high street shopping in a clear and easy to use format with the Casual/Active section being particularly strong.

Site Usability:	★★★★	Based:	UK
Product Range:	★★★★	Express Delivery Option? (UK)	Yes
Price Range:	Medium	Gift Wrapping Option?	Yes
Delivery Area:	Worldwide	Returns Procedure:	Down to you

www.mango.com

Spanish label Mango offers inexpensive, up-to-the minute clothes and accessories which they'll ship to you just about anywhere in the world, so if you don't fancy battling your way through one of their stores you can buy calmly from them here. Their clever, modern website shows you everything at a glance. With jackets at around 60 euros and t-shirts from around 13 euros you can find plenty here to help you get the latest look without breaking the bank. Delivery is from Spain but is usually extremely quick.

Site Usability:	★★★★	Based:	Spain
Product Range:	★★★★★	Express Delivery Option? (UK)	No
Price Range:	Very Good Value	Gift Wrapping Option?	No
Delivery Area:	Worldwide	Returns Procedure:	Down to you

www.marksandspencer.com

You've probably already shopped from Marks & Spencer's huge online range of just about every-thing clothing related, from outerwear, tailoring, casualwear and accessories, lingerie, swimwear, shoes – the list just goes on and on. What's really great about this website now is that the special collections are available too, such as Autograph, Per Una and Limited Collection where you can shop from the more contemporary designs and make your choice from everything available rather than what's just in the small store near you.

Site Usability:	★★★★★	Express Delivery Option? (UK)	Yes
Product Range:	★★★★★	Gift Wrapping Option?	No
Price Range:	Medium/Very Good Value	Returns Procedure:	Free to store or their Freepost service
Delivery Area:	UK		

www.missselfridge.co.uk

An integral part of the high street since the 1960s, Miss Selfridge has always been a mainstay for young, modern style. There's nothing quiet about the clothes on offer, but plenty of information and guidance on how to put together the latest looks and the background to the trends. They do go up to a size 16 but most of the clothes are designed for smaller sizes. They only deliver to the UK and offer express delivery for just £1 more than their standard service.

Site Usability:	★★★★	Based:	UK
Product Range:	★★★★	Express Delivery Option? (UK)	Yes
Price Range:	Very Good Value	Gift Wrapping Option?	No
Delivery Area:	UK	Returns Procedure:	Freepost or to their stores but complicated

www.monsoon.co.uk

With its well known presence on the high street almost everyone has heard of Monsoon, offering attractive, not inexpensive but still good value clothing including some extremely wearable and different occasionwear. Sizing in a lot of cases goes up to a 20. The childrenswear selection is smaller but has the same look with really pretty clothes, mainly for younger girls, including candy coloured skirts and tops, sugar striped swimwear and the prettiest partywear.

Site Usability:	★★★★★	Based:	UK
Product Range:	★★★★★	Express Delivery Option? (UK)	No
Price Range:	Medium/Very Good Value	Gift Wrapping Option?	No
Delivery Area:	UK	Returns Procedure:	Down to you

www.oasis-stores.com

The new Oasis website allows you to shop simply and easily by garment, where you can zoom right in to every detail and find all the information on sizing and fabric you could need. Alternatively you can shop by trend, where all the relevant pieces are brought together for you or visit the new glamorous Vintage collection. The site is really easy to buy from, sizing goes up to a 16 and delivery is UK only.

Site Usability:	★★★★★	Based:	UK
Product Range:	★★★★	Express Delivery Option? (UK)	No
Price Range:	Medium/Very Good Value	Gift Wrapping Option?	No
Delivery Area:	UK	Returns Procedure:	Down to you

www.principles.co.uk

With an easier to wear selection than some of the high street retailers, Principles offer a stylish, well priced collection of separates, dresses and coats on their attractively designed website. They clearly show some of the trends of the season and have picked out pieces that go well together for each look. You'll find dresses, skirts, tops, jeans, knitwear, some very attractive tailoring and occasionwear and a petite collection which goes from size 6 to 16.

Site Usability:	★★★★	Based:	UK
Product Range:	★★★★	Express Delivery Option? (UK)	Yes
Price Range:	Very Good Value	Gift Wrapping Option?	No
Delivery Area:	UK	Returns Procedure:	Freepost or return to store but complicated

www.riverisland.com

If you're looking for the latest combat trousers, sparkly, decorated jeans or flirty tops (and you're no larger than a size 12 in most cases) then take a look round here. They seem to get more modern each season. However, they do have some coats, parkas and jackets that would be wearable for a lot of ages and a casual, modern menswear collection. The site is very quick and easy to use and their help desk with all the delivery information is excellent.

Site Usability:	★★★★★	Based:	UK
Product Range:	★★★★	Express Delivery Option? (UK)	Yes
Price Range:	Medium	Gift Wrapping Option?	No
Delivery Area:	UK	Returns Procedure:	Down to you

www.savagelondon.com

For t-shirt collectors this is the place to visit, with t-shirts and tops of all shapes and sizes and an enormous range of colours. The main point here is that you can customise your t-shirt or hoody (for yourself or whoever you want to give one to). Just select your design, choose your style (raw edge, long sleeve etc) then the colour. On some you can choose the text or word and other embellishment as well. The website is very busy but the instructions are clear once you get the hang of how things work.

Site Usability:	★★★★	Based:	UK
Product Range:	★★★★	Express Delivery Option? (UK)	No
Price Range:	Medium	Gift Wrapping Option?	No
Delivery Area:	Worldwide	Returns Procedure:	Down to you

www.tedbaker.co.uk

Expanding global brand Ted Baker offers well made and innovative clothing on their modern, well photographed and easy-to-navigate website, for women, men and kids. Don't expect cheap here, you won't find it. What you will find is up-to-the minute, mainly understated fashion, totally inline with each season's trends. Also swimwear, underwear, watches, accessories and fragrance.

Site Usability:	★★★	Based:	UK
Product Range:	★★★	Express Delivery Option? (UK)	No but UK delivery is very fast
Price Range:	Medium	Gift Wrapping Option?	No
Delivery Area:	Worldwide	Returns Procedure:	Down to you

www.topshop.co.uk

This is the place to go if you want the latest fashions at the best prices – and definitely the place to go if you can't stand the scrum of the shops. Can't afford Marc Jacobs or Miu Miu? Go straight to Top Shop, and if you can't bear the heaving crowds in the store, desperately seeking the last pair of the latest and absolutely must-have heels in your size, you can order them online and have them sent to you by express delivery. A fashionista could surely ask for no more than this.

Site Usability:	★★★★	Based:	UK
Product Range:	★★★★★	Express Delivery Option? (UK)	Yes
Price Range:	Very Good Value	Gift Wrapping Option?	Yes
Delivery Area:	UK, USA, Australia and ROI	Returns Procedure:	Down to you

www.urbanoutfitters.co.uk

Fast growing, US-based brand Urban Outfitters' young modern website is clearly targeted directly at their 18 to 30-year-old audience with a wide range of chic 'urban styled' clothes and accessories for girls and boys. There's designer wear from Alice McCall and See by Chloe, an eclectic, well priced range of separates, hosiery, scarves and gloves and right through to shoes, jewellery and underwear. Get the look now.

Site Usability:	★★★★★	Based:	UK
Product Range:	★★★★★	Express Delivery Option? (UK)	Yes
Price Range:	Medium	Gift Wrapping Option?	Yes
Delivery Area:	UK	Returns Procedure:	Down to you

www.wallis-fashion.com

Wallis offers a small selection from its stores on the website and just about everything goes up to a size 20, so styles on the whole are easier to wear for most people. They give clear information right from the start about each and every product, right down to washing information, fabric content and sizing, as well as telling you about each season's looks and how to put them together. They aim for 48 hour delivery in the UK with the option of express delivery.

Site Usability:	★★★★★	Based:	UK
Product Range:	★★★	Express Delivery Option? (UK)	Yes
Price Range:	Medium/Very Good Value	Gift Wrapping Option?	No
Delivery Area:	UK	Returns Procedure:	Freepost or return to store

www.warehouse.co.uk

Shop online at Warehouse for the latest trends and stylish must-haves. You'll find excellent seasonal collections as well as Warehouse Maternity, Denim and the Spotlight collection – a glam range of pieces for special occasions. The website is very user friendly and they deliver to all UK and ROI addresses. You can also subscribe to their e-newsletter to be kept up to date with what's new online and be the first to know about their latest news and promotions. Log on now and get shopping!

Site Usability:	★★★★	Based:	UK
Product Range:	★★★★	Express Delivery Option? (UK)	Yes
Price Range:	Very Good Value	Gift Wrapping Option?	No
Delivery Area:	UK and ROI	Returns Procedure:	Freepost or return to store

Chapter 2

Luxury Brands

This is a really dangerous place to check out and the hottest place to find the new looks each season. Here's your virtual Bond Street and the real problem is that unlike the street itself, where if you're anything like me you'll think twice about going into the stores and being stared down by those haughty, beautifully attired shop assistants (apologies if you're not really like that, maybe it's an illusion) here you can see everything that's on offer and spend as much time as you like browsing at any time of day or night.

So what if you're not their beloved size 8 (zero I really have difficulty in thinking about)? So what if you're actually a real life 12 or 14 like me? Take your time and have a look round, particularly at the start of each season, at Marni, Browns, Matches and Diane von Furstenberg. If something takes your fancy place your order fast. It will sell out and they will be unlikely to replace it – after all, you don't want to spot someone else in the same Temperley dress, now do you?

Sites to Visit

www.amandawakeley.com

Amanda Wakeley has launched her new website, where you can order from her luxuriously chic collection of dresses and separates plus accessories such as shoes, belts and stoles. Everything here is in the highest quality fabric, beautifully made, and you can expect to find detailing such as beading, lace edging and silk satin trims.

Site Usability:	★★★★	Based:	UK
Product Range:	★★★★	Express Delivery Option? (UK)	No
Price Range:	Luxury	Gift Wrapping Option	No
Delivery Area:	Worldwide	Returns Procedure:	Down to you

www.dior.com

At luxury brand Christian Dior's online boutique you can purchase from their range of beautiful, covetable handbags, shoes and boots, small leather accessories, scarves, watches and fine jewellery. Prices are steep as you would expect but if you want to be carrying the latest version of their instantly recognisable Gaucho or My Dior handbag on your arm this season you'll no doubt be prepared. Dior have specific websites for overseas shipping so you need to check if they have one for your country.

Site Usability:	★★★★	Based:	UK
Product Range:	★★★★★	Express Delivery Option? (UK)	Yes
Price Range:	Luxury	Gift Wrapping Option?	No but beautiful packaging is standard
Delivery Area:	UK but US and other sites available	Returns Procedure:	Down to you and complicated

www.allegrahicks.com

This is a really beautifully designed website offering some unusual and contemporary clothes and accessories designed by Allegra Hicks, who specialises in translating oriental themes into western style using strong organic patterns and colour. Her fashion collection is aimed at the woman who travels a lot and needs stylish clothes that work in many climates and travel and pack easily.

Site Usability:	★★★★	Based:	UK
Product Range:	★★★★	Express Delivery Option? (UK)	No
Price Range:	Luxury	Gift Wrapping Option	No
Delivery Area:	Worldwide	Returns Procedure:	Down to you

www.brownsfashion.com

The Browns website is not only very clear and easy to navigate but also offers a mouth-watering list of contemporary designers including Lanvin, Balenciaga, Missoni and Paul Smith plus Dolce & Gabbanna, Roberto Cavalli, Ann Demeulemeister and Issa. There are several views of each item plus lots of essential information and size charts. Look here too for your next Luella handbag fix (or Fendi or Marni) or pair of heels (Christian Louboutin or Marc Jacobs).

Site Usability:	★★★★★	Based:	UK
Product Range:	★★★★★	Express Delivery Option? (UK)	No
Price Range:	Luxury/Medium	Gift Wrapping Option?	No
Delivery Area:	Worldwide	Returns Procedure:	Down to you and complicated

www.burberry.com

Now you can buy from Burberry online through its beautifully designed website. You can browse the luxuriously photographed collections including Burberry Prorsum, Burberry London and the Icons Collection then click through to Shop Online and choose from menswear, womenswear, bags and accessories. If you want to see what's coming next you can preview the new collections. Expect superb quality and gorgeous packaging.

Site Usability:	★★★★★	Based:	UK
Product Range:	★★★★★	Express Delivery Option? (UK)	Automatic
Price Range:	Luxury	Gift Wrapping Option?	No
Delivery Area:	UK but US site available	Returns Procedure:	Down to you and complicated

www.dvflondon.com

On Diane von Furstenberg's stylish website you can see all the new collections with ease, from her famous collection of wrap dresses to a modern selection of coats, jackets and separates and a small range of beautifully designed swimwear. If you like the original fabrics she used you can buy from the Vintage collection on offer here, or from the 'Exclusives' collection which you'll only find online and at Matches Fashion.

Site Usability:	★★★★★	Based:	US
Product Range:	★★★★	Express Delivery Option? (UK)	Yes
Price Range:	Luxury/Medium	Gift Wrapping Option?	Yes
Delivery Area:	Worldwide	Returns Procedure:	Down to you/complicated

www.escada.com

You'll probably be surprised at the range of clothes and accessories available on Escada's extremely pretty website, where you'll find both the Escada and Escada Sport brand offering seriously beautiful and seriously expensive cocktail and evening dresses, skirts, jackets, shirts and knitwear plus stylish sporty casualwear, handbags, belts, small leather goods and fragrance. They'll be happy to gift wrap and send your order out on your behalf – if you can bear to give anything here away.

Site Usability:	★★★★★	Based:	EU
Product Range:	★★★★	Express Delivery Option? (UK)	Yes
Price Range:	Luxury	Gift Wrapping Option?	Yes
Delivery Area:	EU	Returns Procedure:	Contact them to arrange

www.lineafashion.com

Linea started life as a boutique in London's Hampstead, offering designer- wear from around the world. The shop is now online, with the range clearly photographed so you can see each item properly. Included are collections from international designers such as Blumarine, Celine, Etro, Gharani Strok, Juicy Couture, Missoni and Emanuel Ungaro plus handbags and shoes by Hogan, Tods and Celine. If you're in a buying mood this could be a very dangerous site to visit.

Site Usability:	★★★★★	Based:	UK
Product Range:	★★★★★	Express Delivery Option? (UK)	Yes
Price Range:	Luxury/Medium	Gift Wrapping Option?	No
Delivery Area:	Worldwide	Returns Procedure:	Down to you/complicated

www.luisaviaroma.com

This excellent luxury online boutique is based, not totally surprisingly, at No 3 Via Roma, Florence, Italy. They offer worldwide shipping on a wonderful range of designers, including Burberry, Chloe, Balenciaga, Lanvin, Narcisco Rodruigez, Roberto Cavalli and Missoni. Prices are exactly as you would expect them to be but the pictures are very clear with several views of each item and the range is exceptional.

Site Usability:	★★★★★	Based:	Italy
Product Range:	★★★★★	Express Delivery Option? (UK)	No
Price Range:	Luxury/Medium/Very Good Value	Gift Wrapping Option?	No
Delivery Area:	Worldwide	Returns Procedure:	Down to you

www.marni.com

Luxury brand Marni has launched its high tech 'virtual store' where all the garments seem to be hanging in mid-air. Everything is very clearly photographed and you can see several views of each. Register with them so that you can create 'My Style Notes', where you can view all the pieces you've selected together in one place and then see if you can resist putting them all in your basket. Be warned that most items don't go beyond size 44/12. This really is high fashion online shopping at its best so take time to look round

Site Usability:	★★★★★	Based:	UK
Product Range:	★★★★	Express Delivery Option? (UK)	Yes
Price Range:	Luxury	Gift Wrapping Option?	No
Delivery Area:	Worldwide	Returns Procedure:	Down to you

www.matchesfashion.com

Luxury designer boutique Matches are famous for offering a unique, personal service together with a mouth-watering choice of designers such as Dolce & Gabbana, Bottega Veneta, Chloe, Christian Louboutin, Lanvin, Marc Jacobs, Missoni and Stella McCartney. You can now find this excellent service and the full range of designers online where you can place your order directly through their website or search through their entire season's Lookbook then call for availability when you find something you like. They'll be delighted to help you choose the essential pieces for each season.

Site Usability:	★★★★★	Based:	UK
Product Range:	★★★★	Express Delivery Option? (UK)	Yes
Price Range:	Luxury	Gift Wrapping Option?	Yes
Delivery Area:	Worldwide	Returns Procedure:	Down to you

www.mytheresa.com

Be sure to click on the English version here unless your German is exceptionally good as that's where this online boutique is based. The talent list here is exceptional with designers such as Anna Sui, Catherine Malandrino, Christian Louboutin, Dolce & Gabanna, Temperley, McQueen and Vera Wang being just a small example. Prices are all in Euros and are totally at the designer end of the spectrum but the choice of clothes, bags, shoes and other accessories is wonderful. Now would my bank manager still speak to me if I bought those Dolce shoes? No, didn't think so.

Site Usability:	★★★★★	Based:	Germany
Product Range:	★★★★★	Express Delivery Option? (UK)	Yes but Germany only
Price Range:	Luxury	Gift Wrapping Option?	Yes
Delivery Area:	Worldwide	Returns Procedure:	Free within 14 days of delivery and contact them first

www.net-a-porter.com

This is the uber fashionista's website, where you'll find the most impressive range of designer clothes and accessories available online and a retailer that's becoming increasingly well known for its clever buying, excellent service and attractive packaging. So if you're looking for something special with a designer label, such as Marc Jacobs, Alexander McQueen, Burberry, Roland Mouret, Alberta Feretti, Marni, Jimmy Choo or Paul Smith (the list goes on and on) you should definitely have a look here.

Site Usability:	★★★★★	Based:	UK
Product Range:	★★★★★	Express Delivery Option? (UK)	Yes
Price Range:	Luxury	Gift Wrapping Option?	Yes
Delivery Area:	Worldwide	Returns Procedure:	Free using their DHL service

www.paulsmith.co.uk

One of the most successful and internationally well known British designers, with several collections including Paul Smith Black, Jeans and fragrance his website is, as you would probably expect, different and idiosyncratic. Here you'll find a selection of his jeans, shoes, knitwear, t-shirts, and accessories plus a small amount of tailoring, and there are several clear views of each item. This is also a great place for gifts for Paul Smith fans.

Site Usability:	★★★★★	Based:	UK
Product Range:	★★★★	Express Delivery Option? (UK)	Yes
Price Range:	Luxury/Medium	Gift Wrapping Option?	Yes
Delivery Area:	worldwide	Returns Procedure:	Down to you

www.pollyanna.com

Here's one of the longest established fashion retailers in the UK with a premium list of designers for men and women including Comme des Garcons, Issey Miyake, Junya Watanabe and Johji Yamamoto plus Jill Sander and Lanvin. Shop on their modern, clean website and choose where to go by designer, garment type or season. This is very much a premium priced fashion forward fix but if these designers are for you you'll be delighted to find them online.

Site Usability:	★★★★	Based:	UK
Product Range:	★★★★	Express Delivery Option? (UK)	No
Price Range:	Luxury/Medium	Gift Wrapping Option?	No
Delivery Area:	worldwide	Returns Procedure:	Within one week of delivery and contact them first

www.room7.co.uk

Room 7 offers you the opportunity of shopping from collection by designers such as Chloe, Goat, Juicy Couture, Marni, and Alexander McQueen. It's a modern, quite starkly designed website with clear clean pictures and different garment views and you're able to see immediately if what you want to buy is available or not. New designers are being added all the time so if this is your style you'll need to check back regularly.

Site Usability:	★★★★	Based:	UK
Product Range:	★★★★	Express Delivery Option? (UK)	No
Price Range:	Luxury/Medium	Gift Wrapping Option?	No
Delivery Area:	Worldwide	Returns Procedure:	Within 7 days of delivery and after you've contacted them

www.shoptommy.co.uk

There's an excellent selection of modern daywear and accessories available from the Tommy Hilfiger website, from cashmere/cotton cable knitwear, jeans and winter jackets and coats to bags and wallets, snow boots and shoes and chic skiwear. There's also a gift section and the option of gift boxing for all items offered. This is a really easy website to shop from and a must to have a look at if you want to add some new casualwear to your wardrobe now.

Site Usability:	★★★★★	Based:	UK
Product Range:	★★★★	Express Delivery Option? (UK)	No
Price Range:	Medium	Gift Wrapping Option?	Yes
Delivery Area:	Worldwide	Returns Procedure:	Down to you

www.temperleylondon.com

There's no doubt that within a very short space of time Alice Temperley has become well known throughout the fashion world for her totally desirable dresses and separates, including her fabulous collection of evening dresses. Although you can only view her clothing online (and I don't expect this to change in the near future) you can buy her accessories, including handbags, gloves, belts and scarves. It's a small collection at present, but one that is bound to grow.

Site Usability:	★★★★★	Based:	UK
Product Range:	★★★	Express Delivery Option? (UK)	Yes
Price Range:	Luxury	Gift Wrapping Option?	No
Delivery Area:	Worldwide	Returns Procedure:	Down to you

www.zenggi.com

Keep your credit cards firmly locked away when you start to look at this Netherlands based website as the temptation levels are extremely high. Zenggi is a new online luxury clothing and accessories store offering a chic, high quality, covetable range. When you click on an item you can see a stylish model pic plus your chosen piece and how to accessorise it. Gift packaging is standard.

Site Usability:	★★★★★	Based:	Netherlands
Product Range:	★★★★	Express Delivery Option? (UK)	No
Price Range:	Luxury	Gift Wrapping Option?	Yes
Delivery Area:	EU	Returns Procedure:	Down to you

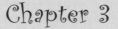

Chapter 3

The Knitwear Store

Do this one just for me: the next time you're out shopping (did I say 'out' shopping?) see if you can find anything quite like the range of knitwear on offer here, at anything like these prices. I'll be astounded if you can.

Most of the yarns used here – particularly cashmere – do not come from Scotland as they used to but from Asia. This has really brought the price down and we're definitely the ones to benefit. You will find Scottish cashmere on some of the websites below and you'll note that the price goes up accordingly. You will also be buying a higher quality product, so the choice is yours; however, as I haven't listed any websites offering really cheap and cheerful cashmere (sorry, you'll have to find those for yourselves) you're safe to pick and choose from the traditional to modern styles in a huge range of colours.

Just one more thing – many of the fashion retailers listed above under Modern Fashion Retailers and Mail Order Specialists also offer excellent knitwear so take a look there too.

Sites to Visit

www.anonymousclothing.com

Knitwear? Underwear? Clothing? I'm not really certain where this collection belongs for sure, so as the way I think of it is as those fine knit, lace trimmed tops, camis and cardis I thought you could read about it here. The name has now changed to Ross and Bute (the designers) for Anonymous and you're bound to have seen them; in a range of sometimes quite unusual colours and with pointelle details and different shaped necklines. Now you can buy all of these online plus the new selection of tunics and dresses.

Site Usability:	★★★★	Based:	UK
Product Range:	★★★	Express Delivery Option? (UK)	Yes
Price Range:	Medium	Gift Wrapping Option?	Yes
Delivery Area:	Worldwide	Returns Procedure:	Email first for returns code then down to you

www.belindarobertson.com

Award winning Belinda Dickson is a knitwear designer whose international reputation for quality, colour and modern eclectic style has earned her the affectionate title of 'Queen of Cashmere'. On her website you'll find her two different labels, the White Label collection, offering affordable but beautifully designed cashmere and her signature 'Cashmere Couture' range of the finest cashmere made exclusively in Scotland and sparkling with Swarovski crystals and satin trims, all available in a wide range of colours.

Site Usability:	★★★★	Based:	UK
Product Range:	★★★★	Express Delivery Option? (UK)	Yes
Price Range:	Luxury/Medium	Gift Wrapping Option?	Yes
Delivery Area:	Worldwide	Returns Procedure:	Down to you

www.brora.co.uk

Brora was established in 1992 with the aim of offering classic fine quality Scottish cashmere with a contemporary twist, with prices that offer real value for money. Although they are not the cheapest they offer some of the best quality available and in designs and a selection of colours that you won't find anywhere else. The pictures are beautifully clear and you'll find them hard to resist. The collection extends to men, children and babies.

Site Usability:	★★★★★	Based:	UK
Product Range:	★★★★	Express Delivery Option? (UK)	Yes
Price Range:	Luxury/Medium	Gift Wrapping Option?	Yes
Delivery Area:	Worldwide	Returns Procedure:	Down to you

www.cashmere.co.uk

Purely Cashmere is one of Scotland's longest standing online cashmere retailers. They offer very high quality single, two and three ply knits for men and women in a good range of colours and there's a combination of truly classic designs and modern styles plus some luxurious throws for the home. They also sell cashmere care products such as Cashmere Wash and clear zipped bags for storing and travelling.

Site Usability:	★★★★	Based:	UK
Product Range:	★★★	Express Delivery Option? (UK)	Yes if an item is in stock
Price Range:	Luxury/Medium	Gift Wrapping Option?	No
Delivery Area:	Worldwide	Returns Procedure:	Down to you

www.claireid.com

A site with a really different, fun and quirky feel offering modern pure cotton knitwear in unusual styles and a good range of colours. There's also a made-to-measure service offered plus a colour advisory service. Some of the pictures are at strange angles, which makes it hard to see the products clearly but everything is designed to be easy to wear and sizing goes from 8 to 24 so whatever your size or shape (or if you're expecting) you may well find something.

Site Usability:	★★★★	Based:	UK
Product Range:	★★★	Express Delivery Option? (UK)	No
Price Range:	Medium	Gift Wrapping Option?	No
Delivery Area:	Worldwide	Returns Procedure:	Down to you

www.crumpetengland.com

Crumpet offers a small range of quite expensive but very beautiful and modern cashmere, ranging from fine almost lingerie inspired pieces to chunky knits. Most items are available in a range of new season's colours and all are very beautifully photographed. There are plenty of places to find your everyday cashmere classics: here you'll find something special and different so take a look.

Site Usability:	★★★★	Based:	UK
Product Range:	★★★	Express Delivery Option? (UK)	No
Price Range:	Luxury/Medium	Gift Wrapping Option?	No
Delivery Area:	Worldwide	Returns Procedure:	Down to you

www.designsoncashmere.com

This company is based in Edinburgh and offers real Scottish cashmere - mostly two ply - so the prices will be more than on some other websites offering single ply cashmere sourced overseas. The styles are mostly classic and the range of colours isn't huge but if you want your cashmere to come from Scotland this could be the place to buy. They'll ship to you all over the world, shipping is free (worldwide) and they offer a currency converter if you're ordering from overseas.

Site Usability:	★★★★	Based:	UK
Product Range:	★★★	Express Delivery Option? (UK)	No but worldwide delivery is free
Price Range:	Luxury/Medium	Gift Wrapping Option?	No
Delivery Area:	Worldwide	Returns Procedure:	Down to you

www.ejk.biz

If you're looking to invest in a new piece of cashmere but want something slightly different then here's the place to look, where Emma Jane Knight's collection is uniquely detailed, high quality (and high end priced) with cashmere sweaters, wraps and jackets in a very good range of colours. You need to download and fill in their order form or call them to order. The styling is really lovely and unusual and the quality quite exceptional so take a good look.

Site Usability:	★★★★	Based:	UK
Product Range:	★★★	Express Delivery Option? (UK)	No
Price Range:	Luxury	Gift Wrapping Option?	No
Delivery Area:	Worldwide	Returns Procedure:	Down to you

www.eric-bompard.com

French knitwear retailer Eric Bompard offers a really pretty and unusual collection with chic styling and some different colours. Remember to click for the English version in the bottom right hand corner unless your French is very good. They have some very attractive designs in a wide range of colours that you won't find anywhere else so do have a look here. They'll ship to anywhere in the EU and you need to allow 6-8 days for delivery.

Site Usability:	★★★★★	Based:	France
Product Range:	★★★★	Express Delivery Option? (UK)	No
Price Range:	Medium	Gift Wrapping Option?	No
Delivery Area:	EU	Returns Procedure:	Down to you

www.johnsmedley.com

John Smedley is a family owned business originally established in 1784 and specialises in the highest quality fine gauge knitwear. It's definitely expensive but unbeatable for quality and fit and whether you want a simple shell to wear underneath a jacket or a modern cut fine merino cableknit top with the perfect neckline and three quarter sleeves it's better to buy just one piece from here than several cheaper versions. Buy two if you can. You really won't regret it.

Site Usability:	★★★★	Based:	UK
Product Range:	★★★	Express Delivery Option? (UK)	No
Price Range:	Luxury/Medium	Gift Wrapping Option?	No
Delivery Area:	Worldwide	Returns Procedure:	Down to you

www.purecollection.com

This is chic, high quality cashmere in a wide range of styles with the emphasis on modern shapes and new season's colours. Alongside their less expensive range they also offer 'Superfine' cashmere at a higher price which is perfect for layering or wearing on its own. The delivery and service are excellent and the prices are very good too. If you want something particular in a hurry, call to make sure it's in stock and you can have it the next day.

Site Usability:	★★★★★	Based:	UK
Product Range:	★★★★	Express Delivery Option? (UK)	Yes
Price Range:	Luxury/Medium	Gift Wrapping Option?	Yes
Delivery Area:	Worldwide	Returns Procedure:	Free

www.isla.uk.com

Isla was set up to provide high quality cashmere accessories primarily in vibrant colours, using Scottish yarn and production techniques. This is not a big collection, but a small lovely choice of scarves and knitted pashminas, mittens (for girls) and beanies (guys) available in colours such as viola, midnight blue, shocking pink and turquoise plus naturals black, white, grey and oatmeal.

Site Usability:	★★★★	Based:	UK
Product Range:	★★★	Express Delivery Option? (UK)	No
Price Range:	Medium	Gift Wrapping Option?	No
Delivery Area:	UK and USA	Returns Procedure:	Down to you

www.spiritoftheandes.co.uk

Spirit of the Andes offers a very good selection of fitted and chunky knitwear in Pima cotton and the finest baby alpaca yarn. The styling and photography are very classic so this is not the place if you're looking for something with a modern twist, however the quality is high and there's an excellent choice of colours. Sizing is from small to extra large.

Site Usability:	★★★★	Based:	UK
Product Range:	★★★	Express Delivery Option? (UK)	No
Price Range:	Medium	Gift Wrapping Option?	No
Delivery Area:	Worldwide	Returns Procedure:	Free

Chapter 4

Tall and Plus Sizes

Although you'll find larger sizes at some of the retailers listed in previous chapterss, these are the places that specialise and have sized up their garments properly. Too often what you're getting is something that's just the same but ... larger, when what you really need is a new pattern with a totally different set of measurements.

Having said that, surprisingly, there are still only a few very good websites offering clothes in larger sizes and hopefully that will change (I seem to have said that before but I don't think anyone was listening). It *should* change so watch this space.

Sites to Visit

www.cinnamonfashion.co.uk

Cinnamon specialises in clothing for sizes 16-34 and stocks casual wear, tailoring and occasion-wear plus sportswear and swimwear. You'll find lots of continental brands such as Chalou, Melli Mel, Doris Streich, Yoek, Samoon and BS Casuals plus designers such as Kirsten Krog and Charles and Patricia Leicester. They're happy if you call them for advice on what works with what and will deliver to you anywhere in the world. Contact them to request express delivery.

Site Usability:	★★★★	Based:	UK
Product Range:	★★★	Express Delivery Option? (UK)	Yes
Price Range:	Medium	Gift Wrapping Option?	No
Delivery Area:	Worldwide	Returns Procedure:	Down to you

www.grayandosbourn.co.uk

This is an excellent selection of designer separates from labels such as Basler and Gerry Weber plus their own well priced Gray and Osbourn range. Most items are available in sizes 12 to 22 and some go up to 26. The range is essentially classic but in tune with each season and you can dress here from holiday/cruise, country weekends, smart tailoring, tops and accessories to really chic eveningwear. Delivery is by courier within 7-10 days and UK and Channel Islands only.

Site Usability:	★★★★★	Based:	UK
Product Range:	★★★★	Express Delivery Option? (UK)	No
Price Range:	Luxury/Medium	Gift Wrapping Option?	No
Delivery Area:	UK	Returns Procedure:	Down to you

www.longtallsally.co.uk

As someone who's always been quite a bit shorter than I'd really like to be, when I click onto this modern, stylish website I always wish that they offered clothes I could wear as well (foolish, I know, but there it is). Here you'll find a range of clothes for women over 5ft 7in from casual to smart and everything in between, also swimwear, maternity wear, shoes and accessories. Everything is beautifully photographed; they'll ship worldwide and offer an express service in the UK.

Site Usability:	★★★★	Based:	UK
Product Range:	★★★★	Express Delivery Option? (UK)	Yes
Price Range:	Medium	Gift Wrapping Option?	No
Delivery Area:	Worldwide	Returns Procedure:	Freepost or return to store but complicated

www.pennyplain.co.uk

Penny Plain (who you've probably already heard of), have a very good, clear website, where you can order their clothes which go from size 10 to size 26. The collection of separates, dresses and eveningwear is essentially classic and combines pretty fabrics with reasonable (although definitely not cheap) prices. There's a small range of attractive shoes as well.

Site Usability:	★★★★★	Based:	UK
Product Range:	★★★★	Express Delivery Option? (UK)	Yes but expensive
Price Range:	Medium	Gift Wrapping Option?	No
Delivery Area:	Worldwide	Returns Procedure:	Down to you

www.rowlandsclothing.co.uk

The first Rowlands shop opened in Bath in 1983 with the aim of providing a range of high quality, reasonably priced, smart casual classic country clothing. From their successful mail order catalogue they've now put their collection online with a simple, easy-to-use website offering smart coats and jackets, dresses and a selection of separates from day to evening. Sizing is 10 to 22 (24 for some items). They aim to deliver within 7–10 days.

Site Usability:	★★★★	Based:	UK
Product Range:	★★★★	Express Delivery Option? (UK)	No
Price Range:	Medium	Gift Wrapping Option?	No
Delivery Area:	UK	Returns Procedure:	Down to you

www.silhouettes.com

Silhouettes is an excellent, US-based fashion retailer who offers its collections in sizes 14 to 38 (UK equivalent 16/18 to 40/42). To make sure you order the correct size you need to use their size chart which gives everything in inches. You'll find smart separates, tailoring, dresses and outerwear. Because you'll be ordering from the US I suggest that you don't go for anything too fitted.

Site Usability:	★★★★	Based:	US
Product Range:	★★★★	Express Delivery Option? (UK)	Yes, Worldwide
Price Range:	Medium	Gift Wrapping Option?	No
Delivery Area:	Worldwide	Returns Procedure:	Down to you

www.spirito.co.uk

This is the top end of the online plus size clothing ranges offering a very high quality selection in sizes 10-20 including smart daywear, knitwear, casualwear and evening wear. Everything is beautifully made in Italy and smartly photographed to make you really want to buy, as you would expect from Artigiano's sister company. Shoes, accessories and jewellery are from the main Artigiano ranges and footwear goes up to a size 9.

Site Usability:	★★★★★	Based:	UK
Product Range:	★★★★	Express Delivery Option? (UK)	Yes
Price Range:	Medium	Gift Wrapping Option?	Yes on some items
Delivery Area:	Worldwide	Returns Procedure:	Free with Royal Mail

Also visit these websites for Tall and Plus Size Clothing:

Website address	You'll find it in
www.dorothyperkins.co.uk	Chapter 1: Fashion Online/The High Street
www.principles.co.uk	Chapter 1: Fashion Online/The High Street
www.wallis-fashion.com	Chapter 1: Fashion Online/The High Street
www.llbean.com	Chapter 5: Shop America
www.eddiebaur.com	Chapter 5: Shop America
www.claireid.com	Chapter 3: The Knitwear Store

Chapter 5

Shop America

There's no doubt that the US is way ahead of the UK in terms of their retailers going online. No, forget I said that, just about ALL major US retailers are online and have been for a while, and most superbrand designers are also willing and able to ship to anywhere - in the States (and sometimes Hawaii, thank you very much).

What many of them won't do is ship to you here and, bearing in mind the size of the US market, that's unlikely to change. Having said that, there are a few great brands and stores that you can buy from, such as Abercrombie and Fitch, American Eagle and, for most products they offer, Neiman Marcus, although you have to phone or fax to order.

When they do ship over here the service is almost unbelievably fast, using 3-5 day UPS or FedEx and is amazingly reliable. Hope that Banana Republic will change its mind soon and go back to shipping to the UK - they used to, and then they stopped, how unfair is that?

Just a word of advice. If you're not sure about the size you're ordering, go up. You're much less likely to have to send back something if it's slightly too big than if it's too small.

For clothing size conversions, US clothes are usually one but can sometimes be two sizes down from the UK. So a US 8 will be a UK 10 or 12. The only way to be sure about clothing measurements is to look at the size guides, measure yourself and then allow a bit. Here are the US/UK/Europe sizing conversions for reference.

Women's clothing size conversions

US	UK	France	Germany	Italy
6	8	36	34	40
8	10	38	36	42
10	12	40	38	44
12	14	42	40	46
14	16	44	42	48
16	18	46	44	50
18	20	50	46	52

Women's shoe size conversions

UK	3.5	4	4.5	5	5.5	6	6.5	7	7.5	8	8.5
EU	36.5	37	37.5	38	38.5	39	40	41	42	43	43.5
US		6	6.5	7	7.5	8	8.5	9	9.5	10	10.5	11

Men's shoe size conversions

UK	7	7.5	8	8.5	9	9.5	10	10.5	11	11.5	12
EU	40.5	41	42	42.5	43	44	44.5	45	46	46.5	47
US	7.5	8	8.5	9	9.5	10	10.5	11	11.5	12	12.5

Sites to Visit

www.uk.abercrombie.com

This is where the young chic American denim brigade shop for their jeans, jackets and tees and now you can buy direct from their UK-based website with all prices shown in pounds and duty included. The style is very 'Casual Luxury' and they even call it that. Take a look around if you can tear yourself away from the outstanding photographs of the most beautiful models (mostly men). Sizing is SMALL particularly for fitted items so, if in any doubt, go up a size. Of course you can now shop in their Savile Row, London, store but if you can't get there ...

Site Usability:	★★★★★	Based:	US
Product Range:	★★★★	Express Delivery Option? (UK)	No
Price Range:	Medium	Gift Wrapping Option?	No
Delivery Area:	Worldwide	Returns Procedure:	Down to you

www.ae.com

Not as expensive as Abercrombie (and not quite so well known, particularly over here), American Eagle offers a wide selection of colourful, young, modern, casual clothing extremely popular across the pond and I wish they were just down the road here, too. Think preppy striped shirts, humorous and sporty t-shirts and great jeans, hoodies and jackets plus some camis and underwear and a good range of shoes. Thankfully they have no problem in shipping to you anywhere in the world using USPS Global Express Mail.

Site Usability:	★★★★★	Based:	US
Product Range:	★★★★	Express Delivery Option? (UK)	No
Price Range:	Medium/Very Good Value	Gift Wrapping Option?	No
Delivery Area:	Worldwide	Returns Procedure:	Down to you

www.brooksbrothers.com

Here you'll find quite expensive, beautifully made classic clothes for both men and women and they have no problem shipping to you anywhere in the world. The quality really is excellent and for a perfect classic cardigan or pair of trousers you'll be hard put to find anywhere better, particularly if you've tried them and know their look. The website is beautifully photographed, easy to navigate and delivery is speedy.

Site Usability:	★★★★★	Based:	US
Product Range:	★★★★★	Express Delivery Option? (UK)	No
Price Range:	Luxury/Medium	Gift Wrapping Option?	No
Delivery Area:	Worldwide	Returns Procedure:	Down to you

www.eddiebaur.com

Eddie Baur is one of those American companies who show how it really should be done. It's attractive to look at, easy to get round, offers great products, good prices (not cheap but good value) and they'll ship to you anywhere in the world. No wonder Vogue US picks some of their products as the 'must haves' of the season. From clothing, to swimwear, performance walking boots, accessories and some very, very good sporting luggage you won't go wrong here.

Site Usability:	★★★★★	Based:	US
Product Range:	★★★★★	Express Delivery Option? (UK)	No
Price Range:	Medium/Very Good Value	Gift Wrapping Option?	No
Delivery Area:	Worldwide	Returns Procedure:	Down to you

www.goclothing.com

You have been warned. There's so much to look at on this website that it takes a while to load and yes, they do ship internationally. You'll almost certainly discover something you like, from C & C California t-shirts to funky belts and bags and a whole host of clothing labels including allen b jeans, Tracy Reese, Catherine Malandrino, Lilly Pulitzer and a lot you'll probably never have heard of.

Site Usability:	★★★★	Based:	US
Product Range:	★★★★★	Express Delivery Option? (UK)	No
Price Range:	Luxury/Medium	Gift Wrapping Option?	yes
Delivery Area:	Worldwide	Returns Procedure:	Down to you

www.grahamkandiah.com

If you're going anywhere hot in the near future you have to take a look at this website now, where you can choose from the most attractive sarongs, kaftans, wraps and bikinis plus t-shirts and totes, all in a wonderful treasure trove of fabrics with names such as Tiger, Riviera, South Beach, Jungle, Havana and Bahia. Yes the retailer is based in the US, but it's quick and easy to order and they'll deliver to you anywhere in the world.

Site Usability:	★★★★	Based:	US
Product Range:	★★★	Express Delivery Option? (UK)	No
Price Range:	Medium	Gift Wrapping Option?	Yes
Delivery Area:	Worldwide	Returns Procedure:	Down to you

www.llbean.com

You'll be hard put to see a more comprehensive collection of very well priced, quality clothing including outerwear, fleece, shirts, trousers and snow sport clothing, luggage, outdoor gear, swimwear, footwear and accessories. They're particularly good for their cold weather shirts which are extremely reasonable. Have a browse. It's hard to get away without buying something.

Site Usability:	★★★★★	Based:	US
Product Range:	★★★★★	Express Delivery Option? (UK)	No
Price Range:	Medium/Very Good Value	Gift Wrapping Option?	No
Delivery Area:	Worldwide	Returns Procedure:	Down to you

www.neimanmarcus.com

Every designer from YSL to Marc Jacobs and accessories from Manolo Blahnik to Tods is offered at this top level US store with a brilliantly laid out website showing beautiful modern pictures of absolutely everything. The downside is you'll have to pay duty on top of the designer prices (if you're not based in the US) but it's worth having a look at some of the American designers and well worth checking out the trends from season to season. If you want to place an international order you need to call them on 1 888 888 4757.

Site Usability:	★★★★★	Based:	US
Product Range:	★★★★★	Express Delivery Option? (UK)	No
Price Range:	Luxury/Medium	Gift Wrapping Option?	Yes
Delivery Area:	Worldwide	Returns Procedure:	Down to you

www.shopbop.com

Here is just about the full collection from Juicy Couture, including the velour and cashmere collections, plus brands such as Diane von Furstenberg, Chip and Pepper, Marc by Marc Jacobs and Seven For All Mankind. Brands that you can find here but you really have to look for them. They offer standard UPS delivery plus the worldwide express service which will only take 2–3 days.

Site Usability:	★★★★★	Based	USA
Product Range:	★★★★★	Express Delivery Option? (UK)	No
Price Range:	Luxury/Medium	Gift Wrapping Option?	No
Delivery Area:	Worldwide	Returns Procedure:	Down to you

www.sillysports.co.uk

Now you can buy your Abercrombie and Fitch t-shirts and American Eagle shorts from one online retailer and, despite the fact that they're based in Florida, they say that you shouldn't be charged duty and all prices here are in sterling. Brands on offer are the aforesaid Abercrombie and American Eagle, Converse, Hollister (A & F again), K-Swiss and Timberland.

Site Usability:	★★★★	Based	USA
Product Range:	★★★★	Express Delivery Option? (UK)	No
Price Range:	Medium	Gift Wrapping Option?	No
Delivery Area:	Worldwide	Returns Procedure:	Down to you

www.sundancecatalog.com

Inspired (and initiated) by Robert Redford, Sundance is a truly American catalogue which has now become a worldwide online store. You'll discover wonderful jewellery by American craftsmen, a wide range of high quality, classic American clothing – including shirts, tops, ts, skirts and trousers, ranch style boots, home accessories (gorgeous quilts and throws) and lots of ideas for gifts.

Site Usability:	★★★★★	Based	USA
Product Range:	★★★★★	Express Delivery Option? (UK)	No
Price Range:	Luxury/Medium	Gift Wrapping Option?	Yes
Delivery Area:	Worldwide	Returns Procedure:	Down to you

www.swimwearboutique.com

This is a really excellent swimwear boutique offering great labels such as Gottex and Gideon Oberson which for some reason are hard to buy here. When you're placing your order you'll notice that one of the clever features of the site is the 'availability' box which shows up as soon as you've chosen your style, size and colour and tells you when you can have your order. They offer quick worldwide delivery but you'll have to pay duty if you're outside the US.

Site Usability:	★★★★★	Based:	US
Product Range:	★★★★	Express Delivery Option? (UK)	No
Price Range:	Medium	Gift Wrapping Option?	No
Delivery Area:	Worldwide	Returns Procedure:	Down to you

www.travelsmith.com

This US-based website must be the ultimate online travel clothing store. They offer a really comprehensive and well priced range of travel clothing and accessories for men and women, from outerwear including washable suede, tailoring and safari jackets to easy care separates, hats, swimwear and luggage. You can't place your order directly online for international delivery but you can fax it to them at 001 415-884-1351 and they'll send it to you anywhere in the world.

Site Usability:	★★★★★	Based:	US
Product Range:	★★★★★	Express Delivery Option? (UK)	No
Price Range:	Medium	Gift Wrapping Option?	No
Delivery Area:	Worldwide	Returns Procedure:	Down to you

www.trunkltd.com

For t-shirt addicts only. This funky US-based websites sells collectible t-shirts, camis and jackets emblazoned with classic rock and roll art – think the Beatles, Alice Cooper, Blondie, Frank Zappa, Fleetwood Mac and Janis Joplin. Be careful before you get too excited, some of these, embellished with Swarovski crystals, are definitely collector's items with steep prices to match. They'll deliver to you anywhere in the world.

Site Usability:	★★★★	Based	US
Product Range:	★★★★	Express Delivery Option? (UK)	No
Price Range:	Luxury/Medium	Gift Wrapping Option?	No
Delivery Area:	Worldwide	Returns Procedure:	Down to you

www.victoriassecret.com

The US-based, mail-order lingerie company that uses world famous models. Seductive pictures of bronzed beauties don't detract from the fact that here is quite possibly the best selection of lingerie in the world and with such good prices you'll probably want to buy here. When you consider the size of the American market it's not surprising that they're so good and it's even better that you can order from anywhere in the world.

Site Usability:	★★★★★	Based:	US
Product Range:	★★★★★	Express Delivery Option? (UK)	No
Price Range:	Very Good Value	Gift Wrapping Option?	Yes
Delivery Area:	Worldwide	Returns Procedure:	Down to you

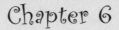

Chapter 6

Sportswear to Look Great In

Some people do look wonderful in sportswear – you know, those little zip up jackets, bare midriffs and pull on trousers; my daughter's one of them. I'm not, unfortunately, so sportswear to me is my unbelievably comfortable Puma Mostros, stretch clothes for the gym when I do go, (which is usually in a panic before going skiing), and the most flattering skiwear that I can find – but no more of that because you won't find that here but in the Sport and Leisure section.

What you will find is an excellent selection of all types of sportswear, including retailers such as Jack Wills and Joules who essentially offer casualwear for the horsy set but also some wonderful fleece and polo shirts; Crew Clothing – like the two I've mentioned before but for sailors, and Wildlife Online which is nothing like its name but has a range from brands such as Armor Lux, Camper, Dockers and Musto

So, couch potato or not, looking great in it or not, here's some really good sportswear, to go to the gym in, do yoga or Pilates in, or just to curl up in in front of the TV. Some of it is extremely stylish and expensive and some very reasonably priced. You can also find very good discounts on sports footwear by major brands such as Nike and Adidas.

Feel like a run, anyone??

Sites to Visit

www.adidas-shop.co.uk

Up until now you've had to go to a general sports store to find Adidas footwear and clothing. Now with this new, modern designed website you can look at everything in one place – but, much better than that, you can also read up on all the latest sports innovations from this famous brand. There's sports clothing and footwear for men, women and kids plus the 'Adidas by Stella McCartney' line.

Site Usability:	★★★★★	Based:	UK
Product Range:	★★★★	Express Delivery Option? (UK)	Yes
Price Range:	Medium	Gift Wrapping Option?	No
Delivery Area:	UK	Returns Procedure:	Down to you

www.asquith.ltd.uk

If you haven't yet given up on your New Year's resolution of getting fitter, or you want something to stimulate you into getting on with it, then have a look here. Asquith offer an unusual collection of clothes for yoga, Pilates (and, yes, lounging around in) in a lovely selection of colours including candy, coral, aqua and dewberry, including wrap tops, capri pants, camisoles and t-shirts. There's excellent information about each item, from what it's made of, to sizing and washing instructions.

Site Usability:	★★★★	Based:	UK
Product Range:	★★★	Express Delivery Option? (UK)	Yes
Price Range:	Medium	Gift Wrapping Option?	No
Delivery Area:	Worldwide	Returns Procedure:	Down to you

www.elliegray.com

This is an excellent sportswear destination, whether you're looking for exercise clothes for the gym or just for relaxing in. Offering brands USA Pro, Pure Lime, Deha and their own, you'll find a selection of hoodies and jackets, sweatshirts, pants, outerwear, sports bras and accessories in a good range of colours and styles. Everything is easy to see and described in detail and, even better, you can immediately see what's in stock.

Site Usability:	★★★★★	Based:	UK
Product Range:	★★★	Express Delivery Option? (UK)	Yes
Price Range:	Medium	Gift Wrapping Option?	No
Delivery Area:	Worldwide	Returns Procedure:	Down to you

www.jackwills.co.uk

If you're missing your Abercrombie/American Eagle fix this year you should take a look at this website, offering 'cool' and idiosyncratic sportswear including jeans, hoodies, fun, printed t-shirts, polo shirts and accessories for girls and guys. Annoyingly you can't find the delivery details until you start to place an order, however this is a well laid out site with clear product pictures so take a look.

Site Usability:	★★★★	Based:	UK
Product Range:	★★★	Express Delivery Option? (UK)	Yes
Price Range:	Medium/Very Good Value	Gift Wrapping Option?	No
Delivery Area:	Worldwide	Returns Procedure:	Use their returns service

www.jdsports.co.uk

As one of the largest UK sports retailers there is, unsurprisingly, a huge range of sports shoes on this website including Nike, Puma, Reebok, Lacoste and Adidas. Their clothing ranges are also extensive and taken from the same brands and the ordering system is extremely easy to use. With each pair of shoes (or each item of clothing) they show you other items to go with. They aim to make delivery within five working days of receipt of your order.

Site Usability:	★★★★★	Express Delivery Option? (UK)	No
Product Range:	★★★★	Gift Wrapping Option?	No
Price Range:	Medium	Returns Procedure:	Down to you
Delivery Area:	UK		

www.joulesclothing.com

Joules is a clothing website with a difference; beautifully photographed and well laid out and there are some excellent fun sporty separates for just about everyone provided you like stripes and colours (although lots of items are available in black/jet as well). It's mainly aimed at the riding fraternity although many of their clothes, particularly the jackets and fleece, have a much wider appeal.

Site Usability:	★★★★	Express Delivery Option? (UK)	Yes – call them
Product Range:	★★★★	Gift Wrapping Option?	No
Price Range:	Medium	Returns Procedure:	Down to you
Delivery Area:	Worldwide		

www.nomadtravel.co.uk

The next time you feel like taking off on safari or into the jungle take a look at this website, which offers a good, highly edited range of efficient and well priced travel clothing including lightweight trousers, zip-offs and vented shirts, base layer fleece and thermals as well as lots of advice on travel health depending on where you're going with particular advice on malaria and also travelling with children. You can place your order to the EU online and elsewhere by contacting them and they offer 48 hour delivery in the UK

Site Usability:	★★★★★	Express Delivery Option? (UK)	48 hour service
Product Range:	★★★★	Gift Wrapping Option?	No
Price Range:	Medium	Returns Procedure:	Down to you
Delivery Area:	Worldwide		

www.puma.com

Puma have now launched their own website so they can offer pretty much their full range to you online. As a great fan of their unbelievably comfortable footwear (so comfortable I've become an addict) this is great news. Whereas on most sports websites you'll find just a small part of the range now you can choose from all the styles and all the colourways. Delivery is within 1–3 days unless you select Royal Mail Special Delivery, in which case you can have your order the day after you place it.

Site Usability:	★★★★★	Based:	UK
Product Range:	★★★★	Express Delivery Option? (UK)	Yes
Price Range:	Medium	Gift Wrapping Option?	No
Delivery Area:	EU most countries	Returns Procedure:	Down to you

www.quba.com

Aimed at the sailing enthusiast, Quba offer an attractive range of jackets, tops, trousers and skirts, for both men and women (skirts for the girls only, of course). If you're looking for casual summer gear this would be a good place to check out, as the shorts, trousers and tops look excellent although they're definitely not cheap. There's a good selection of beachbags and holdalls here as well.

Site Usability:	★★★★	Based:	UK
Product Range:	★★★	Express Delivery Option? (UK)	Yes
Price Range:	Luxury/Medium	Gift Wrapping Option?	No
Delivery Area:	Worldwide	Returns Procedure:	Down to you

www.sport-e.com

Part of Littlewoods Online, this is the place to find discounted sports shoes by Nike, Adidas, Puma, Reebok, Converse and Lacoste. Also sportswear, sports bras and sports equipment. There's a good selection, delivery is free if you spend over £100, and returns are free as well – so if you really don't want to spend too much but you still like to have that 'designer' look you may well find your answer here.

Site Usability:	★★★★★	Based:	UK
Product Range:	★★★★	Express Delivery Option? (UK)	No
Price Range:	Medium/Very Good Value	Gift Wrapping Option?	No
Delivery Area:	UK	Returns Procedure:	Free of charge

www.sheactive.co.uk

Here's a website just for women, covering sports such as fitness, cycling, rock climbing, skiing and swimming. They don't offer any products that are adaptations of men's sportswear and just go for the best that's been specifically designed for women. There's a very good choice, whether you're a dedicated sportswoman or just want the look. Brands include Puma, Adidas, Berghaus, Bolle, Helly Hanson and Salomon.

Site Usability:	★★★★★	Based:	UK
Product Range:	★★★★	Express Delivery Option? (UK)	Yes
Price Range:	Medium	Gift Wrapping Option?	No
Delivery Area:	Worldwide	Returns Procedure:	Free of charge

www.shoe-shop.com

Puma, Asics, Nike, Adidas and Reebok are just some of the many brands you can choose from, whatever your sport. If you're a lounge lizard and just want to look modern (and like being comfortable) you'll find all the latest styles here too. They do sell other types of shoes but their strength is definitely at the sporty end. Beware of wearing your sports shoes too much though, you'll never be happy in your killer heels again.

Site Usability:	★★★★★	Based	UK
Product Range:	★★★★★	Express Delivery Option? (UK)	No
Price Range:	Medium	Gift Wrapping Option?	No
Delivery Area:	Worldwide	Returns Procedure:	Down to you but select their good value returns paid option

www.sportswoman.co.uk

Don't visit this website unless you're feeling energetic (although it could push you in the right direction). Here you can see, beautifully photographed, the Casall range of sportswear, which includes basic activewear, tennis, running, yoga, Pilates and golf clothing plus underwear and accessories such as socks, water bottles and kit bags. In the exercise equipment and accessories section there are gym balls, ab rollers and gloves and more will be added soon.

Site Usability:	★★★★★	Based	UK
Product Range:	★★★★★	Express Delivery Option? (UK)	Yes
Price Range:	Medium	Gift Wrapping Option?	No
Delivery Area:	Worldwide	Returns Procedure:	Down to you

www.sweatybetty.com

Another website to get you going, where you can choose from an excellent and stylish range of clothes for the gym and for yoga, available in basic colours such as black, grey and pink. They also offer sleek (and minimal) beachwear, chic and well priced skiwear plus accessories such as leg and arm warmers and books on yoga. Postage is free on orders over £50 (UK) and they'll deliver worldwide.

Site Usability:	★★★★	Based	UK
Product Range:	★★★	Express Delivery Option? (UK)	No
Price Range:	Medium	Gift Wrapping Option?	No
Delivery Area:	Worldwide	Returns Procedure:	Down to you

www.travellinglight.co.uk

Order your hot weather travel clothing here at any time of the year. There's a very good range for men and women – particularly if you're planning to go trekking or on safari; plus smart/classic, easy-to-wear separates, tailoring and eveningwear. In their casualwear section there are shorts, bermudas and capri pants plus lots of tops and t-shirts. They also have accessories such as lightweight luggage, Bolle and Oakley sunglasses and sun hats.

Site Usability:	★★★★★	Based:	UK
Product Range:	★★★★	Express Delivery Option? (UK)	Yes
Price Range:	Medium	Gift Wrapping Option?	No
Delivery Area:	Worldwide	Returns Procedure:	Free of charge

www.wildlifeonline.com

Wildlife Clothing offer a range of leisurewear, footwear and accessories for people with active lifestyles, bringing together a selection of products from international brands such as Armor Lux from Brittany, Camper and Hispanitas footwear from Spain, Dockers, Merrell and Sebago from the United States, Oska from Germany, Kipling from Belgium and Joules, Jack Wills, Quayside, Orla Kiely, Musto and Seasalt from the UK. Allow 7-10 days for delivery although they aim to dispatch all items much faster.

Site Usability:	★★★★★	Based:	UK
Product Range:	★★★★	Express Delivery Option? (UK)	No
Price Range:	Luxury/Medium	Gift Wrapping Option?	Yes
Delivery Area:	Worldwide	Returns Procedure:	Down to you

www.whitestuff.com

This young, urban clothing company sells casual sporty lightweight gear in the summer months for guys and girls and trendy skiwear in the winter (hence the name). There are colour options for just about all the clothes, from the Flawless T to the Java Jive pant and you can see straight away what's available in stock or what you'll have to wait for. This isn't a huge collection but it's fun and well priced and definitely worth having a look at.

Site Usability:	★★★★	Based:	UK
Product Range:	★★★	Express Delivery Option? (UK)	Yes
Price Range:	Medium/Very Good Value	Gift Wrapping Option?	No
Delivery Area:	Worldwide	Returns Procedure:	Freepost or return to store

Also take a look at the following for Sportswear Online:

Website address   **You'll find it in**
www.figleaves.com   Chapter 7: Lingerie

Chapter 7

Lingerie

Whatever your choice of lingerie you'll find it here, and if that sounds glib it's not meant to be, it's just the truth. So if you want lacy – underwired or not – full cup or half, thong or briefs and see-through or not then, yes, you'll find them here on a range of sites – from Agent Provocateur's glam, sexy website to beautifully photographed (and glam and sexy) Figleaves where the choice is simply mind-blowing.

Ah yes, a word about Figleaves. Assuming you've heard of this mammoth collection of lingerie of all kinds, shapes and sizes; swimwear and cover-ups, sleepwear and men's underwear, you might be tempted to wonder why you would want to shop anywhere else. I can say this easily as I have purchased from Figleaves more times than I care to remember and they are truly a wonderful place to shop. However, do please take a look as well at the beautiful small lingerie boutiques listed here.

You will find some very different products on offer; really chic and minimalist underwear from CKU (my daughter's favourite), suggestive sexiness at Agent Provocateur, stylish camisoles and classic nightwear from Bella di Notte and gorgeous glam from Glamorous Amorous, just to mention a very few.

The real difference about shopping for lingerie online, apart from the obvious benefits of convenience and huge choice, is that you can search on most of these websites by size, thus eliminating that extremely annoying moment when you discover that the bra you've fallen in love with isn't available in your size. Forget about going to another store and searching, with growing frustration; you're almost certain to find it here.

And if, perchance, you're one of those lucky people whose significant other loves to buy beautiful lingerie for you, then you can just leave this book open at the appropriate page featuring *that* website offering *that* (glam and expensive) deep cocoa lace plunge bra – with your note of the style in the margin, of course – and then wait for that pretty, tissue wrapped package to arrive. Simple, really, don't you think?

Sites to Visit

www.agentprovocateur.com

Joseph Corre and Serena Rees opened the first Agent Provocateur shop in December 1994 and have never looked back. The look is overt and sexy and you'll find just that on their extremely unusual website, where their gorgeous lingerie is displayed with attitude on the most perfect bodies. Don't come here if you're looking for something in a size larger than a 36E or if you want a website where ordering is easy; it's not until you've got used to it. Do come here if you love their products and don't want to have to go out to find them.

Site Usability:	★★★	Based:	UK	
Product Range:	★★★★	Express Delivery Option? (UK)	Yes	
Price Range:	Luxury/Medium	Gift Wrapping Option?	No but packaging is very attractive	
Delivery Area:	Worldwide	Returns Procedure:	Down to you	

www.barenecessities.co.uk

An excellent site offering a range of lingerie and swimwear from brands such as Prima Donna, Marie Jo, Aubade, Lejaby, Felina, Gottex, Maryan, Fantasie/Freya, Seaspray and Anita. They keep all items in stock where possible and their size range is from A to H. They also offer mastectomy lingerie and swimwear and are excellent on service so give them a call if you want to ask them any questions

Site Usability:	★★★★	Based:	UK	
Product Range:	★★★★	Express Delivery Option? (UK)	Yes	
Price Range:	Medium	Gift Wrapping Option?	Yes	
Delivery Area:	Worldwide	Returns Procedure:	Down to you	

www.belladinotte.com

This is a very smiley website with very smiley models showing really pretty nightwear, lingerie and tops. Italian silk and wool (washable) blend tops come in modern colours such as chocolate, aubergine and (of course) black. Lingerie is by Chantelle and Lejaby and their range of wool and silk thermals, sleeveless, short sleeved and long sleeved, frequently trimmed in lace and in white, ivory, black and, on occasion, garnet could certainly be worn as tops.

Site Usability:	★★★★	Based:	UK	
Product Range:	★★★★	Express Delivery Option? (UK)	Yes	
Price Range:	Medium	Gift Wrapping Option?	Yes	
Delivery Area:	Worldwide	Returns Procedure:	Down to you	

www.bodas.co.uk

Much loved by glossy magazine fashion editors for its modern minimal style, at Bodas you won't find loads of lace or extra details but just chic, seam-free and form fitting lingerie with a choice of colours, beautifully photographed and including briefs, camisoles, vests, crop tops and a small range of swimwear in season. Just a word of warning, they don't really offer anything much beyond a 36D, so if you're looking for a larger size this is not the place for you.

Site Usability:	★★★★★	Based:	UK
Product Range:	★★★	Express Delivery Option? (UK)	Yes
Price Range:	Medium	Gift Wrapping Option?	No
Delivery Area:	Worldwide	Returns Procedure:	Down to you

www.bonsoirdirect.com

Here's very pretty nightwear from Bonsoir by Post, ranging from soft dreamy cotton to Italian lace and pure silk in a range of colours. Be warned though, if your taste is for black or neutral you won't find much of it here, but colours such as ash, heather, pale blue and white. There's also a small range of loungewear including yoga pants, fluffy towels and bath robes plus scented candles, mules, beaded slippers and bedsocks.

Site Usability:	★★★★★	Based:	UK
Product Range:	★★★★	Express Delivery Option? (UK)	Yes
Price Range:	Medium/Very Good Value	Gift Wrapping Option?	Yes
Delivery Area:	Worldwide	Returns Procedure:	Down to you

www.bravissimo.com

Bravissimo was started to fill the niche in the market created by those who aren't looking for lingerie or swimwear in minute sizes. They offer a wide selection of lingerie in D to JJ cup plus bra-sized swimwear in D to J cup making it the essential site for the fuller figure. You'll find strappy tops and sports bras and fitting advice as well. Their service is really excellent and if you have any queries you can email them and they'll come back to you immediately. They'll ship to you speedily anywhere.

Site Usability:	★★★★★	Based:	UK
Product Range:	★★★★	Express Delivery Option? (UK)	Yes but you need to call them
Price Range:	Medium	Gift Wrapping Option?	No
Delivery Area:	Worldwide	Returns Procedure:	Free

www.carmalondon.com

Carolina Maddox's Carma London online store offers a small and really attractive range of night and loungewear where the attention to detail – lace trims, pretty ribbons and top quality fabric – is what makes the collection special. You'll find cotton voile pjs and kaftans, super-lightweight hoodies and pretty polka-dot chemises, all available in sizes 8-16. If you're ordering from overseas you need to call or email them for a shipping quote.

Site Usability:	★★★★★	Based:	UK
Product Range:	★★★	Express Delivery Option? (UK)	No
Price Range:	Medium	Gift Wrapping Option?	Yes
Delivery Area:	Worldwide	Returns Procedure:	Down to you

www.contessa.org.uk

Contessa has a superb selection of bras and briefs in every colourway and style you can think of. You can choose by brand, style, size or colour or to make matters even easier just click on your size on the home page and everything that they have in stock can be viewed straight away. The

47

emphasis here is very much on price and they frequently have some excellent offers. They'll ship worldwide and gift-wrap your order as well.

Site Usability:	★★★★★	Based:	UK
Product Range:	★★★★	Express Delivery Option? (UK)	Yes
Price Range:	Medium/Very Good Value	Gift Wrapping Option?	Yes
Delivery Area:	Worldwide	Returns Procedure:	Down to you

www.cku.com

This is the website for Calvin Klein's modern, minimal range of underwear and I should tell you right now that if you're anything larger than a D (or in a very few styles a DD) cup you should move on fast. If you're within their size range you'll probably find the collection of beautiful, sexy and not over priced lingerie and basics quite irresistible. There are separate websites for overseas orders so you need to check if they deliver to you.

Site Usability:	★★★★★	Based:	UK
Product Range:	★★★	Express Delivery Option? (UK)	No
Price Range:	Medium	Gift Wrapping Option?	No
Delivery Area:	Worldwide using their country specific sites	Returns Procedure:	Free

www.elingerie.uk.net

This is a really calm, well photographed website that's easy to find your way round, offering brands such as Rigby and Peller, Chantelle, Janet Reger, Huit, Freya, Splendour, Panache and lots more. The products are all very easy to see, although I suggest you search for your size rather than pick on a range and find it's not available for you. There's also lots of help for men buying lingerie as gifts plus a giftwrap service.

Site Usability:	★★★★	Based:	UK
Product Range:	★★★★	Express Delivery Option? (UK)	No
Price Range:	Luxury/Medium	Gift Wrapping Option?	Yes
Delivery Area:	Worldwide	Returns Procedure:	Down to you

www.figleaves.com

If you can't find it here, you may well not be able to find it anywhere else as this is definitely one of the best collections of lingerie, swimwear and sportswear available online. Almost every lingerie brand name is offered, from DKNY, Dolce and Gabbana and Janet Reger to Sloggi, Gossard and Wonderbra and delivery is free throughout the world. All sizes are covered from the very small to the very large and there's a huge choice in just about every category.

Site Usability:	★★★★★	Based:	UK
Product Range:	★★★★★	Express Delivery Option? (UK)	Yes
Price Range:	Luxury/Medium/Very Good Value	Gift Wrapping Option?	Yes
Delivery Area:	Worldwide	Returns Procedure:	Free in the UK

www.fleurt.com

Fleur T is a unique lingerie design house offered in major stores throughout the world such as Barneys in New York and Galleries Lafayette in Paris. The difference here is that each season Fleur

T designs a new collection around a story to encapsulate the mood of that season, with names such as 'Stiletto', 'Kitten', 'Chocolat' and 'Cream Tea'. If you like lingerie that is feminine, quirky and sexy then you should take a look.

Site Usability:	★★★★★	Based:	UK
Product Range:	★★★	Express Delivery Option? (UK)	Yes
Price Range:	Luxury/Medium	Gift Wrapping Option?	Yes
Delivery Area:	Worldwide	Returns Procedure:	Down to you

www.glamonweb.co.uk

This is quite an unusual website with some slightly strange translations (probably due to the fact that they're electronic, rather than done by real people) offering lingerie, hosiery and nightwear by La Perla, Marvel and Malizia. Here's beautiful and luxurious lingerie as you would expect with prices to match and I would suggest that you make sure that you know your La Perla size before you order as the sizing is not standard. If in doubt you can email or call their customer service team.

Site Usability:	★★★★	Based:	UK
Product Range:	★★★★	Express Delivery Option? (UK)	Yes
Price Range:	Luxury/Medium	Gift Wrapping Option?	No
Delivery Area:	Europe	Returns Procedure:	Down to you

www.glamorousamorous.com

You'll find some quite different lingerie here - think animal print and scarlet trim from Fifi Chachnil, sequin and silk camisoles from Guia La Bruna and a lace bustier and thong from Bacirubati and you'll get the kind of idea - extremely glam in other words. There's a Lingerie and Gift Guide with help for men buying presents and everything arrives in a silk organza bag, wrapped in tissue paper scented with Provençal lavender. UK mainland delivery is free.

Site Usability:	★★★★★	Based:	UK
Product Range:	★★★★	Express Delivery Option? (UK)	Yes
Price Range:	Luxury/Medium	Gift Wrapping Option?	Yes
Delivery Area:	Worldwide	Returns Procedure:	Down to you

www.heavenlybodice.com

This is a lingerie website particularly good for gifts and particularly from him to her. You can choose from a wide range of designers, from Charnos and Warners to Naughty Janet and Shirley of Hollywood. There's an excellent selection of bridal lingerie, a separate section for larger sizes, swimwear by Fantasie, Panache and Freya and gifts by price band or in the 'Naughty' category. There's also a gift guide specifically for men.

Site Usability:	★★★★	Based:	UK
Product Range:	★★★★	Express Delivery Option? (UK)	No
Price Range:	Luxury/Medium	Gift Wrapping Option?	Yes
Delivery Area:	Worldwide	Returns Procedure:	Down to you

www.hush-uk.com

Hush-uk.com have a really well designed and beautifully photographed website where there are lots of clothes for going to sleep in or just for lounging around, with nightdresses, pyjamas and gowns, vest tops, t-shirts and sloppy joes and also kaftans and sarongs for the beach and sheepskin slippers. In their gift ideas section you can combine various items to be wrapped up together and they offer gift vouchers as well.

Site Usability:	★★★★	Based:	UK
Product Range:	★★★★	Express Delivery Option? (UK)	Yes
Price Range:	Medium	Gift Wrapping Option?	Yes
Delivery Area:	Worldwide	Returns Procedure:	Down to you

www.janetreger.co.uk

On Janet Reger's beautiful, dark website, there's the most gorgeous selection of lingerie, where the prices are definitely not for the faint hearted. Once you've picked the style you like you can immediately see all the other items in the range plus colourways and size options (don't expect large sizes here). This brand is totally about luxe and glamour so be prepared to spend a small fortune; but on absolutely wonderful quality and style.

Site Usability:	★★★★★	Based:	UK
Product Range:	★★★★	Express Delivery Option? (UK)	Yes
Price Range:	Luxury	Gift Wrapping Option?	Yes
Delivery Area:	Worldwide	Returns Procedure:	Down to you

www.ladybarbarella.com

Specialising in exclusive vintage pieces, decadent silks and burlesque styles, plus designs aimed at the many of us who can't fit into a 32B, at Lady Barbarella you can browse through a delightful selection of less available designers including Damaris Evans, Emma Benham, Frankly Darling, FleurT, Spoylt and Yes Master plus many more. This is a very prettily and cleverly designed website well worth a look if you like something a bit different.

Site Usability:	★★★★	Based:	UK
Product Range:	★★★	Express Delivery Option? (UK)	Yes
Price Range:	Medium	Gift Wrapping Option?	Yes
Delivery Area:	Worldwide	Returns Procedure:	Down to you

www.lasenza.co.uk

La Senza is an own-brand lingerie retailer originally based in Canada and also well established in the United Kingdom. You'll find a large choice of lingerie and nightwear ranging from beautiful basics to seriously sexy styles as well as bra accessories. It's great to know that retailers are actually catering for those who want something larger than a C cup as sizes also go from 30A to 38F. Yes you can buy colours, plunge bras and diamante trimmed bras even if you're a DD or above and you'll also find cleavage enhancers, extra bra straps and strap extenders here.

Site Usability:	★★★★★	Based:	UK
Product Range:	★★★★★	Express Delivery Option? (UK)	Yes
Price Range:	Very Good Value	Gift Wrapping Option?	Yes
Delivery Area:	Worldwide	Returns Procedure:	Down to you

www.luxuryfrenchlingerie.com

There are so many lingerie websites out there now that it must be really difficult to think up a new, clever design. Well Luxury French Lingerie has managed it, with a sleek, black background and intelligent layout. They offer designers such as Aubade, Simone Perele and Lisa Charmel with some styles you're unlikely to find anywhere else, plus a small range of swimwear by Aubade and expensive but beautiful silk nightwear.

Site Usability:	★★★★★	Based:	UK
Product Range:	★★★★	Express Delivery Option? (UK)	No
Price Range:	Luxury	Gift Wrapping Option?	Yes
Delivery Area:	Worldwide	Returns Procedure:	Down to you

www.myla.com

Of course, chocolate body paint may be just what you're looking for, along with some of the more risqué items offered on this sexy lingerie website (I'll say no more) but if what you're looking for is really beautiful feminine lingerie then just click into their lingerie section and ignore the rest. They also offer suspenders, thongs, feather boas, silk mules, camis and baby dolls and sizing goes up to a 36E in some parts of the range.

Site Usability:	★★★★	Based:	UK
Product Range:	★★★	Express Delivery Option? (UK)	Yes
Price Range:	Luxury/Medium	Gift Wrapping Option?	No but packaging is lovely
Delivery Area:	Worldwide	Returns Procedure:	Down to you

www.mytights.co.uk

My Tights have a really great, modern and easy-to-use website, offering the hosiery brands of Aristoc, Charnos, Elbeo, Gerbe, La Perla, Levante and Pretty Polly, to name but a few, plus maternity tights by Spanx and Trasparenze. So, whether you want footless or fishnet tights and stockings, support tights, shapewear, knee highs or suspenders you'll find it all here and, provided you order before 3pm, you'll probably get it the next day.

Site Usability:	★★★★★	Based:	UK
Product Range:	★★★★	Express Delivery Option? (UK)	Yes
Price Range:	Luxury/Medium	Gift Wrapping Option?	No
Delivery Area:	Worldwide	Returns Procedure:	Down to you

www.rigbyandpeller.com

You may know their shop just round the side of Harrods where you can be properly fitted for your next bra and choose from a chic selection of lingerie. If you can't get to Knightsbridge you can now see the range on their website, where they offer a wide range of brands such as Aubade, Lejaby, La Perla alongside their own – plus they offer a superb service. They endeavour to dispatch all orders within 48 hours and will send to you anywhere in the world.

Site Usability:	★★★★	Based:	UK
Product Range:	★★★★	Express Delivery Option? (UK)	Yes
Price Range:	Luxury/Medium	Gift Wrapping Option?	Yes
Delivery Area:	Worldwide	Returns Procedure:	Down to you

www.sassyandrose.co.uk

If you're a collector of gorgeous nightwear (and definitely one of those who likes to look glam when she goes to bed rather than the novelty t-shirt kind) you should have a browse here at a colourful range of camisoles, chemises, nightdresses, kaftans and pjs in high quality but well priced silk and embroidered cotton. If you want delivery outside the UK you need to call them and they aim to ship everything within two days.

Site Usability:	★★★	Based:	UK
Product Range:	★★★	Express Delivery Option? (UK)	No
Price Range:	Medium	Gift Wrapping Option?	No
Delivery Area:	Worldwide	Returns Procedure:	Down to you

www.silkstorm.com

The next time you're looking for something out of the ordinary take a look here at Silk Storm – an online lingerie boutique offering luxury French and Italian brands with collections including Aubade, Valery, Argentovivo, Cotton Club and Barbara. Everything is beautifully photographed and the sizing help is excellent although don't expect anything to go much above a 36D. They're aiming this very much at men buying lingerie for their ladies with sexy pictures and gorgeous gift wrapping.

Site Usability:	★★★★	Based:	UK
Product Range:	★★★	Express Delivery Option? (UK)	Yes
Price Range:	Medium	Gift Wrapping Option?	Yes
Delivery Area:	Worldwide	Returns Procedure:	Down to you

www.sophieandgrace.co.uk

Sophie and Grace offer top quality lingerie, nightwear and swimwear including the bridal ranges of Honeymoon Pearls and Verde Veronica where you'll find garters, bras and briefs, basques and nightgowns with touches such as embroidered lace and pearl straps. This is a very different and luxurious range and you'll no doubt want some to take away on honeymoon as well. Delivery is free and everything is tissue wrapped and gift boxed as a matter of course.

Site Usability:	★★★★	Based:	UK
Product Range:	★★★	Express Delivery Option? (UK)	Yes
Price Range:	Luxury/Medium	Gift Wrapping Option?	Yes
Delivery Area:	UK (Call them for Overseas)	Returns Procedure:	Down to you

www.lingerie-company.co.uk

Based in Hinckley, Leicestershire, this retailer offers lingerie by a multitude of designers including Aubade, Lejaby, Chantelle, Charnos, Fantasie, Passionata, Panache and Triumph. Also Swimwear by Aubade, Freya and Fantasie. A discount of 10% is automatically taken off the retail price on all orders. It is a very simply designed website with an excellent search facility so you can pick exactly what you are looking for. Expect a high level of personal service and quick delivery.

Site Usability:	★★★★	Based:	UK
Product Range:	★★★★	Express Delivery Option? (UK)	Yes but you need to call to request
Price Range:	Medium	Gift Wrapping Option?	No
Delivery Area:	Worldwide	Returns Procedure:	Down to you

www.tightsplease.co.uk

Whether you want fishnets and crochet tights, bright colours, knee highs, stay-ups, stockings or footsies you'll find them all here plus leg warmers, socks and flight socks, maternity and bridal hosiery. This website really caters for all your hosiery needs and with names such as Aristoc, Pretty Polly and Charnos offered you should never run out again. As an extra benefit delivery is free in the UK and takes only 1–2 days.

Site Usability:	★★★★★	Based:	UK
Product Range:	★★★★★	Express Delivery Option? (UK)	Automatic
Price Range:	Luxury/Medium	Gift Wrapping Option?	No
Delivery Area:	Worldwide	Returns Procedure:	Free

www.vollers-corsets.com

This is quite simply an amazing collection of corsets, both for underwear and outerwear. The sexy and feminine designs include ruched velvet, satin, lace, leather, beaded brocade, gold and silver fabric, moire and tartan and with flower, feather, lace and velvet trims. Sizes go from an 18 to 38 waist or you can have a corset specially made for you. There are corsets perfect for weddings and special occasion and most are available in a range of colours.

Site Usability:	★★★★★	Based:	UK
Product Range:	★★★★★	Express Delivery Option? (UK)	Yes
Price Range:	Luxury/Medium	Gift Wrapping Option?	No
Delivery Area:	Worldwide	Returns Procedure:	Down to you

www.wolfordboutiquelondon.com

Wolford are world famous for their top quality hosiery, bodies, tops and lingerie and you can now purchase their collection online, through their London South Molton Street shop. The range includes sexy and beautifully photographed seasonally inspired pieces and is being updated all the time. Wolford are definitely not the cheapest for any part of their range but everything is of the highest quality and well worth an investment.

Site Usability:	★★★★	Based:	UK
Product Range:	★★★★★	Express Delivery Option? (UK)	Yes
Price Range:	Luxury	Gift Wrapping Option?	No
Delivery Area:	Worldwide	Returns Procedure:	Down to you

Also check out these websites for lingerie and swimwear:

Website address	You'll find it in
www.victoriassecret.com	Chapter 5: Shop America

Chapter 8

Resortwear Store

I always leave it too late to buy that perfect resortwear that's going to put me well ahead of the pack on the beach this summer; I leave it too late, find the style that I want and then get really disappointed if it's no longer available in my size. Don't be like me. If you want something different and gorgeous make sure that you allow enough time and buy early.

Bear in mind that swimwear starts arriving in the shops and at the online retailers from as early as January for summer and that the main collections should be in from mid March. If you find a retailer with a style that you like give them a call to make sure that you know when you'll need to buy. You may think that your black bandeau swimsuit from several years back will do for another year but this year give yourself a treat and invest in something new plus kaftan or pareo and accessories.

I've decided that the best policy is to buy one special resort outfit each year and add bits and pieces in from wherever I go. As I'm a black swimwear and gold accessory beach babe (not that anyone calls me that) it's not hard for me to build up a collection that mixes and matches so I can just pick the pieces I want to take with me whenever I'm invited to somewhere delicious and hot – which needless to say isn't often enough.

Don't you get really fed up with hearing from people how they're off to Barbados or the South of France or the Maldives *every* holidays (or so it seems). I certainly do. So I won't bore you with the fact that I'm writing this while sitting in a hotel room in the Bahamas on a trip to celebrate being married to my husband for twenty years. Am I serious? I'll leave it to you to work it out ...

Sites to Visit

www.anula.co.uk

Anula have done the hard work for you when you're looking for all year round resortwear by putting together a range of swimsuits and bikinis with matching and contrasting kaftans, flip-flops, beach bags, baskets and jewellery. This isn't a huge selection but there are some very stylish pieces which work well together.

Site Usability:	★★★★	Based:	UK
Product Range:	★★★	Express Delivery Option? (UK)	Yes
Price Range:	Medium	Gift Wrapping Option?	No
Delivery Area:	Worldwide	Returns Procedure:	Down to you

www.biondicouture.com

If you're going somewhere hot soon you'll need to take a look here, at this luxury travel boutique where you can buy hard-to-find swimwear, beachwear (as in kaftans and sun dresses) and accessories such as silk and cashmere slippers, sandals and travel wallets. Because this is an all year round holiday shop you'll find a good selection whatever time of year you decide to jet off. Check into their trends section first to find out what you *should* be wearing on the beach and then go shop.

Site Usability:	★★★★	Based:	UK
Product Range:	★★★	Express Delivery Option? (UK)	Yes
Price Range:	Medium	Gift Wrapping Option?	No
Delivery Area:	Worldwide	Returns Procedure:	Down to you

www.elizabethhurley.com

You may well have read in the press about the Elizabeth Hurley Beach collection and here it is online. There's wonderful, sexy, stylish swimwear, chic kaftans, dresses and tops and a choice of knitwear and t-shirts. Then there are the totes, sarongs and towels to help complete your look. It's an expensive range but you'll almost certainly want something. There's adorable swimwear for kids as well.

Site Usability:	★★★★	Based:	UK
Product Range:	★★★	Express Delivery Option? (UK)	No
Price Range:	Luxury	Gift Wrapping Option?	No
Delivery Area:	Worldwide	Returns Procedure:	Down to you

www.espadrillesetc.com

Whether or not you're an espadrilles fan, if you're going on holiday you really should take a look at this summer shoe website, where there's every colour, fabric and style you can think of to choose from including soft coloured suede and brightly coloured fabric espadrilles, plus some very pretty sandals, brightly coloured beach bags and totes and children's espadrilles as well. They'll be happy to ship to you anywhere in the world and all the espadrilles are despatched in bright, colourful and transparent shoe bags.

Site Usability:	★★★★	Based:	Spain
Product Range:	★★★	Express Delivery Option? (UK)	No
Price Range:	Medium/Very Good Value	Gift Wrapping Option?	No
Delivery Area:	Worldwide	Returns Procedure:	Down to you

www.heidiklein.com

Heidi Klein offers really beautiful holidaywear all the year round. The range includes chic bikinis and one piece swimsuits, pretty and flattering kaftans, dresses and sarongs plus all the accessories you could need for your next trip away to the sun (flip-flops, hats, bags and more). They offer a same day delivery service in London and express delivery throughout the UK.

Site Usability:	★★★★	Based:		UK
Product Range:	★★★	Express Delivery Option? (UK)		Yes
Price Range:	Luxury/Medium	Gift Wrapping Option?		Yes
Delivery Area:	Worldwide	Returns Procedure:		Down to you

www.kikoy.com

For holidays and trips abroad you'll definitely want to know about this colourful website, offering fine cotton and muslin shorts, kaftans, cover-ups, trousers, hats and bags plus beach towels. There are some excellent summer/holiday gift ideas here but if you see something you want in a hurry give them a call to make sure that they have it in stock. If they do, they'll ship it to you for next day delivery. They're happy to deliver to you anywhere in the world.

Site Usability:	★★★★	Based:		UK
Product Range:	★★★	Express Delivery Option? (UK)		Yes, call them
Price Range:	Medium/Very Good Value	Gift Wrapping Option?		No
Delivery Area:	Worldwide	Returns Procedure:		Down to you

www.obadash.com

Celebrity swimwear designer Melissa Obadash offers beautifully chic one-piece swimsuits and bikinis in her online store, together with cover-ups and kaftans, beach bags, t-shirts in a great choice of colourways plus swimwear for children. You won't find the full range here but a well edited selection and I would expect that the sizing for this designer range will be on the small side so if in doubt order a size up.

Site Usability:	★★★★	Based:		UK
Product Range:	★★★★	Express Delivery Option? (UK)		Yes, call them
Price Range:	Luxury	Gift Wrapping Option?		No
Delivery Area:	Worldwide	Returns Procedure:		Down to you

www.sand-monkey.com

If you fancy a change from run-of-the-mill synthetic flip-flops you should take a look at this collection of 'Sand Monkeys' – leather sandals with cute, stylish and funky finishes including beads and shells, originally designed on a luxury safari camp in Kenya's Masai Mara to be worn by the camp's clients. You can now have them sent to you anywhere in the world and by express delivery if you ask especially nicely.

Site Usability:	★★★★	Based:		UK
Product Range:	★★★	Express Delivery Option? (UK)		Yes on request
Price Range:	Medium	Gift Wrapping Option?		No
Delivery Area:	Worldwide	Returns Procedure:		Down to you

www.louisesandberg.com

There were so many kaftans around last summer that you're almost certainly aware by now that this is a must-have for summer holidays. Whether they're in fashion or not (and I'm sure they will be for a while) they're great for wearing over a swimsuit when you want something to give more cover than a sarong. Here's an excellent collection, long, short, colourful or neutral and beautifully embroidered. You'll definitely find yours here.

Site Usability:	★★★	Based:	UK
Product Range:	★★★	Express Delivery Option? (UK)	Yes
Price Range:	Medium	Gift Wrapping Option?	No
Delivery Area:	Worldwide	Returns Procedure:	Down to you

www.simplybeach.com

At last, a really great website devoted just to swimwear and including designer brands Melissa Odabash, Gideon Oberson and Wahine with swimsuits and bikinis in all shapes and sizes. There's a wide range of accessories as well including cover-ups, towels, beach bags and inflatables and direct links through to their other website where you'll find everything for scuba diving and snorkelling. Get ready for your next beach holiday and take a good look round.

Site Usability:	★★★★★	Based:	UK
Product Range:	★★★★	Express Delivery Option? (UK)	Yes
Price Range:	Medium	Gift Wrapping Option?	No
Delivery Area:	Worldwide	Returns Procedure:	Down to you

www.splashhawaii.com

Not for the faint hearted, this Hawaii based site really only sells bikinis (and diddy ones at that) but there's a very good choice so if you fit into the bikini category it's well worth having a look. Billabong, Roxy and Tommy Hilfiger are just some of the brands available plus US designers you may well not have heard of. They'll ship worldwide but if you take my advice you'll make that special journey and go and collect yours.

Site Usability:	★★★★	Based:	Hawaii
Product Range:	★★★	Express Delivery Option? (UK)	No
Price Range:	Medium	Gift Wrapping Option?	No
Delivery Area:	Worldwide	Returns Procedure:	Down to you

Also check out these websites for resortwear:

Website address	You'll find it in
www.barenecessities.co.uk	Chapter 7: Lingerie
www.bravissimo.com	Chapter 7: Lingerie
www.figleaves.com	Chapter 7: Lingerie
www.heavenlybodice.com	Chapter 7: Lingerie
www.sophieandgrace.co.uk	Chapter 7: Lingerie
www.lingerie-company.co.uk	Chapter 7: Lingerie
www.grahamkandiah.com	Chapter 5: Shop America
www.swimwearboutique.com	Chapter 5: Shop America
www.victoriassecret.com	Chapter 5: Shop America

Chapter 9

Leather, Shearling and Faux Fur

I've given this clothing area a separate place all of its own as, to me, these are not so much items of clothing but investment accessories. A well cut (and good quality) leather or suede jacket, a great pair of jeans, white shirt and, of course, heels and you have a modern, practically undatable look that suits most people and will take you just about anywhere. Don't wear jeans? No matter, substitute a well cut pair of black trousers and you have the same, albeit slightly dressier, effect.

Remember; I said well cut jacket, which doesn't mean the kind of slightly shapeless, too long blazer you might have been wearing a few years back – don't even try to bring that out – buy something shorter, neater and well fitted to your figure, in soft leather or suede. Be prepared to pay a little bit more for quality – the cheaper end of the market is flooded with bad quality skins and you want to steer well away from those.

In terms of shearling (or sheepskin if you prefer), again go for the best quality you can afford and buy a style that's going to last. Although our winters seem to be getting warmer and warmer and you might wonder why you need a shearling coat or jacket at all, when you look at some of the styles below you'll almost certainly be tempted.

My advice, if you're not as yet a leather wearer, is to get a jacket in soft suede and in a dark neutral, like dark brown. Once you've worn it a few times and you realise how versatile it is you may want to expand your collection to a slim coat or a skirt. The two items in my wardrobe I wear probably more than any others are my wonderfully flattering and confidence building jacket and coat in cocoa suede. On television (just had to get that in), at meetings or any other occasion they've never let me down.

Sites to Visit

www.celtic-sheepskin.co.uk

There are some excellent clothes and accessories here, particularly for the winter months, including chic Toscana shearling jackets and coats, gloves, scarves and sheepskin lined boots and slippers, waistcoats and gilets and cute shearling duffles and boots for children. Prices are reasonable and everything's really clearly pictured. If you want to order a coat or jacket you'll probably have to wait a couple of weeks so take a look now.

Site Usability:	★★★★★	Based:	UK
Product Range:	★★★	Express Delivery Option? (UK)	No
Price Range:	Luxury/Medium	Gift Wrapping Option?	No
Delivery Area:	UK	Returns Procedure:	Down to you

www.dlux-ltd.co.uk

Dlux is a boutique mail-order company specialising in beautiful sheepskin and shearling collections. The range is made of the highest quality soft and supple Merino and Toscana skins and there are two sections, which they call Classic and Modern although everything is chic and stylish here whichever you choose. To order you need to download their order form and then email it to them. If you're in the mood for something luxuriously soft and warm this winter take a good look here.

Site Usability:	★★★★	Based:	UK
Product Range:	★★★	Express Delivery Option? (UK)	No
Price Range:	Luxury/Medium	Gift Wrapping Option?	No
Delivery Area:	UK	Returns Procedure:	Down to you

www.ewenique.co.uk

This is a very attractive and comprehensive range of leather, suede and shearling coats and jackets for men and women plus flying jackets and accessories such as scarves and stoles, hats, hide bags, gloves and snuggly slippers. Everything is beautifully photographed with close-ups of the sheepskins so that you can see exactly what you're buying plus there's lots of detailed information about each garment.

Site Usability:	★★★★	Based:	UK
Product Range:	★★★★	Express Delivery Option? (UK)	No
Price Range:	Medium	Gift Wrapping Option?	No
Delivery Area:	Worldwide	Returns Procedure:	Down to you

www.fabulousfurs.com

No, these are not the real thing. You'll almost certainly be fooled when you look at them on this US-based website but everything here is made of the highest quality mod-acrylic fibre which gives them the look and feel of real fur. You can choose from full length coats to modern jackets, fake fur trimmed knits, stoles and wraps and there are luxurious throws for the home as well. You will have to pay duty on anything you buy but for the quality nothing is overpriced.

Site Usability:	★★★★	Based:	US
Product Range:	★★★★	Express Delivery Option? (UK)	No
Price Range:	Luxury/Medium	Gift Wrapping Option?	No
Delivery Area:	Worldwide	Returns Procedure:	Down to you

www.faux.uk.com

If you like to wrap yourself in something soft and furry, but you don't want to wear the real thing then here's a collection of the softest faux fur coats, jackets and shrugs plus gorgeous accessories, cushions and throws. These are perfect additions to winter evenings, whether you choose a jacket to go over your evening dress or an unbelievably soft throw to snuggle up in at home. It's not a huge collection and the pictures could be improved, but the products are well worth a look.

Site Usability:	★★★	Based:	UK
Product Range:	★★★	Express Delivery Option? (UK)	Yes but you need to call them
Price Range:	Medium	Gift Wrapping Option?	No
Delivery Area:	Worldwide	Returns Procedure:	Down to you

www.higgs-leathers.co.uk

This is an unsophisticatedly designed website (although improving all the time) with a really marvellous collection of leather, suede and shearling clothing. They obviously know what they're doing and offer very high quality items at reasonable (though not cheap) prices. Expect to pay around £900 for the best Toscana shearling full length coat. You need to call them to order to ensure that you take the right size.

Site Usability:	★★★★	Based:	UK
Product Range:	★★★★	Express Delivery Option? (UK)	No
Price Range:	Luxury/Medium	Gift Wrapping Option?	No
Delivery Area:	Worldwide	Returns Procedure:	Down to you

www.hyde-online.net

Here's real designer quality, beautifully made leather, suede and shearling from a company that makes for some world famous designers. Nothing here is cheap but you definitely get what you pay for. You may not know the difference between the various types of suede and shearling but they certainly do and only use the highest quality skins. The focus is on modern styling but you'll also find some great classics that'll last you for years.

Site Usability:	★★★★	Based:	UK
Product Range:	★★★★	Express Delivery Option? (UK)	No
Price Range:	Luxury	Gift Wrapping Option?	No
Delivery Area:	Worldwide	Returns Procedure:	Down to you

Chapter 10

Fashion for Bumps

Designer Maternitywear   Maternity Boutiques

Firstly my apologies if you've heard me say this before; you're so lucky to have all these fab maternity boutiques to buy from, with such a wide range of different styles, fabrics and prices – far, far better than when I had my children (yes all those years ago).

Nowadays if you like a chic and minimal, understated style you can find it easily. Alternatively if you want more traditional maternitywear you'll discover that as well and all without having to go anywhere near the shops, which is probably the last thing you want to do when you're expecting.

A little black cocktail dress? No problem. Designer jeans? No problem. Whether you like your clothes to have top designer labels or prefer them to be of the casual, lounge about variety – none of it's a problem.

One thing I would advise is not to leave it too late before buying a couple of chic maternity outfits; far better to be prepared than to make your current jeans last just that little while longer and get more and more uncomfortable wearing them. Buy something gorgeous now, and you can look forward to wearing it, rather than waiting with dread for that moment when simply nothing fits. Listen to me; I know about this, I've been there three times and when I had mine there was nothing like the choice you have now. In fact I feel faint when I think of some of the things I used to wear and no, I'm not going to describe them to you, at least not in this book.

Sites to Visit

Designer Maternitywear

www.apeainthepod.com
This is without a doubt one of the most famous US-based maternity stores, offering both their own well priced range plus designer selections by Tocca, Lily Pulizer, Juicy Couture, Diane von Furstenberg, Betsey Johnson and lots more plus premium denim brands such as Citizens of Humanity and

Paige. Take a look at their Celebrity Red Carpet which includes actresses such as Holly Hunter, Maggie Gyllenhall and Diane Farr wearing their gowns then choose something for yourself.

Site Usability:	★★★★★	Based:	US
Product Range:	★★★★★	Express Delivery Option? (UK)	No
Price Range:	Luxury/Medium	Gift Wrapping Option?	No
Delivery Area:	Worldwide	Returns Procedure:	Down to you

www.blossommotherandchild.com

Blossom caters for the fashion conscious expectant mum, with a collection of glamorous dresses and separates which combine high-end fashion with comfort and functionality. You'll also find customised jeans by brands such as Rock and Republic and James. They use an assortment of luxurious fabrics such as silk-cashmere, voile and jersey and expand the collection continuously.

Site Usability:	★★★★	Based:	UK
Product Range:	★★★★	Express Delivery Option? (UK)	Yes
Price Range:	Luxury/Medium	Gift Wrapping Option?	No
Delivery Area:	Worldwide	Returns Procedure:	Down to you

www.fortyweeks.co.uk

The aim of maternity designer basics retailer Forty Weeks is to offer you contemporary, stream-lined design combined with great fabrics (and reasonable pricing) to create a wardrobe that can be worn before, during and after pregnancy. There's a wide selection of colours and styles which would work perfectly with the more formal pieces of your new wardrobe and, unlike many things you buy now, you'll almost certainly want to wear them afterwards. Take advantage of their home visiting service within the London area.

Site Usability:	★★★★	Based:	UK
Product Range:	★★★	Express Delivery Option? (UK)	No
Price Range:	Luxury/Medium	Gift Wrapping Option?	No
Delivery Area:	Worldwide	Returns Procedure:	Down to you

www.isabellaoliver.com

Isabella Oliver is a maternity wear company for pregnant women who love clothes. Their sexy designs in soft jersey fabrics have signature style details like ruching and wrapping to flatter new curves. Every item comes gift wrapped and their brochure and website include style tips to pick up on the season's trends. You can see each item as a model shot, drawing and also using their really clever and innovative catwalk animation. As well as day and evening separates you can buy lingerie, loungewear, sophisticated sleepwear, chic outerwear, sun and swimwear.

Site Usability:	★★★★★	Based:	UK
Product Range:	★★★★	Express Delivery Option? (UK)	Yes
Price Range:	Luxury/Medium	Gift Wrapping Option?	Yes
Delivery Area:	Worldwide	Returns Procedure:	Free

www.pushmaternity.com

The Push boutique in Islington specialises in designer maternity wear and a high level of customer service. Now you can buy the collection online from labels such as Earl Jean, Tashia, Alex Gore

Brown, Cadeau, Citizens of Humanity, Leona Edmistion (gorgeous jersey dresses) and Juicy Couture. There's maternity hosiery and chic baby bags here as well. Select from express or standard delivery and if you have any queries don't hesitate to give them a call.

Site Usability:	★★★★	Based:	UK
Product Range:	★★★★	Express Delivery Option? (UK)	Yes
Price Range:	Luxury/Medium	Gift Wrapping Option?	No
Delivery Area:	Worldwide	Returns Procedure:	Down to you

Maternity Boutiques

www.bjornandme.com

For choice and value you'd find it hard to beat this website, where the clothes are divided up into sections such as Outdoor and Exercise wear/Formalwear/Petite/Tall and Plus Size. There's also swimwear and lingerie, so whether you're looking for a pair of soft white linen trousers or something for the Oscars, you'll almost certainly find it here - the evening and occasionwear is particularly good. This is international designer styled maternity wear and a very good collection.

Site Usability:	★★★★	Based:	UK
Product Range:	★★★★	Express Delivery Option? (UK)	Yes
Price Range:	Medium	Gift Wrapping Option?	No
Delivery Area:	Worldwide	Returns Procedure:	Down to you

www.bloomingmarvellous.co.uk

There's a wide choice of well priced but good quality clothes for expectant mothers and babies on this fun, colourful website. Whether you're looking for casualwear or city clothes you're sure to find something as they offer a wide range from sophisticated skirts and tops to lots of modern, casual options. There's also information on how to dress with a bump and a monthly newsletter to sign up for so make this one of your first stops for browsing when you're expecting a baby.

Site Usability:	★★★★★	Based:	UK
Product Range:	★★★★★	Express Delivery Option? (UK)	No
Price Range:	Medium/Very Good Value	Gift Wrapping Option?	No
Delivery Area:	Worldwide	Returns Procedure:	Down to you

www.cravematernity.co.uk

Crave Maternity have a well designed, friendly and clearly photographed website offering well cut and versatile separates and dresses in good fabrics and at reasonable prices. You'll find tailoring, eveningwear and casualwear all aimed at the busy woman who wants to carry on with her normal life and look smart throughout her pregnancy and afterwards. This is a website just for maternity clothes so you're not going to be sidetracked by the children's clothes and accessories you'll find on so many other sites.

Site Usability:	★★★★		Based:	UK
Product Range:	★★★		Express Delivery Option? (UK)	No
Price Range:	Medium		Gift Wrapping Option?	No
Delivery Area:	Worldwide		Returns Procedure:	Down to you

www.formes.com

Formes is a French company offering beautifully styled 'designer' pregnancy wear and selling all over the world. You won't find their full collection but an edited range and it's well worth looking through. Unlike a lot of the maternity shops here you'll find all the information you could possibly want, from complete product detailing to fabric content and full measurements plus very clear pictures.

Site Usability:	★★★★★		Based:	UK
Product Range:	★★★★		Express Delivery Option? (UK)	No
Price Range:	Medium		Gift Wrapping Option?	No
Delivery Area:	Worldwide		Returns Procedure:	Down to you

www.jojomamanbebe.co.uk

This is a really pretty website offering a very good choice for expectant mothers, babies and young children. The drop-down menus on the home page take you quickly and clearly to everything you might be looking for, whether it's maternity occasionwear or safety gates for young children. There's a range of underwear and swimwear as well. They have some very good present ideas and offer gift vouchers and boxes as well to make your life easier.

Site Usability:	★★★★★		Based:	UK
Product Range:	★★★★		Express Delivery Option? (UK)	No
Price Range:	Medium		Gift Wrapping Option?	No
Delivery Area:	Worldwide		Returns Procedure:	Down to you

www.kickmaternitywear.com

This is the place to start if you need good maternity working clothes, as the tailoring styles are very good. There are at least three styles of jacket on offer with matching trousers or skirts, great tops and shirts to go with plus excellent separates and knitwear. If you want to invest in a Little Black Dress or other occasionwear you'll find that here as well and there are several options to choose from.

Site Usability:	★★★★★		Based:	UK
Product Range:	★★★★		Express Delivery Option? (UK)	Yes
Price Range:	Medium		Gift Wrapping Option?	No
Delivery Area:	Worldwide		Returns Procedure:	Down to you

www.mamasandpapas.co.uk

This company combines great attention to detail, high quality fabrics and pretty designs in their well priced maternity section, covering everything from eveningwear and separates to sleepwear and swimwear. There's lovely clothing here as well for babies and toddlers plus a wide range of equipment and lots of present ideas. This is really a beautifully photographed website offering loads of advice on what to buy. They only deliver to the UK but you can click through to their US-based site.

Site Usability:	★★★★★	Based:	UK	
Product Range:	★★★	Express Delivery Option? (UK)	No	
Price Range:	Medium	Gift Wrapping Option?	No	
Delivery Area:	UK but US site available	Returns Procedure:	Down to you	

www.seraphine.com

Find excellent maternitywear on this really attractive website where the collection is stylish and different and the prices reasonable. You can choose from the latest looks, maternity essentials and glamorous partywear and as well as all of this there's lingerie by Elle Mcpherson, Nougatine and Canelle, gorgeous layettes for newborn babies and Tommy's Ts. Delivery takes up to five working days; you'll find postage costs for the UK and EU on the website and email them for elsewhere.

Site Usability:	★★★★	Based:	UK	
Product Range:	★★★★	Express Delivery Option? (UK)	No	
Price Range:	Medium/Very Good Value	Gift Wrapping Option?	No	
Delivery Area:	Worldwide	Returns Procedure:	Down to you	

www.tiffanyrose.co.uk

Here you'll find smart and unusual maternitywear including dresses and chic separates. It's quite a small range but very stylish so if you're looking for something for a special occasion you should have a click around. There are also beautiful maternity wedding dresses and a sale area where there are usually some very good discounts. They deliver worldwide and offer a next day and Saturday delivery service for the UK.

Site Usability:	★★★★	Based:	UK	
Product Range:	★★★	Express Delivery Option? (UK)	Yes	
Price Range:	Luxury/Medium	Gift Wrapping Option?	No	
Delivery Area:	Worldwide	Returns Procedure:	Down to you	

www.wondermummy.com

Wondermummy has a special section for businesswear, where there are pinstriped suits, simple tops and skirts, formal trousers and cross over tops in several colours. Although this is very much only part of the range, so many maternity boutiques seem to leave the work angle out altogether that this definitely merits a look. Browse 'Active' as well for reasonably priced easy pieces.

Site Usability:	★★★★	Based:	UK	
Product Range:	★★★	Express Delivery Option? (UK)	Two day delivery is standard	
Price Range:	Very Good Value	Gift Wrapping Option?	No	
Delivery Area:	Most Eu	Returns Procedure:	Down to you	

Also take a look at the following for Maternitywear Online

Website address	You'll find it in
www.marksandspencer.com	Chapter 1: Fashion Online/The High Street
www.dorothyperkins.co.uk	Chapter 1: Fashion Online/The High Street
www.warehousefashion.com	Chapter 1: Fashion Online/The High Street

Chapter 11

Bump Essentials – Lingerie, Swim and Sportswear

I'm not going to bore you with too many comments here as the same comments are true that I made in the section above, only more so, perhaps.

What has changed hugely for the good is that there is so much more than just black and white nursing and maternity lingerie to choose from, you'll probably be surprised at the colours and styles you can find.

Where swimwear is concerned the same isn't yet true and the selection is surprisingly small. I'm sure that that will change as more and more of you buy your maternity gear online. I firmly suggest that you make your feelings known, when you visit an online maternity retailer with a tiny choice of swimwear send them an email asking why they don't offer more choice. Please do. Maybe they'll listen to you and expand their ranges. It's definitely about time they did.

Sites to Visit

www.amoralia.com

This is a small but very cleverly designed selection of lingerie, where you just click on the style you like to see the full range for each one. There are maternity and nursing bras, hipster briefs, French knickers and thongs and each style is available in the sort of colours you don't associate with maternity lingerie, such as blush, lilac, caramel, ivory and lacy black. They'll deliver worldwide.

Site Usability:	★★★★	Based:	UK
Product Range:	★★★	Express Delivery Option? (UK)	No
Price Range:	Medium	Gift Wrapping Option?	No
Delivery Area:	Worldwide	Returns Procedure:	Down to you

www.emily-b.co.uk

Emily B is a new brand of maternity lingerie offering you beautiful luxury bras and briefs and created because of the frustration the founder Emily Barnes experienced after giving birth to her first child in 2002 when she realised that luxury maternity lingerie was extremely hard to find. Here the look is most important, although at the same time her products offer good support, coverage and comfort. You should definitely have a browse round here.

Site Usability:	★★★★	Based:	UK
Product Range:	★★★	Express Delivery Option? (UK)	No
Price Range:	Medium	Gift Wrapping Option?	No
Delivery Area:	Worldwide	Returns Procedure:	Down to you

www.fromheretomaternity.co.uk

If you want to breastfeed your baby wearing a leopard print bra, or something black and unbelievably pretty and lacy then this is the place to look. You can find your basic maternity essentials here as well, but to my mind the site's strength is definitely in the bra department, where you will find styles by Elle McPherson, Bravado, Carriwell and Emma Jane. There's also a small range of swimwear and very attractive nightwear.

Site Usability:	★★★★	Based:	UK
Product Range:	★★★	Express Delivery Option? (UK)	Yes
Price Range:	Medium	Gift Wrapping Option?	No
Delivery Area:	Worldwide	Returns Procedure:	Down to you

www.mothernaturebras.co.uk

There's a good selection of maternity and nursing bras, plus support garments such as baby belts and attractive swimwear from this small online retailer and one that's well worth having a look at. I have to confess that I'm not sure why most nursing bras have to come in white only but if that's what you're happy with then you'll probably like this basic collection, of which the swimwear is the strongest part. The information here is really helpful and if you want some advice you can call them.

Site Usability:	★★★★	Based:	UK
Product Range:	★★★	Express Delivery Option? (UK)	No
Price Range:	Medium	Gift Wrapping Option?	No
Delivery Area:	Worldwide	Returns Procedure:	Down to you

www.white-orchid.com

White Orchid is a small online boutique offering a selection of gorgeous, seductive nightwear with a limited but very attractive maternity line of nightdresses and pyjamas in colours such as palest pink, pale blue and lavender. The prices are quite high but everything here is very high quality and hand finished so if you want to treat yourself, take a look.

Site Usability:	★★★★	Based:	UK
Product Range:	★★★	Express Delivery Option? (UK)	No
Price Range:	Luxury	Gift Wrapping Option?	No
Delivery Area:	Worldwide	Returns Procedure:	Down to you

Also take a look at these websites for Maternity Lingerie and Swimwear:

Website address	You'll find it in
www.agentprovocateur.com	Chapter 7: Lingerie
www.bravissimo.com	Chapter 7: Lingerie
www.figleaves.com	Chapter 7: Lingerie

Section 2
The Accessory Place

The Accessory Place

If you're anything like me this is the hardest place of all to resist. Not only do I want (but can't usually afford) the must-have bag of the season, but somehow accessory purchases are also the ultimate feel-good buys. It doesn't matter if you're having a fat or a thin day, which is most certainly does when you're trying on clothes, a beautiful new accessory just makes you feel that little bit better and, of course, there are so many to choose from.

You can decide to invest in that must have Balenciaga or Marc Jacobs quilted bag and blow it all in one go, or spread out your purchasing over several pieces in the different, new season's colours.

You can find shoes for every occasion from chic (yes still chic) ballet flats in metallics and animal prints, gorgeous Swarovski stone embellished killer heels, round toe, peep toe or pointed toe platforms and pumps and boots to fit everyone, with several new online retailers offering different calf measurements.

Then there's the jewellery; and if you can't go for that five carat diamond ring today you can just stop off at fashion jewellery boutiques such as Butler and Wilson and Lola Rose for an excellent fix – something pretty and modern that'll arrive in just a day, beautifully packaged and a joy to wear. These websites are also, of course, great places for gifts, so while you're shopping for yourself you can buy your best friend's birthday present as well and have it sent out gift wrapped with your own message.

As accessory areas within the large offline stores seem to be diminishing, so they're expanding online so look out for fabulous shades, hip hugging belts (plus the waisted variety), scarves, wraps and all the rest of the pieces that go together to make sure you look (and feel) your best all the time.

Chapter 12

Handbag Temptation

The A List   Carry These Without Breaking the Bank   Bag a Bargain

Every time my husband spots me 'researching' a new designer handbag website he starts to groan, knowing that it will probably mean an investment to add to my collection. For – yes – I am a collector and have been for a while. It's all part of the essential research, you know.

Just joking; I'm not that bad, no really I'm not. It's just that this is my absolute favourite area of shopping online or off. With a great new handbag how can you go wrong?

I'm sure that you've realised by now we're in the age of the monumentally priced designer handbag, as seen on the arms of Paris, Kylie, Elle and Cameron, lauded in the press until you think you can't live without the latest Fendi, Marc Jacobs or Dior – until, that is, you check out the price and discover that it's well in excess of £1000. Yes, really, £1000. Just for a handbag.

So what do you do? Do you give up and carry on with that tote you've been hauling around for the past couple of years? Do you do something that will alienate your bank manager for many months to come? Or do you try and find something a little bit more reasonable that will still make the season's statement but won't cause you any problems? Yes definitely, that's what you should do.

I am a great believer that your handbag says almost more about you than your clothes and that you can get away with simple, well cut, timeless clothes provided you have a good handbag. Take a look at the next few people you meet and see if you don't agree with me. Your handbag makes a statement – make sure it's the right one – it doesn't have to cost the earth.

Here you'll find handbags that fall into three price groups: The A List, where you'll find Gucci, Vuitton, Dior, Luella, Chloe and more and where even if you don't want to shell out the astronomical sums they're asking you should take a look to see the kind of thing that's 'now'.

Then there's Carry These Without Breaking the Bank (a bit long winded, sorry, but I think you'll know what I mean), where you can find sometimes classic and sometimes very modern and utterly gorgeous bags without having to spend too much.

Finally there's Bag a Bargain – just a few retailers offering discounted designer handbags because they're buying from true re-sellers and ends of designer lines. This leads me to a major warning: don't ever be tempted to buy a 'replica' bag and I suggest that you don't buy from auction websites either. You may well be totally disappointed. In any case I think you'll have to agree that there are plenty of great websites here to choose from.

Sites to Visit

The A List

www.anyahindmarch.com

Anya Hindmarch's collection of beautiful, unique and sometimes quirky handbags and small accessories have long been glossy magazine fashion editors favourites. They're totally different and very special, always carrying her signature bow logo somewhere whether they're on her clever picture bags or richly coloured leather tassled Marissa. Her chic Bespoke Ebury handbag is available in several colourways and is only made to order, with your personalised inscription inside.

Site Usability:	★★★★	Based:	UK
Product Range:	★★★	Express Delivery Option? (UK)	No
Price Range:	Luxury	Gift Wrapping Option?	No
Delivery Area:	Worldwide	Returns Procedure:	Down to you

www.forzieri.com

Italian company Forzieri offers handbags and wallets by Dolce & Gabbana, Prada, Tods, Gucci, and Burberry plus superb leather and shearling jackets, an excellent, stylish shoe collection, gloves, leather travel bags and other accessories. There's also a wide choice of reasonably priced high quality Italian brands. Very good descriptions are given about the all the products plus lots of different views so you know exactly what you're buying.

Site Usability:	★★★★★	Based:	Italy
Product Range:	★★★★★	Express Delivery Option? (UK)	Yes
Price Range:	Luxury/Medium	Gift Wrapping Option?	Yes
Delivery Area:	Worldwide	Returns Procedure:	Down to you

www.gucci.com

As one of the ultimate 'superbrand' designers to come online you visit this website at your peril. As you would expect the site is very modern and beautiful (and heartstoppingly expensive) and the products irresistible. You can buy handbags, luggage, men and women's shoes and gifts, such as key rings and lighters. Don't expect them to offer clothes, at least not for a while, as the fit would be very difficult and returns far too high.

Site Usability:	★★★★★	Express Delivery Option? (UK)	Yes
Product Range:	★★★★★	Gift Wrapping Option?	Yes/Automatic
Price Range:	Luxury	Returns Procedure:	Down to you
Delivery Area:	Worldwide most places		

www.jandmdavidson.com

J & M Davidson design and produce beautiful quality and extremely expensive leather goods and clothing including handbags and small accessories in lovely leathers and different colours. Their website is quite simple and the pictures small and not as good as they could be, however, don't be fooled. Anything you buy from them will be real designer quality, superbly made and will last you a long time.

Site Usability:	★★★	Based:	UK
Product Range:	★★★★	Express Delivery Option? (UK)	No
Price Range:	Luxury	Gift Wrapping Option?	No
Delivery Area:	Worldwide	Returns Procedure:	Down to you

www.launer.com

Launer small leather goods (and signature handbags for ladies) are handmade by skilled crafts-people in the softest calf, exotic lizard, ostrich and alligator skin. Every attention is paid to detail, and the gold plated fittings all feature the signature Launer rope emblem. Launer's trademark is understated, elegant and classic. This is not the place for an up-to-the-minute look but for really beautifully made investment pieces that will last a great deal of time.

Site Usability:	★★★★	Based:	UK
Product Range:	★★★	Express Delivery Option? (UK)	No
Price Range:	Luxury/Medium	Gift Wrapping Option?	No
Delivery Area:	Worldwide	Returns Procedure:	Down to you

www.louisvuitton.com

Louis Vuitton's unmistakable, covetable (and luxuriously expensive) handbags are now available online directly through their quick and clear website. So you don't have to go into one of their stores anymore and ask for help and information, you'll find everything you could possibly need to know here, such as interior details, care and sizing. Once you've selected your country you'll find which styles are available to you; simply choose the design you like and go shop.

Site Usability:	★★★★★	Based:	UK
Product Range:	★★★★★	Express Delivery Option? (UK)	Yes
Price Range:	Luxury	Gift Wrapping Option	Automatic
Delivery Area:	Worldwide	Returns Procedure:	Down to you

www.luella.com

Any member of the handbag cognoscenti will tell you that Luella's handbags are all gorgeous and covetable (they're also not over-expensive when you consider some of the prices you can pay for 'must-have' handbags currently). Take a look at her website and you can view the collection with all the colourways, from the well known Stevie and Gisele bags to the studded Joni, Strappy Army and chic Sandhurst. If you see something you like, order it straight away, as they don't carry lots of stock in each colourway.

Site Usability:	★★★★	Based:	UK	
Product Range:	★★★★	Express Delivery Option? (UK)	No	
Price Range:	Luxury/Medium/Very Good Value	Gift Wrapping Option	No	
Delivery Area:	Worldwide	Returns Procedure:	Down to you	

www.luluguinness.com

'Be a glamour girl, put on your lipstick', is the phrase welcoming you to this elegant website, from which exquisite handbags and accessories from famous British designer Lulu Guinness can now be shipped to you wherever you are. With unique styling, sometimes very quirky, sometimes just plain gorgeous and a selection of cosmetic bags in stylish prints to take you anywhere, this is a website you should take a look at if you're in the mood for a treat or special gift.

Site Usability:	★★★★	Based:	UK	
Product Range:	★★★	Express Delivery Option? (UK)	No	
Price Range:	Luxury/Medium	Gift Wrapping Option?	No but everything is beautifully packaged	
Delivery Area:	Worldwide	Returns Procedure:	Down to you	

www.mulberry.com

Mulberry is a truly British luxury brand with an extensive line of highly crafted bags which combine stylish, standout design with the finest leathers and highly wrought detailing. Stuart Vevers, Design Director, has used Mulberry's 1970s Bohemian roots as a reference point in many of his designs and styles like the Bayswater, Emmy and Brooke have become covetable fashion classics for consumers and celebrities alike. Buy one if you can.

Site Usability:	★★★★★	Based:	UK	
Product Range:	★★★★	Express Delivery Option? (UK)	No	
Price Range:	Luxury	Gift Wrapping Option?	No	
Delivery Area:	Worldwide	Returns Procedure:	Down to you	

www.smythson.com

Smythson is famous as the Bond Street purveyor for over a century of absolutely top quality personalised stationery and accessories, including diaries, leather journals, albums, frames and gold edged place cards. They also have a luxurious small collection of handbags, briefcases, wallets and small leather goods at totally frightening prices. You can use their online personalised stationery service or call to order and they'll send you a sample pack from which you can choose your paper and style. Just let them know your choice and you're away.

Site Usability:	★★★★★	Based:	UK	
Product Range:	★★★★	Express Delivery Option? (UK)	No	
Price Range:	Luxury	Gift Wrapping Option?	No	
Delivery Area:	Worldwide	Returns Procedure:	Down to you	

www.tannerkrolle.co.uk

Tanner Krolle, launched in 1856, is one of London's oldest and finest luxury leather goods houses and all of the brand's bespoke bridle leather pieces are still hand-crafted in London. In addition to their traditional luggage Tanner Krolle produces beautiful handbags, shoes and small leather goods. You need to call to order and you can expect excellent service.

Site Usability:	★★★★	Based:	UK
Product Range:	★★★	Express Delivery Option? (UK)	Yes
Price Range:	Luxury	Gift Wrapping Option?	No but luxury packaging is standard
Delivery Area:	Worldwide	Returns Procedure:	Down to you

Also visit these websites for luxury handbags:

Website address	You'll find them in
www.net-a-porter.com	Luxury Fashion Brands
	Miu Miu
	Chloe
	Bottega Veneta
	Marc Jacobs
	Juicy Couture
	Stella McCartney
	Celine
	Fendi
	Jimmy Choo
	Missoni
	Roberto Cavalli
www.paulsmith.co.uk	Luxury Fashion Brands
www.lineafashion.com	Luxury Fashion Brands
	Tod's
	Cesare Paciotti
	Missoni
www.brownsfashion.com	Luxury Fashion Brands
	Chloe
	Fendi
	Marni
	Luella
	Bottega Veneta
	V.B.H

Carry These Without Breaking The Bank

www.angeljackson.co.uk

From the glamorous Ultimate Day Bag in black, cocoa, green or gold, to the woven leather Polanski you'll find an irresistible collection of extremely well priced and well made handbags here, plus weekenders, purses and day to evening clutches. You can see all the items in a lot of detail with close-up and different view photographs. Call them for mail order until their online shopping facility is up and running.

Site Usability:	★★★	Based:	UK
Product Range:	★★★	Express Delivery Option? (UK)	No
Price Range:	Medium	Gift Wrapping Option?	No
Delivery Area:	Worldwide	Returns Procedure:	Down to you

www.alicecaroline.co.uk

Not your usual range of handbags and jewellery here but something just a little bit different to tempt you when you want a new colourful fix but don't want to shell out the earth. There are fabric bags which would be perfect for summer and evenings, with oriental and funky prints such as Glamour Girls and Shoes, pretty gemstone, silver and gold jewellery and they'd all make great gifts for style conscious girls.

Site Usability:	★★★★	Based:	UK
Product Range:	★★★	Express Delivery Option? (UK)	Yes — call them
Price Range:	Medium	Gift Wrapping Option?	No
Delivery Area:	Worldwide	Returns Procedure:	Down to you

www.aspinaloflondon.com

If you're looking for top quality leather and British craftsmanship then take a look at this beautifully designed and photographed website where the product range is growing all the time and now includes chic handbags for day and evening, luxurious travel bags and accessories such as wallets and purses, gloves, cosmetic cases, jewellery rolls and make-up brush sets. This is definitely the place to find gorgeous accessories and excellent gifts as well.

Site Usability:	★★★★★	Based:	UK
Product Range:	★★★★★	Express Delivery Option? (UK)	Yes
Price Range:	Luxury/Medium	Gift Wrapping Option?	Yes
Delivery Area:	Worldwide	Returns Procedure:	Down to you

www.belenechandia.com

Here are soft leather handbags in a choice of colours with names such as Rock Me, Hold Me and Take Me Away by accessory label Belen Echandia. Choose your style of handbag, check out the measurements and detailing and then use their semi-bespoke service to select your particular choice of leather, from croc finish to metallics and brights to neutrals. These are definitely not inexpensive but unique and different, and investments that'll last you for years.

Site Usability:	★★★★	Based:	UK
Product Range:	★★★	Express Delivery Option? (UK)	Yes
Price Range:	Luxury	Gift Wrapping Option?	Yes
Delivery Area:	Worldwide	Returns Procedure:	Down to you

www.billamberg.com

From Bill Amberg's London studio the accessories team design a seasonal collection of very modern bags and luggage in carefully selected fine leathers and suedes with names such as Rocket Bag, Trafalgar Tote and Supernatural. You won't find his full range online but just a small collection which also gives you a very good idea of his individual style. You can also buy jewellery boxes and briefcases here along with his range for the shooting enthusiast.

Site Usability:	★★★	Based:	US
Product Range:	★★★	Express Delivery Option? (UK)	No
Price Range:	Luxury	Gift Wrapping Option?	No
Delivery Area:	Worldwide	Returns Procedure:	Down to you

www.bravida.co.uk

Bravida offers a collection of simple, stylish handbags made by Italian craftsmen in very high quality leather. You may not be buying into a famous brand, but many of the handbags are really chic and with prices starting at around £130 they're very good value. There are contemporary and classic bags plus a small collection of wallets. They'll ship worldwide and offer an express service.

Site Usability:	★★★	Based:	UK
Product Range:	★★★	Express Delivery Option? (UK)	Yes
Price Range:	Medium/Very Good Value	Gift Wrapping Option?	No
Delivery Area:	Worldwide	Returns Procedure:	Down to you

www.ignesbags.com

The next time you're looking for a new handbag, take a look at ignesbags.com, where you can find unique designs in unusual South American leathers. This is a small, high quality collection priced mostly at between £150 and £200 and ranging from large day bags to small, idiosyncratic evening bags with chain handles. Contact them if you want to order from outside the EU.

Site Usability:	★★★★	Based:	UK
Product Range:	★★★	Express Delivery Option? (UK)	No
Price Range:	Medium/Very Good Value	Gift Wrapping Option?	No
Delivery Area:	Worldwide	Returns Procedure:	Down to you

www.kanishkabags.co.uk

This is a lovely, ethnically inspired collection of clothes and accessories and you're unlikely to find it in the shops. You'll discover beaded and quilted handbags (plus straw totes in the summer), unusual and well priced jewellery, beautifully embroidered and colour woven shawls plus beaded silk and cotton kaftans, so if you like something totally unique and different you may find it here.

Site Usability:	★★★★	Based:	UK
Product Range:	★★★	Express Delivery Option? (UK)	No
Price Range:	Medium	Gift Wrapping Option?	No
Delivery Area:	Worldwide	Returns Procedure:	Down to you

www.julieslaterandson.co.uk

You can certainly find these products on other websites (passport covers, address books, purses, luggage tags and the like), however you'd have to search long and hard to find the colour ranges offered here which include pistachio, aubergine, meadow blue, hot pink and carnation. Everything is beautifully pictured in detail so you'll know exactly what you're ordering.

Site Usability:	★★★★	Based:	UK
Product Range:	★★★	Express Delivery Option? (UK)	Yes
Price Range:	Medium	Gift Wrapping Option	Yes
Delivery Area:	Worldwide	Returns Procedure:	Down to you

www.lizcox.com

Liz Cox offers a collection of bags and luggage hand made in her own workshops in the UK using exclusive fabrics, bridle and saddle leathers and incorporating exotic patterns and innovative designs. Her shops are based in Bath and Notting Hill, London and you can now buy a selection of her range online. Prices are definitely not cheap, so make sure you're a colourful patterned bag sort of person before you invest (although you can buy her gorgeous leathers as well here). Call for gift wrapping and express delivery.

Site Usability:	★★★	Based:	UK
Product Range:	★★★	Express Delivery Option? (UK)	Call them
Price Range:	Medium	Gift Wrapping Option?	Call them
Delivery Area:	Worldwide	Returns Procedure:	Down to you but you need to tell them first

www.ollieandnic.com

Ollie & Nic offer a stylish and chic range of accessories at excellent prices including pretty bags for day, evening and holiday, umbrellas, sunglasses, scarves, brooches and other accessories. The collection is very seasonal with new products being introduced all the time and each season will have a specific theme so you can visit this website regularly and you'll never be bored. There are very good gift ideas here for anyone who collection accessories, particularly in the winter season.

Site Usability:	★★★★	Based:	UK
Product Range:	★★★	Express Delivery Option? (UK)	No
Price Range:	Medium	Gift Wrapping Option?	No
Delivery Area:	Worldwide	Returns Procedure:	Down to you

www.orlakiely.com

Orla Kiely designs unique, instantly recognisable clothes and accessories, using bold and colourful patterns that are always fresh and appealing. On her website there is a small selection from her ready-to-wear clothing range, but a much wider choice of her unusual, attractive and highly functional accessories including handbags, purses and luggage.

Site Usability:	★★★★	Based:	UK
Product Range:	★★★	Express Delivery Option? (UK)	No
Price Range:	Medium	Gift Wrapping Option?	No
Delivery Area:	Worldwide	Returns Procedure:	Down to you

www.osprey-london.co.uk

For many years Osprey have created beautifully crafted handbags and small leather accessories in high quality leathers, all designed by Graeme Ellisdon in Florence. The range includes classic and business handbags – but think modern business, so although they'll take all the papers you need to carry, they look like great bags as well – plus the London Collection of contemporary bags in tune with what's happening each season.

Site Usability:	★★★★	Based:	UK
Product Range:	★★★	Express Delivery Option? (UK)	Yes
Price Range:	Luxury/Medium	Gift Wrapping Option?	No
Delivery Area:	Worldwide	Returns Procedure:	Down to you

www.tabitha.uk.com

At Tabitha you can see some covetable, not overpriced but very unusual bags and accessories in a choice of coloured leathers and metallics. There's lots to choose from, from the studded Angel Bag, to the chic Go Less Lightly bag with loads of pockets and buckles and my definite favourite the Lost Weekend Bag, just irresistible in ice white glazed leather. To order you need to complete their online form and email it back to them.

Site Usability:	★★★★	Based:	UK
Product Range:	★★★	Express Delivery Option? (UK)	No
Price Range:	Medium	Gift Wrapping Option?	No
Delivery Area:	Worldwide	Returns Procedure:	Down to you

Bag A Bargain

www.branded.net

Handbags, wallets and purses by Gucci, Christian Dior, Fendi, Dolce & Gabanna and Prada are on offer here, all at discounted prices and from recent seasons' collections. The site is based in London UK and they'll ship all over the world. You always have to be careful when buying discounted designer labels in case they're not the real thing, however there are a number of re-sellers (at present) particularly in Italy who are able to sell on ends of lines and overstocks of real designer products and these are what you'll find here.

Site Usability:	★★★★	Based:	UK
Product Range:	★★★★	Express Delivery Option? (UK)	No
Price Range:	Luxury/Medium	Gift Wrapping Option?	Yes
Delivery Area:	Worldwide	Returns Procedure:	Down to you

www.handbagcrush.co.uk

This company buys from designer reseller to enable you to buy authentic handbags and accessories from designers such as Gucci, Prada, Fendi and Versace. They clearly state the RRP (which I always suggest you should check if you can) plus the discount on offer and there are good, detailed pictures and lots of information. Worth having a look round.

Site Usability:	★★★★	Based:	UK
Product Range:	★★★★	Express Delivery Option? (UK)	Yes
Price Range:	Luxury/Medium	Gift Wrapping Option?	No
Delivery Area:	Worldwide	Returns Procedure:	Down to you

www.koodos.com

New web retailer Koodos offers you the opportunity of buying clothes, shoes and accessories by designers such as Gucci, Prada, Fendi, Feraud, Amanda Wakeley, Beatrix Ong and Nicole Farhi at amazing discounts. You need to check back often to see what's there and if there's something you like; snap it up straight away or you'll get back to it with the frustrating 'just sold out' notice clearly visible. To bring you even more temptation they hold 'Private Sales' of certain designers' new season's collection which you can only take part in if you've registered to be on the guest list.

Site Usability:	★★★★★	Based:	UK
Product Range:	★★★★	Express Delivery Option? (UK)	No
Price Range:	Luxury/Medium	Gift Wrapping Option?	No
Delivery Area:	UK	Returns Procedure:	Down to you

www.yoox.com

At Yoox you'll find end of season designer pieces at very good discounts – usually 50% off the designer's original price. It's a huge site and there are lots of designer clothes and accessories to choose from so it's best to have some sort of idea of what you're looking for before you start. Click on your favourite designer, search for a specific type of item and you're away.

Site Usability:	★★★★★	Based:	USA but use UK website
Product Range:	★★★★★	Express Delivery Option? (UK)	Yes
Price Range:	Luxury/Medium	Gift Wrapping Option?	Yes
Delivery Area:	Worldwide but click on the country for delivery to see that range	Returns Procedure:	Free but there's a $5 restocking fee per item

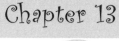

Chapter 13

Kick Your Heels

I was recently on holiday (without my kids, for once) and at a dinner party, when a woman walked in wearing the most delicious pair of shoes. They were dark brown, high heeled with platforms and peep toes and by Michael Kors. She'd bought them in New York.

I have to admit this huge wave of envy that swept over me. They were absolutely gorgeous, so modern, so totally now. The fact that she was at least two sizes smaller than me, about seventeen shades browner than me and that I wouldn't have been able to walk more than a couple of yards in them (I have real trouble with high heels) has nothing to do with it: I WANTED THOSE SHOES.

Anyway; enough of that. There are disastrously priced designer shoes just like handbags and just like handbags there are beautiful, well made and wearable lower priced shoes. I just have to warn you, once you've taken a good look at Gina and Jimmy Choo you may well feel just like I did.

Just in case you're in doubt, once again here are the size conversions for UK, European and US women's shoes

Women's shoe size conversions

UK	3.5	4	4.5	5	5.5	6	6.5	7	7.5	8	8.5
EU	36.5	37	37.5	38	38.5	39	40	41	42	43	43.5
US	6	6.5	7	7.5	8	8.5	9	9.5	10	10.5	11

Sites to Visit

Luxury Heels

www.emmahope.com

On her really pretty new website you can now see the full range of Emma Hope's beautiful designer shoes at real designer prices, so if you're in the mood to invest for your feet this is very much a place to explore. You'll find ballet flats, evening heels and modern platforms in a choice of colours, plus bags and accessories and an elegant wedding collection. Emma Hope is definitely one of the UK's most famous luxury shoe designers so take a look here now.

Site Usability:	★★★★★	Based:	UK
Product Range:	★★★★	Express Delivery Option? (UK)	Yes
Price Range:	Luxury	Gift Wrapping Option?	No
Delivery Area:	Worldwide	Returns Procedure:	Down to you

www.exclusivefootwear.com

Gina, Moschino, Beatrix Ong, Pedro Garcia and Patrick Cox head up the list of designer label footwear you'll find here, alongside Stuart Weitzman and lots of other stylish brands plus a good selection of casual footwear, boots and bridal shoes. The website is extremely quick to browse round with temptation everywhere. Men's ranges include Oliver Sweeney, Jeffery West and Patrick Cox. They ship to many overseas destinations but check to ensure that yours is included.

Site Usability:	★★★★★	Based:	UK
Product Range:	★★★★	Express Delivery Option? (UK)	Yes
Price Range:	Luxury/Medium	Gift Wrapping Option?	Yes
Delivery Area:	Worldwide most countries	Returns Procedure:	Down to you

www.gina.com

Gina was first established in 1954 and named after Gina Lollobridgida. Now it's run by the three Kurdash brothers (the sons of the founder, Mehmet Kurdash) who continue to design totally exquisite shoes, so if you want the couture look and a seriously special pair then click no further. Here you'll find a truly wonderful collection of beautiful, sexy shoes in the softest leather and with out-to-lunch and dinner heels. There's a price to match as you would expect but the shoes are definitely worth it and they'll last a long time. There's also a small selection of handbags.

Site Usability:	★★★★	Based:	UK
Product Range:	★★★★	Express Delivery Option? (UK)	No but 2 days is standard
Price Range:	Luxury	Gift Wrapping Option?	No
Delivery Area:	Worldwide	Returns Procedure:	Down to you

www.jimmychoo.com

Needless to say the new Jimmy Choo website is beautifully and provocatively designed and makes you want to browse right through even though the prices are quite frightening in most cases, to say the least. This is always a totally covetable collection, including diamante encrusted sandals, killer heel peep toe slides, gorgeous boots and wonderful, right on trend handbags.

Site Usability:	★★★★★	Based:	UK
Product Range:	★★★★★	Express Delivery Option? (UK)	Yes
Price Range:	Luxury	Gift Wrapping Option?	Automatic
Delivery Area:	Worldwide	Returns Procedure:	Down to you

www.rupertsanderson.co.uk

Rupert Sanderson, who has designed collections for both Margaret Howell and Jean Muir, offers a collection of timeless, classic hand-made shoes in a very British style. Don't expect to find the latest platforms or wedges here, but there are beautifully designed heels for day and evening in a range of this season's colours plus a small collection of sandals and flats. Prices are high but you're buying investment shoes here that you can expect to last you a while.

Site Usability:	★★★★	Based:	UK
Product Range:	★★★★	Express Delivery Option? (UK)	No
Price Range:	Luxury	Gift Wrapping Option?	Automatic
Delivery Area:	Worldwide	Returns Procedure:	Down to you

Also visit these websites for Luxury Heels:

Website address	You'll find them in
www.brownsfashion.com	Luxury Fashion Brands
	Jill Sander
	Lanvin
	Christian Louboutin
	Salvatore Ferragamo
	Dries van Noten
	Dolce & Gabbana
www.net-a-porter.com	Luxury Fashion Brands
	Miu Miu
	Chloe
	Christian Louboutin
	Jimmy Choo
	Missoni
	Roberto Cavalli
www.paulsmith.co.uk	Luxury Fashion Brands
www.lineafashion.com	Luxury Fashion Brands
	Tod's
	Cesare Paciotti
	Missoni
www.gucci.com	Handbag Temptation/The A List
www.vivaladiva.com	Lulu Guinness
	Beatrix Ong
	Christian Dior
	Sergio Rossi

Affordable Heels

www.bucklesandbows.co.uk

If you're considering investing in a pair of boots but you have the popular problem of most boots being too tight on the calf then have a look at this extremely quick website. First measure the widest part of your calf, click on the boots you like and check which size you should take. Prices are around £100, they offer next day delivery and they'll ship worldwide.

Site Usability:	★★★★★	Based:	UK
Product Range:	★★★	Express Delivery Option? (UK)	Yes
Price Range:	Medium	Gift Wrapping Option?	No
Delivery Area:	Worldwide	Returns Procedure:	Down to you

www.dune.co.uk

Here you can buy from a range of trendy, affordable and stylish shoes and accessories including glitzy sandals, dressy pumps and flats, modern casual shoes and ballerinas and excellent boots. As well as all of this there are handbags, belts and sunglasses. The website is well photographed and easy to use and provided you place your order before 10am you'll receive it the next day.

Site Usability:	★★★★	Based:	UK
Product Range:	★★★	Express Delivery Option? (UK)	Yes
Price Range:	Medium/Very Good Value	Gift Wrapping Option?	No
Delivery Area:	UK	Returns Procedure:	Down to you

www.duoboots.com

If you've ever (like me) gone into a shoe shop, discovered the perfect pair of boots and found that the zip won't do up to the top, you'll welcome this website. Duo Boots offer 21 calf sizes, from 30cm to 50cm. You just select your style and colour from their wide range, check out the pictures which are excellent, then input your normal shoe size and calf measurement.

Site Usability:	★★★★★	Based:	UK
Product Range:	★★★★	Express Delivery Option? (UK)	Yes
Price Range:	Medium	Gift Wrapping Option?	No
Delivery Area:	Worldwide	Returns Procedure:	Down to you

www.faith.co.uk

In 1964 Samuel Faith established Faith shoes with the aim of combining style and affordability and he seems to have succeeded. You'll discover some extremely modern styles here plus some that are far more classic and they're all at very reasonable prices. Faith Solo is the most avent garde part of the collection and there are also some extremely well priced fun leather handbags.

Site Usability:	★★★★	Based:	UK
Product Range:	★★★	Express Delivery Option? (UK)	No
Price Range:	Very Good Value	Gift Wrapping Option?	No
Delivery Area:	UK	Returns Procedure:	Down to you

www.floydshoes.co.uk

You won't find this collection of well priced shoes in any retail outlets (at least not at the time of writing) as they're currently only offered on this website and at regional fairs. All the shoes here are designed by Janice Floyd, who created her company in 2002 with the idea of producing distinctive, fashionable and elegant but fun shoes at an affordable price. There's also a small range of handbags in a selection of great colours.

Site Usability:	★★★★	Based:	UK
Product Range:	★★★	Express Delivery Option? (UK)	No
Price Range:	Medium	Gift Wrapping Option?	No
Delivery Area:	Worldwide	Returns Procedure:	Down to you

www.footlux.com

Footlux is a Spanish based company whose aim is to offer you an eclectic range of footwear and accessories by famous and less well known designers such as Michael Kors, Pedro Garcia, Barbara Bui and Chie Mihara. Don't worry if you don't know some of the designers; there's excellent information about all of them and best of all when you browse the collections you'll discover modern (sometimes quite unusual) designs, always at the forefront of fashion.

Site Usability:	★★★★	Based:	Spain
Product Range:	★★★★	Express Delivery Option? (UK)	Yes
Price Range:	Luxury/Medium	Gift Wrapping Option?	No
Delivery Area:	Most worldwide countries	Returns Procedure:	Down to you with their authorisation code

www.frenchsole.com

If you've been looking for the perfect ballet flat to update your spring/summer or autumn/winter wardrobe you need search no more. French Sole are well known for offering a wide range of styles, from the classic two-tone pump to this season's must-have animal print and metallic versions and each season they bring out new styles. They also offer high quality travel slippers and driving shoes.

Site Usability:	★★★★	Based:	UK
Product Range:	★★★★	Express Delivery Option? (UK)	No
Price Range:	Medium	Gift Wrapping Option?	No
Delivery Area:	Worldwide	Returns Procedure:	Down to you

www.helenbateman.com

Winner at the 2002 Footwear Awards for Customer Service this Edinburgh based shoe designer offers a pretty and unusual selection of shoes for all occasions. There's a great deal of choice from beaded Shantung silk evening shoes and stylish sandals to funky espadrilles in a range of colours. One of the great advantages of ordering shoes here is the amount of information on each style, from fit to fabric and heel height plus different views.

Site Usability:	★★★★★	Express Delivery Option? (UK)	Yes
Product Range:	★★★★	Gift Wrapping Option?	No
Price Range:	Medium	Returns Procedure:	Down to you
Delivery Area:	Worldwide		

www.kurtgeiger.com

Browse the Kurt Geiger online store for shoes and accessories from many of your favourite designers, including Kurt Geiger, Marc Jacobs, Stuart Weitzman KG, Gina and Carvela. With new arrivals daily, you can find styles ranging from young contemporary to modern classic, with the site also featuring a sale area. They currently deliver to the British Isles and Eire, and offer a next day service.

Site Usability:	★★★★★	Express Delivery Option? (UK)	Yes
Product Range:	★★★★	Gift Wrapping Option?	No
Price Range:	Luxury/Medium/Very Good Value	Returns Procedure:	Down to you
Delivery Area:	UK		

www.modainpelle.com

Moda in Pelle offers an excellent range of fashionable and well priced shoes, boots and bags including trendy daytime bags and shoes and a very good evening selection (check out the diamante sandles). They aim themselves at a young, High Street, audience (think River Island, Jane Norman and Morgan) but with their up to the minute styling have a much wider appeal. Their new website allows you to see every detail of the shoes on offer and is well worth a look round.

Site Usability:	★★★★★	Express Delivery Option? (UK)	No
Product Range:	★★★★	Gift Wrapping Option?	No
Price Range:	Very Good Value	Returns Procedure:	Down to you
Delivery Area:	Worldwide		

www.panacheshoes.co.uk

This is a very busy website offering some excellent shoes and accessories from an ecelectic selection of brands ranging from very modern to quite classic. Stuart Weitzman, LK Bennett, Lulu Guinness, YIN and Chie Mihara are just some of the designers on offer, you can see everything very clearly and also check if what you want to order is in stock. UK delivery is free on orders over £100 and if you want overseas delivery you need to call them.

Site Usability:	★★★★★	Express Delivery Option? (UK)	No
Product Range:	★★★★	Gift Wrapping Option?	No
Price Range:	Luxury/Medium	Returns Procedure:	Down to you
Delivery Area:	Worldwide but call for outside UK		

www.plusinboots.co.uk

Here you'll find boots at price levels from £50 to about £200 plus calf measurements from 35cm to 46cm. You need to take a look at their measuring guide as they offer both their own boots and those made by other manufacturers. There are some modern and some very classic styles to choose from plus a small range of shoes.

Site Usability:	★★★	Express Delivery Option? (UK)	Yes, worldwide
Product Range:	★★★	Gift Wrapping Option?	Yes
Price Range:	Medium/Very Good Value	Returns Procedure:	Down to you
Delivery Area:	Worldwide		

www.prettyballerinas.com

Established in 1918 to make ballet shoes Pretty Ballerinas offer a wide selection of colours and prints including animal prints (zebra, leopard, or tiger) metallics, sequins, prints such as purple butterflies and fuchsia, green or blue satin. When you look at the site you need to be aware that all the prices are in Euros so you'll need to do the conversion to pounds, dollars or whatever currency you want to buy in.

Site Usability:	★★★★	Based:	UK
Product Range:	★★★	Express Delivery Option? (UK)	No
Price Range:	Medium	Gift Wrapping Option?	No
Delivery Area:	Worldwide	Returns Procedure:	Down to you

www.rubbersole.co.uk

According to the fashion magazines, Crocs are what you should be wearing on your feet right now and you'll find the full range here. If you think they're a bit too modern for you, on this excellent website you can also order your Havainas flip-flops, stylish Cubanas (flip-flops with heels) and Pare Gabia espadrilles, plus Vans and Converse trainers and Hunter wellies. You can see immediately what's in stock and they offer a speedy delivery service.

Site Usability:	★★★★★	Based:	UK
Product Range:	★★★★★	Express Delivery Option? (UK)	No but delivery is very fast
Price Range:	Medium	Gift Wrapping Option?	No
Delivery Area:	UK	Returns Procedure:	Down to you.

www.scorahpattullo.com

If your taste is for the very (I mean very) high heeled and extremely modern then come and take a look round Scorah Puttullo where their latest collections are just waiting to be delivered to you by high speed courier anywhere in the world. The emphasis is on the latest up to date styles, from flats and sandals to dressy heels so if you're looking for something new this season you may well find it here.

Site Usability:	★★★★	Based:	UK
Product Range:	★★★	Express Delivery Option? (UK)	No but expect two working days
Price Range:	Luxury	Gift Wrapping Option?	No
Delivery Area:	Worldwide	Returns Procedure:	Down to you

www.schuhstore.co.uk

At schuhstore.co.uk there are lots of pairs of shoes from a wide choice of labels to choose from at very good prices. There are always some very modern styles and others rather over colourful but there's such a large range you'll surely discover something to suit. You can select from each range (boots, for example) whether you want high heel, mid heel, low heel or flat and the zoom feature allows you to get really close up to each product. You can also search by brand, style, price and what's new. They offer a 365 day returns policy for shoes returned in perfect condition.

Site Usability:	★★★★	Based:	UK
Product Range:	★★★★★	Express Delivery Option? (UK)	Yes
Price Range:	Medium/Very Good Value	Gift Wrapping Option?	No
Delivery Area:	UK	Returns Procedure:	Down to you

www.shellys.co.uk

Here are the modern (think extremely, in some cases) well priced shoes to go with your next buy from Miss Selfridge, Top Shop or River Island. It's a very clear website and they tell you straight away what's leather and what's not and what's available right now. If you're into the latest 'Babe' platform slingback sandal with mega heels you'll love it here

Site Usability:	★★★★	Based:	UK	
Product Range:	★★★★	Express Delivery Option? (UK)	No	
Price Range:	Medium/Very Good Value	Gift Wrapping Option?	No	
Delivery Area:	UK	Returns Procedure:	Down to you	

www.shoestudio.com

The Shoe Studio Group is a multi-branded fashion footwear retailer on the UK high-street with brands such as Pied a Terre, Kenneth Cole, Bertie, Nine West and Principles. On its clearly photographed website you can buy from most of their modern and well priced brands and find everything from day and evening heels to boots, holiday shoes and flats plus a very good range of handbags. If you want to know what's hot you can click straight through to their 'must have' section for each of the brands where you can buy straight into the latest trends.

Site Usability:	★★★★★	Based:	UK	
Product Range:	★★★★★	Express Delivery Option? (UK)	No	
Price Range:	Medium/Very Good Value	Gift Wrapping Option?	No	
Delivery Area:	UK and Eire	Returns Procedure:	Down to you	

www.ugsandkisses.co.uk

If you're a fan of the extraordinarily comfortable and popular Ugg boot from Australia then you'll definitely need this website, which offers the full range of UGG Australia boots including the Classic short and tall versions and in a choice of colours. They also sell baby Uggs, Snow Joggers, Love from Australia, My Sweet Feet, Simple footwear and their own Ugs & Kisses brand. There's lots of information on how to care for your Uggs including Ugg Shampoo which you can order. Delivery is free in the UK on orders over £45.

Site Usability:	★★★★★	Based:	UK	
Product Range:	★★★	Express Delivery Option? (UK)	No	
Price Range:	Medium	Gift Wrapping Option?	No	
Delivery Area:	Worldwide	Returns Procedure:	Down to you	

www.vivaladiva.com

This is an online store that's growing like topsy with more and more styles and designers being added each season. You'll find couture shoes and boots by Beatrix Ong, Cavalli, Sergio Rossi and Lulu Guinness, their Boutique collection with names such as Amira and Carvela plus much less expensive ranges like Schuh, Moda in Pelle and Converse. It's a fun website to take a look at with a lot of attitude and the shoes are displayed very clearly. Shoes range from £25 to £300. Watch out for new designers being included.

Site Usability:	★★★★★	Express Delivery Option? (UK)	Yes	
Product Range:	★★★★	Gift Wrapping Option?	Yes/Automatic	
Price Range:	Luxury/Medium/Very Good Value	Returns Procedure:	Free of charge by courier or Royal Mail	
Delivery Area:	UK			

Chapter 14

Sunglasses

Sunglasses are another essential accessory that do *so* much more for people than most of them realise. You don't think that all those celebrities are wearing their Gucci, Oliver Peoples, Prada or Chanel shades just to cut out the glare do you? Definitely not.

They're wearing them because they're the latest style, because they flatter their faces and because, by wearing those particular shades, they're recognised as the cognoscenti – the in crowd who know what's hot.

Sunglasses are such an easy way to stay in style and yes, they can be useful as well. Don't go out this summer with the pair that you've been wearing for the past few years. If you can, invest in a new, chic pair that suit your face, cut out the glare and the sun and make you feel great; as a new accessory they're much less expensive than a handbag, after all.

If you're not sure which style will suit you several of the websites below are very good at advising you on what shapes will suit your face. Take a look in the advice sections at www. sunglasses-shop.co.uk (where you can download your own photo and try out different shapes) and www.sunglassesuk.co.uk, where they also give you lots of help.

Your siteguide.com password is SG015. Please use this as the media code when subscribing for your free year's login.

Sites to Visit

www.davidclulow.com

With concessions in Harrods and Selfridges and stores throughout London you'd expect David Clulow to be a great destination shop for contemporary eyewear and you'd be right. Online you'll find Burberry, Gucci, Armani, Oliver Peoples, Ray-Ban and Prada plus sports goggles and glasses by Oakley, Adidas and Bolle. This certainly isn't the largest range of designer sunglasses online but you may well find it easier to choose from a smaller, well edited collection. Take a look at the contact lens prices here too.

Site Usability:	★★★★	Based:	UK
Product Range:	★★★	Express Delivery Option? (UK)	No
Price Range:	Luxury/Medium	Gift Wrapping Option?	No
Delivery Area:	UK	Returns Procedure:	Down to you with their authorisation

www.shadestation.co.uk

For the cooler end of the market have a look round here, where the emphasis is on young, modern styles from brands such as Prada, Police, D & G, Diesel, Gucci and Armani and you'll find watches by some of these names as well. They stock the complete Oakley brand including glasses, accessories, goggles and watches plus replacement lenses and sunglass cases.

Site Usability:	★★★	Based:	UK
Product Range:	★★★	Express Delivery Option? (UK)	Yes
Price Range:	Luxury/Medium	Gift Wrapping Option?	No
Delivery Area:	UK	Returns Procedure:	Down to you

www.ten-eighty.co.uk

By far the best thing about this site is their range of Oakley sunglasses and lenses. Whereas on most sites you'll be offered a style and that's it, here with their help you can create your own, particularly for sports use, and their service is really excellent. Persevere with this site although some of it is hard to read and you do have to scroll around a lot. It will be worth it. If you want extra advice don't hesitate to call them – their service is excellent.

Site Usability:	★★★	Based:	UK
Product Range:	★★★	Express Delivery Option? (UK)	Yes
Price Range:	Luxury/Medium	Gift Wrapping Option?	No
Delivery Area:	UK	Returns Procedure:	Down to you

www.the-eye-shop.com

This website is based in Chamonix in France (where you do need sunglasses a lot of the time, of course) and the list of brand names is fantastic, including Chanel, Dior, Diesel, Bolle, Oakley, Quicksilver and Valentino. They claim to hold almost everything in stock and delivery is free by UPS. You can also choose from a very good selection of sport goggles here from brands such as Cebe, Oakley and Adidas plus binoculars and GPS systems.

Site Usability:	★★★★★	Based:	France
Product Range:	★★★★★	Express Delivery Option? (UK)	No
Price Range:	Luxury/Medium	Gift Wrapping Option?	No
Delivery Area:	Worldwide	Returns Procedure:	Down to you

www.sunglasses-shop.co.uk

The Sunglasses Shop offers you free express UK delivery and you can choose from designer brands Prada, Gucci, Chanel, Versace, Dolce and Gabbana, Dior and many more. They have a very comprehensive and modern range and if you click on the pair you like you not only get a close-up but also detailed pictures showing you what the side hinges and nose piece look like. You can shop by brand and by colour or select from their best sellers.

Site Usability:	★★★★★	Based:	UK
Product Range:	★★★★★	Express Delivery Option? (UK)	Yes
Price Range:	Luxury/Medium	Returns Procedure:	Down to you
Delivery Area:	UK		

www.sunglassesuk.co.uk

Just about every brand of sunglasses is available from this UK site including Gucci, Chloe, Dolce and Gabbana, Moschino, Bolle and Prada. You can check out their best sellers or buy the same pair of sunglasses your favourite celebrity is wearing this year. It's a fun site with lots to see. They don't carry every style in stock and it's best to call them if you find something you really like to make sure it's available now.

Site Usability:	★★★★	Based:	UK
Product Range:	★★★★	Express Delivery Option? (UK)	No
Price Range:	Luxury/Medium	Gift Wrapping Option?	No
Delivery Area:	UK	Returns Procedure:	Down to you

www.technical-gear.com

For sports and technical sunglasses and goggles look no further than this excellent website, where they offer brands such as Oakley, Bolle, Gargoyle, Action Optics and Spy; a full range of goggles for all sports activities and specific advice on which shades you need for driving, skiing, sailing, golf, fishing and many more activities

Site Usability:	★★★★★	Based:	US
Product Range:	★★★★★	Express Delivery Option? (UK)	No
Price Range:	Medium	Gift Wrapping Option?	No
Delivery Area:	Worldwide	Returns Procedure:	Down to you

www.unitedshades.com

This US-based website (now with a European arm) has a comprehensive range of the latest sunglasses. Choose from Versace, Armani, Ferragamo, Givenchy, Gucci, Yves St Laurent and many more. With over twenty-five brands on offer you're sure to find something you like. Delivery is free for most countries – check their Shipping Tariff form to make sure that yours is on there.

Whatever you're thinking of buying you absolutely should have a look at their 'Choose the right sunglasses for your face' area where they give a lot of advice. Everyone who sells sunglass online should be doing this but most of them aren't yet (or they're hiding it) and it's essential if you're going to buy online.

Site Usability:	★★★★★	Based:	EU/US
Product Range:	★★★★	Express Delivery Option? (UK)	Yes
Price Range:	Luxury/Medium	Gift Wrapping Option?	No
Delivery Area:	Worldwide	Returns Procedure:	Down to you

Chapter 15

Jewellery and Watches

Luxury Jewels   Gorgeous and Accessible   Fashion Rocks   Watches

This is not the place to find jewels for less, as although I've divided this section into four for what I hope from their titles are obvious reasons, there are thousands of really, really cheap jewellery websites which you won't find here.

In Luxury Jewels you'll find just that, beautiful, hand crafted pieces that are really special and will last a lifetime. If you're looking for that 5 carat diamond you can find it here and although I'm not really advocating that you buy it online you can if you want to. Just a word of advice: If you do want to buy a special stone online do not buy without speaking to the retailer/diamond merchant and making sure that you are absolutely happy about your purchase.

I was testing out a jewellery website the other day and was amazed that I was allowed to put a £44,000 emerald cut diamond into my 'basket'. Who would ever do such a thing without a great deal of research into the stone itself and who they were buying from? I'm not saying that this particular retailer didn't know what they were doing (and I'm not going to tell you who it was, anyway) but you do need to take care.

Buy from Tiffany, Boodles or Theo Fenell and you'll be buying beautiful quality from a totally trustworthy name. At Astley Clarke you'll find a wide range of prices and some really lovely jewellery from hard to find designers such as Lisa Stewart and Carolina Bucci.

Ok, enough of the luxury jewels, let's move on to the Gorgeous and Accessible variety, which, as I'm sure you've realised, are not (in the main) jewellers at the top end of the market but online retailers offering a wide range, from diamond set jewellery at Blitz and Ice Cool to glamorous gemstone jewellery at Emma Chapman and Kirsten Goss, plus lovely modern pieces at Kabiri and Reglisse. I've mentioned just a few of my favourites but when you have a browse through, you will find a really good choice at all of the websites below, all of which will make perfect gifts or treats for you.

Fashion Rocks is the place to find 'on trend' jewellery to go with the latest fashion looks and you can spend a lot or a little as you choose. They all offer something slightly different and they're all excellent, with a selection over quite a wide price range, although in general they're far more reasonable than the luxury end, of course.

Finally there are watches online, and here you're plunged into choosing between diamond encrusted Cartier, sporty Tag Heuer, chic, modern Gucci and fun Swatch. You won't at the moment find the full ranges online, but what there is is very good and quite enough to give you palpitations at some of the prices - well they do to me, anyway.

Sites to Visit

Luxury Jewels

www.astleyclarke.com

Luxury online jewellery boutique Astley Clarke carries exquisite contemporary fine and designer jewellery collections from all over the world. This is the perfect place to find romantic jewellery gifts or something special for your own jewellery box. With a strong base of celebrity customers including Nicole Kidman, Julia Roberts and Christie Turlington and a gorgeous, modern range this online shop is not to be missed.

Site Usability:	★★★★★	Based:	UK
Product Range:	★★★★★	Express Delivery Option? (UK)	Yes
Price Range:	Luxury/Medium	Gift Wrapping Option?	Yes
Delivery Area:	Worldwide	Returns Procedure:	Down to you

www.boodles.co.uk

Gorgeous modern jewellery: The real thing. Some things you might just imagine buying for yourself and others you'd probably rather have bought for you, like the divine Asscher cut diamond earrings that they don't even tell you the price for. Have a look round anyway, you might just be tempted. I should warn you though, there's almost nothing here for under £1000. Everything is gift wrapped and they'll ship all over the world.

Site Usability:	★★★★	Based:	UK
Product Range:	★★★★	Express Delivery Option? (UK)	Yes
Price Range:	Luxury	Gift Wrapping Option?	Yes
Delivery Area:	Worldwide	Returns Procedure:	Down to you

www.mikimoto-store.co.uk

Mikimoto is a name synonymous with beautiful and luxurious pearls (they've been in business for over 100 years) and now you can buy a selection of their best selling jewellery online. Prices start at around £120 for a pair of timeless pearl studs and go up to around £2000 for their Tahitian pearl and pink sapphire pendants and earrings. Everything is beautifully gift wrapped and you can have your order within 48 hours.

Site Usability:	★★★★★	Based:	UK
Product Range:	★★★★	Express Delivery Option? (UK)	Yes
Price Range:	Luxury/Medium	Gift Wrapping Option?	Yes
Delivery Area:	Worldwide	Returns Procedure:	Down to you

www.theofennell.com

Theo Fennell is famous as the jewellery designer of stars such as Elton John. His modern diamond studded crosses and keys are recognised the world over together with his solid silver Marmite lids and Worcester sauce bottle holders. Nothing on this website is inexpensive but you'll find some extremely beautiful and unique designs and if you buy anything you can be sure it will be exquisitely presented. Browse the site and see if you're tempted.

Site Usability:	★★★	Based:	UK
Product Range:	★★★★	Express Delivery Option? (UK)	No
Price Range:	Luxury	Gift Wrapping Option?	Yes
Delivery Area:	Worldwide	Returns Procedure:	Down to you

www.tiffany.com

Exquisite and expensive: the two words that sum up one of the world's most luxurious jewellery emporiums. Anything in the signature Tiffany blue box is sure to make a perfect present, from the smallest piece of Elsa Peretti or Paloma Picasso jewellery to wonderful classic diamonds and pearls. Beautiful Tiffany glass candlesticks, bowls and stemware, the new Tiffany fragrance in its lovely glass bottle or christening gifts for a new baby; it's all available online.

Site Usability:	★★★★★	Based:	UK
Product Range:	★★★★★	Express Delivery Option? (UK)	Yes
Price Range:	Luxury	Gift Wrapping Option?	Yes/Automatic
Delivery Area:	UK and USA	Returns Procedure:	Down to you

Gorgeous and Accessible

www.absolutepearls.co.uk

This website was originally established in China and has now relocated to the UK to offer you quality cultured pearl necklaces, earrings and bracelets. There's a good selection from simple single strand necklaces to black Tahitian pearl and diamond pendants. If you want information about how to choose pearls and what makes them so special you'll find it in their extremely comprehensive information centre together with suggestions for gifts and their message card service.

Site Usability:	★★★★★	Based:	UK
Product Range:	★★★★	Express Delivery Option? (UK)	Yes
Price Range:	Luxury/Medium	Gift Wrapping Option?	No
Delivery Area:	UK	Returns Procedure:	Down to you

www.bobijou.com

BoBijou is a reasonably priced European designer jewellery brand, offering a collection of chic colourful pieces, designed in-house and hand-made using natural cultured pearls and gemstones with silver and gold. Many designs carry their signature design feature, MLMF (Multi Look Multi Function), so a long design can be a belt, a lariat style necklace, a chunky choker or a bracelet; making them very flexible and giving you more value for money. New styles are added each season.

Site Usability:	★★★★★	Based:	UK
Product Range:	★★★★	Express Delivery Option? (UK)	Yes
Price Range:	Luxury/Medium	Gift Wrapping Option?	No
Delivery Area:	EU	Returns Procedure:	Down to you

www.chapmansjewellery.co.uk

Dower and Hall, Vivienne Westwood, Shaun Leans, Colman Douglas Pearls and Mounir are just some of the designers you'll find here alongside their own range (although the collection changes regularly) and while you can order everything online if you should have a query they have staff who you can call for advice. Some of the pieces are stunningly pretty (as is the website) and there are several very clear views of each.

Site Usability:	★★★★★	Based:	UK
Product Range:	★★★★	Express Delivery Option? (UK)	No
Price Range:	Medium	Gift Wrapping Option?	Yes
Delivery Area:	UK	Returns Procedure:	Down to you

www.dinnyhall.com

Here you can see beautifully designed well priced modern jewellery from one of Britain's foremost jewellery designers. Every piece is hand crafted using traditional jewellery making techniques with high quality silver, gold and precious and semi-precious stones. If you haven't discovered her work up until now this is definitely the time to start collecting. She has a very clear and modern website where you can see all the products in each category at once which is extremely helpful.

Site Usability:	★★★★★	Based:	UK
Product Range:	★★★★	Express Delivery Option? (UK)	No
Price Range:	Medium	Gift Wrapping Option?	Yes
Delivery Area:	Worldwide	Returns Procedure:	Down to you

www.emmachapmanjewels.com

Emma Chapman is a new jewellery designer, based in London, who creates beautiful and glamorous designer gemstone jewellery which is exotic with a contemporary edge. It's a covetable collection grouped by descriptions such as 'Beach Babe', 'Baroque Goddess' and 'Indian Princess'. Everything is individually made and reasonably priced so if you see something you like you need to contact them immediately.

Site Usability:	★★★★	Based:	UK
Product Range:	★★★	Express Delivery Option? (UK)	No
Price Range:	Medium	Gift Wrapping Option?	No
Delivery Area:	Worldwide	Returns Procedure:	Down to you

www.green-frederick.co.uk

If you love beautiful jewellery and the sparkle of diamonds but the real thing is slightly out of your range (like most of us) you'll need to spend some time on this wonderful but unsophisticated website where there are 18ct gold necklaces, bracelets and earrings set with glittering hand cut cubic zirconias plus a wide range of real pearl jewellery. This is not cheap jewellery but superb quality at a very good price and it's very hard to tell the difference between the highest quality zirconias used here and the real thing.

Site Usability:	★★★★	Based:	UK
Product Range:	★★★★	Express Delivery Option? (UK)	Yes
Price Range:	Medium	Gift Wrapping Option?	No
Delivery Area:	Worldwide	Returns Procedure:	Down to you

www.harriet-whinney.co.uk

Harriet Whinney specialises in pearl jewellery made to order and beautiful timeless pearl earrings, necklaces and bracelets. You can select from her ready made range or choose the quality of the pearl you want for your piece of jewellery and then select the type of clasp. There are also some extremely special pieces here such as baroque and South Sea pearls.

Site Usability:	★★★★	Based:	UK
Product Range:	★★★★	Express Delivery Option? (UK)	No
Price Range:	Luxury/Medium	Gift Wrapping Option?	No
Delivery Area:	Worldwide	Returns Procedure:	Down to you

www.icecool.co.uk

At Ice Cool you can select from a range of modern and classic well priced jewels, including diamond studs, tennis bracelets, pendants and rings, mostly set in 18ct gold and with sparkling diamonds. Prices start at around £100. One of the best things here is their Trend section, where you can find out what you should be wearing jewellerywise this year and also Discover Diamonds, where you can read all you could possibly want to know (and more) about what are definitely my favourite stones. They offer a bespoke service as well.

Site Usability:	★★★★★	Based:	UK
Product Range:	★★★★	Express Delivery Option? (UK)	No
Price Range:	Medium	Gift Wrapping Option?	No
Delivery Area:	Worldwide	Returns Procedure:	Down to you

www.kabiri.co.uk

Kabiri is a jewellery shop on London's Marylebone High Street, carrying an eclectic range of modern, international designers such as Wendy Nichol, Adina, Carolina Bucci, Pippa Small and Tracy Matthews. The search facility is excellent; as you can look by designer, type of jewellery and price and as there's so much to see I suggest you use it. Be prepared to spend some time here - with this amount of choice you're bound to find something you like. For express delivery call them.

Site Usability:	★★★★★	Based:	UK
Product Range:	★★★★★	Express Delivery Option? (UK)	No
Price Range:	Luxury/Medium	Gift Wrapping Option?	No
Delivery Area:	Worldwide	Returns Procedure:	Down to you

www.kirstengoss.com

After studying jewellery design in South Africa Kirsten Goss moved to London and launched her own company where she currently creates exclusive, modern collections of jewellery using semi precious stones and sterling silver. Having been featured by *Harpers*, *Elle*, *Glamour* and *In Style* and described as 'the next big thing' by the *Sunday Times* magazine this is definitely one to watch.

Site Usability:	★★★★	Based:	UK
Product Range:	★★★	Express Delivery Option? (UK)	Yes
Price Range:	Medium	Gift Wrapping Option?	No
Delivery Area:	Worldwide	Returns Procedure:	Down to you

www.linksoflondon.com

Links of London are well known for an eclectic mix of jewellery in sterling silver and 18ct gold, charms and charm bracelets, cufflinks, gorgeous gifts and leather and silver accessories for your home. Inevitably each season they design a new collection of totally desirable pieces (in other words, I want them) such as the 'Sweetie Rolled Gold Bracelet', or 'Annoushka' gold and ruby charm. This website is perfect for gifts and if you need something sent in a hurry they offer an express service worldwide.

Site Usability:	★★★★★	Based:	UK
Product Range:	★★★★★	Express Delivery Option? (UK)	Yes
Price Range:	Luxury/Medium	Gift Wrapping Option?	Yes
Delivery Area:	Worldwide	Returns Procedure:	Down to you

www.manjoh.com

On Manjoh's attractively designed contemporary jewellery website, you'll find designers such as Izabel Camille, Benedicte Mouret, Vinnie Day and Scott Wilson and the list is regularly being added to. Most recent additions include DAY Jewels, a luxury jewellery line from Day Birger et Mikkelsen, which they sell exclusively online and ultra fashionable R jewellery. The site also includes monthly features on the latest trends and interviews with designers.

Site Usability:	★★★★★	Based:	UK
Product Range:	★★★	Express Delivery Option? (UK)	Yes
Price Range:	Medium	Gift Wrapping Option?	Yes
Delivery Area:	Worldwide	Returns Procedure:	Down to you

www.murrayforbes.co.uk

Based in Inverness in the Highlands of Scotland, Murray Forbes has an unusual selection of not overpriced jewellery online, comprising earrings, bracelets and necklaces, some quite traditional and some modern, using semi precious stones, pearls, black and white diamonds and 9 or 18ct gold. The pictures are very clear and the details and information excellent. They offer free shipping and shipping insurance in the UK and will deliver worldwide.

Site Usability:	★★★★	Based:	UK
Product Range:	★★★	Express Delivery Option? (UK)	No
Price Range:	Medium	Gift Wrapping Option?	Yes
Delivery Area:	Worldwide	Returns Procedure:	Down to you

www.palenquejewellery.co.uk

Palenque are a young contemporary jewellery company offering a unique collection of earrings, necklaces, bracelets and pendants quite different to what you'll find elsewhere. The range consists of brushed, frosted and polished finishes to both gold and silver, combined with vibrant glass, semi precious stones, sparkling crystals and pearls and is well worth a look

Site Usability:	★★★★	Based:	UK
Product Range:	★★★	Express Delivery Option? (UK)	No
Price Range:	Medium	Gift Wrapping Option?	Yes
Delivery Area:	Worldwide	Returns Procedure:	Down to you

www.pascal-jewellery.com

Here's a collection of timeless stylish jewellery from a retailer that was originally established in Liberty of London about 25 years ago and who you can now find in stores such as Harvey Nichols. As members of the National Association of Goldsmiths you can be sure that you're buying real quality. The collection is updated at least four times a year so you can be tempted regularly and prices start at around £50 (and average about £300).

Site Usability:	★★★★★	Based:	UK
Product Range:	★★★★	Express Delivery Option? (UK)	No
Price Range:	Luxury/Medium	Gift Wrapping Option?	Yes
Delivery Area:	UK	Returns Procedure:	Down to you

www.reglisse.co.uk

For those of you who are looking for something different and unusual take a look round here. This collection of accessories and jewellery, created by an eclectic group of modern luxury designers, includes some really beautiful pieces, such as the lizard embossed calfskin passport cover, assymetric glass wine carafe and crystal and hammered gold necklace. There's a very good choice at a wide range of prices and a speedy delivery service within the UK.

Site Usability:	★★★★	Based:	UK
Product Range:	★★★★	Express Delivery Option? (UK)	Yes
Price Range:	Luxury/Medium	Gift Wrapping Option?	No
Delivery Area:	Worldwide	Returns Procedure:	Down to you

www.selectraders.co.uk

This is a company based in Germany, offering a superb range of pearls including Akoya, South Sea and freshwater with a gorgeous choice of necklaces, earrings, rings, bracelets and pendants. Everything is beautifully and extremely clearly photographed with many views of the same item and you can choose pearls on their own or match them with diamonds and 18ct gold settings. They'll deliver all over the world.

Site Usability:	★★★★	Based:	Germany
Product Range:	★★★★★	Express Delivery Option? (UK)	No
Price Range:	Medium	Gift Wrapping Option?	No
Delivery Area:	Worldwide	Returns Procedure:	Down to you

www.stonedjewellery.co.uk

With its main boutique based in Nottingham, Stoned stocks a unique mix of local designers, directional London studios and Far Eastern pearl specialists. Everything offered is chic, stylish and beautifully photographed, of the highest quality and a mid price range with necklaces starting at around £100 and earrings at £55 (and going up steeply). You'll find designers such as Claire Henry, Dower and Hall and Monica Vinader plus others you probably won't have heard of before.

Site Usability:	★★★★	Based:	UK
Product Range:	★★★	Express Delivery Option? (UK)	No
Price Range:	Medium	Gift Wrapping Option?	Yes
Delivery Area:	UK	Returns Procedure:	Down to you

www.swarovski.com

You've almost certainly heard of Swarovski (and seen those sparkling faceted crystal collectibles and objects). You may also have passed their glorious shops with glittering and stylish jewellery and accessories inside (and I mean really glittering). You'll no doubt be delighted to know that you can buy a wide selection online, all set with their signature crystals and extremely hard to resist.

Site Usability:	★★★★★	Based:	Germany
Product Range:	★★★★★	Express Delivery Option? (UK)	No
Price Range:	Medium	Gift Wrapping Option?	Yes
Delivery Area:	Worldwide	Returns Procedure:	Down to you

www.vanpeterson.com

This is a small collection of extremely modern and unusual jewellery designed by Eric van Peterson, who opened his Walton Street jewellery store in 1981 to offer easily distinguished, modern/ethnic designs. It's certainly a highly edited selection of his range on a very black based website which doesn't make the pieces easy to see, but if you like his style it's certainly worth a look.

Site Usability:	★★★	Based:	UK
Product Range:	★★★	Express Delivery Option? (UK)	No
Price Range:	Medium	Gift Wrapping Option?	No
Delivery Area:	Worldwide	Returns Procedure:	Down to you

Fashion Rocks

www.accessoriesonline.co.uk

Modern designer jewellery by Angie Gooderham, Les Nereides, Butler and Wilson, Tarantino and Kleshna with a varied and attractive, well priced range. Click here when you want your next fashion jewellery fix or when you're looking for a treat for a friend and you'll definitely not be disappointed. Les Nereides in particular are really unusual and pretty, not cheap but always in line with the season.

Site Usability:	★★★★★	Based:	UK
Product Range:	★★★★	Express Delivery Option? (UK)	No
Price Range:	Medium/Very Good Value	Gift Wrapping Option?	No
Delivery Area:	Worldwide	Returns Procedure:	Down to you

www.accessorize.co.uk

Accessorize is the essential destination if you're looking for up to the minute and extremely well priced accessories, including a wide range of jewellery. It's also an excellent place for a gift for an older child or if your early teen and upwards needs (as in I NEED) a new pair of earrings, flip-flops, party slip on shoes, scarf or bag. Not only do the prices make it a great place for gifts but all the products are fun and modern too.

Site Usability:	★★★★★	Based:	UK
Product Range:	★★★★	Express Delivery Option? (UK)	No
Price Range:	Very Good Value	Gift Wrapping Option?	No
Delivery Area:	UK	Returns Procedure:	Down to you

www.butlerandwilson.co.uk

Famous for their signature whimsical fashion jewellery you can now choose from a glamorous and well priced range online of necklaces, bracelets, earrings and brooches. Both costume jewellery and jewellery using semi-precious stones such as rose quartz, agate, amber and jade are available. You can also see the collection of very pretty printed and beaded handbags plus bridal jewellery and accessories.

Site Usability:	★★★★	Based:	UK
Product Range:	★★★★	Express Delivery Option? (UK)	No
Price Range:	Medium	Gift Wrapping Option?	No but everything is beautifully packaged
Delivery Area:	Worldwide	Returns Procedure:	Down to you

www.chezbec.com

For a pretty and well priced jewellery fix from an attractive and helpful website you need look no further. Chez Bec has an unusual selection sourced from designers around the world, incorporating, shells, semi precious stones, pearls, silver and glass beads. Most pieces retail for under £100 and everything is beautifully presented in Chez Bec's fuchsia pink gift boxes.

Site Usability:	★★★★	Based:	UK
Product Range:	★★★	Express Delivery Option? (UK)	No
Price Range:	Medium	Gift Wrapping Option?	No but everything is beautifully packaged
Delivery Area:	Worldwide	Returns Procedure:	Down to you

www.jewel-garden.co.uk

Brand new online jewellery company Jewel Garden offers a very attractive range of well priced jewellery by modern designers that you won't find in the stores. They concentrate on silver and semi-precious stones such as smokey quartz, agate, turquoise and citrine plus pearl, crystal and coloured glass. Combine this with their clear layout, fast worldwide delivery and gift wrapping services and this becomes a very attractive place to shop for gifts or treats.

Site Usability:	★★★★★	Based:	UK
Product Range:	★★★	Express Delivery Option? (UK)	Yes
Price Range:	Medium/Very Good Value	Gift Wrapping Option?	Yes
Delivery Area:	Worldwide	Returns Procedure:	Down to you

www.justdivine.co.uk

Just Divine is a collection of vintage inspired jewellery and gifts designed by Shelley Cooper of the USA, a fashion and jewellery historian whose passion for the past is reflected in her work. If you love vintage style jewellery you'll be spoilt for choice here. The website offers a limited edition of favourites from the huge range of designs in the main collection and highlights select pieces each month.

Site Usability:	★★★★★	Based:	UK
Product Range:	★★★	Express Delivery Option? (UK)	No
Price Range:	Medium	Gift Wrapping Option?	No
Delivery Area:	EU	Returns Procedure:	Down to you

www.lolarose.co.uk

This is a very unusually designed website, where you see all the products as on the pages of a book. However, it's very clever as well, as you can not only see everything very clearly but also view all the different colourways of the necklaces and bracelets made with rose quartz, white jade, green aventurine, mother of pearl and black agate. The prices for these beautifully designed pieces are very reasonable so it's well worth having a look.

Site Usability:	★★★★	Based:	UK
Product Range:	★★★	Express Delivery Option? (UK)	No
Price Range:	Medium	Gift Wrapping Option?	No
Delivery Area:	Worldwide	Returns Procedure:	Down to you

www.piajewellery.com

Pia has a very quick and clever website where you can choose from their creative jewellery by type or browse page by page through their catalogue. The pictures of this modern, well priced jewellery range are extremely clear and definitely make you want to buy. There are natural stones such as carnelian, agate, labradorite and coral mixed with silver all turned into very wearable necklaces, earrings and bracelets. They also offer soft leather handbags, a small of leather and shearling clothing and pretty scarves and shawls.

Site Usability:	★★★★★	Based:	UK
Product Range:	★★★★	Express Delivery Option? (UK)	Yes
Price Range:	Medium	Gift Wrapping Option?	Yes
Delivery Area:	Worldwide	Returns Procedure:	Down to you

www.tictocsnrocks.co.uk

Tictocsnrocks is a collection of modern jewellery and designer watches at a range of prices from a retailer based in Devon. There are watches by Calvin Klein, D&G, Diesel, DKNY and Roberto Cavalli and jewellery by Angie Gooderham, Azuni, Philippe Ferrandis, Pilgrim and Taratata plus lots more. This would make a great place to find an accessory gift as they offer a gift wrapping service and they'll also ship worldwide.

Site Usability:	★★★	Based:	UK
Product Range:	★★★	Express Delivery Option? (UK)	No
Price Range:	Medium	Gift Wrapping Option?	Yes
Delivery Area:	Worldwide	Returns Procedure:	Down to you

www.treasurebox.co.uk

Here you'll find a wealth of costume jewellery from Butler and Wilson, Tarina Tarantino, Angie Gooderham, Juicy Couture, Barbara Easton and Les Nereides to name just a few, with the emphasis on what's in fashion right now. You can select your jewellery to go with each new season's look and they're adding in new designers all the time. This is a really fun website where there's not only a lot of choice but also a great deal of information about the trends the pieces go with.

Site Usability:	★★★★	Based:	UK
Product Range:	★★★★	Express Delivery Option? (UK)	Yes
Price Range:	Medium	Gift Wrapping Option?	Yes
Delivery Area:	Worldwide	Returns Procedure:	Down to you

Watches

www.buyaswatch.co.uk

With names such as Colour The Sky, Chessboard and Black Injection you can imagine the sort of watches you'll find here – fun, different, colourful (in many cases) and modern. You can choose from the range of watches they have in stock for express delivery or check out their themed or limited edition selection. There's even a choice of watches you can load with your next ski pass data which you can use at more than 450 resorts worldwide.

Site Usability:	★★★★★	Based:	UK
Product Range:	★★★★★	Express Delivery Option? (UK)	Yes
Price Range:	Medium/Very Good Value	Gift Wrapping Option?	No
Delivery Area:	UK	Returns Procedure:	Down to you

www.ernestjones.co.uk

Ernest Jones have a really beautifully designed website where you can buy watches by a wide range of premium designers such as TAG Heuer, Gucci, Longines and Rado. The advantage of buying here is that if you have any problems you can choose to visit one of their 190 UK based stores or use the online address. They have a very good gift finder and offer gift packaging and express delivery services.

Site Usability:	★★★★★	Based:	UK
Product Range:	★★★★★	Express Delivery Option? (UK)	Yes
Price Range:	Luxury/Medium	Gift Wrapping Option?	Yes
Delivery Area:	UK	Returns Procedure:	Down to you

www.goldsmiths.co.uk

Here's another well known offline chain of jewellery stores offering a wide range of its products online on a well designed and easy to navigate website. Alongside the jewellery ranges where there's an excellent choice they also have watches by Seiko, Tissot, Longines and Citizen plus fashion brands Gucci, DKNY, Armani, Versace and Burberry. Expect delivery within three days.

Site Usability:	★★★★★	Based:	UK
Product Range:	★★★★★	Express Delivery Option? (UK)	No
Price Range:	Medium	Gift Wrapping Option?	No
Delivery Area:	UK	Returns Procedure:	Down to you

www.thewatchhut.co.uk

Buy your next watch from thewatchhut.co.uk and you'll know that you're buying from an authorised dealer with the full manufacturer's guarantee. On some of the watches there are excellent discounts so it's worth having a good look through the brands on offer such as Ebel, Accurist, Breil, Diesel and Fossil.

Site Usability:	★★★★★	Based:	UK
Product Range:	★★★★	Express Delivery Option? (UK)	Yes
Price Range:	Medium	Gift Wrapping Option?	No
Delivery Area:	UK	Returns Procedure:	Down to you

Chapter 16

Scarves, Shawls, Gloves, Belts and More

So you've done it all; you've gone out and bought that new handbag, designer or otherwise, that you feel totally good about carrying. Your shoes or boots are of the requisite height and colour for the season (and your trousers are long enough, please): Your shades are the same ones that have been seen on several celebrities recently and you're totally happy with your updated look.

Off you go out on the town and from your new glam bag you bring your tired old purse/wallet that you think no one can see and yes, you're probably right but *you* can see it. Does it make you feel good? Thought not.

I know you probably think I'm being really boring and after all, this is a book about where to buy products online, isn't it, not what to buy or not to buy? It's just that having spent so many years in the fashion industry I thought you might like a bit of free advice. Not about what to wear, what styles and shapes to wear and what colours to wear but just a few (hopefully) uplifting suggestions that you can take or leave as you wish.

So turn your handbag upside down and get rid of anything that doesn't belong. Buy yourself a new smart wallet, which doesn't have to be expensive unless you want to buy Gucci, Prada and the like. Invest in a cosmetics purse or make-up bag that'll hold all your bits and pieces and that you can transfer easily from one handbag to another. Buy a great belt and new season's scarf in the right colour for you and then you're really ready to go out on the town.

Sites to Visit

www.aspinaloflondon.com

Here you'll find some really beautiful wallets, vanity cases, make-up bags and travel document holders plus the new range of handbags and travel bags. Each piece is handmade from high quality leathers and beautifully lined and finished. Most items can be personalised and everything can be beautifully gift boxed and sent out with your personal message. This is a collection of elegant, sophisticated, classic and contemporary designs which you can have sent anywhere in the world.

Site Usability:	★★★★★	Based:	UK
Product Range:	★★★★★	Express Delivery Option? (UK)	Yes
Price Range:	Luxury/Medium	Gift Wrapping Option?	Yes
Delivery Area:	Worldwide	Returns Procedure:	Down to you

www.black.co.uk

If you're not a black and neutral person you won't like this website. However, if, like me, you're known for being a black addict you should have a browse through this collection offering beautiful – and beautifully photographed – accessories such as shawls and scarves, gloves, bags, jewellery and belts in (you guessed it) black, grey, cream and beige. Look out for their new swimwear and homeware ranges.

Site Usability:	★★★★	Based:	UK
Product Range:	★★★	Express Delivery Option? (UK)	Yes
Price Range:	Luxury/Medium	Gift Wrapping Option?	Yes
Delivery Area:	Worldwide	Returns Procedure:	Down to you

www.caxtonlondon.com

Take a look round here for a wide choice of high quality accessories, including leather travel wallets, photograph albums, address books and organisers in colours such as cerise, white, sky blue, lilac and lime. You'll also find games such as backgammon and solitaire, silver pens by Lalex and the Mont Blanc Meisterstuck range and delightful baby and christening gifts. Postage within the UK is free and they offer a free gift wrapping service as well.

Site Usability:	★★★★	Based:	UK
Product Range:	★★★★	Express Delivery Option? (UK)	No
Price Range:	Medium/Very Good Value	Gift Wrapping Option?	Yes
Delivery Area:	Worldwide	Returns Procedure:	Down to you

www.cityorg.co.uk

You may well not have heard of this excellent website, offering Filofax organisers and accessories, Cocinelle handbags, wallets and keyrings, Lo Scritto leather bound notebooks in lots of colours, Quo Vadis diaries, Paul Smith handbags and accessories, pens by Cross, Azuni jewellery, Paul Smith and Mont Blanc cufflinks, Leatherman tools and gadgets by Oregon Scientific. The website is easy to get round and the pictures large and clear. This is an excellent place for accessories.

Site Usability:	★★★★	Based:	UK
Product Range:	★★★★	Express Delivery Option? (UK)	Yes
Price Range:	Luxury/Medium	Gift Wrapping Option?	Yes
Delivery Area:	Worldwide	Returns Procedure:	Down to you

www.corneliajames.com

Long standing famous glove maker Cornelia James has now expanded her range to include fashion accessories such as faux fur wraps and gilets, stoles and silk scarves. There's a small but very special selection of gloves to buy online, including leather, snaffled trimmed gloves, sexy lace mittens, opera length satin gloves trimmed with boa feathers and long and short velvet leopard print gloves perfect for Christmas.

Site Usability:	★★★★	Based:	UK
Product Range:	★★★	Express Delivery Option? (UK)	No
Price Range:	Luxury/Medium	Gift Wrapping Option?	No
Delivery Area:	Worldwide	Returns Procedure:	Down to you

www.heroshop.co.uk

There are lots of places you can buy leather goods online, but very few that offer the quality and service you'll find here. It's not a huge range but a selection of classic luggage and weekenders, photo albums, home accessories, document wallets, jewellery boxes and cosmetic bags for her, wet packs for him, plus shooting accessories and luxury dog leads, collars and baskets.

Site Usability:	★★★★	Based:	UK
Product Range:	★★★	Express Delivery Option? (UK)	No
Price Range:	Medium	Gift Wrapping Option?	No
Delivery Area:	Worldwide	Returns Procedure:	Down to you

www.jobuckler.com

If you're one of those people like me who's always looking for the perfect scarf or shawl to add the finishing touch, you should take a look at this small but beautiful collection of scarves and wraps in pleated chiffon. These are definitely statement pieces and are available in different sizes and a very good range of colours from neutrals to brights. Delivery is free in the UK.

Site Usability:	★★★★	Based:	UK
Product Range:	★★★	Express Delivery Option? (UK)	Yes
Price Range:	Medium	Gift Wrapping Option?	No
Delivery Area:	Worldwide	Returns Procedure:	Down to you

www.julieslaterandson.co.uk

Everything on this website is beautifully pictured so you'll know exactly what you're ordering. There's a wonderful selection of leather purses, gifts and travel accessories and you'd have to search long and hard to find the colour range offered elsewhere, which includes pistachio, pale blue, meadow green, hot pink, carnation and royal blue. Delivery is worldwide with an express delivery option for the UK and they'll gift wrap for you as well.

Site Usability:	★★★★	Based:	UK
Product Range:	★★★	Express Delivery Option? (UK)	Yes
Price Range:	Medium	Gift Wrapping Option?	Yes
Delivery Area:	Worldwide	Returns Procedure:	Down to you

www.leatherglovesonline.com

This is a marvellous glove (surprise) retailer where the prices are excellent and they offer a speedy delivery service. You should have a good look round before it gets really cold out there. There are plain leather gloves with silk or cashmere linings, contrast stitched and extra long cuffs, fur and faux fur trims and linings and the warmest of all, gloves lined in shearling.

Site Usability:	★★★★	Based:	US
Product Range:	★★★★	Express Delivery Option? (UK)	No
Price Range:	Medium	Gift Wrapping Option?	No
Delivery Area:	Worldwide	Returns Procedure:	Down to you

www.perilla.co.uk

At Perilla you'll find 'the ultimate treat for feet', a range of high quality British made alpaca socks in a choice of colours and styles, from the deluxe, lightweight City Sock to the sturdier, ribbed Country Sock. You can choose from a selection of gift boxes containing up to five pairs and select the colours and sizes you want to be included. You can also buy luxurious alpaca scarves and wraps, which will be automatically gift wrapped for you so if you're looking for a special gift this could be the perfect place. There are laptop bags and weekenders here too.

Site Usability:	★★★	Based:	UK
Product Range:	★★★	Express Delivery Option? (UK)	Yes
Price Range:	Luxury/Medium	Gift Wrapping Option?	Yes
Delivery Area:	Worldwide	Returns Procedure:	Down to you

www.safigloves.com

I don't know if you're anything like me but the minute it gets cold I have to search through any and all of my winter coats and jackets for the gloves I left behind as, I'm sure you'll agree with me, cold hands are the worst. Anyway, here's a website that'll solve that problem for you with an excellent range, including gloves with fur cuffs and cashmere lining, silk lined gloves, fingerless gloves, driving gloves and gloves for kids of all ages.

Site Usability:	★★★★	Based:	UK
Product Range:	★★★	Express Delivery Option? (UK)	No
Price Range:	Medium	Gift Wrapping Option?	No
Delivery Area:	UK	Returns Procedure:	Down to you

www.trehearneandbrar.com

This must surely be the most beautiful collection of pashminas and shawls available. Don't expect cheap prices here and don't expect to be able to see them all online, either. You need to email them or call for a brochure. (Hopefully they'll be online soon although it would be very difficult to show their constantly changing range). Their collection includes plain, dyed to order, lined and reversible shawls, plus blankets and exquisite beaded shawls and all are of the best quality you can find.

Site Usability:	★★★	Based:	UK
Product Range:	★★★	Express Delivery Option? (UK)	No
Price Range:	Luxury	Gift Wrapping Option?	No
Delivery Area:	Worldwide	Returns Procedure:	Down to you

www.wonderfulwraps.com

Established for over ten years, Wonderful Wraps has featured in major UK retail outlets such as Harrods, Selfridges and Harvey Nichols in London and Saks Fifth Avenue and Neiman Marcus in the US. They offer a collection of sumptuous velvets, silk organzas, chiffons and tulles, satins, faux furs, marabous and other luxury wraps, stoles and capes, with styles ranging from luxurious embroidered organzas to classic angora throws. To place your order you need to call them.

Site Usability:	★★★	Based:	UK
Product Range:	★★★	Express Delivery Option? (UK)	No
Price Range:	Luxury/Medium	Gift Wrapping Option?	No
Delivery Area:	Worldwide	Returns Procedure:	Down to you

www.zocaloalpaca.com

This is a small, fairly new online retailer, specialising in (yes you guessed it) South American Alpaca products from soft and light baby alpaca scarves to brightly coloured striped shawls and chunky wraps. The advantage here is that the products look lovely with a wide choice of colourways, the prices are very reasonable and they offer an express service plus gift wrapping, so if you want to give a pretty scarf or shawl that isn't cheap pashmina you can shop here instead.

Site Usability:	★★★★	Based:	UK
Product Range:	★★★	Express Delivery Option? (UK)	Yes
Price Range:	Medium/Very Good Value	Gift Wrapping Option?	Yes
Delivery Area:	Worldwide	Returns Procedure:	Down to you

Also take a look at these websites for Accessories:

Website address	You'll find it in
www.pickett.co.uk	Chapter 20: Shoes and Leather Accessories

Section 3
Mainly for Men

Mainly for Men

I always have a slight problem here: Should I write to you, the original shopaholic who buys clothes for her man, or should I address him direct?

Well this time I've decided that it's his turn, particularly because the number of online men's retailers has expanded so much and I'm not just going to be talking about shirts, ties and socks (perish the thought) but the full kit including formal tailoring, places where he can buy great country gear (shooting jackets, plus twos and the like) and excellent footwear that you couldn't possibly choose for him.

Having said that, if you're looking for a gift for your man this is also the place to be as there are some high quality accessories, cashmere sweaters and scarves, lighters, cufflinks and belts. Just let him have his own browse round first (or give him his own copy of this book).

Chapter 17

Shirts, Ties, Cufflinks and Belts

You may well have been tempted by now to buy some shirts and ties online. They were the first items of men's clothing to be offered on the web and now that the photography and colour reproduction is so much improved it's even easier to choose.

I always think that men are really lucky from the sizing point of view as a 15.5 collar is always that, no matter who the shirt maker is, all you really need to know are your main measurements and whoever you're buying from should size them the same. So you don't have all the glorious fun that we have, of one designer's size 12 being another's size 8, and so on - can you believe that that really goes on? I assure you that it does, all the time.

So, as long as you know your style (narrow stripes, wide stripes, no stripes, button down, double cuff etc.) you should be fine, and you'll really be spoilt for choice here.

Another great advantage of buying shirts and ties online is that many of the retailers below have quite long periods of discounting which may well not be going on in their shops. So, before you're tempted to your favourite shirtmaker in Jermyn Street, take a look here and make sure that the prices aren't better online. You may be pleasantly surprised.

Sites to Visit

www.ctshirts.co.uk

Charles Tyrwhitt are well known for their colourful and well laid out catalogue and now you can also order all their shirts, handmade shoes, ties and other accessories online. Their website is extremely attractive and easy to navigate and the service offered excellent. A range of shirt qualities and styles are available and they frequently have special offers. There's a good selection of casual shirts and knitwear, tailoring, ladies shirts, cashmere knits and accessories and 'Tiny Tyrwhitt' clothing too.

Site Usability:	★★★★★	Based:	UK
Product Range:	★★★★★	Express Delivery Option? (UK)	Yes
Price Range:	Medium	Gift Wrapping Option?	Yes
Delivery Area:	Worldwide	Returns Procedure:	Down to you

www.coles-shirtmakers.com

Here you'll find high quality shirts with an excellent choice of fabrics and styles and an emphasis on finish. You can order from their standard selection or alternatively have your new shirt made exactly to your measurements (be careful here as of course you won't be able to return a bespoke shirt unless it's faulty). There's a discount system if you spend over a certain amount and a lot of information on how to order the perfect shirt. They also offer ties and cufflinks.

Site Usability:	★★★★	Based:	UK
Product Range:	★★★★	Express Delivery Option? (UK)	Yes
Price Range:	Medium	Returns Procedure:	Down to you
Delivery Area:	Worldwide		

www.curtisanddyer.co.uk

Curtis and Dyer do not have retail outlets and so you may well find that their shirts sell online for quite a lot less than you would expect to pay for the quality. They also give you the opportunity of supplying them with your exact size and specification. Their shirt selector is really excellent. First you choose your fabric, then collar type, cuff type, neck measurement and then input your exact measurements if you want to or use their standard sizing.

Site Usability:	★★★★★	Based:	UK
Product Range:	★★★★	Express Delivery Option? (UK)	No
Price Range:	Medium	Gift Wrapping Option?	No
Delivery Area:	UK	Returns Procedure:	Down to you

www.dariopaganini.it

At this Milan based online retailer you'll find internationally styled shirts created in 100% Egyptian cotton and available in different fits and collar styles. Once you've chosen your style you'll be taken to the different fabrics on offer plus sizing options. This is a really clearly designed website and very different to most online retailers offering men's shirts and accessories.

Site Usability:	★★★★★	Based:	Italy
Product Range:	★★★★	Express Delivery Option? (UK)	No
Price Range:	Medium	Gift Wrapping Option?	No
Delivery Area:	Worldwide	Returns Procedure:	Down to you

www.emmawillis.com

Bespoke shirt-maker Emma Willis trained at the Slade School of Art before starting her business in 1987. Her philosophy is the highest quality make, keeping to the original traditions of English shirt making and using luxurious Italian and Swiss cottons, silks and linens, many of which are exclusive to her collections. Nominated in GQ Style magazine as London's best bespoke shirt maker, if you're seeking the ultimate shirt, this is the place to visit.

Site Usability:	★★★★★	Based:	UK
Product Range:	★★★★	Express Delivery Option? (UK)	No
Price Range:	Luxury	Gift Wrapping Option?	No
Delivery Area:	Worldwide	Returns Procedure:	Down to you

www.gievesandhawkes.com

Situated at Number 1 Savile Row, London and established in 1785, Gieves and Hawkes have always stood for the very best in men's tailoring whether for formal evening wear, suiting or casualwear. On their website you can now not only find out a great deal about the brand, but also choose from their high quality range of shirts, belts and braces, cufflinks, shoes and ties.

Site Usability:	★★★★	Based:	UK
Product Range:	★★★	Express Delivery Option? (UK)	No
Price Range:	Luxury/Medium	Gift Wrapping Option?	Yes
Delivery Area:	EU	Returns Procedure:	Down to you

www.harvieandhudson.com

Harvie and Hudson are a family-owned London shirtmaker and gentlemen's outfitter based in Jermyn Street and Knightsbridge. They offer a wide range of shirts online from deep button down to classic stripe, plain and check shirts, unusual colour combinations and excellent country shirts. You can have your shirt custom made by selecting from their fabrics and then choosing your cuff and collar style and you can order too from ties, links, socks, evening wear shirts and accessories.

Site Usability:	★★★★	Based:	UK
Product Range:	★★★★★	Express Delivery Option? (UK)	No
Price Range:	Medium	Gift Wrapping Option?	No
Delivery Area:	Worldwide	Returns Procedure:	Down to you

www.hilditchandkey.co.uk

Recognised as one of the longest established Jermyn Street retailers of men's shirts and accessories (as well as some women's shirts) Hilditch manages to give you a top of the range shopping experience without your having to leave home. Their shirts are not the cheapest, definitely, but if you order from them you'll be absolutely certain that you'll get the high quality you're paying for. They also offer silk ties and some clothing.

Site Usability:	★★★★★	Based:	UK
Product Range:	★★★★	Express Delivery Option? (UK)	No
Price Range:	Luxury	Gift Wrapping Option?	No
Delivery Area:	Worldwide	Returns Procedure:	Down to you

www.josephturner.co.uk

Joseph Turner offers men's shirts, ties, cufflinks, sweaters, shoes (made by Loake) and accessories with a wide choice in all areas. They also have regular special offers. There's much more information than usual on sizing than at a lot of men's online retailers and they also offer an alterations service. As with all the men's clothing websites they're extremely keen to offer something extra so you'll find cashmere sweaters, socks and belts here as well.

Site Usability:	★★★★★	Based:	UK
Product Range:	★★★★★	Express Delivery Option? (UK)	No
Price Range:	Medium	Gift Wrapping Option?	No
Delivery Area:	UK	Returns Procedure:	Down to you

www.longmire.co.uk

At Longmire you'll find what is probably the best selection of luxury cufflinks available online. Don't expect the inexpensive here as although silver cufflinks start at just over £100, their signature enamel and gold links are over £1000 and art deco inspired 18ct gold 'stirrup' links over £2000 (not to mention the black and white diamond revolver cufflinks which will set you back a mere £5000). This is the place for a really, really special gift.

Site Usability:	★★★★★	Based:	UK
Product Range:	★★★★	Express Delivery Option? (UK)	Yes
Price Range:	Luxury/Medium	Gift Wrapping Option?	No
Delivery Area:	Worldwide	Returns Procedure:	Down to you

www.manning-and-manning.com

This is not a modern, beautifully photographed website but what you will find here are not only classic 'Jermyn Street' style shirts but also their 'Stateside' fit which they recommend for more casual shirts. Here you choose your shirt measurements by going for their standard fit or inputting your own, then you select from a wide range of fabrics and finally the type of fit you want. Prices are high but bearing in mind you'll end up with a totally unique shirt, if you're looking for the very best that's what you'll get.

Site Usability:	★★★	Based:	UK
Product Range:	★★★★★	Express Delivery Option? (UK)	No
Price Range:	Luxury/Medium	Gift Wrapping Option?	No
Delivery Area:	Worldwide	Returns Procedure:	Down to you

www.thomaspink.co.uk

Thomas Pink has a slick and beautifully designed website offering shirts, clothing and accessories for men and women. There's an enormous amount of detail available for every product plus very clear pictures and a speedy search facility by pattern, style and finish. You can also buy scarves, knitwear, accessories and nightwear and you can always be sure that what you'll receive will be a very high quality product, extremely well made and beautifully packaged.

Site Usability:	★★★★	Based:	UK
Product Range:	★★★★	Express Delivery Option? (UK)	Yes
Price Range:	Luxury	Gift Wrapping Option?	Yes
Delivery Area:	Worldwide	Returns Procedure:	Down to you

www.woodsofshropshire.co.uk

This is a shirt retailer with a difference, offering you high quality, mid-priced shirts, free and easy returns, worldwide delivery, extra collar stiffeners with every shirt plus complimentary silk knots with double cuff shirts. Roll your mouse over the shirt and tie pics and home right in on the fabrics. You can buy large size shirts here too up to a collar size 20. A great deal of thought has gone into this website and it shows. Couple that with a well made shirt for £30 (at time of writing) and you have a website well worth a try.

Site Usability:	★★★★	Based:	UK
Product Range:	★★★★	Express Delivery Option? (UK)	No
Price Range:	Medium	Gift Wrapping Option?	No
Delivery Area:	Worldwide	Returns Procedure:	Down to you

Chapter 18

Tailoring and Formalwear

I agree with you that you're unlikely to buy your next bespoke suit online – OK? I'm not that stupid. However, if you were really short of time or simply couldn't get to the shops you *could* order your next two piece or three piece without going anywhere.

If you're even considering doing anything like this you need to ask for a sample of the fabric first – preferably even for a ready made suit although this will almost certainly be more difficult, as this is the area that is hardest to judge from a picture. Please bear in mind that you really do get what you pay for here; if you're looking for a less expensive suit then the best thing you could possibly do would be to go straight to Marks & Spencer where you know the quality will be good and the prices reasonable.

If you're searching for really cheap tailoring you won't find it here as this is not the place for suiting for less. What you will find is a series of retailers offering you everything from good value and quality to top of the range cashmere blends and fine tailoring. The choice is yours.

Sites to Visit

www.austinreed.co.uk

The choice on this website is growing every season and now you can buy men's tailoring, shirts and ties, casual jackets, trousers and knitwear. The photography is very simple compared to most of the other men's websites and some of the products are quite hard to see. Balance this with the fact that you almost certainly already know the name and the quality that it represents and you'll probably want to have a look round.

Site Usability:	★★★	Based:	UK
Product Range:	★★★	Express Delivery Option? (UK)	No
Price Range:	Medium	Gift Wrapping Option?	No
Delivery Area:	UK	Returns Procedure:	Down to you

www.blackstonelewis.co.uk

Blackstone Lewis offers you the facility of designing a bespoke suit online. This may sound daft, but as soon as you visit their website you can tell that they really know what they're talking about. It's a very cleverly laid out site but you'll need quite a lot of time to work through the whole process of choosing your cloth, style of jacket and trouser and all the details such as buttons and pockets. I suggest you ask them for a sample of your chosen cloth/s before you start.

Site Usability:	★★★★★	Based:	UK
Product Range:	★★★★	Express Delivery Option? (UK)	No
Price Range:	Luxury/Medium	Gift Wrapping Option?	No
Delivery Area:	Worldwide	Returns Procedure:	Down to you

www.cromwellandsmith.co.uk

Cromwell & Smith is a Shrewsbury based high quality men's outfitter offering a range of carefully selected suppliers for tailoring, shirts, shoes and casualwear with labels such as Henry Cotton, Hilditch and Key, Bladen, Feraud, Crockett and Jones and Eton Shirts. This is a very well edited collection with simple, clear pictures and several views of each item. Expect quite high prices but excellent quality and service.

Site Usability:	★★★★★	Based:	UK
Product Range:	★★★★	Express Delivery Option? (UK)	No
Price Range:	Luxury/Medium	Gift Wrapping Option?	No
Delivery Area:	Worldwide	Returns Procedure:	Down to you

www.crombie.co.uk

The Crombie name has been synonymous for over 200 years with high quality, hard wearing cloth and while that still continues the Crombie brand has been developed into an excellent collection of clothing for men and women, some of which you can find online. There's an extensive range for men, including the famous Crombie coat, blazers and jackets, shirts, ties and other accessories and some very good gift ideas. For women there's a much smaller range including some leather and suede.

Site Usability:	★★★★	Based:	UK
Product Range:	★★★★	Express Delivery Option? (UK)	No
Price Range:	Luxury/Medium	Gift Wrapping Option?	No
Delivery Area:	Worldwide	Returns Procedure:	Down to you

www.haggarts.com

Haggarts of Aberfeldy are one of the most famous Scottish tweed producers, having been in business since 1801 and they've now put their excellent country clothing catalogue online, so if you're one for the great outdoors (think shooting, hunting, fishing) this website is a must. Traditional coats, sports jackets and shooting waistcoats plus plus twos, moleskins, cords and cavalry twills, hunter boots, caps and hats are just some of the items you can buy here (you can even buy your Sherlock Holmes hat).

Site Usability:	★★★		Based:	UK
Product Range:	★★★		Express Delivery Option? (UK)	No
Price Range:	Medium		Gift Wrapping Option?	No
Delivery Area:	Worldwide		Returns Procedure:	Down to you

www.hawesandcurtis.com

Hawes and Curtis were established in 1913, and are famous for being the creators of the backless waistcoat, which was originally worn under a tailcoat and was renowned for its comfort. Now on their excellently designed website you can choose from their range of classic and fashion shirts, ties, cufflinks, silk knots and boxer shorts. They also offer a range of women's classic, high quality shirts in three different styles.

Site Usability:	★★★★		Based:	UK
Product Range:	★★★		Express Delivery Option? (UK)	No
Price Range:	Medium		Gift Wrapping Option?	Yes
Delivery Area:	Worldwide		Returns Procedure:	Down to you

www.kinlochanderson.co.uk

Really the only place to buy a Scottish Tartan kilt is Scotland but if you can't make it up there then you can order it online from Kinloch Anderson. (Don't mock, my husband's a Scot and looks great in his kilt and now my eldest son has his as well). You need to know which tartan you want to order – yours, of course – and they have an extensive selection to choose from. You can also buy all the necessary accessories including jackets and sporrans, skien dubh's (decorative knives) kilt pins, belts and footwear with kilts, jackets, sashes and accessories for ladies and children as well.

Site Usability:	★★★★		Based:	UK
Product Range:	★★★		Express Delivery Option? (UK)	No
Price Range:	Luxury/Medium		Gift Wrapping Option?	No
Delivery Area:	UK		Returns Procedure:	Down to you

www.milanclothing.com

At Milan Clothing you'll find casual clothing from brands such as Fake London, Paul Smith, Pringle and Paul and Shark. There's a wide selection so you'll no doubt want to take advantage of the speedy search facility where you can search by brand, or type of clothing, or both. The pictures are very simple indeed because the range is changing all the time, but this is a very clear and easy to navigate website and one of the best for casualwear.

Site Usability:	★★★★★		Based:	UK
Product Range:	★★★★★		Express Delivery Option? (UK)	Yes
Price Range:	Medium		Gift Wrapping Option?	No
Delivery Area:	Worldwide		Returns Procedure:	Down to you

www.mossdirect.co.uk

No this is not the place you can hire your dinner jacket, but an offshoot of the famous brand (and men's hire shop) retailing Moss Bros's own brand, plus Savoy Tailors Guild, De Havilland, Pierre

Cardin and Baumler. You won't find an enormous range but a well designed website with some very good special offers and particularly good dress shirts (which is one of the things they're famous for, after all). Delivery is UK only and you need to allow ten days.

Site Usability:	★★★★	Based:	UK
Product Range:	★★★	Express Delivery Option? (UK)	No
Price Range:	Medium	Gift Wrapping Option?	No
Delivery Area:	UK	Returns Procedure:	Down to you

www.newandlingwood.com

In 1865 a Miss New and a Mr Lingwood founded the business which still bears their names. Now based in Jermyn Street, London, they're almost certainly the most traditional of the gentlemen's outfitters, supported by their own workrooms where they make their own bespoke and ready made shirts, the finest quality piped pyjamas and bespoke shoes and boots. Their website offers a selection of classic, casual and fashion shirts, footwear from luxury boots to casual shoes and everything from velvet collared coats to eveningwear accessories. Expect high prices and the very best quality here.

Site Usability:	★★★★	Based:	UK
Product Range:	★★★★	Express Delivery Option? (UK)	No
Price Range:	Luxury	Gift Wrapping Option?	No
Delivery Area:	Worldwide	Returns Procedure:	Down to you

www.pakeman.co.uk

Here's an extensive range of good quality sensibly priced classic clothing from this Cotswold based retailer. For men you can choose from black tie tailoring, suits, flannels, cords, jeans, shirts and ties, belts, shoes, cufflinks and underwear. They offer a next day delivery service for items in stock and the emphasis is on service and quality. This is not a complicated website but one where there is high standard in every area so don't be put off by the simplicity of the pictures.

Site Usability:	★★★★	Based:	UK
Product Range:	★★★★	Express Delivery Option? (UK)	Yes
Price Range:	Medium	Gift Wrapping Option?	No
Delivery Area:	Worldwide	Returns Procedure:	Down to you

www.perlui.co.uk

This is an excellent designer menswear store offering ranges by Lacoste, Ralph Lauren, Tommy Hilfiger, Ted Baker and many more. You'll find good discounts in their end of season sales but otherwise they offer full price new season's stock. The collection is mainly casual and sportswear. You can also order from their Hackett range but you have to call them to do so.

Site Usability:	★★★★	Based:	UK
Product Range:	★★★★	Express Delivery Option? (UK)	No
Price Range:	Luxury/Medium	Gift Wrapping Option?	No
Delivery Area:	Worldwide	Returns Procedure:	Down to you

www.racinggreen.co.uk

Famous for its well priced men's and ladies wear for several years Racing Green has now re-launched its website with a good range of menswear including shirts, tailoring, dinner jackets, dress shirts, shoes and accessories. It's a very easy site to get round and much more classic than it used to be with smart pictures of a wide range of products. The prices are reasonable and the branding is very classy so definitely give it a try.

Site Usability:	★★★★★	Based:	UK
Product Range:	★★★★	Express Delivery Option? (UK)	Yes
Price Range:	Medium/Very Good Value	Gift Wrapping Option?	No
Delivery Area:	UK	Returns Procedure:	Down to you

www.savilerowco.com

This is a really good and fast developing range of menswear with everything you could possibly need, including tailoring (and dinner jackets) a wide range of formal shirts, casual shirts, trousers and sweaters plus a full collection of accessories. The site is very clearly photographed and the order system is really easy. There are also some men's gift ideas here such as cashmere scarves and cufflinks.

Site Usability:	★★★★★	Based:	UK
Product Range:	★★★★★	Express Delivery Option? (UK)	Yes
Price Range:	Medium	Gift Wrapping Option?	No
Delivery Area:	Worldwide	Returns Procedure:	Free

www.tmlewin.co.uk

T M Lewin have one of the easiest sites to get round with simple drop down menus and clear pictures. They also frequently have some very good special offers. You can buy almost everything here, from formal tailoring to casual trousers, a good selection of accessories and there's a wide range of striped, check and solid coloured shirts with simple size and length options.

Site Usability:	★★★★	Based:	UK
Product Range:	★★★★	Express Delivery Option? (UK)	Yes
Price Range:	Medium	Gift Wrapping Option?	No
Delivery Area:	Worldwide	Returns Procedure:	Down to you

Chapter 19

Best of the Casuals

Here you'll find clothes and accessories that'll take you from casual weekends at home to the wilds of Scotland and much further afield and there's a wide range on offer in all areas, from casual sportswear brands such as Quicksilver and Animal to your essential country Barbour. The idea is that whatever you enjoy doing in your free time, you'll find the clothes to go with below.

On some of the more sports orientated websites you can get some good discounts, particularly at sale time but also throughout the year so keep checking back to see what's on offer.

If you're off to somewhere with a very hot climate definitely check out Rohan; who have kitted out my eldest son on his trips to Borneo and India and my husband for the summer in Maryland – the quality is excellent and the clothes are perfect for hot weather. My only advice is not to leave it to the last minute with any of these websites and risk your order not arriving in time for your journey – I've done that quite recently (and yes I was ordering for him and yes I did get into trouble). Oh well.

Sites to Visit

www.countryattire.co.uk

Country Attire offer the best of the range of Barbour outerwear and clothing online, from the traditional wax jackets to quilted and tweed jackets, gilets, footwear and accessories. Although the photographs of some of the products are not as good as they could be the selection is excellent. This website is a must for anyone who lives in the country.

Site Usability:	★★★★	Based:	UK
Product Range:	★★★★	Express Delivery Option? (UK)	Yes
Price Range:	Medium	Gift Wrapping Option?	No
Delivery Area:	Worldwide	Returns Procedure:	Down to you

www.d2-clothing.co.uk

With collections by Diesel, Adidas, Evisu, Firetrap and Fake London this is a really good place for casual clothing. You can choose by item or brand, click on an item and you can immediately see if they have your size in stock. Try here for jeans, casual footwear, a wide selection of urban style jackets, great t-shirts and essential beanies.

Site Usability:	★★★★	Based:	UK	
Product Range:	★★★★	Express Delivery Option? (UK)	No	
Price Range:	Medium	Gift Wrapping Option?	No	
Delivery Area:	UK	Returns Procedure:	Down to you	

www.extremepie.com

There are enough casual/sportswear brands here to answer anyone's needs from famous brands such as O'Neill, Quicksilver, Animal, Vans, Billabong, RipCurl, Addict, Extreme and Reef plus loads more that you may not have heard of. This is definitely a good site for anyone who's addicted to sport, or just wants the sporty look (and for gifts for sporty people). They also sell snowboards, skateboards, wetsuits, accessories and sunglasses by Animal and Roxy.

Site Usability:	★★★★	Based:	UK	
Product Range:	★★★★	Express Delivery Option? (UK)	Yes	
Price Range:	Medium	Gift Wrapping Option?	No	
Delivery Area:	Worldwide	Returns Procedure:	Down to you	

www.fatface.com

When you first take a look at the fatface.com website you may be a little disconcerted. It's certainly not like most others with pictures and type all being used to reinforce Fatface's idiosyncratic 'cool' active style. But it works together. You'll find a wide selection of tops and t-shirts, jackets and fleece, denim and sweats, all in unique fabrics and style and their more often than not muted colour palette.

Site Usability:	★★★★	Based:	UK	
Product Range:	★★★★	Express Delivery Option? (UK)	Yes	
Price Range:	Medium	Gift Wrapping Option?	No	
Delivery Area:	Worldwide	Returns Procedure:	Down to you	

www.hackett.co.uk

Hackett are famous for using Jonny Wilkinson as their model as well as for great quality clothing and you can now buy from a selection of their sportswear, tailoring, shirts and ties, great quality knitwear and outerwear online. In the Rugby Shop you can choose from very good range of striped rugby shirts and you can also visit the Aston Martin Shop, with 'Aston Martin Racing by Hackett' socks, hats and brollies.

Site Usability:	★★★★	Based:	UK	
Product Range:	★★★	Express Delivery Option? (UK)	2 working days	
Price Range:	Medium	Gift Wrapping Option?	No	
Delivery Area:	UK	Returns Procedure:	Down to you/complicated	

www.oki-ni.com

Oki-ni is an independent, London-based design group, working in collaboration with a range of globally renowned brands and designers such as Aquascutum, Adidas, Evisu and Tanner Krolle to create products unique to Oki-ni and only available online from their website. You can choose from footwear, jeans, jackets and accessories all with an unusual designer twist. All items are available in limited numbers so if you see something you like, order it fast.

Site Usability:	★★★★	Based:	UK
Product Range:	★★★	Express Delivery Option? (UK)	No
Price Range:	Luxury/Medium	Gift Wrapping Option?	No
Delivery Area:	UK	Returns Procedure:	Down to you

www.rohan.co.uk

Specialists in easy care (easy wear, easy wash and dry) travel and casual clothing, Rohan offer trousers, shirts, underwear and accessories for men and women. You select depending on the type of activity, clothing or climate and there's a very good selection, lots of information and fast service. If you're planning a visit to the jungle this is an excellent website as you can buy not only your clothing but also clever washbags, microfibre towels, dry wash, travel bottles and lots of other accessories.

Site Usability:	★★★★	Based;	UK
Product Range:	★★★★	Express Delivery Option? (UK)	Yes
Price Range:	Medium	Gift Wrapping Option?	No
Delivery Area:	Worldwide	Returns Procedure:	Down to you

www.routeone.co.uk

Route One is a young, independent store aimed at inline skate and skateboard riders but having such a large selection of shoes, clothing and accessories by brands such as Converse, Atticus, Fenchurch, Billabong and Carhatt (and, I have to confess, loads of others I haven't heard of) it's bound to appeal to anyone who likes a contemporary, sporty look. The service is speedy and reliable.

Site Usability:	★★★★	Based;	UK
Product Range:	★★★★	Express Delivery Option? (UK)	Yes
Price Range:	Medium	Gift Wrapping Option?	No
Delivery Area:	Worldwide	Returns Procedure:	Down to you

www.stoneisland.co.uk

Trendy, relaxed and very well photographed, this website offers Stone Island and C.P casualwear (and some more formal jackets) plus outerwear, jeans, shirts, knitwear and accessories. This is an extremely fast and attractive website to look round. Be warned though; the products are not inexpensive but high quality designer gear, so if you're looking for a cheap pair of casual jeans you'll be disappointed.

Site Usability:	★★★★★	Based:	UK
Product Range:	★★★	Express Delivery Option? (UK)	No
Price Range:	Luxury/Medium	Gift Wrapping Option?	No
Delivery Area:	UK	Returns Procedure:	Down to you

www.theclothesstore.com

Click on the cute icons here to choose the type of clothing you're looking for and select from the excellent collections by Burberry London, Nigel Hall, Lacoste, Puma and One True Saxon and 'Urban Menswear' by Fred Perry, Ben Sherman, Wrangler and Edge. The designer ranges are changing all the time so check back to see whose listed each season. They also offer a good collection from Converse and Kickers.

Site Usability:	★★★★	Based:	Channel Islands
Product Range:	★★★★	Express Delivery Option? (UK)	No
Price Range:	Medium	Gift Wrapping Option?	No
Delivery Area:	Worldwide	Returns Procedure:	Down to you

www.w1style.co.uk

This is an excellent website offering new and current brands such as Quicksilver, Roxy, O'Neill, Bench, Billabong, Diesel and FCUK in an easy to view format. Although most of the items offered are brand new current season's stock (and new stock is regularly being added to the site) there are also some very good reductions. They will ship to North America as well as Europe and all items are shipped from Gibraltar.

Site Usability:	★★★★	Based:	Gibraltar
Product Range:	★★★★★	Express Delivery Option? (UK)	Yes
Price Range:	Medium	Gift Wrapping Option?	Yes
Delivery Area:	EU and North America	Returns Procedure:	Down to you

Also take a look at the following for Casualwear Online:

Website address	You'll find it in
www.orvis.co.uk	Chapter 1: Fashion Online/Mail Order Specialists
www.landsend.co.uk	Chapter 1: Fashion Online/Mail Order Specialists
www.eddiebaur.com	Chapter 5: Shop America
www.llbean.com	Chapter 5: Shop America

Chapter 20

Shoes and Leather Accessories

For some reason people have the idea that buying shoes online is difficult when actually it's even easier than buying clothes – after all, put weight on or take it off, your shoe size doesn't normally change and particularly with men's shoes, if you have a favourite brand, the sizing is even more likely to stay the same. There are also so many high quality brands available; you can see all the styles in one place and many of these retailers offer extremely quick shipping.

You'll also find accessories here that weren't included in the Shirts and Ties chapter as separating the ranges out becomes quite complicated when some of the retailers offering shirts and ties start to offer shoes, wallets, and cufflinks as well.

If you're in the mood to treat yourself you should definitely take a look at Pickett and Dunhill. Both are expensive and both offer marvellous quality, with products that will last and last. Treat yourself or drop hints and make sure you're treated soon.

International shoe size conversion table

UK	7	7.5	8	8.5	9	9.5	10	10.5	11	11.5	12
EU	40.5	41	42	42.5	43	44	44.5	45	46	46.5	47
US	7.5	8	8.5	9	9.5	10	10.5	11	11.5	12	12.5

Sites to Visit

www.bexley.com

This is a French based website (although you'll probably be glad to know that there's an English translation) offering excellent shoes and accessories for men. Clearly and attractively photographed and easy to navigate you can buy socks, formal and casual shoes, ties, shoe trees, polishing kits, belts and gloves at reasonable prices. Average shipping time for Europe is roughly one week and up to two weeks for the rest of the world.

Site Usability:	★★★★	Based:	France
Product Range:	★★★★	Express Delivery Option? (UK)	No
Price Range:	Medium	Gift Wrapping Option?	No
Delivery Area:	Worldwide	Returns Procedure:	Down to you

www.dunhill.com

In 1893 Alfred Dunhill inherited his father's saddlery business on London's Euston Road and developed a luxurious line of accessories. The first collection included car horns and lamps, leather overcoats, goggles, picnic sets and timepieces. Over a hundred years later Dunhill is one of the leading makers of English luxury accessories for men and here you can choose from their range which includes luggage, briefcases, washbags, wallets, diaries and belts, ties and cufflinks.

Site Usability:	★★★★	Based:	UK
Product Range:	★★★	Express Delivery Option? (UK)	No
Price Range:	Luxury	Gift Wrapping Option?	No
Delivery Area:	UK	Returns Procedure:	Down to you

www.dalvey.com

Dalvey of Scotland has created a range of elegant and useful gifts which are attractively displayed on their extremely well laid out website. Suggestions such as beautifully made leather travel clocks and business card cases, cufflinks and cufflink cases, hipflasks and binoculars are all luxuriously presented and would make really lovely gifts. It is a small range but if you're looking for something for the man in your life (and it's something you know he needs or he'll use) then buy here. Most items can be engraved.

Site Usability:	★★★★★	Based:	UK
Product Range:	★★★	Express Delivery Option? (UK)	No
Price Range:	Luxury	Gift Wrapping Option?	No
Delivery Area:	Worldwide	Returns Procedure:	Down to you

www.kjbeckett.com

K J Beckett have a really good selection of branded accessories for men, including Regent Belt Company belts, cufflinks by Simon Carter, Ian Flaherty and Veritas, silk ties, cummerbunds, wallets and handkerchiefs – and that's just a few of the many items they offer. They'll deliver almost anywhere in the world using their priority service and UK delivery is free of charge

Site Usability:	★★★★★	Based:	UK
Product Range:	★★★★★	Express Delivery Option? (UK)	Yes
Price Range:	Luxury/Medium	Gift Wrapping Option?	Yes
Delivery Area:	Worldwide	Returns Procedure:	Down to you

www.oliversweeney.com

Oliver Sweeney is best known for his high quality 'classic with a twist' and fashion forward foot-wear which you can order online here. Alongside these and in the same mode, there are leather wallets and key holders, gloves and belts, edgy attaché cases and weekenders plus a small range of outerwear. If the man in your life is a true traditionalist this is probably not the place but if he's into modern menswear take a look.

Site Usability:	★★★★★	Based:	UK
Product Range:	★★★★	Express Delivery Option? (UK)	No
Price Range:	Luxury/Medium	Gift Wrapping Option?	No
Delivery Area:	Worldwide	Returns Procedure:	Down to you

www.pickett.co.uk

Gloves, wallets, umbrellas, belts, briefcases and stud boxes are just some of the high quality, beautifully made men's accessories available on Pickett's website. If you've ever visited one of their shops you'll know that everything is the best you can buy and most items would make lovely gifts. Couple this with their distinctive dark green and orange packaging and excellent service and you can't go wrong, whatever you choose. There's a gorgeous range of accessories for women, too.

Site Usability:	★★★★★	Based:	UK
Product Range:	★★★★	Express Delivery Option? (UK)	No
Price Range:	Luxury/Medium	Gift Wrapping Option?	No but luxury packaging is standard
Delivery Area:	Worldwide	Returns Procedure:	Down to you

www.pierotucci.com

There's a very good range of briefcases and bags on this Florence based website from hard sided briefcases to slim portfolios, soft travel and duffle bags, wallets and belts. Everything is made in Italy (as you'd expect) and because it's an Italian brand (rather than a 'designer' brand) some of the prices are quite reasonable although you are looking at top Italian quality. The women's collection includes handbags and leather clothing.

Site Usability:	★★★★	Based:	Italy
Product Range:	★★★★	Express Delivery Option? (UK)	Yes
Price Range:	Medium	Gift Wrapping Option?	No
Delivery Area:	Worldwide	Returns Procedure:	Down to you

www.sandstormbags.com

If you're a luxury consumer on the lookout for products that not only work well but have a high degree of authenticity, Sandstorm fits the bill. Sandstorm is the only range of authentic premium safari-style bags out of Africa. These beautiful bags are handcrafted in Kenya and are perfect for your next safari, walking in the Cotswolds or weekend city breaks in five star hotels – they look good anywhere, delivering a striking combination of luxury, style and durability.

Site Usability:	★★★★	Based:	UK
Product Range:	★★★★	Express Delivery Option? (UK)	Yes
Price Range:	Luxury/Medium	Gift Wrapping Option?	No
Delivery Area:	Worldwide	Returns Procedure:	Down to you

www.shiptonandheneage.co.uk

Shipton and Heneage have been trading for over 12 years and offer a very good, high quality collection of over 120 styles of shoe. You choose first from different types such as brogues, country shoes, town shoes, Oxfords, extra wide and loafers and then make your choice from the selection of each that rapidly appears. They also have a range of sailing shoes plus slippers, socks and accessories.

Site Usability:	★★★★★	Based:	UK
Product Range:	★★★★	Express Delivery Option? (UK)	Yes
Price Range:	Medium	Gift Wrapping Option?	No
Delivery Area:	Worldwide	Returns Procedure:	Down to you

www.shoesdirect.co.uk

For reasonably priced smart and casual shoes stop here, where you'll find Loake, Rockport, Gregson, Ecco, Clarks and Barker. Everything is very clearly shown and they couldn't make the order process easier. Some of their shoes go up to a UK size 16 which is really large and if you're in doubt about which size to use their shoe size conversion chart is always available. They'll also tell you which shoes have extra width. Mainland UK deliveries are free for orders over £30.

Site Usability:	★★★★★	Based:	UK
Product Range:	★★★★★	Express Delivery Option? (UK)	No
Price Range:	Medium	Gift Wrapping Option?	No
Delivery Area:	UK	Returns Procedure:	Down to you

www.swaineadeney.co.uk

If you know London well you're bound to have passed the elegant Swaine Adeney Brigg store at 54 St James's Street. Well known as purveyors of the highest quality gentlemen's accessories such as umbrellas with unique handles, wallets, attaché and document cases in a variety of styles and leathers plus wonderful (and wonderfully priced) leather luggage. They have a very good gift selection and many of their items can be personalised.

Site Usability:	★★★★★	Based:	UK
Product Range:	★★★★	Express Delivery Option? (UK)	No
Price Range:	Luxury	Gift Wrapping Option?	No
Delivery Area:	Worldwide	Returns Procedure:	Down to you

www.wellie-web.co.uk

Here's a website with a name that you won't forget quickly but if you're someone who spends a lot of time outdoors, particularly in wet weather, you'll find it indispensable. You can find a cheap pair of wellies here with prices starting at £22 and you'll also find some with flowers all over them (er, maybe not). However, this website specialises in the quality end of the market where a top notch pair of boots can set you back up to £200.

Site Usability:	★★★★	Based:	UK
Product Range:	★★★★	Express Delivery Option? (UK)	Yes
Price Range:	Luxury/Medium	Gift Wrapping Option?	No
Delivery Area:	UK	Returns Procedure:	Down to you

Also visit the following websites for men's shoes and accessories:

Website address	You'll find it in
www.aspinaloflondon.com	Chapter 16: Scarves, Shawls, Gloves, Belts and More
www.ctshirts.co.uk	Chapter 17: Shirts, Ties, Cufflinks and Belts
www.forzieri.com	Chapter 12: Handbag Temptation
www.josephturner.co.uk	Chapter 17: Shirts, Ties, Cufflinks and Belts
www.gucci.com	Chapter 12: Handbag Temptation

Chapter 21

Men's Toiletries and Nightwear

Whatever your favourite aftershave or cologne you'll almost certainly be able to re-order it online, as I don't believe there's a men's fragrance brand you can't find on the web. That may sound a bit too easy to say, and someone may as you're reading this be pointing out to me a totally exclusive brand that I've never heard of and that isn't available online, but if they succeed it'll very much be the exception proving the rule – and I will find someone they can order it from.

Get used to buying this kind of product online, plus your other grooming and shaving kit – it saves masses of time, you know that you won't have to send it back, and you may also find somewhere that sells it cheaper than you can buy it in the shops.

Obviously if you want to try something new then don't shop here, however good the descriptions they're never really quite as they read, but if you're buying more of what you already know don't hesitate for a moment, it's all too easy as you're just about to discover.

Where nightwear is concerned there are only a very few online retailers who are specialists. If you want to see more of a range you could take a look both at the retailers here and also at www.johnlewis.com and www.figleaves.com who both have good collections – with Figleaves, of course, offering a great choice of designers.

Sites to Visit

Men's Toiletries

www.adonisgrooming.com

The first thing you think (or at least, I thought of) when I came across this website was just how easy on the eye it is. Not only that, but Adonis offers an excellent range of grooming products for men, from shaving, hair care and bodycare from brands such as Dermalogica, Clarins for Men and Jose Eisenberg to gifts and accessories; travel kits by California North, Jack Black and 4V00, D R Harris fragrances and Zirh products.

Site Usability:	★★★★★	Based:	UK
Product Range:	★★★★★	Express Delivery Option? (UK)	Yes
Price Range:	Medium	Gift Wrapping Option?	Yes
Delivery Area:	Worldwide	Returns Procedure:	Down to you

www.1001beautysecrets.com/beauty/caswell

I've included this website because here you can buy products from Caswell Massey, one of the America's oldest perfumers. If you'd like to try something different check out their excellent men's range including their Newport, Lime and Verbena fragrances. There's a full range of products from Cologne to soap to shower gel and with everything so smartly packaged they'd make great gifts as well.

Site Usability:	★★★★	Based:	US
Product Range:	★★★★	Express Delivery Option? (UK)	No
Price Range:	Medium	Gift Wrapping Option?	No
Delivery Area:	Worldwide	Returns Procedure:	Down to you

www.aehobbs.com

This is a very simple website from a retailer who's been based in Tunbridge Wells for over 100 years. They offer traditional grooming and toiletry products from brands such as Truefitt and Hill, Woods of Windsor, Mason and Pearson and Kent from their barbershop and Klorane, Perlier and Olverum from their beauty department. They stock Zambesia Botanica as well, which is a special range for people who have very sensitive skin.

Site Usability:	★★★★	Based:	UK
Product Range:	★★★	Express Delivery Option? (UK)	No
Price Range:	Medium	Gift Wrapping Option?	No
Delivery Area:	Worldwide	Returns Procedure:	Down to you

www.carterandbond.com

Carter and Bond was established in 2002 to bring together the very finest male grooming products around. The simple to use secure website is home to over 600 products from more than 40 brands including Molton Brown, American Crew, Baxter of California, Geo F Trumper and Proraso. Whether you're looking for skin care, hair care, fragrance, shaving products or gift ideas you'll find it all here. Orders received by 2.30pm are despatched same day (to anywhere in the world) and gift wrapping is available for just 95p per item.

Site Usability:	★★★★★	Based:	UK
Product Range:	★★★★★	Express Delivery Option? (UK)	Yes
Price Range:	Medium	Gift Wrapping Option?	Yes
Delivery Area:	Worldwide	Returns Procedure:	Down to you

www.hqman.com

If you've spent any time at all at thesiteguide.com you (hopefully) will already have come across wonderful hair and accessories website hqhair.com. Well now they've launched a website specifically for men and excellent it is too. Check out brands such as 4V00, Anthony Logistics, Calmia, Decleor Men, Malin+Goetz and Fred Bennett plus lots more and expect to find the full ranges across body, bath, skincare, haircare and accessories. Good service and speedy delivery are the norm here too.

Site Usability:	★★★★★	Based:	UK
Product Range:	★★★★★	Express Delivery Option? (UK)	No
Price Range:	Luxury/Medium	Gift Wrapping Option?	No
Delivery Area:	Worldwide	Returns Procedure:	Down to you

www.jasonshankey.co.uk

If you're a fan of Tigi, Fudge, NV Perricone, Skin Doctors or Dermalogica products this could well be the place for you and there are lots of other brands as well. The range includes everything from hair and nail care to hair appliances, slimming products, men's grooming and slimming products. Definitely the easiest way to use this website is to know the brand you're looking for, then just click on the list to your left on the home page and you'll be away.

Site Usability:	★★★★	Based:	UK
Product Range:	★★★★	Express Delivery Option? (UK)	Yes
Price Range:	Medium	Gift Wrapping Option?	Yes
Delivery Area:	Worldwide	Returns Procedure:	Down to you

www.mankind.co.uk

This is definitely one of the best men's websites. It's modern, easy to use and has a great range of products, showcasing the very best and most innovative shaving, skin and hair care brands made for men such as Lab Series, Nickel and K2 and offering them in a way that makes buying simple, fast and fun. There are shaving products, skin basics and problem skin solutions as well as gift ideas here. Next day and standard delivery to the UK; worldwide delivery options and gift wrapping are all available.

Site Usability:	★★★★★	Based:	UK
Product Range:	★★★★★	Express Delivery Option? (UK)	Yes
Price Range:	Medium	Gift Wrapping Option?	Yes
Delivery Area:	Worldwide	Returns Procedure:	Down to you

www.murdocklondon.com

Murdock London is a modern men's grooming product retailer with a slick, easy-to-navigate website offering brands such as D R Harris, Caron, Malin+Goetz and Kevin Murphy plus aromatic candles and room scents by Mariage Freres. In their Gift Box section you'll find an excellent selection of pampering, beautifully presented hampers by Edwin Jagger and Santa Maria Novella ranging from around £40 to over £100.

Site Usability:	★★★★★	Based:	UK
Product Range:	★★★★	Express Delivery Option? (UK)	Yes
Price Range:	Luxury/Medium	Gift Wrapping Option?	No but beautifully wrapped gift boxes
Delivery Area:	Worldwide	Returns Procedure:	Down to you

www.trumpers.com

Established in 1875 in Curzon Street, Mayfair, this famous traditional London barber is well known for superb exclusive men's fragrances and grooming products. Think of fragrances such as Sandalwood, Bay Rum and Spanish Leather which all have matching soaps and body washes. Now you can buy the full range online plus an exclusive collection of ties and cufflinks and they'll be delighted to ship to you anywhere in the world.

Site Usability:	★★★★	Based:	UK
Product Range:	★★★★	Express Delivery Option? (UK)	Yes
Price Range:	Luxury/Medium	Gift Wrapping Option?	Yes
Delivery Area:	Worldwide	Returns Procedure:	Free

www.theenglishshavingcompany.co.uk

At The English Shaving Company you'll find the highest quality hand crafted razors and shaving sets plus travel sets, soaps, brushes and aftershaves from Geo Trumper, Edwin Jagger, D R Harris and Molton Brown. You'll can read their 'shaving tutorial' in Useful Information plus razor shaving tips so if you're tired of using your electric razor and want to turn traditional you'll definitely need this site.

Site Usability:	★★★★	Based:	UK
Product Range:	★★★★	Express Delivery Option? (UK)	No
Price Range:	Luxury/Medium	Gift Wrapping Option?	Yes
Delivery Area:	Worldwide	Returns Procedure:	Down to you

Other websites to visit for Mens Toiletries:

Website address	You'll find it in
www.escentual.co.uk	Chapter 33: Fragrance, Bath and Body
www.penhaligons.co.uk	Chapter 33: Fragrance, Bath and Body
www.woodruffs.co.uk	Chapter 33: Fragrance, Bath and Body
www.boots.com	Chapter 37: Modern Skincare and Cosmetics
www.garden.co.uk	Chapter 37: Modern Skincare and Cosmetics

Nightwear

www.derek-rose.com

Long established Savile Row nightwear designer Derek Rose offers an excellent choice of nightshirts, robes, pyjamas, loungewear and boxers for men and robes and gowns for women. In each section there's a selection of mainly traditional fabrics and styles and, particularly if men's nightwear is what you're looking for, you're unlikely to find a better collection anywhere.

Site Usability:	★★★★		Based:	UK
Product Range:	★★★★★		Express Delivery Option? (UK)	No
Price Range:	Luxury/Medium		Gift Wrapping Option?	No
Delivery Area:	Worldwide		Returns Procedure:	Down to you

Also take a look at the following for men's nightwear

Website address	**You'll find it in**
www.figleaves.com	Chapter 7: Lingerie
www.bonsoirdirect.com	Chapter 7: Lingerie
www.thomaspink.co.uk	Chapter 17: Shirts, Ties, Cufflinks and Belts
www.josephturner.co.uk	Chapter 17: Shirts, Ties, Cufflinks and Belts
www.newandlingwood.com	Chapter 18: Tailoring and Formalwear

Chapter 22

Gifts, Gadgets and Experience Days

I'm sure that some of you are going to tell me that these websites offer gift ideas for the girls as well, and yes they do, but you have to admit that they're mainly for the guys, surely. Ok so I might find a pampering day out here and possibly something for my daughter but I'd have no trouble at all in finding presents for my sons, although you have to search for things that they'll use for more than a day or two. I have to confess that I totally object to buying 'gadgets' that get put on one side and then later thrown out.

Do think long and hard before splashing out on expensive 'driving experiences', or any other type for that matter. Too often they're not used (yes I have experience of this). Make sure that the person you're buying for will be delighted with that off road experience and then book the date yourself if necessary.

Sites to Visit

www.chessbaron.co.uk

If you know someone who's a chess enthusiast you'll almost certainly find something for them from this retailer based in Taunton, Somerset offering just artisan made chess boards and pieces so if you're looking for any other type of game you'll need to go somewhere else. There are over 100 sets to choose from, from well priced travel sets retailing for under £50 to exquisitely made rosewood or ebony sets at about £300.

Site Usability:	★★★★★	Based:	UK
Product Range:	★★★★	Express Delivery Option? (UK)	No
Price Range:	Luxury/Medium	Gift Wrapping Option?	No
Delivery Area:	Worldwide	Returns Procedure:	Down to you

www.thegadgetshop.com

Browse their online catalogue for some of the funniest, coolest gadgets you can buy, with everything for the frivolous to the functional, the digital to the downright silly. You'll find Big Boy's Toys, Retro Toys, Fun Stuff, Star Wars and iPod accessories here too. They'll ship all over the world and offer an express delivery service in the UK. This is a particularly good website for mid to older teenagers so if you've one of those to buy for take a good look round.

Site Usability:	★★★★★	Based:	UK
Product Range:	★★★★★	Express Delivery Option? (UK)	Yes
Price Range:	Medium/Very Good Value	Gift Wrapping Option?	Yes
Delivery Area:	Worldwide	Returns Procedure:	Freepost or via their customer services department

www.greatexperiencedays.co.uk

Here if you're looking for a gift for an active person you can choose between driving a Ferrari or Porsche 996, dual control flying lessons or clay pigeon shooting (to name just a few). Alternatively you can organise a pampering day out or simply purchase an original newspaper for the special date. They'll ship (items that can be shipped, of course) anywhere in the world and offer standard or express delivery for gifts and vouchers in the UK.

Site Usability:	★★★★★	Based:	UK
Product Range:	★★★★★	Express Delivery Option? (UK)	Yes
Price Range:	Luxury/Medium	Gift Wrapping Option?	Experiences arrive as a gift pack
Delivery Area:	Worldwide	Returns Procedure:	Down to you

www.theinsideman.com

On a lot of general gift stores they make it too easy to move away from thinking properly about your specific recipient. However, on this website they've covered so many areas for men, such as art and design, leather boxes and trays, smoking accessories, clocks, watches, pens, stationery, sports, games and toiletries that they're created a really excellent specifically men's gift department store where you're unlikely not to find something. Have a look and you'll see what I mean.

Site Usability:	★★★★	Based:	UK
Product Range:	★★★★	Express Delivery Option? (UK)	Yes
Price Range:	Medium	Gift Wrapping Option?	No
Delivery Area:	Worldwide	Returns Procedure:	Down to you

www.iwantoneofthose.co.uk

An irresistible (and very cleverly designed) gift and gadget shop with a huge choice and a very well designed website. You can search by price or product type and there's a wide range of all levels. With excellent animation for most products you can choose from gadgets for garden, kitchen and office plus the inevitable toys and games. They offer same day delivery, free standard delivery on orders over £50 and are happy to ship to you anywhere in the world.

Site Usability:	★★★★★	Based:	UK
Product Range:	★★★★★	Express Delivery Option? (UK)	Yes
Price Range:	Medium/Very Good Value	Gift Wrapping Option?	Yes
Delivery Area:	Worldwide	Returns Procedure:	Down to you

www.microanvica.com

Here's an online site with an offline presence in Tottenham Court Road and Selfridges, offering the latest in computers, cameras and audio equipment including iPod and all the accessories. Expect a very good choice and excellent service - they do know what they're talking about and really want to help. Being a slightly less well known retailer Micro Anvika is a very good place to look if you're trying to buy that hot new product just before Christmas.

Site Usability:	★★★★★	Based:	UK
Product Range:	★★★★	Express Delivery Option? (UK)	Yes
Price Range:	Medium	Gift Wrapping Option?	No
Delivery Area:	Worldwide	Returns Procedure:	Down to you

www.oregonscientific.co.uk

Oregon Scientific, established in the US in 1989, creates electronic products for modern lifestyles. Its innovative range is the combination of cutting-edge US technology and stylish European design. You've no doubt seen their stylish wireless weather stations and thermometers but did you know that you can also find the world's slimmest radio controlled alarm clock or a Barbie B Book learning laptop on this irresistible website, plus loads more ideas ranging from the very reasonable to the really quite expensive.

Site Usability:	★★★★★	Based:	UK
Product Range:	★★★	Express Delivery Option? (UK)	Yes
Price Range:	Luxury/Medium	Gift Wrapping Option?	No
Delivery Area:	UK	Returns Procedure:	Down to you

http://eurostore.palm.com

At this worldwide specialist in hand-held computers you can purchase a wide range of products from the newest state of the art latest compact models to all the essential accessories to link your hand-held to your PC. As the world of hand-held computers seems to develop by the day (and it seems to me you need to be something of a boffin to be able to use them properly), you'll need all the excellent information they give you here. GPS solutions and SmartPhones are available as well.

Site Usability:	★★★★★	Based:	UK
Product Range:	★★★★★	Express Delivery Option? (UK)	Yes
Price Range:	Luxury/Medium	Gift Wrapping Option?	No
Delivery Area:	Worldwide	Returns Procedure:	Down to you

www.paramountzone.com

Paramount Zone offers an extensive and carefully selected choice of gadgets, games, boys' toys, bar items, sports gadgets (a good selection), mp3 players, executive items/toys, bachelor pad stuff, gift ideas, and lifestyle accessories - and these are just some of the items you'll find. The majority of UK address orders are despatched the same day for 1-2 day delivery and they're happy to deliver worldwide.

Site Usability:	★★★★	Based:	UK
Product Range:	★★★★	Express Delivery Option? (UK)	Yes
Price Range:	Luxury/Medium	Gift Wrapping Option?	No
Delivery Area:	Worldwide	Returns Procedure:	Down to you

www.redletterdays.co.uk

One of the best 'Experience' day providers (and you've probably seen their brochures and packs in some of the larger stores), Red Letter Days make it easy for you to choose between flying, driving and some serious adventurers experiences. They also offer some great junior options plus body and soul pampering and luxurious, such as lunch on the Orient Express. Once you've ordered what you want it will be sent out in an attractive gift pack to the recipient.

Site Usability:	★★★★★	Based:	UK
Product Range:	★★★★★	Express Delivery Option? (UK)	Yes
Price Range:	Luxury/Medium	Gift Wrapping Option?	No
Delivery Area:	UK	Returns Procedure:	Down to you

www.sciencemuseumstore.com

Next time you go to London pay a visit to the Science Museum, where you can take a 'Moon Walk', check out the Wild Safari or examine the Spy Car. If you can't get there you can find a number of fun and innovative products at their online shop. A rocket that flies using vinegar and baking soda to demonstrate Newton's Third Law of Motion for example, and a light that floats in mid-air as if by magic. Just two of the interesting and fun gifts they offer.

Site Usability:	★★★★★	Based;	UK
Product Range:	★★★★	Express Delivery Option? (UK)	Yes
Price Range:	Medium	Gift Wrapping Option?	No
Delivery Area:	UK	Returns Procedure:	Down to you

www.shopping-emporium-uk.com

This is a brightly coloured unsophisticated website offering the highest quality Italian made games sets for backgammon, dominoes and solitaire, bridge, roulette, poker and more, contained in unique boxes and travel cases made of mahogany, walnut and high quality leather. They also offer mini football and billiard tables and lots of other games. This is definitely the top end of the market but the prices are not unreasonable for what you're buying.

Site Usability:	★★★★	Based;	UK
Product Range:	★★★	Express Delivery Option? (UK)	Yes
Price Range:	Luxury/Medium	Gift Wrapping Option?	No
Delivery Area:	Worldwide	Returns Procedure:	Down to you

www.trackday-gift-experiences.com

This is different from most of the 'experience' websites in that Trackday only offer driving experiences (at different venues in the South and Midlands) that you can select here for the boy racer in your life – if he hasn't got a fast enough car already. Send him rally driving, 4 × 4 off road, Formula 1 or off in a supercar or even to learn how to manage a skid pan – excellent for everyone, particularly new drivers. You order vouchers, either open or for a particular experience and they're valid for a year.

Site Usability:	★★★★	Based;	UK
Product Range:	★★★	Express Delivery Option? (UK)	Yes
Price Range:	Luxury/Medium	Gift Wrapping Option?	No
Delivery Area:	UK	Returns Procedure:	Down to you

www.thesharperedge.co.uk

Originally in the mobile phone industry, this retailer branched out into up-to-the-minute gadgets and gifts several years ago and specialises in keeping you up to date with the latest ideas on the market. It's a really excellent store offering you clever and unusual suggestions plus innovative household accessories and a good place to look if you need a last minute present as they despatch aiming for next day delivery and offer to wrap your present as well.

Site Usability:	★★★★	Based:	UK
Product Range:	★★★★	Express Delivery Option? (UK)	Yes
Price Range:	Medium	Gift Wrapping Option?	Yes
Delivery Area:	Worldwide	Returns Procedure:	Down to you

Chapter 23

Cigars, Pens and Small Accessories

I have to confess that I'm becoming less and less tolerant about smoking, at least smoking that affects me, so I for one am not sorry about smokeless public places. Having said that; my husband smokes a pipe and definitely enjoys the occasional cigar. Here you'll find my two favourite places for buying cigars, where I can promise you you'll find excellent service and in one case particularly, very good prices. Take a look and see.

Where pens are concerned all the brands are available online, including Mont Blanc, Yard O'Led, Faber Castell, Cross and Lamy. They not only make excellent gifts but for those who spend a lot of time at their desks are essential, much utilised tools. A great pen is a pleasure to use. I just wish someone wouldn't keep 'borrowing' mine.

On swiftly to small accessories which mainly fall into the small leathers category and you'll find stud boxes, photo frames and document wallets plus in some cases briefcases and a selection for girls. These are very good gifts to have sent out for you and often free monogramming is offered as well.

Sites to Visit

Cigars

www.simplycigars.co.uk
This is my favourite UK based website offering cigars and humidors plus some very attractive accessories and gifts, wines and spirits. The cigars are expensive as you would expect, however the site is beautifully designed with clever drop down menus and I know from experience that if you need a last minute gift for a smoker (or wine lover) they will do their utmost to get it to you on time so do have a look.

Site Usability:	★★★★★	Based:	UK
Product Range:	★★★★★	Express Delivery Option? (UK)	Yes
Price Range:	Luxury/Medium	Gift Wrapping Option?	No
Delivery Area:	Worldwide	Returns Procedure:	Down to you

www.topcubans.com

Buying cigars in the UK is an extremely expensive experience particularly as you can buy from abroad and make a huge saving on superb quality products. Here is a wide choice, recommendations and advice you can trust and the delivery service is excellent. Not only that but if you're a smoker you'll be bombarded with regular special offers and even recipes to match the time of year. This is a cigar smoker's paradise.

Site Usability:	★★★★★	Based:	Switzerland
Product Range:	★★★★★	Express Delivery Option? (UK)	No
Price Range:	Luxury/Medium	Gift Wrapping Option?	No
Delivery Area:	Worldwide	Returns Procedure:	Down to you

Pens and Small Accessories

www.davidhampton.com

If you like to carry your cash and cards around in a superb quality leather wallet or purse then this is the site for you. David Hampton of London has been supplying luxury leather goods to top hotels throughout the world for the last 20 years, and now, for the first time, you can get your hands on some of their exquisitely crafted accessories online, made out of the finest hides and available in colours such as aubergine and straw in addition to traditional black and brown.

Site Usability:	★★★★	Based:	UK
Product Range:	★★★	Express Delivery Option? (UK)	No
Price Range:	Medium	Gift Wrapping Option?	No but gift boxing is automatic
Delivery Area:	Worldwide	Returns Procedure:	Down to you

www.filofax.co.uk

Your Filofax is now available in many different colours, sizes and styles; including mini, pocket, A5 and A4, black, red, pink, purple, pale blue and denim and on this website you can see each and every one, plus all the refills and accessories such as calculators and pens. Together with this you can download their address software and also buy the luxury range of Yard O'Led pens, making this a very good website for gifts.

Site Usability:	★★★★★	Based:	UK
Product Range:	★★★	Express Delivery Option? (UK)	Yes
Price Range:	Medium	Gift Wrapping Option?	No
Delivery Area:	Worldwide	Returns Procedure:	Down to you

www.h-s.co.uk

This is a name you may well never have heard of, but Harrison and Simmonds have been in business since 1928 offering pipes, cigar humidors and accessories and luxury gifts from companies such as Dalvey. There's also a wide range of Mont Blanc pens and accessories which you need to call them to order, plus chess sets, Hunter pocket watches and shooting sticks. They're happy to ship to you anywhere in the world and if you call them for advice you'll receive excellent service.

Site Usability:	★★★★	Based:	UK
Product Range:	★★★★	Express Delivery Option? (UK)	Yes
Price Range:	Luxury/Medium	Gift Wrapping Option?	No
Delivery Area:	Worldwide	Returns Procedure:	Down to you

www.mrpen.co.uk

Mr Pen has a clear website offering different ranges of pens, including Cross and Sheaffer plus the gorgeously packaged Mount Everest Legacy. An engraving service is available for most pens for a small charge and gift-wrapping is free. Cut glass inkwells, general cartridges and pen repairs are also available. If you're looking for a special nib then call them and you can expect a really personal service.

Site Usability:	★★★	Based:	UK
Product Range:	★★★★	Express Delivery Option? (UK)	Yes
Price Range:	Luxury/Medium	Gift Wrapping Option?	Yes
Delivery Area:	Worldwide	Returns Procedure:	Down to you

www.penandpaper.co.uk

So what's different about this website, when you can find most of the same pens elsewhere? Well apart from being well laid out and offering free delivery on orders over £50 they also have a section for different and hard to find pens including left handed pens and the unusual Yoro pen. For gift ideas as well as the colourful Cross Morph Pens they offer a very good range of the Fisher Space Pens including lacquered Bullet Pens in bronze, Orange Slush, Purple Passion and Rainbow; Shuttle retractable pens, YK3 and Zero Gravity pens.

Site Usability:	★★★★	Based:	UK
Product Range:	★★★★	Express Delivery Option? (UK)	No
Price Range:	Luxury/Medium	Gift Wrapping Option?	No
Delivery Area:	Worldwide	Returns Procedure:	Down to you

www.penshop.co.uk

This is a really attractive website offering one of the best selections of luxury pens including Yard-o-Led's beautiful sterling silver fountain pens, ballpoints and pencils, Faber Castell pens in wood and silver, Mont Blanc (you need to phone to order), and Porsche Design steel pens. They also offer Lamy, Rotring, Shaeffer and Waterman, aim to send out the day you order and they'll deliver worldwide. There's a repairs service as well.

Site Usability:	★★★★	Based:	UK
Product Range:	★★★★	Express Delivery Option? (UK)	Yes
Price Range:	Luxury/Medium	Gift Wrapping Option?	No
Delivery Area:	Worldwide	Returns Procedure:	Down to you

www.peterdraper.co.uk

Offering Porsche design, Caran D'Ache and Lalex pens plus Parker, Waterman, Lamy and Cross, Filofax organisers and pen refills Peter Draper has an unsophisticated website but one where you can expect to find very good service – free delivery on all orders over £25 and worldwide shipping. This is the kind of retailer where if you have a query you can call up and speak to someone who really knows what they're talking about and can give you good advice, particularly if you're looking for a special gift.

Site Usability:	★★★	Based:	UK
Product Range:	★★★★	Express Delivery Option? (UK)	No
Price Range:	Luxury/Medium	Gift Wrapping Option?	No
Delivery Area:	Worldwide	Returns Procedure:	Down to you

www.old.co.uk

Robert Old has a really attractive and easy to navigate website, offering a high quality range of men's gifts and accessories including cashmere sweaters and scarves, leather gifts from cufflink boxes to travel alarm clocks, classic English briefcases and weekenders and shoes by Crockett and Jones. There's lots of clear information about each item and although standard delivery is the norm, they switch to express delivery towards Christmas.

Site Usability:	★★★★	Based:	UK
Product Range:	★★★★	Express Delivery Option? (UK)	Yes
Price Range:	Medium	Gift Wrapping Option?	No
Delivery Area:	Worldwide	Returns Procedure:	Down to you

Also check out these websites for pens and accessories:

Website address	You'll find it in
www.aspinaloflondon.com The Bank	Chapter 12: Handbag Temptation/Carry These Without Breaking
www.forzieri.com	Chapter 12: Handbags Temptation/The A List
www.gucci.com	Chapter 12: Handbags Temptation/The A List
www.pickett.co.uk	Chapter 20: Shoes and Leather Accessories

Section 4
Babies, Kids and Teens

Babies, Kids and Teens

Because there are so many great online retailers in this section offering an enormous range of products it simply wasn't possible to list them all here, so if you want to take a look at every single one you'll need to invest in your very own copy of *The Shopaholic's Guide to Buying for Mother and Child Online.*

To help you get the best out of this area I've picked my top ten favourites in each one - that's not to say that the ones that aren't here aren't good; they certainly are, but I wanted you give you the best choice in the smallest amount of space, if you know what I mean.

Buying for babies, kids and teens online is such a boon. Having had three children myself very (very) close together, I know just how hard it is to try and visit the shops with them in tow. One or all of them is likely (simultaneously or independently) to be hungry, tired, whiney or in a feisty, fighting mood, picking rows with you or one another just when you're trying to have a quiet conversation with a friend or a helpful shop assistant, and you immediately lose complete track of what you were saying or trying to achieve.

You may resolutely try and carry on but I recommend taking them home, having a strong drink, waiting until they're asleep and then buying online - but I would, wouldn't I?

For babies and kids you'll find clothes, accessories, toys and equipment here including some excellent sport and skiwear, trampolines, dressing up clothes and everything for parties.

For older children who are reaching that cross-over point when they think they're no longer children you could, for clothes and accessories, also check out The High Street section in Chapter 1. My daughter is now just about seventeen (depending when you're reading this book - she could even be driving - help!) but for at least five years she's considered herself far too old for kids' clothing and has preferred to take a look, and spend my money, at places like Miss Selfridge, Top Shop and River Island.

You may think that she started rather young, but you just try and stop yours when they reach that age. My belief is that it's much better to let them browse the more grown up styles with you beside them than to say a firm NO until they're old enough to go on their own and start buying things that will make you gasp. I'm afraid that they do that anyway in their drive to experiment but you have to do what you can.

So, have a look at the websites here and don't take your little ones out to the shops any more. You really don't need to. Think of the stress you'll save.

Chapter 24

Baby and Toddler Clothes

You'll find two types of childrenswear retailers here; those that offer a selection of designers, such as Jean Bourget, Chipie, AraVore and Ikks, and those who offer their own brand – Rachel Riley and Marie Chantal are just two examples of those.

There's also a wide range of prices and everything from beautiful, hand made party dresses to essential waterproofs for tinies.

Take a look at Chapter 24 for baby and toddler clothes too, as many of the websites there cater for the full range of ages from newborns right up to age 14 (and sometimes higher).

Sites to Visit

www.balloonsweb.co.uk

Just looking at the pictures on this website, in the Catamini and Pamplona sections particularly, makes you want to buy something as they're absolutely enchanting. Balloonsweb specialises in designer children's clothing for the aforesaid brands, and also Miss Sixty, Chipie, Jean Bourget, Ikks and Timberland. This is a really excellent children's website offering clothes and accessories from newborn to 14 years, plus pretty baby gifts and christening wear.

Site Usability:	★★★★★	Based:	UK
Product Range:	★★★★★	Express Delivery Option? (UK)	No
Price Range:	Luxury/Medium	Gift Wrapping Option?	No
Delivery Area:	Worldwide	Returns Procedure:	Down to you

www.boutiqueenfant.com

Boutique Enfant offers a collection of cashmere knitwear for 6 month to 12 year old babies and children in a rich and vibrant colour selection for older children and marshmallow colours for the baby range. The emphasis is on traditional designs and you can mix and match from the range of knits as well as buy blankets and toys. If you're looking for a special present; they offer a high quality gift wrapping service and they'll ship worldwide. There are exquisite hand smocked girls' dresses here as well.

Site Usability:	★★★★★	Based:	UK
Product Range:	★★★★	Express Delivery Option? (UK)	No
Price Range:	Luxury	Gift Wrapping Option?	Yes
Delivery Area:	Worldwide	Returns Prodecure	Down to you

www.kentandcarey.co.uk

Kent and Carey have been in the business of supplying beautifully made, classic children's clothes for over 15 years. For babies there are cute babygros and really sweet nightwear in pretty fabrics. For slightly older girls; Peter Pan printed tops, tiered skirts and print tied trousers and for boys check shirts, long shorts and traditional 'grown up style' knitwear. The pictures are lovely and the prices are good as well.

Site Usability:	★★★★	Based:	UK
Product Range:	★★★	Express Delivery Option? (UK)	No
Price Range:	Medium	Gift Wrapping Option?	No
Delivery Area:	Worldwide	Returns Procedure:	Down to you

www.littlefashiongallery.com

Little Fashion Gallery is based in France and has a range of beautiful, luxury clothes and accessories for children aged 0-6. As well as offering brands such as American Apparel, Antik Batik, Caramel Baby and Child and Bonnie Baby this is an excellent destination for gifts which they're happy to ship worldwide. You can also read their Little Fashion Gallery magazine online which tells you all about the childrenswear trends for the season and has a variety of other articles.

Site Usability:	★★★★	Based:	France
Product Range:	★★★★★	Express Delivery Option? (UK)	No
Price Range:	Luxury	Gift Wrapping Option?	No
Delivery Area:	Worldwide	Returns Procedure	Down to you

www.littletrekkers.co.uk

If this is the moment when you realise your newly walking (and getting into things and splashing in puddles) toddler is going to be getting wet and dirty from now on you definitely ought to take a look here. You'll find extremely good value waterproofs, from splashsuits, jackets and dungarees, to skiwear and fleece for babies and kids up to age 8. There's also weatherproof and summer pool footwear and lots of other ideas for babies and young children.

Site Usability:	★★★★★	Based:	UK
Product Range:	★★★★	Express Delivery Option? (UK)	Yes
Price Range:	Medium/Very Good Value	Gift Wrapping Option?	No
Delivery Area:	Worldwide	Returns Procedure:	Down to you

www.mariechantal.com

This is an exquisite collection of baby and children's wear designed by Marie Chantal of Greece. As you would expect the prices are quite steep, but you'll be hard put to find this quality of fabric and modern use of colour and design in many other children's stores. The clothing is available in two sections; babies, and toddlers (although some of these go up to age 8). If you want something really special you should have a look here.

Site Usability:	★★★★	Based:	UK
Product Range:	★★★★	Express Delivery Option? (UK)	No
Price Range:	Luxury/Medium	Gift Wrapping Option?	No
Delivery Area:	Worldwide	Returns Procedure:	Down to you

www.masterandmiss.com

AraVore, Cut 4 Cloth, D'Arcy Brown, Ikks, Mini a Ture and Tiny Tulips are some of the original children's clothing brands offered here, with the range extending from baby clothes to children up to 10 years. There's lots to choose from, including colourful knitwear, traditional separates and some really pretty nightwear from 18 months to 8 years.

Site Usability:	★★★★	Based:	UK
Product Range:	★★★★	Express Delivery Option? (UK)	Yes
Price Range:	Luxury/Medium	Gift Wrapping Option?	No
Delivery Area:	UK	Returns Procedure:	Down to you

www.muddypuddles.com

Waterproofs, wellies, thermal socks and booties, hats, gloves, brollies for tinies, ski wear and even a wellie peg is to be found on this innovative and clever site aimed at children up to five with a very few items going up to eight (such as ski tops). This is an absolutely essential website for just about anyone with young children so take a good look round, as you could easily give some of the flowered wellies, funny socks and bootees as gifts.

Site Usability:	★★★★	Based:	UK
Product Range:	★★★★	Express Delivery Option? (UK)	No
Price Range:	Medium/Very Good Value	Gift Wrapping Option?	No
Delivery Area:	Worldwide	Returns Procedure:	Down to you

www.rachelriley.com

The next time you're asked where someone could find a really special outfit for your little one, point them in the direction of Rachel Riley, where you'll discover a truly lovely collection for infants, teens and grown ups as well. Everything there is exquisite with a marvellous attention to style and detail and as you'd expect, nothing is inexpensive. So if you can't afford to kit out your child totally from here, at least you can ask a Godmother or granny to contribute something really special.

Site Usability:	★★★★	Based:	UK
Product Range:	★★★★	Express Delivery Option? (UK)	Yes
Price Range:	Luxury	Gift Wrapping Option?	No
Delivery Area:	Worldwide	Returns Procedure:	Down to you

www.thekidswindow.co.uk

The Kids Window is a real children's department store, offering children's clothing brands from designers such as Catfish, Inside Out, Marie Chantal and Budishh, a full range of baby equipment, activity toys such as trampolines, swings and slides and lots of toys and games. You can search on this website by age, gender, season and brand. or click through to each section of the range.

Site Usability:	★★★★★	Based:	UK
Product Range:	★★★★★	Express Delivery Option? (UK)	Yes
Price Range:	Luxury/Medium	Gift Wrapping Option?	Yes
Delivery Area:	Worldwide	Returns Procedure:	Down to you

www.weegooseberry.com

Wee Gooseberry have definitely aimed themselves at the tiny end of the designer market, with most of their clothes going up to 24 months. There's a wonderful choice of brands including Levi, Catamini, Bob and Blossom (love it), Ellepi, Kidorable rainwear (love that too), Mini Mink, Ickle Pickle and Snuggle Sac. They also have fancy dress costumes for tinies, a wide range of shoes and some lovely gift ideas. Buy from them.

Site Usability:	★★★★★	Based:	UK
Product Range:	★★★★★	Express Delivery Option? (UK)	Yes
Price Range:	Luxury/Medium	Gift Wrapping Option?	Yes
Delivery Area:	Worldwide	Returns Procedure:	Down to you

Also take a look at these websites for Baby and Toddler Clothes:

Website address	You'll find it in
www.bloomingmarvellous.co.uk	Chapter 10: Fashion for Bumps
www.jojomamanbebe.co.uk	Chapter 10: Fashion for Bumps
www.mamasandpapas.co.uk	Chapter 10: Fashion for Bumps

Chapter 25

Baby Accessories and Equipment

The benefits of being able to shop online for baby accessories and equipment are probably greater than in almost any other area, as there are so many essential items you need such as car seats, travel systems or buggies and safety equipment.

Yes you can see quite a good range at some of the larger baby stores on the high street but what you can do here – very easily – is price comparison shop. So find the make and model that you like best and then go seeking out the best deal.

It's really easy to do this using price comparison websites such as Kelkoo and if you're not sure how to make it work for you just visit Chapter 89 of this book where you'll find all the information you need.

Sites to Visit

www.babycare-direct.co.uk

One of the first places to check out on this friendly website is the Babylist section, where you'll find helpful lists of what you'll need to have ready when your baby arrives (and what you will probably want to take with you to hospital). Then click through to Baby on the Move, with its wide range of clearly pictured and described buggies, prams and travel systems, Safety Equipment, where they offer everything you'll need, Feeding Time, Bedtime, Bath and Changing. This is an excellent website and there are some very good prices as well.

Site Usability:	★★★★★	Based:	UK
Product Range:	★★★★★	Express Delivery Option? (UK)	No
Price Range:	Medium	Gift Wrapping Option?	Yes
Delivery Area:	Worldwide	Returns Procedure	Down to you

www.babycity.co.uk

Designed in pale pink and blue, Baby City is a calming, well laid out website offering lots of products including baby clothes and accessories, monitors and safety equipment such as cot nets and toy ties and totally useful but quite hard to find products such as nappy wrappers (!), steam sterilisers and bottle warmers and a range of products for premature babies. There are lots of gift ideas here as well.

Site Usability:	★★★★★	Based:	UK
Product Range:	★★★★	Express Delivery Option? (UK)	No
Price Range:	Medium	Gift Wrapping Option?	Yes
Delivery Area:	Worldwide	Returns Procedure	Down to you

www.babygurgles.co.uk

I have to say that I thought you had just about enough baby equipment websites to browse through when I came to this website, but when I read the question 'What is a Buggy Snuggle?' in the margin I knew you'd want to know as well and it is, of course, a cute version of just what you'd expect it to be available in lots of different prints. There are other lovely things here, such as The Bug in a Rug Baby Wrap, Miracle swaddling blanket, Wheelie Bug toddler rides and lots of other basic and essential equipment. Take a look.

Site Usability:	★★★★★	Based:	UK
Product Range:	★★★★	Express Delivery Option? (UK)	No
Price Range:	Medium	Gift Wrapping Option?	No
Delivery Area:	UK	Returns Procedure	Down to you

www.baby-pages.co.uk

Baby Pages offers you the choice of prams and travel systems by Silver Cross, Bebe Confort, Quinny, Micralite, Bugaboo and Britax plus accessories such as bags, buggy liners and blankets, buggy pods, baby hoodies, sheepskin liners and rain hoods. There's also a very good range of car seats right up to 12 years and furniture ranges by Boori and Kidsmill.

Site Usability:	★★★★★	Based:	UK
Product Range:	★★★★★	Express Delivery Option? (UK)	Most items are sent for UK next day delivery
Price Range:	Luxury/Medium	Gift Wrapping Option?	No
Delivery Area:	UK	Returns Procedure:	Down to you

www.kiddies-kingdom.com

This is a really well laid out website which helps you get to the product you're looking for with no fuss. So you can choose from High Chairs, Prams and Pushchairs, Buggy Boards and Travel Systems, Moses Baskets, Cots and Cribs, Furniture and Monitors and much, much more. They offer all the premium brands and there's free delivery in the UK if you spend over £50, which you're almost certain to do.

Site Usability:	★★★★★	Based:	UK
Product Range:	★★★★★	Express Delivery Option? (UK)	Yes automatic
Price Range:	Luxury/Medium	Gift Wrapping Option?	No
Delivery Area:	UK	Returns Procedure:	They collect most items

www.kiddicare.com

Kiddicare is a large independent retailer of baby and nursery equipment and nursery furniture and claim to keep everything in stock ready to send out to you. You can buy Avent sterilisers and feeding bottles, Grobags, buggies and travel cots, high chairs, rockers and baby swings plus equipment for the home including playpens, stair gates, cots, changing units and nursery furniture. Delivery is free to most of the UK and takes about four working days.

Site Usability:	★★★★★	Based:	UK
Product Range:	★★★★★	Express Delivery Option? (UK)	No
Price Range:	Medium	Gift Wrapping Option?	No
Delivery Area:	UK	Returns Procedure:	Down to you

www.mothercare.com

It's really hard to know where to put Mothercare, as it offers such a wide range of everything for mothers, babies and young children, including some incredibly well priced maternity wear, pushchairs, buggies and all sorts of travel systems, everything (and I mean everything) you could need for the nursery plus feeding and safety equipment, toys and gifts. The emphasis here is on simplicity and good pricing, there are excellent check lists for hospital bags, babies first wardrobe and travel solutions and a great deal more information as well.

Site Usability:	★★★★★	Based:	UK
Product Range:	★★★★	Express Delivery Option? (UK)	No
Price Range:	Very Good Value	Gift Wrapping Option?	No
Delivery Area:	UK – enquire for overseas orders	Returns Procedure:	Down to you or to store

www.preciouslittleone.com

Here's an excellent baby equipment website offering, amongst other things, footmuffs, pushchairs and accessories with plenty of details to help you choose. There are also car seats and a very good range for the nursery including the high quality Saplings range of furniture, most of which will take your child from baby to older years. You can buy giant themed sticker sets for room decorating here too

Site Usability:	★★★★★	Based:	UK
Product Range:	★★★★	Express Delivery Option? (UK)	No
Price Range:	Medium	Gift Wrapping Option?	No
Delivery Area:	Worldwide	Returns Procedure:	Down to you

www.thebaby.co.uk

Don't be put off by the tremendous range here, including Mountain Buggy Prams, Simon Horn and Wigwam Kids furniture, Stevenson Rocking Horses and so much more. Whatever you're looking for, for your baby or child you'll probably find it, whether you need travel accessories, full room sets or baby accessories such as high chairs and monitors. They offer a next day delivery service and will ship worldwide, although some items are restricted by weight.

Site Usability:	★★★	Based:	UK
Product Range:	★★★★★	Express Delivery Option? (UK)	Yes
Price Range:	Luxury/Medium	Gift Wrapping Option?	No
Delivery Area:	Worldwide	Returns Procedure:	Down to you

www.twoleftfeet.co.uk

This is a fantastic baby equipment website claiming to offer the largest selection in the UK. Browse through their sections offering cots and baby bedding, pushchairs, prams and the latest buggies, car seats, cribs and rocking horses and just about everything in between. Premium brands include Silver Cross, Bebe Confort, Chicco, Britax and Maclaren. You'll also find lovely children's furniture here.

Site Usability:	★★★★★	Based:	UK
Product Range:	★★★★★	Express Delivery Option? (UK)	Yes
Price Range:	Medium	Gift Wrapping Option?	No
Delivery Area:	Most EU plus the USA	Returns Procedure:	Down to you

Also take a look at these websites for Baby Accessories and Equipment:

Website address
www.mamasandpapas.co.uk
www.johnlewis.com

You'll find it in
Chapter 10: Fashion for Bumps
Chapter 44: The Kitchen

Chapter 26

Baby and Pre-School Toys

oys for gifts, toys for treats and toys to help them start learning are all available here from this selection of online retailers who not only offer you a comprehensive selection but also give you lots of help before you buy on what type of toy is suitable for each age group.

If you're buying a gift you can almost always find a great deal of help and advice so that if you don't have kids yourself you won't make the mistake of buying something (horrors) far too young or much too old for the recipient.

If you're thinking of spending quite a bit and you're not quite sure what to buy my advice would be to give the mother a call and make sure that your giftee (is there such a word?) doesn't already have what you're considering. Think of the disappointment you'll avoid.

Sites to Visit

www.babydazzlers.com

This company aims to offer you toys that combine the elements of fun with teaching, so as well as lots of toys and craft kits to buy there's a great deal of advice on what you should be choosing (and what your child should be doing) at each stage from birth to five years. It's a really excellent resource as well as a great shop and I just wish they'd been around when I had my kids.

Site Usability:	★★★★★	Based:	UK
Product Range:	★★★★★	Express Delivery Option? (UK)	Yes but call them
Price Range:	Medium	Gift Wrapping Option?	Yes
Delivery Area:	UK and call for overseas	Returns Procedure:	Down to you

www.beyondtherainbow.co.uk

This is a marvellous website to have a look round for toys and games for your pre-schooler. Not only is it colourful, fun and well laid out, but there's a really wide selection, in sections such as Bashing and Banging (great for small boys), Pull and Push Along Toys and Activity Toys as well as the straightforward learning variety. There are also some great wall charts to help to learn to tell the time and to spell, plus the Maths Bus. Delivery is free on orders over £50.

Site Usability:	★★★★★	Based:	UK
Product Range:	★★★★★	Express Delivery Option? (UK)	Yes
Price Range:	Luxury/Medium	Gift Wrapping Option?	No
Delivery Area:	UK	Returns Procedure:	Down to you

www.elc.co.uk

The baby and toddler section at the Early Learning Centre's colourful website is well worth having a look round, as you'll find a wide range perfect for starting your baby off, including bath toys, Blossom Farm baby toys, buggy and cot toys and just about every other type of baby toy you can think of. They make it easy for you to choose as, as well as selecting by type of toy you can choose by themes such as Action and Adventure and Art and Music.

Site Usability:	★★★★★	Based:	UK
Product Range:	★★★★★	Express Delivery Option? (UK)	Yes
Price Range:	Medium/Very Good Value	Gift Wrapping Option?	No
Delivery Area:	UK	Returns Procedure:	Free – collection or freepost

www.gamleys.co.uk

Action Man, Bratz Dolls, Dora the Explorer (love that one), Little Tikes, My Little Pony, Peppa Pig, Pixel Chix (!?) Pocoyo, Polly Pocket and Power Rangers are just some of the brands on offer here. Then for tinies there are pre-school toys by Fisher Price, Mega Bloks, Teletubbies and Tomy. Provided you stick to the clear menus of categories and brands you shouldn't get lost; go off on a tangent and you almost certainly will be.

Site Usability:	★★★★★	Based:	UK
Product Range:	★★★★★	Express Delivery Option? (UK)	No
Price Range:	Medium	Gift Wrapping Option?	No
Delivery Area:	UK	Returns Procedure:	Down to you

www.izziwizzikids.co.uk

I really like this website. When you reach one of those moments when you just can't look at another hugely colourful and busy online retailer where there's (probably) too much choice, you can calm down here. Izzi Wizzi specialise in toys for babies up to one year old. For each product, (Tooting Teddy or Old MacDonald's Noisy Barn, for example) they give you just the right amount of information. You can browse by age, product type or category and they deliver throughout the EU.

Site Usability:	★★★★★	Based:	UK
Product Range:	★★★	Express Delivery Option? (UK)	Yes
Price Range:	Medium	Gift Wrapping Option?	No
Delivery Area:	EU	Returns Procedure:	Down to you

www.theentertainer.com

This is one of the largest independent toy retailers in the UK with a huge range and an excellent, easy to navigate website where you can search by brand, type of toy, age group or price. Once you've decided what you want to buy and registered both your address and any addresses where you want your orders despatched to, you simply select from the standard or express delivery services, give your payment details and you're done.

Site Usability:	★★★★★	Based:	UK
Product Range:	★★★★★	Express Delivery Option? (UK)	Yes
Price Range:	Medium	Gift Wrapping Option?	No
Delivery Area:	Worldwide	Returns Procedure:	Down to you

www.toysbymailorder.co.uk

Toys by Mail Order specialises in toys, gifts, games, nursery items and jigsaw puzzles for children of all ages. You can search the range of wooden toys and soft toys for baby and toddler gifts, the many items stocked for older boys and girls plus traditional family games. They offer fast delivery, a gift wrapping service and personalised messages for special occasions. As well as all this you'll find Manhattan bootees, puppets, dolls, puzzles and games for when they're a little older.

Site Usability:	★★★★	Based:	UK
Product Range:	★★★★★	Express Delivery Option? (UK)	Yes 2 day service
Price Range:	Medium	Gift Wrapping Option?	No
Delivery Area:	Worldwide	Returns Procedure:	Down to you

Also take a look at these websites for Baby and Pre-School Toys:

Website address	You'll find it in
www.amazon.co.uk	Chapter 71: Books, Music and Movies

Chapter 27

Furniture and Nursery Bedding

It would be all too easy to get carried away here, particularly if you want to totally redecorate a room in your house for your tiny. You could invest in (apart from the new carpet and curtains, of course) the cot, the bedding, the furniture from changing table to beautifully handpainted chests of drawers and wardrobes and all the gorgeous accessories from cushions to bean bags, floor mats and play pens.

I would, however, just ask you to stop and think for a moment before you splash out. I would recommend decorating your tiny's room and buying for it in a way that will last you slightly longer, so that when he or she is old enough to appreciate their surroundings they won't be asking you to change everything again.

There are so many different ways of doing this – yes of course buy gorgeous baby print curtains as they're easy to change later on, plus the accessories to go with; ditto, but in terms of furniture I would think slightly ahead and buy versatile furniture that perhaps isn't quite so babyish.

These are just my thoughts, and of course it's all up to you. Sorry, Kirstie, I promise to get those stars off your bedroom window sometime soon.

Sites to Visit

www.aspaceuk.com

At Aspace you can shop by range (Astor, Vermont, Porterhouse, Mill Tree, Key West, Captain's Girl, Boomsbury, Hudson) or by type of furniture, such as single or bunk beds, desks, wardrobes and chests, duvet sets, mattresses, sleeping bags, bean bags and cushions. In each section there's a great deal to see at a wide range of prices but there's also a lot of information and help on how to put ranges together.

Site Usability:	★★★★	Based:	UK
Product Range:	★★★★★	Express Delivery Option? (UK)	No
Price Range:	Luxury/Medium	Gift Wrapping Option?	No
Delivery Area:	UK	Returns Procedure:	They'll collect

www.gltc.co.uk

Here's great range of ideas for babies and young children of all ages including Fairy Ballerina and Sports Champion duvet sets and accessories, reasonably priced traditional children's furniture, innovative storage ideas, playtables, bunk beds, baby and toddler sleeping bags and themed furniture. There's the Squishy, Squirty Bath Book, Jungle soft toy Bowling Set and Toy House Play Mat too plus loads more clever suggestions.

Site Usability:	★★★★	Based:	UK
Product Range:	★★★★	Express Delivery Option? (UK)	Yes
Price Range:	Medium	Gift Wrapping Option?	No
Delivery Area:	Worldwide	Returns Procedure:	Down to you

www.helenbroadhead.co.uk

If you like something completely different then take a look round here, where Helen Broadhead offers her totally original and hand painted range of furniture. What you need to do first is look on her designs page and choose from the collection including Under the Sea, Teddy Bears, Jungle, Tank, Pirates or Fairy, then select the piece of furniture you'd like which range from tables and chairs to mirrors and chests. Nothing is overpriced and most items would make lovely gifts.

Site Usability:	★★★★	Based:	UK
Product Range:	★★★★	Express Delivery Option? (UK)	No
Price Range:	Medium	Gift Wrapping Option?	Yes
Delivery Area:	Worldwide but call for overseas deliveries	Returns Procedure:	No returns for bespoke items unless they're faulty

www.kidsrooms.co.uk

Kids Rooms specialises in children's furniture and accessories for children's bedrooms, nurseries and playrooms. The range includes children's beds, wardrobes, chest of drawers, bedside cabinets, children's tables and chairs, toy boxes, bedding, bookends, height charts and much more. The website is attractive and easy to navigate and the product range is growing all the time.

Site Usability:	★★★★★	Based:	UK
Product Range:	★★★★	Express Delivery Option? (UK)	No
Price Range:	Medium	Gift Wrapping Option?	No
Delivery Area:	UK	Returns Procedure:	Down to you

www.linenstore.co.uk

This is another place you may or may not want to let your children loose at (well certainly not with your credit card, anyway). There's an amazing range of children's and nursery bedlinen and accessories, including Dennis the Menace, Scooby Doo, RAF, Cosmic Spaceboy and Thomas the Tank (for boys, of course) alongside Magical Fairy, Tinkerbell, Dora the Explora and Party Girl for girls plus loads (and I mean loads) more. For the nursery there are pretty designs from Lollipop Lane plus borders and curtains to match.

Site Usability:	★★★★	Based:	UK
Product Range:	★★★★★	Express Delivery Option? (UK)	No
Price Range:	Medium/Very Good Value	Gift Wrapping Option?	No
Delivery Area:	UK but there's www.andyslinens.com for USA	Returns Procedure:	Down to you

www.nurserywindow.co.uk

Once you arrive at this website you'll find it very hard to leave. There are some seriously lovely things here for children's rooms, from unusual bedding, Moses baskets and high quality cots and furniture to gift baskets for new babies and everything is beautifully photographed. Just click on the area of their online shop you're interested in, enter, and you'll certainly be hooked. You can also buy matching fabric to the bedlinen. Nothing is cheap but it's all beautiful quality.

Site Usability:	★★★★★	Based:	UK
Product Range:	★★★★	Express Delivery Option? (UK)	No
Price Range:	Luxury/Medium	Gift Wrapping Option?	No
Delivery Area:	UK	Returns Procedure:	Down to you

www.thechildrensfurniturecompany.co.uk

It's well worthwhile having a good look round and investing here, as these are not children's things for the short term, but pieces of furniture that will last and last with childish accents that you can remove and change, such as bunks that can be debunked and safety rails removed; engraved panels which can be swapped for plain ones and brightly-coloured panels which flip to reveal more muted tones. When you take a good look you'll fully understand why they've been awarded the Guildmark by The Worshipful Company of Furniture Makers.

Site Usability:	★★★★★	Based:	UK
Product Range:	★★★★★	Express Delivery Option? (UK)	No
Price Range:	Luxury/Medium	Gift Wrapping Option?	No
Delivery Area:	UK	Returns Procedure:	They charge a collection fee if you change your mind

www.tuttibambini.co.uk

Tutti Bambini offers a range of coordinating nursery furniture including cribs, cots, cot beds, wardrobes, dressers, toy boxes, shelves and cot top changers. They also sell glider chairs, wooden toys and quality mattresses which are available in four sizes. Their cot top changers are designed to fit onto the top of a cot or cot bed and have raised sides and a padded, vinyl, wipe clean surface. Take some time when you're looking here as this is a very good collection at a wide range of prices.

Site Usability:	★★★★★	Based:	UK
Product Range:	★★★★★	Express Delivery Option? (UK)	Yes for some items
Price Range:	Luxury/Medium	Gift Wrapping Option?	No
Delivery Area:	UK	Returns Procedure:	Down to you

www.vipkids.co.uk

VIP Kids specialises in the design, manufacture and import of high quality imaginative children's beds, chairs, bedroom furniture, toys, nursery furniture and accessories. You'll find collections featuring the 1930s reproduction Ferrari F2 Retro Racers. fantastic children's room lighting, hand-crafted upholstered loose cover armchairs, fun light switch covers and wooden mobiles. Children's beds range from toddler beds to mid sleeper and four poster styles.

Site Usability:	★★★★★	Based:	UK
Product Range:	★★★★★	Express Delivery Option? (UK)	No
Price Range:	Luxury/Medium	Gift Wrapping Option?	No
Delivery Area:	UK	Returns Procedure:	Down to you

www.vivababy.com

Themes here to choose from go under the headings such as Summer House, Nautilus, Roses, Tom's Cabin, Flower Power, Sleeping Beauty and Football – does that give you some kind of idea? Beware letting your child choose from this website, you may well end up with a Kontiki bunk bed instead of the traditional style you were aiming for, or the amazing Nautilus bed/play area. There's a lot of fun to be had with this delightful range which offers bedlinen and accessories to match.

Site Usability:	★★★★★	Based:	UK
Product Range:	★★★★★	Express Delivery Option? (UK)	No
Price Range:	Luxury/Medium	Gift Wrapping Option?	No
Delivery Area:	Worldwide	Returns Procedure:	They will collect.

Also take a look at these websites for children's furniture and bedlinen:

Website address	You'll find it in
www.thewhitecompany.com	Chapter 41: In the Bedroom
www.thekidswindow.com	Chapter 24: Baby and Toddler Clothes

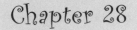

Chapter 28

Clothing to Age 11

I know, I know, you're going to tell me I can't count, but when I went through the websites here I found it impossible to leave any of them out. That's just how good they are. I was astounded by the amount of choice and thought enviously (though fleetingly) of the narrow choice available in the shops when my kids were young.

Most of these kids' fashion retailers also offer clothes for tinies, so when you're going through you can shop for all the age groups making life even easier: lucky you.

Sites to Visit

www.caramel-shop.co.uk

If you're looking for childrenswear you must take a look here, as Caramel have one of the most attractive websites and best collections around. The clothes are designed for babies and children aged two to twelve and you can also buy shoes, boots and socks. Each part of the range is divided into themes so you can clearly see what works together and you never feel swamped by the amount of choice.

Site Usability:	★★★★★	Based:	UK
Product Range:	★★★★★	Express Delivery Option? (UK)	Yes
Price Range:	Luxury/Medium	Gift Wrapping Option?	Yes
Delivery Area:	Worldwide	Returns Procedure:	Down to you

www.childrenssalon.co.uk

This is a family run business operating out of their shop in Kent and offering designer children's clothes from 0 to 12 years from labels such as Oilily, Bench, Oxbow, Gabrielle, Elle, Cacharel, Kenzo, Dior and loads more (and I mean loads). They also have the Petit Bateau range of underwear for boys and girls, nightwear and dressing up clothes and they specialise in a gorgeous range of christening gowns and accessories.

Site Usability:	★★★★★	Based:	UK
Product Range:	★★★★	Express Delivery Option? (UK)	Yes
Price Range:	Luxury/Medium	Gift Wrapping Option?	No
Delivery Area:	Worldwide	Returns Procedure:	Down to you

www.clothes4boys.co.uk

Here you'll find, yes you guessed it, clothes just for boys, from 2-14 years old and including designers Ripcurl, Salty Dog, Eager Beaver, Regatta and Flyers. There really is a great choice with casual clothes from t-shirts to boarding trousers and football trousers plus an excellent sale shop and some fun swimwear. You can select to view their range by age or by designer.

Site Usability:	★★★★★	Based:	UK
Product Range:	★★★★	Express Delivery Option? (UK)	No
Price Range:	Medium	Gift Wrapping Option?	No
Delivery Area:	Worldwide	Returns Procedure:	Down to you

www.cosyposy.co.uk

This well thought out childrenswear website has gone straight into my list of favourites, as it's attractive to look at, easy to navigate and offers an original and reasonably priced range for boys and girls from 2 to 6 plus a separate babies' collection. Brands include Inch Blue, Cacharel, Elizabeth James and Butterscotch. There are also some very good gift ideas for new babies and children including gift sets and toys and you can buy gift vouchers which can be sent out on your behalf.

Site Usability:	★★★★★	Based:	UK
Product Range:	★★★★★	Express Delivery Option? (UK)	Yes
Price Range:	Medium	Gift Wrapping Option?	Yes
Delivery Area:	Worldwide	Returns Procedure:	Down to you

www.kidscavern.co.uk

Kids Cavern is one of the top children's designer stores in the North West of England and their website covers childrenswear over three departments from newborn to 3 years, 4-10 years and 11-16 years. Designers offered include Timberland, Moschino, DKNY, Burberry, Armani, Miniman, Dior and many more, and they'll ship worldwide although outside the UK and USA you need to email them to find out how much your postage will cost.

Site Usability:	★★★	Based:	UK
Product Range:	★★★★	Express Delivery Option? (UK)	Yes
Price Range:	Medium	Gift Wrapping Option?	No
Delivery Area:	Worldwide	Returns Procedure:	Down to you

www.mischiefkids.co.uk

At Mischief Kids you can find a great really good selection of designer clothing for kids, from labels such as Emile et Rose, Ikks, Mim-Pi, Marese, Trois Pommes and Quicksilver. Click on the brand you're interested in and you can immediately see everything they're offering plus what's available right now (although this could be simplified). This is an excellent website for children's clothing and one that your kids will enjoy looking through too, for its fun and quirky design.

Site Usability:	★★★★	Based:	UK
Product Range:	★★★★★	Express Delivery Option? (UK)	Yes
Price Range:	Luxury/Medium	Gift Wrapping Option?	No
Delivery Area:	Worldwide	Returns Procedure:	Down to you

www.mittyjames.com

Mitty James offers luxuriously soft towelling beach robes and holiday wear for babies, kids, children and teenagers along with traditional cotton swimwear and classic daywear. Once you're on this website it's difficult to leave without buying something, particularly if you're just off on holiday, as the pictures are filled with prettily coloured childrenswear perfect for holiday and beach. Call for express delivery.

Site Usability:	★★★★★	Based:	UK
Product Range:	★★★	Express Delivery Option? (UK)	Yes if you call them
Price Range:	Medium	Gift Wrapping Option?	No
Delivery Area:	Worldwide but call them outside the UK	Returns Procedure:	Down to you

www.petitpatapon.com

I'm sure that my kids were never as well behaved as the ones in the pictures here, where delightful girls and boys in gorgeous clothes are happily playing and laughing and modelling. The range goes from newborn layettes to babies and then toddler boys and girls up to age 5. Finally there's a girls' range up to age 14 and all the prices are reasonable. Remember to click on your currency first.

Site Usability:	★★★★★	Based:	France/USA
Product Range:	★★★★★	Express Delivery Option? (UK)	No
Price Range:	Medium/Very Good Value	Gift Wrapping Option?	No
Delivery Area:	Worldwide	Returns Procedure:	Down to you

www.pleasemum.co.uk

This is a company that was established in London in 1971, aiming to provide fashionable, unique and high quality children's clothing. They now offer their excellent own brand collections online for children up to age 12/13, and there are some really gorgeous outfits here, particularly for girls, plus designer childrenswear by Moschino, D & G, Armani, Versace and Roberto Cavalli. Do not expect to save money when you visit this website, it's definitely not cheap.

Site Usability:	★★★★	Based:	UK
Product Range:	★★★★	Express Delivery Option? (UK)	No
Price Range:	Luxury/Medium	Gift Wrapping Option?	No
Delivery Area:	Worldwide	Returns Procedure:	Down to you

www.raindrops.co.uk

At Raindrops there's a range of Scandinavian designed rainwear for children up to about age 9, including well priced fleece lined rain jackets, dungarees in a wide choice of colours and waterproof all in ones. There's also a very good choice here of high quality more general outerwear, from a country that's well known for its love of the outdoors and wet weather gear.

Site Usability:	★★★★	Based:	UK
Product Range:	★★★	Express Delivery Option? (UK)	Yes
Price Range:	Very Good Value	Gift Wrapping Option?	Yes
Delivery Area:	Worldwide	Returns Procedure:	Down to you

www.tansen.co.uk

Tansen is an eclectic, pretty and different range of clothes and accessories for women, girls and boys inspired by the East, with designs following the traditions and beauty of Nepal, India and Japan incorporating embroidery and vibrant colours, fabrics such as silk saris, chiffon, cord and cotton, hand knit and crochet and prints embellished with sequins, beads and jewels. There are some really gorgeous things here, particularly for little girls, which would make lovely gifts.

Site Usability:	★★★★	Based:	UK
Product Range:	★★★★	Express Delivery Option? (UK)	Yes
Price Range:	Medium	Gift Wrapping Option?	No
Delivery Area:	Worldwide	Returns Procedure:	Down to you

www.teddywear.com

Teddywear is a small internet boutique selling high quality children's clothes including brands such as Balu, Catimini, Marese, Miniman, Little Darlings, SULK, Chipie, Lili Gaufrette, Babar, Timberland, DKNY, Diesel, Confetti, and Pampolina. You can search by age or brand and as they update their stock regularly keep coming back to see what's available. There's a really good selection up to age 9/10 as well as a baby section.

Site Usability:	★★★★	Based:	UK
Product Range:	★★★★	Express Delivery Option? (UK)	No
Price Range:	Luxury/Medium	Gift Wrapping Option?	No
Delivery Area:	Worldwide	Returns Procedure:	Down to you

www.theirnibs.com

The approach at Their Nibs is to offer a truly distinctive children's clothing collection to fill the gap between the national chains and independent retailers who stock all the usual brands. The collection, which includes lots of prints, is continually updated and inspiration comes from a variety of sources including their own in-house 'vintage' collection. There are some very pretty clothes for children aged 0–8 including perfect dresses for little flowergirls.

Site Usability:	★★★★★	Based:	UK
Product Range:	★★★★	Express Delivery Option? (UK)	No
Price Range:	Medium	Gift Wrapping Option?	No
Delivery Area:	Worldwide	Returns Procedure:	Down to you

www.wildchildfashions.com

With labels such as Lacoste, Paul Smith, Ted Baker, Hackett, Timberland, Diesel, DKNY, Nike and Guess you'll probably have to fight to keep your children off this website and warn your bank manager if you fail. Wildchild are a fairly new childrenswear company aiming to appeal to both children and parents (is such a thing possible?) and offer their ranges for girls and boys up to mid teens.

Site Usability:	★★★★★		Based:	UK
Product Range:	★★★★		Express Delivery Option? (UK)	Yes
Price Range:	Luxury/Medium		Gift Wrapping Option?	No
Delivery Area:	Worldwide		Returns Procedure:	Down to you

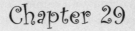

Chapter 29

General Toy Shops

These are the places you can find just about everything, whether it's a specific type of toy you already know about or you just want to have a browse for some new ideas. Sometimes the home pages are so busy you really don't know where to start but take a moment, look for the menu and get going.

I find it much easier to shop here than in a toy store and although you may well say that's because I've had lots of practice, and I have, it's more because I personally hate crowded shops filled with yelling kids, particularly at times when I'm desperately looking for something to buy quickly. I just want to get out of there as fast as I can. So no longer do I go out searching for that elusive shop assistant - I can find everything I need, and all I need to know - right here.

Sites to Visit

www.brainydays.co.uk

To be quite honest, although this is a really good, fun children's toy and gift website, I'm not sure why it's aimed at the 'brainy' ones. There's a wide selection here of items such as Pocoyo bean bag toys, Corolle of France dolls, gorgeous Lilliputian interactive soft toys from Belgium, Cambridge electronic kits (ok so these are quite clever) and their bestselling Golden Coin Maker Kit. There's a lot to choose from so have a browse.

Site Usability:	★★★★	Based:	UK
Product Range:	★★★★★	Express Delivery Option? (UK)	No
Price Range:	Medium	Gift Wrapping Option?	No
Delivery Area:	Worldwide but outside Europe postage is very high	Returns Procedure:	Down to you

www.dollshouse.com

Whether you're new to the world of dolls' houses or a dedicated miniaturist, the Dolls' House Emporium should fill you with inspiration. The site features fully decorated dolls' houses and

167

thousands of miniatures in colour co-ordinated room sets plus carpets and flooring, lighting and wallpapers. You can also see a selection of 1:12 scale dolls' houses shown open and fully furnished to give you ideas.

Site Usability:	★★★★★	Based:	UK
Product Range:	★★★★	Express Delivery Option? (UK)	No
Price Range:	Luxury/Medium	Gift Wrapping Option?	No
Delivery Area:	Worldwide	Returns Procedure:	Down to you

www.gamleys.co.uk

Action Man, Bratz Dolls, Dora the Explorer (love that one), Little Tikes, My Little Pony, Peppa Pig, Pixel Chix (!?) Pocoyo, Polly Pocket and Power Rangers are just some of the brands on offer here. Then for tinies there are pre-school toys by Fisher Price, Mega Bloks, Teletubbies and Tomy. Provided you stick to the clear menus of categories and brands you shouldn't get lost; go off on a tangent and you almost certainly will be.

Site Usability:	★★★★★	Based:	UK
Product Range:	★★★★★	Express Delivery Option? (UK)	No
Price Range:	Medium	Gift Wrapping Option?	No
Delivery Area:	UK	Returns Procedure:	Down to you

www.hamleys.co.uk

If you've ever visited this world famous Regent Street toy emporium (I hate the word but it's the only way to describe this store) you'll know that there's a huge range of gadgets, games, soft toys, puzzles, stocking fillers and every toy you can think of at all price levels and for all ages. In fact it's a disastrous place to take more than one child at a time as there's so much to see. There's a highly edited range on their website although the list of products on offer is growing all the time.

Site Usability:	★★★★★	Based:	UK
Product Range:	★★★★	Express Delivery Option? (UK)	No
Price Range:	Luxury/Medium	Gift Wrapping Option?	No
Delivery Area:	Worldwide	Returns Procedure:	Down to you

www.lambstoys.co.uk

This is another of those toy websites that offers so many brands it's hard to know where to start. To help you I'll tell you that they have an excellent range of Meccano, Hornby and Scalextric, Lego, Schleich Models, Flashing Storm scooters and Power Rangers. Then for little girls there's Zapf Baby Annabel, Chou Chou and Colette plus Miss Milly and My Model makeup and hair styling sets (and lots more). Phew.

Site Usability:	★★★★★	Based:	UK
Product Range:	★★★★★	Express Delivery Option? (UK)	Yes
Price Range:	Medium	Gift Wrapping Option?	No
Delivery Area:	Worldwide	Returns Procedure:	Down to you

www.lilyandagathe.com

Based in the Catalan region of France bordering on Spain, Lily and Agathe is a small English/ French speaking company with a love of all things beautiful, charming and vintage. Here you'll discover exceptional and timeless gifts and toys with a lean towards nostalgia. Many of the items here are one-offs so if you see something you like buy it quick, and if you like the overall idea keep checking back.

Site Usability:	★★★★	Based:	UK
Product Range:	★★★★	Express Delivery Option? (UK)	No
Price Range:	Medium	Gift Wrapping Option?	Yes
Delivery Area:	Worldwide	Returns Procedure:	Down to you

www.mailorderexpress.com

Mail Order Express claims to be the largest toy website in Europe and who am I to argue? It's a hugely busy site with loads of offers and pre-order invitations on the home page but where, thankfully, you can shop by categories such as Music, Gadgets, Party, Science, Toy Vehicle, Dolls and Accessories or by brand. Take a look for yourself.

Site Usability:	★★★★	Based:	UK
Product Range:	★★★★★	Express Delivery Option? (UK)	Yes
Price Range:	Medium/Very Good Value	Gift Wrapping Option?	No
Delivery Area:	Worldwide	Returns Procedure:	Down to you

www.sayitwithbears.co.uk

This is one of those websites that obviously started off doing one thing and then branched out, because you can not only find bears here, but Labradors, elephants, rabbits, cats and Dalmatians, plus lots of other dogs. So if you know someone who collects soft toys or needs a feel-good gift you should take a look. Oh yes, and you can buy Lovvie Bears, Thank you Bears and Anniversary Bears as well.

Site Usability:	★★★★	Based:	UK
Product Range:	★★★★★	Express Delivery Option? (UK)	Yes
Price Range:	Medium	Gift Wrapping Option?	Yes
Delivery Area:	Worldwide	Returns Procedure:	Down to you

www.theentertainer.com

This is one of the largest independent toy retailers in the UK with a huge range and an excellent, easy to navigate website with 'More Toys, More Value and More Fun' as their motto. Here you can search by brand, type of toy, age group or price and you can choose from so many, including Baby Annabel, Dr Who, Hornby, Mattel, Nintendogs and Playmobil. Find something you like and you'll be offered lots more like it, helping you to narrow down your choice quickly.

Site Usability:	★★★★★	Based:	UK
Product Range:	★★★★★	Express Delivery Option? (UK)	Yes
Price Range:	Luxury/Medium	Gift Wrapping Option?	No
Delivery Area:	Worldwide	Returns Procedure:	Down to you

www.toysdirecttoyourdoor.co.uk

Some general toy websites make you (me in any case) want to run away, they're so busy on the home page. On this website you're immediately drawn in, from the train running across the top of the screen to the clear menu, information and special offer details. They sell Playmobil, Thomas trains, Sylvanian Families, Lego and Duplo, Brio, Schleich animals and much more.

Site Usability:	★★★★★	Based:	UK
Product Range:	★★★★★	Express Delivery Option? (UK)	No
Price Range:	Medium	Gift Wrapping Option?	No
Delivery Area:	Worldwide	Returns Procedure:	Down to you

www.toysbymailorder.co.uk

Toys by Mail Order specialise in toys, gifts, nursery items and jigsaw puzzles for children of all ages. The menus are easy to use as once you've clicked on Online Shop you can see all the brands and all the different types of toy, such as baby toys, puzzles, soft toys and arts and crafts. There's also a selection of games ranging from Early Learning Games to Murder Mystery. They offer fast delivery, a gift wrapping service and personalised messages for special occasions.

Site Usability:	★★★★	Based:	UK
Product Range:	★★★★★	Express Delivery Option? (UK)	Yes 2 day service
Price Range:	Medium	Gift Wrapping Option?	No
Delivery Area:	Worldwide	Returns Procedure:	Down to you

Chapter 30

Hobbies, Models, Puzzles and Games

Having had two boys (sorry, do I keep going on about that?) I know only too well that this is a fantastic area to buy from for rainy days. We had countless holidays when, if they couldn't go outside and weren't allowed to watch endless tv, all they complained about was being bored: a visit down to the model shop always solved that one.

As good model shops are few and far between, your time may well be short and that rainy day is frequently unexpected, my advice is to always have something up your sleeve to take care of those occasions. Have a look round here and if yours are anything like my children, make sure you spend the same on both.

Sites to Visit

www.airfix.com

Just about every boy has at some time made an Airfix model (or usually part made and left). The joy of opening all those tiny tins of paint and spending hours making a mess and sticking all those bits together seems totally irresistible. Well here it all is online; on a very simple site where you can order all the kits with just a few clicks and there's everything from a supercharged 1930 Bentley to a Tiger Moth with clear details for them all.

Site Usability:	★★★★★	Based:	UK
Product Range:	★★★★★	Express Delivery Option? (UK)	No
Price Range:	Luxury/Medium	Gift Wrapping Option?	No
Delivery Area:	Worldwide	Returns Procedure:	Down to you

www.barneys-newsbox.co.uk

Many of the online retailers offering jigsaw puzzles are based in the Lake District – why? Well I would have thought it obvious, my having been there so many times when it has rained. If you're into jigsaws they're the perfect answer to a rainy day, for sure. Anyway, here you'll find mainly fairly large to extremely large puzzles, starting at 500 pieces and going up to 1500. The Bright Ideas animal puzzles are so lovely it's tempting even for me to give it a go.

Site Usability:	★★★★★	Based:	UK
Product Range:	★★★★★	Express Delivery Option? (UK)	No
Price Range:	Luxury/Medium	Gift Wrapping Option?	No
Delivery Area:	Worldwide	Returns Procedure:	Down to you

www.boogaloo.co.uk

At Boogaloo (love that name) there's a very good range of Hornby Railway sets and accessories, from the Steam Driven Train Set with teak coaches at just under £500 to the Local Freight Starter Set at £39.99 and everything in between. Then you'll find Digital Scalextric, jigsaw puzzles and essential carry cases, arts and crafts and lots of gadget gift ideas such as electronic backgammon and crossword puzzle solvers. Take a look.

Site Usability:	★★★★★	Based:	UK
Product Range:	★★★★★	Express Delivery Option? (UK)	Yes
Price Range:	Luxury/Medium	Gift Wrapping Option?	Yes
Delivery Area:	Worldwide for most items excluding US	Returns Procedure:	Down to you

www.farscapegames.co.uk

You may be looking for a complete travel games compendium or just a new reasonably priced backgammon set and whether your favourite game is Mah Jong, dominoes, monopoly or bridge you're sure to find what you're seeking here. This without having to go to your local store and decide whether you should be in the children's section or somewhere else, then finding that, after all, there are only a couple of options for your chosen game.

Site Usability:	★★★★★	Based:	UK
Product Range:	★★★★	Express Delivery Option? (UK)	Yes
Price Range:	Medium	Gift Wrapping Option?	No
Delivery Area:	Worldwide	Returns Procedure:	Down to you

www.lego.com

Lego kits seem to have become more and more complicated and you practically need an engineering degree to build some of them (well I never was very good at that sort of thing). Let your son on this website if you dare. Everything is brilliantly shown, including Star Wars, Lego Sports, building sets, Robotics and the very latest editions. You can take the Club tour, order the magazine or click on to the Games Page.

Site Usability:	★★★★★	Based:	UK
Product Range:	★★★★★	Express Delivery Option? (UK)	Yes
Price Range:	Medium	Gift Wrapping Option?	No
Delivery Area:	Worldwide	Returns Procedure:	Down to you

www.modelhobbies.co.uk

Model Hobbies are the perfect place for the model enthusiast. They have an extremely well laid out website and offer models by over 50 different manufacturers plus all the paints, tools and brushes you could possibly need. There are miniature soldiers here as well. They cleverly highlight the newest kits to hit the market so that you keep coming back for more and you can buy gift vouchers too.

Site Usability:	★★★★★	Based:	UK
Product Range:	★★★★★	Express Delivery Option? (UK)	No
Price Range:	Luxury/Medium	Gift Wrapping Option?	No
Delivery Area:	Worldwide	Returns Procedure:	Down to you

www.modelrockets.co.uk

You can buy model cars, tanks and planes from several different websites but there are very few specialising in rockets. By rockets I mean real enthusiasts' stuff, from starter sets and ready to fly kits to competition standard models. Don't be fooled into thinking that the rockets themselves are inexpensive, by the time you've invested in the engine and all the bits and pieces you can spend a small fortune. They can give hours of fun however, until they blow themselves to bits or land on the back of a lorry, never to be seen again (yes that one happened to us).

Site Usability:	★★★★	Based:	UK
Product Range:	★★★★	Express Delivery Option? (UK)	No
Price Range:	Luxury/Medium	Gift Wrapping Option?	No
Delivery Area:	Worldwide	Returns Procedure:	Down to you

www.otherlandtoys.co.uk

Otherland Toys offers a wide selection particularly good for boys. I suggest when you're looking round that you click on 'only show items in stock' as there's so much to choose from anyway and at least you'll not be looking at what they don't have. There are remote control cars at all levels, excellent gadgets, Meccano Magic and lots of outdoor ideas. Make sure you have your cup of coffee with you when you start, you'll need it.

Site Usability:	★★★★★	Based:	UK
Product Range:	★★★★★	Express Delivery Option? (UK)	Yes, Fedex Worldwide
Price Range:	Luxury/Medium/Very Good Value	Gift Wrapping Option?	Yes
Delivery Area:	Worldwide	Returns Procedure:	Down to you

www.slotcity.co.uk

Slot City is one the largest independent retailers of slot cars in the UK and Europe and you can only buy from them online. They offer the full range of Scalextric plus other brands such as Carrera from Germany and SCX for Spain - household names in their own countries but almost impossible to find here until now. You'll also find Hornby and Carrera model kits. Everything is ready for immediate delivery unless you're told otherwise on the website.

Site Usability:	★★★★	Based:	UK
Product Range:	★★★★★	Express Delivery Option? (UK)	No
Price Range:	Luxury/Medium	Gift Wrapping Option?	No
Delivery Area:	All EU countries and the USA	Returns Procedure:	Down to you

Chapter 31

Dressing Up, Magic Tricks and Party Accessories

When I was a child (yes me, this time) my parents had a friend who was a member of the 'Magic Circle', the most prestigious society of magicians. I'll never forget the wonder and fascination of some of the things he could do and needless to say, he never got away with coming to visit without putting on a performance, however small.

I'm not suggesting that your children should aspire to the same levels, but I'm sure that it's much easier for them to read about and learn magic tricks today than it was then – there's so much information available and so many trick sets to buy. Just take a look below and you'll see what I mean.

Regarding choice and information the same applies to dressing up, as you can order from an amazing array of costumes for kids of all ages, from enchanting fairies and ballerinas to the more grown up Superman or Cleopatra. There's a good range of prices here so have a look at as many of the sites as you can before choosing and then don't forget to buy that essential dressing up box to keep it all together in.

Sites to Visit

www.a2z-kids.co.uk

Choose from Historical Costumes, Girls' Party Costumes, Books, Rhymes and Fairytales, Christmas and Nativity, Animals and Creatures such as Scooby Doo and Dinosaur, Superman Returns, Disney, and toddler and infant costumes. The menus here are particularly good and although you can find the same types of costumes elsewhere, you can narrow down your search on this website very fast.

Site Usability:	★★★★★	Based:	UK
Product Range:	★★★★	Express Delivery Option? (UK)	Yes
Price Range:	Medium	Gift Wrapping Option?	No
Delivery Area:	Worldwide	Returns Procedure:	Down to you

www.charliecrow.com

This is a fun website for kids' dressing up costumes of all kinds and there are some great extras here as well, including party games with instructions, recipes for nibbles like Cheesy Straws, Self Portrait Pizzas (!) and Swamp Jelly, some daft stories and a really helpful party planner to try and keep you sane.

Site Usability:	★★★★★	Based:	UK
Product Range:	★★★★★	Express Delivery Option? (UK)	Yes
Price Range:	Medium	Gift Wrapping Option?	No
Delivery Area:	Worldwide	Returns Procedure:	Down to you

www.costumecrazy.co.uk

If your child fancies himself in a Zoot Suit or as a Clone Trooper at the next fancy dress party he goes to then this is the place. For girls there are the Country and Western or Spiderella outfits and needless to say there are simply loads more to choose from. There are angel and fairy wings, wands and halos, witches broomsticks, devil horns and Cleopatra's snake. There'll definitely be a problem here when it's 'make your mind up time'.

Site Usability:	★★★★★	Based:	UK
Product Range:	★★★★★	Express Delivery Option? (UK)	Yes
Price Range:	Medium	Gift Wrapping Option?	No
Delivery Area:	Worldwide	Returns Procedure:	Down to you

www.dudethatscoolmagic.co.uk

You'll probably have to keep this book close to hand to be able to remember the name of this website, well I certainly would, and this online store is worth remembering as it's bursting with magic tricks, card tricks, street magic, close up magic tricks, props and magic illusions for both the beginner and more experienced 'magician'. It's a colourful website and includes an excellent section on children's magic shows as well.

Site Usability:	★★★★★	Based:	UK
Product Range:	★★★★★	Express Delivery Option? (UK)	Yes
Price Range:	Medium	Gift Wrapping Option?	No
Delivery Area:	Worldwide	Returns Procedure:	Down to you

www.greatlittleparties.co.uk

They've definitely made an effort here to get away from totally theme driven party supplies (although ultimately it's best to do that here as well and yes there are lots to choose from, from Peter Pan and Noddy to Thomas the Tank, Fifi and the Flowerpots). Alongside these you can also order party music cds, party games, books (party food recipes and planning a party), birthday cake candles and gift wrap. So this is definitely a one stop shop. There are christening party supplies here as well.

Site Usability:	★★★★★	Based:	UK
Product Range:	★★★★★	Express Delivery Option? (UK)	Yes
Price Range:	Medium	Gift Wrapping Option?	No
Delivery Area:	EU	Returns Procedure:	Down to you

www.hopscotchdressingup.co.uk

Hopscotch have definitely got the children's dressing up market sewn up with their lovely bright website full of dressing up box clothes for children from angels and fairies to witches and wizards, cowboys and indians to kings and queens and everything in between. There's no question that if your child has been asked to a fancy dress party and is determined to really look the part you absolutely have to visit Hopscotch.

Site Usability:	★★★★★	Based:	UK
Product Range:	★★★★★	Express Delivery Option? (UK)	Yes
Price Range:	Medium/Very Good Value	Gift Wrapping Option?	No
Delivery Area:	Worldwide	Returns Procedure:	Down to you

www.magictricks.co.uk

You'll find some wonderful ideas for gifts here, from the Cyclopedia of Magic, Wizard School Video and dvd, card magic sets, pub tricks (??) and the Ultimate Magic Trick Set – a compilation of some of the greatest close-up magic tricks ever invented – and this is just a very small selection of what's on offer. You can also buy gift vouchers and lots of their own brand products at all price levels.

Site Usability:	★★★★	Based:	UK
Product Range:	★★★★	Express Delivery Option? (UK)	No
Price Range:	Medium	Gift Wrapping Option?	No
Delivery Area:	Worldwide	Returns Procedure:	Down to you

www.ollipops.com

I suppose that puppets aren't strictly dressing up but rather than put them in toys and gifts I thought that this was where they belonged. At Ollipops there's a lovely range of glove puppets, from animals such as squirrel, toad and white rabbit, all beautifully dressed, the fabulous dragon puppet, finger puppets, long sleeved puppets and much, much more including their best selling Rabbit in a Lettuce. Take a look.

Site Usability:	★★★★	Based:	UK
Product Range:	★★★★★	Express Delivery Option? (UK)	No but delivery is free for most items
Price Range:	Medium	Gift Wrapping Option?	No
Delivery Area:	Worldwide	Returns Procedure:	Down to you

www.partyark.co.uk

Let's move away for a moment from the huge, multi choice, online party retailers for everyone from 0-80 (although they are great) and settle here, on this prettily designed website just for tinies. You have the option of choosing each item to go with your theme, be it Dancing Fairies or Knights and Dragons or you can go straight to Party Packs where they've done it all for you. There are tips and advice, planning help and absolutely everything to make your life easier.

Site Usability:	★★★★★	Based:	UK
Product Range:	★★★★★	Express Delivery Option? (UK)	Yes
Price Range:	Medium	Gift Wrapping Option?	No
Delivery Area:	Worldwide	Returns Procedure:	Down to you

www.partydelights.co.uk

This is a really fun and colourful website and it's very well laid out so although you're bombarded with choice you shouldn't find it too difficult to shop even though it's for adults too. Click to the Party Planner at the foot of the left hand margin, make your list then get going. As on most of these websites the range of themes is astonishing so you definitely need to know whether you're going for a Fairy Princes, Safari or Happy Feet party. Once you've done that everything is together in one place and life becomes simple.

Site Usability:	★★★★★	Based:	UK
Product Range:	★★★★★	Express Delivery Option? (UK)	Yes
Price Range:	Medium	Gift Wrapping Option?	No
Delivery Area:	Worldwide	Returns Procedure:	Down to you

Chapter 32

Dance and Craft Supplies

For those of you with would-be ballerinas in the family, jazz or tap dancers, rather than seek out your local dance shop for their new costumes and shoes, take a look round here. There's a really good selection and whereas you may find difficulty in getting a specific size offline (and what a pain to have to order it and then wait) you're bound to be able to order every size from these websites.

The only thing that I would say is that for special shoes make sure that your child is properly measured first. It's fine to order a leotard that's slightly too small or too big and then have to change it, but in the case of shoes you can do so much damage to feet by having the wrong size that no matter how much of a hurry you're in you need to do things properly.

Also here you'll find a small but very good range of craft supplies, for knitters, dressmakers, embroiderers and more.

Sites to Visit

Dance

www.dancedepot.co.uk

This is a great place for dancewear, where you'll find brands such as Pineapple, Capezio and Bloch and everything from RAD approved examination leotards and skirts, jazz shoes, boots and warm-up clothes to stage and character shoes, a range of costumes and Snazaroo and Charles Fox make-up. There are also enchanting tutus for those mini wannabe ballet girls.

Site Usability:	★★★★★	Based:	UK
Product Range:	★★★★	Express Delivery Option? (UK)	No
Price Range:	Medium	Gift Wrapping Option?	No
Delivery Area:	UK	Returns Procedure:	Down to you

www.dancedirectworld.com

For anyone who's into (or just starting) ballet or jazz this is a lovely, essential website. The pictures of the dancing girls on the front lead you straight in to a wonderful selection of leotards, skirts and tutus, tights, leggings and warm up gear plus tops and pants for jazz, soft and pointe ballet shoes and a selection of sneakers.

Site Usability:	★★★★	Based:	UK
Product Range:	★★★★	Express Delivery Option? (UK)	No
Price Range:	Medium	Gift Wrapping Option?	No
Delivery Area:	Worldwide	Returns Procedure:	Down to you

Craft Suppliers

www.johnsoncrafts.co.uk

Cross stitch, knitting and crochet, tapestry and decoupage are just some of the crafts you'll find here, where there's a wide range of kits including Brambly Hedge, Farm Animals and Charlie 'n Friends (cross stitch), simple and quite complicated tapestry sets, knitting and crochet, threads and accessories and everything you could need to get going. Call them if you have any queries - it would be helpful if they had a rating for how complicated each item is but they don't (yet).

Site Usability:	★★★★	Based:	UK
Product Range:	★★★★★	Express Delivery Option? (UK)	No
Price Range:	Medium	Gift Wrapping Option?	No
Delivery Area:	Worldwide	Returns Procedure:	Down to you

www.yorkshireartstore.co.uk

Discover a wonderful treasure trove of artists' and craft supplies, from paints, pencils, brushes and inks to clay, craft paper and adhesives plus fabric art and needlecraft equipment. There are also accessories including frames, tapestry wools, stranded cotton and fantasy threads. This is not one of the most highly sophisticated websites but it's easy to use and quick to order from. Expect a high level of service and speedy delivery and call them if you need advice.

Site Usability:	★★★★	Based:	UK
Product Range:	★★★★	Express Delivery Option? (UK)	No
Price Range:	Medium	Gift Wrapping Option?	No
Delivery Area:	UK	Returns Procedure:	Down to you

Also take a look at the following for Craft Supplies:

Websites Address	**You'll find it in**
www.carnmeal.co.uk	Chapter 73: Ribbon and Wrap
www.jaycotts.co.uk	Chapter 73: Ribbon and Wrap
www.lakelandlimited.co.uk	Chapter 44: The Kitchen

Section 5
Pamper Yourself

Pamper Yourself

This is an extremely dangerous area to go shopping online in so be warned. (I think I said that before somewhere, but anyway, now I'm saying it again.) Whatever your pampering requirements you'll find them here, plus lots to explore, to discover for the first time and to be dreadfully tempted by.

So whether you're looking for your favourite skincare and cosmetic brand or a new, special treatment that you can only normally find in salons, essential aromatherapy oils, luxurious fragranced candles or organic skincare lines you'll find them all here.

I know only too well that some of you will want to point out to me that you can't yet find the full range of modern US brands online but as you can find Bobbi Brown, Laura Mercier and Nars (Space NK), Benefit, Pout, Bloom and Philosophy and the others will surely be available very soon, you shouldn't worry too much.

Chapter 33

Fragrance, Bath and Body

This is an area where the true shopaholic in me always comes out, despite the fact that most fragrances in their strongest versions always make me sneeze - exceptionally annoying, I know.

However, when we're talking about bath and body products, there you've really got me. I like to buy the products I know and love, and then again, I also like to find something new: not necessarily the obvious choices by the major brand names, but less well known, equally gorgeous shower gels and body lotions by makes such as l'Occitane, Cote Bastide and Czech and Speake.

Everyone knows what my particular favourite brand is at any given time as that's what I'll be giving for birthdays and other present giving occasions - provided I'm sure they'll suit the recipient, of course.

So you too can have a field day here and buy yourself something special and new - alternatively buy a gift for a friend who needs a boost. In my opinion these products rarely fail.

Sites to Visit

www.arranaromatics.com

If you want to find something a little unusual, beautifully presented and well priced then look no further than Arran Aromatics where you can discover bath and body products, candles and much more with names such as After the Rain, Angelica, Bay Citrus and Parfumeur. The packaging is very pretty and you can select from individual items such as living fragrances, shower gels and bath soak grains or their excellent gift boxes.

Site Usability:	★★★★★	Based:	UK
Product Range:	★★★★	Express Delivery Option? (UK)	Yes
Price Range:	Medium/Very Good Value	Gift Wrapping Option?	No
Delivery Area:	Worldwide	Returns Procedure:	Down to you

www.bathandunwind.com

Bath & Unwind specialise in luxury products that help you to relax (and unwind) after a hard day's work. They aim to provide the highest quality bath and spa products from around the world including brands such as Aromatherapy Associates, Korres, Nougat, Burt's Bees and Jane Packer. Delivery is free (UK) provided you spend over a certain amount and they'll ship to you anywhere in the world. They also have a gift selector and an express service for the next time you forget that special present.

Site Usability:	★★★★	Based:	UK
Product Range:	★★★★	Express Delivery Option? (UK)	Yes
Price Range:	Medium	Gift Wrapping Option?	No
Delivery Area:	Worldwide	Returns Procedure:	Down to you

www.beautybay.com

This is a beautifully laid out website offering just about every fragrance with bath and body products to match and a small range of cosmetics and skincare, plus jewellery and fragrance giftsets (excellent for presents). Delivery is free on orders over £30, they'll ship to just about anywhere in the world and offer a next day service as well. What's particularly good here is that on many of the products you'll find yourself spending less than you expect. What more could you want?

Site Usability:	★★★★★	Based:	UK
Product Range:	★★★★	Express Delivery Option? (UK)	Yes
Price Range:	Luxury/Medium/Very Good Value	Gift Wrapping Option?	No
Delivery Area:	Worldwide	Returns Procedure:	Down to you

www.crabtree-evelyn.co.uk

Well known and sold throughout the world, Crabtree & Evelyn offer a wide range of bath, body and spa products from classic fragrances such as Lily of the Valley to the ultra modern La Source and brand new India Hicks' Island Living collection. Everything is cleverly and attractively packaged and offered here on their well designed and easy to use website. Particularly good as gifts are their pretty boxes containing miniatures of their most popular products.

Site Usability:	★★★★★	Based:	UK
Product Range:	★★★★★	Express Delivery Option? (UK)	No
Price Range:	Medium	Gift Wrapping Option?	No
Delivery Area:	Worldwide	Returns Procedure:	Down to you

www.cologneandcotton.com

This is a very special website offering some unusual and hard to find bath and body products and fragrance by Diptyque (If you haven't already tried their candles you really should, they're gorgeous), Cath Collins, La Compagnie de Provence and Cote Bastide. There are also fragrances by Annik Goutal, Coudray and Rosine and for the bathroom they have lovely fluffy towels and bathrobes.

Site Usability:	★★★★★	Based:	UK
Product Range:	★★★★	Express Delivery Option? (UK)	Yes
Price Range:	Luxury/Medium	Gift Wrapping Option?	Yes
Delivery Area:	Worldwide	Returns Procedure:	Down to you

www.comptoir-sud-pacifique.com

Comptoir Sud Pacifique is a brand synonymous with escape, exotism and sun, so if you feel the need for an exotic change of scenery just click through here and let your senses take you away. Choose from Vanilla, Spicy, Fruity, Woody, Floral and Fresh Waters fragrances and candles such as Muscade Orange, Vanille Apricot and Aqua Motu. You can order as you go round the website or from a list by clicking on Buy Online. All prices are in Euros.

Site Usability:	★★★★	Based:	UK
Product Range:	★★★★	Express Delivery Option? (UK)	No
Price Range:	Medium	Gift Wrapping Option	No
Delivery Area:	France	Returns Procedure:	Down to you

www.escentual.co.uk

Escentual carry what is probably the widest range of fragrance for men and women in the UK. Choose a fragrance or fragrance linked bath and body product and then search for it on this site - you're almost certain to find it. Bath and body products include Burberry, Bvlgari, Calvin Klein, Gucci, Guerlain, Rochas and Versace plus Crabtree and Evelyn, Tisserand and I Coloniali. Delivery is free on orders over £30 and they also offer free gift wrapping.

Site Usability:	★★★★★	Based:	UK
Product Range:	★★★★★	Express Delivery Option? (UK)	Yes
Price Range:	Luxury/Medium/Very Good Value	Gift Wrapping Option?	Yes
Delivery Area:	Worldwide	Returns Procedure:	Down to you

www.florislondon.com

Here's one of the oldest and most traditional perfumers, having been established originally in 1730. You'll find favourites Lavender, China Rose, Gardenia and Stephanotis and more modern fragrances Night Scented Jasmin, Bouquet de la Reine and No 89. The updated packaging is lovely and for each fragrance there's a full range of bath and body products plus special wrapped sets for Christmas.

Site Usability:	★★★★★	Based:	UK
Product Range:	★★★★★	Express Delivery Option? (UK)	Yes
Price Range:	Luxury/Medium	Gift Wrapping Option?	Yes
Delivery Area:	Worldwide	Returns Procedure:	Down to you

www.harrods.com

Personally I think that Harrods deserves a prize for taking the plunge and going online where other major department stores 'fear to tread' - I'm sure you can guess who I mean. The range available is growing all the time and is very well presented. Currently the strongest area is definitely beauty where the bath and body ranges include REN, Floris, Korres, Acqua di Parma and Vie Lux. Buy from them and encourage them to put more of their shop online.

Site Usability:	★★★★★	Based:	UK
Product Range:	★★★★	Express Delivery Option? (UK)	No
Price Range:	Luxury/Medium	Gift Wrapping Option?	No
Delivery Area:	Worldwide	Returns Procedure:	Down to you

www.jomalone.co.uk

This has to be one of my personal favourites, where you can buy Jo Malone's beautifully packaged range of luxurious fragrances plus bath and body products with names like Pomegranate Noir and Blue Agava & Cacao. You'll also find her cleansers, serums and moisturisers, facial finishers such as mascara and lip gloss and irresistible travel sets. New products are being developed all the time which make this a great place for feel good treats and gifts you won't want to part with. The service is excellent and if you need a last minute gift this is definitely the place.

Site Usability:	★★★★★	Based:	UK
Product Range:	★★★★★	Express Delivery Option? (UK)	Yes
Price Range:	Luxury	Gift Wrapping Option?	Yes
Delivery Area:	Worldwide	Returns Procedure:	Down to you

www.kennethturner.com

White Flowers, Wild Garden, Magnolia Grandiflora and Rose (plus his Original fragrance) are some of the fragrances you'll find on this pretty website, presented as candles, tea lights, shower gel and body lotions, room colognes and pot-pourri. His packaging, in flower printed blue and white boxes turn his products into perfect gifts and you'll find travel sets and prepared gift boxes here as well.

Site Usability:	★★★★	Based:	UK
Product Range:	★★★	Express Delivery Option? (UK)	Yes
Price Range:	Luxury/Medium	Gift Wrapping Option?	Yes
Delivery Area:	Worldwide	Returns Procedure:	Down to you

www.laboutiquedelartisanparfumeur.com

If you're not already aware of this gorgeous collection of French fragrance and bath and body products by L'Artisan Parfumeur, with names such as Mure et Musc (blackberry and musk) Figuier and Orchidee Blanche then now's the time to discover a new beautifully presented range and order it online. You'll also find unusual ideas such as their blackberry shaped glass bottle, scented silk peonies and terracotta amber balls, all of which make exceptional gifts.

Site Usability:	★★★★	Based:	UK
Product Range:	★★★	Express Delivery Option? (UK)	Yes
Price Range:	Luxury	Gift Wrapping Option?	Automatic
Delivery Area:	Worldwide	Returns Procedure:	Down to you

www.lessenteurs.com

Les Senteurs is a famous parfumery based in London, offering different and unusual fragrance, bath and body products and an excellent service. Brands they offer are Creed, Annick Goutal, Diptyque, E Coudray, Serge Lutens, Carons and Parfums Historique to name but a few and the ranges are split into categories, such as fragrance, bath and body or fragrance notes, such as citrus, oriental or fruity. To help you make your choice they offer a sample service, where for a small charge they'll send you a small sample of each of your chosen fragrances.

Site Usability:	★★★	Based:	UK
Product Range:	★★★★	Express Delivery Option? (UK)	No
Price Range:	Luxury/Medium	Gift Wrapping Option?	Yes
Delivery Area:	Worldwide	Returns Procedure:	Down to you

www.miam-miam.co.uk

I had to find this one out. Dorothy Day of miam-miam tells me that the name is the French equivalent of our 'yummy'. 'Because everything in my shop is yummy'. Take note, if you're passing through Edinburgh visit her shop, it certainly looks lovely. Anyway, you can buy your L'Occitane products from here wherever you are in the world, along with gorgeous hand stitched quilts from Une Histoire Simple and Blanc d'Ivoire and decorative wall clocks by Roger Lascelles.

Site Usability:	★★★★	Express Delivery Option? (UK)	Yes
Product Range:	★★★	Gift Wrapping Option?	Yes
Price Range:	Medium	Returns Procedure:	Down to you
Delivery Area:	Worldwide		

www.millerharris.com

If you'd like to give someone a gorgeous fragrance or bath and body product which is not so well known, then Miller Harris may have the answer. This is a small, independent company which specialises in blending its own fragrances, with enticing names such as Tangerine Vert, Fleur Oriental and Terre de Bois. In each one you'll find not only the Eau de Parfum, but bath and body products and candles as well.

Site Usability:	★★★★	Based:	UK
Product Range:	★★★	Express Delivery Option? (UK)	Yes
Price Range:	Luxury/Medium	Gift Wrapping Option?	Yes
Delivery Area:	Worldwide	Returns Procedure:	Down to you

www.moltonbrown.co.uk

The range of Molton Brown's bath, skincare, makeup and spa products seems to increase daily and you want to try every single one. The packaging is lovely and the products not only look and smell wonderful but they are not overpriced. Delivery is quick and you quite often get sent delicious trial sized products with your order. A great site for gifts, travel size products and that extra body lotion and bath gel you simply won't be able to resist.

Site Usability:	★★★★★	Based:	UK
Product Range:	★★★★★	Express Delivery Option? (UK)	No
Price Range:	Medium	Gift Wrapping Option?	Yes
Delivery Area:	Worldwide	Returns Procedure:	Down to you

www.ormondejayne.com

Sometimes you feel that you'd really like to find a new range of fragrance and candles, one that most people haven't heard of but one that's still totally luxurious and beautifully presented. That's exactly what you'll find here, with a unique range of fragrances such as the citrussy Osmanthus and floral Champaca. There are bath and body products to complement the fragrances plus the most beautiful candles and everything is gorgeously packaged.

Site Usability:	★★★★	Based:	UK
Product Range:	★★★	Express Delivery Option? (UK)	Yes
Price Range:	Luxury	Gift Wrapping Option?	Yes
Delivery Area:	Worldwide	Returns Proce dure:	Down to you

www.parfumsdorsay.co.uk

Here you'll find a very small, beautifully photographed range of fragrance, soaps and scented candles from long established fragrance house Parfums d'Orsay of France. If you already know the fragrances you'll be delighted that they're now available here and if you haven't tried them before email and ask for the sample of your choice – you'll find they're very special. Gift wrapping was not available at time of writing but may be now.

Site Usability:	★★★★★	Based:	UK
Product Range:	★★★	Express Delivery Option? (UK)	Yes – call
Price Range:	Luxury/Medium	Gift Wrapping Option?	No
Delivery Area:	UK	Returns Procedure:	Down to you

www.penhaligons.co.uk

Penhaligons offers fragrance, candles and bath and body products for perfect and luxurious gifts for men and women. Choose from classics Lily of the Valley, Elizabethan Rose or Bluebell or the more modern and spicy Malabah, Artemesia or LP No 9. Each fragrance is matched up to its own shower gel, soap, body lotion and candle. Gift-wrapping is gorgeous, free and they deliver worldwide.

Site Usability:	★★★★★	Based:	UK
Product Range:	★★★★★	Express Delivery Option? (UK)	Yes
Price Range:	Luxury	Gift Wrapping Option?	Automatic
Delivery Area:	Worldwide	Returns Procedure:	Down to you

www.scentstore.co.uk

This website is well worth checking out if you know exactly which fragrance you want to buy as you can find some excellent discounts. So although you won't find every product in each range, it's a good idea to have a look here in case your favourite is on offer. Brands for men include Lacoste, Hugo Boss, Burberry and Tommy Hilfiger and for women Gucci, Ralph Lauren and Issey Miyake.

Site Usability:	★★★★★	Based:	UK
Product Range:	★★★★	Express Delivery Option? (UK)	Yes
Price Range:	Medium/Very Good Value	Gift Wrapping Option?	No
Delivery Area:	Worldwide	Returns Procedure:	Down to you

www.skye-soap.co.uk

Here's a really beautifully designed website offering natural aromatherapy soaps produced on the Isle of Skye. There isn't a huge range of products but if you like lovely, natural soaps and oils you'll want to buy from here, not only for yourself but also for your friends from their selection of attractively packaged gift boxes. You'll discover fragrances such as Lavender, Lemon and Lime, Geranium, Patchouli, Sandalwood, Tea Tree and Orange for the soaps and essential oils plus gifts of bath bombs and soaks.

Site Usability:	★★★★	Based:	UK
Product Range:	★★★	Express Delivery Option? (UK)	No
Price Range:	Medium/Very Good Value	Gift Wrapping Option?	No
Delivery Area:	Worldwide	Returns Procedure:	Down to you

www.strawberrynet.com

Check to see if your favourite product is available on this Hong Kong based website where shipping is free and most products are discounted. There's a really huge range of designers, so big it's not worth trying to list. To be clear, as this site is based overseas you may well get charged duty. However, delivery to anywhere in the world is free of charge and the discounts can be very good.

Site Usability:	★★★	Based:	Hong Kong
Product Range:	★★★★★	Express Delivery Option? (UK)	No
Price Range:	Medium/Very Good Value	Gift Wrapping Option?	Yes
Delivery Area:	Worldwide	Returns Procedure:	Down to you

www.thesanctuary.co.uk

Just looking at this spa website makes you feel more relaxed, with its shades of blue background and the attractive, simple packaging of pampering products such as Sanctuary Salt Soak, Body Polisher and Eastern Massage and Body Oil. You can buy the full range of Sanctuary products here plus Gift Vouchers and information on treatments at the Covent Garden spa. For International orders you need to give them a call.

Site Usability:	★★★★	Based:	UK
Product Range:	★★★★	Express Delivery Option? (UK)	Yes
Price Range:	Medium/Very Good Value	Gift Wrapping Option?	Automatic
Delivery Area:	Worldwide	Returns Procedure:	Down to you

Chapter 34

Healthcare and Contact Lenses

on't skip past this chapter, thinking that it's too mundane; it will really make your life easy, give you more time to shop for real goodies *and* save you money as well.

Think ahead for your medicine cupboard and bathroom essentials and order them all at once from somewhere like boots.com or pharmacy2u.co.uk. You may find that you're not necessarily saving money here unless you're buying something like the antihistamine Benadryl in the middle of the summer when there are lots of special offers; but you will find that it's helpful to be able to buy everything together so you don't run out of your regular over-the-counter-medicines, toothbrushes and tissues.

It slightly surprises me that you can buy prescription medicines here as well, although the system, as it has to be, is slightly complicated (and if anyone's trying to make it really easy make sure that they're a registered chemist first). Having tested this out when my son needed malaria tablets for a trip to Borneo I know exactly how it works: First get your prescription. Then place your order on one of the Chemists' websites below. After that you need to send them the prescription and they in return will send you your order.

This works well on two counts: firstly if you find it difficult to get to a chemist, and secondly if you want a better price for a specific drug, as I found for Malarone. The difference was quite a lot and well worth having so give this a try.

Where contact lenses are concerned I have to say that anyone buying them from their local optician without checking the prices here must actually want to pay more, because they surely are. I'll say no more than that, other than to tell you that my son buys (actually of course I buy) his daily lenses online and we wouldn't dream of paying the prices on the high street. Check these websites out and you'll see exactly what I mean.

Sites to Visit

www.auravita.com

Claiming to stock over 20,000 products (phew) you'll find everything here from Nurofen to eyelash curlers, homeopathy remedies, health foods and drinks and sport supplements and vitamins. There's also a wide choice of cosmetics including Elizabeth Arden, Kanebo, Clarins, Lancôme, Christian Dior lipstick and nail polish and Max Factor. It's a confusing website to go round, so make use of the Brand search and Store Guide facilities near the top of the home page.

Site Usability:	★★★	Express Delivery Option? (UK)	No
Product Range:	★★★★★	Gift Wrapping Option?	No
Price Range:	Medium/Very Good Value	Returns Procedure:	Down to you
Delivery Area:	Worldwide		

www.bs4health.com

The B & S House of Health takes itself extremely seriously, with a mission statement that sets out exactly what it is trying to do: offer you very high quality vitamins and supplements from sources that it has found to be totally reliable. Click on each area and you get a full list of subsections describing exactly what you'll find and what the products are for, which then links through to each individual product and the buying facility. This is an excellent, clear and informative website.

Site Usability:	★★★★	Express Delivery Option? (UK)	No
Product Range:	★★★★	Gift Wrapping Option?	No
Price Range:	Medium	Returns Procedure:	Down to you
Delivery Area:	Worldwide		

www.chemistdirect.co.uk

Chemist Direct operates out of London and is a member of the National Pharmaceutical Association. There's a wide range of products here from vitamins and health supplements, baby products, toiletries, holiday and sun care. They're also happy to fulfill your prescriptions for you, either private or NHS and their prices are excellent (always check against an offline chemist if you're not sure about the price). You send payment to them online and your prescription by post after which they'll immediately despatch your order to you.

Site Usability:	★★★★	Express Delivery Option? (UK)	Yes
Product Range:	★★★★	Gift Wrapping Option?	No
Price Range:	Medium	Returns Procedure:	Down to you
Delivery Area:	UK		

www.contactsdirect.co.uk

Here's another contact lens retailer trying to get your business away from your local supplier and they should certainly be considered. Remember that when you do order your contacts online and you need a check-up or a new prescription you'll probably have to pay a fee. Even so you'll save lots of money by buying online. The prices are keen and you can expect a speedy service.

Site Usability:	★★★★★	Express Delivery Option? (UK)	No
Product Range:	★★★★	Gift Wrapping Option?	No
Price Range:	Medium	Returns Procedure:	Free
Delivery Area:	UK		

www.goldshield.co.uk

As well as all the vitamins and supplements you would expect from a health food store, here you can also buy food and snacks, such as assortments of fruit and nuts, crystallised ginger, dried fruit, pistachios and pumpkin seeds and everything for making your own yoghurt, plus not quite so 'healthy' (but very tempting) snacks including chocolate coated ginger and brazils. There's lots of information on all the different sections here plus health books.

Site Usability:	★★★★	Express Delivery Option? (UK)	No
Product Range:	★★★★	Gift Wrapping Option?	No
Price Range:	Medium	Returns Procedure:	Free
Delivery Area:	Worldwide		

www.goodnessdirect.co.uk

There's really a vast range here with 3000+ health foods, vitamins and items selected for those with special dietary needs. You can search for foods that are dairy free, gluten free, wheat free, yeast free and low fat plus organic fruit, vegetables (in a selection of boxed choices), fish and meat. You'll also find frozen and chilled foods, so you can do your complete shopping here. Don't be worried by the amount of choice, the website is very easy to get round and order from.

Site Usability:	★★★★	Based:	UK
Product Range:	★★★★★	Express Delivery Option? (UK)	No
Price Range:	Medium	Gift Wrapping Option?	No
Delivery Area:	UK	Returns Procedure:	Down to you

www.lensway.com

Lensway are one of the best online places to buy contact lenses (and I've tested them many times). The prices are just about the best you'll find online, the website is very easy to use and your lenses arrive incredibly fast. You can buy most types from daily to monthly lenses by Johnson & Johnson, Acuvue, Bausch and Lomb and others.

Site Usability:	★★★★	Based:	Sweden
Product Range:	★★★★★	Express Delivery Option? (UK)	No but fast delivery is automatic
Price Range:	Medium/Very Good Value	Gift Wrapping Option?	No
Delivery Area:	Worldwide	Returns Procedure:	Down to you

www.marnys.co.uk

On this website you can find organic products such as Muesli, toasted sesame seeds, brown lentils, texturised soya, flax seeds, pumpkin and sunflower seeds as well as salt crystal lamps. There's also a wide range of supplements, vitamins and minerals divided into sections such as Royal Jelly, Korean Ginseng and Bee Pollen as specific products and Weight Control, Cardiovascular System and Hormonal System as separate areas.

Site Usability:	★★★★	Based:	Spain	
Product Range:	★★★★★	Express Delivery Option? (UK)	No but fast delivery is automatic	
Price Range:	Medium	Gift Wrapping Option?	No	
Delivery Area:	Worldwide	Returns Procedure:	Down to you	

www.pharmacy2u.co.uk

All your regular medicines and healthcare essentials are available on this site plus plenty of advice and suggestions. If you can't be bothered or don't have the time to go out to the chemist then this is definitely the site for you. It's very clear and well laid out and I doubt if there would be anything you couldn't find. You can also arrange for your prescriptions to be filled. They are members of the Royal Pharmaceutical Society of Great Britain and the National Pharmaceutical Association.

Site Usability:	★★★★★	Express Delivery Option? (UK)	No	
Product Range:	★★★★★	Gift Wrapping Option?	No	
Price Range:	Medium	Returns Procedure:	Down to you	
Delivery Area:	Worldwide for most products			

www.thefitmap.com

Do you really want to know how fit you are (and do something about it)? Thefitmap.com gives you loads of information on where to find a personal trainer, diet and fitness news and health club reviews and if you really want to get going click to subscribe on the Fitness Training Planner and get your own schedule against which you can then plot your success (or not). This is maybe not quite the same as having your personal trainer banging on the door to take you through your paces but certainly an incentive worth trying out.

Site Usability:	★★★★★

www.travelpharm.com

TravelPharm is an independent private pharmacy and a member of the National Pharmaceutical Association. You can buy first aid and medical kits, total sun block, travel sickness tablets, water purification tablets and flight socks on this well designed website. As a registered pharmacy they can also provide you with pharmacy only medication such as malaria tablets and they offer up-to-the-minute details of vaccinations and anti-malarial requirements for your destination as a free of charge service.

Site Usability:	★★★★★	Express Delivery Option? (UK)	No	
Product Range:	★★★★★	Gift Wrapping Option?	No	
Price Range:	Medium	Returns Procedure:	Down to you	
Delivery Area:	UK			

You'll also find healthcare products at the following websites:

Website address	You'll find it in
www.boots.com	Chapter 37: Modern Skincare and Cosmetics
www.garden.co.uk	Chapter 37: Modern Skincare and Cosmetics

Chapter 35

Hair, Nails and Beauty Accessories

anger: stop and shop here at your peril; it's easy to go mad without realising. With websites such as HQ Hair and Look Fantastic pretending just to be hair websites and branching out into wonderful and hard to find make-up and beauty accessories, once you've ordered that extra large bottle of your favourite shampoo you may well browse the aisles (so to speak) for Philosophy bath and body products, Urban Decay cosmetics, Jonny Loves Rosie hair ties and the latest deepest red nail polish, filling your basket – literally – as you go. Then you have the fright at the check-out page, or I nearly always do.

These websites are not just incredibly useful but fun to visit too, offering speedy, reliable and excellent service and in most cases delivering to you the day after you've placed your order. As I said, take care – that super Parlux Turbo compact hair dryer comes in red, pink, purple and chocolate brown as well. Very hard to resist.

Sites to Visit

www.beautysleuth.co.uk

Beauty Sleuth offers a wide range of products on their attractively designed website. They also have Air Stocking – (spray it on and your legs look as if you're wearing stockings), Tweezerman products, Mister Mascara's mascaras and eyelash curlers, ID Essentials make-up brushes and GHD straighteners and accessories. This is a very well edited range so it shouldn't take you long to find what you're looking for.

Site Usability:	★★★★★	Based:	UK
Product Range:	★★★	Express Delivery Option? (UK)	Yes
Price Range:	Medium	Gift Wrapping Option?	No
Delivery Area:	UK	Returns Procedure:	Down to you

www.beverlybeaute.com

Once you've taken a good look here you may well decide to order your nail products from this US-based retailer. They stock the full range of Jessica, Opi, Essie, Seche and Creative plus less well known brands Star Nail, Qtica and Gena and everything at a very good discount. You can also order from the Thalgo range of Marine Algae and plant based products here. Delivery is fast and there's a standard charge of £3 but don't forget you may have to pay duty.

Site Usability:	★★★★★	Based:	US
Product Range:	★★★★★	Express Delivery Option? (UK)	No
Price Range:	Very Good Value	Gift Wrapping Option?	No
Delivery Area:	Worldwide	Returns Procedure:	Down to you

www.corioliss.co.uk

For high tech hair straighteners and dryers that you may well not have come across before take a look here. There are wide-plate, wet and dry and cordless irons plus the new C2 range which, they claim, kills the bacteria in your hair, the Infralite high speed hair dryer plus their folding travel dryers in purple, silver, gold and white. The irons are definitely the best part of the range and I'm definitely not showing this website to my daughter – they're expensive (but marvellous, I'm sure).

Site Usability:	★★★★	Based:	UK
Product Range:	★★★	Express Delivery Option? (UK)	No
Price Range:	Luxury/Medium	Gift Wrapping Option?	No
Delivery Area:	Worldwide	Returns Procedure:	Down to you

www.hqhair.com

If you haven't used it already you should really try this fun and incredibly useful website, where along with a huge range of excellent modern beauty products and cosmetics and absolutely everything you could need for your hair including Blax, Nexxus and Paul Mitchell products, you'll also discover Anya Hindmarch, Kate Spade and Lulu Guinness exquisite cosmetic bags, (perfect for presents and also for treats); also lots of beauty accessories including high quality makeup and hair brushes.

Site Usability:	★★★★★	Based:	UK
Product Range:	★★★★	Express Delivery Option? (UK)	Most orders take 24–48 hours
Price Range:	Luxury/Medium	Gift Wrapping Option?	No
Delivery Area:	Worldwide	Returns Procedure:	Down to you

www.johnmasters.co.uk

Here you'll find an excellent range of organic hair care (and skincare) from Lavender and Rosemary or Honey and Hibiscus shampoo to Rosemary and Peppermint Detangler and Bourbon, Vanilla and Tangerine Hair Texturiser. His range of skincare includes face washes and cleansers, serums and body milks with fragrances such as Blood Orange and Vanilla, Lavender, and Green Tea and Rose. The packaging is simple and chic and delivery is free within the UK (at time of writing).

Site Usability:	★★★★	Based:	UK
Product Range:	★★★	Express Delivery Option? (UK)	No
Price Range:	Medium	Gift Wrapping Option?	No
Delivery Area:	Worldwide	Returns Procedure:	Down to you

www.johnnylovesrosie.co.uk

Famous for their chic, modern collection of hair accessories, Johnny Loves Rosie has now branched out into a collection of small, beautifully detailed bags, flip-flops and pretty bead jewellery. There's a small selection online, but how can you resist their carved marigold bobby pins, crystal hair clips and flower clips and elastics, featuring orchids, buttercups, hyacinths and carnations, in a variety of colours? They're simply a must for any hair conscious girl.

Site Usability:	★★★★	Based:	UK
Product Range:	★★★★	Express Delivery Option? (UK)	No
Price Range:	Medium	Gift Wrapping Option?	No
Delivery Area:	Worldwide	Returns Procedure:	Down to you

www.justbeautifully.co.uk

This is a recent addition to the haircare online retailers list and a really great website, offering the full range of my favourite hair dryers by Parlux, which comes in colours such as pink, red and chocolate as well as black, of course; straighteners by Coriolis, T3 and Kodo Creative; manicure and pedicure tools and lots of other beauty treats. It's a very well laid out website and I would definitely give them a try.

Site Usability:	★★★★★	Based:	UK
Product Range:	★★★★	Express Delivery Option? (UK)	No
Price Range:	Medium	Gift Wrapping Option?	No
Delivery Area:	UK	Returns Procedure:	Down to you

www.kaven.co.uk

This site offers skincare from Guerlain, Decleor, and Guinot plus St Tropez self tanning products and the full range of Jessica nail care although the colours are hard to see if you're not sure exactly which one you want. It's a quick and easy site to order from with details and pictures of each and every item. Guerlain makeup is also available. If you have any queries you can call them and they're always delighted to help.

Site Usability:	★★★★	Based:	UK
Product Range:	★★★★	Express Delivery Option? (UK)	Yes
Price Range:	Medium	Gift Wrapping Option?	Yes
Delivery Area:	Worldwide	Returns Procedure:	Down to you

www.lookfantastic.com

Here's a marvellous selection of hair care products from well-known brands such as Kerastase, Paul Mitchell, Tigi and Redken, plus nailcare by Essie, Opi, Jessica and Nailtiques. In the Beauty Accessories section they offer straighteners, dryers, brushes and clippers by GHD, Babyliss, T3 and Icon and if you haven't discovered GHD ceramic brushes yet you can order them here. Try them, they're excellent. Provided you join their club you can take advantage of the very good discounts on offer.

Site Usability:	★★★★	Based:	UK
Product Range:	★★★★★	Express Delivery Option? (UK)	Yes
Price Range:	Medium/Very Good Value	Gift Wrapping Option?	No
Delivery Area:	Worldwide	Returns Procedure:	Down to you

www.martynmaxey.co.uk

There are lots of hair care websites springing up but this is definitely one of the best designed. They offer products by J F Lazartigue, GHD Babyliss, Kerastase, Philip Kingsley and Sebastian plus skincare by MD Formulations, Murad and Prevage together with cosmetics by ID Bare Escentuals, which is a really great new range. Sign up to become a member and take advantage of their discounts.

Site Usability:	★★★★★	Based:	UK
Product Range:	★★★★★	Express Delivery Option? (UK)	Yes
Price Range:	Medium	Gift Wrapping Option?	No
Delivery Area:	UK	Returns Procedure:	Down to you

www.nailsbymail.co.uk

Calling themselves 'The UK's leading nail boutique' Nails by Mail offer products by Essie and Seche (and if you haven't yet tried the truly marvellous Seche Vite quick dry you should) together with colours, treatments, files and buffers making this is an excellent well priced site for all the elements necessary for keeping your nails in top shape. If you need any advice you can give them a call and their Nail Technicians will be happy to help.

Site Usability:	★★★★	Based:	UK
Product Range:	★★★★★	Express Delivery Option? (UK)	No
Price Range:	Medium	Gift Wrapping Option?	No
Delivery Area:	UK	Returns Procedure:	Down to you

www.nailsinc.com

If you've visited the US you'll know that there are several nail bars in each and every shopping mall no matter how big or small and much of the time you don't even have to book, you can just walk in on a whim. The UK has taken a long time to catch up but now with Nails Inc. you can visit one of their 35 locations in the UK for an excellent, speedy manicure and you can also buy their products online, from high quality treatments and gift sets to their outlet store offering goodies for less.

Site Usability:	★★★	Based:	UK
Product Range:	★★★	Express Delivery Option? (UK)	No
Price Range:	Medium	Gift Wrapping Option	No
Delivery Area:	UK	Returns Procedure:	Down to you

www.saloneasy.com

This is the place to find your professional standard hairdryer by Parlux (they're really excellent, come in a fab range of colours and are not overpriced), hair straighteners and stylers and a wide range of hair brushes. This site is aimed at the professional so there are a wide range of salon products that you almost certainly won't be interested in but the prices for the dryers and brushes are some of the best you'll find and the service is speedy.

Site Usability:	★★★	Based:	UK
Product Range:	★★★★	Express Delivery Option? (UK)	No
Price Range:	Medium	Gift Wrapping Option?	No
Delivery Area:	UK	Returns Procedure:	Down to you

www.salonlines.co.uk

Here's another hair product website offering a very good range of Schwarzcopf hair care products plus Tigi and Joico, GHD straighteners and ceramic brushes and loads of other beauty products including specialist hair treatments and some grooming products. You can go to their advice section and find out about how to deal with specific problems or you can email their expert and ask for help. They're happy to ship all over the world, offer an express delivery option and bulk shipping discount.

Site Usability:	★★★★	Based:	UK
Product Range:	★★★★	Express Delivery Option? (UK)	Yes
Price Range:	Medium	Gift Wrapping Option?	No
Delivery Area:	Worldwide	Returns Procedure:	Down to you

www.screenface.com

The next time you want to buy a new set of makeup brushes have a good look here before you rush off and spend hundreds of pounds on some of the major brands. The selection is huge and very well priced and you can also buy makeup bags and cases, professional makeup and tweezerman products. Some of the pictures are not very clear (if they're there at all) but you can send off for their catalogue.

Site Usability:	★★★	Based:	UK
Product Range:	★★★★	Express Delivery Option? (UK)	No
Price Range:	Very Good Value	Gift Wrapping Option?	No
Delivery Area:	UK	Returns Procedure:	Down to you

www.smoothgroove.co.uk

Star hairdresser Daniel Hersheson has salons in Conduit Street, London and Harvey Nichols. You can now find his high quality range of styling tools online at www.smoothgroove.co.uk. There are Ceramic Ion brushes in five sizes, a smoothing iron and waving tongs and his professional hairdryer which he states is the most powerful tool of its kind available (and so it should be at around £90).

Site Usability:	★★★★	Based:	US
Product Range:	★★★	Express Delivery Option? (UK)	No
Price Range:	Luxury	Gift Wrapping Option?	No
Delivery Area:	Worldwide	Returns Procedure:	Down to you

www.themakeupbrushcompany.co.uk

Make-up artist to the stars Christine Allsopp has created this website not just to offer a small but excellent range of brushes and brush sets, but also to give you lots of information on how to use your brushes to get the best effect and with online video clips of actresses and models applying their make-up (expertly, of course). In order to get the best out of this website you need to buy something, which gives you the pass through to all the information.

Site Usability:	★★★	Based:	UK
Product Range:	★★★	Express Delivery Option? (UK)	Yes
Price Range:	Medium	Gift Wrapping Option?	No
Delivery Area:	Worldwide	Returns Procedure:	Down to you

Also take a look at these websites for Hair, Nails and Beauty Accessories:

Website address	You'll find it in
www.jasonshankey.co.uk	Chapter 21: Men's Toiletries and Nightwear
www.zpm.com	Chapter 87: General Travel Planning

Chapter 36

Scented Candles

I'm not one of those people who loves to have a deep bath surrounded by beautiful, lit, fragranced candles. I always think that I should be, it sounds such a wonderful way to relax, but as I'm usually in a rush I just about manage to pour in my favourite gel and leave it at that. One of these days …

I do love to be given beautifully packaged candles – I've said as much to my family when they're in one of their 'oh she's sooo difficult to buy for' moods and then they go off and buy me a book, instead. Now I've nothing against books, I'm a book addict; but please, please, please next time go and buy me that wonderful John Galliano candle for Diptyque. I have to confess having bought one as a Christmas gift for someone last year, but I haven't yet managed to talk myself into giving it away. It's sitting there, wrapped in its pink and green tissue paper and just waiting for me to open it and light it. Think I'll go and do that as soon as I've finished writing this.

Anyway, buy these lovely treats for yourself or for a friend or colleague. Buy the mini versions and take them travelling with you. Surround yourself with them the next time you have a bath and you have the time to truly relax. You go on and do that and I'll go and open that candle. Bye for now.

Sites to Visit

www.ancienneambiance.com

The Ancienne Ambiance concept of antiquity-inspired luxury goods has been designed and developed by Adriana Carlucci, a graduate of the London College of Fashion with a degree in product development. She began by creating a unique collection of six glass encased candles, each featuring fragrances evocative of an ancient culture together with elegant hand-crafted packaging. You'll also discover small inserts made of authentic hand-made Egyptian papyrus which carry the description and the ancient associations of each scent used.

Site Usability:	★★★★	Based:	UK
Product Range:	★★★	Express Delivery Option? (UK)	Yes
Price Range:	Medium	Gift Wrapping Option?	Yes
Delivery Area:	Worldwide	Returns Procedure:	Down to you

www.kiarie.co.uk

Kiarie has one of the best ranges of scented candles, by brands such as Geodosis, Kenneth Turner, Manuel Canovas, Creation Mathias, Rigaud and Millefiori – there are literally hundreds to choose from at all price levels (this site is very fast, so don't panic) and you can also choose your range by price, maker, fragrance, colour and season. Once you've made your selection you can ask them to gift wrap it for you and include a hand written message.

Site Usability:	★★★★★	Based:	UK
Product Range:	★★★★★	Express Delivery Option? (UK)	Yes
Price Range:	Medium	Gift Wrapping Option?	Yes
Delivery Area:	Worldwide	Returns Procedure:	Down to you

www.naturalmagicuk.com

Unlike almost all conventional candles (which contain paraffin wax and synthetic oils), Natural Magic candles are made from clean, pure vegetable wax, scented with the best quality organic aromatherapy oils. They're also twice the size of the average candle (1kg) with 3 wicks and up to 75 hours of burn time. Each candle has a specific theraputic task, such as uplifting, inspiring, soothing and de-stressing and all are beautifully packaged and perfect for treats and gifts.

Site Usability:	★★★★★	Based:	UK
Product Range:	★★★	Express Delivery Option? (UK)	Yes
Price Range:	Medium	Gift Wrapping Option?	No
Delivery Area:	Worldwide	Returns Procedure:	Down to you

www.parkscandles.com

Parks Candles have an easy to get round website offering a beautiful range of scented candles in decorative containers. Three wick candles in silver bowls, perfumed candles in glass containers with silver lids and scented dinner candles in green, burgundy or cream are just some of the selection. Delivery is excellent and the prices are less than you find in most shops.

Site Usability:	★★★★★	Based:	UK
Product Range:	★★★	Express Delivery Option? (UK)	Automatic
Price Range:	Medium	Gift Wrapping Option?	No
Delivery Area:	Worldwide	Returns Procedure:	Down to you

www.timothyhan.com

If you haven't already come across these luxurious candles then take a look now. Timothy Han has a small but gorgeous range, including aromatherapy candles with names such as Orange Grapefruit and Clove, Lavender, and Scent of Fig and his unfragranced candles which are perfect for entertaining. You can also buy his candles in Bill Amberg's specially created leather travel case. Call for urgent deliveries.

Site Usability:	★★★★★	Based:	UK
Product Range:	★★★	Express Delivery Option? (UK)	Yes but call them
Price Range:	Luxury/Medium	Gift Wrapping Option?	Yes
Delivery Area:	Worldwide	Returns Procedure:	Down to you

www.truegrace.co.uk

If you want to pamper someone with something small and beautiful and you don't want to spend a fortune you should choose from the gorgeous candles here. All beautifully wrapped and in glass containers, you'll find the 'Never a Dull Day' range in pretty printed boxes with fragrances such as Vine Tomato, Stem Ginger and Hyacinth and 'As it Should Be', the slightly more simply (but equally attractively) boxed candle in 37 fragrances including Citrus, Cappucino and Raspberry. Try them.

Site Usability:	★★★★	Based:	UK
Product Range:	★★★★	Express Delivery Option? (UK)	No
Price Range:	Medium	Gift Wrapping Option?	No
Delivery Area:	Worldwide	Returns Procedure:	Down to you

Chapter 37

Modern Skincare and Cosmetics

This is an excellent place to buy skincare and cosmetics (but skincare, mainly) that are very hard to find in the stores as well as those that you know and love. It's not the place to try out an expensive new product unless you email first and ask for try-out samples.

I have no doubt that all the products here are excellent but needless to say they won't all be right for you. With some wonder-creams now retailing at well over £100 a pot it makes sense to test them first on your skin, no matter how tempting they sound and look. If it sounds odd for me to be advising you like this I can assure you it's because of expensive mistakes I've made in the past which I want to prevent you making now.

Where cosmetics are concerned my cautious words are really about colour. Even though colour reproduction has improved dramatically over the past few years be very careful before investing in the new hot green, purple or blue, they may not be quite as you see them on screen – neutrals are far easier. When you're looking at foundations and blushers be especially careful – in the same way that you have to be aware of shop lighting when trying to match colours to your skin in store, this is an area that can so easily go wrong.

To be totally honest I think, having made several mistakes, that you need to test base colours in daylight, in the shops. Even a small added amount of yellow from your screen or artifical light will completely change what you see. So buy the colours you know are right for you online and try out new ones offline. Yes I actually said go shop, but then if I didn't in this case you'd surely think I was daft.

Sites to Visit

www.beautique.com

Beautique is a brand new beauty and hair website, divided into three sections: Learn, where you can find tips and advice written by industry experts in all areas of beauty and hair; Buy, where you can order all the products offered; and Experience, showcasing treatments, spas and salons in the UK and around the world, with personal recommendations and reviews. Brands include Aveda, Bumble and Bumble, Carole Franck, Dr Hauschka, Guerlain and J C Brosseau. It's beautifully designed and well worth having a look round

Site Usability:	★★★★★	Based:	UK
Product Range:	★★★★★	Express Delivery Option? (UK)	Yes
Price Range:	Luxury/Medium	Gift Wrapping Option?	No
Delivery Area:	UK	Returns Procedure:	Down to you

www.benefitcosmetics.co.uk

You can find Benefit cosmetics in the major stores but you'll be hard put to see this complete range anywhere else online, and with tempting products such as Benetint, Lip Plump, Super Strength Blemish Blaster and Ooh La Lift how can you resist buying from this veritable candy store for the face? There's the cleverly packaged makeup, foundations, concealers and glitters, bodycare, skincare, accessories and a great gift selection.

Site Usability:	★★★★★	Based:	UK
Product Range:	★★★★	Express Delivery Option? (UK)	Yes
Price Range:	Medium	Gift Wrapping Option?	Yes
Delivery Area:	Worldwide	Returns Procedure:	Down to you

www.blisslondon.co.uk

Sign up for Bliss Beaut e-mails and stay in the 'Glow'. Does that give you some idea of the tone from beauty online from New York and London's hottest spa? If you don't have the time to visit the spas themselves you can at least now buy the products online and relax at home with your own treatments, shower gels and shampoos with simple names like Body Butter, Rosy Toes and Glamour Glove Gel. Some of the products are reasonably priced but you'll also find some of their marvellous anti-ageing products will set you back a bit. It'll be worth it though.

Site Usability:	★★★★	Based:	UK
Product Range:	★★★	Express Delivery Option? (UK)	Yes
Price Range:	Medium	Gift Wrapping Option?	No
Delivery Area:	Worldwide	Returns Procedure:	Down to you

www.bobbibrown.co.uk

Just occasionally a website appears that I know I'm going to be using a lot as it's one I've been waiting for. This is definitely one of those because quite frankly, I'm a Bobbi Brown addict. In my opinion they have the some of the best colours and tools you can find and (unfortunately for my bank balance) they seem to manage to create something I really can't resist each season. If you haven't yet tried this excellent all-American cosmetics and skincare company I suggest you get going as you've been missing some of the best products available anywhere.

Site Usability:	★★★★★	Based:	UK
Product Range:	★★★★★	Express Delivery Option? (UK)	Yes
Price Range:	Medium	Gift Wrapping Option?	No
Delivery Area:	UK this website	Returns Procedure:	Down to you

www.boots.com

Not only can you buy your basic bathroom cupboard items here, plus fragrance from most of the major brands, but from their Brand Boutique you can also buy the full ranges from Chanel, Clarins, Clinique, Dior, Estée Lauder, Elizabeth Arden and Lancôme plus ultra modern brands Ruby and Millie, Urban Decay and Benefit. Delivery is free when you spend £40 and returns are free too. Their excellent service is simply not publicised enough.

Site Usability:	★★★★★	Express Delivery Option? (UK)	Yes
Product Range:	★★★★★	Gift Wrapping Option?	Yes
Price Range:	Luxury/Medium/Very Good Value	Returns Procedure:	Free
Delivery Area:	UK		

www.clinique.co.uk

If you're a dedicated Clinique follower then this is the site for you, where not only can you purchase replacements for all your favourite products, but you can also read all about what's new, visit their Gift Centre to order special sets and accessory kits and join Club Clinique, where you can register for fast checkout, free samples with your orders, 'Beauty Scoops' and expert advice. Delivery is to the UK only but there's an express service and gift wrap option.

Site Usability:	★★★★★	Based:	UK
Product Range:	★★★★★	Express Delivery Option? (UK)	Yes
Price Range:	Medium	Gift Wrapping Option?	Yes
Delivery Area:	UK	Returns Procedure:	Down to you

www.cosmeticsalacarte.com

Christina Stewart and Lynne Sanders, both creative cosmetic chemists, founded Cosmetics à la carte 30 years ago – the first made-to-measure make-up range. If you can't get to their Knightsbridge store you can order this range of 'makeup to fit' online with easy to see wide choices of colours for face, cheek, lip and eye products (including their wonderful Lip Glass) plus 'Skin Basics' skin treats and a great selection of brushes and other beauty accessories.

Site Usability:	★★★★	Express Delivery Option? (UK)	No
Product Range:	★★★★	Gift Wrapping Option?	No
Price Range:	Medium	Returns Procedure:	Down to you
Delivery Area:	Worldwide		

www.esteelauder.co.uk

As you'd expect, Estée Lauder have a really beautiful website and although you can buy their products from other online retailers here there are lots of extra goodies, such as information on the latest products and best sellers and where you can find (offline, of course) their free gifts and brow bars around the country. They offer express and Saturday delivery services plus gift wrapping.

Site Usability:	★★★★★	Express Delivery Option? (UK)	Yes
Product Range:	★★★★	Gift Wrapping Option?	Yes
Price Range:	Luxury/Medium	Returns Procedure:	Down to you
Delivery Area:	Worldwide		

www.garden.co.uk

The Garden Pharmacy's list of top brands seems to be growing by the day. Here you'll find Chanel, Elizabeth Arden, Lancôme, Revlon, Clinique and Clarins online together with Vichy, Avene, Caudalie and Roc and spa products by I Coloniali, L'Occitane, Roger et Gallet and Segreti Mediterranei (and no doubt a few more will have appeared by the time you read this). The list of fragrances they offer is huge. They also offer free gift wrapping and 24 hour delivery.

Site Usability:	★★★★	Based:	UK
Product Range:	★★★★★	Express Delivery Option? (UK)	Yes
Price Range:	Luxury/Medium/Very Good Value	Gift Wrapping Option?	Yes
Delivery Area:	Worldwide	Returns Procedure:	Down to you

www.lancome.co.uk

Although you can buy all the products from this world famous skincare and cosmetics company online from other retailers, now you can buy them directly from Lancôme on their clear, stylish website. If you're a Lancôme addict this is surely the site to visit as you can immediately find out about the latest products, take a look at their best sellers and find out about gifts and special events taking place offline.

Site Usability:	★★★★★	Based:	UK
Product Range:	★★★★★	Express Delivery Option? (UK)	Yes
Price Range:	Luxury/Medium	Gift Wrapping Option?	No
Delivery Area:	UK	Returns Procedure:	Down to you

www.maccosmetics.co.uk

You've seen their cosmetics in all the best beauty stores and now you can buy them online, direct from their ultra chic website. Shop by category – lips, eyes, nails, skincare, etc. – or from one of their collections, with names such as Viva Glam, Barbie Loves Mac, Untamed, Rockocco or Technacolour – and these change each season. Click on 'What's New' to discover the latest treats and tips or go through to 'Looks' to discover how they're created (and buy the products, of course). Be warned, it's extremely hard to leave without buying.

Site Usability:	★★★★★	Based:	UK
Product Range:	★★★★★	Express Delivery Option? (UK)	Yes
Price Range:	Medium	Gift Wrapping Option?	No
Delivery Area:	UK	Returns Procedure:	Down to you

www.nevertoobusytobebeautiful.com

I find this website quite confusing; however, stick to the product list on the left and you'll be OK. There's an excellent range of cosmetics (in 'makeup') from blushers, concealers and cream foundation to glitter eye shadows and metallic loose powder. What makes everything really special is the packaging, which is totally unique. Think foundation bottles decorated with Moroccan metal and blushers in jewelled pots and you'll get the idea.

Site Usability:	★★★	Based:	UK
Product Range:	★★★★	Express Delivery Option? (UK)	Yes
Price Range:	Medium	Gift Wrapping Option?	No
Delivery Area:	Worldwide	Returns Procedure:	Down to you

www.pixibeauty.com

Pixi is an independent British beauty company consisting of cosmetics and skincare ranges and beauty accessories. It was started by three sisters, Sara, Sophia and Petra, two of whom are makeup artists and the third a skin therapist, so you're definitely in the hands of experts. In their words the range is 'magical, individual, feminine, small, cute, playful, free spirited, mischievous, friendly, colourful, cheeky, unique, illusive and tempting.' Irresistible (my word).

Site Usability:	★★★★	Based:	UK
Product Range:	★★★	Express Delivery Option? (UK)	No
Price Range:	Medium	Gift Wrapping Option?	No
Delivery Area:	Worldwide	Returns Procedure:	Down to you

www.pout.co.uk

Pout is the perfect place for beauty junkies who want to enjoy and have fun with cosmetics. The whole range is clever and light-hearted through tongue-in-cheek product names such as 'Bite my Cherry' and 'Saucy Sadie' and packaging inspired by the founders' favourite items of underwear, gaining Pout the reputation as 'the underwear of make-up'. If this sounds slightly silly, don't be fooled, it's a really gorgeous, cleverly packaged range of cosmetics, makeup bags, great gifts and excellent beauty accessories. Take a look round now.

Site Usability:	★★★★★	Based:	UK
Product Range:	★★★★★	Express Delivery Option? (UK)	Yes
Price Range:	Medium	Gift Wrapping Option?	Yes
Delivery Area:	Worldwide	Returns Procedure:	Down to you

www.powderpuff.net

Next time you go looking to buy one of your regular beauty essentials have a look at this website, offering free delivery in the UK and a huge selection of products. It's been called 'The Daddy of all Beauty Sites' and you'd find it hard to disagree. You'll find brand names such as Lancôme, Clarins, Clinique and YSL plus GHD, Kinerase and Fudge together with skincare, cosmetics and fragrance and mostly at very good prices. They'll also deliver worldwide.

Site Usability:	★★★★	Based:	UK
Product Range:	★★★★	Express Delivery Option? (UK)	Yes
Price Range:	Medium/Very Good Value	Gift Wrapping Option?	Yes
Delivery Area:	Worldwide	Returns Procedure:	Down to you

www.procosmetics.co.uk

There are four main brands available from this new skincare and cosmetics website – Nouba; with its excellent range of cosmetics and make-up brushes and bags, Algodermia for marine based skincare, 3 Lab for specialist treatments and Lucky Chick for really fun and well priced spa treats (think Lucky Lips Vanilla Lip Shine and Foot Fetish Spearmint Foot & Leg Cream). Take a look now.

Site Usability:	★★★★★	Based:	UK
Product Range:	★★★★	Express Delivery Option? (UK)	No
Price Range:	Medium	Gift Wrapping Option?	No
Delivery Area:	Worldwide	Returns Procedure:	Down to you

www.spacenk.co.uk

Nars, Stila, Darphin, Laura Mercier, Eve Lom, Diptyque, Frederic Fekkai and Dr Sebagh are just some of the 60 plus brands offered on the website of this retailer, famous for bringing unusual and hard to find products to the UK (so you don't have to go to New York any more to buy your Frederic Fekkai shampoo: shame). They're also an excellent place for gifts as they offer a personalised message and gift wrapping service and next day delivery if you need it. It's a well designed and easy to navigate website with very clear pictures.

Site Usability:	★★★★★	Based:	UK
Product Range:	★★★★	Express Delivery Option? (UK)	Yes
Price Range:	Luxury/Medium	Gift Wrapping Option?	Yes
Delivery Area:	Worldwide	Returns Procedure:	Down to you

www.urbanapothecary.co.uk

Whether you're looking for a pampering gift or something for yourself you'll almost certainly like this website which is easy to use and well photographed. Choose from Beauty, Skincare, Haircare, Candles and Home Fragrance or Gifts and Accessories from brands such as Korres, Sohum or This Works. Alternatively shop by brand or by scent, check out their recommendations or take advantage of free gifts and special offers. Whatever; you'll have a fun time browsing here.

Site Usability:	★★★★★	Based:	UK
Product Range:	★★★★★	Express Delivery Option? (UK)	Yes
Price Range:	Medium	Gift Wrapping Option?	No
Delivery Area:	UK	Returns Procedure:	Down to you

www.xen-tan.co.uk

If you want to know everything there is to know about the hot new self tan product from the US then this is the website to visit. So read all about it then choose from their Body Scrub, Tan Extender, Lotion, Mousse and Mist, plus the Perfect Bronze Compact. There's also an excellent application advice section to help you get the perfect fake tan.

Site Usability:	★★★★★	Based:	UK
Product Range:	★★★	Express Delivery Option? (UK)	No
Price Range:	Medium	Gift Wrapping Option?	No
Delivery Area:	EU	Returns Procedure:	Down to you

Chapter 38

Natural and Organic Beauty

Green, eco-friendly and organic are the buzz words right now in every area of your life, from clothing to homewares, baby and beauty products.

I'm not sure that I want to buy a sweatshirt made out of recycled cardboard - sorry, but I'm being totally honest here - which is why you won't find such items in this book, but I'm happy to do my bit where possible by buying into some of the gorgeous skincare, cosmetics and other beauty products here because they are just that - gorgeous.

If you're into all things natural this is a great place for beauty and one where you'll find aromatherapy oils, herbal supplements, natural soaps and organic bath oils. Make sure before you buy that you really do know how natural and organic whatever you have selected is. The most honest retailers are those who give you lots of information; 'totally organic' just doesn't cut it with me - just how 'natural' is that? I suspect some retailers will be jumping on the organic band wagon because they can see that these new products sell, rather than because they care.

Also be aware that truly organic products are unlikely to have the shelf life of the non-organic variety as they won't contain the non-natural preservatives that make them last. If in doubt, call the retailer and ask.

Sites to Visit

www.airandwater.co.uk

Here you can find out about the properties of essential oils with their natural soaps, beauty products, aromatherapy boxes, carrier and massage oils; enhance your home with oil burners, incense, resins, candles and vaporisers and find Bach flower remedies and the Rescue Remedy range of herbal supplements. Air and Water's suppliers include Edom Health and Beauty products, Meadows Aromatherapy and Arran Aromatics.

Site Usability:	★★★★	Based:	UK
Product Range:	★★★★	Express Delivery Option? (UK)	Yes
Price Range:	Medium	Gift Wrapping Option?	No
Delivery Area:	EU	Returns Procedure:	Down to you

www.baldwins.co.uk

G. Baldwin & Co. is London's oldest and most established Herbalist and if you pay a visit to their shop you'll find that it still has a nostalgic atmosphere of stepping back in time, with wooden floors, high old fashioned counters and shelves stacked with herbs, oils and ointments. You can shop online from the complete ranges of both Bach Flower Remedies and the Australian Bush Flower Essences, their own brand aromatherapy oils, natural soaps, creams and bath accessories and herbs, seeds, roots and dried flowers.

Site Usability:	★★★★	Based:	UK
Product Range:	★★★★	Express Delivery Option? (UK)	Yes
Price Range:	Medium	Gift Wrapping Option?	No
Delivery Area:	Worldwide	Returns Procedure:	Down to you

www.beauty-republic.com

Beauty Republic sources natural beauty secrets from all over the world and they offer a range of specialised products such as Black Palm Natural Soap, Hi Shine hair products, Lullaby Lavender, Kosmea natural skin care and Rainforest Remedies. For each and every product they tell you what it does, what's in it and how to use it so if you've never come across it before you may well be tempted to give it a try.

Site Usability:	★★★★★	Based:	UK
Product Range:	★★★★	Express Delivery Option? (UK)	Yes
Price Range:	Medium	Gift Wrapping Option?	Yes
Delivery Area:	Worldwide	Returns Procedure:	Down to you

www.bodyshop.co.uk

Alongside all the gorgeous luxury skincare and cosmetic brands you can now find online there's The Body Shop, well known for so many years and now with a beautifully laid out, fun to use website offering all their well priced ranges of skincare, bath and body products and cosmetics, such as their Ultra Smooth Foundation, Aloe Soothing Night Cream and Relaxing Lavender Massage Oil. There are lots of gift ideas as well, and with everything you can trust Body Shop's mandate of shunning animal testing and protecting the planet.

Site Usability:	★★★★★	Based:	UK
Product Range:	★★★★★	Express Delivery Option? (UK)	Yes
Price Range:	Very Good Value	Gift Wrapping Option?	No
Delivery Area:	UK but there are overseas transactional websites	Returns Procedure:	Down to you

www.freshsoapdeli.com

The handmade soap deli is a speciality soap, bath and body company producing a therapeutic range of products using high quality essential oils, tailor-made fragrances and herbal extracts to create a range which includes 'freshly cut off the block' soaps, wonderful Lemon Sherbet, Cherry and Lavender bath bombes, Mango Body Butter, Strawberry Body Polish and gifts such as the Tutti Frutti Soap Kebab. You'll definitely have fun choosing here.

Site Usability:	★★★★	Based:	UK
Product Range:	★★★	Express Delivery Option? (UK)	No
Price Range:	Medium	Gift Wrapping Option?	No
Delivery Area:	EU	Returns Procedure:	Down to you

www.fushi.co.uk

Fushi was established just over four years ago as a lifestyle brand of holistic health and beauty products. Expanding on the philosophy that inner health promotes outer well-being, Fushi has developed a range of natural products including herbal remedies, cosmetic ranges and aromatherapy oils, most of which are organic. Use their product finder to treat specific ailments or select by product range. There's lots of information so be prepared to spend some time.

Site Usability:	★★★★★	Based:	UK
Product Range:	★★★★	Express Delivery Option? (UK)	No
Price Range:	Medium	Gift Wrapping Option?	No
Delivery Area:	Worldwide	Returns Procedure:	Down to you

www.jowoodorganics.com

Available only in her boutique and online, Jo Wood offers a range that contains the highest possible percentage of organic ingredients from accredited sources. You'll find bath oils, body lotions and soaps plus natural soy wax candles all exquisitely presented in glass bottles and jars. Note that because of the lack of chemical ingredients here your products need to be stored out of sunlight and to be used within nine months.

Site Usability:	★★★★	Based:	UK
Product Range:	★★★	Express Delivery Option? (UK)	1–2 working days
Price Range:	Luxury/Medium	Gift Wrapping Option?	No
Delivery Area:	Worldwide	Returns Procedure:	Down to you

www.highlandsoaps.com

On this really attractive website you'll find a wide range of handmade soaps from the Highlands of Scotland, beautifully packaged and with names like May Chang and Lime, and Rosehip and Patchouli. Alternatively there's Mango Butter, Wild Nettle and Heather and exfoliating soaps with natural loofah (I'll definitely be trying one of those!). They offer bath bombes, body crème and luxurious hand wash plus gift boxes and bath accessories and their services include overseas shipping and gift wrapping.

Site Usability:	★★★★★	Based:	UK
Product Range:	★★★	Express Delivery Option? (UK)	No
Price Range:	Medium	Gift Wrapping Option?	Yes
Delivery Area:	Worldwide	Returns Procedure:	Down to you

www.loccitane.com

L'Occitane is another brand you're sure to have heard of, offering products ranging from personal care to home fragrance and all manufactured in traditional ways using natural ingredients, primarily from Provence. The range includes fragrance, body and hand care, bath and shower products, skin care, hair care and home fragrance with Verbena Harvest, Eau d'Ambre, Lavender, Oranger and Green Tea forming the bases for Eau de Toilette, soaps, hand creams, shower gels and shampoos.

Site Usability:	★★★★★	Based:	UK
Product Range:	★★★★★	Express Delivery Option? (UK)	Yes
Price Range:	Medium	Gift Wrapping Option?	Yes
Delivery Area:	Worldwide	Returns Procedure:	Down to you

www.lovelula.com

There's a huge amount of information available here on Love Lula's organic apothecary website, from which natural products to buy for stress, acne, chapped lips and stretch marks to the online skincare consultation and 'Ask Lula' email option. There are lots of products to choose from, including gifts and special ranges for mother and baby, and everything's very clear and easy to see.

Site Usability:	★★★★★	Based:	UK
Product Range:	★★★★★	Express Delivery Option? (UK)	Yes
Price Range:	Medium	Gift Wrapping Option?	No
Delivery Area:	Worldwide	Returns Procedure:	Down to you

www.mandala-aroma.com

Mandala Aroma is a luxury organic aromatherapy company set up by ex-fashion buyer and qualified aromatherapist Gillian Kavanagh. Here you'll discover bath oils, body treatment oils and aromatherapy candles all under the headings of Wisdom, Love, Courage and Strengh. Click on the item of your choice and you'll find out more about its ingredients and benefits.

Site Usability:	★★★★★	Based:	UK
Product Range:	★★★	Express Delivery Option? (UK)	No
Price Range:	Medium	Gift Wrapping Option?	No
Delivery Area:	Worldwide	Returns Procedure:	Down to you

www.mysanatural.com

Quite a lot of online retailers offering natural and environmentally friendly products think that we want to see them looking as natural as possible. Personally I don't think we do – buying lotions and potions online should always be a treat. Here at Mysa both the natural and treat elements meet beautifully – think Pink Grapefruit Hand and Body Lotion, Ginger Loofah Soap or Sweet Jasmine Body Scrub and you'll get the idea. Packaging is chic and minimal and there are great gift sets here too.

Site Usability:	★★★★★	Based:	UK
Product Range:	★★★	Express Delivery Option? (UK)	Yes
Price Range:	Medium	Gift Wrapping Option?	No
Delivery Area:	Worldwide	Returns Procedure:	Down to you

www.musthave.co.uk

Musthave offers the best in natural and organic skincare, bodycare, fragrance and cosmetics sourced from suppliers around the world. You'll find REN, Paul & Joe, Anthony Logistics, Cowshed, Jo Wood Organics, Headonism Organic Haircare, Living Nature and Abahna alongside brands you probably already know such as Nailtiques, Phyto and Caudalie. The information is extremely clear here and written by professional beauty therapists. You can browse by brand, product type or skin and hair type.

Site Usability:	★★★★★	Based:	UK
Product Range:	★★★★★	Express Delivery Option? (UK)	Yes
Price Range:	Medium	Gift Wrapping Option?	Yes
Delivery Area:	Worldwide	Returns Procedure:	Down to you

www.naturalcollection.com

All the products on this website are seriously natural, from fairly traded laundry baskets to organic cotton bedlinen. They also have a Personal Care selection which includes brands such as Organic Options (natural soaps), Faith in Nature (aromatherapy body care) Barefoot Botanicals (skin and body care) plus lots of natural pampering products and gift ideas. In their Wellbeing section you'll find Sage Organics vitamins and minerals and Bath Indulgence Spa sets.

Site Usability:	★★★★★	Based:	UK
Product Range:	★★★★★	Express Delivery Option? (UK)	Yes
Price Range:	Medium	Gift Wrapping Option?	No
Delivery Area:	Worldwide	Returns Procedure:	Down to you

www.nealsyardremedies.com

This is probably one aromatherapy and herbal remedy retailer you have heard of. From the first shop located in Neal's Yard in the heart of London's Covent Garden, Neal's Yard Remedies has grown into one of the country's leading natural health retailers. On their attractive website you can buy a wide range of their products, from aromatherapy, body care, luxurious bath products and homeopathic remedies plus attractively packaged gift sets.

Site Usability:	★★★★★	Based:	UK
Product Range:	★★★★	Express Delivery Option? (UK)	Yes
Price Range:	Medium	Gift Wrapping Option?	No
Delivery Area:	Worldwide	Returns Procedure:	Down to you

www.nicetouch.co.uk

Nice Touch offers REN, Aromatherapy Associates, Dermalogica, Trilogy botanical skincare, Xen-Tan self tanning range, St Tropez, Pacifica soy candles and prettily packaged earth friendly baby products. They pride themselves in helping you make informed choices about the products that you put on your skin as there's all the information you need about each brand including the ingredients of the products, their suitability for your skin type and the ethics of the companies who make them. It's an excellent website.

Site Usability:	★★★★★	Based:	UK
Product Range:	★★★★	Express Delivery Option? (UK)	No
Price Range:	Medium	Gift Wrapping Option?	No
Delivery Area:	Worldwide	Returns Procedure:	Down to you

www.origins.co.uk

You may well have heard of Origins; specialists in natural skincare using aromatic plants, earth and sea substances and other resources to produce products as close to nature as they can be. Now you can buy the full range online, including their luxurious Ginger Souflée Whipped Body Cream, Jump Start Body Wash and Pomegranate Wash cleanser. You really do want to try them all.

Site Usability:	★★★★★	Based:	UK
Product Range:	★★★★	Express Delivery Option? (UK)	Yes
Price Range:	Luxury/Medium/Very Good Value	Gift Wrapping Option?	No
Delivery Area:	UK	Returns Procedure:	Down to you

www.potions.org.uk

Potions & Possibilities produce natural toiletries and aromatherapy products, ranging from soaps and bath oils to restorative balms and creams. Everything is blended and created using the highest quality essential oils, and you can find their award winning products in Bloomingdales (in the US) and Fenwicks in the UK among other stores and, of course, online. Resist if you can or choose from bath sizzlers, bath and shower gels, shampoos, fragrance and gift collections.

Site Usability:	★★★★	Based:	UK
Product Range:	★★★	Express Delivery Option? (UK)	Yes
Price Range:	Medium	Gift Wrapping Option?	No
Delivery Area:	Worldwide	Returns Procedure:	Down to you

www.primrose-aromatherapy.co.uk

This attractively laid out website is just about aromatherapy and the selection of Essential Oils is huge, with pictures of the fruits, flowers and herbs themselves rather than dinky little bottles. For each product there's a great deal of information on their properties and how to use them. They will ship all over the world and you need to contact them if you want courier delivery.

Site Usability:	★★★★	Based:	UK
Product Range:	★★★	Express Delivery Option? (UK)	Yes
Price Range:	Medium	Gift Wrapping Option?	No
Delivery Area:	Worldwide	Returns Procedure:	Down to you

www.pureskincare.co.uk

All of the products here are 100% natural and suitable for vegetarians. There's also brief information next to each brand name to show which brands are organic or contain organic ingredients, rather than those which are purely 'natural'. Brands available include Balm Balm, Akamuti, Aubrey Organics, Dr Bronner, Suki and Trovarno Organics and products range from general skin and hair care to specialist skincare and travel sizes.

Site Usability:	★★★★★	Based:	UK
Product Range:	★★★★	Express Delivery Option? (UK)	No
Price Range:	Medium	Gift Wrapping Option?	No
Delivery Area:	UK	Returns Procedure:	Down to you

www.rose-apothecary.co.uk

Here's a natural beauty website with a difference. It offers lots of their own, unique, really prettily packaged products such as Rose Petal Bath and Shower Creme, Lavender Shampoo and luxurious gift boxes plus J & E Atkinson, fragrances I Coloniali, Rice and Segreti Mediterranei, Yardley English Lavender, 4711 Cologne and Soir de Paris. Their aromatherapy products – remedy oils and creams and massage oils – are all blended in house.

Site Usability:	★★★★	Based:	UK
Product Range:	★★★★	Express Delivery Option? (UK)	No
Price Range:	Medium	Gift Wrapping Option?	No
Delivery Area:	Worldwide	Returns Procedure:	Down to you

www.theorganicpharmacy.com

The Organic Pharmacy is dedicated to health and beauty using organic products and treatments. Fully registered with The Royal Pharmaceutical Society of Great Britain, they choose to specialise in herbs, homeopathy and organic skincare. They promise no artificial preservatives, colourings or fragrances and everything they offer is hand made in small batches. Look for cosmetics, skincare and gorgeously fragranced candles here plus mother and baby care.

Site Usability:	★★★★★	Based:	UK
Product Range:	★★★★	Express Delivery Option? (UK)	No
Price Range:	Luxury/Medium	Gift Wrapping Option?	No
Delivery Area:	Worldwide	Returns Procedure:	Down to you

www.youraromatherapy.co.uk

This is a really clear and modern aromatherapy website, where you can immediately see all the products on offer, including essential and massage oils, aromatherapy kits, candles and accessories, vaporisers and ionisers and body care for all the family. They have a very good gift section and an attractive selection of candles.

Site Usability:	★★★★★	Based:	UK
Product Range:	★★★★	Express Delivery Option? (UK)	No
Price Range:	Medium	Gift Wrapping Option?	No
Delivery Area:	Worldwide	Returns Procedure:	Down to you

Chapter 39

The Beauty Specialists

This is where we move away from the big brand name skincare companies to smaller, less well known retailers who are just waiting to offer you their specialist knowledge: beauticians such as Amanda Lacey, Eve Lom and Rebecca Korner plus salon only brands Dermalogica, Elemis and Ren.

On many of these websites you can also find products by brands such as Burt's Bees, Fake Bake and l'Occitaine and I have to confess I think that having such a range of different brands on offer just makes them all so much more interesting.

As usual I would suggest that you ask for samples before going for broke to make sure that your new skincare suits your complexion. You'll also find that as most of these websites are run by experts you can get some excellent advice and answers to any questions you may have.

Sites to Visit

www.amandalacey.com

Amanda Lacey is known for her luxurious facials, using the purest most special oils. Known as 'The English rose of skincare' and fast becoming a firm favourite among stars of stage and screen, you can buy into her skincare regimen online, which includes her classic Cleansing Pomade and Oils of Provence, Protecting Day Moisturiser and Restoring Mandarin Mask. Everything is beautifully presented and packaged and extremely hard to resist.

Site Usability:	★★★★	Based:	UK
Product Range:	★★★	Express Delivery Option? (UK)	No
Price Range:	Medium	Gift Wrapping Option?	No
Delivery Area:	Worldwide Most Countries	Returns Procedure:	Down to you

www.beautyandtheeast.co.uk

This is one of those online retailers offering a wide range of specialist products where if you use one or more you'll surely like to shop. On its attractive website you can buy Aveda, Blinc Mascara,

Burt's Bees, Elemis, Fudge, Molton Brown and Dr Lewinn's Ultra R4 Restorative Cream. There's plenty of detail and clear pictures to help you choose if you want to try something new.

Site Usability:	★★★★	Based:	UK
Product Range:	★★★★	Express Delivery Option? (UK)	No
Price Range:	Medium	Gift Wrapping Option?	No
Delivery Area:	UK but ask for overseas delivery	Returns Procedure:	Down to you

www.beautyexpert.co.uk

Here you'll find beauty products by Caudalie, Aromatherapy Associates, Fudge, L'Occitaine, NV Perricone, Phytomer and Ren, plus lots more. Most of these are not ranges that you'll find in the shops, but specialist products from salons and spas. There's lots of specialist advice on the Advice Line run by beauty therapists if you should have a query and an excellent selection of starter kits if you want to try a new product.

Site Usability:	★★★★	Based:	UK
Product Range:	★★★	Express Delivery Option? (UK)	Yes
Price Range:	Medium	Gift Wrapping Option?	Yes
Delivery Area:	Worldwide	Returns Procedure:	Down to you

www.beautyflash.co.uk

Beauty Flash offers the full range from Dermalogica, including masques and moisturisers, specialist treatments and treatment foundations (although you really need to know your colour before you buy these), spa body products and sun care. They have the Skin Doctors range of professional strength skincare with lots of information and advice, Fake Bake and St Tropez tanning products, Air Stockings and Dermablend Cover Creme.

Site Usability:	★★★★	Based:	UK
Product Range:	★★★★	Express Delivery Option? (UK)	Yes
Price Range:	Medium	Gift Wrapping Option?	Yes
Delivery Area:	UK	Returns Procedure:	Down to you

www.beautynaturals.com

This is a family run business offering a comprehensive and affordable collection of high quality, natural health and beauty products, inspired by Martha Hill, who launched her own herbal based, cruelty free skin care products over 30 years ago. The Beauty Naturals collection encompasses all aspects of natural beauty and includes skincare, cosmetics, hand and nail care and bath and body products plus a wide range of specialist products by unusual and hard to find brands.

Site Usability:	★★★★	Based:	UK
Product Range:	★★★★★	Express Delivery Option? (UK)	Yes
Price Range:	Medium	Gift Wrapping Option?	No
Delivery Area:	UK	Returns Procedure:	Down to you

www.beautyxposure.com

Beauty Xposure is a Dermalogica skin care salon based in Hertfordshire, and on their clear and cleanly designed website they offer three ranges for you to buy online: Dermalogica skin care system, Fake Bake – a really great fake tan that will last up to a week and was recently voted best self tanner in the New York Times) and the Nailtiques nail care system. If you're not sure which Dermalogica products you should order just fill in their questionnaire and they'll give you lots of advice.

Site Usability:	★★★★	Based:	UK
Product Range:	★★★	Express Delivery Option? (UK)	Yes
Price Range:	Medium	Gift Wrapping Option?	Yes
Delivery Area:	UK	Returns Procedure:	Down to you

www.drhauschka.co.uk

You may well have read about Dr Hauschka's natural skincare products through its press celebrity connections. When you look at the products online you'll find that they're not overpriced and there's lots of information about each one, not just what it's for, but also how to use it plus a full list of ingredients. When you find something you like, check to see if a trial/travel size is offered before you splash out.

Site Usability:	★★★★	Based:	UK
Product Range:	★★★	Express Delivery Option? (UK)	Yes
Price Range:	Medium	Gift Wrapping Option?	Yes
Delivery Area:	UK but there are international websites	Returns Procedure:	Down to you

www.espaonline.com

ESPA was created to bring together the best of ancient and modern therapies with the finest quality ingredients and skin care advances. This is a lovely light and modern website offering their famous range of aromatherapy products from specific beauty treatments to bath and body products and luxury gifts, with everything formulated from the highest quality organically grown plants. So if you're feeling stressed, this would definitely be a good place to start.

Site Usability:	★★★★★	Based:	UK
Product Range:	★★★★	Express Delivery Option? (UK)	No
Price Range:	Medium	Gift Wrapping Option?	No but there are special gift sets
Delivery Area:	Worldwide	Returns Procedure:	Down to you

www.evelom.co.uk

This is surely one of the most famous names in modern skincare, based on Eve Lom's belief that the best skincare is quite simply total cleansing using natural products and her famous polishing cloth. You may not be able to get to her for a personal facial but at least now you can find her products to buy online. The range is small and definitely not cheap but you'll know that you're buying the very best.

Site Usability:	★★★★	Based:	UK
Product Range:	★★★	Express Delivery Option? (UK)	Yes
Price Range:	Luxury	Gift Wrapping Option?	No
Delivery Area:	Worldwide	Returns Procedure:	Down to you

www.kornerskincare.com

Created by Australian Rebecca Korner, Korner Skincare is a product range formulated in Paris, using rare plant, marine and mineral extracts with cell restructuring and regenerating properties sourced from around the world. The range includes Radiate Presence day cream, Look Famous purifying mask and Seem a Dream cleansing wash and for each product there's plenty of seductive information to make you want to give them a go.

Site Usability:	★★★★	Based:	UK
Product Range:	★★★	Express Delivery Option? (UK)	No
Price Range:	Medium	Gift Wrapping Option?	No
Delivery Area:	Worldwide	Returns Procedure:	Down to you

www.laline.co.uk

Laline is new range of bath, bodycare and home accessories, hand-made with natural oils and fragrances such as Shea butter, aloe and citrus oils, all sourced in France and beautifully packaged. The range includes soaps, body creams and souffles, body oils, face masks plus products for men, babies and home and prices start from around £4. There are always some lovely, well priced gift ideas here for all occasions.

Site Usability:	★★★★	Based:	UK
Product Range:	★★★	Express Delivery Option? (UK)	Yes
Price Range:	Medium/Very Good Value	Gift Wrapping Option?	No but gift sets are available
Delivery Area:	EU	Returns Procedure:	Down to you

www.lizearle.com

Liz Earle has a beautiful website offering her 'Naturally Active Skincare' – a pampering range of skin, body and sun care products. She's particularly well known for her cleanse and polish hot cloth cleanser and well priced but excellent special treatments and moisturisers. Shimmer products for body and lips, Vital Aromatherapy Oils and travel mini-kits from the wide range are just some of the temptations on offer and the lovely packaging is an extra bonus.

Site Usability:	★★★★	Based:	UK
Product Range:	★★★★	Express Delivery Option? (UK)	Yes
Price Range:	Very Good Value	Gift Wrapping Option?	Yes, everything is beautifully packaged
Delivery Area:	Worldwide	Returns Procedure:	Down to you

www.salonskincare.com

Some of the brands you'll find here such as Elemis, Decleor, Gatineau and Phytomer are not hard to find on the web and others, such as luxury skincare brand Carita, Baxter of California, Max Benjamin (candles) and MD Formulations are not readily available. Couple this with the extremely well thought out design of this website and this becomes and essential beauty destination if you like salon brand products. You can also buy Dermalogica, Fake Bake, Molton Brown and Nailtiques here plus Klein-Becker Strivectin SD, the stretch mark turned anti-wrinkle wonder cream.

Site Usability:	★★★★★	Based:	UK
Product Range:	★★★★★	Express Delivery Option? (UK)	Yes
Price Range:	Luxury/Medium	Gift Wrapping Option?	No
Delivery Area:	Worldwide	Returns Procedure:	Down to you

www.karinherzog.co.uk

'We didn't just jump on the oxygen band wagon we created it', they say here; where you can order from this range of oxygen skincare from Switzerland. If you're not quite sure (and the products aren't cheap), go for one of their trial packs and kits, such as the Congestion Charge, which aims to help skins with acne and dull, excessively oily skin or the energising Detox in a Box. There's a lot to read here and you may well be tempted.

Site Usability:	★★★★	Based:	UK
Product Range:	★★★★	Express Delivery Option? (UK)	No
Price Range:	Luxury	Gift Wrapping Option?	No
Delivery Area:	UK	Returns Procedure:	Down to you

www.skinstore.co.uk

What's great about this website offering the latest anti-ageing treatments and innovative skin and body products such as StriVectin, MD Skincare, Rodan and Fields and Sovage is that you can access their online chat facility and 'talk' to an expert before you buy to help to make sure that what you're buying will be right for you. There's a huge range here plus lots of information so if anti-aging is what you're looking for you should definitely have a look.

Site Usability:	★★★★★	Based:	UK
Product Range:	★★★★★	Express Delivery Option? (UK)	No
Price Range:	Luxury/Medium	Gift Wrapping Option?	No
Delivery Area:	EU	Returns Procedure:	Down to you

www.thebeautyroom.com

You may already have come across the French salon brands Gatineau, Phytomer and Mary Cohr and on this website you can order from their full ranges of skincare including anti-ageing creams, cleansers, toners, moisturisers and exfoliators plus the Mary Cohr/Masters Colours extensive collection of cosmetics. These are expensive products and this website will work best for those who have already tried them, although there's lots of information and advice if you want to invest in a something new.

Site Usability:	★★★★	Based:	UK
Product Range:	★★★	Express Delivery Option? (UK)	Yes
Price Range:	Medium	Gift Wrapping Option?	No
Delivery Area:	No	Returns Procedure:	Down to you

www.thisworks.com

Here you'll find soothing, natural and gently scented products for bath and body with unusual names such as Energy Bank, Deep Calm Bath and Shower Oil, Muscle Therapy, Enjoy Really Rich Lotion or Hot Stone Essences, and all have been created by Vogue beauty expert Kathy Phillips.

The collection also includes bath and shower gels, moisturisers, lovely gift ideas and an irresistible travel pouch designed by Orla Kiely containing eight miniature This Works products.

Site Usability:	★★★★	Based:	UK
Product Range:	★★★	Express Delivery Option? (UK)	No
Price Range:	Medium	Gift Wrapping Option?	Yes
Delivery Area:	Worldwide	Returns Procedure:	Down to you

www.timetospa.com

Time to Spa offers Elemis face and body products, La Therapie solutions for acne, scarring and hyper-pigmentation and Steiner Haircare. This is not a retailer so much as a beauty salon, where you can register with them for an online consultation by one of their team of therapists on your beauty regimen, find out about food and fitness for health and have your beauty questions answered. If you purchase from their online shop you'll find lots of gift ideas, excellent Elemis travel collections and gift wrapping.

Site Usability:	★★★★	Based:	UK
Product Range:	★★★	Express Delivery Option? (UK)	Yes
Price Range:	Luxury/Medium	Gift Wrapping Option?	Yes
Delivery Area:	Worldwide	Returns Procedure:	Down to you

www.yearsyounger.co.uk

I have to confess to having been a bit sceptical when I first looked at this website but it certainly didn't take me long to be converted as the advice here is intelligent, practical and easy to read. Years Younger is all about helping to make you look and feel younger and offers lots of advice on skincare, make-up, hair care, style and fashion – how to find the right hair colour, for example, or how to apply makeup properly. You can buy products such as GHD straighteners, Natural Elements skincare and Glominerals cosmetics as well.

Site Usability:	★★★★★	Based:	UK
Product Range:	★★★★	Express Delivery Option? (UK)	Yes
Price Range:	Medium	Gift Wrapping Option?	No
Delivery Area:	UK	Returns Procedure:	Down to you

www.zelens.co.uk

You may not have heard of this line of hi tech skin care products: Zelens is a very small, expensive and specialist range of Day, Night and Eye creams, formulated by leading skin ageing and cancer specialist, Dr Marko Lens. They have two ranges – Skin Science, which is a natural cellular protector and rejuvenation cream, and Fullerene C60, an extremely potent anti-oxidant. There's a great deal of product information on the website but if you want to know more I suggest that you give them a call.

Site Usability:	★★★★	Based:	UK
Product Range:	★★★	Express Delivery Option? (UK)	No
Price Range:	Luxury	Gift Wrapping Option?	No
Delivery Area:	Worldwide	Returns Procedure:	Down to you

Chapter 40

Spas and Pamper Days Out

Here you'll find some real treats for yourself, whether you just want a day to de-stress or a week away on your own. Be slightly wary of buying for someone else unless you're absolutely sure that your gift will be used and if you want to give a spa day as a present I suggest that you book it and go along as well. If I'm repeating myself I apologise – I just know that these can be really expensive presents and think how upsetting it would be if your gift went to waste. Yes it's happened in my family – not with spa days out but with driving days out, twice, and I wouldn't want it to happen to you.

One way you can never go wrong, in my opinion, is to give someone a gift voucher for their favourite local salon. So rather than giving them a manicure or massage they can choose for themselves which treatment they go for. As another of my 'please buy this for me rather than a piece of kitchen equipment' presents I really, really know about this.

Sites to Visit

www.leadingspasoftheworld.com

All you need to know here is when you want to go (did I say this was for a gift? I must have been mad), roughly where you want to go, i.e. which country, and you're away. Use their excellent search facility to find the most luxurious spas throughout the world, where you can choose from spas with hydrotherapy, Ayurvedic spas, spas with Yoga, Pilates and Tai Chi or somewhere gorgeous to just relax and be pampered. If you are going to choose one of these as a gift, make absolutely sure you're free to go as well.

Site Usability:	★★★★★	Price Range:	Luxury
Product Range:	★★★★★	Delivery Area:	Worldwide

www.spabreak.co.uk

Dedicated to UK spas only, Spa Break offers excellent and comprehensive information on luxury spas all over the country. There's plenty of advice and pictures to help you make up your mind where you want to go, and once you've decided you can purchase a gift voucher for a specific monetary value or type of break, which will be sent to you or whoever you want together with the relevant colour brochure.

Site Usability:	★★★★★	Delivery Area:	UK
Product Range:	★★★★	Based:	UK
Price Range:	Luxury/Medium		

www.spafinder.com

This is much more than just a global spa locator. Here you can easily discover spas anywhere in the world offering the specific services you require and contact them directly through the website's links. You can see so many wonderful pictures of each spa that, if you're anything like me, you'll want to book something immediately. You can order the Worldwide Spa Directory here or the Luxury Spa Finder Magazine, check out day spa deals and group specials and buy vouchers to spas throughout Europe. Next time you need a bit of pampering definitely take a look here.

Site Usability:	★★★★★	Delivery Area:	Worldwide
Product Range:	★★★★★	Based:	UK
Price Range:	Luxury/Medium		

www.thanksdarling.com

Yes thanks indeed, here are some wonderful pampering spa breaks and days out, mainly in the south of England, where on ordering you (or your chosen recipient) are sent an open dated voucher pack for the break you've chosen, whether it's a 'Special Chill Out Spa Break for Two' or just a 'Luxury Pamper Day'. You'll no doubt be extremely popular if you give one of these as a gift for someone and hopefully you'll be invited along.

Site Usability:	★★★★	Delivery Area:	UK
Product Range:	★★★★	Based:	UK
Price Range:	Luxury/Medium	Express Delivery Option? (UK)	No

www.thespasdirectory.com

Whatever you're looking for, whether it's a relaxing and pampering day out, a Pilates class or fitness advice you'll find it here on thespadirectory's advanced search facility. There's almost too much to choose from as the site covers the whole world. Does it make you feel better or worse to discover that the spa of your dreams is in Baja, Mexico? However, you'll surely find one nearer to home while you wait for your chance to leap on a plane. The site is very clean and clear and there are full profiles with pictures on every spa listed and a direct link through to each spa's website.

Site Usability:	★★★★	Delivery Area:	Worldwide
Product Range:	★★★★	Based:	UK
Price Range:	Luxury/Medium	Express Delivery Option? (UK)	No

Section 6
At Home

At Home

This section is for everything 'At Home', from lighting, pretty home accessories and storage ideas right up to your next whirlpool bath and set of kitchen table and chairs.

Because the internet allows you to see so many different ranges of products together; you can visit small craft retailers buried in deepest Suffolk (for example) right up to large department stores and everything in between.

You may prefer to traipse round the bathroom shops to find your new chic stone sunk glass basin and accessories but needless to say I definitely wouldn't. Even if you end up not actually placing your order online I'd suggest that you have a good look at what's available as you can see far more options for everything than you could in a week in the shops, (unless you totally wore yourself out, of course). The same is true for modern and traditional dining room and conservatory furniture, beds and bedding, kitchen appliances and accessories, table linens, glassware and place settings.

Just a word here on the appliance front: don't forget that when you've decided on the make and model you want you should do a price comparison check. I hope, because I've been going on about it so much, that you'll automatically compare prices, but just in case …

Happy home shopping.

Chapter 41

In the Bedroom

Bedlinen and Accessories   Bedroom Furniture

I can never quite decide if I'm a Toile de Jouey person or a minimal white bedlinen person – there are so many beautiful duvet and quilt covers to choose from it makes it very hard to be certain. What it usually comes down to for me, particularly because I have a large family and we like to have friends to stay, is a combination of quality and price. What I buy has to have the right unfussy look (well you don't call Toile de Jouey fussy, surely?) be of a good quality and a reasonable price.

Thankfully now there are lots of online retailers who have realised that most of us don't want to spend over £100 for our next duvet cover and are offering high quality at good prices. Take a look at www.thewhitecompany.com and also www.kingofcotton.com and you'll see what I mean.

When we're talking about bedroom furniture there's a different story to tell. If you want your cupboards totally built in then I suggest that you take a look round at what's available online and decide on the style, but you'll probably want someone to come out and do all the measuring up etc. If it's beds and bedroom furniture, however, you can of course do the measuring yourself and order online, only calling for advice if you need to.

There is such a marvellous choice here, from antique repro to traditional and contemporary styles and beds from the extremely reasonable kind to the sky's-the-limit kind. Don't forget to check when you're ordering that your new bed includes the mattress as often you have to order that separately. My daughter, having finally persuaded me into buying her a new bed, chose a beauty (not extravagant, just extremely well thought out for at 16-year-olds room) and totally within her budget. I'm sure you've guessed what I'm going to say next; no, it didn't include the mattress and yes, I have given in. I'm far too much of a softy as my kids, if they're being honest, will admit. Oh well.

Sites to Visit

Bedlinen and Accessories

www.armoirelinen.com

The next time you're buying bedlinen for your yacht, stop off here and take a look (and yes I am being serious). Armoire have created a range of luxe bedlinen specifically for yachts and five star hotels and now you can buy into their collection of pure linen and heirloom Egyptian cottons plus blankets, robes and towels. Having said that you're definitely not going to be surprised that the prices here are steep; neither should you be surprised that the quality is fabulous and that everything can be monogrammed.

Site Usability:	★★★★★	Based:	UK
Product Range:	★★★	Express Delivery Option? (UK)	No
Price Range:	Luxury	Gift Wrapping Option?	No
Delivery Area:	Worldwide	Returns Procedure:	Down to you

www.baer-ingram.com

Baer and Ingram design and print their own exclusive fabrics which you can order online. The collection includes florals, Toile de Jouey, patchwork, polka dots and stripes in a choice of colourways. You'll also find some lovely gifts and home accessories such as lighting, painted furniture, tablelinen and presents for tinies. You can order most of their products online but if you want something made to order, such as blinds, headboards, curtains or cushions you need to give them a call.

Site Usability:	★★★★	Based:	UK
Product Range:	★★★★	Express Delivery Option? (UK)	No
Price Range:	Luxury/Medium	Gift Wrapping Option?	No
Delivery Area:	Worldwide	Returns Procedure:	Down to you

www.biju.co.uk

Luxurious bathrobes and towels, cashmere blankets (at a faint inducing price) and throws and a wonderful collection of table linen, Missoni tableware, mats and trays are just some of the items you can choose from on this treasure trove of a website where they also offer enchanting children's bedding and bedroom accessories. There's so much here that you need to have time for a good browse. They also offer a personalisation embroidery service on their bathrobes and towels to help you create totally individual gifts.

Site Usability:	★★★★	Based:	UK
Product Range:	★★★★	Express Delivery Option? (UK)	No
Price Range:	Luxury/Medium	Gift Wrapping Option?	No
Delivery Area:	Worldwide	Returns Procedure:	Down to you

www.cathkidston.co.uk

Cath Kidston started her company over ten years ago in a small shop in Notting Hill, selling second-hand furniture and vintage fabrics. She soon began to design her own fabric and wallpaper, creating signature floral prints which have come to stand for her unique look. On her colourful website you'll see some really pretty and different bedlinen and bedspreads with pattern names such as 'New Bubbles' and 'Vintage Posy' plus crochet blankets and even sleeping bags.

Site Usability:	★★★★	Based:	UK
Product Range:	★★★★	Express Delivery Option? (UK)	Yes
Price Range:	Medium	Gift Wrapping Option?	Yes
Delivery Area:	Worldwide	Returns Procedure:	Down to you

www.designersguild.com

You'll find Tricia Guild's gorgeously coloured bedlinen here both for grown-ups and children, plus very different towels, bedspreads and throws, small leather goods and Fragrant Home from Designers Guild – a beautiful collection of home fragrance and luxury body products. If you haven't come across Designers Guild until now but you like pretty, colourful designs then take a look here.

Site Usability:	★★★★	Based:	UK
Product Range:	★★★	Express Delivery Option? (UK)	Yes
Price Range:	Luxury/Medium/Very Good Value	Gift Wrapping Option	Yes
Delivery Area:	UK	Returns Procedure:	Down to you

www.egyptiancottonstore.com

If you like beautiful bedlinen you'll love this attractively presented website, where you can buy top quality Egyptian Cotton (of course) duvet covers and sheets, goosedown and cotton duvets and pillows, nursery bedding, towels and bathrobes plus elegant table linen. Delivery is free in the UK and they'll ship worldwide. Everything here is expensive, but then for the quality you would expect it.

Site Usability:	★★★★★	Based:	UK
Product Range:	★★★	Express Delivery Option? (UK)	Yes
Price Range:	Luxury	Gift Wrapping Option	Yes
Delivery Area:	Worldwide	Returns Procedure:	Down to you

www.hibiscushome.com

Here you'll find an eclectic mix of luxury soft furnishings, full of colour and detail such as embroidery, beads and sequins with inspirations from countries such as India and Morocco. The website is divided into sections with titles such as Beach Boutique, Coco Morocco, Samiksha and Shanghai Chic and there are gorgeous treats to be found in each one. Luxury gift wrapping is standard.

Site Usability:	★★★★	Based:	UK
Product Range:	★★★	Express Delivery Option? (UK)	No
Price Range:	Medium	Gift Wrapping Option?	Yes
Delivery Area:	Worldwide	Returns Procedure:	Down to you

www.kingofcotton.co.uk

If you haven't already come across this website you'll probably be delighted to do so now, particularly if you have several bedrooms in your house, like high quality bedlinen (and towels) but don't want to pay the earth – the best for less, as it were. At King of Cotton you'll find bedlinen, duvets, pillows and mattress covers, towels and robes at really good prices and the service is excellent. Bear in mind that the initial prices don't include VAT and contact them if you want express delivery.

Site Usability:	★★★★★	Based:	UK
Product Range:	★★★★	Express Delivery Option? (UK)	No
Price Range:	Medium/Very Good Value	Gift Wrapping Option?	No
Delivery Area:	Worldwide	Returns Procedure:	Down to you

www.lumadirect.com

If your preference for your bedroom is pretty colours and florals then don't shop here. If, however, you prefer soft stylish neutrals then this is an excellent website for you, where all the fabrics are luxurious organic cottons, environmentally-friendly linens and silks and pure wools, including pashmina, merino and angora. Contact them for EU deliveries.

Site Usability:	★★★★★	Based:	UK
Product Range:	★★★★	Express Delivery Option? (UK)	Yes
Price Range:	Medium	Gift Wrapping Option?	No
Delivery Area:	EU	Returns Procedure:	Down to you

www.maisoncollection.com

Maison offer a really pretty collection of plain and patterned high quality and traditionally styled bed linen and bedspreads with detailing such as embroidery, hemstitching and lace edging. For some of the designs you'll find accessories such as lavender bags, tissue box holders and laundry bags. There's also a very feminine choice of gifts such as lace covered clothes hangers and fine linen guest towels plus lovely children's bed linen.

Site Usability:	★★★★★	Based:	UK
Product Range:	★★★★★	Express Delivery Option? (UK)	Yes
Price Range:	Medium	Gift Wrapping Option?	No
Delivery Area:	Worldwide	Returns Procedure:	Down to you

www.monogrammedlinenshop.co.uk

For the past 25 years The Monogrammed Linen Shop has provided classical and contemporary household linens to customers from all over the world. They only use the most beautiful laces and embroideries together with the finest cottons, linens, and silks to produce luxurious bedlinen, table linen and nightwear. They also offer perfect ideas for gifts for all occasions and offer an exquisite babywear collection going up to age 4. Their monogramming service rarely takes more than ten working days.

Site Usability:	★★★★	Based:	UK
Product Range:	★★★★	Express Delivery Option? (UK)	No
Price Range:	Luxury/Medium	Gift Wrapping Option?	No
Delivery Area:	Worldwide	Returns Procedure:	Down to you

www.reallylindabarker.co.uk

Click on 'Sleeping' on this busy website and you'll find a small but prettily edited range of bedlinen and bedspreads, throws, cushions, lamps and porcelain and attractive bedroom furniture. Everything is designed to work together in a very attractive, light and modern style which is 'reallylindabarker' and all in her modern, natural style. In the 'Living' section there are lamps, mirrors, cushions, clocks and storage ideas for the rest of your home.

Site Usability:	★★★★★	Based:	UK
Product Range:	★★★	Express Delivery Option? (UK)	Yes
Price Range:	Medium	Gift Wrapping Option?	No
Delivery Area:	Worldwide but phone if delivery is for overseas	Returns Procedure:	Down to you

www.thelaundry.co.uk

The Laundry's exclusive collection covers everything from bedwear to bedlinen, linen cupboard accessories to laundry room essentials and everything in between. Their philosophy is to blend contemporary with vintage to create a highly individual look. This is not a large range but something quite unusual; take their pretty zinnia print and mix it with their spot printed pure cotton and you'll get the idea.

Site Usability:	★★★★	Based:	UK
Product Range:	★★★	Express Delivery Option? (UK)	No
Price Range:	Medium	Gift Wrapping Option?	No
Delivery Area:	Worldwide but phone if delivery is for overseas	Returns Procedure:	Down to you

www.thelinenworks.com

The Linen Works specialises in products from Northern Europe made mainly from natural materials. You'll find olivewood utensils, lightweight enamelware from Austria, super soft pure virgin wool rugs and throws from Germany and eiderdowns from France. New for autumn is their own range of bolsters, tablecloths and oilcloths produced from their French fabric collection. This is a beautifully and simply laid out website and very easy to get round.

Site Usability:	★★★★★	Based:	UK
Product Range:	★★★★	Express Delivery Option? (UK)	No
Price Range:	Medium	Gift Wrapping Option?	Yes
Delivery Area:	Worldwide	Returns Procedure:	Down to you

www.thewhitecompany.com

Here's absolutely everything you need for stylish bedrooms, with a collection of beautifully made contemporary bed linen (think white, cream, natural and pale blue) and luxurious throws and blankets from cashmere to quilted velvet in colours such as pebble, willow, chocolate and taupe. They also offer luxury duvets and pillows and bedroom accessories such as rugs, mirrors and toiletries. There are lots of ideas for the rest of your home as well, plus lounge wear, gorgeous toiletries and candles and other gifts.

Site Usability:	★★★★★	Based:	UK
Product Range:	★★★★★	Express Delivery Option? (UK)	Yes
Price Range:	Medium	Gift Wrapping Option?	Yes
Delivery Area:	Worldwide	Returns Procedure:	Down to you

www.tonderandtonder.co.uk

This is a small but extremely pretty collection of pure cotton bedlinen and accessories, all designed by Hannah Tonder. The colours she offers are cool and crisp blue, taupe and pink incorporated into traditional designs such as Ticking Stripe, Cotton Lavender, Zig Zag or pure white. You can also order her enchanting baby quilts and towel sets. Nothing is overpriced, you need to ask specially for express delivery and she'll ship worldwide.

Site Usability:	★★★★	Based:	UK
Product Range:	★★★	Express Delivery Option? (UK)	Yes
Price Range:	Medium	Gift Wrapping Option?	No
Delivery Area:	Worldwide	Returns Procedure:	Down to you

www.volgalinen.co.uk

The Volga Linen Company is a family run, British company that sells an exquisite collection of pure linen from Russia. The collection consists of table linen, bed linen, ready to hang curtains and a children's range and accessories. They produce plain weaves, fabric with drawn thread work embroidery, damasks, and richly coloured paisleys. Also take a look at their new clothing range online.

Site Usability:	★★★★	Based:	UK
Product Range:	★★★	Express Delivery Option? (UK)	No
Price Range:	Luxury	Gift Wrapping Option?	Yes
Delivery Area:	Worldwide	Returns Procedure:	Down to you

Bedroom Furniture

www.alexandermiles.co.uk

Here you'll find the forefront of design in bedroom furniture with beautiful contemporary timber designs in beech, oak or walnut; wrought iron, and glass and steel beds, beds in leather and fabric and modern divans. As these are unique designs made with the highest quality materials you wouldn't expect to find anything other than high prices here so if you're on a tight budget I wouldn't waste your time. If you like the style here you'll find bedroom and modern occasional furniture as well.

Site Usability:	★★★★★	Based:	UK
Product Range:	★★★★	Express Delivery Option? (UK)	No
Price Range:	Luxury	Gift Wrapping Option?	No
Delivery Area:	UK	Returns Procedure:	In agreement with them

www.bedworld.net

Choose from a huge range of beds from this online retailer, from cheap and cheerful to beautifully crafted bateau lit and beds up to superking size with all grades of mattresses. Nineteen brand names are offered including the well known such as Silentnight, Hypnos and Slumberland and some lesser known brands. They also have a twenty-four hour delivery service on some mattresses and UK delivery is free on orders over £300.

Site Usability:	★★★★★	Based:	UK
Product Range:	★★★★★	Express Delivery Option? (UK)	No
Price Range:	Luxury/Medium	Gift Wrapping Option?	No
Delivery Area:	UK — free to most UK postcodes	Returns Procedure:	They will collect

www.cannockbeds.co.uk

There's a really good selection of beds here, from wooden, brass and leather bedsteads to a small range of excellent styles for children. You'll find single up to king-size beds and you can choose from the different qualities of mattress available (and if you need a mattress in a hurry you can order it for next day delivery). Once you've picked your new bed you can choose from the extensive range of furniture to go with it, including bedside tables, blanket boxes, mirrors and wardrobes.

Site Usability:	★★★★★	Based:	UK
Product Range:	★★★★★	Express Delivery Option? (UK)	Some items
Price Range:	Luxury/Medium	Gift Wrapping Option?	No
Delivery Area:	UK most postcodes	Returns Procedure:	They will collect/7 day home trial

www.indigofurniture.co.uk

Indigo is based in Matlock, Derbyshire and specialises in solid wood and leather furniture for bedroom, living room and dining room, some of which is made from oak beams recycled from factories and old mills. Perfect furniture, in fact, if you live in a loft or a barn. The excellent news here is that you can buy just about everything online and they're pictured it in such a way that you can see several views of each item. If only more people did that.

Site Usability:	★★★★★	Based:	UK
Product Range:	★★★★★	Express Delivery Option? (UK)	No
Price Range:	Luxury/Medium	Gift Wrapping Option?	No
Delivery Area:	UK most postcodes	Returns Procedure:	They will collect

www.pinehouse.co.uk

This is a cleverly designed website where you first select the room in which you're looking for your new furniture (living room, kitchen, bedroom etc.), then select the item you need, at which point you'll be offered thumbnails of everything in that range (and there's a really large choice). Once you've chosen (a table, for example) you can select your finish from those shown online. If this all sounds complicated it really isn't but there is a great deal to choose from for every room in the house so be prepared to spend a while.

Site Usability:	★★★★★	Based:	UK
Product Range:	★★★★★	Express Delivery Option? (UK)	No
Price Range:	Luxury/Medium	Gift Wrapping Option?	No
Delivery Area:	UK	Returns Procedure:	In agreement with them

www.pineonline.co.uk

This site is perfect if you're looking for well priced beds and bedroom furniture with a wide range from traditional styles to four poster beds and children's bunk beds. There's a good selection of furniture to match most beds plus a small range of mattresses, duvets and pillows and bedlinen by Esprit. They'll deliver free using their own courier service to most places in the UK and delivery time is normally 14–21 days.

Site Usability:	★★★★★	Based:	UK
Product Range:	★★★★★	Express Delivery Option? (UK)	No
Price Range:	Medium/Very Good Value	Gift Wrapping Option?	No
Delivery Area:	UK	Returns Procedure:	In agreement with them

www.seventh-heaven.co.uk

A comprehensive website for antique style beds and bedding where you can choose from standard, four poster and half tester beds in brass and iron and timber, Louis XV or country style beds and daybeds. The prices are what you would expect for the quality of the workmanship. The look is traditional and solid so if you're into contemporary styling this won't be for you. However, the extensive range of bedlinen covers everything from the chic and modern to pretty and old fashioned.

Site Usability:	★★★★★	Based:	UK
Product Range:	★★★★★	Express Delivery Option? (UK)	No
Price Range:	Luxury	Gift Wrapping Option?	No
Delivery Area:	Worldwide	Returns Procedure:	In agreement with them

www.featherandblack.com

A wide selection of traditional beds and bedroom furniture where you can choose from wood finish (cherry, oak, maple or painted) or metal, leather and upholstered styles and there are some good ideas for storage as well. You'll also find mattresses and a range of bedlinen in designs exclusive to Feather and Black which they'll ship to you by next day delivery. If you want any advice you can call them to discuss your requirements. They offer a full assembly service and they'll even take the packaging materials away with them.

Site Usability:	★★★★★	Based:	UK
Product Range:	★★★★★	Express Delivery Option? (UK)	On some items
Price Range:	Luxury/Medium	Gift Wrapping Option?	No
Delivery Area:	UK	Returns Procedure:	Down to you

www.treatyourhome.com

This is a really busy, Irish-based furniture website with an excellent range of furniture for the home, from beds and bedroom furniture (including children's bunks), dining tables and chairs, conservatory and garden furniture and sofas and sofa beds. Delivery is free to most places in the UK and Ireland on orders over £500. Use their live online support if you want immediate advice and be prepared to spend quite a lot of time at this home department store.

Site Usability:	★★★★★	Based:	UK
Product Range:	★★★★★	Express Delivery Option? (UK)	No
Price Range:	Luxury/Medium	Gift Wrapping Option?	No
Delivery Area:	UK and Ireland	Returns Procedure:	In agreement with them

Chapter 42

Bath Time

Towels and Bathroom Accessories

Bathroom Fittings

I'm only going to say one thing about towels and that's to advise you to buy the very best that you can afford. Ignore those amazingly cheap offers; you'll definitely get what you pay for. My wretched family like to have clean towels every day (the kids, that is) and I've totally failed to convince them that it would be helpful, well brought up and tidy (what sort of a word is that?) if they picked their towels up and hung them over our huge, old-fashioned bathroom radiator to dry. Pick them up? No surely not. Towels are meant to be wrapped around oneself after a shower and then dropped, surely?

So back to quality. The best ones wash better, keep their colour better and stay fluffy longer, it's as simple as that. So it's a truly false economy to go for cheap and cheerful. The number of washes our towels get enables me to tell you this with great authority.

Bathroom accessories and fittings are rather like those for the bedroom. There are lots to choose from and it's well worth having an explore here. Thankfully it's the kind of explore you can do with a cup of coffee at your side, no heavy handbag over your shoulder and just a mouse and a screen to hand. Doesn't this make life easier? I defy you to tell me it doesn't.

Sites to Visit

Towels and Bathroom Accessories

www.christy-towels.com

The Christy at home website is really beautifully designed – clean, clear and modern – and definitely makes you want to buy. Don't think of Christy just for towels, although there's a wide colour range to choose from, but look also at their high quality bedlinen in mostly neutral shades and cotton blends and other products including robes, cushions, throws and contemporary bathroom accessories.

Site Usability:	★★★★	Express Delivery Option? (UK)	No
Product Range:	★★★	Gift Wrapping Option?	No
Price Range:	Medium	Based:	UK
Delivery Area:	UK	Returns Procedure:	Down to you

www.gaiamdirect.co.uk

Gaiam is a fusion of the words 'Gaia' (the name of Mother Earth from the Minoan civilisation in ancient Crete) and 'I am', to remind us that we are all interconnected with the Earth, air and water. All the furniture and accessories here are made from natural materials and alongside some lovely gift ideas and hard-to-find skincare there are organic cotton towels and robes, matresses, pillows and duvets. Call for overseas delivery.

Site Usability:	★★★★★	Express Delivery Option? (UK)	Yes
Product Range:	★★★★	Gift Wrapping Option?	No
Price Range:	Medium	Based:	UK
Delivery Area:	Worldwide	Returns Procedure:	Down to you

www.towels.co.uk

This is an offshoot of excellent home accessories website Biju.co.uk, where you can find a really attractively photographed range of bathrobes, from the expensive hand made English variety to simple well priced waffle robes (and children's bathrobes); towels in a wide selection of colours and textures and other tempting bathroom treats. It's a very well laid out website with easy access to all the information you could need.

Site Usability:	★★★★	Based:	UK
Product Range:	★★★★	Express Delivery Option? (UK)	No
Price Range:	Luxury/Medium	Gift Wrapping Option?	No
Delivery Area:	Worldwide	Returns Procedure:	Down to you

Also visit these websites for Towels and Bathroom Accessories

Website Address	You'll Find it in
www.thewhitecompany.com	Chapter 41: In the Bedroom
www.johnlewis.com	Chapter 44: The Kitchen
www.kingofcotton.co.uk	Chapter 41: In the Bedroom

Bathroom Fittings

www.bathroomheaven.com

This is a seriously large online bathroom shop but what is so good here is the 'quick find' menu on the right of the home page, taking you in just one click to the product you're looking for. There's pretty well everything here you could possibly need, from traditional to modern bathrooms (and a small range of modern accessories) and each item had been beautifully and stylishly photographed.

Site Usability:	★★★★★	Based:	UK
Product Range:	★★★★★	Express Delivery Option? (UK)	Yes for some items
Price Range:	Luxury/Medium	Gift Wrapping Option?	No
Delivery Area:	UK	Returns Procedure:	In agreement with them

www.bathroomluxury.co.uk

This is not the world of your basic plastic bath but an entirely different place. Here you'll find only high quality and elegance for that 'interior designed' look. Freestanding 'designer' baths with luxurious brassware, deluxe 11 jet whirlpool baths to massage your stress away each day and taps from the extremely modern to Victoriana are all available, with excellent clear photographs and drawings and full details and dimensions. A lovely site

Site Usability:	★★★★★	Based:	UK
Product Range:	★★★★	Express Delivery Option? (UK)	No
Price Range:	Luxury/Medium	Gift Wrapping Option?	No
Delivery Area:	UK	Returns Procedure:	In agreement with them

www.czechandspeake.com

Czech & Speake are a worldwide luxury brand of bathroom & kitchen fittings and accessories, creating unique and timeless products that combine authentic English traditional style and modern design. You can only view their products online (and then call them to order) but you can buy their marvellous aromatic fragrances and shaving requisites, all of which are perfect for gifts. Choose from Cuba, Neroli, No 88, Oxford and Cambridge as bath oils, colognes and aftershaves.

Site Usability:	★★★★	Based:	UK
Product Range:	★★★	Express Delivery Option? (UK)	No
Price Range:	Luxury/Medium	Gift Wrapping Option?	No
Delivery Area:	Worldwide	Returns Procedure:	Down to you

www.heals.co.uk

I'm sure you'll have heard of this famous store on Tottenham Court Road in London, famous for their contemporary styling for furniture and accessories throughout the home, most of which are exclusive to Heals. Shelves, cup holders, shower curtains, towel rails and medicine cabinets are just some of the items you can buy here alongside bathroom storage, toiletries, towels and robes.

Site Usability:	★★★★	Based:	UK
Product Range:	★★★★★	Express Delivery Option? (UK)	Yes
Price Range:	Medium	Gift Wrapping Option?	No
Delivery Area:	UK	Returns Procedure:	Down to you

www.plumbworld.co.uk

Calling themselves 'The UK's largest online specialist retailer of bathrooms', this busy website offers a huge choice from the very modern to the traditional and from budget prices up to their luxury whirlpool bath. As well as baths of all styles and descriptions you'll find mirrors, bathroom furniture, extractor fans, bathroom scales and plumbing equipment. They deliver to anywhere in the UK including the Channel Isles.

Site Usability:	★★★★★	Based:	UK
Product Range:	★★★★★	Express Delivery Option? (UK)	No
Price Range:	Luxury/Medium	Gift Wrapping Option?	No
Delivery Area:	UK	Returns Procedure:	Email them for a returns number first

www.premierbathrooms.co.uk

Premier Bathrooms specialise in easy access and assisted entry baths incorporating hydrotherapy for the less able. They're part of a family group of companies and have been in existence since 1985. They operate worldwide. You need to click on the Contact link and get them to call you in order to discuss what you're looking for with one of their advisers, to make sure that you buy the right product both for you and for your home.

Site Usability:	★★★★	Based:	UK
Product Range:	★★★	Express Delivery Option? (UK)	No
Price Range:	Luxury/Medium	Gift Wrapping Option?	No
Delivery Area:	UK	Returns Procedure:	In agreement with them

www.taps4less.co.uk

You know that moment when your showerhead stops working properly on your traditional style bath and you don't have a clue where to go to get a replacement – let alone one that isn't going to take a great deal of time and mean searching in a huge warehouse-like shop? Well, here's the answer and in a very short space of time you'll find what you're looking for and it'll arrive at your door. The same goes for all sorts of taps, heated towel rails, tiles and ceramics and lots of other bathroom accessories. Delivery is free.

Site Usability:	★★★★★	Based:	UK
Product Range:	★★★★★	Express Delivery Option? (UK)	No
Price Range:	Medium	Gift Wrapping Option?	No
Delivery Area:	UK	Returns Procedure:	Down to you

www.victorianbathrooms.com

If you're a traditionalist and like the old fashioned style of bathroom you'll really like this Yorkshire based website, where you'll find a very good selection of cast iron roll-top baths, old-fashioned style mixer taps and some whirlpool baths. They frequently have some excellent special offers from across their range and if you live in Yorkshire they'll come out and re-enamel your bath for you.

Site Usability:	★★★★★	Based:	UK
Product Range:	★★★★★	Express Delivery Option? (UK)	No
Price Range:	Luxury/Medium	Gift Wrapping Option?	No
Delivery Area:	UK	Returns Procedure:	In agreement with them

www.victoriaplumb.com

After some of the very busy bathroom websites listed above this one is a joy to visit, it's laid out so that you can get from one product to another with ease, and everything is beautifully photographed too. You can choose from individual products with a range taking you from Edwardian roll-top baths to modern high jet shower units plus bathroom furniture, mirrors and accessories from the well priced to the luxury. You'll also find a very good choice of small bathroom accessories.

Site Usability:	★★★★★	Based:	UK
Product Range:	★★★★★	Express Delivery Option? (UK)	No
Price Range:	Luxury/Medium	Gift Wrapping Option?	No
Delivery Area:	UK	Returns Procedure:	Larger pieces in agreement with them

Chapter 43

Living Space –
Furniture and Accessories

Furniture – Tableware and Tablelinen – Decorative Accessories

It seems to me that very few people have a 'dining room' as such nowadays, preferring to use the extra room as a study or sitting room and having family meals and informal dinners in the kitchen - we certainly do. Such was definitely not the case when I was a child, with formal meals the norm, but nowadays we would much prefer to entertain the hoards casually, still creating a pretty table with candles and attractive glasses and dinnerware but without so much of the fuss. You may be like us or you may still prefer the formal approach, either way there are tables and chairs of all possible styles available to see and buy online, from reproduction antique refectory tables to the most modern glass and wrought iron. I have to say that I love the look of a glass table but think that trying to keep it finger-mark free would be just too much of a bore. Over to you on that one.

Just one word here - make absolutely sure that you've measured up if you're buying a new sofa, dining table or any other piece of furniture online. These are costly items to ship out to you and the last thing you want is to have to try and persuade a bad tempered driver to take your new leather sofa back because it doesn't fit (I'm not saying that they're all bad tempered but I think in this circumstance it might be justified). If I'm telling you to do something you would do automatically I apologise, but I thought it should be said.

Where tableware and linens are concerned you can choose from all the major brands such as Wedgwood, Waterford and Villeroy and Boch to Provencal styles and you can even order from Provençe-based online retailers. Once again there's just so much to see.

This is of course also an excellent area for gifts - so when you've exhausted the options in Section 9 The Gift Shop, you can have a browse round here too.

Sites to Visit

Furniture

www.barkerandstonehouse.com

There's furniture here (plus home accessories) for every room in your house, from dining room and living room to bedroom and home office so have a good look round. There's also a wide range of styles from modern to traditional although the emphasis is definitely modern. The strength of this retailer particularly lies in the amount of assistance they offer; you can call them for advice on any of their products and they also provide UK wide delivery using their own fleet of vans and trained drivers.

Site Usability:	★★★★★	Based:	UK
Product Range:	★★★★★	Express Delivery Option? (UK)	No
Price Range:	Luxury/Medium	Gift Wrapping Option?	No
Delivery Area:	UK	Returns Procedure:	In agreement with them

www.darlingsofchelsea.co.uk

If your taste is for leather sofas and chairs of the highest quality you should have a look round this website, whose creators have been in the business of making such furniture for over forty years. Most items, with the exception of their Italia range, are handmade in the UK using solid hardwood frames, aniline leathers for the contemporary range and European hides for the traditional styles. They aim to deliver in five to seven weeks and it's a worldwide service. You'll also find study chairs, sofa beds and leather bean bags here.

Site Usability:	★★★★★	Based:	UK
Product Range:	★★★★★	Express Delivery Option? (UK)	No
Price Range:	Luxury/Medium	Gift Wrapping Option?	No
Delivery Area:	Worldwide	Returns Procedure:	In agreement with them

www.herringport.co.uk

Based in Gorleston-on-sea, this high quality furniture company (originally boat builders) specialises in superb pine, walnut and cherry, ash and oak furniture for kitchen, living and dining. Refectory tables, hand-painted kitchen dressers and wardrobes and four poster beds are just some of the items available here, all beautifully photographed. Most prices are on application so be prepared for them to be high although whatever you select will be an investment.

Site Usability:	★★★★	Based:	UK
Product Range:	★★★★	Express Delivery Option? (UK)	No
Price Range:	Luxury/Medium	Gift Wrapping Option?	No
Delivery Area:	UK	Returns Procedure:	In agreement with them

www.holloways.co.uk

This is a family business based in Worcestershire offering high quality willow, rattan, iron and glass traditional and contemporary conservatory furniture. There's a wide selection of styles, including Lloyd Loom, Plantation, Heritage (very beautiful and classic) and Java and the ranges include sofas, chairs, dining tables and coffee tables. Once you've decided which style you want they'll help you choose the fabric as well, and then you have to wait for about six weeks for delivery.

Site Usability:	★★★★★	Based:	UK
Product Range:	★★★★	Express Delivery Option? (UK)	No
Price Range:	Luxury/Medium	Gift Wrapping Option	No
Delivery Area:	UK	Returns Procedure:	Down to you in agreement with them

www.jwminteriors.com

Here you'll find furniture for everywhere in the home, from rustic French styling to hand painted finishes and solid pine and oak. The range is excellent so expect to spend some time here. As well as all of this you'll find genuine Lloyd Loom furniture from Spalding in Suffolk. This is available in about 27 different weaves and colours so you need to call them to ask for a brochure in order to see the different colourways. They deliver free of charge to anywhere in the UK on orders over £1000.

Site Usability:	★★★★★	Based:	UK
Product Range:	★★★★★	Express Delivery Option? (UK)	No
Price Range:	Luxury/Medium	Gift Wrapping Option?	No
Delivery Area:	UK	Returns Procedure:	Down to you

www.marston-and-langinger.com

With stores in London and New York, Marston and Langinger has the enviable reputation as a market leader in the manufacture of custom-made timber-and-glass conservatories, poolhouses and garden rooms. On their attractive website you can order from their range of furniture, lighting, garden tools, accessories, textiles, and Marston & Langinger's own-label domestic paint. Make sure you've plenty of time before you stop off here, there's a great deal of this beautiful collection to browse through.

Site Usability:	★★★★★	Based:	UK
Product Range:	★★★★★	Express Delivery Option? (UK)	No
Price Range:	Luxury/Medium	Gift Wrapping Option?	No
Delivery Area:	Worldwide	Returns Procedure:	Down to you

www.myakka.co.uk

Myakka is a family run business, specialising in hand crafted, solid wood furniture, unique home accessories and beautiful soft furnishings. The furniture ranges are Shaker, Classic, Contemporary, Mallani and Thakat and include some really attractive trunk tables and sideboards. In the textiles section you'll find rugs and gorgeous Indian fabric cushions, plus gift ideas such as vases and bowls, incense burners and wooden tile boxes.

Site Usability:	★★★★	Based:	UK
Product Range:	★★★	Express Delivery Option? (UK)	No
Price Range:	Luxury/Medium	Gift Wrapping Option?	No
Delivery Area:	Worldwide	Returns Procedure:	In agreement with them

www.okadirect.com

Oka has a really beautifully designed and photographed website where you'll find some inspirational ideas for your home and lovely gifts. Browse through their roomsets and pick out the individual items that would enhance your existing decor, or go for broke and buy them all. From throws, cushions, quilts and rugs to porcelain vases and elegant furniture there's a wealth of items to choose from.

Site Usability:	★★★★★	Based:	UK
Product Range:	★★★★★	Express Delivery Option? (UK)	Yes for Central London only
Price Range:	Medium	Gift Wrapping Option?	No
Delivery Area:	Worldwide	Returns Procedure:	Down to you

www.shimu.co.uk

Shimu offers the simple elegance of classical Chinese furniture based on the clean styles of the Ming Dynasty, with each item being hand made by craftsmen in their workshop in Shanghai. There are some quite large pieces of furniture here but also beautifully finished trunks and chests at not unreasonable prices and other small accessories. Allow 30 days for delivery and call them for overseas shipping.

Site Usability:	★★★★	Based:	UK
Product Range:	★★★★	Express Delivery Option? (UK)	No
Price Range:	Luxury/Medium	Gift Wrapping Option?	No
Delivery Area:	Worldwide	Returns Procedure:	In agreement with them

www.sofaworkshop.co.uk

Sofa Workshop has been in existence since 1985. 'We love sofas', is their motto and they certainly seem to, with a very high quality range of sofas in all shapes and sizes and with a huge range of covers from casual fabrics, to leather and classic designs and prices from around £300 to over £1500. They also have accessories such as bean bags, cushions, throws and benches. With a five year guarantee, free UK delivery and interest free credit available this site must be worth a serious look if you're looking for a new sofa.

Site Usability:	★★★★★	Based:	UK
Product Range:	★★★★★	Express Delivery Option? (UK)	No
Price Range:	Luxury/Medium	Gift Wrapping Option?	No
Delivery Area:	UK	Returns Procedure:	In agreement with them

www.touchstoneinteriors.com

For home accessory gifts or something special and new for your own home this is a lovely place to shop. The website is very clearly laid out so you can easily get to whatever you're looking for, be it soft furnishings, bathroom accessories, modern mirrors or cookware. The pictures are excellent and there's an enormous amount to choose from so allow yourself plenty of time.

Site Usability:	★★★★★	Based:	UK
Product Range:	★★★★★	Express Delivery Option? (UK)	Yes
Price Range:	Luxury/Medium	Gift Wrapping Option?	No
Delivery Area:	UK	Returns Procedure:	In agreement with them and within 7 days

Also take a look at the following for furniture online

Website Address	**You'll find it in**
www.lauraashley.com	Chapter 1: Fashion Online
www.johnlewis.com	Chapter 44: The Kitchen

Tableware and Tablelinen

www.emmabridgewater.co.uk

Emma Bridgewater is well known for her high quality pottery and clever and attractive designs such as Polka Dots, Hugs and Kisses and Hearts as well as her mug collections which include dogs, cats, birds and flowers. Every season she's bringing out new products, such as cutlery, glass, preserves and teas, all with her signature script. Almost every kitchen has one or two pieces of her pottery, the only question is; can you resist the urge to collect?

Site Usability:	★★★★★	Based:	UK
Product Range:	★★★★	Express Delivery Option? (UK)	Yes
Price Range:	Medium	Gift Wrapping Option?	Yes
Delivery Area:	Worldwide	Returns Procedure:	Down to you

www.davidmellordesign.com

David Mellor, Royal Designer for Industry, has an international reputation as designer, manufacturer and shopkeeper. Born in Sheffield, he has always specialised in metalwork and has often been described as 'the cutlery king'. On his website there's a selection of his modern stainless steel cutlery, plus contemporary high quality glass and tableware, kitchen tools and equipment.

Site Usability:	★★★★★	Based:	UK
Product Range:	★★★★	Express Delivery Option? (UK)	Yes
Price Range:	Luxury/Medium	Gift Wrapping Option?	Yes
Delivery Area:	Worldwide	Returns Procedure:	Down to you

www.dartington.co.uk

From bowls and vases to ice buckets, decanters, jugs and glassware Dartington have created the modern options to match contemporary design in your home or to make excellent gifts (particularly for wedding presents). The prices are reasonable and you can be certain that anything you order will be very well made. They'll deliver to you anywhere in the world: 7–14 days for overseas, and faster within the UK.

Site Usability:	★★★★★	Based:	UK
Product Range:	★★★	Express Delivery Option? (UK)	No
Price Range:	Medium	Gift Wrapping Option?	No
Delivery Area:	Worldwide	Returns Procedure:	Down to you

www.finetable.co.uk

FineTable offer a unique selection of linen and design-led dining accessories from across Europe from companies large and small, including unusual candles and candlesticks (with names such as 'single tangle' and 'tangelarbra'), Volga table linen, Carrol Boyes cheese knives and Julien Macdonald glass. Most items are available by mail order but you have to phone or email to place your order.

Site Usability:	★★★	Based:	UK
Product Range:	★★★	Express Delivery Option? (UK)	No
Price Range:	Medium	Gift Wrapping Option?	No
Delivery Area:	UK	Returns Procedure:	Down to you

www.french-brand.com

This is a France based retailer offering you all those home accessories you saw on your last trip but weren't able to sneak into your suitcase. Gorgeous and colourful table linen from Les Olivades and Jaquard Francais (and lots more), quilted cushions by Souleido and toiletries and home fragrance by Manuel Canovas and Jardin Secret are just some of the things you can order online. There's also a fantastic range of bed linen by designers such as Descamps and colourful beach towels as well.

Site Usability:	★★★★	Based:	France
Product Range:	★★★★★	Express Delivery Option? (UK)	No
Price Range:	Luxury/Medium	Gift Wrapping Option?	No
Delivery Area:	Worldwide	Returns Procedure:	Down to you

www.purpleandfinelinen.co.uk

At Purple and Fine Linen their pure linen tablecloths, placemats, napkins and runners are designed to offer a look of timeless luxury and simple elegance. As well as traditional white and ivory you can choose from their range in deep chilli red and damson (purple), which would be lovely for Christmas. These are definitely investment table linens and very beautiful.

Site Usability:	★★★★★	Based:	UK
Product Range:	★★★	Express Delivery Option? (UK)	Yes
Price Range:	Luxury/Medium	Gift Wrapping Option?	No
Delivery Area:	Worldwide	Returns Procedure:	Down to you

www.smallislandtrader.com

Small Island Trader is an excellent company (with an excellent website) offering not only china and glass from a wide range of designers and manufacturers but also kitchen equipment from juicers and steamers to copper and Le Creuset pots and pans, Sabatier knives, baking trays, and the Eva

Solo's range of kitchen and living products. Needless to say they can't carry everything they offer in stock and delivery time is very much dependent on what you order. Allow at least 28 days.

Site Usability:	★★★★★	Based:	UK
Product Range:	★★★★★	Express Delivery Option? (UK)	No
Price Range:	Luxury/Medium	Gift Wrapping Option?	No
Delivery Area:	Worldwide	Returns Procedure:	Down to you

www.tainpottery.co.uk

If you've paid a visit to the Scottish Highlands recently you'll certainly have come across this really attractive, country style hand painted pottery, depicting fish and fruit designs on warm and atmospheric backgrounds. You can find some lovely gifts here or put together a complete dinner service for yourself and you can be sure that what you buy is very special and different. They're happy to ship all over the world and you need to allow at least 7 days in the UK for your order to arrive.

Site Usability:	★★★★	Based:	UK
Product Range:	★★★	Express Delivery Option? (UK)	No
Price Range:	Medium	Gift Wrapping Option?	No
Delivery Area:	Worldwide	Returns Procedure:	Down to you

www.thefrenchhouse.net

As you would expect all the products here are from France; from tableware, linen and cutlery, to toiletries by Christian Lenart and Savon de Marseilles and elegant Anduze garden pots. Also a selection of pretty bedlinen in traditional French designs such as Toile de Jouey, Fleurs de Champs and Monogram. The descriptions and information on every item are clear and well written and everything is beautifully photographed. This website only delivers to the UK other than by special arrangement.

Site Usability:	★★★★	Based:	UK
Product Range:	★★★	Express Delivery Option? (UK)	No
Price Range:	Medium	Gift Wrapping Option?	No
Delivery Area:	UK	Returns Procedure:	Down to you

www.welch.co.uk

Robert Welch trained as a Silversmith at Birmingham College of Art. He then moved to the Royal College of Art in 1952, where he specialised exclusively in stainless steel production design. In 1965 he was awarded Royal Designer for Industry. Together with his son, William, he has designed some unusual home accessories which you can buy from their website, including candlesticks, bathroom accessories, flatware and pewter. Don't miss his hourglass salt and pepper holders.

Site Usability:	★★★★★	Express Delivery Option? (UK)	No
Product Range:	★★★	Gift Wrapping Option?	No
Price Range:	Luxury/Medium	Based:	UK
Delivery Area:	Worldwide	Returns Procedure:	Down to you

Also visit these websites for Tableware and Tablelinen

Website Address	You'll find it in
www.thewhitecompany.com	Chapter 41: In the Bedroom
www.johnlewis.com	Chapter 44: The Kitchen
www.volgalinen.com	Chapter 41: In the Bedroom

Decorative Accessories

www.abentleycushions.co.uk

If you're someone who likes to surround themselves with beautiful cushions you should definitely have a browse round this website, where there's an amazing choice including tapestry, quilted, velvet, woven and faux fur; plus plaids, animal and wildlife designs. They also offer wallhangings, throws, draught excluders and tapestry bags.

Site Usability:	★★★★	Based:	UK
Product Range:	★★★	Express Delivery Option? (UK)	No
Price Range:	Medium	Gift Wrapping Option?	No
Delivery Area:	Worldwide	Returns Procedure:	Down to you

www.alisonhenry.com

These are seriously gorgeous modern accessories, mainly in neutral colours, which would make superb gifts for weddings and other important occasions, or when you feel in the need of adding something really special to your home. There's a cut crystal fragrance bottle filled with Alison's signature bath oil, pure cashmere cushions and double sided throws plus other beautifully photographed objects.

Site Usability:	★★★★	Based:	UK
Product Range:	★★★	Express Delivery Option? (UK)	No
Price Range:	Luxury/Medium	Gift Wrapping Option?	No
Delivery Area:	UK	Returns Procedure:	Down to you

www.cabane.co.uk

Here's another website offering a wide selection of ideas for the home, influenced by traditional French style yet with a practical modern twist. Think of simply furnished cabins with crackling log fires, perched high on hillsides or wooden beach houses; full of light and you'll get the mood that's being created here. You'll find pretty bedspreads, cushions and blankets, Savon de Marseilles soaps and candles, colourful linen and cotton napkins and tablecloths.

Site Usability:	★★★★	Based:	UK
Product Range:	★★★★	Express Delivery Option? (UK)	Yes
Price Range:	Medium	Gift Wrapping Option?	No
Delivery Area:	Worldwide	Returns Procedure:	Down to you

www.casacopenhagen.com

Danish designer Theresa Bastrup Hasman has brought together a beautiful collection of cushions and soft furnishings grouped into categories with names such as Moroccan Nights, Indian Fairy Tales and Paisley Flowers. There's also a small section for children and they offer a bespoke service as well. Everything is made especially for you so you need to allow four weeks for delivery.

Site Usability:	★★★★	Based:	UK
Product Range:	★★★	Express Delivery Option? (UK)	No
Price Range:	Luxury/Medium	Gift Wrapping Option?	No
Delivery Area:	Worldwide	Returns Procedure:	Down to you

www.chelseatextiles.com

Chelsea Textiles re-creates antique fabrics, cushion designs and furnishing accessories with patterns such as embroidered vines, Indo China, and Heather Voile for the fabrics, and animals (mainly dogs and cats) and insects (butterflies, dragonflies and bees) for the embroidered cushions and bags alongside gorgeous roses, florals and vines. You do have to call them or e-mail to order at present but if you're looking for a special fabric or gift you could well find it here.

Site Usability:	★★★	Based:	UK
Product Range:	★★★	Express Delivery Option? (UK)	No
Price Range:	Medium	Gift Wrapping Option?	No
Delivery Area:	Worldwide	Returns Procedure:	Down to you

www.clarissahulse.com

Ferns, pampas grass and acacia, Narnia and Magic Roundabout are just some of the designs Clarissa Hulse has created to use on cushions and wallpaper in her online store. Her colours are modern and range from neutrals – brown, stone and cream – to hazy purple and dark red. It's a small and very different collection but extremely attractive. Check out also the stationery collection, featuring Clarissa's designs on beautiful silk covered notebooks and photo albums – perfect for presents.

Site Usability:	★★★	Based:	UK
Product Range:	★★★	Express Delivery Option? (UK)	No
Price Range:	Medium	Gift Wrapping Option?	No
Delivery Area:	Worldwide	Returns Procedure:	Down to you

www.davidlinley.com

As you would expect, this is a really beautiful website offering you the opportunity to buy David Linley designed accessories online including frames, vases, lamps, candlesticks, home fragrance, jewellery boxes and cushions. Everything is beautifully photographed and there are some gorgeous gift ideas here – just receiving one of his dark blue boxes makes you feel special straight away. Prices start at about £55 for his key rings and head off upwards steeply.

Site Usability:	★★★★★	Based:	UK
Product Range:	★★★★	Express Delivery Option? (UK)	Yes
Price Range:	Luxury	Gift Wrapping Option?	No but packaging is lovely
Delivery Area:	Worldwide	Returns Procedure:	Down to you

www.dianaforrester.co.uk

On Diana Forrester's website there's a very good choice of quite unusual gifts and decorative accessories for the home and garden mainly from France and also from other parts of the world, ranging from a cute mouse salt and pepper set to vintage style French storage jars, unusual vases and photo frames, fine porcelain and an original espresso set. You can also see pictures from Diana's shop which will definitely make you want to go there.

Site Usability:	★★★	Based:	UK
Product Range:	★★★	Express Delivery Option? (UK)	No
Price Range:	Medium	Gift Wrapping Option?	Yes
Delivery Area:	Worldwide	Returns Procedure:	Down to you

www.dibor.co.uk

Dibor is an independent UK-based company offering continental style furniture, home accessories and gifts. For your bedroom they have a selection of delightful French-inspired hand painted furniture, including cupboards, chests of drawers and pretty bedside tables, plus small accessories such as jewelled perfume bottles, French photo frames and Victorian Rose covered toiletry bags.

Site Usability:	★★★	Based:	UK
Product Range:	★★★	Express Delivery Option? (UK)	Yes
Price Range:	Medium	Gift Wrapping Option?	No
Delivery Area:	Worldwide	Returns Procedure:	Down to you

www.dutchbydesign.com

Dedicated to Dutch design, here you'll discover beautiful, modern home accessories from designers that Dutch by Design believe could become the interior design classics of tomorrow. Simplicity, clarity and often a sense of humour are the hallmarks of what they offer and the range includes mirrors, clocks, vases, throws and attractive lighting plus some very good gift ideas.

Site Usability:	★★★★★	Based:	UK
Product Range:	★★★★	Express Delivery Option? (UK)	No
Price Range:	Medium	Gift Wrapping Option?	No
Delivery Area:	Worldwide	Returns Procedure:	Down to you

www.horn-trading.co.uk

OK, so now for something totally different. Here's a Western style collection of furniture, including a cowhide and steer horn chair and cowhide shelf, soft furnishings, (yes you guessed it, cowhide covered cushions and rugs) and accessories and gifts such as bronco or cactus decorated china, western style cushions, hides, mats and cowhide bags and purses. The company is based in Battle, Sussex, but everything is sourced in the US.

Site Usability:	★★★★	Based:	UK
Product Range:	★★★	Express Delivery Option? (UK)	No
Price Range:	Medium	Gift Wrapping Option?	Yes
Delivery Area:	UK	Returns Procedure:	Down to you

www.interiors-tides.co.uk

Driftwood pebbles, shell tie-backs and pot-pourri are just a few of the delightful accessories and gifts available here, plus pretty beach-house style furniture, bathroom accessories including sponge bags, candles and soaps, kitchen and garden accessories from galvanised watering cans to ceramic measuring cups. They aim to ship everything to you within seven days but delivery is UK only.

Site Usability:	★★★★	Based:	UK
Product Range:	★★★★	Express Delivery Option? (UK)	No
Price Range:	Medium	Gift Wrapping Option?	No
Delivery Area:	UK	Returns Procedure:	Down to you

www.lavenderandsage.co.uk

Lavender & Sage was founded by Mayke Hogestijn, an interior designer who has worked in both England and France and who has sourced a range of beautiful and well made home accessories. Browse through her prettily designed website to find items such as embroidered cushions and organdie curtains, French tableware and 'Grand Hotel' luxury towels, traditional bedlinen and unusual lanterns. She also offers the Senteurs du Sud toiletry and home fragrance ranges. Just about everything here would make lovely gift or treat for your home.

Site Usability:	★★★★	Based:	UK
Product Range:	★★★★	Express Delivery Option? (UK)	No
Price Range:	Medium	Gift Wrapping Option?	No
Delivery Area:	Worldwide	Returns Procedure:	Down to you

www.lyttonandlily.co.uk

This is another wonderful home accessories website where there's so much to see you almost don't know where to start. For the kitchen there's colourful enamelware, Cath Kidston china and bistro cutlery; for the bathroom there are Comptoire Grande towels and Branche d'Olive toiletries; for the bedroom there are Monsoon Home and Comptoir bedlinens and throws; and candles, clocks and mirrors for the living room. Thankfully the website is extremely easy to navigate and very well photographed.

Site Usability:	★★★★★	Based:	UK
Product Range:	★★★★★	Express Delivery Option? (UK)	Yes
Price Range:	Luxury/Medium	Gift Wrapping Option?	No
Delivery Area:	Worldwide but you need to call or email	Returns Procedure:	In agreement with them

www.mithus.co.uk

This online home accessory retailer offers mainly Scandinavian style accessories including chic tablelinens, candleholders and vases, photo frames, cushions, and rugs plus an excellent selection of dinner and pillar candles in an unusual range of colours. For Christmas there are wreaths and garlands, enchanting lights and candles and traditional decorations.

Site Usability:	★★★★	Based:	UK
Product Range:	★★★★	Express Delivery Option? (UK)	No
Price Range:	Medium	Gift Wrapping Option?	No
Delivery Area:	UK	Returns Procedure:	Down to you

www.pier.co.uk

Based on the famous US furniture and accessories retailer Pier One Imports everything here is attractive and well priced and you'll discover lovely gifts and accessories from all over the world. The range is very extensive; you could furnish an entire room in your house with their stylish, modern and traditional furniture or just choose from their wide selection of textiles, glassware and lighting. They're excellent for presents and bring out a special catalogue each Christmas to complement the website.

Site Usability:	★★★★★	Based:	UK
Product Range:	★★★★★	Express Delivery Option? (UK)	No
Price Range:	Medium/Very Good Value	Gift Wrapping Option?	No
Delivery Area:	Worldwide	Returns Procedure:	Call to arrange collection or return small goods by post

Also take a look at the following websites for Decorative Accessories

Website Address	You'll find it in
www.grahamandgreen.co.uk	Chapter 78: Home Accessory Gifts

Chapter 44

The Kitchen

Equipment and Accessories

Home Appliances (including TV and Hi Fi)

Here's another of those areas where there's almost too much choice – too many great kitchen emporiums offering you everything you could possibly need and probably quite a few things you wouldn't dream of buying, for every size of kitchen and every style of cook. Having said that; if you're a busy person these websites will be a real boon.

Although the main tableware section is in Chapter 43, you'll also find some here, for the most part less expensive everyday options, plus small appliances and accessories by the likes of Dualit and Alessi, Magimix and Krups.

Because most of the large home appliances online retailers also offer TV and Hi Fi, this is the place to look for those as well. Once again this is a 'department' where you need to use those price comparison websites to make sure you get the best deal. When purchasing larger appliances it's very important to find out

a) is delivery included in the price?
b) will they take your old appliance away if you want them to?
c) will they install your new one? and
d) will they take all the packing materials away with them?
e) And last but not least will they carry your new 52-inch plasma TV up the stairs to your sitting room/TV room?

Find the make and model you want, then use one of the price comparison websites mentioned in Chapter 89. Then, when you think you've found the best price call the retailer and ask the essential questions. Make sure that you get your answers confirmed by email – some people will do anything to close a deal (not everyone; most are totally above board but you don't want to get any bad news *after* you've paid).

Sites to Visit

Kitchen Equipment and Accessories

www.cooksknives.co.uk

Essential for any cooking enthusiast is a set of really good quality sharp knives and you'll definitely find them here. You can buy individual knives or sets by Global, Henckels, Sabatier, Haiku and Wusthof (and more), professional knife sharpeners and OXO 'good grip' tools. You will pay quite a lot for a really good set of knives and knife block but they will last you for years and be worth every penny. These are excellent gifts for real cooks.

Site Usability:	★★★★★	Based:	UK
Product Range:	★★★★★	Express Delivery Option? (UK)	No
Price Range:	Luxury/Medium	Gift Wrapping Option?	No
Delivery Area:	EU	Returns Procedure:	Down to you

www.conran.com

Conran are famous for their modern, colourful and well priced furniture and accessories which you can now buy online through their website. Discover their modern take on everything from kitchen accessories, candles and soft furnishings, lighting, clocks and gifts. Oh yes, and you can book your next Conran restaurant meal here as well.

Site Usability:	★★★★★	Based:	UK
Product Range:	★★★★	Express Delivery Option? (UK)	No
Price Range:	Medium/Very Good Value	Gift Wrapping Option?	Yes
Delivery Area:	Worldwide	Returns Procedure:	Down to you

www.cookware.co.uk

A same day despatch online cook shop offering a wide range of high quality items, including chopping boards, every kitchen utensil you can think of, pan racks and trolleys and clever storage solutions, plus bar accessories and everything for baking. There's also electrical equipment by Dualit, KitchenAid, Magimix and Krups. A great deal of care has gone into this website with lots of information and clear pictures. Well worth a browse.

Site Usability:	★★★★★	Based:	UK
Product Range:	★★★★★	Express Delivery Option? (UK)	Yes
Price Range:	Medium	Gift Wrapping Option?	No
Delivery Area:	UK	Returns Procedure:	Down to you

www.cucinadirect.co.uk

Here's another excellent retailer offering everything for the kitchen beautifully displayed, including knives, pots and pans, bar tools, glasses and serving dishes, picnic equipment, housekeeping items and a gift selection. You'll also find a small but very high quality range of electrical appliances,

253

with Dualit toasters and kettles and KitchenAid mixers just a couple of the items you can order to be shipped to anywhere in the world.

Site Usability:	★★★★★	Based:	UK
Product Range:	★★★★	Express Delivery Option? (UK)	Yes
Price Range:	Medium	Gift Wrapping Option?	Yes
Delivery Area:	Worldwide	Returns Procedure:	Down to you

www.diningstore.co.uk

You'll find some quite different products on this website, such as the ZapCap bottle opener, Escali Cibo nutritional scale and CaddyO bottle chiller alongside their designer kitchen and tableware with collections from Eva Solo, Cuisinox Elysee, Le Creuset, Mauviel, Couzon and Jura. This is not the normal kitchen and cookware selection so have a look round, you're certain to discover something very different as well as some great gifts for the enthusiastic cook.

Site Usability:	★★★★	Based:	UK
Product Range:	★★★	Express Delivery Option? (UK)	No
Price Range:	Medium	Gift Wrapping Option?	No
Delivery Area:	Europe	Returns Procedure:	Down to you

www.divertimenti.co.uk

This famous London based cookery equipment site offers over 5000 items from hand painted tableware including decorated and coloured pottery from France to a really comprehensive range of kitchen essentials including knives, boards and bakeware, Italian products such as parmesan graters and ravioli trays, copper bowls and pans and children's baking sets. There's also a wedding gift, knife sharpening and copper re-tinning service. This has always been and still remains one of the best kitchen and dining shops around.

Site Usability:	★★★★	Based:	UK
Product Range:	★★★★	Express Delivery Option? (UK)	No
Price Range:	Medium	Gift Wrapping Option?	No
Delivery Area:	Worldwide	Returns Procedure:	Down to you

www.dualit.com

If you know you like the brand and you'd like to choose from the complete range (rather than the edited range you'll find on some other websites) then you should visit this site. Dualit are surely the best known manufacturers of high quality toasters and they also sell kettles, hand mixers, coffee grinders and scales, all to the highest specifications. You can buy spare parts and accessories for all their equipment here as well which are usually hard to find elsewhere.

Site Usability:	★★★★	Based:	UK
Product Range:	★★★	Express Delivery Option? (UK)	No
Price Range:	Luxury/Medium	Gift Wrapping Option?	No
Delivery Area:	UK	Returns Procedure:	Down to you

www.evertrading.co.uk

After twelve years of supplying interior design shops with gorgeous home accessories Evertrading have opened their own online shop, where you can buy their range of elegant and contemporary hand engraved glassware, chenille and faux fur throws, pretty cushions, modern cutlery and unusual storage suggestions. Their plain and coloured glassware in a variety of styles is definitely the main part of the collection and you could find some very lovely gifts here, including wedding gifts.

Site Usability:	★★★★	Based:	UK
Product Range:	★★★	Express Delivery Option? (UK)	No
Price Range:	Medium	Gift Wrapping Option?	No
Delivery Area:	Worldwide	Returns Procedure:	Down to you

www.johnlewis.com

Needless to say you'll find all the essentials here for your kitchen and for everywhere else in your house – all the tableware, kitchen accessories and equipment you could need from fluffy towels in a huge range of colours and simple and stylish bathroom storage to modern furniture, beds and bedding and on through to mirrors and lighting, garden furniture and even flowers. This is definitely one of the best sites on the web, offering a service to match.

Site Usability:	★★★★★	Based:	UK
Product Range:	★★★★★	Express Delivery Option? (UK)	Yes
Price Range:	Medium	Gift Wrapping Option?	No
Delivery Area:	UK	Returns Procedure:	Call them to collect or return goods to store

www.lakelandlimited.co.uk

You've probably already heard of this marvellous colourful, fun and innovative kitchen collection. There's a huge range on offer, regularly updated, with something for just about every occasion and every room in the house. You'll find every kind of kitchen utensil plus boards and storage solutions, foils, cleaning products and waste bags and a whole host of other useful and original products. There are lots of ideas for eating outside and picnics as well, plus foodie gifts at Christmas. Have a browse.

Site Usability:	★★★★★	Based:	UK
Product Range:	★★★★★	Express Delivery Option? (UK)	Yes
Price Range:	Medium/Very Good Value	Gift Wrapping Option?	No
Delivery Area:	UK	Returns Procedure:	Down to you

www.rickstein.com

You may well have heard of Rick Stein – eaten at his restaurant in Padstow if you're very lucky or bought or cooked from one of his many excellent recipe books. Now at his online shop you can order the items in his cook shop such as cooking utensils and original tea towels; send one of his hampers as a gift, buy his Chilli Chutney, tapenade or home made Florentines, choose from his personal wine selection or buy gift vouchers. There's a really good collection here and some great gift ideas for the cook, but of course only if he or she likes fish.

Site Usability:	★★★★★	Based:	UK
Product Range:	★★★★	Express Delivery Option? (UK)	No
Price Range:	Luxury/Medium	Gift Wrapping Option?	No
Delivery Area:	Worldwide for most items	Returns Procedure:	Down to you

www.silvernutmeg.com

An A–Z of high quality kitchen equipment, with professional quality cookware, kettles, knives, pasta makers, toasters, pancake pans, workstations and bread making machines being just a few from brands such as Cuisinart, Gaggia and Magimix. You can also take a look through their home interiors section for candles, rugs, floor cushions and planters. The pictures are very clear although you do have to click on a basic list first to get to them.

Site Usability:	★★★★	Based:	UK
Product Range:	★★★★★	Express Delivery Option? (UK)	No
Price Range:	Luxury/Medium	Gift Wrapping Option?	No
Delivery Area:	Worldwide	Returns Procedure:	Down to you

www.thecookingshop.co.uk

There are a lot of kitchen equipment shops online offering you every tool and gadget you can think of but this one is particularly well designed and easy to use. You can select from an excellent range of pots, pans, bakeware and other kitchen equipment plus some unusual tableware including an Eastern dining section with chopsticks, mats, bowls and accessories. They also offer recipe suggestions, household hints and tips and decorative ideas for the table.

Site Usability:	★★★★★	Express Delivery Option? (UK)	No
Product Range:	★★★★	Gift Wrapping Option?	No
Price Range:	Medium	Returns Procedure:	Down to you
Delivery Area:	Worldwide		

www.thecookskitchen.com

A vast selection of products is available on this attractively designed site which promises to dispatch just about all of its products to you anywhere in the world. Coffee makers, butchers blocks, knives, recipe books, saucepans and basic kitchenware are just a few of the items available. In their country kitchen department you'll find old fashioned enamelware, farmhouse crockery and traditional style kettles to sit on your Aga.

Site Usability:	★★★★★	Based:	UK
Product Range:	★★★★	Express Delivery Option? (UK)	No
Price Range:	Medium	Gift Wrapping Option?	Yes
Delivery Area:	Worldwide	Returns Procedure:	Down to you

Also visit these websites for Kitchen and Dining Accessories

Website Address	You'll find it in
www.heals.co.uk	Chapter 42: Bath Time
www.thewhitecompany.com	Chapter 41: In the Bedroom

Home Appliances (including TV and Hi Fi)

www.buyersandsellersonline.co.uk

When it comes to buying electrical appliances you want to be sure to get the best price you can and a reliable service. Buyers and Sellers have been in business since 1954 and certainly offer very keen prices on all top names such as Admiral, Neff, Miele, Siemens and Rangemaster and specialise in American makes of fridges and washing machines. Make sure you check out their prices if you're looking for something new for your kitchen.

Site Usability:	★★★★	Based:	UK
Product Range:	★★★★	Returns Procedure:	Discuss with them
Price Range:	Luxury/Medium/Very Good Value		
Delivery Area:	UK		

www.dabs.com

Dabs are simply huge, with an enormous choice of products for computing, home entertainment, in-car products (including the dreaded in car theatre system that the kids can all fight over) and photo and video. When you're comparing prices Dabs will almost always come up with a very good one, if not the cheapest. They're extremely reliable and their delivery is far cheaper than on most sites.

Site Usability:	★★★★★	Based:	UK
Product Range:	★★★★★	Express Delivery Option? (UK)	Yes
Price Range:	Luxury/Medium/Very Good Value	Returns Procedure:	Down to you
Delivery Area:	UK		

www.electricshop.com

At electricshop you'll find two main ranges; domestic appliances for kitchen and laundry including a comprehensive range of American fridges with built in ice makers, and computing, photographic and audio visual products such as plasma screen TVs, Panasonic and Sony cameras and camcorders, Sony laptops and portable audio. They also have appliance spares for kitchen and laundry, vacuum bags, light bulbs and AV leads and offer free delivery within the UK.

Site Usability:	★★★★	Based:	UK
Product Range:	★★★★★	Returns Procedure:	Discuss with them
Price Range:	Luxury/Medium/Very Good Value		
Delivery Area:	UK		

www.pantheronline.co.uk

Based in London, this company specialises in the sale of top brand high technology consumer electronics, domestic appliances, photographic equipment and communications. You can buy just about everything for the kitchen including coffee makers and washing machines, all you need for your home cinema including plasma TVs and DVD recorders (as opposed to just players) a small range of Hi Fi and digital cameras by Olympus, Panasonic and Sony.

Site Usability:	★★★★★	Based:	UK
Product Range:	★★★★	Express Delivery	No
Price Range:	Luxury/Medium/Very Good Value	Returns Procedure:	Discuss with them
Delivery Area:	UK		

www.qed-uk.com

This is another electrical retailer appearing to offer you just about every product under the sun and on an uncluttered and clear website. On the household side there are washing machines and dryers, vacuum cleaners fridges, freezers, ovens, dishwashers and small appliances by manufacturers such as Miele, Bosch and AEG. There's also home cinema and Hi Fi equipment by Philips, Panasonic and loads more plus computers and accessories by Acer, Apple, HP, IBM and Sony.

Site Usability:	★★★★	Based:	UK
Product Range:	★★★★	Express Delivery	No
Price Range:	Luxury/Medium/Very Good Value	Returns Procedure:	Discuss with them
Delivery Area:	UK		

www.thedac.co.uk

The Discount Appliance Centre claim to have the largest selection of 'Free Standing' and 'Built In' appliances: The company catchphrase is 'Names you recognise, prices you won't' and with leading brands such as AEG, Bosch, Miele, Siemens, Neff and Zanussi; if you're looking for an electrical appliance you should certainly check out the prices here. They also have Rangemaster range cookers, American style refrigeration and Siemens top-of- the-range washing machines.

Site Usability:	★★★★★	Based:	UK
Product Range:	★★★★★	Express Delivery	No
Price Range:	Luxury/Medium/Very Good Value	Returns Procedure:	Discuss with them
Delivery Area:	UK		

Essential Appliance Accessory Websites

www.vacuumbags2u.co.uk

This may sound like a very boring website but if you regularly have to go to the shops to buy your replacement vacuum bags (and who wants to do that?) this will make your life easier. All types of bags for just about every make of vacuum cleaner are available here and delivery is extremely quick and efficient.

Site Usability:	★★★★	Based:	UK
Product Range:	★★★★	Express Delivery	No
Price Range:	Medium/Very Good Value	Returns Procedure:	Discuss with them
Delivery Area:	UK		

www.gbbulbs.co.uk

For light bulbs look no further than this website when you want to stock up and order using their easy selector which also shows you clearly the different types of bulb fittings. You'll find every type of light bulb from incandescent, to halogen, photo optic, fluorescent, energy saving and high intensity alongside sunbed tubes and daylight bulbs. They offer a 24/48 hour national delivery service.

Site Usability:	★★★★	Based:	UK
Product Range:	★★★★★	Express Delivery	Yes
Price Range:	Medium/Very Good Value	Returns Procedure:	Discuss with them
Delivery Area:	UK		

Chapter 45

Office Stationery and General Supplies

You don't need a lot of choice here, which is why I've only given you the two websites that I use all the time for office essentials. If you use up a lot of printer paper, your kids are always asking for new pens, rulers and calculators before each start of term, and you're always needing new printer cartridges and the like then these are the places to buy from.

Here you can find everything in one place, delivery is fast, the prices are good and you're saved from giving each of your kids a basket in the shop and telling them to go and get what they need, which usually leads to enormous expense, at least it always does in my family. Staples offer a next day delivery service for just about everything which is an added joy.

Sites to Visit

www.euroffice.co.uk

This is an excellent place to look for your essential pen and paper supplies and computer essentials – they say that they offer the cheapest prices going but always check and compare. It's a very busy website with a huge range of products so it's always better to shop here when you know exactly what you want to try and avoid getting sidetracked.

Site Usability:	★★★★		Based:	UK
Product Range:	★★★★★		Express Delivery:	Yes
Price Range:	Medium/Very Good Value		Returns Procedure:	Down to you
Delivery Area:	UK			

www.staples.co.uk

Buy all your stationery and computer requirements quickly and easily online, with everything from files to office furniture, high quality writing paper and the best priced copy paper. Once you've created your list you can store it so make sure that you order the right toner cartridge for your printer each time without having to look for it. This is also an excellent place for school supplies.

Site Usability:	★★★★	Based:	UK
Product Range:	★★★★★	Express Delivery	Yes
Price Range:	Medium/Very Good Value	Returns Procedure:	Down to you
Delivery Area:	UK		

Chapter 46

Fabrics, Paints and Wallpapers

This is a slightly tricky area for online shopping as you're unlikely to want to go straight ahead and buy; you need to see samples of everything first. Thankfully the websites here offering serious interiors' options are well aware of that and offer an excellent service, with samples of fabrics and wallpapers, paint colour charts (which in my opinion only help start you on the road) and mini pots of paints to help you make your final decision.

One of the benefits of having a browse round here is that there are some excellent roomsets to take a look at. Where they're offering to make bespoke curtains you can see exactly how your chosen fabric will look made up and what your new sofa will look like *in situ* (or their *situ*). Be careful again about measurements when commissioning bespoke curtains and blinds here, you really don't want to get it wrong.

Sites to Visit

Fabrics

www.borderlinefabrics.com

Borderline create inspired textile collections mainly produced from archive sources originally based around 19th century documents and textile samples from their own archives, and more recently including the retro designs of Enid Marx, Florence Broadhurst, E.Q. Nicholson, Nancy Nicholson, Calkin James and Cressida Bell on fabrics as well as wallpapers. Most of the fabrics are screen printed on a variety of natural base cloths in the UK. You can order cuttings first and then the fabric lengths you need.

Site Usability:	★★★★	Based:	UK
Product Range:	★★★★	Express Delivery Option? (UK)	No
Price Range:	Luxury/Medium	Gift Wrapping Option?	No
Delivery Area:	UK	Returns Procedure:	Down to you but no returns on specially cut fabrics.

www.elanbach.com

This is a pretty website run by a family business offering lovely traditional Welsh fabrics which they design and print using the latest digital technology. You can buy the fabrics themselves by the metre, have them make up curtains and blinds for you using their online measuring calculator or buy cushions, bags and boxfiles. Your order can take up to ten days to arrive (longer for curtains and blinds) and they're happy to ship to you anywhere in the world. Take a look at their hotel website and you'll see how the fabrics look in place but don't start there or you'll never escape, it looks so enticing.

Site Usability:	★★★★★	Based:	UK
Product Range:	★★★★	Express Delivery Option? (UK)	No
Price Range:	Medium	Gift Wrapping Option?	No
Delivery Area:	Worldwide	Returns Procedure:	Down to you

www.fabricsandpapers.com

Fabricsandpapers.com is a new online shop where you can buy thousands of fabrics and wallpapers for upholstery, curtains, bedspreads and cushions from leading British and European design houses. Use their design board to see various schemes for different types of room that they've put together and if you order everything they've chosen you'll get a 20% discount. There are lovely fabrics for children in particular and a lighting range as well.

Site Usability:	★★★★★	Based:	UK
Product Range:	★★★★★	Express Delivery Option? (UK)	No
Price Range:	Medium	Gift Wrapping Option?	No
Delivery Area:	Worldwide	Returns Procedure:	Down to you

www.interiorsathome.co.uk

This is a fabrics and interiors accessory website offering blinds, ready-made curtains and tie backs plus an unexpectedly wide range of high quality fabrics, linings and trimmings. They also offer home accessories such as bedspreads, duvet covers and throws, cushions and cushion pads (for those places where they only sell you the covers) and an exceptional range of wall hangings. They offer an advice service if you want some help with your décor, and they'll also try and source fabrics for you that are not included on their site.

Site Usability:	★★★★	Based:	UK
Product Range:	★★★★	Express Delivery Option? (UK)	No
Price Range:	Medium	Gift Wrapping Option?	No
Delivery Area:	UK	Returns Procedure:	Down to you

www.laragrace.co.uk

This is a beautifully designed website from a company offering you the opportunity to order their designer curtain and upholstery fabrics online. The extensive range includes Linen Union, vintage style florals, patchworks, nursery fabrics, toile fabrics plus their range of Checks and Stripes. You can order samples first and then if there's no one in your area to make up your curtains for you they'll do that too. Samples are expensive but the price is refunded when you order.

Site Usability:	★★★★	Based:	UK
Product Range:	★★★★	Express Delivery Option? (UK)	No
Price Range:	Medium	Gift Wrapping Option?	No
Delivery Area:	UK	Returns Procedure:	No refund on specially cut fabrics

www.montgomerycurtainsdirect.co.uk

There aren't a great number of places you can buy curtains online, mainly because it's difficult to show them well, however here they've managed it. You first need to select your colour scheme then the specific fabric, which they have available in different sizes. Click on the one you choose and you'll see what it looks like made up. It's a simple, clever and easy to use system. The range isn't huge but what's there is excellent and you can order valances, cushion covers and fabrics as well.

Site Usability:	★★★★★	Express Delivery Option? (UK)	No
Product Range:	★★★★	Gift Wrapping Option?	No
Price Range:	Medium	Returns Procedure:	Down to you
Delivery Area:	UK		

www.pretavivre.com

This is an excellent interiors website offering curtains and tie-backs, fabrics by the metre, blinds, poles, bedlinen and quilts. The ordering system is quite confusing as you can't see what you're ordering while you do it but the products are lovely and there's lots of information available including a simple and clear measuring guide for curtains and blinds. You can browse through their gallery to get some ideas and you can also order samples here.

Site Usability:	★★★★★	Express Delivery Option? (UK)	No
Product Range:	★★★★★	Gift Wrapping Option?	No
Price Range:	Medium/Very Good Value	Returns Procedure:	Down to you
Delivery Area:	UK		

www.queenshill.com

Queenshill is a family run business offering a lovely selection of fabrics, wallpapers, gifts and home accessories from brands such as Mulberry, GP and J Baker, Harlequin and Fired Earth. The selection of mouth-watering gift ideas includes Mulberry candles, pot-pourri, cushions and throws and James Brindley's range of faux fur (think leopard, llama, bear and cheetah) throws, cushions and hot water bottle covers. Resist if you can. You can request free samples of fabrics to help you finalise your choice.

Site Usability:	★★★★★	Express Delivery Option? (UK)	No
Product Range:	★★★★★	Gift Wrapping Option?	No
Price Range:	Luxury/Medium	Returns Procedure:	Down to you
Delivery Area:	Worldwide		

www.thecottonmill.com

There's a lot to see at the Cotton Mill, as you could easily be sidetracked by the duvets and covers, throws and cushions, although there isn't necessarily a huge choice in each area. Where the range *is* large, however, is in curtains: so click there, choose your colour scheme and then the fabric and size. There's a guide to how to measure your window for ready-made curtains and there's a selection of Sanderson fabrics to choose from as well.

Site Usability:	★★★★★	Express Delivery Option? (UK)	No
Product Range:	★★★★	Gift Wrapping Option?	No
Price Range:	Medium	Returns Procedure:	Down to you
Delivery Area:	Worldwide		

Paints and Wallpapers

www.designerpaint.co.uk

From the same family as wallpapersdirect.co.uk comes this excellent website, offering you a wide choice of high quality paints from makers such as Farrow and Ball, Cole and Son, Designers Guild and Zoffany. For a very small sum you can buy the colourcard pack which includes all the makes (highly recommended) and you can explore all the colour areas in their Colour Picker. If you're looking for an antique style you can visit their Heritage Library and they'll advise on paints for a specific era. Whatever kind or colour of paint you're looking for, you'll almost certainly find it here.

Site Usability:	★★★★★	Based:	UK
Product Range:	★★★★★	Express Delivery Option? (UK)	No
Price Range:	Luxury/Medium	Gift Wrapping Option?	No
Delivery Area:	UK	Returns Procedure:	Down to you

www.farrow-ball.com

Farrow & Ball is the last remaining traditional paint and wallpaper manufacturer in Britain. Their complete online service enables you to learn more about their high quality paints and papers, to request samples and colour cards, buy their products, answer your technical queries, and of course, ask for their advice. They'll deliver to you wherever you are in the world and offer an express delivery service for the UK.

Site Usability:	★★★★★	Based:	UK
Product Range:	★★★★★	Express Delivery Option? (UK)	Yes
Price Range:	Luxury/Medium	Gift Wrapping Option?	No
Delivery Area:	Worldwide	Returns Procedure:	Down to you

www.grahamandbrown.com

Graham and Brown offer you the opportunity of buying innovative and dramatic wallpapers online by designers such as Laurence Llewelyn-Bowen, Linda Barker and students from the Royal College of Art. Take a look at their roomsets and you can quickly judge if there's a paper there for you. Alternatively you can invest in one of their stunning Wall Art canvases, buy from their chic storage range and order wallpaper samples. They deliver to the UK, US and Canada and some EU countries.

Site Usability:	★★★★★	Based:	UK
Product Range:	★★★★	Express Delivery Option? (UK)	No
Price Range:	Luxury/Medium	Gift Wrapping Option?	No
Delivery Area:	UK, US, Canada and some EU	Returns Procedure:	Down to you

www.thelittlegreene.com

Here you can choose your high quality paints. Order their colour card first (you have to pay a small charge but it's hand made using their exact colours, so I suppose it's fair) then choose your colour and type of paint from acrylic to oil based – they give you advice on which type of paint for which surface. You can also download their Point and Paint software which enables you to visualise your new colour scheme on screen.

Site Usability:	★★★★	Express Delivery Option? (UK)	Yes
Product Range:	★★★★	Gift Wrapping Option?	No
Price Range:	Luxury/Medium	Returns Procedure:	Paints mixed specially for you are not returnable unless
Delivery Area:	EU		faulty

www.wallpaperdirect.co.uk

Here's a very good selection of wallpapers, all of which you can order online, from designers such as Graham and Brown, Sanderson, William Morris, Osborne and Little and Cath Kidston. The only problem really with this is that there's so much choice you need to have at least some idea of what you're looking for before you start. They have a really good 'Design Ideas' section, where you can select from 'Fresh Air and Muddy Boots', 'Country Cottage', 'City Living', 'Kids' and 'Grand Elegance'. Click on any one and you'll get ideas on how to decorate your chosen room. They also sell all the tools you'll need for the job and offer you guidance on how to wallpaper a room.

Site Usability:	★★★★★	Express Delivery Option? (UK)	No
Product Range:	★★★★★	Gift Wrapping Option?	No
Price Range:	Luxury/Medium	Returns Procedure:	Down to you, subject to a re-stocking charge
Delivery Area:	Worldwide but email for overseas postage quote		

Chapter 47

Lighting

People's taste in lighting differs enormously so it's just as well there's so much choice online. Having said that, you'll almost certainly have more problems choosing here than walking into your local lighting emporium and having just a few from which to select. Here there are literally hundreds in just about every style.

Although yes, you can find all the traditional styles of lighting here, one of the things I enjoy the most is discovering so many places that have something just that little bit different, that you almost certainly wouldn't be able to find in the shops. There's a wide range of prices here from well priced modern desk lighting to expensive Venetian glass chandeliers so make sure that you know what you're looking for when you start out or you could easily get distracted.

Sites to Visit

www.ascolights.co.uk

So you're looking for a new lamp for your recently decorated living room? Or do you have a friend who's getting married and you want to give her something other than the tableware and household goods off her wedding list? If either is the case you could take a look at this lighting website where there are lots of mainly contemporary ideas at not unreasonable prices from modern table and desk lighting to floor standing uplighters. If your order is in stock you can have it the following day.

Site Usability:	★★★★★	Based:	UK
Product Range:	★★★★★	Express Delivery Option? (UK)	Yes
Price Range:	Medium	Gift Wrapping Option?	No
Delivery Area:	UK	Returns Procedure:	Down to you

www.besselink.com

For really beautiful lighting stop here: This may well not be the place from which you're going to replace all your lighting in your home but it's one where you'll find some really beautiful and unusual ideas. Click through to their ceramics, urns and balusters and in particular their lamps with decorated figures; I think you'll see exactly what I mean. They're not cheap but very, very special and would make excellent presents as well. They offer a worldwide delivery service for all their lights.

Site Usability:	★★★★★	Based:	UK
Product Range:	★★★★★	Express Delivery Option? (UK)	No
Price Range:	Luxury/Medium	Gift Wrapping Option?	No
Delivery Area:	Worldwide	Returns Procedure:	Down to you some pieces in agreement with them

www.christopher-wray.com

This is one of the best known UK-based lighting stores and the only downside to their website is that you can't order directly online (at time of writing, maybe you can now) but you have to call them. Bearing in mind the huge choice here that's probably not too much to ask. The site is extremely quick to get round and offers everything from desk and table lighting, brass wall lights, traditional chandeliers and picture lights. Accessories include candle tubes, chandelier chains, switches, oil burner parts and bulbs.

Site Usability:	★★★★★	Based:	UK
Product Range:	★★★★★	Express Delivery Option? (UK)	No
Price Range:	Luxury/Medium	Gift Wrapping Option?	No
Delivery Area:	Worldwide	Returns Procedure:	Down to you some pieces in agreement with them

www.designer-lighting.com

If you're looking for lighting and want something a little unusual and modern then this is your place. The range, which includes everything from fabulous barleytwist arm chandeliers to modern picture lighting (plus fibre optics, downlighters, garden lighting, track lights, spot lights and kids' lighting from flying planes to bugs and dinosaurs) is huge so allow time to have a good look round. You need to allow eight days for delivery to the UK and three weeks for international orders.

Site Usability:	★★★★★	Based:	UK
Product Range:	★★★★★	Express Delivery Option? (UK)	No
Price Range:	Luxury/Medium	Gift Wrapping Option?	No
Delivery Area:	Worldwide	Returns Procedure:	Down to you

www.italian-lighting-centre.co.uk

All the lights on this website are designed and manufactured by Italian companies and although you'll be buying from a British company they'll be shipped to you straight from the manufacturer; so if you order a craftsman made light you may well have to wait a few weeks, but it'll be well worth it. You'll find a wide range, from the gorgeous and breathtakingly priced Murano chandeliers to more reasonable and classic floor and table lights and they'll deliver anywhere in the world.

Site Usability:	★★★★★	Based:	UK
Product Range:	★★★★★	Express Delivery Option? (UK)	No
Price Range:	Luxury/Medium	Gift Wrapping Option?	No
Delivery Area:	Worldwide	Returns Procedure:	Down to you

www.jim-lawrence.co.uk

Jim Lawrence is a designer who creates traditional ironwork lighting re-worked into modern/ classic and unusual styles. His chandeliers, for example, are totally different to anything you can find elsewhere but you'll also find lanterns, table lights, candelabra and wall lights and you can choose from a range of finishes such as polished, matt black, gold or verdigris. You can also buy the bulbs and fittings to go with his lights.

Site Usability:	★★★★★	Based:	UK
Product Range:	★★★★	Express Delivery Option? (UK)	No
Price Range:	Luxury/Medium	Gift Wrapping Option?	No
Delivery Area:	Worldwide	Returns Procedure:	Down to you

www.thelightingsuperstore.co.uk

If you want a mammoth choice, free UK delivery and excellent prices take a look round here. This is an extremely busy website showing you every type of lighting from spotlights to table lamps, garden lighting and pendant lights, Tiffany lamps and children's lighting and in most cases you can choose from modern, contemporary, and traditional styles. They also have a selection of billiard and snooker lights at a range of prices.

Site Usability:	★★★★★	Based:	UK
Product Range:	★★★★★	Express Delivery Option? (UK)	Yes
Price Range:	Medium/Very Good Value	Gift Wrapping Option?	No
Delivery Area:	UK	Returns Procedure:	Down to you

Chapter 48

Wall Hangings and Pictures

I'm always very impressed when I visit people's houses and all their pictures and photos are beautifully placed around the house with family portraits elegantly displayed and prints and paintings in just the right place to catch the light. I'm afraid I'm definitely not that person and wonder just where they get the time to be so organised. In fact most visitors to our house wouldn't know what the rest of the family looked like at all (since they were toddlers at least) had it not been for my eldest son giving me one of those fantastic digital photo frames and loading it with all our latest pictures.

Sorry, I seem to have gone off on a bit of a tangent there but I'm sure you know what I mean. On the websites below you'll find great posters for kids' rooms, wonderful tapestries to hang over your fireplace or on that huge spare wall in your home, and framed prints of famous paintings to hang anywhere you like. The framing services in particular are really good, as you can choose everything from one place and it'll be sent to you, fully prepared in just a very short space of time. Much better than having to go out, buy your print, bring it home and then take it to your local picture frame shop. You can do that, of course, if you really want to – but again, you can do it all here too.

Sites to Visit

www.artrepublic.com

There's a huge range here of well presented posters and prints by artists such as Matisse, Hockney, Chagalle, Warhol and many, many more. You can search by artist, title or style or just browse through the range until you find something to suit. Delivery is free and, if you want framing, they give you the choice of aluminum or wood frames. There's also comprehensive information on exhibitions all over the world.

Site Usability:	★★★★★	Based:	UK
Product Range:	★★★★★	Express Delivery Option? (UK)	No
Price Range:	Medium	Gift Wrapping Option?	No
Delivery Area:	Worldwide	Returns Procedure:	Down to you

www.haywoods-tapestries.com

There's a lovely selection here of tapestries and wall hangings that are not overpriced. You can order mainly from stock and many of the pieces are available in a choice of sizes. This collection of tapestries is reproduced from originals dating back to medieval times, many of which are now on display in famous museums throughout the world. You can expect to receive your delivery within 14 days and they welcome overseas enquiries.

Site Usability:	★★★★★	Based:	UK
Product Range:	★★★★★	Express Delivery Option? (UK)	No
Price Range:	Luxury/Medium	Gift Wrapping Option?	No
Delivery Area:	Worldwide	Returns Procedure:	Down to you

www.northerntapestries.com

Northern Tapestries offer a wide range of tapestries and wall hangings covering subjects (which you pick from) such as floral, courtly elegance, castles and chateaux, hunting scenes and medieval. They really are excellently displayed. You click on the one you want to see in detail to get quite a large picture with dimensions etc. They are based in British Columbia so you may well have to pay duty – however the prices are good and shipping via Air Express is free.

Site Usability:	★★★★★	Based:	British Columbia
Product Range:	★★★★★	Express Delivery Option? (UK)	No
Price Range:	Medium	Gift Wrapping Option?	No
Delivery Area:	Worldwide	Returns Procedure:	Down to you

www.postershop.co.uk

Choose from their selection of lithographics by artists such as Bacon, Braque and Miro, art prints and posters by Kandinsky, Delaunay or Cocteau, plus a huge range of etchings and screen prints. There are also some particularly good sport prints including sailing ships, surfing and fishing. Once you've chosen your poster or print you have the option of taking it to the virtual framing studio or just sending it straight to your shopping cart.

Site Usability:	★★★★★	Based:	UK
Product Range:	★★★★★	Express Delivery Option? (UK)	No
Price Range:	Medium	Gift Wrapping Option?	No
Delivery Area:	Worldwide	Returns Procedure:	Down to you

www.pushposters.com

Pushposters.com almost certainly offer the largest range of music posters in the world, featuring over 1500 different artists from all genres of music ranging from the smallest independent bands right up to the best selling stadium acts. They also have related t-shirts, hoodies, caps and hats, calendars, keyrings, wallets, bags and other accessories for the modern music addict. There's really an amazing selection here so check it out.

Site Usability:	★★★★★	Based:	UK
Product Range:	★★★★★	Express Delivery Option? (UK)	No
Price Range:	Medium	Gift Wrapping Option?	No
Delivery Area:	Worldwide	Returns Procedure:	Down to you

www.tapestries-inc.com

This is a marvellous tapestry website based in the US who are happy to ship worldwide. It's well worth having a look round as what you have here are the highest quality hand woven tapestries in a wonderful choice of designs. There's also a wealth of information on what to look for when choosing a tapestry and how to install a tapestry, which makes this site indispensable. Email them if you have any queries.

Site Usability:	★★★★★	Based:	UK
Product Range:	★★★★★	Express Delivery Option? (UK)	No
Price Range:	Luxury/Medium	Gift Wrapping Option?	No
Delivery Area:	Worldwide	Returns Procedure:	Down to you

www.worldgallery.co.uk

World Gallery have a huge, easily searchable, interactive database and deliver prints, posters and frames worldwide. Choose from the selection by artist, subject and style; such as classic, contemporary, modern or impressionist. Once you've decided on your picture you can select your mount and frame online and see exactly what the finished product will look like. This is a really excellent website – try it and you'll see.

Site Usability:	★★★★★	Based:	UK
Product Range:	★★★★★	Express Delivery Option? (UK)	No
Price Range:	Medium/Very Good Value	Gift Wrapping Option?	No
Delivery Area:	Worldwide	Returns Procedure:	Down to you

Chapter 49

Carpets and Rugs

I'm not suggesting for a moment that you're going to order your next bedroom carpet online, in the same way that you're not going to order your new fitted kitchen. Online shopping may well get to those places eventually but not only is it not there yet but I don't believe that we are either.

What you may well do is take a look at the carpet makes and styles that are available and then send off for samples and find out where you can order (and get your carpet fitted properly). You can also get a very good idea of price so that when you come to make your final decision you won't get any surprises.

Rugs are totally different and you may be tempted to order a rug or two online (well maybe only one if it's oriental). Here there's everything from sheepskin, cowhide, sisal and patterned rugs to absolutely top-of-the-range Chinese and Bokhara rugs and most of these websites have been cleverly designed so that you can get up close to the patterns and colours.

Although colour reproduction isn't perfect, and of course in this area you aren't going to get any samples, delivery is usually very quick and you can change your rug if it isn't quite right for the designated room.

Sites to Visit

www.axminster-carpets.co.uk

Although you have to actually order through a stockist this is such a clever website in terms of choosing your new carpet I've included it here. You can search their portfolio by colour, texture, range and style. Click on style, for example, then from floral, classic, plain etc. Once you've selected your chosen pattern you can send it through their home decorator facility where you choose a type of room and then change the colour of the walls and main furnishings and get a good idea of how it would look (sorry if this sounds complicated, it definitely isn't and it's extremely clever).

Site Usability:	★★★★★	Based:	UK
Product Range:	★★★★★	Express Delivery Option? (UK)	No
Price Range:	Medium/Very Good Value	Gift Wrapping Option?	No
Delivery Area:	Worldwide	Returns Procedure:	Down to you

www.funkyrugs.co.uk

Moving away for a moment from traditional pattern rugs take a look at these modern designs; perfect for contemporary interiors. You can choose from their Ultra Funky rugs, modern wool rugs, shaggy rugs, leather rugs, skins and hides and loads more. One of the strongest parts of this collection must surely be the natural rugs, where you can select from sisal, coir, bamboo and seagrass with different edgings for simple and striking interiors. They'll ship worldwide and delivery within the UK is free.

Site Usability:	★★★★★	Based:	UK
Product Range:	★★★★★	Express Delivery Option? (UK)	No
Price Range:	Medium	Gift Wrapping Option?	No
Delivery Area:	Worldwide	Returns Procedure:	Down to you — some rugs are non returnable

www.hillco.co.uk

This is quite a different sort of website, offering the very highest quality of rugs available at some stratospheric prices; up into the thousands of pounds, although of course not all of them are as much. These rugs are all replicas of old rugs, made by skilled craftsmen on looms owned and overseen by the retailers, who are obviously experts. Take a look at their question and answer section to find out more about the rugs on offer and you'll be able to see the difference, when browsing through the site, between these and other much cheaper versions.

Site Usability:	★★★	Based:	UK
Product Range:	★★★★	Express Delivery Option? (UK)	No
Price Range:	Luxury	Gift Wrapping Option?	No
Delivery Area:	Worldwide	Returns Procedure:	Down to you in agreement with them

www.rugsdirect.co.uk

A rug can add so much atmosphere to a room as I'm sure you'll agree and if you haven't inherited a few from your great grandmother you can choose from the very good selection on this website, from traditional patterned rugs (think Chinese or Turkish in deep dark rich colours) to extremely modern designs, such as animal prints and abstracts. Thank goodness, too, that this is a site that actually gives you immediate information on ordering and delivery – why don't they all do that? You'll also be able to buy stair rods and rug underlay here.

Site Usability:	★★★★★	Based:	UK
Product Range:	★★★★★	Express Delivery Option? (UK)	Yes
Price Range:	Luxury/Medium	Gift Wrapping Option?	No
Delivery Area:	Worldwide	Returns Procedure:	Down to you

www.lounge-about.com

No ordinary rug company this, but one where you'll find cowhide rugs in a variety of colours plus zebra and tiger cowhide. Once you've chosen a design you can ask them to send you pictures of a selection of hides so that you can choose the exact one you want – extremely important as of course they're all different. You can buy cowhide cushions backed in suede and gorgeous leather beanbags here as well.

Site Usability:	★★★★★	Express Delivery Option? (UK)	No
Product Range:	★★★★★	Gift Wrapping Option?	No
Price Range:	Medium/Very Good Value	Returns Procedure:	Down to you
Delivery Area:	Worldwide		

www.therugcollection.co.uk

The Rug Collection has over 8000 rugs available to buy online and offers UK delivery. Their range is handpicked from around the globe and includes everything from Belgian Wilton, hand-made Tibetan and Kadian hand-knotted Nepalese rugs to shaggy and Harlequin Chinese rugs, hallway runners and rugs for your bathroom. Even though the choice is so large the website is extremely easy to navigate and there's lots of information about particular types of rugs, sizing and colour options.

Site Usability:	★★★★★	Based:	UK
Product Range:	★★★★★	Express Delivery Option? (UK)	No
Price Range:	Luxury/Medium	Gift Wrapping Option?	No
Delivery Area:	UK and ask them for a quote for overseas delivery	Returns Procedure:	Down to you

www.therugcompany.co.uk

The Wonderland Rug Company, based in the North East of England, have been importing and retailing a comprehensive range of rugs for nearly twenty years. There are Indian Jalna and plain rugs, a Bokhara collection from Pakistan and beautiful soft coloured Chinese rugs, plus classic rugs from Turkey and Afghanistan and a small selection of children's rugs. There's also lots of information on buying a rug, how to choose and what to look for. Delivery is worldwide and they will normally dispatch to you within 48 hours.

Site Usability:	★★★★	Based:	UK
Product Range:	★★★★★	Express Delivery Option? (UK)	No
Price Range:	Luxury/Medium	Gift Wrapping Option?	No
Delivery Area:	Worldwide	Returns Procedure:	Down to you

www.uniqueorientalcarpets.com

There are all sorts of extra gimmicks on this website. Skip past their intro and click onto 'Travels of an Oriental Carpet', to hear the company's owner talk you through how carpets are made and the centuries of culture behind them. Then just select the style and type of carpet you're looking for and you can turn over the 'stack' of rugs you'll be shown until you find one you like and use their magnifier to get close up to the colours and design. There isn't a huge range here but what there is is beautifully demonstrated.

Site Usability:	★★★★★	Based:	UK
Product Range:	★★★	Express Delivery Option? (UK)	No
Price Range:	Luxury/Medium	Gift Wrapping Option?	No
Delivery Area:	UK	Returns Procedure:	Down to you

Chapter 50

Storage Solutions

All those with a tidy, well organised household – hands up please! If that's you, you're going to love the websites below as you can find somewhere to put everything neatly.

I really wish my household was like that. It's no use telling me that I wasn't strict enough with my kids when they were young, I know that already and unfortunately I also married – er how shall I put it? One of the less tidy kinds of men. That doesn't sound too mean, does it? It was far too late to train him, I'm afraid.

Anyway back to you; if you're like some of my friends with their ridiculously tidy houses well done you and if you're looking for more storage options you'll find them below. Enough said and yes I am very, very jealous, but you probably realised that already.

Sites to Visit

www.freyadesign.co.uk

If you're looking for a gorgeous gift for a small person, or just want to start your children off on the tidy trail early, then take a look here at these pretty hand-painted toy and keepsake boxes for boys and girls. They can be personalised with names or messages, and there are keepsake boxes for new babies and weddings, money boxes and hand-painted door signs available here too. Call them for worldwide delivery.

Site Usability:	★★★★	Based:	UK
Product Range:	★★★	Express Delivery Option? (UK)	No
Price Range:	Medium	Gift Wrapping Option?	No
Delivery Area:	Worldwide	Returns Procedure:	Down to you

www.mujionline.co.uk

You must have heard of Muji, the Japanese-based company offering functional and marvellous value products for the home and office including stationery, cookware, bags, luggage and accessories, travel sized bottles and excellent storage solutions. There's so much to see on this website it'll take you a while to get round and like me you'll probably be amazed by some of the prices. Don't expect anything elaborate – Muji is famous for stylish simplicity in all areas and excellent value.

Site Usability:	★★★★★	Based:	UK
Product Range:	★★★★★	Express Delivery Option? (UK)	No
Price Range:	Very Good Value	Gift Wrapping Option?	No
Delivery Area:	Worldwide	Returns Procedure:	Down to you

www.originalbooks.net

So you're one of those people who like to keep their papers, CDs and even the TV remote control tidied up and elegantly stored – then this is the place for you. You'll find every kind of storage covered in what looks like antique embossed leather but which is actually a special resin. They offer booksafes, box files and journals, drinks accessories, photo frames and much more and they'll deliver worldwide.

Site Usability:	★★★★	Based:	UK
Product Range:	★★★★	Express Delivery Option? (UK)	No
Price Range:	Medium	Gift Wrapping Option?	No
Delivery Area:	Worldwide	Returns Procedure:	Down to you

www.somersetlevels.co.uk

This is a small company specialising in high quality basketware, so if you're looking for a new linen or log basket (or a dog basket for yours to chew his or her way through, and there are loads), this would be a very good place to start. As well as willow baskets made in their own workshop they also offer an extensive range of basketware handmade by craftspeople from all across the globe in weaving materials such as rush, seagrass and cane.

Site Usability:	★★★★	Based:	UK
Product Range:	★★★	Express Delivery Option? (UK)	No
Price Range:	Medium	Gift Wrapping Option?	No
Delivery Area:	Worldwide	Returns Procedure:	Down to you

www.theholdingcompany.co.uk

If you've suddenly decided that it's time you went for the tidy, well organised look you'll definitely need this website, where you'll find every type of storage for the home, including bathroom space-savers - laundry baskets, hooks (yes they're actually for hanging your robe on rather than dumping it on the floor) trolleys, corner shelves and shaving mirrors (not storage, but hey). Chic and clever storage for everywhere you can think of, in fact. The only problem is you'll have to get everyone else to use it as well.

Site Usability:	★★★★	Based:	UK
Product Range:	★★★★★	Express Delivery Option? (UK)	No
Price Range:	Medium	Gift Wrapping Option?	No
Delivery Area:	UK	Returns Procedure:	Down to you

www.toytidy.co.uk

You're going to love this website, believe me, as along with all the different storage ideas for children you can also find some excellent toy boxes which would be perfect for dressing up paraphernalia. There are solid wood and fabric covered boxes plus, and most specially, beautiful hand painted personalised boxes covered with fairies, teddies or trains. Expensive, I know, but absolutely gorgeous.

Site Usability:	★★★★	Based: UK	
Product Range:	★★★★	Express Delivery Option? (UK)	No
Price Range:	Luxury/Medium	Gift Wrapping Option?	No
Delivery Area:	UK	Returns Procedure:	Down to you

Also take a look at the following for storage solutions:

Website Address	You'll find it in
www.johnlewis.co.uk	Chapter 44: The Kitchen
www.lakelandlimited.co.uk	Chapter 44: The Kitchen

Chapter 51

The Garden: Equipment, Furniture and Barbecues

Plants and Seeds

Gardening Gifts and Accessories

Pet Accessories and Petfood

As this is such a huge area of online shopping and one that is growing really fast (no pun intended) I'm not going to give you a comprehensive list of the websites available here, it just wouldn't be possible as they deserve a book all to themselves (yes just keep an eye out for that one, I'm sure you can have it soon).

What I have done is selected some of the best websites for you in each area so that you can get a taste of what's available. Although having said that on these websites alone you can find everything from the latest Australian barbecues to hedge trimmers, ride-on lawn mowers and general garden tools.

Where pets are concerned if you're not a pet owner you'll doubtless want to move straight on to the next chapter, however if you live in the country, have one or two (or several) large dogs then you'll be overjoyed to know that you no longer have to go out to your local pet store and carry that huge bag of dog food to the car and then into your house. You can just order it here and have it delivered straight to your door.

Online supermarkets such as Ocado and Tesco carry certain ranges of pet food and treats but here you'll find everything and quite often at some good prices. This may not be a shopaholic's paradise but you, like me, will almost certainly find it useful.

Sites to Visit

Equipment, Furniture and Barbecues

www.bbqworld.co.uk

This is another excellent place to look for your next barbecue. Here you'll find not only the Weber range, but also Buschbeck masonry barbecues and fireplaces, Dancook plated steel fireplaces and BBQ covers plus a selection of Napoleon and Electrolux gas barbecues. There are lots of accessories as well from the basic essentials such as tongs and forks to the very superior Weber Q rolling duffle, gas canisters, rotisseries and griddles and patio coolers. Well worth a look if you're looking for something a bit different.

Site Usability:	★★★★★	Based:	UK
Product Range:	★★★★	Express Delivery Option? (UK)	Two day service
Price Range:	Luxury/Medium	Gift Wrapping Option?	No
Delivery Area:	EU	Returns Procedure:	Down to you

www.birstall.co.uk

Here you can buy just about everything for the garden and gardening enthusiast, from seeds to recliners, barbecues to poultry houses and swimming pool lighting. There are so many products bursting out from the site that it looks a bit confusing but it's well worth the effort. As far as gifts are concerned they sell high quality Felco secateurs, decorative brass Haws watering cans and Leatherman knives plus loads of other ideas.

Site Usability:	★★★★	Based:	UK
Product Range:	★★★★	Express Delivery Option? (UK)	No
Price Range:	Medium	Gift Wrapping Option?	No
Delivery Area:	Worldwide	Returns Procedure:	Down to you

www.gardencentredirect.co.uk

This is another of those extremely comprehensive garden websites where there's a wide choice – from garden sheds, summer houses and log cabins to wheelbarrows, ladders and pruners, trimmers, shredders and brushcutters. You can enlarge everything to see it really clearly and they have a lot of special deals. Delivery is free to the UK mainland and they tell you how long all the items will take to reach you.

Site Usability:	★★★★★	Based:	UK
Product Range:	★★★★★	Express Delivery Option? (UK)	No
Price Range:	Medium	Gift Wrapping Option?	No
Delivery Area:	UK	Returns Procedure:	Down to you but within 7 days

www.greenfingers.co.uk

Calling themselves the Garden Superstore and with good reason, Greenfingers has a well laid out website that's easy to use, as all the departments are very clearly listed on the home page. So you can choose from Garden Furniture, Water Butts, Plant Care, Barbecues, Garden Lighting, Pots and Planters (and much more) and be taken to exactly what you're looking for. You need to allow 10-14 days for delivery but give them a call if you're in a hurry.

Site Usability:	★★★★★	Based:	UK
Product Range:	★★★★★	Express Delivery Option? (UK)	No
Price Range:	Medium	Gift Wrapping Option?	No
Delivery Area:	UK	Returns Procedure:	Down to you

www.grovelands.com

Grovelands are a large garden centre in Berkshire who've managed to transfer just about all their products onto their website. You'll find a wide range of barbecue equipment including brands like Weber and The Australian Barbecue Company, garden furniture from the highest quality teak to well priced garden sets and equipment from pond pumps to propagators. There's also an excellent range of gifts plus Christmas trees, lights and ornaments. Delivery is free to the UK and they'll also ship most items worldwide.

Site Usability:	★★★★	Based:	UK
Product Range:	★★★★	Express Delivery Option? (UK)	Yes
Price Range:	Medium	Gift Wrapping Option?	No
Delivery Area:	Worldwide	Returns Procedure:	Down to you

www.flamingbarbecues.co.uk

Flaming Barbecues offer everything from a wide range of gas, charcoal and portable barbecues by Outback, BillyOh, Big K, Landman, Weber, Beefeater and Sunshine to outdoor heating, smokers and all you could need in the way of accessories. They also offer free delivery to the UK mainland. You can buy barbecues at all price levels here, take their recommendations and find some very good discounts and ends of lines as well. Before your next cookout definitely take a look.

Site Usability:	★★★★★	Based:	UK
Product Range:	★★★★★	Express Delivery Option? (UK)	No
Price Range:	Luxury/Medium/Very Good Value	Gift Wrapping Option?	No
Delivery Area:	UK	Returns Procedure:	Down to you

www.gardenfurnitureworld.co.uk

Garden Furniture World specialises in furniture by Hartman, whose ranges and sets include rattan, wrought iron and teak in a very good choice of modern and traditional styles at a wide range of prices. There's also an excellent collection of cushions by Benetton, parasols which you can order separately and teak oil and furniture cleaner.

Site Usability:	★★★★	Based:	UK
Product Range:	★★★★	Express Delivery Option? (UK)	No
Price Range:	Luxury/Medium	Gift Wrapping Option?	No
Delivery Area:	UK	Returns Procedure:	Down to you

www.indian-ocean.co.uk

If you haven't come across them before, Indian Ocean are retailers of the highest quality teak garden furniture, from dining sets for twelve to occasional tables, chairs, loungers and parasols and decorative garden seats. They also offer superb bathroom furniture and accessories, a range of cushions (for the garden chairs) outdoor lighting and, recently launched, their range of indoor dining furniture. They'll deliver worldwide but call them if you want a delivery outside the UK.

Site Usability:	★★★★	Based:	UK
Product Range:	★★★★	Express Delivery Option? (UK)	No
Price Range:	Luxury	Gift Wrapping Option?	No
Delivery Area:	Worldwide	Returns Procedure:	Down to you in agreement with them

www.ukcamping.co.uk

This is mainly, as you would expect, a site for camping enthusiasts and sells a wide range of tents, sleeping and cooking equipment. They also have a very good range of high quality picnic chairs and tables so they're well worth having a look at if you're about to replace yours. If you need anything in a hurry give them a call to check that what you want is in stock and, if it is, you can probably have it the next day.

Site Usability:	★★★★	Based:	UK
Product Range:	★★★★	Express Delivery Option? (UK)	Yes if you request it
Price Range:	Medium/Very Good Value	Gift Wrapping Option?	No
Delivery Area:	UK	Returns Procedure:	Down to you

www.worldofweber.co.uk

I have to confess that we are definitely Weber addicts, barbecuing as we do right through the summer practically every evening and having started out with the small version and now graduated to the full size (lazy) gas type. They also have a marvellous portable gas barbecue which we used at Henley last year to feed a ravenous crew for about a week (which happened to include my son). So, on this website you'll find the full range. It's not the most sophisticated website but it offers exceptional barbecues (and no they're not paying me to say all that).

Site Usability:	★★★★	Based:	UK
Product Range:	★★★★	Express Delivery Option? (UK)	Yes
Price Range:	Luxury/Medium	Gift Wrapping Option?	No
Delivery Area:	UK	Returns Procedure:	Down to you

Also take a look below at the following for Equipment, Furniture and Barbecues:
www.crocus.co.uk

Plants and Seeds

www.ashridgetrees.co.uk

Here you can select from a full list of shrubs, trees, hedging, roses and fruit trees which are offered from the beginning of May for delivery starting in November; the start of the 'bare-root' season. They don't have masses of stock and everyone is dealt with on a first-come, first-served basis so if you see something you like, order it early or they may run out. If you need advice you can call them and if you're interesting in buying beautifully wrapped, container-grown trees as gifts you can visit their sister website at www.ashridgetreegifts.co.uk.

Site Usability:	★★★★	Based:	UK
Product Range:	★★★★	Express Delivery Option? (UK)	No
Price Range:	Medium	Gift Wrapping Option?	No
Delivery Area:	UK	Returns Procedure:	Down to you

www.crocus.co.uk

Crocus is one of the best gardeners' websites. It not only offers you attractive flowers and plants, giving you more information than most about them, but just about everything else you might need for the garden, all presented in a really attractive and informative way. If you want some advice they're just waiting to give it and they'll always have clever ideas for gifts for occasions such as Mother's Day and Easter. Take a look round now, it's definitely *the* gardener's paradise online.

Site Usability:	★★★★★	Based:	UK
Product Range:	★★★★★	Express Delivery Option? (UK)	Yes
Price Range:	Medium	Gift Wrapping Option?	No
Delivery Area:	UK	Returns Procedure:	Down to you

www.davidaustin.com

David Austin is famous for developing new types of English Roses, with his first, 'Constance Spry', launched in 1963. On his website you can find many varieties, including Modern Hybrid Tea Roses and Floribundas, Climbing Roses, Ramblers, Modern Shrub Roses and Wild Species Roses. You'll also find his new fragrant English Roses created specially for the home. You can order his gift boxed container roses and exquisite rose bouquets here as well for UK delivery.

Site Usability:	★★★★★	Based:	UK
Product Range:	★★★★	Express Delivery Option? (UK)	Yes
Price Range:	Luxury/Medium	Gift Wrapping Option?	Yes for Container Roses
Delivery Area:	Worldwide except container roses and bouquets	Returns Procedure:	Down to you

www.dobies.co.uk

Currently Dobies offer a range of plants and seeds of over 1500 items. You can buy just about every kind of flower and vegetable seed, easy-grow flower plants, vegetable plants, potatoes, fruit bushes and trees, bulbs, perennials, roots and shrubs plus a range of garden equipment. As well as all of this there's lots of information about what you should be growing now – both outdoors and in containers, and how to grow from seed. Delivery is 3-5 days from order other than for seasonal items.

Site Usability:	★★★★★	Based:	UK
Product Range:	★★★★★	Express Delivery Option? (UK)	No
Price Range:	Medium	Gift Wrapping Option?	No
Delivery Area:	UK	Returns Procedure:	Down to you but within 7 days

www.duchyofcornwallnursery.co.uk

This is a unique nursery, offering for sale some 4000 varieties of plants, including many rarely available elsewhere, with the majority grown on site. On this extremely attractive website you can download the full product and price list or visit the plant shop, offering a wide range, beautifully photographed and with detailed descriptions. You can also order Duchy of Cornwall toiletries, Originals (biscuits, preserves and more), hampers and their own high quality range of tools.

Site Usability:	★★★★★	Based:	UK
Product Range:	★★★★★	Express Delivery Option? (UK)	No
Price Range:	Medium	Gift Wrapping Option?	No
Delivery Area:	UK	Returns Procedure:	Down to you

www.naturescape.co.uk

Here you'll find only wild flower plants to buy online from Naturescape's excellent catalogue including native grown collections of wildflowers and grasses, seed collections, meadows, lawns, climbers, wild rose plants, shrubs, trees, hedge plants, pond, marsh, bulbs, corms and more. To see the plants and their descriptions properly you need to click on 'more information' but once you've done that everything is very clear. There's also a section on how to clean and store wild flowers and you can buy books, posters and gift vouchers too.

Site Usability:	★★★★	Based:	UK
Product Range:	★★★★	Express Delivery Option? (UK)	No
Price Range:	Medium	Gift Wrapping Option?	No
Delivery Area:	UK	Returns Procedure:	Down to you

www.plantconnection.com

Plant Connection offer a wide range of bedding and young plants together with a specialist range of organic vegetables and herbs. The different plant categories are very clearly displayed and once you click on the area you're interested in you'll fine even more choice. I have to say that I find the pictures a little on the small side but with the excellent range available together with lots of advice you may well find what you're looking for here.

Site Usability:	★★★★	Based:	UK
Product Range:	★★★★★	Express Delivery Option? (UK)	No
Price Range:	Medium	Gift Wrapping Option?	No
Delivery Area:	UK	Returns Procedure:	Down to you

www.thecuttinggarden.com

Sarah Raven specialises in teaching people how to grow flowers that can be cut and used indoors and her first book, *The Cutting Garden*, won The Specialist Garden Book of the Year Award. On her colourful and attractively designed website you'll find a wonderful collection of seeds, seedlings and bulbs, her books and annual diary (a great gift) plus plenty of other ideas such as florists' scissors, flower arranging gloves and outdoor tableware and glass.

Site Usability:	★★★★	Based:	UK
Product Range:	★★★★	Express Delivery Option? (UK)	No
Price Range:	Medium	Gift Wrapping Option?	No
Delivery Area:	UK	Returns Procedure:	Down to you

www.plantpress.com

Not so much a plant shop (well actually it isn't) more of an online plant encyclopedia. This is free to use and you can search either from their A-Z list of plants or by using Plant Search, with all or part of a plant's name. Currently the resource covers over 5000 plants with 14,000 images and there are full descriptions and details of all the plants included. This is well worth a look and far, far quicker to access than those hugely heavy books in (usually) very small print.

Gardening Gifts and Accessories

www.baileys-home-garden.co.uk

Baileys offer a truly eclectic mix of home and garden accessories, from pretty Welsh blankets and paint buckets, to big sinks, garden lighting, Bailey's Bath Soak and Carrot Hand Cream. There are ideas for junior gardeners' gifts from tools, watering cans and buckets (all in a gorgeous cherry red) and vintage style garden forks, pots and twine reels. To order anything on their website you need to phone them – hopefully that will change soon.

Site Usability:	★★★★	Based;	UK
Product Range:	★★★	Express Delivery Option? (UK)	No
Price Range:	Medium	Gift Wrapping Option?	No
Delivery Area:	UK	Returns Procedure:	Down to you

www.bradleysthetannery.co.uk

Bradleys are an independent leather tannery based in Shropshire and specialising in the design and manufacture of a unique, high quality range of garden, gift, leisurewear and lifestyle products. Everything is handmade in the UK using traditional methods and local craftsman and all the leathers are tanned in-house. If I were a gardener I'd definitely want a pair of their unique gloves or leather trimmed topiary shears which come in a range of colours.

Site Usability:	★★★★	Based;	UK
Product Range:	★★★	Express Delivery Option? (UK)	No
Price Range:	Medium	Gift Wrapping Option?	No
Delivery Area:	Worldwide	Returns Procedure:	Down to you

www.franceshilary.com

Here's a wonderful place to find gifts for the gardener in your life produced by a husband and wife team inspired by visits to long established working gardens around the country. The products combine practicality with style and most would make excellent presents although if you're the gardener in your family you'll no doubt want a treat as well. There are beautifully made, classic tools, gloves, aprons and wonderful boots, dibbers, tampers and twine plus carefully thought out gift sets.

Site Usability:	★★★★★	Based:	UK
Product Range:	★★★★	Express Delivery Option? (UK)	No
Price Range:	Medium	Gift Wrapping Option?	Yes
Delivery Area:	Worldwide	Returns Procedure:	Down to you

www.gardentrading.co.uk

There's a very wide range of prices here as Garden Trading offer some unusual pieces of furniture such as the 'Broomstick Bench' right through to interesting canisters and glassware and the Lisa Stickley collection of cushions, enamel mugs and matchbox covers. There are suggestions in their 'Gift Ideas' section but personally I would recommend having a browse round the whole site as there's a lot to see.

Site Usability:	★★★★	Based:	UK
Product Range:	★★★★	Express Delivery Option? (UK)	No
Price Range:	Medium/Very Good Value	Gift Wrapping Option?	No
Delivery Area:	UK	Returns Procedure:	Down to you

www.grandillusions.co.uk

Grand Illusions offer a great deal to look at on their attractive website but it's very easy to get round and the pictures are really clear. You can choose from their ranges of reasonably priced accessories, including candelabra, storm lanterns, votive glasses, French scented candles and guest soaps plus a wide selection of small pretty items for outdoors from traditional watering cans, to bird feeders, glass carriers and sconces.

Site Usability:	★★★★	Based:	UK
Product Range:	★★★★	Express Delivery Option? (UK)	No
Price Range:	Medium	Gift Wrapping Option?	No
Delivery Area:	UK	Returns Procedure:	Down to you

www.plants4presents.co.uk

Plants make wonderful gifts on most occasions. And, whereas that wonderful bunch of flowers will be gone within a week, plants will last much, much longer. Here you can order from a really good selection including pink roses, early Clematis, fruiting lemon and kumquat trees, jasmine, azaleas and beautiful Moth Orchids. Each plant is hand-wrapped and packed with care instructions and a handwritten full-size greeting card.

Site Usability:	★★★★★	Based:	UK
Product Range:	★★★★	Express Delivery Option? (UK)	Yes
Price Range:	Medium	Gift Wrapping Option?	Yes
Delivery Area:	UK	Returns Procedure:	Down to you

www.plantstuff.com

This is not – as it sounds to me it should be – a plant website, but a great place to find lifestyle products and gardening gifts. It's beautifully laid out and easy to navigate and you can buy braziers and hammocks, candles in metal pots, slate cheeseboards, lead ducks and Hunter clogs and wellies. There's also a wonderful gardener's hamper although most gardeners would almost certainly have some of the items included already. Returns are free.

Site Usability:	★★★★★	Based:	UK
Product Range:	★★★★	Express Delivery Option? (UK)	No
Price Range:	Medium	Gift Wrapping Option?	No
Delivery Area:	EU	Returns Procedure:	Free of charge

www.rhs.org.uk

On the Royal Horticultural Society's website you can become a member of the RHS or make someone else a member; which provides their monthly magazine, reduced entry into RHS flower shows and free entry into RHS and partner gardens. You can click through to RHS Shopping Online which will invite you to the Wisley Bookshop (where you'll find gifts as well as books) and to their other online shopping areas. Alternatively you can go straight through to their main directory which links to other gardening websites.

Site Usability:	★★★★	Based:	UK
Product Range:	★★★	Express Delivery Option? (UK)	No
Price Range:	Medium	Gift Wrapping Option?	No but they will send some items as gifts for you
Delivery Area:	Worldwide	Returns Procedure:	Down to you

www.rkalliston.com

This is a really exceptional website offering perfect gifts for the gardener, from wasp catchers and storm lanterns to dibbers and twine, hammocks (to rest in after a hard day) and fairy vases as well as gardeners' gift sets, china for alfresco dining and pretty flower baskets, and these are just a few of the eclectic collection of gardening items available here.

Site Usability:	★★★★★	Based:	UK
Product Range:	★★★★	Express Delivery Option? (UK)	Yes
Price Range:	Medium	Gift Wrapping Option?	No
Delivery Area:	Worldwide	Returns Procedure:	Down to you

www.thegluttonousgardener.co.uk

Beautifully packaged and hand tied with raffia, here's a wide selection of well photographed gifts for any of your friends who like to garden and eat as well. So you'll find sloe gin accompanying young sloe trees, a bottle of Macon with a white grape vine and champagne with terracotta pots planted with sage, thyme, oregano and rosemary. This really is an excellent website and something just that little bit different.

Site Usability:	★★★★★	Based:	UK
Product Range:	★★★★	Express Delivery Option? (UK)	Yes
Price Range:	Medium	Gift Wrapping Option?	Yes
Delivery Area:	UK	Returns Procedure:	Down to you

www.treesdirect.co.uk

Fruit and nut trees, ornamentals and aromatic, evergreen bays are just some of the unusual gift ideas you can find here. The trees are chosen for their colour, blossom, shape and size to suit

287

all types of gardens and patios and they arrive dressed in a hessian sack tied with green garden string, planting instructions and hand written message card. You can request that your tree arrives on a specific date and if you want advice just give them a call.

Site Usability:	★★★★	Based;	UK
Product Range:	★★★★	Express Delivery Option? (UK)	Yes
Price Range:	Medium	Gift Wrapping Option?	No
Delivery Area:	Europe	Returns Procedure:	Down to you

Pet Accessories and Petfood

www.barkerandball.com

With all the incredibly busy pet supermarkets which you can find online it's a real pleasure to come across one which is slightly different – in this case just for dogs. If you like to spend just that little bit extra and enjoy something a bit different just take a look at their selection of 'nest' beds, colourful dog bowls and toys and doggy gift ideas including fun ID tags. UK delivery is free on orders over £70.

Site Usability:	★★★★★	Based:	UK
Product Range:	★★★	Express Delivery Option? (UK)	Yes worldwide express delivery
Price Range:	Medium	Gift Wrapping Option?	No
Delivery Area:	Worldwide	Returns Procedure:	Down to you

www.petcompany.co.uk

Whether you have cats, dogs, birds, fish or other small animals you'll find everything you need right here, at this online pet superstore; from dog food, treats, dog beds and toys to cat beds, food and litter, fish feeders, DVDs, books and much more. It's a very colourful and friendly website with a speedy delivery service and they make it easy for you go get straight to the product you're looking for.

Site Usability:	★★★★★	Based:	UK
Product Range:	★★★★★	Express Delivery Option? (UK)	No but speedy delivery is standard
Price Range:	Medium	Gift Wrapping Option?	No
Delivery Area:	EU	Returns Procedure:	Down to you

www.petspantry.tv

Here you can find one of the best online ranges for dogs, cats, fish and small animals plus wildbird and reptile(!) food and equipment, horse food, supplements and grooming products and lovely animal themed birthday and greeting cards. Also flea sprays and powders, grass seed, rose food, stain and odour removers and everything to get rid of vermin, although I have to say I prefer to leave that to the experts, coward that I am.

Site Usability:	★★★★★	Based:	UK
Product Range:	★★★★★	Express Delivery Option? (UK)	No
Price Range:	Medium	Gift Wrapping Option?	No
Delivery Area:	Worldwide	Returns Procedure:	Down to you

www.petsparade.com

Pets Parade offer a wide range of equipment and accessories for dogs, including hard-to-find traditional wicker dog baskets (which we gave up when our new puppy chewed through two in quick succession), cats, birds, fish and other small animals. Within each type of pet's section there are lots of articles giving advice on various aspects of breed and care, and also links to other pet minded websites such as grooming, insurance services and kennel directories, making this much more than just a one-stop pet shop.

Site Usability:	★★★★★	Based:	UK
Product Range:	★★★★★	Express Delivery Option? (UK)	No
Price Range:	Medium	Gift Wrapping Option?	No
Delivery Area:	UK	Returns Procedure:	Down to you

www.petplanet.co.uk

This is another excellent pet supermarket and one which I have to admit I've used many times with excellent results. It's a busier website than some but, as long as you immediately click through to the type of animal you're buying for, you should be fine. Register with them and they'll store the details of your previous purchases to make it really easy for repeat orders. You'll also find help with pet insurance, information about various breeds and, probably most useful of all, locate a vet within a short distance of wherever you are.

Site Usability:	★★★★★	Based:	UK
Product Range:	★★★★★	Express Delivery Option? (UK)	Yes
Price Range:	Medium	Gift Wrapping Option?	No
Delivery Area:	Europe	Returns Procedure:	Down to you

Food and Drink

Food and Drink

What can I say here that you haven't heard me say before? That is, of course, presuming that you've already read one of my books.

What? You still go out to the supermarket, load up your trolley and take everything home in the back of your car?

You really like doing that? It gives you pleasure to take your two tinies along with you and have them complain (being polite here) the whole time you're shopping?

You like carrying all those bags into the house while at the same time trying to stop your dog, cat, toddler escaping out of the front door?

Sorry about that but I just had to get it out of my system, again. I know that there are still people who don't shop online and who think that the internet is some kind of dangerous place.

'I'm too old to learn to use the web', a sixty-something lady said to me the other day as I muttered darkly under my breath about my eighty-six-year-old mother-in-law who mastered her computer, email and internet when she was past her eightieth birthday.

Where food and drink are concerned not only is the very best of everything at your fingertips, with far, far more choice than you could ever see anywhere else, but you don't have to go out to the shops to get it – it all comes to you.

Not just supermarket shopping but the best wines, champagnes and spirits, Aberdeen Angus beef, fish just about straight out of the sea, (brill, cod and Dover Sole to lobster, crab and mussels), organic fruit and vegetables, freshly baked bread, cheese from France, Italy and the UK of course, plus wonderful freshly baked cakes are all to be found online.

I quite understand those who want to choose their fruit and veg themselves and visit their local bakery for their bread. I also understand wanting to support your local butcher provided you get a really good service and reasonable prices as we do (Hopper and Babb – you're just the best) but I don't understand why you'd exhaust yourself driving a trolley round a supermarket anymore, I really don't. Perhaps if you have a little look below you'll see what I mean.

Chapter 52

The Bakery

As I've mentioned above, ordering fresh bread and cakes online may seem to be a step too far and this was definitely the case a couple of years ago. Now there are some excellent places who will send their bread and cakes out to you by express delivery so that they're perfect when they get to you. You can also order from the bakery section of your online supermarket and hope that the bread will have been baked the same day.

Some of the best places for ordering bakery goods are the organic foodstores, particularly those who offer weekly box delivery, so check out those websites and slip a few loaves in with your next order.

On the subject of cakes there are now some wonderful online bakeries, with two in particular that I have used many times: megrivers.com and bettysbypost.co.uk. So the next time you really don't want to make your Christmas cake or Easter Simnel cake you can order from them and be sure that they will be, well, certainly as good as my home made ones are. If you're ordering seasonal cakes do make sure that you order early enough as they will run out.

You can also order last minute birthday cakes to be sent out for you, wonderful muffins, brownies and flapjacks and even a Hansel and Gretel house cake, complete with handmade sugared flowers. Then there are luscious chocolate cakes, carrot cakes, cinnamon and orange cakes ... but I'll stop there, just in case I'm making you too hungry.

Sites to Visit

www.bakinboys.co.uk

There's a great deal going on on this website, but click quickly through to 'Buy Stuff' and you'll find a really great selection of flapjacks, muffins, cookies, cakes, hand cooked crisps and Belgian waffles all available in boxes or packs of twelve upwards for next day delivery. You can find nutritional information on all their products and everything is nut free. So, as they say, 'say it with flour'.

Site Usability:	★★★		Based:	UK
Product Range:	★★★		Express Delivery Option? (UK)	Yes
Price Range:	Medium		Gift Wrapping Option?	No
Delivery Area:	UK		Returns Procedure:	Down to you

www.bettysbypost.co.uk

At bettysbypost.com you can order hand decorated Christmas cakes in a variety of sizes, their family recipe Christmas pudding with fruit soaked in brandy and ale and seasonal favourites such as Simnel cake Christmas tea loaf, panettone and stollen. Chocolate ginger, miniature Florentines and peppermint creams are just a few of the goodies on offer in their confectionary section and you'll also find lovely stocking fillers for children and preserves for the Christmas larder.

Site Usability:	★★★★★		Based:	UK
Product Range:	★★★★		Express Delivery Option? (UK)	No
Price Range:	Medium		Gift Wrapping Option?	No
Delivery Area:	Worldwide		Returns Procedure:	Down to you

www.beverlyhillsbakery.com

If you live outside London don't even think of looking at the full range here, as you'll probably be really disappointed when you realise that they can't deliver to you. Do however click through to the selection that they will send to you anywhere in the UK (and overseas, in some cases), which includes their carrot cake, apple and cinnamon cake and pear and ginger cake or one of their attractive gift tins containing delicious mini muffins, cookies and brownies.

Site Usability:	★★★★		Based:	UK
Product Range:	★★★		Express Delivery Option? (UK)	No
Price Range:	Medium		Gift Wrapping Option?	No
Delivery Area:	Worldwide for some items.		Returns Procedure:	Down to you

www.botham.co.uk

Here you'll find a simple collection of cakes for Christmas and other occasions which you can personalise with your own message or buy un-piped. All cakes are hand decorated and iced so they ask you to give them plenty of notice. They do, however, keep a short order iced fruit cake, piped with Happy Birthday for you to buy by quick delivery. You may well also be tempted by the plum bread, biscuits and preserves on this website.

Site Usability:	★★★		Based:	UK
Product Range:	★★★		Express Delivery Option? (UK)	No
Price Range:	Medium		Gift Wrapping Option?	No
Delivery Area:	Worldwide		Returns Procedure:	Down to you

www.caketoppers.co.uk

On this website you can order a birthday cake to be sent for next day delivery (just in case you've forgotten to get one ready in time), send your own photo to be used on a cake, order a Christmas cake to be sent to anywhere in mainland UK and choose from traditional sponge and iced fruit cakes to be sent on the date of your choosing. They also offer mini decorated cupcakes and shortbread with your choice of photo.

Site Usability:	★★★★	Based:	UK
Product Range:	★★★	Express Delivery Option? (UK)	Yes
Price Range:	Medium/Very Good Value	Gift Wrapping Option?	No
Delivery Area:	UK	Returns Procedure:	Down to you

www.cheesecake.co.uk

There's everything here for cheesecake addicts (and I definitely have one in my house) from Chocolate Toffee Walnut Smash and Raspberry Split to Charlie's Original New York New York double baked and far too many more to list. You can order yours personalised for birthdays and other celebrations, there are special cakes for Valentine's Day and weddings and you can have them pre-sliced too. If you want to buy one as a gift, get them to send it out for you with a card.

Site Usability:	★★★★	Based:	UK
Product Range:	★★★★	Express Delivery Option? (UK)	Yes
Price Range:	Medium	Gift Wrapping Option?	No
Delivery Area:	UK	Returns Procedure:	Down to you

www.collinstreet.com

This is a really, really bad website to visit if you're on a diet. The Collins Street Bakery is based in Texas and sells the most delicious, fruit and nut filled, luxury fruit cakes, pecan cakes (think Apple Cinnamon and Pineapple Pecan) you've ever tasted. Don't get too excited about the toffee, cookies and cheesecake here as those items they'll only ship to the US. The cakes, however, they'll ship to anywhere in the world so take care if you have a really sweet tooth.

Site Usability:	★★★★★	Based:	US
Product Range:	★★★	Express Delivery Option? (UK)	No
Price Range:	Medium	Gift Wrapping Option?	No
Delivery Area:	Worldwide	Returns Procedure:	Down to you

www.homefayrelimited.co.uk

Specialists at producing cakes, chutneys and jams for events such as farmers markets, Home Fayre are now offering you the opportunity of buying their wonderful looking and extremely well priced products from home (so the next time you have a tea party you can really fool someone). Their every day cakes include chocolate, cinnamon and raison, coffee and walnut and they also offer birthday and Christmas cakes. You can also buy Tipsy Strawberry and Plum and Ginger jams and totally naughty sweets such as fudge, nut crunch and coconut ice.

Site Usability:	★★★★	Based:	UK
Product Range:	★★★	Express Delivery Option? (UK)	No
Price Range:	Medium/Very Good Value	Gift Wrapping Option?	No
Delivery Area:	UK	Returns Procedure:	Down to you

www.jane-asher.co.uk

I'm sure you've heard of Jane Asher, actress, film star, writer, lifestyle expert and cake designer extraordinaire, but did you also know that you could buy some of her marvellous cakes online? Well now you do. Just click through to her website and her Mail Order cake section and you'll find a choice of about 40 different designs for all sorts of different occasions. You can choose from three sizes of cake and sponge or fruit filling. UK delivery only, and you need to allow up to ten days for your cake to arrive.

Site Usability:	★★★★★	Based:	UK
Product Range:	★★★★	Express Delivery Option? (UK)	No
Price Range:	Luxury	Gift Wrapping Option?	No
Delivery Area:	UK	Returns Procedure:	Down to you

www.megrivers.com

An extremely tempting website offering 'home made' beautifully decorated cakes, biscuits and traybakes (flapjacks, chocolate brownies and the like). Their traditional fruit cake is extremely good and made well in advance so if you can't be bothered to bake yourself definitely shop here. Having ordered from them several times myself I can assure you that everyone who tastes their products will be delighted and their service is excellent. Overseas delivery by request.

Site Usability:	★★★★★	Based:	UK
Product Range:	★★★	Express Delivery Option? (UK)	No
Price Range:	Medium	Gift Wrapping Option?	Yes
Delivery Area:	UK and overseas by request	Returns Procedure:	Down to you

www.need-a-cake.co.uk

This family run cake company will send out most of their cakes to you anywhere in the UK. Because they have so many designs you need to call them to order and confirm prices. They also offer a good range of cake making accessories such as cake tins and forcing bags if you do want to make your own. Their Christmas cakes appear on their website from the end of October so check back if you want to take a look at these.

Site Usability:	★★★	Based:	UK
Product Range:	★★★	Express Delivery Option? (UK)	No
Price Range:	Medium/Very Good Value	Gift Wrapping Option?	No
Delivery Area:	UK	Returns Procedure:	Down to you

www.saralouisekakes.co.uk

If you know someone who has a sweet tooth and needs cheering up you could consider sending them a Hansel and Gretel House cake, decorated in white and pink buttercream and handmade sugared hearts and flowers; alternatively a box of boozy triple chocolate and cherry brownies covered in chocolate fudge icing and decorated with milk chocolate curls. Have I got your attention yet? Thought so. You'll probably want to order some for yourself as well.

Site Usability:	★★★★	Based:	UK
Product Range:	★★★	Express Delivery Option? (UK)	No
Price Range:	Medium	Gift Wrapping Option?	No
Delivery Area:	UK	Returns Procedure:	Down to you

www.theorganiccakecompany.co.uk

There isn't a huge selection here, but when you read about their chocolate cake made with a fresh cream and rum ganache containing 36% chocolate, and their New England home style carrot and walnut cake with its lemon cream cheese topping, if you're anything like me you'll want to have a taste. You buy them as slices, cakes or large traybakes and you need to call or email them to order. All cakes are despatched by next day courier.

Site Usability:	★★★	Based:	UK
Product Range:	★★★	Express Delivery Option? (UK)	Yes
Price Range:	Medium	Gift Wrapping Option?	No
Delivery Area:	UK	Returns Procedure:	Down to you

www.thecakestore.com

The Cake Store offers a range of cakes of different sizes and decorations and for different types of occasion including, of course, Christmas. Prices include delivery and you need to allow 7-10 days for your order to arrive. Every cake is hand crafted and specially made for you from their choice of fun and different designs and they also offer beautiful wedding cakes. At time of writing most are only available for within the M25.

Site Usability:	★★★	Based:	UK
Product Range:	★★★★	Express Delivery Option? (UK)	No
Price Range:	Luxury/Medium	Gift Wrapping Option?	No
Delivery Area:	UK	Returns Procedure:	Down to you

Chapter 53

The Butcher

I have to say that we as a family are exceptionally lucky and our marvellous butcher delivers to us every day. If this is not the case with you then I would definitely take a look at the websites included here where there's a truly excellent selection of meat available to order including home made sausages, Angus beef, oven ready grouse, partridge and turkey, venison, goose, lamb and pork.

If you browse through the various online butchers you'll find quite a range of prices, sometimes due to the size of the retailer (as in some cases you're ordering from individual farms and collectives who are usually less expensive) and of course sometimes due to the quality of the meat.

Very often delivery is quite steep so it pays to order quite a lot and put some in your freezer – please don't do what we do though, which is to forget to label everything and then discover we've left it too long. I'm sure you won't, that's just us being disorganised.

Sites to Visit

www.blackface.co.uk

Heather bred Blackface lamb, organic lamb, haggis, iron-age pork, oven-ready grouse, partridge and bronze turkeys are all available to order online on this site based in Scotland. Note that deliveries and availability depend on seasonality and you may have to wait for some products. Delivery is free and if you want to order your Christmas turkey from them this year they'll send them out by carrier to you a few days before Christmas.

Site Usability:	★★★★	Based:	UK
Product Range:	★★★	Express Delivery Option? (UK)	No
Price Range:	Medium	Gift Wrapping Option?	No
Delivery Area:	UK	Returns Procedure:	Down to you

www.broughs.com

On Broughs' unsophisticated website you can buy, amongst other things, excellent good value beef and award winning sausages. Here are just some of the awards they've won, which they're keen (and rightly so) to tell you about: Britain's Best Pork Sausage, Venison red wine sausage – Gold 'Q Butcher' Award, Birkdale Traditional Sausage – Gold Star & trophy and they've also been voted one of the top three small butchers in the UK.

Site Usability:	★★★	Based:	UK
Product Range:	★★★★	Express Delivery Option? (UK)	No
Price Range:	Medium/Very Good Value	Gift Wrapping Option?	No
Delivery Area:	UK	Returns Procedure:	Down to you

www.donaldrussell.com

This is a superb website from an excellent butcher, beautifully photographed and laid out and extremely tempting. You can buy just about every type of meat here, from goose and game (in season) to pork, beef and lamb plus natural fish and seafood. Most of the pictures show the products as you'd like them to arrive on your plate and you can either buy from their ready prepared dishes such as Salmon en Croute or Bolognese sauce or you can follow their excellent recipes.

Site Usability:	★★★★★	Based:	UK
Product Range:	★★★★★	Express Delivery Option? (UK)	No
Price Range:	Luxury	Gift Wrapping Option?	No
Delivery Area:	UK	Returns Procedure:	Down to you

www.eversfieldorganic.co.uk

Eversfield Organic is an 850 acre organic farm nestling deep in the heart of the West Devon countryside and farmed to the highest Soil Association standards. Aberdeen Angus Beef, Romney Marsh sheep and Large Black pigs are prepared in the traditional manner by their professional butchers, guaranteeing extremely tasty and tender cuts of meat.

Site Usability:	★★★★★	Based:	UK
Product Range:	★★★★	Express Delivery Option? (UK)	No
Price Range:	Medium	Gift Wrapping Option?	No
Delivery Area:	UK	Returns Procedure:	Down to you

www.griffithsbutchers.co.uk

This butcher is based in Somerset and offers next day delivery on a selection of meat boxes, with names such as Winter Warmer (steak and kidney and stewing steak), Christmas Hamper pack with (yes you guessed it) a 7kg turkey, bacon, chipolatas and honey roast ham and Family Gold pack, with Somerset beef and chicken supremes. They also offer seasonal game, barbecue meats and home made sausages.

Site Usability:	★★★	Based:	UK
Product Range:	★★★★	Express Delivery Option? (UK)	Yes
Price Range:	Medium	Gift Wrapping Option?	No
Delivery Area:	UK	Returns Procedure:	Down to you

www.healfarm.co.uk

You won't find a lot of pretty pictures on this simple site offering a wide choice of beef, lamb, pork, poultry, sausages and burgers at reasonable prices, just an excellent selection and very good service. You can order your Bronze and ready stuffed turkey here and specify the size by the kilo. You'll also find recipes, advice on roasting meat and Aga cookery information.

Site Usability:	★★★★★	Based:	UK
Product Range:	★★★★	Express Delivery Option? (UK)	No
Price Range:	Medium	Gift Wrapping Option?	No
Delivery Area:	UK	Returns Procedure:	Down to you

www.lanefarm.co.uk

Lane Farm is a family run farming business based in the Suffolk countryside, which produces quality pork products from their own home produced pork. You can order sausages with names like Winter Warmer and Italian Spice and Garlic, stir fry pork strips, lemon and pepper steaks and Suffolk Roast (stuffed with apricots and wrapped in bacon), plus their own, sweet cured bacon and gammon. To order you need to call, fax or email them.

Site Usability:	★★★	Based:	UK
Product Range:	★★★	Express Delivery Option? (UK)	No
Price Range:	Medium	Gift Wrapping Option?	No
Delivery Area:	UK	Returns Procedure:	Down to you

www.meats.co.uk

You'll find very good value meat on this website, available for next day delivery provided you order before 10am and if you spend over £75. They offer beef, lamb, poultry, pork and game such as wood pigeon, partridge and venison plus York ham, pancetta (which is often hard to find) and black pudding. As you click on a type of meat you'll find a recipe idea alongside the excellent pictures.

Site Usability:	★★★★	Based:	UK
Product Range:	★★★★	Express Delivery Option? (UK)	No
Price Range:	Medium	Returns Procedure:	Down to you
Delivery Area:	UK		

www.realmeat.co.uk

The Real Meat Company supplies meat and poultry from traditional farmers with a nationwide delivery service. You can order your turkey from them for Christmas from mid-November. Their minimum order value is £35 and you specify the day you want your delivery. Remember to allow them enough time in the run up to Christmas.

Site Usability:	★★★★	Based:	UK
Product Range:	★★★★	Express Delivery Option? (UK)	No
Price Range:	Medium	Gift Wrapping Option?	No
Delivery Area:	UK	Returns Procedure:	Down to you

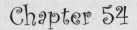

Chapter 54

The Cheese Shop

Here's a real cheese lover's paradise – the place to order your cheeses made all over Europe, from cheese shops based in both the UK and abroad.

Be prepared to spend a bit more here than you would in your local supermarket as these cheeses are definitely a cut above most of what you would find there. Be prepared also, when you're putting these wonderful sounding cheeses in your basket, for a shock when you get to the till. It's all too easy to go mad – if you love your cheese of course.

On most of these websites you can organise a regular delivery, order a complete cheese board for a large party and read all their information about lesser known cheeses you might not otherwise be tempted to try.

As is the case with most of the 'foodie' websites here, they're often being run by real experts who know and love their products so you can definitely trust their judgement.

Sites to Visit

www.cheese-board.co.uk

This is a really beautifully laid out website offering a mouth-watering array of cheese from all over Europe plus recipes for dishes such as Swiss fondue, Baked Vacherin (try it, it's wonderful), warm goats cheese salad and gruyere cheese straws. They also offer a small selection of wines to complement the cheeses, unusual cheese knives as gift suggestions, olive oils and Italian antipasti.

Site Usability:	★★★★★	Based:	UK
Product Range:	★★★★★	Express Delivery Option? (UK)	Yes
Price Range:	Medium	Gift Wrapping Option?	No
Delivery Area:	UK	Returns Procedure:	Down to you

www.fromages.com

Fromages.com is based as you might expect in France and ships its French cheeses to most countries in the world in 24 hours. For a really grown up cheese board you can choose their Party

301

Cheese Board containing their selection of ten cheeses including some well known and some you'll probably never have heard of. Alternatively you can choose your own selection from their list.

Site Usability:	★★★★★	Based:	France
Product Range:	★★★★★	Express Delivery Option? (UK)	Yes
Price Range:	Medium	Gift Wrapping Option?	No
Delivery Area:	Worldwide	Returns Procedure:	Down to you

www.norbitoncheese.co.uk

Sometimes a website is designed in such a way that you just have to go in and have a browse and I warn you, this is one of those. Whether you're specifically looking for Explorateur from France, Keen's Farmhouse Cheddar, or Irish Cashel Blue, or if you just want to have a look round, you're bound to find a) what you're searching for and b) something else as well. All the cheeses are beautifully photographed and there's a great deal of information: where they're from, how to store them and which wines will go with.

Site Usability:	★★★★★	Based:	UK
Product Range:	★★★★★	Express Delivery Option? (UK)	No
Price Range:	Medium	Gift Wrapping Option?	No
Delivery Area:	Worldwide	Returns Procedure:	Down to you

www.teddingtoncheese.co.uk

Every type of cheese you could possibly want and some new ones you won't have tried before are offered on this easy to use website. Buy your cheese by weight from a small piece to enough to feed a large party. Their offer includes accessories for raclette and fondue plus a selection of very unusual cheese knives. You'll find a monthly cheese board selection, gifts of cheese and wine or port and delivery worldwide.

Site Usability:	★★★★★	Based:	UK
Product Range:	★★★★★	Express Delivery Option? (UK)	Yes to Mainland UK
Price Range:	Luxury/Medium	Gift Wrapping Option?	No
Delivery Area:	Worldwide	Returns Procedure:	Down to you

www.paxtonandwhitfield.co.uk

This famous cheese company has a mouth-watering online shop and offers overnight delivery. You can buy speciality British, French and Italian cheeses here and join the Cheese Society to receive their special selection each month. They also sell biscuits, chutneys and pickles, York ham and pates, beautifully boxed cheese knives and stores, fondue sets and raclette machines.

Site Usability:	★★★★★	Based:	UK
Product Range:	★★★★	Express Delivery Option? (UK)	Yes
Price Range:	Luxury/Medium	Gift Wrapping Option?	No
Delivery Area:	Worldwide	Returns Procedure:	Down to you

www.thecheesesociety.co.uk

Although you can find other European cheeses here, the vast majority of those on offer are of the specialist, unpasteurised variety which they source throughout the England and France. There are some excellent gift selections, with which they can include a handwritten card with your personal message. If you want to just give them a call they'll be delighted to give you advice on choosing old favourites and making new discoveries. Free UK delivery on orders over £20.

Site Usability:	★★★★★	Based:	UK
Product Range:	★★★★★	Express Delivery Option? (UK)	Yes
Price Range:	Luxury/Medium	Gift Wrapping Option?	No
Delivery Area:	Worldwide	Returns Procedure:	Down to you

www.finecheese.co.uk

You'll discover a wonderful selection of cheeses at Fine Cheese, all beautifully photographed to make them look even more tempting, and one of the problems is that once you start ordering here you'll never be able to buy cheese at your supermarket again – it's simply not as good (usually). You can also buy Italian Antipasto, Spanish Tapas and some French products plus chocolates and nibbles.

Site Usability:	★★★★★	Based:	UK
Product Range:	★★★★★	Express Delivery Option? (UK)	Yes
Price Range:	Medium	Gift Wrapping Option?	No
Delivery Area:	UK	Returns Procedure:	Down to you

Chapter 55

The Fishmonger

Unlike meat, cheese, fruit and veg and fresh bread, which you can still find reasonably easily in the shops, fish has all but disappeared from the high street, other than the basic fish you can buy in your supermarket. Sometimes this is quite good quality, most times it has been frozen and is a long way away from the fish you'll find at these online retailers which is fresh, tasty and more or less straight from the sea.

There are types of fish here you probably won't have seen anywhere for years plus incredible shellfish (and you can order your lobsters live, if you want) with crab, oysters, mussels and scallops just waiting to be delivered to your door in special cooling containers.

If you have any doubt about the way your fish will be transported (though most online fishmongers offer you plenty of information as this is fundamental to their business) give them a call and make sure that you are satisfied that when the fish leaves them it will be totally fresh, and that it will arrive with you the next day. This way, you have the option of eating it immediately or putting it in your freezer.

These websites also give you plenty of places to order a variety of smoked fish including farmed and wild smoked salmon (and there's a huge difference in both the taste and the price), fish pates, kippers and lots of other fishy specialities. Just a word on smoked salmon; make sure if you're ordering a whole side that you know if it will be hand sliced or unsliced. There's nothing worse than unwrapping your fish thinking that you have an easy starter for lots of people and then discovering that you have to slice it yourself – I know, we've done that one too.

Sites to Visit

www.deadfreshfish.co.uk

Although I thought that at first the name of this website sounded rather offputting, when you click on to it and see what they have to offer I think that you, like me, will change your mind. You can choose how you like to have your fish prepared by this family fishmonger who buys most of their fish from Brixham in Devon, whether you prefer it scaled, trimmed and/or filleted. Fish on offer depends on the season but includes cod, brill, monkfish and John Dory and shellfish such as Canadian lobster, crab and mussels.

Site Usability:	★★★	Based:	UK
Product Range:	★★★★	Express Delivery Option? (UK)	No
Price Range:	Medium	Gift Wrapping Option?	No
Delivery Area:	UK	Returns Procedure:	Down to you

www.fishworks.co.uk

From their premises in Brixham Fishworks buy from fishermen in Dartmouth, Scotland, the East Coast, France, Italy (and as far away as the Maldives for fresh tuna), which means that you have access to one of the widest ranges of fish and shellfish available in the UK. You can choose from shellfish such as wild caught white prawns and Pallourde Clams, fresh fish from Brixham Lemon Sole to Gilthead Bream and loads in between. There's lots of advice here too on preparation and cooking your fish.

Site Usability:	★★★	Based:	UK
Product Range:	★★★★	Express Delivery Option? (UK)	Yes
Price Range:	Medium	Gift Wrapping Option?	No
Delivery Area:	UK	Returns Procedure:	Down to you

www.foweyfish.com

Fowey fish are retail and wholesale fishmongers. Fresh supplies come into their shop every day and they operate a nationwide mail order service for fresh fish, shellfish and some specialist fine wines including the much sought after and hard to find Cloudy Bay. They despatch four days a week, Monday to Thursdays, for next day delivery all over the UK. This is a simply designed website but you know that the fish will be fresh and there's an excellent choice.

Site Usability:	★★★	Based:	UK
Product Range:	★★★★	Express Delivery Option? (UK)	No
Price Range:	Medium	Gift Wrapping Option?	No
Delivery Area:	UK	Returns Procedure:	Down to you

www.gallowaysmokehouse.co.uk

Nestling on the banks of Wigtown Bay is the Galloway Smokehouse, home of prize winning smoked salmon, trout, seafood and game all waiting for you to order online. From the simple kipper to the grand salmon a huge variety of smoked food is on offer and both hot and cold smoked foods are available as well such as kippers, smoked mackerel and even smoked cheese.

Site Usability:	★★★★★	Based:	UK
Product Range:	★★★★	Express Delivery Option? (UK)	Yes
Price Range:	Medium	Gift Wrapping Option?	No
Delivery Area:	Worldwide	Returns Procedure:	Down to you

www.lochfyne.com

You may well have eaten in one of their chain of seafood restaurants which are excellent and not overpriced but you may not know that you can buy a selection of their goods online from their beautifully laid out and photographed website. They offer fresh and smoked trout and salmon, oysters, mussels and langoustine plus Glen Fyne beef, pork, lamb and venison and lots of other goodies such as pates and gift boxes.

Site Usability:	★★★★★	Based:	UK
Product Range:	★★★★★	Express Delivery Option? (UK)	No
Price Range:	Luxury/Medium	Returns Procedure:	Down to you
Delivery Area:	EU		

www.martins-seafresh.co.uk

Buy your fresh fish direct from Cornwall on this simple website. The fish they offer includes sea bass, sea bream, brill and cod through to salmon, skate and Dover sole. There's a wide choice of shellfish as well from crevettes and Cornish lobsters to scallops and oysters and in the smoked department you'll find mussels, salmon and eel plus chicken and goose.

Site Usability:	★★★★	Based:	UK
Product Range:	★★★★★	Express Delivery Option? (UK)	Yes
Price Range:	Medium	Gift Wrapping Option?	No
Delivery Area:	UK	Returns Procedure:	Down to you

www.skye-seafood.co.uk

Isle of Skye Smokehouse is a small dedicated producer supplying traditionally smoked fish to some of the finest hotels in Scotland and now they're happy to sell to you directly online. If you didn't know it already, smoked Scottish wild salmon is completely different to the farmed variety. Once you've tried wild salmon you'll probably never look back although it frequently costs twice as much. It would be certainly worth it for a treat the next time you want something really special.

Site Usability:	★★★★	Based:	UK
Product Range:	★★★	Express Delivery Option? (UK)	Yes
Price Range:	Luxury/Medium	Gift Wrapping Option?	No
Delivery Area:	Worldwide	Returns Procedure:	Down to you

www.smokedsalmon.co.uk

At the Inverawe Smokehouse you'll find classic smoked salmon and trout, smoked Wild Atlantic salmon, gifts, hampers and gourmet boxes. In their deli section they offer smoked pates, cod's roe and salmon and lumpfish caviar. As well as the above, hiding in the 'Larder' section, you'll find beef and pies, shortbread and fruit cakes, pickles, chutneys and jellies and cheeses.

Site Usability:	★★★★	Based:	UK
Product Range:	★★★★★	Express Delivery Option? (UK)	Yes
Price Range:	Luxury/Medium	Gift Wrapping Option?	No
Delivery Area:	EU	Returns Procedure:	Down to you

www.thefishsociety.co.uk

Here you can choose from over two hundred kinds of fish and seafood, all of which will be delivered frozen. There's everything from organic salmon to Dover sole, turbot and tuna plus wild smoked salmon, gigantic prawns and dived scallops. They also have a range of fish recipe books and accessories such as fish kettles and claw crackers. Deliveries are twice a week on Wednesday and Friday, delivery is £5 on orders from £65 to £100 and free after that.

Site Usability:	★★★★★	Based:	UK
Product Range:	★★★★★	Express Delivery Option? (UK)	No
Price Range:	Medium	Gift Wrapping Option?	No
Delivery Area:	UK	Returns Procedure:	Down to you

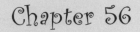

Chapter 56

Gourmet Food/Deli

So what would you like to order today? Some Parma ham, perhaps? A little caviar for a special occasion dinner? Fish pate or a home made pie? Certainly; no problem at all for any or all of it.

The number of online retailers and countries you can shop from here is quite astounding; you wouldn't find anything like this amount of choice anywhere outside the magical food halls of Harrods and Selfridges in London. On some of these websites you can order everything you need for your next gourmet meal, from home made puddings to a whole ham and on others just perfect accompaniments to a smart drinks event; Tapas, spicy peanuts, chorizo sausage or all the ingredients for a dish of delicious antipasti.

As delivery is quite often expensive I suggest you have a look round and decide which onlne retailer suits the type of occasion you're looking to buy for and then try to buy everything from one place. Then the next time you can try somewhere else. On the other hand you simply may not be able to resist trying out a few.

Sites to Visit

www.authenticfoodandwine.com

There are a wide range of products here so it's difficult to know if this retailer should be described as a wine merchant, butcher, fromagerie, or deli – I think food and wine hall probably sums it up the best. Take a look and you'll find a choice of extremely well photographed products including English asparagus (seasonal), Lowland lamb, extra virgin olive oil, preserves by The Wooden Spoon and their own selection of wines and champagnes plus wild and farmed smoked salmon, Marasu's chocolates and lots of gift hampers.

Site Usability:	★★★★★	Based:	UK
Product Range:	★★★★★	Express Delivery Option? (UK)	48 hour weekday service
Price Range:	Luxury/Medium	Gift Wrapping Option?	No
Delivery Area:	UK	Returns Procedure:	Down to you

www.carluccios.com

You may have been lucky enough to eat in one of his restaurants or to receive some of wonderful regional Italian delicacies as a gift. Even if you haven't done either of the above you can now buy from Antonio Carluccio's beautifully presented range online, which includes pasta, olive oil, antipasti and confectionery. Everything is packaged beautifully with lots of information about where the product originated and what you can use it for. Buy for yourself or give it away. It's a delight, either way.

Site Usability:	★★★★★	Based:	UK
Product Range:	★★★	Express Delivery Option? (UK)	No
Price Range:	Luxury/Medium	Gift Wrapping Option?	No
Delivery Area:	UK	Returns Procedure:	Down to you

www.caspiancaviar.co.uk

If caviar is something that you really enjoy but you can't buy the real thing where you live then take a look at this website which offers Beluga, Oscietre and Sevruga caviar right up to 500g tins although thankfully, bearing in mind the price, you can also order their 50g tins. To go with your caviar celebration you can buy crystal caviar bowls, vodka shot glasses, horn spoons, vodka and blinis.

Site Usability:	★★★★	Based:	UK
Product Range:	★★★	Express Delivery Option? (UK)	Yes
Price Range:	Luxury	Gift Wrapping Option?	No
Delivery Area:	EU	Returns Procedure:	Down to you

www.deliinthenook.co.uk

The Deli in the Nook is based in Leicester, and stocks a superb range of antipasti, olives, infused oils and vinegars, balsamics and extra virgin olive oils, pate, pasta, tins and jars of authentic Italian and French produce, hand made chocs, biscuits, chutneys, salsas and sauces, preserves, nibbles, goodies and lots more, if all that wasn't enough already. They'll customise gift parcels for you together with your personalised message and aim to despatch all orders within 24 hours.

Site Usability:	★★★★	Based:	UK
Product Range:	★★★★	Express Delivery Option? (UK)	Yes
Price Range:	Medium	Gift Wrapping Option?	Yes
Delivery Area:	UK	Returns Procedure:	Down to you

www.dukeshillham.co.uk

Dukeshill was founded over 20 years ago with the aim of producing the very best hams, cured the 'old fashioned' way (where flavour and texture are more important than speed or yield). Today you can also buy bacon and other cured meats, fish terrines and smoked salmon, regional cheeses, condiments, preserves and mouth-watering looking cakes. Once you've ordered your ham you'll no doubt be tempted by the rest – I certainly was.

Site Usability:	★★★★★	Based:	UK
Product Range:	★★★★	Express Delivery Option? (UK)	Yes
Price Range:	Medium	Gift Wrapping Option?	No
Delivery Area:	UK	Returns Procedure:	Down to you in agreement with them

www.efoodies.co.uk

This is an extremely tempting website where you can order the highest quality olive oil and balsamic vinegar, British and French cheese, caviar, foie gras, black and white truffles and truffle oil, spices, mushrooms and champagne. Everything is beautifully photographed with lots of information about every product – where it comes from and what makes it special. The prices here are good, particularly when you consider the quality of what you're buying. They offer gift vouchers as well.

Site Usability:	★★★★★	Based:	UK
Product Range:	★★★★	Express Delivery Option? (UK)	Yes
Price Range:	Luxury/Medium	Gift Wrapping Option?	No
Delivery Area:	UK	Returns Procedure:	Down to you

www.elanthy.com

If your normal thought when buying olive oil is to buy Italian you should have another think. Elanthy supply (with free UK delivery) the highest quality olive oil from Greece. The service is really excellent and the prices will probably take you by surprise, particularly if, like us, you use quite a lot. You can also buy balsamic vinegar and Maldon sea salt here, plus Pommery mustard and olive oil based soaps. Give them a try.

Site Usability:	★★★★	Based:	UK
Product Range:	★★★	Express Delivery Option? (UK)	Yes
Price Range:	Medium	Gift Wrapping Option?	No
Delivery Area:	UK	Returns Procedure:	Down to you

www.esperya.com

This is an Italian website offering quick delivery throughout Europe. They offer olive oil, wine, honey, pasta, rice, desserts, charcuterie, cheeses, preserves and seafood – from all the different regions of Italy. As you click through to each product you find a wealth of information; how Pecorino cheese is made for example, where exactly it comes from and how to use it, or Navelli saffron, its history and which dishes it's best suited for. If you like Italian food this is a real paradise.

Site Usability:	★★★★★	Based:	Italy
Product Range:	★★★★	Express Delivery Option? (UK)	Yes
Price Range:	Medium	Gift Wrapping Option?	No
Delivery Area:	Europe	Returns Procedure:	Down to you

www.formanandfield.com

Forman & Field is a luxury delicatessen specialising in traditional British produce from small independent producers. There's a delicious selection of luxury cakes and puddings, smoked salmon, ham and cheeses all beautifully photographed and extremely hard to resist. Don't miss their home made, award winning fish pates and pies, perfect for the next time you're entertaining. They offer speedy delivery to UK, Ireland and the Channel Isles

Site Usability:	★★★★★	Based:	UK
Product Range:	★★★★★	Express Delivery Option? (UK)	Yes
Price Range:	Luxury/Medium	Gift Wrapping Option?	No
Delivery Area:	UK	Returns Procedure:	Down to you

www.frenchgourmetstore.com

Here you'll discover a marvellous choice of regional gourmet products from France all prepared according to traditional recipes and including mushrooms and truffles, mustards, oils and vinegars and gorgeous chocolates. They also have a small but excellent range of hampers and gift baskets. They're actually based in the UK, will ship to you anywhere in the world and offer an express service.

Site Usability:	★★★★★	Based:	France
Product Range:	★★★★	Express Delivery Option? (UK)	Yes
Price Range:	Luxury/Medium	Gift Wrapping Option?	No
Delivery Area:	Worldwide	Returns Procedure:	Down to you

www.iberianfoods.co.uk

Do you like Spanish food? If so then this is a great website to have a look around, offering a great choice of products from Spain such as serrano ham, chorizo and other cured meats and fish, herbs and spices and Spanish cheese. You can also shop from their range of tapas and paella dishes, cookers and ingredients, plus there's a lot of information on where to find good Spanish restaurants in the UK and a Spanish food glossary.

Site Usability:	★★★★	Based:	Spain
Product Range:	★★★★	Express Delivery Option? (UK)	No
Price Range:	Medium	Gift Wrapping Option?	No
Delivery Area:	UK	Returns Procedure:	Down to you

www.mortimerandbennett.co.uk

This online deli is crammed full of speciality foods from around the world, many of which are exclusive to them. You'll find an extensive range of cheeses, breads, oil and charcuterie, as well as a selection of fun foodie gifts such as the La Maison du Miel honey, Italian flower jellies and gold and silver buttons. There's also panettone from Turin, extra virgin olive oil from New Zealand and biscuits from Sardinia; lots to choose from and all easy to see.

Site Usability:	★★★★★	Based:	UK
Product Range:	★★★★	Express Delivery Option? (UK)	Yes
Price Range:	Luxury/Medium	Gift Wrapping Option?	No
Delivery Area:	UK	Returns Procedure:	Down to you

www.savoria.com

Savoria is an online retailer run by obviously passionate 'foodies' offering you the very best from all over Italy, including cheese, meat, pasta, olive oil and antipasti. There's lots of friendly information about each product and which part of the country it comes from plus suggestions for use. Delivery comes to you direct from Italy – orders placed by Sunday night are delivered by the end of the following week. They'll deliver to most EU countries.

Site Usability:	★★★★★	Based:	UK
Product Range:	★★★★★	Express Delivery Option? (UK)	No
Price Range:	Luxury/Medium	Gift Wrapping Option?	No
Delivery Area:	EU	Returns Procedure:	Down to you

www.stickytoffeepudding.net

For lovers of sticky toffee pudding this must surely be the most effortless way of getting hold of some and you'll be buying it from the world famous Cartmel Village Shop in Cumbria. Strangely at a time when websites are trying to offer you everything and more the Sticky Toffee Pudding (plus sauce of course) is the only product available here. Try some. Forget that 'a moment on the lips means a lifetime on the hips' and buy the largest size for 9 people (if you can bear to share it) for £14.95 including postage.

Site Usability:	★★★★	Based:	UK
Product Range:	★★	Express Delivery Option? (UK)	No
Price Range:	Medium	Gift Wrapping Option?	No
Delivery Area:	Worldwide	Returns Procedure:	Down to you

www.valvonacrolla-online.co.uk

Valvona & Crolla is an independent family business based in Edinburgh, specialising in gourmet Italian products plus their excellent range of good value, quality Italian wines from artisan producers and progressive co-operatives. In 2005 they won the *Which?* award for the Italian Specialist Wine Merchant so if you're fond of Italian wines take a good look at their collection. In their wonderful deli you'll find a wide choice including prosciutto and pancetta, cheeses, smoked salmon and all your larder essentials.

Site Usability:	★★★	Based:	UK
Product Range:	★★★★	Express Delivery Option? (UK)	Yes
Price Range:	Luxury/Medium	Gift Wrapping Option?	No
Delivery Area:	UK	Returns Procedure:	Down to you

www.windsorfarmshop.co.uk

Order your wild boar or Duchy chicken liver pate here as just a couple of the mouth-watering options from their delicatessen department, plus a wide variety of meat, fish, dairy, bakery and other products Nothing here is inexpensive but everything is really excellent quality. They don't deliver everything to everywhere in the UK (particularly their bakery items) and they only stock fresh food in the correct season so before you get your hopes up, check exactly what's available to you.

Site Usability:	★★★★★	Based:	UK
Product Range:	★★★★	Express Delivery Option? (UK)	No
Price Range:	Luxury/Medium	Gift Wrapping Option?	No
Delivery Area:	UK or local depending on the item.	Returns Procedure:	Down to you

Chapter 57

Organics Online

This is an area that as I've said before is growing really fast, partly as we want to eat more naturally and partly as we become more aware of, and care for, our environment.

Some of the online retailers here offer just fish or meat, whilst others offer quite unexpected products as well such as freshly baked bread, home made jams, chutneys and sauces and fruit and veg. You'll also find milk, cheeses and eggs, organic wine plus gluten-, wheat- and yeast-free products so this is an excellent place to shop for someone with allergies to those ingredients.

I don't know if you've noticed but organic foods in supermarkets seem to be extraordinarily expensive and frankly I haven't worked out why, other than that they think they have you as a captive market. If you take a look at the websites below you'll see that you definitely aren't anyone's captive market, you can buy from a lot of different places with really high quality products and at much better prices which is, in my opinion, just as it should be.

Sites to Visit

www.abel-cole.co.uk

Abel & Cole deliver delicious boxes of fresh organic fruit and veg, organic meat, sustainably sourced fish and loads of other ethically produced foods, buying as much as possible from UK farms. They offer regular selection boxes of fresh produce, and providing you live in the South of England then you can order all of their other food and drink too, including locally baked bread. For those who live outside the main area they offer two selections of organic fruit and vegetables.

Site Usability:	★★★★	Based:	UK
Product Range:	★★★	Express Delivery Option? (UK)	No
Price Range:	Medium	Gift Wrapping Option?	No
Delivery Area:	UK	Returns Procedure:	Down to you

www.caleyco.com

Caledonian Foods represent a collective of top quality Scottish suppliers and aims to bring you real fresh food, full of flavour, of the highest quality with complete traceability and provenance. With a network of over 100 independent food producers all their food is fresh, free range, organic and wild. You can select from meat and game, fish and shellfish such as oysters, smoked salmon and hand dived scallops, cheeses, deserts and truffles, wines, whiskies and gifts.

Site Usability:	★★★★★	Based:	Scotland
Product Range:	★★★★	Express Delivery Option? (UK)	No
Price Range:	Medium	Gift Wrapping Option?	No
Delivery Area:	UK	Returns Procedure:	Down to you

www.freshfood.co.uk

This is a prize-winning nationwide delivery service of organic and wild harvested foods, and the best way for you to buy from them is to join their box scheme, where you take out a weekly subscription to one or several of their selections. Of course you can cancel this at any time. There is fresh produce such as fruit and veg, meat, fish, game, smoked products, wine and bread – plus lots of recipe ideas. From wild Scottish Salmon to pizzas, if it's organic it'll be here.

Site Usability:	★★★★	Based:	UK
Product Range:	★★★★	Express Delivery Option? (UK)	No
Price Range:	Medium	Gift Wrapping Option?	No
Delivery Area:	UK	Returns Procedure:	Down to you

www.goodnessdirect.co.uk

There's really a vast range here with 3000+ health foods, vitamins and items selected for those with special dietary needs. You can search for foods that are dairy free, gluten free, wheat free, yeast free and low fat plus organic fruit, vegetables (in a selection of boxed choices), fish and meat. You'll also find frozen and chilled foods so you can do your complete shopping here. Don't be worried by the amount of choice, the website is very easy to navigate and order from.

Site Usability:	★★★★	Based:	UK
Product Range:	★★★★★	Express Delivery Option? (UK)	No
Price Range:	Medium	Gift Wrapping Option?	No
Delivery Area:	UK	Returns Procedure:	Down to you

www.graigfarm.co.uk

Now in its 19th year, Graig Farm Organics is an award winning pioneer of organic meats and other organic foods in the UK. The range is now very extensive, and includes meat (organic beef, lamb, mutton, pork, chicken and turkey, as well as local game and goat meat) ready meals, fish, baby food, dairy, bread, groceries, vegetables and fruit, soups and salads, alcoholic drinks, a gluten-free range, and even pet food, plus herbal remedies and essential oils.

Site Usability:	★★★★	Based:	UK
Product Range:	★★★★	Express Delivery Option? (UK)	No
Price Range:	Medium	Gift Wrapping Option?	No
Delivery Area:	UK	Returns Procedure:	Down to you

www.organics-4u.co.uk

Organics4u supply top quality organic vegetables, fruit and dry goods direct to your home or place of work anywhere in the UK. Their fruit and vegetables are delivered in boxes of different sizes, and you can choose to have them delivered weekly, fortnightly or monthly. They also offer dry goods boxes, containing items such as pasta, spices, pulses and oil although you can buy these products separately if you want to.

Site Usability:	★★★★	Based:	UK
Product Range:	★★★	Express Delivery Option? (UK)	No
Price Range:	Medium	Gift Wrapping Option?	No
Delivery Area:	UK	Returns Procedure:	Down to you

www.rhug.co.uk

This organic online farm offers meat produced on the Rhug Estate Farm in Corwen, North Wales including Welsh lamb, beef and chicken plus groceries such as herbs and spices, cheese and excellent looking cookies. They also have non organic sausages and savoury and sweet hand-made pies available such as plum, and steak and ale. Delivery is free on orders over £100.

Site Usability:	★★★★	Based:	UK
Product Range:	★★★★	Express Delivery Option? (UK)	No
Price Range:	Medium	Gift Wrapping Option?	No
Delivery Area:	UK	Returns Procedure:	Down to you

www.riverford.co.uk

Riverford Organic Vegetables is situated along the Dart Valley in Devon and delivers fresh organic vegetable boxes direct from the farm to homes across the South of the UK. They started organic vegetable production in 1987 and have become one of the country's largest independent growers, certified by the Soil Association. Simply enter your postcode to check that they deliver to your area then select which of their fruit and vegetable boxes is most suitable for you.

Site Usability:	★★★★	Based:	UK
Product Range:	★★★★	Express Delivery Option? (UK)	No
Price Range:	Medium	Gift Wrapping Option?	No
Delivery Area:	UK (South)	Returns Procedure:	Down to you

www.somersetorganics.co.uk

Depending on the season, Somerset Organics provide their own organic Angus beef, Rare Breed Berkshire Pork and Organic Lamb, all of which they farm at Gilcombe Farm. They also stock a full range of meat and poultry reared on local organic farms plus non organic free range meats. The dairy range includes stilton, brie and vintage cheddar plus milk and cream and you can order your fruit and veg boxes here as well.

Site Usability:	★★★★	Based:	UK
Product Range:	★★★★	Express Delivery Option? (UK)	No
Price Range:	Medium	Gift Wrapping Option?	No
Delivery Area:	UK	Returns Procedure:	Down to you

www.thelocalfoodcompany.co.uk

Fresh, Devon organic (and non-organic) foods are offered here including bread rolls, cakes and biscuits (with some gluten free), cheeses, deli and fresh meat boxes, smoked salmon and duck, fruit and veg, drinks, and lots of other delicious sounding goods. For most items they tell you which farm was the supplier and give you some information about them which is excellent. They offer hamper and gift ideas plus household and non food items as well.

Site Usability:	★★★	Based:	UK
Product Range:	★★★★	Express Delivery Option? (UK)	No
Price Range:	Medium	Gift Wrapping Option?	No
Delivery Area:	UK	Returns Procedure:	Down to you

www.thesussexwinecompany.co.uk

The Sussex Wine Company is an independent online wine merchant listing quality wine and spirits from around the world, all produced with attention to detail both in the vineyard and the winery. Their organic wines start from £5.95 and some of the estates listed are Albet I Noya of Spain, Battle of Bosworth of Maclaren Vale in Australia, Bodegas Vina Ljalba of Rioja in Spain and Touchstone Organic from Argentina. They aim for next day delivery where possible.

Site Usability:	★★★★★	Based:	UK
Product Range:	★★★★	Express Delivery Option? (UK)	Yes whenever possible
Price Range:	Luxury/Medium	Gift Wrapping Option?	No
Delivery Area:	UK	Returns Procedure:	Down to you

www.westcountryorganics.co.uk

There's a wide choice of organic food and drink here from meat, vegetables and fruit, beer, wine and vegetarian products to pies, tofu, fish and cheese. This is an easy to navigate though unsophisticated website, so don't expect lots of beautiful 'foodie' pictures. However, with such an excellent selection of, in particular, vegetables which you order using their box service, you should have a look round and give them a try.

Site Usability:	★★★★	Based:	UK
Product Range:	★★★★	Express Delivery Option? (UK)	You set the day for delivery
Price Range:	Medium	Gift Wrapping Option?	No
Delivery Area:	UK	Returns Procedure:	Down to you

Chapter 58

Speciality Foods, Herbs and Spices

There's quite a mixture of different products in this chapter – all special in their own way but quite, quite different to each other.

This is the place to buy your highest quality black peppercorns in bulk (well if you're anything like me you will), your extra strong chillies and chilli sauces, all the spices you could think of, and everything you need for your next home made Chinese, Japanese or Indian meal.

One of the best things here is that you're not limited to those silly little jars that only last a fraction of a second (at least they do in our household) but you can buy enough to last you a while, frequently at much better prices than you can find offline.

If you're not sure what any particular ingredient is, these websites are just waiting to tell you more than you could ever want to know, and they'll give you recipes for using them as well.

Sites to Visit

www.bartspicesdirect.co.uk

Bart is a well known name for herbs and spices and now you can visit their online food hall and buy everything in just a few clicks. They offer a very good range, including their basic collection, plus spice blends such as Creole and Cajun seasoning, coconut and chillies and Thai and fish sauces. You can also dip into their deli and find Amarillo chillies and chilli flakes, curry powder and Harissa paste, saffron and star anise.

Site Usability:	★★★★	Based:	UK
Product Range:	★★★	Express Delivery Option? (UK)	No
Price Range:	Medium	Gift Wrapping Option?	No
Delivery Area:	UK	Returns Procedure:	Down to you

www.culpeper.co.uk

Founded in 1927 by herbalist and writer Hilda Leyel, Culpeper is now the oldest chain of herbal shops in the UK. There's a diverse range of products on their website including candles and skincare as well as the mainstream range of herbs and spices, sauces, chutneys and mustards. Oh yes, and if you have a sweet tooth you'll also find Culpeper sweets, honeys and preserves. This is a really attractive website and they'll deliver to you worldwide.

Site Usability:	★★★★★	Based:	UK
Product Range:	★★★★	Express Delivery Option? (UK)	Yes
Price Range:	Medium	Gift Wrapping Option?	No
Delivery Area:	Worldwide	Returns Procedure:	Down to you

www.hot-headz.com

If you like your dishes to be spiced up and you like the unusual on your table then take a look at this site offering hot everything from sauces, salsas and 'pepperphernalia'. Try 'Ass Kickin' Peach Rum Salsa' or 'Crazy Charlie' marinade and stir-fry. Be warned, their 'Mega Death' sauce must be diluted. Don't even think of trying it without and don't think it'll be fun to play a trick on someone and get them to try this neat. It can burn your mouth. Seriously.

Site Usability:	★★★	Based:	UK
Product Range:	★★★	Express Delivery Option? (UK)	No
Price Range:	Medium	Gift Wrapping Option?	No
Delivery Area:	UK	Returns Procedure:	Down to you

www.japanesekitchen.co.uk

The Japanese Kitchen is based in The Japanese Culture Shop in London and for your next sushi party you should definitely take a look at their online shop where you'll discover all the essential ingredients of Japanese cuisine. These include miso pastes, sushi ingredients, Udon & Soba noodles, Panko breadcrumbs, mirin, pickles, ginger, green teas, confectionery, rice crackers, seaweeds, soy sauces and wasabi. It may be simpler to visit your nearest Yo! Sushi – but far more fun to make your own.

Site Usability:	★★★★	Based:	UK
Product Range:	★★★★	Express Delivery Option? (UK)	No
Price Range:	Medium	Gift Wrapping Option?	No
Delivery Area:	Worldwide	Returns Procedure:	Down to you

www.natco-online.com

If you're fond of Indian food and you already cook it yourself or you'd like to try, then take a look at this brightly coloured website specialising in everything for Indian cuisine, including spices and chutneys, curry mixes and curry kits and all types of speciality Indian groceries. They also give some simple curry recipes to complement the curry kits they offer and you can click through their links page to find more recipes and information.

Site Usability:	★★★	Based:	UK
Product Range:	★★★★	Express Delivery Option? (UK)	No
Price Range:	Medium	Gift Wrapping Option?	No
Delivery Area:	Worldwide	Returns Procedure:	Down to you

www.thespiceshop.co.uk

The Spice Shop offers a range of over 2,500 herbs and spices - one of the widest available in the UK. Many chefs and famous TV cooks frequent the shop and draw upon owner Birgit Erath's skills as a source of inspiration and recipe ideas. To make life easy, they have put together a number of spice bundles that relate to TV cooks and their programmes. So if you are following Delia Smith or Jamie Oliver at the moment then in the Celebrity Cooks section below you can order all the recommended spices in one easy package.

Site Usability:	★★★★	Based:	UK
Product Range:	★★★	Express Delivery Option? (UK)	No
Price Range:	Medium	Gift Wrapping Option?	No
Delivery Area:	Worldwide	Returns Procedure:	Down to you

www.saltpepper.co.uk

What's really special about this website, other than the friendly way in which it all comes across, is the amount of information given on every item it sells. That's not to say that there's too much, but everything is written by someone who obviously not only knows their products, but also enjoys using them. So. You'll find salts and peppers, a wide choice of mills, pestles and mortars plus herbs and spices, spice grinders, spice boxes and gift sets.

Site Usability:	★★★★	Based:	UK
Product Range:	★★★★	Express Delivery Option? (UK)	Yes
Price Range:	Medium	Gift Wrapping Option?	Yes
Delivery Area:	UK	Returns Procedure:	Down to you

www.simplyspice.co.uk

Here's one of the widest ranges of authentic Indian foods and spices you can find online including appetisers and snacks, beans, lentils, chutneys, curry pastes, sauces, Masalas, curry mixes, nuts, dried fruit, oils. ghee, pickles, rice, flour, sweets and desserts. So the next time you consider giving an Indian themed dinner party take a good look round here. This is a very well laid out website with lots of information about Indian culture as well.

Site Usability:	★★★★	Based:	UK
Product Range:	★★★★	Express Delivery Option? (UK)	No
Price Range:	Medium	Gift Wrapping Option?	No
Delivery Area:	UK	Returns Procedure:	Down to you

www.steenbergs.co.uk

Steenbergs have an excellent website offering a wide choice of organic salts and peppers, herbs and spices from succulent vanilla to the heady Herbes de Provence. Most of the herbs and spices are offered in three or four different sizes of jars but if you want a specially large quantity of their highest quality Tellicherri Garbled Extra Bold black peppercorns for example, then just send them an email or call them. There's also a small selection of Fairtrade tea and accessories such as unusual salt and pepper mills.

Site Usability:	★★★★★	Based:	UK
Product Range:	★★★	Express Delivery Option? (UK)	Yes
Price Range:	Medium	Gift Wrapping Option?	No
Delivery Area:	Worldwide	Returns Procedure:	Down to you

www.spice-master.com

There's a great selection of herbs and spices from around the world here, where you're best to know what you're looking for first and use their search facility if you want to find something quickly. There are dried herbs and spices, pickles, chutneys and pastes, specific areas for Thai, Malay and Chinese foods and spices, fresh chillies, garlic and ginger, all types of salts and peppers and nuts, pulses and lentils. I'll say it again. You really need to know what you want and then search. You'll see why.

Site Usability:	★★★★	Based:	UK
Product Range:	★★★★★	Express Delivery Option? (UK)	Yes
Price Range:	Medium	Gift Wrapping Option?	No
Delivery Area:	Worldwide	Returns Procedure:	Down to you

www.spicesofindia.co.uk

Everything you'd expect is here for great Indian cooking including an excellent choice of (well photographed) pulses and lentils, pickles and chutneys, appetisers, drinks and beverages. They also offer kitchen and tableware such as balti dishes and pickle servers plus gift baskets such as The Pickle Basket and Deluxe Indian Spice Basket. One of the great things about this website is the amount of information, plus their constantly updated recipe section.

Site Usability:	★★★★	Based:	UK
Product Range:	★★★★★	Express Delivery Option? (UK)	No
Price Range:	Medium	Gift Wrapping Option?	No
Delivery Area:	Worldwide	Returns Procedure:	Down to you

www.wingyip.co.uk

You've probably already tasted their ingredients in your local Chinese restaurant and now you can buy everything you need to create the perfect Chinese meal at home. Select from their sauces, seasonings. condiments, rice, noodles, tinned and preserved foods and buy from their well priced steamers and woks, Chinese tableware and cookbooks. You can also use their Easy Shop to take you straight to the most popular items (as there really is a lot to choose from).

Site Usability:	★★★★	Based:	UK
Product Range:	★★★★	Express Delivery Option? (UK)	Yes
Price Range:	Medium	Gift Wrapping Option?	No
Delivery Area:	Worldwide	Returns Procedure:	Down to you

Chapter 59

Supermarkets

I'm sure that I don't need to say a great deal here as I said it all at the beginning of this section. If you haven't yet tried the online supermarkets and you're still doing your weekly shop then please give these websites a try.

To make life easy first of all you need to make your 'favourites' list. Write down everything you buy each week. Turn on your computer (yes we are getting back to basics here), sign up, click on 'Groceries' and start entering your products. Don't even think of giving up half way as you'll lose everything you've put in, so go right down to the bottom of your list.

If they ask you to book a delivery slot first you can do this even if you're just trying out the system and cancel it later. Once you've done this and entered your shopping list you should check out. That way your list will be held as your 'favourites' and the next time you visit it will be there waiting for you.

As I said, if you don't want to go ahead this time you can cancel your order, or change your delivery slot, or change the items you've ordered right up to the day before your order is scheduled to arrive. Don't listen to anyone who tells you that they tried online supermarket shopping and it didn't work, it was late or they sent the wrong things. They probably haven't ordered online for the past couple of years as during that time the supermarket ordering systems have improved dramatically.

I tell you all this with the voice of great authority as you could now only drag me into a supermarket in an absolute emergency. I have three children, two large dogs (and a husband) and we frequently have a full house of people needing to be fed.

Get me to a supermarket? Not on your life. Get me to my computer, fast.

These are the sites to visit and they all only deliver in the UK. I have to say that for basic products I use Tesco the most with Ocado a close second particularly when I want special things. They are both absolutely excellent and many times I can place my order for next day delivery (except at Christmas, of course, when I can place my initial order weeks in advance). The three that I would recommend are: www.ocado.com; www.sainsbury.co.uk; and www.tesco.com

Note that Tesco is also trying to sell you everything else, from books, DVDs and flowers to mobile phones. Start with the groceries. The service is great.

Chapter 60

Tea and Coffee

I'm one of those very odd people who can't drink coffee stronger than a few grains of instant in a cup and I don't like strong tea either – I've even been known to drink hot water. I'm sure you're already wincing.

Fear not though, I've found you lots of wonderful places you can buy your next Jamaican Blue Mountain Coffee fix plus every other type of coffee and tea you've ever heard of and lots you almost certainly haven't.

These websites are all run by coffee enthusiasts, so you can find out a great deal about the coffee beans you're buying, how you should have them ground and even the best time of day to drink them. The same goes for tea, whether you want your cup of traditional Earl Grey or specialised leaves such as Lapsang Souchong and the latest fruit infusions.

You can also buy coffee makers here from cafetières to the most high tech espresso machines (for which you can pay a small fortune) plus coffee grinders, milk frothers, teapots and cups, many of which make excellent gifts for the coffee lover in your family.

Sites to Visit

www.coffeebypost.co.uk

This is definitely a website for the real coffee connoisseur, as Coffee by Post only offer slow roasted beans from 100% Arabica coffee. So if you think you're being asked to pay a little more, remember that you're buying the best. You can order everything from Columbia Supremo to Italian Dark Espresso Roast, flavoured coffees such as Amaretto and Havana Rum plus accessories such as cafetières, grinders and the clever Bialetti Grillo Stove Top Espresso Maker.

Site Usability:	★★★★★	Based:	UK
Product Range:	★★★★	Express Delivery Option? (UK)	Yes
Price Range:	Medium	Gift Wrapping Option?	No
Delivery Area:	UK	Returns Procedure:	Down to you

www.drury.uk.com

Drury have over 60 years' experience in blending fine quality teas and roasting the world's finest gourmet coffees. Established in central London in 1936 they remain a family-owned business and supply a huge variety of coffee, both beans and ground. They also offer espresso machines, coffee makers and accessories and are waiting to offer you advice. You can choose from an extensive range of leaf teas and tea bags too including black, green, herbal or flavoured and from the finest English Breakfast to aromatic Earl Grey and Lapsang.

Site Usability:	★★★	Based:	UK
Product Range:	★★★★	Express Delivery Option? (UK)	No
Price Range:	Medium	Gift Wrapping Option?	No
Delivery Area:	UK	Returns Procedure:	Down to you

www.fortnumandmason.com

With its famous name and lovely packaging anything from Fortnum and Mason is a pleasure to buy and receive. Their website now offers tea, coffee, hampers, confectionery, ham and cheeses to name but a few and most items can be delivered all over the world. Don't expect anything to be cheap as here we're talking about real luxury but don't let that put you off. The teas and coffees are beautifully packaged and so make great gifts as well.

Site Usability:	★★★★	Based:	UK
Product Range:	★★★★	Express Delivery Option? (UK)	No
Price Range:	Luxury	Gift Wrapping Option?	No
Delivery Area:	Worldwide	Returns Procedure:	Down to you

www.hasbean.co.uk

If you'd like to be sure that your coffee beans have been specifically roasted for you then buy here, as your coffee will arrive with the 'roasted on' date so you can be sure it'll be extra fresh. There's a wide variety of coffee available from Jamaican Blue Mountain Top to Brazil CO_2 Decaffinated plus every type of coffee maker, grinder and pot you can think of and a great deal of information on which coffee to buy if you're not sure. This is a wonderful website for real coffee enthusiasts.

Site Usability:	★★★★	Based:	UK
Product Range:	★★★★★	Express Delivery Option? (UK)	No
Price Range:	Medium	Gift Wrapping Option?	No
Delivery Area:	Worldwide	Returns Procedure:	Down to you

www.nespresso.com

If you've already bought one of the coffee machines that takes the Nespresso capsules, or if you're thinking of buying one, this is the place you can buy both and you'll need to order your replacement capsules here as well. It sounds a nuisance but it couldn't be easier. They're based in Beauchamp Place in London and will deliver to you extremely fast. There's a very good selection of coffees from the very strong to decaf (and strong decaf) plus a selection of accessories.

Site Usability:	★★★★★	Express Delivery Option? (UK)	Yes
Product Range:	★★★	Gift Wrapping Option?	No
Price Range:	Luxury/Medium	Returns Procedure:	Down to you
Delivery Area:	Worldwide		

www.realcoffee.co.uk

The original founders of the Roast & Post Coffee Company were in the coffee business for over 150 years and owned coffee trading companies and estates in Kenya, Tanzania and Uganda, so now they're using the knowledge and expertise perfected over three generations in roasting and blending the finest coffees in the world. You can buy organic and Fairtrade coffees as well as their blended and premium collections and read lots of information about each one. Tea and coffee making equipment is available here too.

Site Usability:	★★★★	Based:	UK
Product Range:	★★★★	Express Delivery Option? (UK)	Yes
Price Range:	Medium	Gift Wrapping Option?	No
Delivery Area:	Worldwide	Returns Procedure:	Down to you

www.thebeanshop.com

With its clear, well photographed website and excellent selection of coffee, tea and hardware this is a very good place to come to order your next cup. There's a lot of information about all the different ranges plus clear roast/body/acidity/strength ratings so you can see straight away what you're buying. You can also buy espresso machines, coffee grinders, tea pots, milk frothers and unusual (and humorous) mugs and cups.

Site Usability:	★★★★★	Based:	UK
Product Range:	★★★★	Express Delivery Option? (UK)	Yes
Price Range:	Luxury/Medium	Gift Wrapping Option?	No
Delivery Area:	Worldwide	Returns Procedure:	Down to you

www.whittard.co.uk

Famous for fine tea and coffee since 1886, Whittard of Chelsea offers a wide range of teas and coffees (choose from Monsoon Malabar, Old Brown Java and Very Very Berry Fruit Infusion) and also offers instant flavoured cappuccinos plus coffee and tea gifts. They have a very high quality hot chocolate to order here and you'll also find machines, grinders, roasters and cafetières, accessories and equipment spares as well as very attractive ceramics, fine bone chine and seasonal hampers.

Site Usability:	★★★★	Based:	UK
Product Range:	★★★★	Express Delivery Option? (UK)	No
Price Range:	Medium	Gift Wrapping Option?	No
Delivery Area:	Worldwide	Returns Procedure:	Down to you

Chapter 61

Wine, Champagne and Spirits

There are definitely times when you want to go out and buy that special bottle from your local wine merchant, probably because you need it urgently and don't have time to order online. I really can't think of any other reason for buying wines and spirits offline. Your local store may have quite a good selection, but do the people who work there really know what they're talking about? You're really taking pot luck here as sometimes they do and sometimes they don't, in which case you're probably going to make your decision based on price, which is not the best way to buy.

I have to exclude Majestic from my comments above as I find that whichever branch you go to they're enthusiastic, helpful and knowledgeable. If you order from them online you can sometimes have your order delivered the same day – you can't ask for more than that.

A number of the online wine merchants below (most of which have shops as well) are at the higher end of the range and you won't necessarily get the best deal. What you will get is a choice of the very best wines and champagnes available in the UK. Some will ask you to buy a case and others will sell you just a few bottles so make sure which service the website you're visiting offers before you get too excited about that bottle of Pomerol.

If you know exactly which wine you're looking for take a visit to wine-searcher.com, where you can find out who is selling it, where they are, and how much they're asking. It's a really good facility but please bear in mind that the prices don't include VAT, nor will they include special offers from retailers such as Majestic, Oddbins or Laithwaites.

Sites to Visit

www.ballsbrothers.co.uk

Balls Brothers is a long established business having shipped and traded wines for over 150 years. You'll discover a handpicked selection of over four hundred wines and you can be sure that everything has been carefully chosen from the least expensive (reds starting at around £4.50 a bottle) right up to Chateaux Palmer Margaux at over £100. The search facility is quite difficult to use as you can't see the complete list so just input the type or colour of wine you're looking for and you'll get a selection.

Site Usability:	★★★	Based:	UK
Product Range:	★★★★	Express Delivery Option? (UK)	No
Price Range:	Luxury/Medium	Gift Wrapping Option?	No
Delivery Area:	Worldwide	Returns Procedure:	Down to you

www.bbr.com

Berry Bros. & Rudd is Britain's oldest wine and spirit merchant having traded from the same shop for over 300 years. Today members of the Berry and Rudd families continue to own and manage the business and their website is a surprisingly busy one. You can not only find out about the wines you should be drinking now but you can also start a BBR Cellar Plan, use their Wedding List services and join their Wine Club.

Site Usability:	★★★★★	Based:	UK
Product Range:	★★★★★	Express Delivery Option? (UK)	Yes
Price Range:	Luxury/Medium	Gift Wrapping Option?	No
Delivery Area:	Worldwide	Returns Procedure:	Down to you

www.cambridgewine.com

This is a really beautifully designed website from a Cambridge based independent wine merchant and a site that's a pleasure to browse through. You can choose by category and by country, select from their mixed cases and promotional offers and take advantage of their gift and En Primeur services. It's the perfect website if you want one that isn't too busy and where it's very easy to place your order.

Site Usability:	★★★★★	Based:	UK
Product Range:	★★★★★	Express Delivery Option? (UK)	No
Price Range:	Luxury/Medium	Gift Wrapping Option?	Yes
Delivery Area:	UK	Returns Procedure:	Down to you

www.champagnewarehouse.co.uk

Here is an attractive website from a retailer established just a few years ago to offer personally selected, top quality champagnes throughout the UK. You can buy your champagne by the bottle, six pack or case and prices start at around £14.00 a bottle. They also offer tasting cases containing two different champagnes. The selection of champagnes changes from month to month as their orders arrive in their warehouse.

Site Usability:	★★★★	Based:	UK
Product Range:	★★★	Express Delivery Option? (UK)	No
Price Range:	Medium/Very Good Value	Gift Wrapping Option?	No
Delivery Area:	UK	Returns Procedure:	Down to you

www.everywine.co.uk

Everywine is a wine retailer combining an excellent search facility, wines from the reasonably priced to the extremely expensive and some very good deals as well. You do need to buy by the case here but if you want a mixed case then you just click through to their sister site at www. booths-wine.co.uk. This is another award winning wine merchant as they won the International Wine Challenge Regional Wine Merchant of the Year 2005.

Site Usability:	★★★★	Based:	UK
Product Range:	★★★★★	Express Delivery Option? (UK)	No
Price Range:	Medium	Gift Wrapping Option?	No
Delivery Area:	UK	Returns Procedure:	Down to you

www.justerinis.com

It's quite a surprise when you first visit this long established wine merchant to be asked where you are and how old you are: definitely a first for me online. Anyway, once you're past that you can pay a proper visit to this gorgeous website where the wines are definitely expensive but you'll only find the best, plus lots of advice on what you're buying and how to look after it. Your order request is sent to one of their brokers, who will then contact you regarding availability and delivery. If there's something you're considering buying, don't delay.

Site Usability:	★★★★	Based:	UK
Product Range:	★★★★	Express Delivery Option? (UK)	No
Price Range:	Luxury/Medium	Gift Wrapping Option?	No
Delivery Area:	Worldwide on application	Returns Procedure:	Down to you in agreement with them

www.laithwaites.co.uk

Laithwaites are an excellent, family run online (and offline) wine merchant with a really personal and efficient service and a very good choice at all price ranges. They offer wines and champagnes, mixed cases, a wide range of fortified wines and spirits and there's also a clever food matching service plus all the other options you would expect including bin ends, mixed case offers and wine plans.

Site Usability:	★★★★★	Based:	UK
Product Range:	★★★★	Express Delivery Option? (UK)	No
Price Range:	Luxury/Medium/Very Good Value	Gift Wrapping Option?	No
Delivery Area:	UK	Returns Procedure:	Down to you

www.laywheeler.co.uk

Based in Colchester and specialising in Bordeaux and Burgundy, Lay and Wheeler are also agents for wine producers in Australia, California, South Africa and other areas. There's wide range of wine on offer on this busy website plus assistance if you need it. You can choose from their current offers or the full wine list, use their gift service, view the tastings programme and find out about their Bin Club and Wine Discovery Club as well.

Site Usability:	★★★★	Based:	UK
Product Range:	★★★★	Express Delivery Option? (UK)	No
Price Range:	Luxury/Medium	Gift Wrapping Option?	No
Delivery Area:	UK	Returns Procedure:	Down to you

www.majestic.co.uk

You've definitely heard of Majestic, but have you tried their online ordering service, which takes away all the hassle of having to go there, load up and then carry everything from your car when you get home? Not only do they make ordering really easy and offer the best prices on bulk orders but your nearest branch will give you a call once you've placed your order and bring it to you exactly when you want it. You can order right up to Christmas too.

Site Usability:	★★★★★	Based:	UK
Product Range:	★★★★★	Express Delivery Option? (UK)	Yes if you request it by phone
Price Range:	Luxury/Medium/Very Good Value	Gift Wrapping Option?	No
Delivery Area:	UK	Returns Procedure:	Down to you

www.oddbins.co.uk

The main difference between buying from Oddbins and buying from Majestic is that at Oddbins you don't have to buy 12 bottles and you can still take advantage of lots of their special offers. So if you just want a couple of bottles at a good price (or even two bottles of their Batard Montrachet at £84 each) you should take a look here. It's a cheerful, colourful and easy to get round website and you can also use their weddings and party services.

Site Usability:	★★★★★	Based:	UK
Product Range:	★★★★★	Express Delivery Option? (UK)	No
Price Range:	Luxury/Medium/Very Good Value	Gift Wrapping Option?	No
Delivery Area:	UK	Returns Procedure:	Down to you

www.tanners-wines.co.uk

You'll find a comprehensive range of wine, champagne, liqueurs and spirits on this clear and well laid out site. Tanners are a traditional style wine merchant with a calm style (very different from the 'full on' style of Majestic and Oddbins') offering an excellent service and reasonable prices plus lots of advice and information about everything on offer. So you may not always find the cheapest deals here, but you'll certainly enjoy buying from them.

Site Usability:	★★★★★	Based:	UK
Product Range:	★★★★	Express Delivery Option? (UK)	No
Price Range:	Luxury/Medium	Gift Wrapping Option?	No
Delivery Area:	UK	Returns Procedure:	Down to you

www.thesecretcellar.co.uk

This is an independent wine merchant offering a hand-picked selection of wines, some of which are easy to find elsewhere and some which are not. It's well worth having a look round as not only are there some interesting wines on offer, but the website is very clear and uncluttered and offers lots of useful information which I not only found helpful (and I'm no expert here) but also made me want to buy. They also offer a next day delivery service provided you order by 2.30pm.

Site Usability:	★★★★★	Based:	UK
Product Range:	★★★★	Express Delivery Option? (UK)	Yes
Price Range:	Medium	Gift Wrapping Option?	No
Delivery Area:	UK	Returns Procedure:	Down to you in agreement with them

www.thewhiskyexchange.com

Although you can buy blended and some single malt whiskies from just about every supermarket and wine merchant, if you want a really good selection of specialist whisky you need to have a look here. They offer a very good range of from the reasonably priced to the not so reasonably priced and include help and advice for the drinker, collector and the investor. Their list of single malts is amazing and prices go up to (don't faint) over £2000 but of course there are plenty between £20 and £25.

Site Usability:	★★★★★	Based:	UK
Product Range:	★★★★★	Express Delivery Option? (UK)	No
Price Range:	Luxury/Medium	Gift Wrapping Option?	No
Delivery Area:	Worldwide	Returns Procedure:	Down to you

www.whiskyshop.com

Shop for your malt whisky here by area (if you really know what you're doing) and choose from Speyside, Highland, Islands and Islay. Alternatively choose from their top ten whiskies or simply enter the brand you're looking for. Don't forget to compare prices to make sure that you're getting the best deal, particularly if you're buying something expensive. There is a good range, from Macallan 1951 at £1,500 and Glenfarclas 30 year old at £93 to more regular varieties (and prices).

Site Usability:	★★★★	Based:	UK
Product Range:	★★★★	Express Delivery Option? (UK)	Yes
Price Range:	Luxury	Gift Wrapping Option?	No
Delivery Area:	Worldwide	Returns Procedure:	Down to you

www.wine-searcher.com

Looking for a particular vintage of Pomerol? Or just Oyster Bay Chardonnay? With prices differing by as much as 40% you need this fantastic worldwide wine comparison website if you're considering buying more than a single bottle of wine. Do register for the pro-version to get all the benefits.

There are literally hundreds of wine merchants online all over the world. and it's simply not possible to list all the good ones. Wine-searcher will take you to many you've never heard of so take a good look at the sites you visit, make sure they're secure, compare the prices and enjoy.

Section 8
Sport and Leisure

Sport and Leisure

This is another area of online shopping where there's a tremendous amount of choice in each area. I've listed here for you my favourite websites for each type of sport and leisure activity, not too many for each one (particularly as each online retailer offers such a wide range), just the pick of the bunch.

As a non totally sporty person (my children will tell you that that's putting it mildly) you might wonder how I can tell you - probably more sporty than me - where to go to find the best equipment and accessories, but believe me I can. Firstly there are five skiers, one oarsman, one rugby player (but four rugby addicts), one hiker and camper, two tennis players, three golfers, two scuba divers, two intermittent gym goers, two horseriders, five table tennis players, three trampoliners, four billiards and three darts players, one musician (me) one artist (not me) and three photographers in my family. All from just the five of us: Not bad, eh?

With larger pieces of equipment it's back to my favourite mantra 'don't forget to check out your price comparison websites before buying'. It's no good me trying to give you all the places you can buy your next Concept II rower; it just wouldn't be possible. What you need to do is select the one you want and then find out who will offer it to you at the lowest price, while not losing sight of the delivery service you want.

No doubt you'll be coming back to me to tell me all about your favourite sport that I've missed out - and if you do I'll gladly add it in for you next time. For now you'll have to put up with the following:

- Fitness and Yoga Equipment
- Outdoor Equipment and Games
- Walking, Climbing and Camping
- Snowsports and Watersports
- Fishing, Golf and Horseriding
- Tennis, Cricket, Rugby and Football
- Everything for the Photographer
- For the Artist and Musician
- Tickets and Subscriptions
- Books, Music, Movies and Games

Chapter 62

Fitness Equipment

If you're creating a basic gym at home, as we have, I would say go for a small number of the best pieces of kit you can afford to start with, rather than try and get everything for the lowest price. That way each piece will last you for a long time and, hopefully, do the best job. In ours we started with a cross trainer and a rower plus gym balls and weights and I have to say that although they're used intermittently they're very good and they'll definitely last a while. We won't discuss the fact that I'm still not allowed to buy a treadmill as, I'm told regularly, I can easily run round the garden (which I hate doing as the ground isn't level). Oh well …

If you have an oarsman in your family (as I did before he went to uni) ask him which rowing machine he would like otherwise *he won't use the one you buy.* Trust me on this.

Here are websites for buying yoga essentials and a huge range of fitness equipment and as I've said, if you're investing in a premium piece of kit, please check the prices first.

Sites to Visit

www.agoy.com

Agoy is an extremely attractive website dedicated to yoga products from modern bags and mats in a wide range of styles and colours to starter kits, which include a bag, mat, belt and DVD at various price levels. This is a very small collection at the moment but as the products are quite different to those you can find elsewhere it's worth a look. In their yoga holidays section they direct you to an agency who can tell you all about wellbeing escapes.

Site Usability:	★★★★	Based:	UK
Product Range:	★★★	Express Delivery Option? (UK)	No
Price Range:	Medium	Gift Wrapping Option?	No
Delivery Area:	UK	Returns Procedure:	Down to you in agreement with them

www.fitness-superstore.co.uk

You can see exactly why this fitness equipment retailer calls itself the largest supplier of specialist fitness equipment in the UK – you'd be hard put to find a better range of top brand equipment. Kit out your home gym from their selection of treadmills, elliptical trainers, rowing machines, bikes, multigyms, toners, dumbells, ab trainers and gym balls. You can also buy boxing kit, table tennis tables and other sports equipment here.

Site Usability:	★★★★★	Based:	UK
Product Range:	★★★★★	Express Delivery Option? (UK)	No
Price Range:	Medium	Gift Wrapping Option?	No
Delivery Area:	UK	Returns Procedure:	Down to you in agreement with them

www.gymworld.co.uk

This is another fitness store where you can buy just about everything from treadmills to elliptical cross trainers and rowers to to multi gyms. Then there are the weights, mats, benches and stability balls. Alongside all of this Gym World offer Jacques crocquet sets, multi-games tables, go-karts and sledges, rehabilitation and mobility aids, yoga and Pilates gear, pool tables and massage couches. Most items can be shipped to the EU – if you have a query call them.

Site Usability:	★★★★★	Based:	UK
Product Range:	★★★★★	Express Delivery Option? (UK)	No
Price Range:	Medium	Gift Wrapping Option?	No
Delivery Area:	Most items throughout EU	Returns Procedure:	Down to you in agreement with them

www.physicalcompany.co.uk

This is a less sophisticated online fitness equipment store than some you'll find but as they're my 'local' as it were I can assure you that they really know their stuff. Particularly useful is the information on the latest equipment which you can see straight away on their home page so take a look there first, then click through to Products and order all your gym essentials. They don't offer the larger pieces of equipment but are excellent for items such as gym balls, benches, rebounders, dumbells and mats. Expect excellent service.

Site Usability:	★★★★★	Based:	UK
Product Range:	★★★	Express Delivery Option? (UK)	Yes
Price Range:	Medium	Gift Wrapping Option?	No
Delivery Area:	UK	Returns Procedure:	Down to you in agreement with them

www.yogamatters.com

Yoga Matters is run by a group of enthusiastic yoga practitioners based in North London, and while you won't find an enormous range you can be sure that what's there has been extremely well thought out. They offer a selection of mats and bags, latex resistance bands and Pezzi gym balls plus clothing by Asquith London, prAna and more, also a good selection of books and DVDs. They're happy to deliver to you worldwide.

Site Usability:	★★★★	Based:	UK
Product Range:	★★★	Express Delivery Option? (UK)	Yes
Price Range:	Medium	Gift Wrapping Option?	No
Delivery Area:	Worldwide	Returns Procedure:	Down to you

www.yogastudio.co.uk

This is one of the largest collections of yoga kit available online with a wide range of products which you can buy individually (such as mats, belts and bags) and a selection of kits, from basic starter kits for yoga and Pilates right up to Wai Lana's Little Yogis Kit – the complete kit for mini yogis. Then you can buy stability balls and cushions and books and DVDs on yoga and Pilates for beginners, in pregnancy and for weight loss.

Site Usability:	★★★★	Based:	UK
Product Range:	★★★★	Express Delivery Option? (UK)	No
Price Range:	Medium	Gift Wrapping Option?	No
Delivery Area:	UK	Returns Procedure:	Down to you

Chapter 63

Outdoor Equipment and Games (including Trampolines, Slides and Swings)

It was quite difficult to know just how much to include in this section, and what really belonged in the kids' area, so I decided that to simplify matters (for me, at least), I'd put it all together.

I know that slides, swings and sandpits are really for kids only but trampolines? Having recently seen seven eighteen year old boys having a relaxing time on our large trampoline I decided that to limit them to kids would be wrong, so here they are, with all the rest.

Then there are outdoor games such as croquet, go-karts from kids' versions to really expensive more adult makes, sledges, rounders sets, badminton nets and lots more and who uses them will, in my opinion, depend more on how old they feel than on how old they actually are.

I recently watched (yes I know, I'm lazy) a group ranging in age from 11 to 60 playing touch rugby in my sister-in-law's garden – how do you define that age group, I wonder?

Sites to Visit

www.activekid.co.uk

Active Kid offers pretty well the full range of TP Toys' climbing frames, sandpits, slides, swings, trampolines (including nets and accessories and wooden playsets). These are all large items it's so much better to order online (how did you do it before?) as not only do they get delivered –

hopefully right to your garden – but you can easily access all the information you need without having to wait for a shop assistant to come and help you.

Site Usability:	★★★★★	Based:	UK
Product Range:	★★★★★	Express Delivery Option? (UK)	No
Price Range:	Medium	Gift Wrapping Option?	No
Delivery Area:	UK	Returns Procedure:	Down to you

www.activitytoysdirect.co.uk

This is an unsophisticated but extremely easy to use website where you'll find (you probably guessed) activity toys, including lots of ideas for garden fun such as netball sets, fun rides and aqua slides, swing and slide combinations, foldaway trampolines with net protection for very young children, plus the full size versions, table tennis tables and climbing frames.

Site Usability:	★★★★	Based:	UK
Product Range:	★★★	Express Delivery Option? (UK)	Yes
Price Range:	Medium/Very Good Value	Gift Wrapping Option?	No
Delivery Area:	UK	Returns Procedure:	Down to you

www.adventuretoys.co.uk

Here you'll find a good range of climbing frames, trampolines and swing sets, and also lots of ride-on tractors and cars, sand and water tables, mini picnic tables, basketball sets, play houses, netball goals, practice tennis nets and trikes. Phew. Brands they carry include Brio, Little Types, TP Toys, Supertramp and Winther. This website is well worth having a good look round.

Site Usability:	★★★★★	Based:	UK
Product Range:	★★★★★	Express Delivery Option? (UK)	Yes
Price Range:	Medium	Gift Wrapping Option?	No
Delivery Area:	UK	Returns Procedure:	Down to you

www.enchanted-wood.co.uk

At Enchanted Wood you can order the very good range of Kettler pedal go-karts and trikes plus Kingswood and Sherwood wooden play systems and accessories. Then for rainy days there's lots of Lego to choose from, from introduction Lego Duplo to Mega Vehicle sets for ages 8+ plus everything Playmobile from Costruction and Everyday Living to Playmobile for tinies.

Site Usability:	★★★★	Based:	UK
Product Range:	★★★★	Express Delivery Option? (UK)	No
Price Range:	Medium	Gift Wrapping Option?	No
Delivery Area:	UK	Returns Procedure:	Down to you

www.gardenadventure.co.uk

This is the serious end of the activity 'toy' online retailers, where you can not only buy a fantastic range of Dino go-karts up to the top of the range Black Magic BF5 at just under £900 plus the Dino pedal powered train and tender but also use their services to build (and buy from them) a wide range of log cabins, wooden play houses and adventure climbing frames. If you want something really special this would be a good place to look.

Site Usability:	★★★★	Based:	UK
Product Range:	★★★★★	Express Delivery Option? (UK)	No
Price Range:	Luxury/Medium	Gift Wrapping Option?	No
Delivery Area:	UK	Returns Procedure:	Down to you in agreement with them

www.gardengames.co.uk

Whether you're looking for trampolines, climbing frames, swings and slides, junior and full sized croquet sets, snooker and pool tables, table tennis tables, aqua slides or an old fashioned wooden sledge you'll find everything on this friendly website. All the items are very well photographed, they offer speedy UK delivery and will also ship to the USA, Canada and Spain.

Site Usability:	★★★★★	Based:	UK
Product Range:	★★★★	Express Delivery Option? (UK)	Yes
Price Range:	Medium	Gift Wrapping Option?	No
Delivery Area:	UK, USA, Canada and Spain	Returns Procedure:	Down to you

www.greatoutdoortoys.co.uk

Alongside the usual outdoor activity kit such as climbing frames and trampolines, here you can buy go-karts, by Puky (I know) and In Car, both made in Germany. The ranges go from the entry versions at about £200 to the top of the range In Car Centurian or Puky Panther at just below £500. You can also buy accessories such as extra seats, flashing lights and trailers.

Site Usability:	★★★★★	Based:	UK
Product Range:	★★★★	Express Delivery Option? (UK)	No
Price Range:	Luxury/Medium	Gift Wrapping Option?	No
Delivery Area:	UK	Returns Procedure:	Down to you

www.mastersgames.com

At Masters Traditional Games you'll find a wide range of indoor and outdoor games made in high quality materials such as Chinese Checkers with a solid teak board and hand crafted bagatelle boards. You'll also find outdoor draughts, table football, bar billiards, table tennis, roulette, croquet, rounders and bar games such as skittles, Aunt Sally and bar billiards.

Site Usability:	★★★★	Based:	UK
Product Range:	★★★★	Express Delivery Option? (UK)	Yes if you contact them
Price Range:	Medium	Gift Wrapping Option?	No
Delivery Area:	Worldwide	Returns Procedure:	Down to you

www.outdoortoystore.co.uk

If your tiny has been begging you to get her the Double Seat Ride On Pink Princess Jeep or a Bounce House Castle and Slide then you've definitely come to the right place, as although you'll find an excellent range of trampolines and nets, swings and slides here, there are also some very different products you won't find everywhere. For outdoor activity toys this is a great place to start.

Site Usability:	★★★★★	Based:	UK
Product Range:	★★★★★	Express Delivery Option? (UK)	No
Price Range:	Luxury/Medium	Gift Wrapping Option?	No
Delivery Area:	UK	Returns Procedure:	Down to you

www.towerstoys.co.uk

If the bright orangeness (is there such a word?) of this website doesn't stop you in your tracks take a good look round, as there's an amazing range of toys, from sandpits, goal posts and ride-on tractors to Jacques croquet sets, rounders kits, sandpit excavators, pedal go-karts and snow toys from simple sledges to the Berg steerable, Snowxpress Max. Ask for a delivery quote outside UK mainland.

Site Usability:	★★★★	Based:	UK
Product Range:	★★★★	Express Delivery Option? (UK)	No
Price Range:	Luxury/Medium	Gift Wrapping Option?	No
Delivery Area:	UK	Returns Procedure:	Down to you

www.trampledunderfoot.co.uk

These are real trampoline experts offering Jumpking Trampolines and Bazoongi plus a full range of accessories such as safety nets, covers and ladders. They also sell mini trampolines, bounce boards, bouncy castles, trampoline parts and replacement pads and springs. There's an excellent buying guide which will help you decide which trampoline will be right for you and how to make it as safe as possible.

Site Usability:	★★★★★	Based:	UK
Product Range:	★★★★	Express Delivery Option? (UK)	Yes
Price Range:	Luxury/Medium	Gift Wrapping Option?	No
Delivery Area:	Worldwide	Returns Procedure:	Down to you

Chapter 64

Walking, Climbing and Camping

Ok this is definitely not my area although (and my kids refuse to believe me) I did go on quite a few camping holidays when I was much, much younger. I have two children who would really rather not have to sleep in a tent, thank you very much, and one older son who's quite happy to do so and has gone on long treks to India and Borneo, not to mention cold and wet forays to the Lake District with his school CCF.

The thing I'm absolutely sure of is that you want to have the best kit possible, whether it's boots for walking on the moors in Scotland, a rucksack or a tent; you need to get it right. The fact that we've ended up with at least four sizes of rucksack and a huge box of camping paraphernalia which has firm instructions on it '*throw away at your peril*', has nothing to do with it. I know for certain, because I was there and I paid, that a great deal of thought and care went into every single piece. Quality is really important here and can make all the difference between comfort and misery.

Sites to Visit

www.allweathers.co.uk

Their name really defines the product on this easy to use website which is perfect for the hiker and camper or really anyone who spends a lot of time braving the elements. With brands such as Hi-Tec and Berghaus you know you're in safe hands purchasing your rucksacks, tents, hiking boots, travel equipment and travel clothing. They also stock a very comprehensive range of Barbour jackets from the classic Beaufort jacket to the top of the range aged waxed cotton needlecord Beauchamp. Prices are very competitive and include postage.

Site Usability:	★★★★★	Based:	UK
Product Range:	★★★★★	Express Delivery Option? (UK)	Yes
Price Range:	Medium	Gift Wrapping Option?	No
Delivery Area:	UK	Returns Procedure:	Down to you

www.completeoutdoors.co.uk

Everything for walking, trekking, rambling, camping, climbing, and many other activities is available here with a wide range of tents, rucksacks, sleeping bags, navigation equipment, boots, walking poles, and general camping accessories from well known brands such as Paramo, Berghaus, Brasher, Meindl, Bushbaby, Victorinox, Leki, Karrimor, Leatherman, Rohan, Nomad Medical, Regatta. There's lots more plus a good gift section.

Site Usability:	★★★★	Based:	UK
Product Range:	★★★★★	Express Delivery Option? (UK)	No
Price Range:	Medium	Gift Wrapping Option?	No
Delivery Area:	UK	Returns Procedure:	Down to you

www.cotswoldoutdoor.com

This is one of the very best websites for camping, hiking and adventure holiday equipment including tents, sleeping bags, clothing, hiking boots, rucksacks, travel equipment and gadgets and tools from brands such as The North Face, Osprey and Gerber. Service is friendly and speedy and they support youth adventure holidays and treks such as World Team Challenge.

Site Usability:	★★★★	Based:	UK
Product Range:	★★★★★	Express Delivery Option? (UK)	Yes if you call them
Price Range:	Medium	Gift Wrapping Option?	No
Delivery Area:	Worldwide	Returns Procedure:	Down to you

www.blacks.co.uk

If you or any member of your family has ever taken part in any major outdoor excursions you'll probably already have visited Blacks, where they offer a well priced (rather than 'designer') range of clothing and accessories and good value skiwear in season. You'll find waterproof jackets and trousers, lots of fleece, tents, poles, footwear and socks and great gifts such as Cybalite torches, Kick and Huntsman knives and tools and Garmin compasses.

Site Usability:	★★★★★	Based:	UK
Product Range:	★★★★★	Express Delivery Option? (UK)	No
Price Range:	Medium/Very Good Value	Gift Wrapping Option?	No
Delivery Area:	UK	Returns Procedure:	Down to you

Also take a look at the following for walking, climbing and camping clothes and equipment:

Website Address	You'll find it in
www.ellis-brigham.com	Chapter 65: Snowsports and Watersports
www.snowandrock.com	Chapter 65: Snowsports and Watersports
www.patagonia.com	Chapter 65: Snowsports and Watersports

Chapter 65

Snowsports and Watersports

If you're lucky enough to have a family where everyone enjoys skiing, my advice is to make it your definite 'family' holiday each year if you can. Having seen my kids disappear off into the wilds of Africa or on Rugby trips to Canada in the summer I know that family beach holidays, unless there's a really active element such as scuba diving or golf and tennis, are about to become a thing of the past.

If it's skiing we're offering there's no question that all three are there, ready, packed and waiting to leave and I suspect, from talking to other families, that this is likely to continue, with various hangers-on, for a long while to come.

Where skiing kit is concerned I have some quite strong advice, based on my experience. You can buy your skis at home. You can buy all your clothes – your jacket, high tech ski pants, thermals and socks here too (and again quality really matters). But if you're thinking of investing in a pair of boots, buy them when you arrive, on your first day, which gives you time to try them out, wear them in and get the shop to change them if they're wrong. I've seen so many people travel out with a new pair of boots only to spend the whole holiday in agony. Listen to me; I know about this and yes, I bought mine there, not here.

With watersports I suggest that you hire the really high tech gear unless sailing and scuba diving are something you're going to be doing a great deal of. Once you're ready to buy take advice from the experts at the online retailers below, they really know their stuff; well they would do, wouldn't they? They spend every available minute either on or under the water.

And if it's just nautical style clothing you're after, or good quality deck shoes then you'll find it easy to kit yourself out without looking for your nearest boating store (particularly if you don't live near the water). This is what these retailers are so good at, now they can offer you their specialised clothing and equipment wherever you are in the world.

Sites to Visit

Snowsports

www.boardsonline.co.uk

Although you can buy some clothing here, this is a website for the real enthusiast and where, although you can buy from a small selection of skateboards and wakeboards, the real business is snowboarding. Boards by Santa Cruz, Wild D and Endeavour are available along with boots, bindings, protection, snowboard clothing and beanies.

Site Usability:	★★★★	Based:	UK
Product Range:	★★★★	Express Delivery Option? (UK)	No
Price Range:	Medium	Gift Wrapping Option?	No
Delivery Area:	UK	Returns Procedure:	Down to you

www.edge2edge.co.uk

The next time you're planning a skiing or snowboarding trip you should take a look round this website, where they have an excellent list of brands such as Exus, Burton and Forum (snowboarding boots) and Atomic, Head and Nordica (skiing) with top line boards and skis to go with them. They also have some excellent discounts plus rental packages at good prices and offer roof boxes and racks for your car in case you're driving to the slopes.

Site Usability:	★★★★★	Based:	UK
Product Range:	★★★★	Express Delivery Option? (UK)	No
Price Range:	Medium	Gift Wrapping Option?	No
Delivery Area:	Worldwide	Returns Procedure:	Down to you

www.ellis-brigham.com

On its wonderful, clearly photographed website for mountaineers and skiers, Ellis Brigham offers brands such as The North Face, Patagonia, Ice Breaker and Lowe Alpine. Every possible type of equipment is very clearly shown and there are some good sporting gift ideas as well including items by Leatherman, Victorinox, Maglite and Toollogic. In the ski section you'll find clothing by lots of different makes; colourful beanies, humorous ski socks and boots and skis by all the great brands.

Site Usability:	★★★★★	Based:	UK
Product Range:	★★★★★	Express Delivery Option? (UK)	No
Price Range:	Luxury/Medium	Gift Wrapping Option?	No
Delivery Area:	Worldwide	Returns Procedure:	Down to you

www.littlesky.co.uk

Little Sky specialises in children's branded surf, ski and fashion wear plus footwear & accessories for kids 0-16 years. On their website there's a really good range of functional, fashionable and technical wear from brands such as Quiksilver, Roxy, Billabong, O'Neill, Animal, Oxbow, Timberland, Kookai, Elle, Reef, Columbia, Trespass and Brugi. In the summer you can find all you need for your holiday in the sun from bikinis, boardshorts and funky shirts to UV suits and footwear and in winter they focus on skiwear and accessories.

Site Usability:	★★★★★	Based:	UK	
Product Range:	★★★★	Express Delivery Option? (UK)	Yes	
Price Range:	Medium	Gift Wrapping Option?	No	
Delivery Area:	EU	Returns Procedure:	Down to you	

www.patagonia.com

As the sports that Patagonia specialises in are Alpine skiing, rock climbing, Nordic climbing and fly fishing you won't be surprised that this is a collection of really high tech/high insulated products. What is surprising (to me, at least), is that they've produced a really excellent range for infants and children too, with jackets, vests, fleece, base layers, all-in-ones and gloves for ages from 3 months to 14. Nothing is inexpensive but you can be sure you're buying the best.

Site Usability:	★★★★★	Based:	UK	
Product Range:	★★★★★	Express Delivery Option? (UK)	Yes	
Price Range:	Luxury	Gift Wrapping Option?	No	
Delivery Area:	Worldwide	Returns Procedure:	Down to you	

www.snowandrock.com

Snow and Rock is a well known retailer for skiers, snowboarders and rock climbers with a full range of equipment and clothing and accessories by brands such as Animal, Billabong, Ski Jacket, Helly Hanson, O'Neill, Quicksilver, Salomon and Oakley. There's also lots of advice on what to buy and on fit. In the gift and gadget section you'll find ideas including books and films, watches, two-way radios, solar chargers and compasses.

Site Usability:	★★★★★	Based:	UK	
Product Range:	★★★★★	Express Delivery Option? (UK)	Yes	
Price Range:	Luxury/Medium/Very Good Value	Gift Wrapping Option?	No	
Delivery Area:	Worldwide	Returns Procedure:	Down to you	

www.simplypiste.com

This is one of a rapidly growing chain of online sporting retailers that includes simplyscuba and simplybeach. At simplypiste there's an excellent, well laid out collection for men, women and children (and you can actually click straight through to the children's skiwear section, which makes a change). Find ski suits, jackets, salopettes, ski pants, base layer and baby skiwear there, plus lots of accessories such as gloves and goggles which you have to look for in their separate sections.

Site Usability:	★★★★★	Based:	UK	
Product Range:	★★★★	Express Delivery Option? (UK)	Yes	
Price Range:	Medium	Gift Wrapping Option?	No	
Delivery Area:	Worldwide	Returns Procedure:	Down to you	

www.waterproofworld.co.uk

Whether or not you want to start your toddler off fishing or skiing at an early age (in which case they'll definitely need the waders here) you can find all types of great waterproofs too from fun raincoats and jackets, excellent skiwear by Trespass and Dare2Be, Togz child all in one waterproofs, Kiba dungarees and waterproof trousers and finally the essential waders which go from a shoe size 24 to 38.

Site Usability:	★★★★	Based:	UK
Product Range:	★★★★	Express Delivery Option? (UK)	Yes if you call them
Price Range:	Medium	Gift Wrapping Option?	No
Delivery Area:	EU	Returns Procedure:	Down to you

Watersports

www.chandlerystore.co.uk

Musto, Henri Lloyd, and Gill are the three main brands on offer here for the sailor, including clothing, accessories, footwear and luggage ranges. You'll also find deck shoes and chandlery, Kahuna watches, Leatherman knives, Silva compasses and charts and marine books, plus the clever Sea Shore 6 speed Marine folding Bike which stows away on board or in the boot of your car.

Site Usability:	★★★★	Based:	UK
Product Range:	★★★★	Express Delivery Option? (UK)	No
Price Range:	Medium	Gift Wrapping Option?	No
Delivery Area:	Europe	Returns Procedure:	Down to you

www.compass24.com

Here's a modern, well designed site with an enormous and easy to view range of sailing clothing and equipment from anchoring and mooring products to boat fittings and boarding ladders. They also have some very good special offers. They call themselves Europe's largest marine mail-order store and when you visit their website you'll find out why.

Site Usability:	★★★★★	Based:	UK
Product Range:	★★★★★	Express Delivery Option? (UK)	2 day service
Price Range:	Medium	Gift Wrapping Option?	No
Delivery Area:	Worldwide	Returns Procedure:	Down to you

www.crewclothing.co.uk

This is a really attractive and modern website with a constantly expanding range, offering all the Crew gear from the full collection of sailing inspired clothing to lots of other choices including hard wearing footwear, faux fur jackets and gilets and excellent travel bags, gloves, hats and socks. They offer standard and next day UK delivery and same day in central London if you order by 12pm.

Site Usability:	★★★★	Based:	UK
Product Range:	★★★★	Express Delivery Option? (UK)	Yes
Price Range:	Medium	Gift Wrapping Option?	No
Delivery Area:	Worldwide	Returns Procedure:	Down to you

www.henrilloydstore.co.uk

As you would expect from his world famous sailing brand, Henri Lloyd has a beautifully designed website offering an increasing range of casual/sailing clothing and accessories including men's and ladies' clothing, footwear, luggage and specific branded marinewear. The technical sailingwear is excellent and although the collection is quite small you can be sure that everything is of the highest quality.

Site Usability:	★★★★	Based:	UK
Product Range:	★★★	Express Delivery Option? (UK)	No
Price Range:	Medium	Gift Wrapping Option?	No
Delivery Area:	UK	Returns Procedure:	Down to you

www.marinestore.co.uk

At Marine Store's online chandlery aimed at the real sailor there's all you could need from children's life jackets to the latest electronic aids. You won't find much designer-brand gear here, just a really comprehensive selection of what the sailor and boat owner might require including books and charts, deck hatches, fenders and buoys, lighting, paint and antifouling, rope and bungees. They offer a next day service for items in stock and if you want to order from overseas you should call them.

Site Usability:	★★★★★	Based:	UK
Product Range:	★★★★★	Express Delivery Option? (UK)	Yes
Price Range:	Medium	Gift Wrapping Option?	No
Delivery Area:	Worldwide	Returns Procedure:	Down to you

www.nautical-living.co.uk

This is not so much a sailing store but a great place to find gifts for anyone who likes the nautical lifestyle. There are sailing themed cupboards, coffee tables and lamps, mirrors, duvet covers, fabrics, picture frames, towels, pegs, light pulls and lots more and it's all beautifully photographed. They also offer an interior design service which is particularly well priced for kids' rooms.

Site Usability:	★★★★★	Based:	UK
Product Range:	★★★★	Express Delivery Option? (UK)	No
Price Range:	Medium	Gift Wrapping Option?	No
Delivery Area:	UK	Returns Procedure:	Down to you

www.rocktheboatclothing.co.uk

This website is essential for anyone who rows, offering all the gear (apart from the boat and blades, of course) the absolutely essential waterproof splash tops, hoodies and jackets, the lycra (yes I know) leggings and shorts plus neckwarmers, hats and pogies (for the hands). Then there are the wonderful, funny t-shirts and tops that only those who have oarsmen in their families will understand with slogans such as Ergo, Ergoing, Ergone and Going Forwards Backwards. All great gifts for the rower you know.

Site Usability:	★★★★	Based:	UK
Product Range:	★★★★	Express Delivery Option? (UK)	Yes
Price Range:	Medium	Gift Wrapping Option?	No
Delivery Area:	EU	Returns Procedure:	Down to you

www.roho.co.uk

If you're into watersports or you know someone who is then this is definitely the site for you, offering clothing and equipment for scuba, windsurfing, waterskiing, kayaking, surfing, sailing and jetskiing. It's an easy to navigate site with clear pictures of every item offered. If you want to learn to scuba they have their own purpose-built dive centre with lecture rooms and an indoor pool. They also run windsurfing, kitesurfing and snowboarding courses. That's if you live or travel to anywhere near Huddersfield, of course.

Site Usability:	★★★★	Based:	UK
Product Range:	★★★★	Express Delivery Option? (UK)	Yes
Price Range:	Medium	Gift Wrapping Option?	No
Delivery Area:	EU	Returns Procedure:	Down to you

www.simplyscuba.co.uk

Selling itself as the UK's online dive store, Simply Scuba offers not only excellent equipment and accessories but information about diving courses at all levels, equipment servicing and advice on where you can dive all over the world. This is one of a growing group of websites including Simply Beach, where you can expect the product range, advice and service to be very good.

Site Usability:	★★★★	Based:	UK
Product Range:	★★★★	Express Delivery Option? (UK)	Yes
Price Range:	Medium	Gift Wrapping Option?	No
Delivery Area:	Worldwide	Returns Procedure:	Down to you

www.turn-turtle.com

Turn Turtle is a clear and easy to navigate website with a wide selection of clothes and accessories designed initially for the sailor but which would be excellent in most cold, wet weather conditions. It carries the full range of Musto, Henri Lloyd and Gill from technical jackets and fleece to salopettes and thermal shorts, deckshoes, boots and luggage plus Garmin GPS systems and lots of gift ideas and accessories as well.

Site Usability:	★★★★★	Based:	Channel Islands
Product Range:	★★★★	Express Delivery Option? (UK)	No
Price Range:	Luxury/Medium	Gift Wrapping Option?	No
Delivery Area:	Worldwide	Returns Procedure:	Down to you

Chapter 66

Fishing, Golf and Horseriding

Here are three sports taken up by my family with great enthusiasm (and I'll admit that I used to ride but have given up, too little control – me over the horse, I mean). So I'm now a fishing widow, a golf widow and a riding widow too – all fine by me as it means the family are happy and occupied for hours on end and I can spend my time how I please, which is usually writing for you.

If you're an aficionado of any of the above sports you'll love the websites below, where you can buy all the paraphernalia that you need, much of which seems to need replacing or adding to as the season approaches – and most of which costs a small fortune. If you're looking for a gift for a fisherman, golfer or rider you'll find some great ideas below but I would advise caution: don't shell out on the latest rod, set of clubs or saddle for your pony owning friend, as you're bound to choose the wrong one. If you want to give a great gift, give a gift voucher which can be spent as the recipient chooses or buy something small and clever from the products offered by the websites below.

Sites to Visit

Fishing

www.fishit.com

Fishit is a Swedish based website which is probably one of the easiest to navigate and most pleasant on the eye of the fishing equipment sites. Offering brands such as Broman, Jaxon, Stroft, Wiggler, Zalt, Tuf-Line and Fladen there's a wide selection of equipment, clothing and footwear some of which would make excellent gifts for the fishing enthusiast. Allow two weeks for delivery.

Site Usability:	★★★★★	Based:	Sweden
Product Range:	★★★★	Express Delivery Option? (UK)	No
Price Range:	Medium	Gift Wrapping Option?	No
Delivery Area:	Worldwide	Returns Procedure:	Down to you

www.fly-fishing-tackle.co.uk

From a full range of rods and reels by manufacturers such as Snowbee, Fulling Mill, Loop and Fladen to waders, hats, caps and gloves, everything for the keen fisherman is available here. If you're looking for a gift go past the fly tying kits unless you're sure they'll be welcome and concentrate more on fly boxes, tackle bags and rod carriers or fly tying tools, lamps and magnifiers.

Site Usability:	★★★★	Based:	UK
Product Range:	★★★★	Express Delivery Option? (UK)	Yes
Price Range:	Luxury/Medium	Gift Wrapping Option?	No
Delivery Area:	Worldwide	Returns Procedure:	Down to you

www.gifts4fishing.co.uk

This is a really good website offering gifts for fishermen that don't get in the way of the rods, reels and flies. You'll find sterling silver fish cufflinks, Barbour scarves and hip flasks, humorous mugs, limited edition prints, note cards, barware, Richard Wheatley fly boxes and silk ties. They use first class post for all deliveries and ship worldwide.

Site Usability:	★★★★	Based:	UK
Product Range:	★★★	Express Delivery Option? (UK)	Yes
Price Range:	Medium	Gift Wrapping Option?	No
Delivery Area:	Worldwide	Returns Procedure:	Down to you

www.johnnorris.co.uk

John Norris of Penrith offers lots of choices for the fisherman including equipment and accessories by Snowbee, Orvis, Musto, Barbour and Le Chameau and lots more. They also offer a full range of shooting accessories from gun cases and shooting sticks to gun cleaning kits and they're happy to ship worldwide. If you have any queries on their products don't hesitate to call them.

Site Usability:	★★★★★	Based:	UK
Product Range:	★★★★★	Express Delivery Option? (UK)	Yes, worldwide express is available
Price Range:	Medium	Gift Wrapping Option?	No
Delivery Area:	Worldwide	Returns Procedure:	Down to you

www.orvis.co.uk

Orvis has always been at the forefront, particularly in the US, of fly-fishing tackle and shooting accessories. Now that they've opened up properly in the UK you can buy all their equipment online plus their excellent luggage and travel clothing, dog leads, collars and 'feeding stations' and a wide range of clothing. Going back to fishing: from rods to reels, lines to waders there's an excellent choice and everything is really clearly photographed and described.

Site Usability:	★★★★★	Based:	UK
Product Range:	★★★★★	Express Delivery Option? (UK)	Yes
Price Range:	Medium	Gift Wrapping Option?	No
Delivery Area:	EU this website	Returns Procedure:	Down to you

www.scottcountry.co.uk

Fishing and general hard wearing outdoor clothing and accessories, boots, waders and shooting supplies are available on this website which rather than being dedicated to a specific sport offers just about everything for the great outdoors. If they cover one area better than others it would have to be for the shot, as here you can find shot gun and air rifle accessories, clay pigeon traps, shooting sticks and hip-flasks.

Site Usability:	★★★★	Based:	UK
Product Range:	★★★★★	Express Delivery Option? (UK)	Yes
Price Range:	Medium	Gift Wrapping Option?	No
Delivery Area:	Worldwide some products	Returns Procedure:	Down to you

www.tackleshop.co.uk

TackleShop was established in 1999 and has grown quickly to become one of the UK's busiest on-line fishing tackle stores. If you're interested in carp fishing, coarse fishing, game, match, pike, pole or sea fishing you must take a look round as the product range is extremely comprehensive. There's also a good selection of clothing and accessories plus reasonably charged worldwide delivery. If you're a fishing fan (or you know someone who is) you'll almost certainly find something here.

Site Usability:	★★★★★	Based:	UK
Product Range:	★★★★★	Express Delivery Option? (UK)	No but delivery is speedy
Price Range:	Medium	Gift Wrapping Option?	No
Delivery Area:	Worldwide	Returns Procedure:	Down to you

Golf

www.118golf.co.uk

With its excellent delivery service offering standard, express and Saturday delivery plus international delivery, and its diverse range of products for the golfer this would be an excellent website for to look for your next set of clubs or for golfing gifts. Check through their golf accessories where you'll find the range from Callaway and Nike, golf gadgets including swing trainers and ball retrievers, DVDs and books. There's also a gift finder which offers you a selection depending on how much you want to spend.

Site Usability:	★★★★★	Based:	UK
Product Range:	★★★★★	Express Delivery Option? (UK)	Yes
Price Range:	Luxury/Medium	Gift Wrapping Option?	No
Delivery Area:	Worldwide	Returns Procedure:	Down to you

www.clickgolf.co.uk

This is a very quick and easy site to use, although like most of the golfing websites it's very busy and offers a huge range of products which at first sight look almost too much. You can find top brand names such as Callaway and Mizuna and some very good special offers here as well, so check for discounted equipment first if it's a new set of clubs you're after. To make the site easier to use just click on the main category menu at the top of the home page (or on the left) and go from there.

Site Usability:	★★★★★	Based:	UK
Product Range:	★★★★★	Express Delivery Option? (UK)	Yes
Price Range:	Luxury/Medium	Gift Wrapping Option?	No
Delivery Area:	EU	Returns Procedure:	Down to you

www.county-golf.co.uk

There's a great selection for the golfer at keen prices together with an express delivery option and free delivery (at time of writing) on orders over £50. If you need professional advice you just click on their 'Ask an Expert' link to get the phone number or email address (although I'm sure that calling would be far more helpful). With brands such as Mizuna, Callaway, Adams, Adidas, Bay Hill and Ashworth they must definitely be worth a look round.

Site Usability:	★★★★★	Based:	UK
Product Range:	★★★★★	Express Delivery Option? (UK)	Yes
Price Range:	Luxury/Medium	Gift Wrapping Option?	No
Delivery Area:	EU	Returns Procedure:	Down to you

www.gleneagles.com

I probably don't need to tell you that this is a five star hotel and championship golf course and it offers five star products in its shop: so it's expensive. But if you want something really special then this could be a good place to visit (online, I mean). I wouldn't, personally, go for the Gleneagles embroidered clothing unless whoever you're searching for a gift for had actually played there; however, take a quick look at the accessories and you may find something that'll be a success.

Site Usability:	★★★★	Based:	UK
Product Range:	★★★	Express Delivery Option? (UK)	No
Price Range:	Luxury/Medium	Gift Wrapping Option?	No
Delivery Area:	Worldwide	Returns Procedure:	Down to you

www.hattiesmart.com

Hattie Smart designs golf gloves, but not just any old golf gloves - these are designer golf gloves, made from the finest leather and available in a range of colours including pistachio, violet, fuchsia and cranberry for women and kangaroo, bay leaf and vanilla for men. All the gloves are very reasonably priced and arrive beautifully packaged so they'd be the perfect gift for your golf playing friend or relative.

Site Usability:	★★★★	Based:	UK
Product Range:	★★★	Express Delivery Option? (UK)	No
Price Range:	Medium	Gift Wrapping Option?	Yes
Delivery Area:	Worldwide	Returns Procedure:	Down to you

www.onlinegolf.co.uk

Online Golf is another retailer offering everything for the golfer and delivering throughout Europe. It's a typical sports website with loads and loads of products and brand names from Nike, Wilson, Adidas and Pringle to name but a few. Ladies' and men's golf clubs and bags, gold balls, clothing, shoes and other accessories are all available here and there's a very good range for junior golfers.

Site Usability:	★★★★★	Based:	UK
Product Range:	★★★★★	Express Delivery Option? (UK)	Yes
Price Range:	Medium	Gift Wrapping Option?	No
Delivery Area:	EU	Returns Procedure:	Down to you

www.planetgolfuk.co.uk

At Planet Golf there's a really good selection for men and women plus alongside all the adult clubs, accessories and clothing there's a good junior selection too, which not only includes Hippo, US Kids and Hawk junior club sets but also clothing by Demon (polo shirts, fleece lined sweaters and t-shirts), shoes, brollies and other accessories. There are kids' waterproofs and windvests here as well.

Site Usability:	★★★★★	Based:	UK
Product Range:	★★★★★	Express Delivery Option? (UK)	No
Price Range:	Medium	Gift Wrapping Option?	No
Delivery Area:	Worldwide	Returns Procedure:	Down to you

Horseriding

www.colemancroft.com

Coleman Croft are master saddlers established over 25 years ago and now offering on their website riding clothing, rugs, saddles, bridles and tack and safety equipment. They also sell Barbour jackets and Hunter wellington boots. They try and keep everything you see in stock so delivery is speedy and they're happy to ship worldwide.

Site Usability:	★★★★	Express Delivery Option? (UK)	No
Product Range:	★★★★	Gift Wrapping Option?	No
Price Range:	Medium	Returns Procedure:	Down to you
Delivery Area:	Worldwide		

www.dragonflysaddlery.co.uk

Here you can choose from army camouflage jods (!), Buddies jods and Saddlehuggers in loads of different colours from pink and blue to the more traditional neutrals. Then there are long and short jodhpur boots, body protectors, wellies, muck boots and rain proof jackets. The website is for all ages although in some cases it's hard to locate the kids' riding essentials as they're hidden within the sizing categories. There's a good choice though so it's worth a look.

Site Usability:	★★★	Express Delivery Option? (UK)	No
Product Range:	★★★★	Gift Wrapping Option?	No
Price Range:	Medium	Returns Procedure:	Down to you
Delivery Area:	Worldwide		

www.loddonequestrian.com

The clear menu on the left hand side of their home page makes this website extremely easy to use (and easier than many). Just click through to body protectors, bits or riding jackets and you can immediately see what's available although the pictures are not very clear. There a good choice of riding equipment and clothing here for all ages.

Site Usability:	★★★★	Express Delivery Option? (UK)	Yes – call to request
Product Range:	★★★★	Gift Wrapping Option?	No
Price Range:	Medium	Returns Procedure:	Down to you
Delivery Area:	Worldwide		

www.mad4ponies.com

This is a great site for pony mad children as unlike lots of other equestrian websites aimed at all riders of all ages this website is just for kids (girls really) aged 5-16 who love to ride. They have funky pink or purple nubuck jodhpur boots, glitter whips, vibrant grooming kits, sparkly diamante hat covers, colourful jodhpurs and bright and brilliant products for your favourite pony. There's also pony themed gear for school bags, bedrooms, the bathroom and casual wear.

Site Usability:	★★★★	Based:	UK
Product Range:	★★★	Express Delivery Option? (UK)	Yes
Price Range:	Medium	Gift Wrapping Option?	No
Delivery Area:	Worldwide (email for a delivery quote for overseas)	Returns Procedure:	Down to you

www.saddler.co.uk

At Saddler there's a very good choice of adult and junior Barbour jackets from the standard waxed jacket to the essential padded, cord collar jacket in lots of colours from burnt orange to apple green. There are also show jackets by Just Togs, hats by FBI Champion and Just Togs, jods by Gorringe in some great colours plus long and short boots, jackets and body protectors. As the place where my daughter has always shopped for her riding kit (offline) I know you can expect great service here.

Site Usability:	★★★★	Based:	UK
Product Range:	★★★★	Express Delivery Option? (UK)	No
Price Range:	Medium	Gift Wrapping Option?	No
Delivery Area:	Worldwide	Returns Procedure:	Down to you

www.tackshack.co.uk

This is an extremely comprehensive and very well laid out horse and rider website with an excellent choice of products including country and equestrian wear for adults and children, long and short jodhpur boots and wellingtons. For the horse there's a full range of saddlery, rugs for summer and winter, all you need for the stable yard plus feed supplements and medications. The drop-down menus make it easy to find what you're looking for and the pictures are very clear. This is one of the best equestrian websites.

Site Usability:	★★★★★	Based:	UK
Product Range:	★★★★★	Express Delivery Option? (UK)	No
Price Range:	Medium	Gift Wrapping Option?	No
Delivery Area:	Worldwide	Returns Procedure:	Down to you

www.theequestrianstore.com

This well designed and easy to navigate website offers express worldwide delivery and sells just about everything for horse and rider. You'll find a comprehensive clothing section offering jodhpurs and hard hats, jackets and boots and in the horse section all you need including saddles, bridles, horse rugs and accessories. Their gift, books and DVD section should give you some great ideas for gifts for the rider.

Site Usability:	★★★★	Based:	UK
Product Range:	★★★★	Express Delivery Option? (UK)	Yes
Price Range:	Medium	Gift Wrapping Option?	No
Delivery Area:	Worldwide	Returns Procedure:	Down to you

www.thelwell-horsey-gifts.com

Norman Thelwell's wonderfully funny cartoons first appeared in Punch magazine over 40 years ago. His portrayals of country life, sporting pursuits and in particular horses and riders are known and loved the world over. This is not a sophisticated website with sophisticated pictures but if you know someone, whatever age, who rides or loves horses (and has a sense of humour, of course) you'll doubtless find a gift for them from cards, diaries, gift wrap and pictures to 'get off my foot!' socks, printed t-shirts, The Riding Academy money box and cross stitch kits.

Site Usability:	★★★	Based:	UK
Product Range:	★★★★★	Express Delivery Option? (UK)	Yes
Price Range:	Luxury	Gift Wrapping Option?	No
Delivery Area:	Worldwide	Returns Procedure:	Down to you

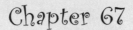

Chapter 67

Tennis, Cricket, Rugby and Football

I'm not even going to bother to tell you that these are not my sports, although I do occasionally play tennis really badly, but cricket and rugby???

But, I have kids who have played: cricket a while back, football casually still and rugby extremely seriously. The kit for all, thank goodness, is not as mind-blowingly expensive as for some other sports but, according to the players I know, the right kit is essential. On the websites below you'll find everything you/they require I have no doubt, although I'm definitely not going to tell you what to buy. That's your problem.

Sites to Visit

Tennis

www.pwp.com

Calling itself 'Europe's No 1 racket specialist for Tennis, Squash and Badminton' you can see the reason clearly when you browse round this site. There's a great deal for the tennis player with rackets by Wilson, Dunlop, Head, Slazenger and Prince, tennis shoes, well priced tennis balls and lots of accessories including the ITP series of DVDs. If you're thinking of buying a gift for a player you would need to know exactly what they want or you could, of course, buy them the huge Wilson logo umbrella.

Site Usability:	★★★★	Based:	UK
Product Range:	★★★★★	Express Delivery Option? (UK)	No
Price Range:	Luxury/Medium	Gift Wrapping Option?	No
Delivery Area:	Worldwide	Returns Procedure:	Down to you

www.racquetlink.com

This is another excellent tennis website retailing racquets by Prince, Wilson, Babolat and Yonex amongst others, ball baskets and ball lobbers by Lobster, Tennis Tower and Shotmaker and everything else for the tennis enthusiast. They also have a Unique Gifts section where you'll find things like tennis bookends, coin trays, bottle openers and letter racks and they offer gift certificates as well.

Site Usability:	★★★★★	Based:	UK
Product Range:	★★★★★	Express Delivery Option? (UK)	Yes
Price Range:	Luxury/Medium	Gift Wrapping Option?	No
Delivery Area:	Worldwide	Returns Procedure:	Down to you

Cricket

www.owzat-cricket.co.uk

Here are bats by Gunn and Moore, Kookaburra and Gray-Nichols plus loads of other brands; gloves, pads, kitbags, body protection, accessories and balls. This is a website obviously designed for real cricketers and they're proud of the fact that they've sold to some of the world's top players such as Phil Defreitas, Karl Krikken and Paul Franks. You'll definitely find something for the cricketer including junior players, for whom they have an excellent range.

Site Usability:	★★★★★	Based:	UK
Product Range:	★★★★★	Express Delivery Option? (UK)	Yes
Price Range:	Medium	Gift Wrapping Option?	No
Delivery Area:	Europe	Returns Procedure:	Down to you

www.cricketbits.co.uk

This is the one stop shop for cricket novelties and gifts with best sellers such as a cricket-ball clock, cricket letter rack and a framed limited edition picture commemorating The Birth of the Ashes in 1882 showing the handwritten batting orders, scorecard and original scorers sheet. There are simply loads of ideas from the very cheap and cheerful to the not so cheap (although most things are well priced), so take a look around here for stocking fillers and attractive gifts for all ages of cricketer.

Site Usability:	★★★★	Based:	UK
Product Range:	★★★★	Express Delivery Option? (UK)	No
Price Range:	Medium/Very Good Value	Gift Wrapping Option?	No
Delivery Area:	UK	Returns Procedure:	Down to you

www.newitts.co.uk

Aerobics, archery, athletics, badminton, baseball, basketball, bikes and billiards are the first eight items on the sports menu here where there's almost everything for every sport you can think of. OK, trampolining, tennis, swimming, cricket, rugby and football are just a few more. In the Back to School section you can buy mouthguards, football shirts, rugby shorts, gloves and boots, headguards and kit bags.

Site Usability:	★★★★	Based:	UK
Product Range:	★★★★★	Express Delivery Option? (UK)	Yes
Price Range:	Medium	Gift Wrapping Option?	No
Delivery Area:	Worldwide	Returns Procedure:	Down to you

Rugby and Football

www.cartoonstock.com

There are great gifts for the sportsman here as Cartoonstock is a searchable database of over 60,000 quality illustrations and cartoons by over 290 of the world's best cartoonists. Once you've chosen your area, e.g. sporting, you just have to put the type of sport (football for example) into their search box and click 'search'. You'll then have loads of cartoons to choose from which you can add to your shopping basket and once you've done that you can choose whether you want your selected cartoon as a print, on a mug, t-shirt or mouse mat.

Site Usability:	★★★★	Based:	UK
Product Range:	★★★★★	Express Delivery Option? (UK)	No
Price Range:	Medium/Very Good Value	Gift Wrapping Option?	No
Delivery Area:	Worldwide	Returns Procedure:	Down to you

www.kitbag.com

Kitbag is one of the best websites for football and rugby clothing, equipment and accessories. It's clear and quick to get round, has a really wide range of products and offers fast delivery. They keep well up to date with the latest kit from your favourite team and offer a full range of shoes and balls from all the top brands. As they ship worldwide and offer European shirts as well there's a quick currency converter ready and waiting for you to use and you can choose from Royal Mail standard or Special deliveries.

Site Usability:	★★★★★	Based:	UK
Product Range:	★★★★★	Express Delivery Option? (UK)	Yes
Price Range:	Medium	Gift Wrapping Option?	No
Delivery Area:	Worldwide	Returns Procedure:	Down to you

www.rugbymegastore.com

This is just as it sounds, a huge, busy website offering a total range for the rugby player including bags, balls, team kit, books and rugby boots by brands such as Mizuno, Puma, Adidas and Nike plus team t-shirts, protection, videos and news direct from the BBC. In the gift and souvenirs section you'll find ideas such as limited edition prints and signed photos and rugby balls and World Cup souvenirs.

Site Usability:	★★★★	Based:	UK
Product Range:	★★★★★	Express Delivery Option? (UK)	No
Price Range:	Medium	Gift Wrapping Option?	No
Delivery Area:	UK	Returns Procedure:	Down to you

www.rugbystore.co.uk

This one's strictly for the boys (I hope) and there's a tremendous range, so if you've a young rugby enthusiast in the family you'll not only find some great kit here but some excellent gift ideas as well. They stock Kooga, Armourfit and Canterbury (CCC) in the general range plus junior rugby shirts for most of the teams. Needless to say there's all the adult rugby kit here too.

Site Usability:	★★★★★	Based:	UK
Product Range:	★★★★★	Express Delivery Option? (UK)	No
Price Range:	Medium/Very Good Value	Gift Wrapping Option?	No
Delivery Area:	Worldwide	Returns Procedure:	Down to you

www.rugbyrelics.com

Rugby Relics are a family business based in Neath in North Wales where you'll find the most amazing collection of rugby gifts and memorabilia. If you want to buy a gift for a rugby mad friend there's probably no better place to visit, you'll almost certainly choose something from their collection of official programs, prints and clothing or by clicking through to their sister website rugbygifts.com.

Site Usability:	★★★	Based:	UK
Product Range:	★★★	Express Delivery Option? (UK)	Yes
Price Range:	Medium	Gift Wrapping Option?	No
Delivery Area:	Worldwide	Returns Procedure:	Down to you

Chapter 68

Everything for the Photographer

I'm sure you'll agree with me that there are really two kinds of photographer: the serious kind who, like my husband, like to have all the kit; the camera with various lenses and other essentials. Then there's the non-serious kind like my daughter and myself who enjoy using a high quality mega-pixel camera which happens to come in a slim, mini size and in a gorgeous bright colour which fits into our handbags – or beach bags, ski jacket pocket etc. – with ease.

Whichever you are there's loads to choose from here and I suggest that if you're going for one of the new compact cameras you shouldn't be swayed by the colour but go for the highest number of megapixels you can afford and a decent sized memory card.

Spend some time working out how to download your pics onto your computer and if you want to change them/join pictures together etc. buy Adobe Photoshop Elements which is a brilliant piece of software for picture management. Then get yourself (or give someone as an extra special present) a digital photo frame from one of the websites below, on to which you can download all your favourite pictures and see them as often as you want to, rather than spending all those hours with a photo album and glue – which I have to confess I never had the patience for.

Yes gone are the days, for most of us at least, of having to take reels of film to the developer and then wondering what to do with the results. It's all brilliantly easy now, not just to take better pics, but to send them to friends, store them and look at them frequently.

You'll find everything you need below, other than the software – and the computer of course. For Photoshop just pay a visit to www.amazon.co.uk or www.software.co.uk and you'll find the best prices.

Sites to Visit

www.cameras.co.uk

This website will certainly take you to the places where you can buy your chosen digital camera for less, but it is, first and foremost, a review and advice centre on digital photography in general and on all the new camera ranges. Once you've had a good read and selected your camera it will then give you the price comparisons for the retailers offering that specific model and you can see some amazing differentials in price. It's a very good place to check out if you're not sure which camera you want to buy or you want to compare prices.

Site Usability:	★★★	Based:	UK
Product Range:	★★★★	Express Delivery Option? (UK)	No
Price Range:	Luxury/Medium/Very Good Value	Gift Wrapping Option	No
Delivery Area:	UK	Returns Procedure:	Down to you in agreement with them

www.cameraking.co.uk

There are lots of places you can buy a camera online but you might like to take a look here as this is a great place for real enthusiasts. They not only offer a huge range of cameras and show you straight away what's in stock, but the menu is very clear and there are some excellent accessories including camera bags, cases and tripods of all shapes and sizes. I wouldn't recommend that you come here if you're looking for the latest pink pocket sized marvel, but for real equipment this is a great place.

Site Usability:	★★★★★	Based:	UK
Product Range:	★★★★★	Express Delivery Option? (UK)	Yes
Price Range:	Luxury/Medium/Very Good Value	Gift Wrapping Option	No
Delivery Area:	UK	Returns Procedure:	Down to you

www.cameras2u.com

This is an excellent website to find your next camera, where you'll find all the new models at very good prices. Compare their prices on a comparison website such as kelkoo.co.uk and you'll find they're nearly always the lowest. There's a lot of advice on digital photography in general such as linking up with your PC and printer plus photo-taking tips. Couple this with free UK next day delivery on orders over £100 placed before 1pm and this is definitely somewhere you should visit.

Site Usability:	★★★★	Based:	UK
Product Range:	★★★★	Express Delivery Option? (UK)	Yes
Price Range:	Luxury/Medium/Very Good Value	Gift Wrapping Option	No
Delivery Area:	UK	Returns Procedure:	Down to you in agreement with them

www.digitalfirst.co.uk

Here you'll find the latest cameras from all the major brand names including Pentax, Canon, Nikon, Olympus and Fuji, plus scanners and printers. It's an extremely quick and easy website to get round with clear pages and easy buying instructions. They also offer two years warranty, 3 months free helpline, a gift wrapping service and free shipping to the UK mainland.

Site Usability:	★★★★	Based:	UK
Product Range:	★★★★	Express Delivery Option? (UK)	No
Price Range:	Luxury/Medium/Very Good Value	Gift Wrapping Option	Yes
Delivery Area:	Worldwide	Returns Procedure:	Down to you

www.digitalframesdirect.com

Having been given one of these frames by my son for Christmas (yes, lucky me), I can definitely recommend them as a gift for any photographer – they beat sticking pictures into albums as far as I'm concerned, are easy to update with your latest pics and provide a constant reminder of the people, places and events you want to keep in mind. Here you'll find a very good choice in a range of sizes right up to ten inches plus a selection of memory cards.

Site Usability:	★★★★★	Based:	UK
Product Range:	★★★★	Express Delivery Option? (UK)	Yes
Price Range:	Medium	Gift Wrapping Option	No
Delivery Area:	UK	Returns Procedure:	Down to you

www.expansys.co.uk

This website specialising in wireless technology is an excellent place to find out about the latest mobile phones, smartphones, and pocket PCs plus GPS navigation systems. In their Digital Camera department you can immediately see the best sellers (and how long you'll have to wait for delivery) then browse their list which is clearly sub-sectioned by brand. For some excellent gifts check out the Ora and Cullmann tripods and accessories, they're just that little bit different.

Site Usability:	★★★★★	Based:	UK
Product Range:	★★★★★	Express Delivery Option? (UK)	Yes
Price Range:	Luxury/Medium	Gift Wrapping Option	No
Delivery Area:	Worldwide	Returns Procedure:	Down to you

www.fotosense.co.uk

Fotosense offers an excellent range of the latest cameras plus everything you need for digital video, MP3 players, binoculars, printers and studio lighting from a list of over 50 manufacturers as well as one of the largest photographic accessory lists available in the UK. If you need advice on what to buy you can just give them a call and they'll be delighted to help. They only deliver to the UK but offer extremely fast delivery options.

Site Usability:	★★★★★	Based:	UK
Product Range:	★★★★★	Express Delivery Option? (UK)	Yes
Price Range:	Luxury/Medium/Very Good Value	Gift Wrapping Option	No
Delivery Area:	Worldwide	Returns Procedure:	Down to you in agreement with them

www.pixmania.co.uk

Pixmania has a wonderfully slick, colourful and user friendly website and tells you straight away about their best sellers and the newly released models. You can become a VIPix and receive a discount and free delivery for a year, plus 20% off extended warranties or give one of their gift certificates. The range of products is huge and very much specialises in the latest 'must-have' camera. They're also nearly always one of the best for price.

Site Usability:	★★★★★	Based:	France
Product Range:	★★★★★	Express Delivery Option? (UK)	Yes
Price Range:	Medium/Very Good Value	Gift Wrapping Option	No
Delivery Area:	Worldwide	Returns Procedure:	Down to you

Chapter 69

For the Artist and Musician

I f you're in a mad rush for that new canvas or specific colour you're no doubt going to go out (or be dragged out) and find it because you'll no doubt need it *immediately*. However, when you have a little more time to plan, or you keep regular supplies, do look at the art websites below as you'll not only be able to order absolutely everything you need, and sometimes at some very reasonable prices, but also some very good gift sets too.

Having said that, these are not gift websites. Instead, you'll find endless selections of proper artists' supplies from canvases and boards to oils, watercolours, pencils and acrylics. If you have a budding artist in the family, as I do, be careful about letting them loose here, you may end up a great deal poorer than you intended.

On to musicians: you may think it strange that I'm recommending you buy musical instruments online, but if you compare some of the prices with those out 'in the real world' I think you'll get quite a surprise. Until now you'd be lucky if your town had a really good instrument store and if there was one you could bet that it would be the only one. The web, of course, has changed all of that and introduced a far greater element of competition which should be great for you. You can buy the same makes, brand new and second hand instruments, sheet music and much more here. Check with your local store against the prices here and you'll see what I mean.

Don't think for a moment, please, that I'm trying to see off your local music store – I just object to paying more than I need to. You can always ask them to match a price that you find here and then it's up to you where you buy from. Music shops tend to be run by musicians who I support wholeheartedly (having been one myself to some extent), but then so do the websites here. Decisions, decisions … yours this time, thankfully.

Sites to Visit

Art

www.artboxdirect.co.uk

Artboxdirect offers discount art supplies, providing artists with a wide range of art materials from Windsor & Newton and Daler Rowney. There are good discounts off the prices of all paints and brushes, pastels, sets, pads and cases. It's best if you already know which colours you want to order although you can download the full colour charts for each range of paints should you need to.

Site Usability:	★★★★	Based:	UK
Product Range:	★★★★	Express Delivery Option? (UK)	No
Price Range:	Medium/Very Good Value	Gift Wrapping Option?	No
Delivery Area:	Europe	Returns Procedure:	Down to you

www.artist-supplies.co.uk

Staedtler, Derwent, Sennelier and Windsor and Newton are just a few of the brands on this website offering a full range of artists' materials including easels, paints (oil, acrylic or watercolour), paper and board, canvases, brushes and folios. They also have a well stocked crafts section with calligraphy, candle making, glass painting, needlecraft and stencilling so there's something for everyone and some very good gift ideas too.

Site Usability:	★★★	Based:	UK
Product Range:	★★★★★	Express Delivery Option? (UK)	Yes
Price Range:	Medium	Gift Wrapping Option?	No
Delivery Area:	Worldwide	Returns Procedure:	Down to you

www.lawrence.co.uk

Here are grown-up artists' materials for the grown-up artist. They carry a huge range and offer a full advisory service and quick delivery. You can buy acrylics, art boards, glass paints and palettes, gold and silver leaf, papers cards and envelopes, everything for printmaking plus storage and packaging (and loads more). You can also buy gift vouchers for the artist in your life or choose from their suggestions.

Site Usability:	★★★★	Based:	UK
Product Range:	★★★★★	Express Delivery Option? (UK)	No
Price Range:	Luxury/Medium	Gift Wrapping Option?	No
Delivery Area:	Worldwide	Returns Procedure:	Down to you

www.stencil-library.co.uk

The Stencil Library is generally accepted as being one of the world's leading stencil design companies offering over 3,500 different styles which you can order online, including traditional, modern,

Indian, Shaker and children's designs, plus brushes, paint, tools for gilding and decoupage and a wide range of general supplies. This site is a must if you're thinking of stencilling anything, anywhere.

Site Usability:	★★★★	Based:	UK
Product Range:	★★★★★	Express Delivery Option? (UK)	Yes
Price Range:	Medium	Gift Wrapping Option?	No
Delivery Area:	Worldwide	Returns Procedure:	Down to you

Music

www.dawsonsonline.com

Once you arrive at this website you need to choose to begin with whether you want to go to the piano and orchestral instrument department where you'll find an excellent range including sheet music, or through to rock and hi tech, which offers electric and acoustic guitars, microphones, mixers, synthesisers and the like. It's an extremely well laid out website, all prices and delivery times are very clearly shown and they carry a full range of accessories.

Site Usability:	★★★★★	Based:	UK
Product Range:	★★★★★	Express Delivery Option? (UK)	No
Price Range:	Luxury/Medium	Gift Wrapping Option?	Yes
Delivery Area:	UK	Returns Procedure:	Down to you

www.musicroom.co.uk

Established in 1995, Musicroom is a global retailer, shipping products out to over 100 countries and offering one of the largest selections of sheet music, song books, books about music and tutor methods in the world. At Christmas time they offer a gift selection, including Christmas music, learning guides for different instruments, CDs and instrument accessories. It really is an excellent website so if you know any young musicians do stop off here.

Site Usability:	★★★★★	Based:	UK
Product Range:	★★★★	Express Delivery Option? (UK)	No
Price Range:	Luxury/Medium	Gift Wrapping Option?	No
Delivery Area:	Worldwide	Returns Procedure:	Down to you

www.signetmusic.com

This is quite a confusing site to look at probably because the range is so big but if you're in the market for a new or second hand musical instrument you must look here as the prices can be very good. Because there's such a wide choice it's very helpful that they have a manufacturer index showing almost 100 brands so you can go easily to the make and product you're looking for. They offer online live support (which you may well need) and worldwide delivery for just about everything.

Site Usability:	★★★	Based:	UK
Product Range:	★★★★	Express Delivery Option? (UK)	Yes
Price Range:	Luxury/Medium	Gift Wrapping Option?	No
Delivery Area:	Worldwide	Returns Procedure:	Down to you

www.themusiccellar.co.uk

Choose from a fantastic selection of musical instruments on this clear and easy to navigate website, from clarinets to grand pianos to acoustic and electric guitars. They offer a repair service and you can buy sheet music here as well. The instruments are discounted (check the price with your local supplier and/or a price comparison website to make sure) but some of the prices look excellent. Prices for UK shipping are supplied online but you need to call them for overseas.

Site Usability:	★★★★★	Based:	UK
Product Range:	★★★★★	Express Delivery Option? (UK)	No
Price Range:	Luxury/Medium	Gift Wrapping Option?	No
Delivery Area:	Worldwide	Returns Procedure:	Down to you

www.woodwindandbrass.co.uk

Woodwind and Brass have a really attractive website which draws you in to their wide range of products, including saxophones from Yanagisawa and Selmer, clarinets from Buffet, LeBlanc and Jupiter, flutes & piccolos from Trevor J James and Buffet, bass clarinets from Jupiter and Besson, and bassoons from Oscar Adler. Accessories include mouthpieces, reeds, stands, gig bags, cases and care and maintenance materials.

Site Usability:	★★★★★	Based:	UK
Product Range:	★★★★★	Express Delivery Option? (UK)	No
Price Range:	Luxury/Medium	Gift Wrapping Option?	No
Delivery Area:	Worldwide	Returns Procedure:	Down to you

Chapter 70

Tickets and Subscriptions

Gone are the days when you had to queue on the telephone to book your theatre tickets. Gone also are the days when you could phone most theatres direct to book your favourite seats. Nowadays you're almost pushed to order online and you have to be really, really careful to ensure that you get the seats you want, and not just the ones they want to sell you.

However, on many theatre booking sites you can see exactly what you're booking from the online seating plan and in some cases you can also check your seat numbers before you confirm your booking. In this way booking is much, much easier than before. This also applies to opera tickets and some concert venues so you can reserve your seats with confidence.

Where there is any doubt about where you'll be sitting don't, if at all possible, use that ticketing agency. Try another.

Subscriptions are another matter, of course, and you can book your best friend's birthday subscription to Vogue, Glamour or Golf Monthly with impunity. Nothing could be easier and the service is excellent. You can also get discounts on your annual subscriptions by checking out the codes in the advertisements in the glossies so look out for those, the discounts are really good. Don't buy an annual subscription without checking that you can get it discounted. You most likely can.

Sites to Visit

www.aloud.com

Aloud specialises in Rock and Pop Concert Tickets and the alphabetic index in the left hand column on the homepage on this website allows you to quickly choose from their Hot New Tickets or Best Seller collections. Ordering is clear and easy although they only tell you the area your seats will be in rather than the row. From their Merchandise Shop, also accessible from the home page, you can buy t-shirts and posters with lots of choices available to give as gifts or keep yourself.

Site Usability:	★★★★	Based;	UK
Product Range:	★★★★★	Express Delivery Option? (UK)	No
Price Range:	Luxury/Medium/Very Good Value	Gift Wrapping Option?	No
Delivery Area:	UK		

www.barbican.org.uk

Open 363 days a year, the Barbican presents a uniquely diverse programme of world-class performing and visual arts encompassing all forms of classical and contemporary music, international theatre and dance and a cinema programme which blends first-run films with special themed seasons. On this website there's lots of information about all the productions together with a ticket booking facility and you can also find out about the restaurants and bars.

Site Usability:	★★★★	Based;	UK
Product Range:	★★★★★	Express Delivery Option? (UK)	No
Price Range:	Medium	Gift Wrapping Option?	No
Delivery Area:	UK		

www.discountpublications.co.uk

If you'd like to give the gift of a magazine subscription then take a look at this website, where you'll find subscriptions for less, including *Vogue*, *Vanity Fair*, *Tatler*, *Red*, *FHM* and *GQ*, *House and Garden*, *The World of Interiors* and most other glossy publications available at much lower prices than you'd pay if you bought them each month. You can also send your subscription with a personalised message and gift certificate and delivery is to the UK only.

Site Usability:	★★★★	Based;	UK
Product Range:	★★★★	Express Delivery Option? (UK)	No
Price Range:	Medium/Very Good Value	Gift Wrapping Option?	No
Delivery Area:	UK		

www.eno.org

It's really easy to book your tickets for the English National Opera on this modern website so you can pay a visit to their newly refurbished home in St Martin's Lane in London. You can also find out about special events such as family events and singing courses, take advantage of their special ticket offers, read reviews and learn about regional tours.

Site Usability:	★★★★	Based;	UK
Product Range:	★★★	Express Delivery Option? (UK)	No
Price Range:	Medium	Gift Wrapping Option?	No
Delivery Area:	UK		

www.glyndebourne.co.uk

Here's the website for the most famous opera house in the country with members being able to book their tickets about six months in advance. Now with their new website where you can find out about all the performance and book any available seats it should be much easier to get there. Don't forget to take your picnic and your brolly as it rains (often); however, the new opera house offers covered trestle tables if you don't want to risk the weather but you need to get there early if you want to bag one.

Site Usability:	★★★★★	Based;	UK
Product Range:	★★★	Express Delivery Option? (UK)	No
Price Range:	Luxury/Medium	Gift Wrapping Option?	No
Delivery Area:	UK		

www.magazine-group.co.uk

With over 400 titles on offer and some very good discounts you could find something for just about everyone here, from the sportsman (*Rugby World*, *Dive*, *Inside Edge*, *The Angler*), food and drink lover (*Olive*, *Good Food*, *Decanter*), home interiors enthusiast (*Beautiful Homes*, *Elle Decoration*) and fashion addict (*Vogue*, *Harpers & Queen* and *In Style*). It's a really comprehensive selection and once you've placed your order you can ask them to send you a gift card to forward on to the recipient.

Site Usability:	★★★★★	Based;	UK
Product Range:	★★★★★	Express Delivery Option? (UK)	No
Price Range:	Medium	Gift Wrapping Option?	No
Delivery Area:	UK		

www.magazinesofamerica.com

Some magazines frankly don't travel well, you read them when you're abroad and when you bring them home they just seem somehow wrong. Personally I think it's different with some of the US publications, such as *American Vogue*, *Glamour* and *House Beautiful* which complement their UK counterparts. Be warned, some of the subscriptions here are extremely expensive; however, delivery is included in the price.

Site Usability:	★★★★	Based;	US
Product Range:	★★★★	Express Delivery Option? (UK)	No
Price Range:	Medium	Gift Wrapping Option?	No
Delivery Area:	Worldwide		

www.npg.org.uk

The National Portrait Gallery houses a unique record of men and women who created – and are creating – Britain's history and culture. It holds ten major events each year such as 'Self Portrait – Renaissance to Contemporary' and 'Photographs 1850-2000'. It also holds its primary collection of over 10,000 portraits, from Gainsborough to Cecil Beaton. Pay a visit to the online shop and take out a subscription to the Gallery, or look through their selection of high quality side-tied notebooks, art books, prints, mugs and gifts.

Site Usability:	★★★★	Based;	UK
Product Range:	★★★	Express Delivery Option? (UK)	No
Price Range:	Medium	Gift Wrapping Option?	No
Delivery Area:	Worldwide		

www.nt-online.org

The website for London's National Theatre gives full details and cast lists for all productions plus an online ticket booking facility. Find out about the restaurants as well and make your reservation for lunch or dinner and have a browse through their bookshop where you'll find books on theory, history, criticism and practical help about theatre.

Site Usability:	★★★★	Based;	UK
Product Range:	★★★	Express Delivery Option? (UK)	No
Price Range:	Medium	Gift Wrapping Option?	No
Delivery Area:	Worldwide		

www.royalacademy.org.uk

Treat yourself or someone special to a year's membership of The Royal Academy, in its beautiful buildings just off Piccadilly. You can also buy individual tickets to the fabulous exhibitions held here, such as CHINA: The Three Emperors or Andrew Lloyd Webber's personal art collection (sorry if you missed that, it was wonderful). Alternatively pay a visit to their online shop where you'll find cards, limited edition prints, lifestyle gifts, diaries and calendars.

Site Usability:	★★★★	Based;	UK
Product Range:	★★★	Express Delivery Option? (UK)	No
Price Range:	Medium	Gift Wrapping Option?	No
Delivery Area:	Worldwide		

www.royalopera.org

The Royal Opera House has for some while had a really elegant website. Once you've read about the different productions and reviews you can select the one you want to see, then the date and the type of seating and when you find seats available you'll know the actual row and seat number so you'll have no doubt at all about where you'll be sitting. Hopefully all ticket websites will offer this service soon.

Site Usability:	★★★★	Based;	UK
Product Range:	★★★	Express Delivery Option? (UK)	No
Price Range:	Luxury/Medium	Gift Wrapping Option?	No
Delivery Area:	UK		

www.seetickets.com

From the X Factor Live to Billy Elliot to Bryn Terfel at Christmas you can book just about everything here, plus events such as the Good Food Show and Clothes Show Live, sporting events such as the Horse of the Year show and the Grand Prix, comedy shows and classical music performances. It's an attractive website to get round and although you can't see exactly where you'll be sitting when you order your tickets they give you a clearer idea than on some others. They also suggest places to stay.

Site Usability:	★★★★★	Based;	UK
Product Range:	★★★★★	Express Delivery Option? (UK)	No
Price Range:	Luxury/Medium	Gift Wrapping Option?	No
Delivery Area:	UK		

www.subscription.co.uk

Here you'll find a vast range of titles to subscribe to, including *Vogue*, *Vanity Fair*, *Tatler*, *Harper's Bazaar*, *In Style* and *Red* plus other titles such as *House and Garden*, *Country Living* and *Mother and Baby*. What you won't find are the special offers available through the magazines themselves, so I suggest you buy a single issue to give you the relevant offer code as there are quite significant discounts to be found. You then quote this code when placing your order.

Site Usability:	★★★★★	Based;	UK
Product Range:	★★★★★	Express Delivery Option? (UK)	No
Price Range:	Medium	Gift Wrapping Option?	No
Delivery Area:	Worldwide		

www.ticketmaster.co.uk

Music, theatre and sport tickets are available on this – the original ticket website. Seating plans for the different venues are easy to see and tickets are quick and easy to book although do make sure you're happy with your seats for certain before you book. If you want standing room tickets to see Robbie Williams, seats for England v Barbarians at Twickenham or Firework and Music tickets at Hampton Court or tickets for pretty well anything else then this is your site. Gift vouchers are on offer too, and they also have links to websites offering you travel, places to stay and eat plus 'What's On in Europe'.

Site Usability:	★★★★★	Based;	UK
Product Range:	★★★★★	Express Delivery Option? (UK)	No
Price Range:	Luxury/Medium	Gift Wrapping Option?	No
Delivery Area:	UK		

Chapter 71

Books, Music and Movies

I think that just about everyone has by now caught on to the fact that the web is the best place to buy books, DVDs, CDs and the like - everyone, that is, except those who still refuse to use a computer (and there are still some of those around I believe, which completely astounds me).

Anyway, books are less expensive online, it's easier to find what you're looking for and although you may have to wait a day or so you save so much time buying this way that a short wait is a small price to pay. The same is true of movies and music and even more so where price is concerned.

Don't think for a minute that I don't drop into my local bookstore for a browse from time to time, usually when I'm passing, nor that I buy all my books online. When I'm travelling or I have a specific need for something to read (a wait of an hour or so for my daughter when she's shopping with friends, for example) I'll go to the nearest store and buy a book. However, given the chance and because I love to read, I'll have a small stack of books ready and waiting for when I finish the one I'm currently reading. I hate not having something new to hand.

Where movies are concerned I always buy online as the prices are so much better. Recently I watched *Philadelphia* (Tom Hanks, Joanne Woodward, Antonio Banderas) for the first time with my eldest son. Afterwards I was talking to him about Joanne Woodward and Paul Newman and he didn't recall ever seeing one of Paul Newman's films; I was horrified. So it was straight off to the web and *Butch Cassidy*, *The Verdict*, *Cool Hand Luke* and *The Road to Perdition* (no I never do anything by halves) were on their way to me along with other books and films I simply couldn't resist.

That is the main problem, of course; the temptation, but think how long it would have taken you to get hold of all those films in the 'old days' (before the www). You'd probably have given up.

Sites to Visit

Books

www.amazon.co.uk

At Amazon you can buy not only books but so much more, including your new Kenwood food mixer or digital camera, baby products and tools for your garden, which can make life rather confusing. They have probably the most comprehensive range of books, music, movies and games available anywhere, frequently at the best price and their service is excellent.

Site Usability:	★★★★★	Based:	UK
Product Range:	★★★★★	Express Delivery Option? (UK)	Yes
Price Range:	Medium/Very Good Value	Gift Wrapping Option?	Yes
Delivery Area:	Worldwide	Returns Procedure:	Down to you

www.abebooks.co.uk

This is the worldwide marketplace for rare, second-hand and out-of-print books. You just need to know the title or the author and if it's available it'll be found immediately. You can then narrow your search to see only first editions, or signed copies, among other options. For special gifts this would be an excellent website as you can choose from a selection of real collectors' items, alternatively you can simply track down that book you lost some years ago and always wanted to read again.

Site Usability:	★★★★★	Based:	UK
Product Range:	★★★★★	Express Delivery Option? (UK)	No
Price Range:	Luxury/Medium	Gift Wrapping Option?	No
Delivery Area:	Worldwide	Returns Procedure:	Down to you

www.best-book-price.co.uk
www.bookbrain.co.uk

These are two excellent places where you can compare book prices and see who has the book you're looking for in stock to send out immediately. They're both very easy to use. They're not really for buying ordinary paperbacks, although you can use them for that if you want to but when you've found a special hardback that you want to give as a gift next week and you're being quoted 4–6 weeks delivery, you may be able to find another bookshop who has it ready to send out. At the same time you can also compare the prices from all the bookstores.

www.blackwell.co.uk

If you prefer a less busy book website then pay a visit to Blackwell's of Oxford, established in 1879 and an online store for over ten years. What you'll find here is a really excellent and more personal service with a clear path through to the various departments: Fiction, Leisure and Life-style, Science, Humanities, Arts, Medical, Business Finance and Law. There are some good discounts to be found and shipping is free to the UK on orders over £20.

Site Usability:	★★★★★	Based:	UK
Product Range:	★★★★★	Express Delivery Option? (UK)	Yes
Price Range:	Luxury/Medium	Gift Wrapping Option?	No
Delivery Area:	Worldwide	Returns Procedure:	Down to you

www.bookgiant.com

Next time you're looking for a new book take a quick look at bookgiant.com. They don't have anything like the range of some other bookstores but what they do have are very good offers, with special editions (usually small hardbacks) of brand new titles at up to 60% off the normal price. Postage and packing are free if you order three items or more, otherwise it's just £1 and you need to register to order (so they can send you regular updates and keep your details to make your next order even quicker).

Site Usability:	★★★★★	Based:	UK
Product Range:	★★★	Express Delivery Option? (UK)	No
Price Range:	Very Good Value	Gift Wrapping Option?	No
Delivery Area:	Worldwide	Returns Procedure:	Down to you

www.borders.co.uk

Here you can sign up for Borders Email, which means that you'll be the first to find out about their in-store promotions, take part in their competitions, find out about events near you and join their new Book Group. If you want to order a book online you can just click straight through to their partner website at www.amazon.co.uk.

Site Usability:	★★★★	Based:	UK
Product Range:	★★★★★	Express Delivery Option? (UK)	Yes
Price Range:	Medium/Very Good Value	Gift Wrapping Option?	Yes
Delivery Area:	Worldwide through amazon.co.uk	Returns Procedure:	Free

www.bookdepository.co.uk

The Book Depository claims to be the fastest growing book distributor in Europe and there's certainly a huge selection available through their easy to navigate website. This is also one of the best places to search out books you've been unable to find elsewhere. If you just want a browse here you can take a look at their editors' Blogs and catch up on the latest book news and reviews. They offer free delivery to most countries worldwide.

Site Usability:	★★★★★	Based:	UK
Product Range:	★★★★★	Express Delivery Option? (UK)	No
Price Range:	Medium/Very Good Value	Gift Wrapping Option?	No
Delivery Area:	Worldwide	Returns Procedure:	Down to you but contact them first by email link

www.compman.co.uk

This site started off as a computer books website and has moved into general educational books and fiction. So you can buy the latest John Grisham alongside Selected Papers on Particle Image Velocimetry: help! The site is very clearly laid out and you can see exactly what's in stock or on

374

limited availability. Some of the discounts are very good. Standard delivery is 1-2 days and is free on orders over a small amount which varies.

Site Usability:	★★★★	Based:	UK
Product Range:	★★★	Express Delivery Option? (UK)	Yes
Price Range:	Medium	Gift Wrapping Option?	No
Delivery Area:	Worldwide	Returns Procedure:	Down to you

www.hatchards.co.uk

Hatchards, booksellers since 1797, is the oldest surviving bookshop in London and is now based in its luxurious quarters at 187 Piccadilly, right next door to Fortnum and Mason. Not only do they offer a very good choice of titles in hardback and paperback, from fiction, children's books, art and architecture, biography, food and wine, gardening, history and humour but they also specialise in signed and special editions and what they call VIPs (Very Important Publications); their recommendations for the season.

Site Usability:	★★★★★	Based:	UK
Product Range:	★★★★★	Express Delivery Option? (UK)	Yes
Price Range:	Luxury/Medium	Gift Wrapping Option?	No
Delivery Area:	Worldwide	Returns Procedure:	Down to you

www.jonkers.co.uk

Jonkers specialise in modern first editions, fine illustrated books, classic children's fiction and nineteenth century literature. So if you have a goddaughter who might appreciate a first edition of Michael Bond's Paddington Goes to Town you'll find it here, plus AA Milne, Enid Blyton, Lewis Carroll and many more. Because some of these books are very expensive and precious (up into the £1000s) you can't order online but need to phone them using their freephone number.

Site Usability:	★★★★	Based:	UK
Product Range:	★★★	Express Delivery Option? (UK)	No
Price Range:	Luxury	Gift Wrapping Option?	No
Delivery Area:	Worldwide	Returns Procedure:	Down to you

www.play.com

See below for their full entry under Music, Movies & Games but do note they also have an impressive books selection with very competitive prices and speedy delivery.

www.thebookplace.com

If you want a new bookshop to look at you could have a browse on this very clear site, which offers an extremely wide range and shows availability as soon as you search for your book. They also have a good selection of signed copies which would make excellent gifts and you can read the weekly press reviews on the latest releases. Postage is £2.75 per single book order plus £0.50 for each additional book and they also offer worldwide shipping and express delivery.

Site Usability:	★★★★	Based:	UK
Product Range:	★★★★	Express Delivery Option? (UK)	Yes
Price Range:	Medium	Gift Wrapping Option?	Yes
Delivery Area:	Worldwide	Returns Procedure:	Down to you

www.redhouse.co.uk

Red House specialises in children's books for all ages; from babies to young adults. They produce a catalogue each month featuring an introduction from a leading author, and their bright and colourful website carries a wide selection of handpicked books which is updated regularly. There's even a safe, fun online community for children including competitions, things to do and a moderated message board. Every book is discounted and P & P is free when you buy four or more books.

Site Usability:	★★★★	Based:	UK
Product Range:	★★★★	Express Delivery Option? (UK)	Yes
Price Range:	Medium/Very Good Value	Gift Wrapping Option?	No
Delivery Area:	UK	Returns Procedure:	Down to you

www.waterstones.com

Waterstone's website is extremely clear and easy to use and a lot less cluttered than many of the online bookstores. You can browse categories from the home page menu which includes areas such as Business, Finance and Law, Computing, Education and Comics and Graphic Novels alongside the more usual Fiction, Children's Books, Food and Drink and Sport. Delivery is free on orders over £15 within the UK and they offer surface or courier services for international orders.

Site Usability:	★★★★★	Based:	UK
Product Range:	★★★★★	Express Delivery Option? (UK)	Yes
Price Range:	Medium	Gift Wrapping Option?	Yes
Delivery Area:	Worldwide	Returns Procedure:	Down to you

www.whsmith.co.uk

On WHSmith's easy-on-the-eye website you can buy books (often at very good discounts), all the latest DVDs, music and computer games plus a small selection from their stationery ranges. There's also a wide range of gift ideas, including original historic newspapers and commemorative sporting books and you can subscribe at a discount to all your favourite magazines. The difference here from a lot of book/music/games websites is that it's clear and simple to get round but also has an excellent choice.

Site Usability:	★★★★★	Based:	UK
Product Range:	★★★★★	Express Delivery Option? (UK)	No
Price Range:	Medium	Gift Wrapping Option?	No
Delivery Area:	UK	Returns Procedure:	Down to you

Music, Movies and Games

www.best-cd-price.co.uk

Know the CD you want to buy but want to make sure you get the best price? Use this price comparison website, which not only shows where you'll find the best deal but includes the postage details as well so you absolutely know where you are. This website is almost unbelievably quick to use and you can use it for DVDs and games as well. As an example, if you do a search on

Take That, Beautiful World, you'll be given eleven places where you can buy it online, with prices from £8.79 to £12.60. Quite a difference, I'm sure you'll agree.

www.cdwow.com

You'll find some of the best prices around here and again this site covers all mediums from CDs and DVDs to computer games. Because their prices are so good it would be worth purchasing gift vouchers here as you can be sure that the recipient will get a good deal, whatever they choose to spend them on. They offer free delivery worldwide for all items and regular special offers.

Site Usability:	★★★★★	Based:	UK
Product Range:	★★★★★	Express Delivery Option? (UK)	No
Price Range:	Medium/Very Good Value	Gift Wrapping Option?	No
Delivery Area:	Worldwide	Returns Procedure:	Down to you

www.dvdpricecheck.co.uk

If you're looking for a DVD this is the place to start as you can see what's available throughout all the world regions. With so many places to buy films online it's hard to know without spending hours which is the best site and with different sites charging different amounts things get even worse. So here it is: the website that'll compare the worldwide prices for you. Just key in your title and region (UK is Region 2) and you'll get all the answers.

Many of the websites they offer don't charge you delivery on top so you can order from as many as you want and as often as you like. Sounds tempting? It's hard to know when to stop.

www.game.co.uk

Whether you have an Xbox 360, Wii, PSP, Nintendo DS Lite (or whatever the latest gaming station is), you'll find a huge range of games here for all of them plus the consoles themselves and accessories. I have to be careful here as things will no doubt have moved on by the time you're reading this so check out this site to find out what's new and hot. They also offer a reward points system – a very good idea as loyalty to game sites is thin on the ground due to the amount of competition.

Site Usability:	★★★★★	Based:	UK
Product Range:	★★★★★	Express Delivery Option? (UK)	Yes for the UK
Price Range:	Medium/Very Good Value	Gift Wrapping Option?	No
Delivery Area:	Worldwide	Returns Procedure:	Down to you

www.hmv.co.uk

The HMV shops on Oxford Street and within Selfridges are usually the first places that my kids want to hit on a trip to London and I quite understand why, because no matter if you're looking for chart CDs or DVDs or something a bit harder to find, they're bound to have it. Up till now their online store has not matched their offline presence but that's all now changed. The website is super easy to navigate and there's an excellent choice. As they're a retailer you're almost bound to know you may well want to buy here.

Site Usability:	★★★★★	Based:	UK
Product Range:	★★★★★	Express Delivery Option? (UK)	Yes and Worldwide Express
Price Range:	Medium/Very Good Value	Gift Wrapping Option?	No
Delivery Area:	Worldwide	Returns Procedure:	Down to you

www.uk.gamestracker.com

However much you may dislike those extremely noisy (and too often violent) computer games, you won't want your precious ones spending more of their not-so-hard-earned pocket money than they need to. If you want to get them the latest game for Christmas or they want to choose one themselves then send them to Games Tracker, where you/they can compare the prices with all the retailers for any specific game and get the deal of the moment.

Site Usability:	★★★★★	Based:	UK
Product Range:	★★★★★	Express Delivery Option? (UK)	No
Price Range:	Medium/Very Good Value	Gift Wrapping Option?	No
Delivery Area:	Worldwide	Returns Procedure:	Down to you

www.play.com

Music, movies, games and books all at very good prices with delivery included are available from this Channel Islands based website. They offer a huge range of films on DVD, CDs and games for all systems plus special offers such as two DVDs for £12, 30% off specific boxed sets and 40% off a wide choice of current releases. Because delivery is included you can order individual items as often as you want to rather than having to group orders together to save on postage.

Site Usability:	★★★★★	Based:	Channel Islands
Product Range:	★★★★★	Express Delivery Option? (UK)	No
Price Range:	Medium/Very Good Value	Gift Wrapping Option?	No
Delivery Area:	Worldwide	Returns Procedure:	Down to you

www.sendit.com

The difference here – as this is yet another website offering games consoles, games, DVDs and computer peripherals and software – is the service. Not only do they offer a courier service within the UK to make sure your order arrives when you need it, free UK delivery and speedy worldwide delivery but also gift certificates and gift wrapping on most items with which they can include your personal message – and you can even choose your wrapping paper.

Site Usability:	★★★★★	Based:	Northern Ireland
Product Range:	★★★★★	Express Delivery Option? (UK)	Yes
Price Range:	Medium/Very Good Value	Gift Wrapping Option?	Yes
Delivery Area:	Worldwide	Returns Procedure:	Down to you

www.virginmegastores.co.uk

On their sleek gunmetal grey website Virgin make it easy for you to order all the latest releases and pre-order the next 'must-have' CDs, DVDs and games. They don't, as most music websites do, always give you the full and discounted price information and they may not be the cheapest but if you compare prices you'll find they're not the top end either. The benefit here is that all the information is very clear and that UK delivery is free of charge.

Site Usability:	★★★★★	Based:	UK
Product Range:	★★★★★	Express Delivery Option? (UK)	No
Price Range:	Medium/Very Good Value	Gift Wrapping Option?	No
Delivery Area:	UK and ROI	Returns Procedure:	Down to you

Section 9
The Gift Shop

The Gift Shop

We seem – or at least I seem – to be buying more and more gifts for people – for Christmas and birthdays (OK I accept those two) then on to Valentine's Day, Mother's Day, Easter, Anniversaries ... I'm sure you can think of some more.

Gift buying is one of the fastest growing areas of online shopping – and it's not really surprising, is it? I mean it's just all too easy; just find a gift online, click a few times, offer your credit card, arrange gift wrap, express delivery and a card with your personal message and you're done.

Should it be that easy? I'm one of those people who think that a lot of gift givers spend too little time thinking about the recipient and too much time buying what *they* like (and I'm sure you've heard me say this before). Where the internet really helps is that it saves you all the frustration of searching offline and possibly grabbing something you think 'will do' at the last minute. Now you have extra time to consider who you're buying for, what they like, and to find something really right for them.

On the websites below there are thousands of gift options so you need to spend a little time narrowing down your options before you go shopping.

Websites are not repeated here from other places in this book, so once you've decided on a specific area you should have a look in the dedicated chapter above as many of the websites there also offer express delivery and gift wrap. Too many options? So sorry, not much I can do about that.

Chapter 72

Cards and Balloons

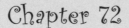

Y-ou can buy individual cards here and have them sent out on your behalf (although I don't recommend you do that one with the kids; they'll always suss you out).

You can also download your favourite photograph on to a card in a couple of seconds, add your own wording, change the text and choose which size you want sent and when you want it to arrive. You can buy excellent Christmas cards and have them all personalised for you – and sent out for you if you really want to. You can use the reminder services you'll find on most of these websites to keep your birthday and special event diaries, even choosing how far in advance you want to be notified about your mothers'/granny's special day. Do you get the idea, yet?

These websites make it so easy for you to make sure that you do the right thing at the right time that the temptation is to totally rely on them, and then when your computer crashes (as mine did last week) you'll overlook the fact that without your email you simply won't remember. Anything. So use them as a back-up service and then the system usually works superbly.

If you haven't yet sent balloons to someone I can tell you now that they're usually a great success (when sent to a child, teen, student and the like). We've now reached the stage where two of my children expect me to send them balloons on their birthdays. The other one hates and detests them after the time I sent him an extra large box that sat outside his door and chimed 'happy birthday' every time it was opened by others, which was frequently.

Sites to Visit

www.ballooninabox.co.uk

If you want to escape from the traditional and to surprise someone then why not send a balloon in a box, which you can send with your personal message or anonymously? The large box arrives and when opened out floats a huge balloon with Happy Birthday or Good Luck (or whatever occasion you're aiming at) printed on it. Having sent these on many occasions I know that you can never fail to please.

Site Usability:	★★★★	Delivery Area:	UK
Product Range:	★★★	Based:	UK
Price Range:	Medium	Express Delivery Option? (UK)	Yes

www.charitycards.co.uk

On this site there are some lovely cards for every type of occasion plus thank-you cards and luxury Christmas cards, Advent calendars and stocking fillers (for girls). You can also order your printed Christmas cards here and if you buy ten or more cards shipping is free. When you're ordering Christmas cards you can buy books of Christmas stamps at the checkout.

Site Usability:	★★★★★	Delivery Area:	Worldwide
Product Range:	★★★★★	Based;	UK
Price Range:	Medium	Express Delivery Option? (UK)	Yes

www.clintoncards.co.uk

Here you can order a card to be sent to you to send to the recipient or for Clinton to personalise on your behalf. You can also use their reminder service for future birthdays and anniversaries. It's quite an attractive and unusual website with links to other gift websites on the home page plus information about who did what on the day you've chosen to visit the site.

Site Usability:	★★★★★	Delivery Area:	Worldwide
Product Range:	★★★★	Based:	UK
Price Range:	Medium	Express Delivery Option? (UK)	Yes

www.moonpig.com

This is definitely one of my favourites – there are more than enough different types of cards here for whenever you might need them and they'll personalise them for you and send them out within 24 hours. It's a very good site, quick and easy to navigate with some excellent cards for birthdays where you can change the name and date to that of the recipient. They really are funny (provided you want funny) and there's everything else as well. Expect a very good and reliable service.

Site Usability:	★★★★★	Delivery Area:	Worldwide
Product Range:	★★★★★	Based:	UK
Price Range:	Medium	Express Delivery Option? (UK)	Yes

www.royalmail.com

Go to their 'Buy Online' section and order your books of stamps here (or your Special Editions or ready stamped envelopes). You do have to order quite a number of stamps at a time when you buy them online but it's the easiest way if you're going to be posting a lot of mail in the near future. Alternatively download 'SmartStamp', which allows you to print your postage directly onto your envelopes from your own printer.

Site Usability:	★★★★★	Based:	UK
Product Range:	★★★★★	Express Delivery Option? (UK)	Yes
Delivery Area:	UK		

www.sharpcards.com

Cards for anniversaries, weddings, Easter, Valentine's Day, birthdays or Christmas with hand written greetings and sent out for you are all waiting for you here. They also have an address book and reminder service so you won't ever forget that birthday or anniversary again. The site is very clear and easy to use but the range of cards is not as large as on some others so have a look round at several before choosing.

Site Usability:	★★★★★	Delivery Area:	Worldwide
Product Range:	★★★★	Based:	UK
Price Range:	Medium	Express Delivery Option? (UK)	Yes

www.skyhi.co.uk

Sky Hi balloons will deliver anything from a single balloon in a box with your message to a huge bouquet of balloons. They also offer a same day delivery service which, although expensive, can be a lifesaver if you've forgotten an important event and want to make a statement. They're very reliable too which is essential if you're going for the last minute panic send and you'll find balloons here for just about every type of occasion.

Site Usability:	★★★★	Delivery Area:	UK
Product Range:	★★★★	Based:	UK
Price Range:	Medium/Very Good Value	Express Delivery Option? (UK)	Yes

Chapter 73

Ribbon and Wrap

Trying to buy 'wrapping supplies' (sounds good, doesn't it?) online can be a very frustrating experience unless it's at Christmas. I personally get very annoyed by the fact that I can buy wonderful presents, but then have to struggle out to the shops to buy a roll of wrapping paper – why isn't someone doing it properly online yet? If they are, and you know of them, please, please let me know, they've obviously gone straight past me.

For the time being the choice of ribbons is wonderful as you'll see below, and don't become confused by the fact that most of these websites offer an amazing variety of craft products as well. Click straight through to the ribbons section and you'll see what I mean.

Sites to Visit

www.carnmeal.co.uk

This site is a must for anyone who has more than a few presents to wrap up. They specialise in a wide choice of beautiful ribbons and craft accessories for all occasions (and particularly weddings) and rather than buying those small irritating balls of gold and silver ribbon, here you can choose from wired and unwired ribbons, organzas and tartans in lots of different widths and a wide selection of colours. Most ribbons are available in 25 metre lengths.

Site Usability:	★★★	Based:	UK
Product Range:	★★★★★	Express Delivery Option? (UK)	No
Price Range:	Medium/Very Good Value	Gift Wrapping Option?	No
Delivery Area:	Worldwide	Returns Procedure:	Down to you

www.jaycotts.co.uk

Online haberdashers and sewing machine retailers Jaycotts offer a great deal more than ribbons, as you can buy all your sewing essentials and accessories here. However, click through to Haberdashery and then Ribbons and choose from double faced satin, taffeta, tartan, gold edged satin and gold and silver lame, all sold by the metre. Orders over £25 have free delivery.

Site Usability:	★★★★★	Based:	UK
Product Range:	★★★	Express Delivery Option? (UK)	No
Price Range:	Medium/Very Good Value	Gift Wrapping Option?	No
Delivery Area:	Worldwide	Returns Procedure:	Down to you

www.millcrofttextiles.co.uk

Millcroft supply general haberdashery items and textiles worldwide, specialising in the bridal industry. They also have a small but lovely selection of ribbons including taffeta, tartan and metallic lame in lots of different colours all of which they show very clearly. You can choose from different widths and lengths although the reels usually start at 20 metres. When you're buying these quantities prices are inevitably much better than you'll find in the shops so buy to use throughout the year.

Site Usability:	★★★★	Based:	UK
Product Range:	★★★★	Express Delivery Option? (UK)	No
Price Range:	Medium/Very Good Value	Gift Wrapping Option?	No
Delivery Area:	Worldwide	Returns Procedure:	Down to you

www.mjtrim.com

This is a marvellous ribbon and trimming store based in the US. It really is well worth taking a look as not only are the prices very good but the choice is quite spectacular, and includes ribbons for Christmas, weddings and other occasions plus trims such as beaded appliqué motifs (think flowers, hearts, bugs and animals), beads, feather and faux fur trims and buttons and tassels. If you're ordering from outside the US you need to fax your order and allow extra time.

Site Usability:	★★★★★	Based:	US
Product Range:	★★★★★	Express Delivery Option? (UK)	No
Price Range:	Medium/Very Good Value	Gift Wrapping Option?	No
Delivery Area:	Worldwide	Returns Procedure:	Down to you

www.nspccshop.co.uk

You can often find some really attractive Christmas ornaments, crackers, decorations and well priced gift suggestions in the NSPCC catalogue each year and when you know that you're giving for such a good cause it makes sense to buy here. There's also usually a wide selection of Christmas Cards, excellent gift wrap, ribbons and calendars.

Site Usability:	★★★★★	Based:	UK
Product Range:	★★★★★	Express Delivery Option? (UK)	No
Price Range:	Medium/Very Good Value	Gift Wrapping Option?	No
Delivery Area:	UK	Returns Procedure:	Down to you

www.nationaltrust-shop.co.uk

The National Trust shop online always has one of the best selections of high quality wrapping paper and gift tags. When you click through to their online shop you'll find not just a wide choice of designs but you can also buy your wrap in different lengths right up to 20 metres; ideal if you've lots of gifts to organise. You'll also find crackers at a range of prices, Christmas cards and gift ideas and ordering is very quick and easy.

Site Usability:	★★★★★	Based:	UK
Product Range:	★★★★	Express Delivery Option? (UK)	No
Price Range:	Medium/Very Good Value	Gift Wrapping Option?	No
Delivery Area:	UK	Returns Procedure:	Down to you

www.thewrappingco.com

Here's a small collection of very beautiful but quite expensive wrap, ribbon and cards which would be suitable if you have just a few presents you want to wrap superbly. They also give suggestions on which ribbon to use with which paper. The website doesn't keep its Christmas selection up all the year round so you need to visit them in October for the full range, although you can of course use them at any time of year for other occasions.

Site Usability:	★★★★	Based:	UK
Product Range:	★★★	Express Delivery Option? (UK)	No
Price Range:	Luxury/Medium	Gift Wrapping Option?	No
Delivery Area:	UK	Returns Procedure:	Down to you

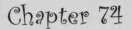

Chapter 74

The Chocolate Lover's Paradise

Don't look round here if you've just decided to go on a diet or to cut down on your chocolate intake as it could lead to disaster. From wonderfully named treats such as Chilli Tickles and Heavenly Honeycomb Bars to handmade truffles in an enormous range of flavours, there's a truly mouth-watering choice. Thank goodness I'm not a chocoholic myself (although like just about everyone I indulge occasionally and I'll freely admit that I'm a real nut addict so I'm not trying to be smug, you understand).

What you will find below are totally out of the ordinary chocolates alongside the regular varieties, so you can really play the one-upmanship game when it comes to giving chocolates as gifts – no more just picking up a box at your local supermarket – order from here and you'll end up with something delicious and special and quite possibly unheard of by the recipient. Yes you will have to pay a little more, probably, but it will only be a little and you'll have a gift that's just that bit different. Don't forget to order some essential 'tasting' chocolates for yourself at the same time. Just to make sure they're OK, of course.

Sites to Visit

www.brownes.co.uk

Brownes offer luxurious hand-made chocolates in four sizes of boxes, from a small selection to their 1kg presentation box, plus after dinner 'mint chasers', buttered brazils, party crackers, dusted almonds and chocolate covered raisins. They all look totally delicious and once you reach this website you'll almost certainly want to give them a try.

Site Usability:	★★★★★	Based:	UK
Product Range:	★★★	Express Delivery Option? (UK)	No
Price Range:	Medium	Gift Wrapping Option?	No
Delivery Area:	Worldwide	Returns Procedure:	Down to you

www.chococo.co.uk

This is a small husband and wife led team based in Purbeck in Dorset. Passionate about proper chocolate, they've developed their own, totally unique, award winning range of fresh chocolates in vibrant, stylish packaging. Alongside their celebration hampers and chunky chocolates you'll find goodies such as Chilli Tickles and Raspberry Riots. There are always wonderful ideas for Easter including giant goodie boxes, chocolate hens and wonderfully colourful eggs for adults and kids.

Site Usability:	★★★★	Based:	UK
Product Range:	★★★	Express Delivery Option? (UK)	Yes
Price Range:	Medium	Gift Wrapping Option?	No
Delivery Area:	Europe	Returns Procedure:	Down to you

www.chocolatebuttons.co.uk

LET YOUR CHILDREN ON THIS WEBSITE AT YOUR PERIL. From old fashioned sherbet to Toblerone, chocolate coins, novelties and gifts, jelly beans and natural candy canes this site is a cornucopia of irresistible sweets. Not only that, but you can buy in quantity. They won't stop you from buying one bag of chocolate Victorian coins, but why not buy 30 – surely you'll find a use for them?

Site Usability:	★★★★	Based:	UK
Product Range:	★★★★	Express Delivery Option? (UK)	Yes
Price Range:	Medium/Very Good Value	Gift Wrapping Option?	Yes for their gift packs
Delivery Area:	Worldwide	Returns Procedure:	Down to you

www.chocolatetradingco.com

Here's a mouth-watering selection of chocolates, from Charbonel et Walker serious chocolate indulgences and chocoholics' hampers to funky and fun chocolates such as chocolate sardines and Jungle Crunch. They'll send your chocolates out for you with a personalised gift card and also offer you lots of information on how to tell when you're tasting the highest quality chocolate.

Site Usability:	★★★★★	Based:	UK
Product Range:	★★★★	Express Delivery Option? (UK)	Yes
Price Range:	Medium	Gift Wrapping Option?	Yes
Delivery Area:	UK	Returns Procedure:	Down to you

www.cocoaloco.co.uk

Started in 2005, Cocoa Loco is a small family business based in Partridge Green, West Sussex, dedicated to making hand made organic chocolates from high quality ingredients. Try treats such as Organic Dark Chocolate Covered Ginger and Mango, Orange and Hazelnut Milk Chocolate Truffles, the Hot and Spicy Special (with Chocolate Chilli Brownies) or jumbo chocolate buttons. Everything can be sent out in a (recyclable) box with the message of your choice.

Site Usability:	★★★★	Based:	UK
Product Range:	★★★	Express Delivery Option? (UK)	Yes
Price Range:	Medium	Gift Wrapping Option?	No
Delivery Area:	Worldwide	Returns Procedure:	Down to you

www.darksugars.co.uk

Dark Sugars hand make rich chocolate truffles with flavours such as apricot and brandy, cardamom and orange, dry apple cider and cinnamon. Then there are the chocolate dipped liqueur-soaked dried fruits – prunes in Armagnac, cherries in cherry brandy and peaches in schnapps – and for each there is a choice of box or packet size. You can also buy the highest quality cooking chocolate and cocoa here – the essential ingredients which they use themselves.

Site Usability:	★★★★★	Based:	UK
Product Range:	★★★	Express Delivery Option? (UK)	No
Price Range:	Medium	Gift Wrapping Option?	No
Delivery Area:	Worldwide	Returns Procedure:	Down to you

www.hotelchocolat.co.uk

This is a really lovely and well designed website with a large selection of beautifully packaged chocolates. Send someone a Chocogram Delux, Champagne Truffles, their Seasonal Selection or let them choose for themselves. They also have some unusual goodies such as Happy Eggs (for Easter), Strawberries in White Chocolate, Christmas Crates, Chocolate Logs, Goody Bags and Rocky Road Slabs. Resist if you can.

Site Usability:	★★★★★	Based:	UK
Product Range:	★★★★★	Express Delivery Option? (UK)	Yes
Price Range:	Luxury/Medium	Gift Wrapping Option?	No
Delivery Area:	Worldwide	Returns Procedure:	Down to you

www.leonidasbelgianchocolates.co.uk

For the ultimate in Belgian chocolates click through to this dedicated website and make your choice. First you select the size of box you want to order and then choose from the chocolate menu with possibilities such as Butter Creams, General Assortment, milk or dark chocolates, Neapolitans and Liqueurs, all of which will be boxed up and despatched to wherever you want.

Site Usability:	★★★★	Based:	UK
Product Range:	★★★	Express Delivery Option? (UK)	Yes
Price Range:	Luxury	Gift Wrapping Option?	No
Delivery Area:	UK	Returns Procedure:	Down to you

www.montezumas.co.uk

Montezumas produce a range of around 40 different hand made truffles, with names such as Caribbean Rhythm, Irish Tipple and Lost in Space. You can order by selecting one of their ready made collections or choose your own from the complete list. Buy organic cocoa drinking chocolate, fantastic fudge and chocolate hampers here too.

Site Usability:	★★★★	Based:	UK
Product Range:	★★★	Express Delivery Option? (UK)	Yes
Price Range:	Luxury	Gift Wrapping Option?	No
Delivery Area:	Worldwide	Returns Procedure:	Down to you

www.thankheavenforchocolate.co.uk

In the Chocolate Shop at thankheavenforchocolate.co.uk there are decorative chocolate hampers, selections of Belgian chocolates, gorgeous special chocs for Valentine's Day, handmade boxes of chocolate truffles and cute chocolate novelties such as Saddleback Piglets and Happy Ducks. This isn't a huge selection but a very well thought out range and prices include free postage plus gift presentation and a card so that you can have your choice sent on your behalf to anywhere in the UK.

Site Usability:	★★★★★	Based:	UK
Product Range:	★★★★	Express Delivery Option? (UK)	Yes
Price Range:	Luxury/Medium	Gift Wrapping Option?	Yes
Delivery Area:	UK	Returns Procedure:	Down to you

www.thehouseofchocolates.co.uk

If your taste is for the top brand chocolates such as those from Godiva and Ackerman to Charbonel et Walker and Neuhaus then this is the place for you. There's a lot to choose from – a chocolate heart box or chocolate covered crystalised ginger from Charbonel, Ackerman's luxurious truffles, luxury boxes from Godiva and Duchy of Cornwall Chocolate Mint Thins. There's quite a wide price range from the reasonable to the truly expensive and you'll find diabetic, Kosher and dairy free chocolates as well.

Site Usability:	★★★★★	Based:	UK
Product Range:	★★★★	Express Delivery Option? (UK)	Yes
Price Range:	Luxury/Medium	Gift Wrapping Option?	No but beautifully presented
Delivery Area:	Worldwide	Returns Procedure:	Down to you

www.theobroma-cacao.co.uk

Forget your usual last minute hunt for a chocolate egg this Easter and click straight through here, where you can order fine hand-crafted chocolates developed by specialist patissier Philip Neal. You can buy wonderful gift selections from seasonal boxes to heart shaped gifts for Valentine's Day as well, but I would suggest that (at the right time of year, of course) you take a good look at his Marbled Finished and 'Spun' eggs, prettily wrapped mini eggs and unique red hand-painted eggs. Definitely one for grown-up chocoholics.

Site Usability:	★★★★★	Based:	UK
Product Range:	★★★★	Express Delivery Option? (UK)	No
Price Range:	Luxury/Medium	Gift Wrapping Option?	No
Delivery Area:	UK	Returns Procedure:	Down to you

www.thorntons.co.uk

Thorntons are ideal for Easter, birthdays, anniversaries and weddings or simply when you want to treat yourself. You can buy their delicious chocolate hampers, choose 800g of continental chocolates or one of the classic boxes and you'll also find gifts to add such as wine, flowers and Steiff bears. As well as all of this they have a small collection of cards which they'll personalise for you and send out with your gift.

Site Usability:	★★★★★	Based:	UK
Product Range:	★★★★★	Express Delivery Option? (UK)	Yes
Price Range:	Medium/Very Good Value	Gift Wrapping Option?	No
Delivery Area:	Worldwide for most products	Returns Procedure:	Down to you

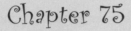

Chapter 75

Flowers

As with chocolates there are lots of excellent flower websites, some where they'll ship internationally for you, some that are well priced and others that are definitely not. Most of them have a truly gorgeous selection and they're just beginning to get the idea that they need to offer something a little bit different, rather than the same bouquets and arrangements as everyone else.

Although flowers are the easy option for thank-yous and celebrations, when have you ever received some and not been delighted? Never? I thought so. I find that they're always uplifting and although they don't last very long, for the short time they're at their best they'll brighten up any room.

A number of these websites offer you other gift ideas to go with your flowers such as teddy bears and chocolates. Personally I'd rather just send, or receive, a really beautiful hand-tied bunch of flowers and forget the extras but needless to say it's totally up to you.

Two of my favourites are definitely www.janepackerdelivered.com and www.imogenstone.com (and if someone's prepared to spend a lot: www.jwflowers.com) but have a look through for yourself and make your choice.

Sites to Visit

www.bloom.uk.com

If you're fed up of throwing out dead flowers and having to spend real money to replace them then take a look at this website: offering the new generation of silk flowers online. They are incredibly real looking in most cases (you may well have admired some in a friend's house without realising they were silk; I certainly have) and they offer all types of arrangements from Dorset cream roses and cabbages to orchids and seasonal arrangements.

Site Usability:	★★★★★	Delivery Area:	UK
Product Range:	★★★★	Based:	UK
Price Range:	Medium	Express Delivery Option? (UK)	Yes

www.designerflowers.org.uk

At Designer Flowers all the arrangements are created by their own florists and delivered direct by courier in secure boxes to London and the UK. You can also include Champagne, Belgian chocolates and soft toys and choose from their selection of special occasion bouquets. Prices are not inexpensive and delivery is extra at £4.50. You can order from them for next day delivery or if your order is really urgent they'll use their network of florists (rather than their own) to provide a same day delivery service.

Site Usability:	★★★★★	Delivery Area:	UK
Product Range:	★★★★	Based:	UK
Price Range:	Luxury/Medium	Express Delivery Option? (UK)	Yes

www.flowersdirect.co.uk

You'll find a good collection of hand tied and traditional bouquets here (and you can select the size you want to send) with a same day delivery option if you order before 2pm, Monday to Saturday. Choose one of their exotic arrangements if you want to give something a bit different with names such as Oriental Orchids and Exotic Paradise and you can include extras such as wine and champagne, spirits, chocolates, balloons and cuddly toys.

Site Usability:	★★★★	Delivery Area:	UK
Product Range:	★★★★	Based:	UK
Price Range:	Medium	Express Delivery Option? (UK)	Yes

www.flowerworksoxford.co.uk

Flowerworks offer a nationwide delivery service and the facility to select from their favourite seasonal bouquets or to design your own. To do this you just have to answer their questions: How would you like your flowers to be arranged – flamboyantly or compactly? In what style would you like them to be – vibrant, classic or exotic? Then you provide information on colour choice, price and the recipient and leave the rest to them.

Site Usability:	★★★★	Delivery Area:	UK
Product Range:	★★★	Based:	UK
Price Range:	Luxury/Medium	Express Delivery Option? (UK)	Yes

www.imogenstone.co.uk

Imogen Stone is an exclusive online florist and luxury gift store, creating beautiful floral designs using the finest fresh flowers combined with scented herbs and interesting foliages. Their flower and plant collection includes hand-tied bouquets, Fairtrade flowers, scented flowers and seasonal plants plus special designs for Valentine's day, Mothers' day, Easter and Christmas. You can include Rococo Chocolate Truffles, Abahna Toiletries, Nougat and LSA vases with your order. Call before 1pm for same day delivery.

Site Usability:	★★★★★	Delivery Area:	Worldwide
Product Range:	★★★★	Based:	UK
Price Range:	Luxury/Medium	Express Delivery Option? (UK)	Yes

www.janepackerdelivered.com

Here are the most beautifully presented, modern flowers to send as a gift or, if you want to give yourself a treat, to yourself. The range in her stores is much larger than what's offered online, but here you'll find roses, hyacinths, pink parrot tulips, orchids and mixed bouquets all presented in her unique, chic style. You can buy Jane Packer's books, fragranced bath and body gifts, champagne and chocolates and gift vouchers here as well.

Site Usability:	★★★★★	Delivery Area:	UK
Product Range:	★★★	Based:	UK
Price Range:	Luxury/Medium	Express Delivery Option? (UK)	Yes

www.jwflowers.com

Visit this website if you want to buy something really special and not if you want 'flowers for less', as you'll expect to pay upwards of £60 for an arrangement or bouquet. Having said that, the flowers here are really exquisite, with unusual combinations (such as pale pink hyacinths, white ranunculas and Candy Bianca roses, or burnt orange Adrema tulips with china grass loops and Guelda roses) used to create designs you won't find anywhere else.

Site Usability:	★★★★	Delivery Area:	UK
Product Range:	★★★	Based:	UK
Price Range:	Luxury	Express Delivery Option? (UK)	Yes

www.lambertsflowercompany.co.uk

On this stylishly designed website Lamberts offer a small but cleverly thought out collection of bouquets and arrangements. There are gorgeous new baby gifts, special flowers for Valentines day and other occasions plus teddies, chocolates and vases. Lamberts also specialise in wedding flowers, including bouquets, church and reception arrangements and buttonholes plus stylish arrangements for the home.

Site Usability:	★★★★★	Delivery Area:	UK
Product Range:	★★★★	Based:	UK
Price Range:	Luxury/Medium	Express Delivery Option? (UK)	No

www.moysesstevens.co.uk

Since 1876 when Miss Moyses and Mr Stevens started their business Moyses Stevens have been known for the artistry and quality of their floristry. They choose their in house florists specifically for their originality and capacity to inspire, and create designs that are innovative, stylish and fun. Expect to find inspirational flowers, fresh, full of life and wonderful to receive. You can order orchids and small plants here too and set up an address book to make your life really easy the next time you want to order.

Site Usability:	★★★★★	Delivery Area:	UK
Product Range:	★★★★	Based:	UK
Price Range:	Luxury/Medium	Express Delivery Option? (UK)	Yes for some bouquets provided you order early enough

www.sylviahague.com

I think that you'll have to admit, as I have, that these flowers look unbelievably real, even though you and I will know that they're all made of silk. You can select from her orchids and roses for smaller arrangements plus wonderful looking blue hydrangeas, green cymbidiums or wild amaryllis for fireplaces or as show pieces. All orders are specially made although you should receive delivery within five days. There's also plenty of information on how to keep your flowers looking fresh.

Site Usability:	★★★★	Based:	UK
Product Range:	★★★	Express Delivery Option? (UK)	No
Price Range:	Medium	Gift Wrapping	Yes
Delivery Area:	UK		

www.vivelarose.com

Using mainly Tea-Hybrid roses for their beautiful full blooms and long stems Vive la Rose adapt their unique bouquets to the latest trends in interiors. The roses travel in special hydrating travel packs and are delivered by courier, enabling them to offer a next day delivery service within the UK. Don't expect a vast selection here; just really beautiful bouquets in a variety of colours that you won't find anywhere else. They offer a wedding flower service as well.

Site Usability:	★★★★★	Based:	UK
Product Range:	★★★	Express Delivery Option? (UK)	Yes
Price Range:	Medium	Gift Wrapping	No
Delivery Area:	UK		

www.worldofroses.com

Yes this is the place to find the most outstanding roses of all varieties, from climbing and floribundas to ground cover and hybrid tea varieties. However, don't expect to find your standard hand tied bunches here as these are gorgeous roses for planting in your garden. You can order them in pots, bare root or gift wrapped and select the date that you want them delivered. If you want something totally unique you can name your own rose here as well.

Site Usability:	★★★★★	Delivery Area:	UK
Product Range:	★★★★★	Based:	UK
Price Range:	Medium	Express Delivery Option? (UK)	No

Chapter 76

Gifts of Food and Drink

I used to be against giving 'hampers' as gifts as I felt, and probably still do in most cases, that they were just a selection of small quantities of expensive items and that you paid a huge amount for the packaging. Now you can put your hampers together yourself and choose what you want to include, and there are some really good delis creating excellent baskets and hampers that they have really put some thought into. I am beginning to change my mind.

Make sure when you're choosing not only that the hamper is presented really attractively, but also that it contains an exclusive selection of mouth-watering products rather than lots of tiny packets and tins. That's my advice, at least, totally based on what I would like to receive or would give.

Sites to Visit

www.agold.co.uk

Here you can order the Brushfield Basket, containing hand baked lemon biscuits, plum bread, Spyder Cream Soda and Darlington's lemon curd, the Hawksmoore Hamper with Fentiman's hot ginger beer, poacher's relish and a selection of cheeses or the Regency Hamper containing cheese, pork pies, sloe gin and lots of other delicious sounding goodies. Alternatively you can select from their excellent online deli and choose exactly what you want to send (which I always prefer). Allow at least five days for delivery.

Site Usability:	★★★★	Based:	UK
Product Range:	★★★★	Express Delivery Option? (UK)	No
Price Range:	Medium	Gift Wrapping Option?	No
Delivery Area:	UK	Returns Procedure:	Down to you

www.bayley-sage.co.uk

Bayley and Sage are a top quality delicatessen based in Wimbledon. On their website you can't actually visit the deli, but you can buy one of their well put together gift selections, with names like Sweet Sensation (jelly beans, chocolate brownies, mini cakes and marshmallows etc.) or Gentleman's Selection (wine, coffee, marmalade, nuts and Gentlemen's Relish). Everything is very clearly photographed and the prices are reasonable.

Site Usability:	★★★★	Based:	UK
Product Range:	★★★★	Express Delivery Option? (UK)	No
Price Range:	Medium	Gift Wrapping Option?	No
Delivery Area:	UK	Returns Procedure:	Down to you

www.butlerswines.co.uk

Butlers specialise in high quality wine and champagne gifts and offer more reasonable prices than most, in that you can see the price of each individual bottle, add the gift packaging and then the handmade truffles. Personally I think this is better than putting everything together and hoping that you won't notice the price but obviously it'll take a few more clicks. There's a good choice of hampers as well plus express delivery.

Site Usability:	★★★★★	Based:	UK
Product Range:	★★★★	Express Delivery Option? (UK)	Yes
Price Range:	Medium	Gift Wrapping Option?	No
Delivery Area:	UK	Returns Procedure:	Down to you

www.claire-macdonald.com

There are so many online retailers who offer you (frequently very good) selections of food and drink put together by totally anonymous people that I always find it a joy to discover a real name, someone who has taken the trouble to create their own range and isn't afraid to announce themselves. Claire Macdonald is one, who offers her gifts of food and wine such as The Chocolate Pudding Collection, Savoury Sauces and Chocolate Fudge, all beautifully packaged in signature dark green gift boxes. Buy from her.

Site Usability:	★★★★	Based:	UK
Product Range:	★★★	Express Delivery Option? (UK)	No
Price Range:	Medium	Gift Wrapping Option?	No
Delivery Area:	Worldwide	Returns Procedure:	Down to you

www.forgoodnesscake.co.uk

The next time you're considering sending flowers to someone as a thank-you gift have a look at this website and you may well be persuaded to send something entirely different. The Classic Box from For Goodness Cake arrives brimming with dainty fairy cakes, prettily packaged in a high quality, pale blue box and tied with fuchsia ribbon. They're freshly baked so you need to eat them quickly, but having received one myself, recently, I can assure you that that won't be a problem. There are ideas for children and weddings plus seasonal suggestions as well.

Site Usability:	★★★★★	Based:	UK
Product Range:	★★★	Express Delivery Option? (UK)	48 hours if you order by midday
Price Range:	Medium	Gift Wrapping Option?	Packaging is lovely
Delivery Area:	UK	Returns Procedure:	Down to you

www.jeroboams.co.uk

This is a seriously beautifully photographed website from a luxury cheese specialist, deli and fine wine importer based in South Kensington. On this site you can order from their cheese selections or gifts of food and wine which include port with stilton, vodka and caviar or whisky and cheddar; choose from one of their luxury hampers or from their list of wines, champagnes and spirits. This would be an excellent place to find a gift for a real food or wine lover although it's definitely at the luxury end.

Site Usability:	★★★★	Based:	UK
Product Range:	★★★	Express Delivery Option? (UK)	No
Price Range:	Luxury/Medium	Gift Wrapping Option?	No
Delivery Area:	UK	Returns Procedure:	Down to you

www.fruit-4u.com

This company will put together the most mouth-watering mix of fresh fruit and present it beautifully in a basket so that you can send it as a gift, with names such as the Exotic Fruit Basket and the Supreme Fruit Basket both packed with perfect Class 1 seasonal fruits. You can also add cheese, wine, teddies and champagne to your selected basket.

Site Usability:	★★★★	Based:	UK
Product Range:	★★★	Express Delivery Option? (UK)	Yes
Price Range:	Medium	Gift Wrapping Option?	No
Delivery Area:	UK	Returns Procedure:	Down to you

www.gogofruitbasket.com

Gogofruitbaskets offer free delivery in mainland UK and you can buy, alongside the fruits, all sorts of 'hampers' including 'Pink Fizz', 'Strawberries and Chocs', 'Cheese and Wine' (plus grapes and clementines), 'Mighty Fruit n Muffin', fruit with The Fabulous Bakin' Boys muffins and shortcake and 'Big Fat Thank You'; forget the fruit here, this is muffins, caramel slices, macaroons, flapjack bars, caramelts and cup cakes.

Site Usability:	★★★★	Based:	UK
Product Range:	★★★	Express Delivery Option? (UK)	Yes
Price Range:	Medium	Gift Wrapping Option?	No
Delivery Area:	UK	Returns Procedure:	Down to you

www.gorgeous-food.co.uk

Here's a really attractive website, using traditional script and clear pictures to make you want to stay and browse. They offer a selection of hampers, from Decadence, Luxury and Indulgence to themed selections such as Afternoon Tea, Chocoholic, Spanish and Chilli Lover and for each one you not only see the filled hamper, but also each individual ingredient as well as the list of what's included. In the 'Other Goodies' section you'll find Booja Booja truffles (!), Catalan Mountain Honey and lots more.

Site Usability:	★★★★★	Based:	UK
Product Range:	★★★★	Express Delivery Option? (UK)	Yes
Price Range:	Luxury/Medium	Gift Wrapping Option?	No
Delivery Area:	UK	Returns Procedure:	Down to you

www.justchampagne.co.uk

So you're not going to be surprised to find champagne here, I suspect. You may be surprised that you'll find not 'just' champagne (could it ever be 'just'?) but champagne gifts with chocolate truffles, picnic bags, teddies and sterling silver cufflinks plus wonderful large bottles such as the Jeroboam (3 litres), Methuselahs (6 litres) and Nebuchadnezzar (15 litres). That one's definitely mine – anyone want to share?

Site Usability:	★★★	Based:	UK
Product Range:	★★★★★	Express Delivery Option? (UK)	Yes
Price Range:	Luxury/Medium	Gift Wrapping Option?	No
Delivery Area:	Most EU and USA	Returns Procedure:	Down to you

www.lewisandcooper.com

Lewis and Cooper are a family run business offering a marvellous selection of hampers for all tastes and price levels. You can choose one of their ready selected hampers or pick the items that you want included. Some of items include Cropwell Bishops Stilton, Inverawe Smoked Salmon and pears in caramel sauce alongside the finest York ham, handmade plum puddings and Yorkshire Moors honey on the comb.

Site Usability:	★★★★★	Based:	UK
Product Range:	★★★★	Express Delivery Option? (UK)	Yes
Price Range:	Luxury/Medium	Gift Wrapping Option?	No
Delivery Area:	UK	Returns Procedure:	Down to you

www.lordswines.co.uk

There's a good selection of food and wine gifts here, from beautifully packaged bottles of wine and champagne to more traditional ideas such as port and stilton and champagne and chocolates plus excellent hampers, particularly at Christmas. Most gifts can be personalised; not just the card but the box as well, and they'll even produce a special wine or champagne bottle label for you.

Site Usability:	★★★★★	Based:	UK
Product Range:	★★★★	Express Delivery Option? (UK)	Yes
Price Range:	Luxury/Medium	Gift Wrapping Option?	Yes
Delivery Area:	UK	Returns Procedure:	Down to you

www.nextday-champagne.co.uk

There are lots of places you can buy champagne online, so these days a retailer has to offer something a little bit different to catch your attention. Here at nextday-champagne.co.uk you can order from their standard range of champagnes which they'll send out with your message, together with everything from a teddy bear to a Christmas pudding. You can also choose from their Lanson

399

vintage selection and design your own personalised label. Prices are steep but if you're looking for a luxury gift; take a look round.

Site Usability:	★★★★★	Based:	UK
Product Range:	★★★★	Express Delivery Option? (UK)	Next working day if you order before 3pm
Price Range:	Luxury/Medium	Gift Wrapping Option?	No
Delivery Area:	UK	Returns Procedure:	Down to you

www.theheavenlyhampercompany.co.uk

The aim of Heavenly Hampers is to offer food and wine gifts that you won't find anywhere else. The collection isn't huge, but they've definitely found some interesting products to include such as red chilli jelly, aubergines stuffed with anchovies and onions marinated in balsamic vinegar. Combine these with their excellent presentation and speedy service and you may well find the answer to your next gift giving problem here.

Site Usability:	★★★★	Based:	UK
Product Range:	★★★	Express Delivery Option? (UK)	Yes
Price Range:	Luxury/Medium	Gift Wrapping Option?	No
Delivery Area:	UK	Returns Procedure:	Down to you

www.whiskhampers.co.uk

Whisk Hampers have drawn on over 15 years' experience in the restaurant and fine food retail business to bring you a range of stylish, modern food gifts. All of these are 'natural', avoiding artificial additives and preservatives, carefully packaged on striking black shred with a quotation postcard based on the contents and with your personalised message included. Choose from excellent champagnes and wines plus hampers with names such as Kitchen Confidential, Dressing to Impress and Instant Karma.

Site Usability:	★★★★	Based:	UK
Product Range:	★★★	Express Delivery Option? (UK)	Yes
Price Range:	Luxury/Medium	Gift Wrapping Option?	No
Delivery Area:	UK	Returns Procedure:	Down to you

www.woodenwinebox.co.uk

Provided you place your order before 2.30pm, The Wooden Wine Box Company will ensure that it arrives on the next working day. Take a look through their well photographed and easy to navigate website for wine and champagne gifts which, for a change, do not include teddies, chocolates and flowers but just high quality, hand picked wines and champagnes. All the gifts are packed into pine gift boxes and can be sent out with your personal message. Delivery is to the UK and business addresses in the EU.

Site Usability:	★★★★★	Based:	UK
Product Range:	★★★★	Express Delivery Option? (UK)	Yes
Price Range:	Luxury/Medium	Gift Wrapping Option?	No
Delivery Area:	UK and EU business addresses	Returns Procedure:	Down to you

Chapter 77

Pamper Someone

If you want to find a girly gift for someone of just about any age you should have a look here where you'll find, alongside the usual bath and body products, pretty boutiques where you can discover a unique piece of jewellery, something unusual for the home or that make-up clutch as well.

Most of these websites, along with their attractive ranges, offer the full gamut of gift services including express delivery, gift wrapping, and attaching a card with your personal message, so they're excellent if you've left that special gift to the last minute as well.

There are so many websites in this book that are good for this type of present giving that you really do need to look elsewhere as well if you have the time – in Section 5 for scented candles, wonderful shower gels, body lotions and hand-made soaps, and also in the Boutique section of Chapter 1 – Fashion Online.

What the websites below are so very good at is saving you time – you'll almost certainly find something in just a very few clicks.

Sites to Visit

www.austique.co.uk

Here's a very attractive and well designed website offering a bit of everything; accessories, lingerie, Rococo chocolates, modern jewellery and unusual bathroom treats such as Limoncello Body Butter and Arnaud Chamomile and Lavender Bubble Bath. The range changes frequently depending on the season. Services include gift wrapping, express delivery and international orders by special request.

Site Usability:	★★★★	Based:	UK
Product Range:	★★★	Express Delivery Option? (UK)	Yes
Price Range:	Medium	Gift Wrapping Option?	Yes
Delivery Area:	Worldwide	Returns Procedure:	Down to you

www.bootik.co.uk

On this well laid out website you'll find lots of gift ideas, from pretty, well priced jewellery set with semi precious stones, beaded bags and attractive cosmetic bags, bath and body products, unusual cushions and tableware and a small and very different (but not so inexpensive) collection of clothes. Most of the items here can't be found elsewhere so it could be well worth having a look round.

Site Usability:	★★★	Based:	UK
Product Range:	★★★	Express Delivery Option? (UK)	Yes
Price Range:	Medium	Gift Wrapping Option?	Yes
Delivery Area:	Worldwide	Returns Procedure:	Down to you

www.boutiquetoyou.co.uk

Boutique to You specialise in personalised gifts, gadgets and jewellery perfect for lots of different occasions. They've also been responsible for introducing some cult jewellery brands from the USA including Mummy & Daddy Tags, Lisa Goodwin New York, and Fairy Tale Jewels. On their website there's a wish-list facility so you can send 'wish mails' to your nearest and dearest with hints of what you'd like to receive and they're also introducing their own loyalty scheme.

Site Usability:	★★★	Based:	UK
Product Range:	★★★★	Express Delivery Option? (UK)	No
Price Range:	Medium	Gift Wrapping Option	Yes
Delivery Area:	Worldwide	Returns Procedure:	Down to you

www.cowshedproducts.com

Recognised for their fun, quirky, bovine-inspired names such as, Dirty Cow Hand Wash, Until the Cows Come Home Gift Set, and Grumpy Cow Uplifting Candle (so you really do need to know who you're giving them to), Cowshed products contain therapeutic blends of herbal infusions and high quality pure essential oils from around the world. The names derive from the original Cowshed spa at Babington House in Somerset. There's a cute Baby Cow range here as well plus attractively packaged candles and gift sets.

Site Usability:	★★★★★	Based:	UK
Product Range:	★★★★	Express Delivery Option? (UK)	Yes if you ask them
Price Range:	Medium	Gift Wrapping Option	No
Delivery Area:	UK and USA (separate site)	Returns Procedure:	Down to you

www.devon-house.co.uk

Here you'll find lovely fragrance, bath and body products and candles by Abahna, Cowshed, Geodosis and Lafco NY plus Serge Bensimon stationery and a small range of homeware. It's a very attractive website and everything is clearly photographed but it does take quite a while to get round. Be patient as there's a good range of pampering gifts here.

Site Usability:	★★★★	Based:	UK
Product Range:	★★★★	Express Delivery Option? (UK)	No
Price Range:	Medium	Gift Wrapping Option	No
Delivery Area:	Worldwide	Returns Procedure:	Down to you

www.parseme.com

Based in Kensington Church Street, London, Parseme offers an exclusive range of natural home fragrance and bath and body care products including scented candles, shower gels, body oils and room sprays in fragrances such as Lavande, Vanille, Verveine and Gardena Blossom. They also offer wonderful, simply and beautifully boxed pot-pourri in Fleurs Sauvages, Symphonie de Couleurs, Champe de Lavande and Les Orangerais all of which would make beautiful gifts.

Site Usability:	★★★★★	Based:	UK
Product Range:	★★★★	Express Delivery Option? (UK)	Yes
Price Range:	Medium	Gift Wrapping Option?	Yes
Delivery Area:	Worldwide	Returns Procedure:	Down to you

www.savonneriesoap.com

This is a really beautiful website with an extremely luxurious feel where you can buy exquisitely packaged hand made soaps (think Flower Garden and Honey Cake), bath and body products such as Geranium and Bergamot Oil, perfect gift boxes and The Naughty Weekend Kit – take a look and you'll find out. Be warned, the photography alone makes you want to buy something immediately.

Site Usability:	★★★★★	Based:	UK
Product Range:	★★★	Express Delivery Option? (UK)	No
Price Range:	Luxury/Medium	Gift Wrapping Option?	No
Delivery Area:	Worldwide	Returns Procedure:	Down to You

www.serendipbeauty.com

Next time you're looking for a pampering beauty/gift website which is also a pleasurable and relaxing shopping experience then click onto this new website. Products on offer include Burt's Bees, Cowshed, Croft+Croft, Fruits and Passion, Jane Packer, Korres, Manuel Canovas and Tocca and if that's not enough there are lots of pretty gift sets to choose from plus really cute make-up bags and wash bags by Zoe Phayre-Mudge.

Site Usability:	★★★★★	Based:	UK
Product Range:	★★★	Express Delivery Option? (UK)	No
Price Range:	Medium	Gift Wrapping Option?	No
Delivery Area:	Worldwide	Returns Procedure:	Down to you

www.simplyroses.co.uk

There are perfect gifts here for anyone who loves roses and also being pampered as this is a hand-picked collection of luxurious rose-inspired products, each one selected to complement the natural beauty of a Simply Roses bouquet (which you need to call them to order). Online you can choose from rose scented foaming bath oil, candles and prettily packaged soaps, pomanders, savon de Marseilles and bath truffles. At the moment you need to send a cheque with your order.

Site Usability:	★★★	Based:	UK
Product Range:	★★★	Express Delivery Option? (UK)	No
Price Range:	Medium	Gift Wrapping Option?	Automatic
Delivery Area:	Worldwide	Returns Procedure:	Down to You

www.thehambledon.com

The Hambledon is a lifestyle shop based in Winchester, who have successfully managed to transfer most of their gorgeous products online, on a pretty and easy to use website. You'll find fragrance and bath and body products by Miller Harris and Wickle, candles by Tocca and REN skincare. There's also a wide selection of gifts. Call them if you want overseas deliveries.

Site Usability:	★★★★	Based:	UK
Product Range:	★★★	Express Delivery Option? (UK)	No
Price Range:	Medium	Gift Wrapping Option?	No
Delivery Area:	Worldwide	Returns Procedure:	Down to you

www.theluxurycandlecompany.com

Candles are always, to my mind, an excellent gift. They're pampering and lovely to receive and to use, particularly when they're as beautifully packaged as they are here. At The Luxury Candle Company there are fragrances such as geranium, orange, lavender and ylang ylang presented in four sizes of candles from the Piccolo to the Grande and all are reasonably priced. The next time you're thinking of sending some flowers to someone, take a look here as well.

Site Usability:	★★★★★	Based:	UK
Product Range:	★★★	Express Delivery Option? (UK)	Yes
Price Range:	Medium	Gift Wrapping Option?	Yes
Delivery Area:	UK	Returns Procedure:	Down to you

www.therenovationstore.co.uk

Don't be confused by the name here – this website is about beautiful pampering gifts by brands such as Nougat, Gianna Rose Atelier, Abahna and Lothantique, then there are wonderful slippers by Ciciabella (I couldn't begin to describe them; you need to take a look) The Laundress New York luxury detergents, accessories for everywhere in your home and pretty nursery ideas. I challenge you to visit this attractively photographed website and not buy something. Gift wrapping is free.

Site Usability:	★★★★★	Based:	UK
Product Range:	★★★★★	Express Delivery Option? (UK)	No
Price Range:	Medium	Gift Wrapping Option?	Yes, Free
Delivery Area:	Worldwide	Returns Procedure:	Down to You

www.woodruffs.co.uk

This fragrance and gift retailer offers an excellent range of bath, body and fragrance products by Roger et Gallet, Diptyque, Kenneth Turner, Crabtree & Evelyn, Floris, Cath Collins and Jane Packer, to name but a few. They'll deliver anywhere in the world, offer an express delivery service for the UK and are happy to gift wrap for you. They have unusual accessory ideas as well.

Site Usability:	★★★★★	Based:	UK
Product Range:	★★★★	Express Delivery Option? (UK)	Yes
Price Range:	Medium	Gift Wrapping Option?	Yes
Delivery Area:	Worldwide	Returns Procedure:	Down to you

Also take a look at the websites in Section 5 for pampering gifts

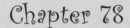

Chapter 78

Home Accessory Gifts

One of my main rules when writing this book was to try to keep each website down to one mention no matter how many places they seemed to fit perfectly, so this has been a very difficult chapter to write as there are so many wonderful home accessories in Chapter 43 which would make lovely gifts.

This is just your quick shop, if you like, where if you're looking for something unusual for someone and you don't want to have to browse through very many websites, you're bound to find the answer. If you have the time take a look at them all and add the ones you really like and will probably use a great deal in the future to your favourites list.

I think that giving home accessories has to be a balance between what *you* like and therefore are happy to give (in terms of style, rather than price) and the home style of the person you're buying for. Don't even think of buying something for someone's home unless you're sure it's their type of thing, or it'll just end up in that present drawer waiting to be given away again. Take a good look round their home and then keep it in mind when you're next buying – they're sure to be delighted with what you give.

Sites to Visit

www.amara.co.uk

This is a really lovely home accessories and gift website with some quite unusual products, such as the deliciously scented and beautifully packaged Gianna Rose Atelier soaps (robin's egg soaps in a porcelain dish and ducks in a gift box are just two), Millefiori candles, Mulberry Home and de Le Cuona throws and shawls, Missoni tableware and lots of other ideas. It's a beautifully designed website and you can see all the products very clearly.

Site Usability:	★★★★★	Based:	UK
Product Range:	★★★★	Express Delivery Option? (UK)	Yes
Price Range:	Medium	Gift Wrapping Option?	Yes
Delivery Area:	Worldwide	Returns Procedure:	Down to you

www.bombayduck.co.uk

This is a very pretty home gifts and interiors website with a wide range of ideas from their own beautifully packaged candles to candy coloured leather accessories, crystal glass chandeliers, vintage style bathroom accessories and printed cushions. There's a wealth of gift suggestions, some expensive – their gorgeous vintage style chandelier at £275 – and others extremely reasonable. They also have a special Christmas area which you can browse in season.

Site Usability:	★★★★	Based:	UK
Product Range:	★★★★	Express Delivery Option? (UK)	Yes
Price Range:	Luxury/Medium	Gift Wrapping Option?	No
Delivery Area:	Worldwide	Returns Procedure:	Down to you

www.brissi.co.uk

Brissi began life as an interiors store in Marlborough, Wiltshire and has now grown up to have two stores in London plus an excellent online shopping facility. Although many of the products on offer have a retro feel the overall mood is chic and modern with beautifully clear photography and mainly neutral colours. The range includes crystal perfume bottles, black and white Limoges tableware and classic glass. In their Gifts section you can shop by recipient or by price and although they don't offer gift wrapping as such everything is sent out ribbon tied in tissue paper.

Site Usability:	★★★★★	Based:	UK
Product Range:	★★★★	Express Delivery Option? (UK)	Yes
Price Range:	Luxury/Medium	Gift Wrapping Option?	No
Delivery Area:	Worldwide	Returns Procedure:	Down to you

www.coffeeandcream.co.uk

This is a beautifully calm website to visit, offering attractively photographed and unusual home accessories, mainly in neutral shades. Think animal print candles, faux fur throws, smoky glasses, almond coloured velvet quilts, black ceramic canisters and pale French Provençal cushions. For anyone who likes natural colours and five star chic in their home, this is the place to find it.

Site Usability:	★★★★	Based:	UK
Product Range:	★★★	Express Delivery Option? (UK)	No
Price Range:	Luxury/Medium	Gift Wrapping Option?	Automatic
Delivery Area:	Worldwide	Returns Procedure:	Down to you

www.grahamandgreen.co.uk

Graham & Green is a long established retailer of home and lifestyle products including candles, tableware, silk cushions, pretty etched glasses and duvet covers and quilts. They're quite hard to really categorise as the products are so wide-spread but if I tell you that some of their bestsellers are bevelled mirrors, Chinese lanterns, lavender scented bags and Penguin (as in the book) mugs you'll probably get the idea.

Site Usability:	★★★★	Based:	UK
Product Range:	★★★	Express Delivery Option? (UK)	Yes
Price Range:	Medium	Gift Wrapping Option?	No
Delivery Area:	UK	Returns Procedure:	Down to you

www.in2decor.com

In2decor is a very easy to get round home accessory and gifts website where you can choose from one of the prettiest selections of traditional style cushions, Venetian glass mirrors, unusual vases and candle holders (such as the monkey nuts candle holder I'm after) and Chinese influenced porcelain. This is a very good place to find gifts, the choice isn't enormous but what is there is very different and attractive.

Site Usability:	★★★★★	Based:	UK
Product Range:	★★★★	Express Delivery Option? (UK)	No
Price Range:	Medium	Gift Wrapping Option?	No
Delivery Area:	UK	Returns Procedure:	Down to you

www.janconstantine.com

This is a collection of hand embroidered fabric, cushions and lavender bags with themes such as Bees and Bugs, Seaside Collection, Botanical, Rose and Classic, described as 'designed for today and destined to be the heirlooms of the future'. These are unique textiles and accessories which you'll probably want to collect and you'll find extremely hard to give away, although their present giving potential is excellent.

Site Usability:	★★★★	Based:	UK
Product Range:	★★★	Express Delivery Option? (UK)	Yes
Price Range:	Medium	Gift Wrapping Option?	No
Delivery Area:	Worldwide	Returns Procedure:	Down to you

www.laprovence.co.uk

La Provence sell beautiful French cloths, fabrics, Lampe Berger and designer giftware in its shops and online. It's a really pretty collection with wonderful gifts for girls, including Swarovski crystal adorned heart necklaces, chic hand-painted porcelain, exquisite glassware and Margaret Loxton limited edition prints of French scenes. They ship free of charge to mainland UK on all items except Lampe Berger Perfumes.

Site Usability:	★★★★★	Based:	UK
Product Range:	★★★★	Express Delivery Option? (UK)	No
Price Range:	Medium	Gift Wrapping Option?	No
Delivery Area:	UK	Returns Procedure:	Down to you

www.locketts.co.uk

Locketts of Hungerford offer a high quality range of modern and traditional photograph albums plus photo frames which range from glass and silver to leather and padded travel frames, most of which are made in their own workshops in the UK. They also have social and sporting books, leather games sets such as cards and backgammon and easel picture stands. Use them also if you need to have faded photographs restored.

Site Usability:	★★★★	Based:	UK
Product Range:	★★★★	Express Delivery Option? (UK)	No
Price Range:	Medium	Gift Wrapping Option?	No
Delivery Area:	Worldwide	Returns Procedure:	Down to you

www.ninacampbell.com

As you would expect, the website of well known interior designer Nina Campbell is really beautifully designed. On it you can choose from a range of her home accessories, including glassware, linens, patterned lambswool throws, small items such as match strikers and pretty bonbon bowls. You can also order her stunningly packaged home fragrance collection which includes candles and room sprays.

Site Usability:	★★★★	Based:	UK
Product Range:	★★★	Express Delivery Option? (UK)	No
Price Range:	Luxury/Medium	Gift Wrapping Option?	No
Delivery Area:	Worldwide	Returns Procedure:	Down to you

www.objects-of-design.com

Here you'll find British designed and made gift and home accessory ideas, with everything either being made in small runs or specially for you. There's the Penguin collection of mugs, Emily Readett-Bayley bookends, wonderful Ferguson's Irish Linen and Phil Atrill crystal stemware and that's just a small selection to give you an idea. You can search by product type or by supplier and create a wish list as you go. You could spend a great deal of time here and you'll find gifts for everyone.

Site Usability:	★★★★	Based:	UK
Product Range:	★★★★★	Express Delivery Option? (UK)	Yes
Price Range:	Medium	Gift Wrapping Option?	Yes
Delivery Area:	Worldwide	Returns Procedure:	Down to you

www.oldeglory.co.uk

Having spent a great deal of time in the US due to the fact that my mother-in-law lives in Maryland, I've become really attached to the old style quilts, shaker boxes and cushions. For that reason I'm delighted to have found this website, established by an American who moved to the UK with her British husband and decided to bring a New England country store with her. For the quilts you'll have to wait a while as they are hand made and for other items you can immediately see the stock availability. If you need something urgently give them a call and email them for international delivery prices.

Site Usability:	★★★★	Based:	UK
Product Range:	★★★★	Express Delivery Option? (UK)	No
Price Range:	Medium	Gift Wrapping Option?	No
Delivery Area:	Worldwide	Returns Procedure:	Down to you

www.polly-online.co.uk

Whereas on some websites you have to search for information about delivery and gift wrapping, at polly-online it's all clearly laid out for you as are the items on offer so buying is far easier. There's an eclectic, contemporary collection here – unusual sculptures and modern jewellery sit side by side with funky lighting, 'sculpted' cushions and pretty, reasonably priced sets of tableware, making this a good place for wedding gifts as well as gifts for other occasions.

Site Usability:	★★★★★	Based:	UK
Product Range:	★★★	Express Delivery Option? (UK)	No
Price Range:	Medium	Gift Wrapping Option?	Yes
Delivery Area:	Worldwide	Returns Procedure:	Down to you

Chapter 79

Gifts For New Babies and Christening Gifts

You may have gathered by now that I have three children, now all in their upper teens so you probably think that their arrivals and christenings took place so long ago that I couldn't possibly remember. Well, there are lots of things that I have, thankfully, forgotten - the sleepless nights, for example - but I can tell you that there is still a beautiful glossy dark red carrier bag in the bottom of one of my cupboards full of - you've probably guessed it - christening gifts.

Please don't think what an ungrateful person I am, or what am I doing hiding the children's gifts from them - neither is the case. It's just that these are gifts that the children will not use. Have looked at and politely admired several times, but have no interest in.

So, my advice on giving gifts to new babies and at christenings is to give something that you can be pretty sure will be used - hung in the nursery (clocks and pictures), worn when they're slightly older (charm bracelets and silver pendants) or drunk with you when they're much, much older (vintage port). Even something beautiful they can wear now (provided it washes, of course). Avoid the silver napkin rings, egg cups and pushers and expensive baby china however much they appeal to you.

You'll get so much more pleasure down the years from seeing your gift used and loved. Believe me - I really do know about these things.

Sites to Visit

www.andreabrierley.com

This is a lovely place to buy something special and quite different. Andrea Brierley has created a range of prints of illustrated names decorated with gorgeous colourful designs of animals, roundabouts, farmyards, fairytale castles and the like. They're not expensive and something you can't buy anywhere else. She'll also undertake an original watercolour commission for you if you get in touch with her. You need to email or call to order.

Site Usability:	★★★★	Based:	UK
Product Range:	★★★	Express Delivery Option? (UK)	No
Price Range:	Medium	Gift Wrapping Option?	No
Delivery Area:	UK	Returns Procedure:	Down to you

www.aspenandbrown.co.uk

On their pale blue, prettily designed website, Aspen & Brown offer a range of gifts. In the Christening section there are lots of very reasonably priced ideas, from personalised blankets, baby shoes and silver bangles to charm bracelets, hand painted initial canvases and named pictures. My advice would be to stay with the personalised items and the silver as there's a great choice and these are definitely the most special and unique.

Site Usability:	★★★★★	Based:	UK
Product Range:	★★★★★	Express Delivery Option? (UK)	No
Price Range:	Medium/Very Good Value	Gift Wrapping Option?	No
Delivery Area:	UK	Returns Procedure:	Down to you

www.babas.uk.com

All of Babas' beautiful handmade baby bedding and accessories are individually made for you and packed in their own unique calico packaging. You can choose sets for cribs, cots and Moses baskets or sleeping bags and towels in their range of contemporary designs with names such as Noah's Ark, Teddy Triplets and Splashy Duck. Everything is really beautiful and different from what you'll find elsewhere and perfect for baby gifts.

Site Usability:	★★★★	Based:	UK
Product Range:	★★★	Express Delivery Option? (UK)	No
Price Range:	Medium	Gift Wrapping Option?	Yes
Delivery Area:	Worldwide	Returns Procedure:	Down to you

www.babygiftgallery.co.uk

The range of baby gifts on offer here on this attractive website is huge so be prepared to take your time. In particular take a look at the christening gifts of sterling silver bangles, Doudou et Compagnie House of Barbotine Gift Boxes, Emile et Rose, keepsake boxes and photo albums. Then you might want to browse through baby gift boxes which you can customise yourself and babywear by Bob and Blossom, Emile et Rose, Inch Blue, Little Blue Dog, Toby Tiger and more.

Site Usability:	★★★★★	Based:	UK
Product Range:	★★★★★	Express Delivery Option? (UK)	Yes – call them
Price Range:	Luxury/Medium	Gift Wrapping Option?	Yes
Delivery Area:	Worldwide	Returns Procedure:	Down to you

www.babiesbaskets.com

Babiesbaskets is a retailer offering (you guessed) 'basket' gift sets for new babies and they go right up to the luxury end of the spectrum although prices start off quite reasonably. There's the 'Loveheart' baby basket containing a babygro, cardigan, pram shoes, fleece and photo album and the ultimate 'Fudge' baby basket which offers as well a cableknit blanket, a hand embroidered towel and babygro and handmade photo album. Everything is beautifully packaged.

Site Usability:	★★★★	Based:	UK
Product Range:	★★★★	Express Delivery Option? (UK)	Yes
Price Range:	Luxury/Medium	Gift Wrapping Option?	Yes
Delivery Area:	Worldwide	Returns Procedure:	Down to you

www.bellini-baby.com

Every time I think 'that's enough, no more baby gift websites' I come across another that you simply have to know about and this is one of those. Perfect for luxury, expensive gifts, Bellini Baby offers you the opportunity of buying absolutely beautiful baskets and hampers (most of which include champagne, so they're for you too) with Takinou of France soft toys, Bebe-Jou soft cotton terry baby dressing gowns, pampering essentials and chocolates, all gorgeously wrapped and hand tied with ribbon.

Site Usability:	★★★★★	Based:	UK
Product Range:	★★★★	Express Delivery Option? (UK)	They aim for next day for all UK orders
Price Range:	Luxury	Gift Wrapping Option?	Yes
Delivery Area:	Worldwide	Returns Procedure:	Down to you

www.hickorydickory.co.uk

Discovering a website like this one – attractive, easy to use and with clever ideas – is a real joy, particularly when it's for children. At Hickory Dickory you can order pretty handmade children's room accessories including mobiles, height charts, name plates, clocks and mirrors, all of which can be personalised with a name or date and would make perfect and different gifts for christenings, birthdays and other special occasions. Call them for overseas delivery.

Site Usability:	★★★★	Based:	UK
Product Range:	★★★	Express Delivery Option? (UK)	No
Price Range:	Medium	Gift Wrapping Option?	Yes
Delivery Area:	Worldwide	Returns Procedure:	Down to you

www.littlepresentcompany.co.uk

There are quite a variety of gifts on offer here for all sorts of occasions including christenings and birthdays. Go straight to the christening gifts section, where there are screen printed photograph albums, children's sized traditional wooden chairs, silver spoons and bowls and gorgeous horn and silver accessories which they'll want to use later on. In my opinion you couldn't go wrong with the beautiful hammered silver bowl they have here and which I haven't seen anywhere else, the only problem is you'll probably want to use it first.

Site Usability:	★★★★★	Based:	UK
Product Range:	★★★★	Express Delivery Option? (UK)	Yes
Price Range:	Luxury/Medium	Gift Wrapping Option?	No but they will engrave items for you
Delivery Area:	UK	Returns Procedure:	Down to you

www.morelloliving.co.uk

I was delighted to find this really beautifully designed website, where you can browse a range of well photographed, clear pictures of lovely accessories and gifts for children including knitted animals, finger puppets, wooden letters, photo frames, scented candles and much more. Take a look round now, as from the personalised paintings to the Create-it Fairy Princess kit I'm sure you'll be as enchanted as I was.

Site Usability:	★★★★★	Based:	UK
Product Range:	★★★★★	Express Delivery Option? (UK)	No
Price Range:	Medium	Gift Wrapping Option?	No
Delivery Area:	UK	Returns Procedure:	Down to you

www.nurserywindow.co.uk

Once you arrive at this website you'll find it very hard to leave. There are some seriously lovely things here for children's rooms, from unusual bedding, Moses baskets and high quality cots and furniture to gift baskets for new babies and everything is beautifully photographed. Just click on the area of their online shop you're interested in, enter, and you'll certainly be hooked. Nothing is cheap but it's all beautiful quality.

Site Usability:	★★★★★	Based:	UK
Product Range:	★★★★	Express Delivery Option? (UK)	No
Price Range:	Luxury/Medium	Gift Wrapping Option?	No
Delivery Area:	UK	Returns Procedure:	Down to you

www.thewoolcompany.co.uk

There's no question that most people give silver for christenings or beautiful baby clothes. Here's something slightly different that will almost certainly be used for a long time. The Wool Company's 100% pure new merino wool blankets have whip-stitched edges and come in a variety of colours polar ice check (soft blue) and natural cream to wonderful guava check and carmine red. You can also buy nursery sheepskin here and pastel checked 'cuddle' blankets plus blankets for the home.

Site Usability:	★★★★★	Based:	UK
Product Range:	★★★	Express Delivery Option? (UK)	No
Price Range:	Medium	Gift Wrapping Option?	No
Delivery Area:	UK	Returns Procedure:	Down to you

www.timetin.com

If you want to give something completely different from the normal run of baby gifts take a look here. You can use your baby Timetin to gather information on what life was like around the time of your baby's birth, remind yourself of the names you considered and make predictions on how you think he or she will develop. The Timetin contains a specially designed 'Time Book', reminder card, sealing labels, Message for the Future envelope and advice on what to put in the tin.

Site Usability:	★★★★	Based:	UK
Product Range:	★★★	Express Delivery Option? (UK)	No
Price Range:	Medium	Gift Wrapping Option?	No
Delivery Area:	Worldwide	Returns Procedure:	N/A unless faulty

Also take a look at the following Websites for Gifts for New Babies and Christening Gifts:

Website address	You'll find it in
www.aspinaloflondon.com	Chapter 16: Scarves, Shawls, Gloves, Belts and More
www.mariechantal.com	Chapter 24: Baby and Toddler Clothes
www.murrayforbes.co.uk	Chapter 15: Jewellery and Watches
www.rachelriley.com	Chapter 24: Baby and Toddler Clothes
www.linksoflondon.co.uk	Chapter 15: Jewellery and Watches
www.tiffany.com	Chapter 15: Jewellery and Watches

Chapter 80

For New Mums

Inevitably your first thought on buying a present for a new mum will be to buy some flowers – that's what nearly everyone does. I don't think you can go really wrong there – but I'd suggest you don't send them to the hospital; you wait a few days and send them to her home so that when everyone else's flowers have faded yours will be there, fresh and beautiful.

I do think that there is something to be said for giving something other than flowers though, as a gorgeous pampering gift will last and be uplifting for much longer. Now that most of the good gift websites will delivery speedily and gift wrap including a card with your own message, there are lots to choose from. Start with the websites below to get some ideas and then have a quick look at www.cologneandcotton.com, www.thewhitecompany.com (two of my personal favourites) for some other excellent possibilities.

Sites to Visit

www.arenaflowers.com

Arena Flowers offer a pretty selection of hand tied floral arrangements as new baby gifts which you can accompany with a teddy bear, Prestat chocolates or a balloon and as there's such a wide range over all the categories I suggest that you select by flower type or by the amount you want to spend. They offer a free UK next day delivery service plus a same day service throughout the UK (which is free in London and the South East).

Site Usability:	★★★★★	Based:	UK
Product Range:	★★★★★	Express Delivery Option? (UK)	Yes
Price Range:	Medium	Gift Wrapping Option?	No
Delivery Area:	UK	Returns Procedure:	Down to you

www.babeswithbabies.com

This is definitely a lovely place to buy a gift for a new mum (or if you are one, to treat yourself). They offer pretty polka dot mama and baby pyjamas, chic nursing tops, Superfluffy alpaca slippers, pampering gift sets and incredibly elegant baby bags as just some of their ideas. You can book baby portrait sessions and buy gift vouchers here as well.

Site Usability:	★★★★★	Based:	UK
Product Range:	★★★★	Express Delivery Option? (UK)	Yes but call to arrange
Price Range:	Medium	Gift Wrapping Option?	Automatic
Delivery Area:	Worldwide	Returns Procedure:	Down to you

www.dreambabyuk.co.uk

There are lots of different types of new and expecting mum gifts on this website, so whether she's into natural, spa or the beautifully fragranced type of pampering you'll find it here. There's also the Booties Keepsake Book which comes in blue or pink (of course), Beatrix Potter My First Year book and Natalia New Parent Survival Kit. There are also lots of other gift ideas including teddies and champagne, new baby gifts and food hampers.

Site Usability:	★★★★★	Based:	UK
Product Range:	★★★★	Express Delivery Option? (UK)	Yes
Price Range:	Luxury/Medium	Gift Wrapping Option?	No
Delivery Area:	Worldwide except for container roses and bouquets	Returns Procedure:	Email them first

www.myfirstday.co.uk

There are so many wonderful gifts you can choose as a memento of a baby's birth, most of which fit into a specific category such as flowers, hampers or silver. Here's something totally different and very unusual which I personally think is a lovely idea: each day since mid-summer's day 2005, landscape photographer Gavan Goulder has taken stunning photographs of the Cornish coastline, so you can buy a beautifully framed photograph to mark the day of your (or a friend's) baby's birth. Take a look and see.

Site Usability:	★★★★★	Based:	UK
Product Range:	★★★	Express Delivery Option? (UK)	No
Price Range:	Luxury/Medium	Gift Wrapping Option?	No
Delivery Area:	Worldwide	Returns Procedure:	Down to you

Also check out these websites for Gifts for New Mums:

Website Address	**You'll find them in**
www.cologneandcotton.com	Chapter 33: Fragrance, Bath and Body
www.janepackerdelivered.com	Chapter 75: Flowers
www.kennethturner.com	Chapter 33: Fragrance, Bath and Body
www.laline.co.uk	Chapter 39: The Beauty Specialists
www.lambertsflowercompany.co.uk	Chapter 75: Flowers
www.thewhitecompany.com	Chapter 41: In the Bedroom

Plus the other websites in

Chapter 75: Flowers
Chapter 33: Fragrance, Bath and Body

Chapter 81

Gifts for Kids

This is a very small selection of websites offering gifts for kids. Why – you may well ask. Well one of the improvements I was determined to make with this book was to try to offer you each website only once, even though it would fit into more than one place, and to tell you exactly where to go to find the rest.

So rather than repeat all the great kids' websites here, I would ask you please, having had a browse below, to turn your book to Chapter 29, where you'll find numerous other excellent children's websites, offering not just a large (in some cases enormous) choice of gift options but also all the services you could possibly want, such as gift wrapping and express delivery. Take a look now.

Sites to Visit

www.funkymoose.co.uk

FunkyMoose offers a range of home and lifestyle products and gifts for children sourced from all over the world, with each having being hand picked for its quality, usefulness and individuality. You can expect to find cutting edge design side by side with traditional craftsmanship and there's a great deal to browse through from bedroom furniture and bedding to beach accessories and new babies' gift baskets. The website is extremely clear with all the information you need available from the home page.

Site Usability:	★★★★★	Based:	UK
Product Range:	★★★★	Express Delivery Option? (UK)	Yes
Price Range:	Medium	Gift Wrapping Option?	Yes
Delivery Area:	Worldwide	Returns Procedure:	Down to you within 7 days of receipt

www.jigsaw-puzzles-online.co.uk

Personally I've never had the patience to tackle mega jigsaw puzzles but I know that there are those who do, and who keep them out year round for rainy day entertainment. This site is aimed at puzzle enthusiasts of all ages as it caters for everyone with 60 piece puzzles for children and going to right up to the (horrendous to me) 13,000 piece puzzle by Clementoni – I wouldn't know where to start, would you?

Site Usability:	★★★★★	Based:	UK
Product Range:	★★★★★	Express Delivery Option? (UK)	Yes
Price Range:	Luxury/Medium	Gift Wrapping Option?	No
Delivery Area:	Worldwide	Returns Procedure:	Down to you

www.lilyandagathe.com

Based in the Catalan region of France bordering on Spain, Lily and Agathe is a small English/French speaking company with a love of all things beautiful, charming and vintage. Here you'll discover exceptional and timeless gifts and toys with a lean towards nostalgia. Many of the items here are one-offs so if you see something you like buy it quick, and if you like the overall idea keep checking back.

Site Usability:	★★★★	Based:	France
Product Range:	★★★★	Express Delivery Option? (UK)	No
Price Range:	Medium	Gift Wrapping Option?	Yes
Delivery Area:	Worldwide	Returns Procedure:	Down to you

www.littlefolk.co.uk

This is an excellent place for unusual gifts for kids as just about everything in the kids' section would make a great present – they have some lovely, well priced personalised t-shirts, aged from 3 to 14, with the Little Folk (Twirl the Little Ballerina, Fizzly the Little Fairy and Squirt the Little Elephant as just a few) plus the alphabet letter and name of your choice. There are also personalised bags, bedding, place settings and pictures too.

Site Usability:	★★★★★	Based:	UK
Product Range:	★★★	Express Delivery Option? (UK)	Yes for some items
Price Range:	Medium	Gift Wrapping Option?	No
Delivery Area:	UK	Returns Procedure:	Down to you

www.sayitwithbears.co.uk

Sayitwithbears.co.uk is one of those websites that obviously started off doing one thing and then branched out, because you can not only find bears here, but Labradors, elephants, rabbits, cats and Dalmatians, plus lots of other dogs. So if you know someone who collects soft toys or needs a feel-good gift you should take a look. Oh yes, and you can buy Lovvie Bears, Thank you Bears and Anniversary Bears as well.

Site Usability:	★★★★	Based:	UK
Product Range:	★★★★★	Express Delivery Option? (UK)	Yes
Price Range:	Medium	Gift Wrapping Option?	Yes
Delivery Area:	Worldwide	Returns Procedure:	Down to you

Also take a look at the following chapters for more gifts for kids:

Chapter 26: Baby and Pre-school toys
Chapter 63: Outdoor Equipment and Games
Chapter 29: General Toy Stores
Chapter 30: Hobbies, Models, Puzzles and Games

Chapter 82

General Gift Stores

I've never been very good at finding presents in general gift stores, always preferring to shop somewhere specific depending on who I'm seeking out a gift for. Having said that there are some very good suggestions here and I would advise that you have a look round at what they have to offer before you next need an emergency gift so that you'll know straight away where to go.

The two areas that they're really best at are pampering gifts and home accessory ideas and they frequently have items to buy that you're unlikely to find anywhere else (or without looking very hard), such as Churchill China – with images painted by Sir Winston Churchill – the Forget-me-not Pocket Garden and Rosanna's J'adore Shoes espresso cup set. Those are just three from an extremely wide selection. Get to know what's where and you'll be able to find special gifts in an instant.

Sites to Visit

www.aspinaloflondon.com

If you're looking for top quality leather and British craftsmanship then take a look at this beautifully designed and photographed website where the product range is growing all the time and there really is something for just about everyone, with gift wrapping and personalisation just two of the services offered. There are chic handbags, luxurious travel bags and accessories such as wallets and purses, gloves, cosmetic cases, jewellery rolls and make-up brush sets and for men there are briefcases, belts, stud boxes and much more. You'll also find ideas for christenings, weddings and other occasions. Take a look now.

Site Usability:	★★★★★	Based:	UK
Product Range:	★★★★★	Express Delivery Option? (UK)	Yes
Price Range:	Luxury/Medium	Gift Wrapping Option?	Yes
Delivery Area:	Worldwide	Returns Procedure:	Down to you

www.coxandcox.co.uk

This Cox and Cox website is divided up into sections such as A Decorative Home, A Creative Diva, Any Excuse for a Party and Children's Corner. In each of the sections you'll find appropriate ideas such as soft furnishings and pictures, linen ribbon and coloured tissue paper, outdoor table clips and tea light holders and gumball machines and butterfly garlands. They'll send this eclectic mix to you anywhere in the world and if you want something urgently you need to call them.

Site Usability:	★★★	Based:	UK
Product Range:	★★★	Express Delivery Option? (UK)	Yes
Price Range:	Medium	Gift Wrapping Option?	No
Delivery Area:	Worldwide	Returns Procedure:	Down to you

www.erinhousegifts.co.uk

This retailer offers a wide choice of gifts including Halcyon Days Enamels, Churchill China (which uses images painted by Sir Winston Churchill) Franz Porcelain and jewellery, delightful Winnie the Pooh classics, the extraordinary Yoro pen and pens by Swarovski. Then there are Country Artists', Lilliput Lane and Wild World figurines plus fun Happy Cats tableware. They're happy to deliver all over the world.

Site Usability:	★★★★	Based:	UK
Product Range:	★★★★	Express Delivery Option? (UK)	No
Price Range:	Medium	Gift Wrapping Option?	Yes
Delivery Area:	Worldwide	Returns Procedure:	Down to you

www.giftinspiration.com

Based in Wiltshire this website claims to be the UK's leading gift delivery service. They certainly have a good selection (think The Espresso Hamper, Hot Chocolate Cup and Saucer Gift Box, Hunter leather covered flask and cups and silver Aspirin Cufflinks) and if you needed a gift in a hurry I would definitely have a look as they offer all the right services - gift wrapping including your personal message and express delivery.

Site Usability:	★★★	Based:	UK
Product Range:	★★★★	Express Delivery Option? (UK)	Yes
Price Range:	Medium	Gift Wrapping Option?	Yes
Delivery Area:	UK	Returns Procedure:	Down to you

www.bitsnstuff.co.uk

The amount of choice you'll find at this gifts for all ages website offering products you'll be hard put to find elsewhere is quite amazing. As a few examples there are hand smocked dresses for children, personalised keepsake boxes and pegboards, decorative silver bottle stoppers and elegant lead crystal decanters. Prices run from the extremely reasonable to hundreds of pounds. This would be a very good place to have a browse *before* you have your next gift giving panic as although the menus are extremely clear there really is a great deal to see.

Site Usability:	★★★★	Based:	UK
Product Range:	★★★★★	Express Delivery Option? (UK)	No
Price Range:	Luxury/Medium/Very Good Value	Gift Wrapping Option?	No
Delivery Area:	Worldwide	Returns Procedure:	Down to you

www.notonthehighstreet.com

There's almost an impossible amount of choice on this website acting as a marketplace for a group of small manufacturers and designers who'll supply you direct. Most of it is reasonably priced and most items are perfect for gifts. You'll find jewellery, scarves and shawls, pretty evening and day handbags, Cote Bastide and Willow bath and body products, unusual camisoles and t-shirts, albums and keepsake boxes plus a selection of home accessories.

Site Usability:	★★★	Based:	UK
Product Range:	★★★★★	Express Delivery Option? (UK)	No
Price Range:	Medium/Very Good Value	Gift Wrapping Option?	No
Delivery Area:	UK	Returns Procedure:	Down to you

www.oliverbonus.co.uk

Voted Best Gift Retailer for 2006 this is a very well designed and easy to use website with a lovely range of products (just as you would expect). They offer some extremely well attractive jewellery and accessories, gifts for the 'domestic goddess', ideas for the garden and leather albums, notebooks and address books. Delivery is free on orders over £50 and where items are in stock they'll despatch the same day. Contact them for overseas deliveries.

Site Usability:	★★★★	Based:	UK
Product Range:	★★★	Express Delivery Option? (UK)	Yes
Price Range:	Medium	Gift Wrapping Option?	No
Delivery Area:	Worldwide	Returns Procedure:	Down to you

www.nationaltrust-shop.co.uk

This is a real treasure trove of well priced gifts and stocking fillers such as pretty floral notecards, chocolate éclairs in pretty boxes, humorous t-shirts and giant crosswords. You can buy Christmas cards and good value wrap and ribbon here too and take advantage of their free gift-wrapping and personalisation service. Orders may take up to 21 days as deliveries come from The National Trust's various suppliers so allow extra time.

Site Usability:	★★★★★	Based:	UK
Product Range:	★★★	Express Delivery Option? (UK)	No
Price Range:	Medium/Very Good Value	Gift Wrapping Option?	Yes
Delivery Area:	UKI	Returns Procedure:	Down to you

www.sogifted.co.uk

So Gifted is a general gift website offering ideas for everyone including christening gifts (pretty photo albums and a christening keepsake box) weddings, educational and general gifts for young children and unusual gifts for the home and garden. You'll also find the exquisite range of Rosanna and Café Paris china of beautifully boxed espresso cups, dessert plates and Haute Shoes tea for two which you'll probably want to keep for yourself.

Site Usability:	★★★	Based:	UK
Product Range:	★★★	Express Delivery Option? (UK)	Yes
Price Range:	Medium	Gift Wrapping Option?	No
Delivery Area:	Worldwide	Returns Procedure:	Down to you

Chapter 83

Wedding Gifts

There will always be wedding guests (the really well behaved ones) who are delighted to stick to your list. And there will be others (difficult, like me) who prefer to buy something different and more personal. The gifts that Andrew and I were given that stick most in my mind are of course the ones that we use the most often, the beautiful Italian pewter engraved serving dish which always comes out when I make Tarte Tatin and the Georgian champagne flutes which started our collection of a particular shape of glass. Not that we drink enough champagne, of course. Does anyone?

If you're going to buy from a list then you won't want to look at the websites below now, but you might like to keep them in mind for other special celebrations such as silver wedding anniversaries, as they would be equally good there, or any other occasion where you want to give something memorable.

These websites specialise in the beautiful and the unusual, from antique glass to wonderful modern silver and stylish, and not too expensive home accessories. Ok so you may not be buying something from 'The Wedding List' but you'll definitely be buying something you'll be remembered for.

Sites to Visit.

www.albumania.com

Here's a website where you can find a totally unique kind of present. At Albumania you design your own photo album, box file, guest book, wine book, address book or diary. You just download a photograph (digitally), choose the colour of binding and ribbon, all online and then you can see exactly what the cover of your book will look like. While you're ordering you have the option of adding extra pages and adding a ribbon tied card with your personal message. All the books are gift boxed and take about two weeks.

Site Usability:	★★★★★		Based:	UK
Product Range:	★★★		Express Delivery Option? (UK)	No
Price Range:	Medium		Gift Wrapping Option?	No
Delivery Area:	Worldwide		Returns Procedure:	Down to you

www.antique-glass.co.uk

For a silver wedding gift for someone who you know loves beautiful glass look here, at this website tried and tested by my family several times and where you'll find unique alternatives to the traditional modern silver that many will give. If you're not sure what you're doing give them a call (you cannot order directly online), particularly if you know that the recipient already collects antique glass, and they'll give you the best advice on what to buy for the amount you want to spend.

Site Usability:	★★★★		Based:	UK
Product Range:	★★★★		Express Delivery Option? (UK)	No
Price Range:	Luxury/Medium		Gift Wrapping Option?	No
Delivery Area:	Worldwide		Returns Procedure:	In agreement with them

www.braybrook.com

If you're looking for a really special present then have a browse round this excellent website offering hand made fine silver designed by British master silversmiths and where you can expect to find an extremely personal service. Prices for gifts range upwards from £65, from beautifully coloured glass and silver bowls to gorgeous designs by leading silversmiths for over £1000 and a wide selection at under £200. They offer worldwide delivery, gift wrapping and express delivery.

Site Usability:	★★★★		Based:	UK
Product Range:	★★★★★		Express Delivery Option? (UK)	Yes
Price Range:	Luxury/Medium		Gift Wrapping Option?	Yes
Delivery Area:	Worldwide		Returns Procedure:	Down to you

www.culinaryconcepts.co.uk

Going round the shops looking for a different wedding gift (when you don't want to buy into the wedding list) is sometimes very difficult because classic gifts may well clash with what's already been chosen. Here you'll find some new and clever design ideas including unusual cheese knives and servers, hammered stainless steel bowls and plates and table accessories such as unique sugar and olive bowls, wine buckets and vases.

Site Usability:	★★★★		Based:	UK
Product Range:	★★★★		Express Delivery Option? (UK)	No
Price Range:	Medium		Gift Wrapping Option?	No
Delivery Area:	Worldwide		Returns Procedure:	Down to you

www.juliannebalai.com

Julianne Balai originally specialised in jewellery and glass design and includes as her stockists Harvey Nichols, Liberty and Harrods. On her clear and simple website you can discover her unusual (and expensive) glass art including hand made coloured glass decanters and unique vases, embossed leather photo frames and stylish coffee plungers, all of which would make excellent wedding gifts and that you would be unlikely to come across elsewhere.

Site Usability:	★★★★	Based:	UK
Product Range:	★★★★	Express Delivery Option? (UK)	No
Price Range:	Luxury/Medium	Gift Wrapping Option?	No
Delivery Area:	UK	Returns Procedure:	Down to you

www.mulberryhall.co.uk

Mulberry Hall offers you the opportunity of buying online some of the ranges that they hold in their York shop including brands such as Baccarat, Herend, Lladro, Royal Copenhagen and Waterford. This would be a great place to find gifts for all sorts of occasions and particularly for weddings as there's a beautiful collection of traditional and modern items for the home and they offer a free of charge gift wrapping service.

Site Usability:	★★★★★	Based:	UK
Product Range:	★★★★★	Express Delivery Option? (UK)	No
Price Range:	Luxury/Medium	Gift Wrapping Option?	Yes
Delivery Area:	Worldwide	Returns Procedure:	Down to you

www.smallislandtrader.com

Small Island Trader is an excellent company offering not only china, glass and silver from a wide range of designers and manufacturers including Waterford, Villeroy & Boch and Spode but also kitchen equipment from juicers and steamers to copper and Le Creuset pots and pans, Sabatier knives, baking trays, and unusual kitchen products and homewares. You can order items separately or you may find that the couple you're buying for has selected to use their excellent wedding list service and you can choose from that.

Site Usability:	★★★★★	Based:	UK
Product Range:	★★★★★	Express Delivery Option? (UK)	No
Price Range:	Luxury/Medium	Gift Wrapping Option?	No
Delivery Area:	Worldwide	Returns Procedure:	Down to you

www.thebridagiftbox.co.uk

This is a very attractive website offering (you guessed it) lots of ideas for weddings including jewellery and tiaras for the brides, a wide selection of favours, gifts for pages and bridesmaids and well priced and attractive wedding gift suggestions. Everything is beautifully photographed, the website is easy to navigate and you can use their Wish Mail service to send yourself (or someone else) a reminder if you've seen something you really like.

Site Usability:	★★★★	Based:	UK
Product Range:	★★★★	Express Delivery Option? (UK)	Yes
Price Range:	Medium	Gift Wrapping Option?	No
Delivery Area:	UK	Returns Procedure:	Down to you

www.theolivegrove.co.uk

The Olive Grove online is home to an expanding range of beautiful interior and garden accessories from a number of independent designers alongside leading brands such as Mulberry Home. If you're looking for a slightly unusual wedding gift you would do well to have a look round here, where you can choose from iron candlesticks, glass ice buckets, slate cheeseboards and Mulberry's gorgeous cushions and willow baskets.

Site Usability:	★★★★	Based:	UK
Product Range:	★★★★★	Express Delivery Option? (UK)	Yes
Price Range:	Medium	Gift Wrapping Option?	Yes
Delivery Area:	Europe	Returns Procedure:	Down to you

www.tjklondon.com

At TJK London you'll discover a selection of classic and contemporary silver, wood and leather gifts including jewellery, cufflinks, photo albums and frames designed in-house and sterling silver marmite and jam jar lids, also really lovely glass match strikers/tea light holders with silver hallmarked collars. A bonus here is that everything is automatically gift-wrapped and for a small charge they will also engrave items for you.

Site Usability:	★★★★	Based:	UK
Product Range:	★★★	Express Delivery Option? (UK)	Yes
Price Range:	Luxury/Medium	Gift Wrapping Option?	Luxury packaging is standard
Delivery Area:	Worldwide	Returns Procedure:	Down to you

www.silversmiths.co.uk

Pruden & Smith make beautiful contemporary silver tableware that is spun, hand-raised or forged using traditional silversmith techniques and with their famous hammered finish. This really is modern silver at its best and there's a wide range to choose from. You can't buy directly through the website at the moment but need to email or call them with your enquiry – a small price to pay for such a special range.

Site Usability:	★★★★	Based:	UK
Product Range:	★★★★★	Express Delivery Option? (UK)	Yes for items in stock
Price Range:	Luxury/Medium	Gift Wrapping Option?	Ask them
Delivery Area:	Worldwide	Returns Procedure:	Down to you

Chapter 84

The One Stop Christmas Shop

Inevitably Christmas is the one time you really don't want to *have* to go out and shop; your kids are home from school and want lots of entertaining; you've been invited to several parties and maybe you're giving one yourself; you have an endless stream of people coming to visit, all of whom expect to be fed and you've decided that you'd like to do something special with the Christmas tree this year. All of that putting aside the fact that you may need to work right up to Christmas, too.

I hope that by the time you've reached this section of the book you'll already be taking advantage of the fact that you can have most of your food delivered (well all, actually, but there may be some things you prefer to see and choose yourself). Plus the fact that with the great selection of gifts here, not just in the Gifts section but throughout the book, you shouldn't be battling your way through the crowds to do your Christmas shopping. Yes, ok, you'll have had to do it a little bit earlier than usual to make sure that everything arrives with you on time, but provided you've done that you can relax in the knowledge that it's all going to come to you.

In this chapter I've brought together all my favourite online retailers who offer either specific Christmas essentials, such as crackers, tree lights, trees and decorations plus your Christmas cake, pudding and turkey. Then there are those who provide the finishing touches such as gorgeous table linens, candles and other decorative ideas plus food and drink extras.

Below you'll find websites divided into the following categories:

Christmas cakes and food (including the turkey)
The Christmas Table – candles, crackers, linens and more
Christmas trees, decorations and lighting.

For the following you need to go to other places in the Guide:

Wines, champagne and spirits	Chapter 61
Extra Christmas food	Chapters 51–61
Tea and Coffee	Chapter 60
Christmas Cards	Chapter 72
Ribbon and Wrap	Chapter 73

You can select your presents from the gift websites in Section 9 as well as having a look through some of the other more specific websites in this Guide such as Jewellery (chapter 15), Lingerie (Chapter 7) and Fragrance, Bath and Body (Chapter 33). You'll also find other wonderful food websites in the main food section from Chapter 52 onwards.

The only thing I would say is this. The postal and courier services have improved by leaps and bounds to try to keep pace with our love of online ordering. However, no one is infallible so please allow just that little bit of extra time. Yes, you can have things delivered right up to Christmas and all the retailers should tell you their last ordering days very clearly but don't put these too much to the test. For peace of mind give them an extra few days (or couple of weeks) if you can, to make sure they can get their deliveries out to you on time.

After all, the whole idea of this is not just to give you all that extra choice but also to remove the stress of shopping for Christmas – you want to have some nails left to paint, after all, don't you?

Sites to Visit

Christmas Cakes

www.bettysbypost.com

At bettysbypost.com you can order hand decorated Christmas cakes in a variety of sizes, their family recipe Christmas pudding with fruit soaked in brandy and ale and seasonal favourites such as Christmas Tea Loaf, Panettone and Stollen. Chocolate ginger, miniature Florentines and Peppermint Creams are just a few of the goodies on offer in their confectionary section and you'll also find lovely stocking fillers for children and preserves for the Christmas larder.

Site Usability:	★★★★★	Based:	UK
Product Range:	★★★★	Express Delivery Option? (UK)	No
Price Range:	Medium	Gift Wrapping Option?	No
Delivery Area:	Worldwide	Returns Procedure:	Down to you

www.botham.co.uk

Here you'll find a simple collection of cakes for Christmas and other occasions which you can personalise with your own message or buy un-piped. All cakes are hand decorated and iced so they ask you to give them plenty of notice. They do, however, keep a short order iced fruit cake, piped with Happy Birthday for you to buy by quick delivery. You may well also be tempted by the plum bread, biscuits and preserves on this website and they're happy to ship to you anywhere in the world

Site Usability:	★★★★	Based:	UK
Product Range:	★★★★	Express Delivery Option? (UK)	No
Price Range:	Medium	Gift Wrapping Option?	No
Delivery Area:	Worldwide	Returns Procedure:	Down to you

www.megrivers.com

This is an extremely tempting website offering 'home made' beautifully decorated cakes, biscuits and traybakes; flapjacks, chocolate brownies and Bakewells. Their traditional fruit cakes and Christmas cakes, including a chocolate Christmas cake, are lovely to look at and taste delicious (and I know, I've tried them). If you can't be bothered or don't have the time to bake yourself this Christmas definitely shop here. You won't be disappointed.

Site Usability:	★★★★★	Based:	UK
Product Range:	★★★	Express Delivery Option? (UK)	No
Price Range:	Medium	Gift Wrapping Option?	No
Delivery Area:	Worldwide	Returns Procedure:	Down to you

www.savoirdesign.com

Alongside the wonderful wedding cakes you can order from Savoir Design, for Christmas you can order their traditional fruit cake, either finished with fruit, nuts and gold leaf, or alternatively iced and piped with Merry Christmas. You can also order gift packaged mini mince pies, chocolate truffles and chocolate dipped orange slices.

Site Usability:	★★★★	Based:	UK
Product Range:	★★★	Express Delivery Option? (UK)	No
Price Range:	Luxury/Medium	Gift Wrapping Option?	No
Delivery Area:	UK	Returns Procedure:	Down to you

Online Delis

www.authenticfoodandwine.com

There are a wide range of products here, so it's difficult to know if this retailer should be described as a wine merchant, butcher, fromagerie, or deli – I think food and wine hall probably sums it up the best. Take a look and you'll find a choice of extremely well photographed products including English asparagus (seasonal), Lowland lamb, extra virgin olive oil, preserves by The Wooden Spoon and a very good selection of wines and champagnes, plus wild and farmed smoked salmon, Marasu's chocolates and lots of gift hampers.

Site Usability:	★★★★★	Based:	UK
Product Range:	★★★★★	Express Delivery Option? (UK)	48 hour weekday service
Price Range:	Luxury/Medium	Gift Wrapping Option?	No
Delivery Area:	UK	Returns Procedure:	Down to you

www.formanandfield.com

Forman & Field is a luxury delicatessen specialising in traditional British produce from small independent producers. You'll find a delicious selection of luxury cakes and puddings, smoked salmon, ham and cheeses all beautifully photographed and extremely hard to resist. Don't miss their home made, award winning fish pates and pies, perfect for the next time you're entertaining. They offer speedy delivery to UK, Ireland and the Channel Isles.

Site Usability:	★★★★★	Based:	UK
Product Range:	★★★★★	Express Delivery Option? (UK)	Yes
Price Range:	Luxury/Medium	Gift Wrapping Option?	No
Delivery Area:	UK	Returns Procedure:	Down to you

www.paxtonandwhitfield.co.uk

You can buy a mouth-watering selection of speciality British, French and Italian cheeses here and join the Cheese Society to receive their special selection each month. They also sell biscuits, chutneys and pickles, York ham and pates, beautifully boxed cheese knives and stores, fondue sets and raclette machines. This is really the place find all the cheeses you need here for Christmas plus some excellent gifts for cheese lovers.

Site Usability:	★★★★★	Based:	UK
Product Range:	★★★★	Express Delivery Option? (UK)	Yes
Price Range:	Luxury/Medium	Gift Wrapping Option?	No
Delivery Area:	Worldwide	Returns Procedure:	Down to you

Specialist Food Suppliers

www.canapeum.com

You know, those delicious little bite size nibbles that you have at drinks parties that used to be quite simple and now are more and more complicated, using ingredients such as lobster, foie gras, tapenade and pastrami. At Canapeum you just calculate how many canapes you need then choose which ones you want to order. Prices range from reasonable to quite expensive but when you think of all that fiddling in the kitchen you won't have to do at your next party you may well think them worth a go.

Site Usability:	★★★	Based:	UK
Product Range:	★★★★	Express Delivery Option? (UK)	No
Price Range:	Luxury/Medium	Gift Wrapping Option?	No
Delivery Area:	UK	Returns Procedure:	Down to you but only if there's a problem

www.christmasdinnercompany.co.uk

If you really don't have the time to order all your Christmas ingredients online and prepare your feast yourself then let The Christmas Dinner Company do everything for you. They'll select the best ingredients – a Kelly Bronze turkey, Duchy Originals stuffings and cocktail sausages, Joubere gravy, cranberry sauce and Mrs Ray's Christmas pudding and pack them off to you with ready peeled spuds, brandy butter and mince pies. Cooking guidelines, a suggested time plan and recipe leftover ideas are included too.

Site Usability:	★★★★	Based:	UK
Product Range:	★★★	Express Delivery Option? (UK)	No
Price Range:	Luxury	Gift Wrapping Option?	No
Delivery Area:	UK	Returns Procedure:	Down to you but only if there's a problem

www.donaldrussell.com

This is a superb website from an excellent butcher, beautifully photographed and laid out and extremely tempting. You can buy just about every type of meat here, from free range goose and game (in season) to pork, beef and lamb plus natural fish and seafood. Most of the pictures show the products as you'd like them to arrive on your plate and you can either buy from their ready prepared dishes such as Salmon en Croute, Smoked Salmon Pate or Bolognese sauce or you can follow their excellent receipes.

Site Usability:	★★★★★	Based:	UK
Product Range:	★★★★★	Express Delivery Option? (UK)	No
Price Range:	Luxury/Medium	Gift Wrapping Option?	No
Delivery Area:	UK	Returns Procedure:	Down to you

www.dukeshillham.co.uk

Dukeshill was founded over 20 years ago with the aim of producing the very best hams, cured the 'old fashioned' way (where flavour and texture are more important than speed or yield). Today, alongside their hams, you can also buy bacon and other cured meats, fish terrines and smoked salmon, regional cheeses, condiments and preserves and mouth-watering looking cakes. Once you've ordered your ham you'll no doubt be tempted by the rest – I certainly was.

Site Usability:	★★★★★	Based:	UK
Product Range:	★★★★	Express Delivery Option? (UK)	Yes
Price Range:	Medium	Gift Wrapping Option?	No
Delivery Area:	UK	Returns Procedure:	Down to you in agreement with them

www.frenchgourmetstore.com

Here you'll discover a marvellous selection of regional gourmet products from France, all prepared according to traditional recipes and including mushrooms and truffles, mustards, oils and vinegars and gorgeous chocolates. They also have a small but excellent range of hampers and gift baskets. They're actually based in the UK, will ship to you anywhere in the world and offer an express service.

Site Usability:	★★★★★	Based:	France
Product Range:	★★★★	Express Delivery Option? (UK)	Yes
Price Range:	Luxury/Medium	Gift Wrapping Option?	No
Delivery Area:	Worldwide	Returns Procedure:	Down to you

www.lakelandlimited.co.uk

If you thought (as I always have) that Lakeland was about gifts and gizmos for the kitchen and home and clever picnic and tableware then think again. A selection of chocolates, Bay Tree Turkish Delight, Apricots in Moscato, Candied Fruits, Marrons Glace, olive oils, jalapeno spiced nuts plus the famous Australian Celebration Cake are just some of the goodies they offer at Christmas. Couple this with Lakeland's emphasis on quality and service and you certainly won't go wrong when you place an order here.

Site Usability:	★★★★★	Based:	UK
Product Range:	★★★★★	Express Delivery Option? (UK)	Yes
Price Range:	Medium/Very Good Value	Gift Wrapping Option?	No
Delivery Area:	Worldwide	Returns Procedure:	Down to you

Christmas Puddings

www.georgieporgiespuddings.co.uk

These traditional Christmas puddings are made with all the ingredients you'd expect from the home-made variety, including currants, sultanas, raisins and orange peel, brandy, rum and spices. They're available in a choice of sizes, from a tiny one person pudding to one large enough to feed fifteen. Other puddings and deserts on offer are Cider and Apple, Orange and Cointreau, Lemon and Pimms, treacle sponge and Spotted Dick. This one's definitely not good for the diet.

Site Usability:	★★★★	Based:	UK
Product Range:	★★★	Express Delivery Option? (UK)	No
Price Range:	Medium	Gift Wrapping Option?	No
Delivery Area:	UK	Returns Procedure:	Down to you

www.thecarvedangel.com

At thecarvedangel.com you'll find their famous Christmas pud, which you can order in three sizes to feed up to a dozen people. All the puddings are traditionally presented in a re-usable earthenware bowl that is dishwater and microwave safe and then hand tied with a muslin cloth and ribbon with cooking instructions attached. You can buy your brandy butter here as well. Allow at least 14 days for delivery

Site Usability:	★★★★	Based:	UK
Product Range:	★★★	Express Delivery Option? (UK)	No
Price Range:	Medium	Gift Wrapping Option?	No
Delivery Area:	UK	Returns Procedure:	Down to you

Turkeys

www.kelly-turkeys.com

Recommended as the turkey du jour by celebrity chefs, you can order your traditionally farmed Kelly Bronze turkey directly from their website. Select your turkey by weight on their order form and it will be delivered to you, close to Christmas, in their insulated cool boxes. There are lots of recipes and advice on storing, preparing and cooking your turkey plus delicious suggestions on how to use it afterwards.

Site Usability:	★★★★	Based:	UK
Product Range:	★★★	Express Delivery Option? (UK)	No
Price Range:	Medium	Gift Wrapping Option?	No
Delivery Area:	UK	Returns Procedure:	Down to you

www.realmeat.co.uk

The Real Meat Company supplies excellent quality meat and poultry from traditional farmers with a nationwide delivery service. You can order your turkey from them for Christmas from mid-November. Their minimum order value is £35 and you can specify the day you want your delivery. Remember to allow them enough time in the run up to Christmas.

Site Usability:	★★★	Based:	UK
Product Range:	★★★	Express Delivery Option? (UK)	No
Price Range:	Medium	Gift Wrapping Option?	No
Delivery Area:	UK	Returns Procedure:	Down to you

Also take a look at the websites in the Food and Drink Section for other places to find food for Christmas.

The Christmas Table

Living in a 17th Century farmhouse as we do, our Christmas table is always of the traditional kind although we've moved away from the green and gold towards white candles, white and gold crackers and white china which is definitely a refreshing improvement.

Christmas is a time when, if you're allowed to by your family, you can experiment, and it can be great fun as by spending just a little extra you can create a totally different look. If you steer well away from Christmas themed cloths, napkins and crockery (please, please do), you can also invest in items that will look really special during the season, and then work for you all the year round.

We tend to have a very tall tree, as we have a pipe sunk into the floor of our barn specially to hold it (thank goodness my mother-in-law gave us that idea before the flooring was finished). What a difference it makes – no more balancing the tree in a large pot or yards of red tissue paper round the base. In it goes, all sixteen or so feet of it and with no more than a few small bits of wood to act as wedges there it stays.

Sites to Visit

Candles

www.candle-city.co.uk

There are lots of places you can buy candles online but few with as comprehensive selection as you'll find here, with a very good range of Price's dinner candles, plus Yankee Candles, Colonial, Pintail (those little tins of fragranced candles), Claremont and May and more.

Site Usability:	★★★	Based:	UK
Product Range:	★★★★	Express Delivery Option? (UK)	No
Price Range:	Medium	Gift Wrapping Option?	No
Delivery Area:	Worldwide	Returns Procedure:	Down to you

www.candlesontheweb.co.uk

This is a very unsophisticated candle website but offering an amazing range of dinner candles and tea lights, church and pillar candles, hand dipped beeswax candles and a gold and silver range. They also have a very good choice of extra large candles which you can pay a fortune for elsewhere and a Christmas collection which includes gold and beaded candles and Christmas fragrances.

Site Usability:	★★★	Based:	UK
Product Range:	★★★★	Express Delivery Option? (UK)	No
Price Range:	Medium/Very Good Value	Gift Wrapping Option?	No
Delivery Area:	UK	Returns Procedure:	Down to you

www.onestopcandleshop.co.uk

Here you'll find very well priced dinner candles in a wide choice of colours including gold and silver, tea lights (again available in gold and silver as well as plain and scented ranges), a huge selection of candle holders for all sizes of candles, from individual holders to multi candle sconces and some gift ideas. They offer express and standard delivery to the UK mainland so it you live in the Highlands and Islands you need to call them for delivery.

Site Usability:	★★★	Based:	UK
Product Range:	★★★	Express Delivery Option? (UK)	Yes
Price Range:	Medium/Very Good Value	Gift Wrapping Option?	No
Delivery Area:	UK	Returns Procedure:	Down to you

www.parkscandles.com

This is quite a small website offering a beautiful range of scented candles in decorative containers, triple wick candles in silver bowls and perfumed candles in glass containers some of which would look lovely on a Christmas table. They also offer scented dinner candles in green, burgundy and cream and nothing here is overpriced. Expect speedy delivery and excellent service.

Site Usability:	★★★★	Based:	UK
Product Range:	★★★	Express Delivery Option? (UK)	Yes
Price Range:	Medium	Gift Wrapping Option?	No
Delivery Area:	Worldwide	Returns Procedure:	Down to you

www.thecandlecollection.co.uk

This is an elegantly designed website with a good range of candles by Price, Arco, Parks, Kenneth Turner and Shearer in just about every colour you could need. They also offer decorative candles (perfect for gifts) and tea light holders and all the essentials including tapers, lamp oil, alcohol gel and Parks of London refills. They'll ship worldwide.

Site Usability:	★★★★	Based:	UK
Product Range:	★★★★★	Express Delivery Option? (UK)	Yes
Price Range:	Medium	Gift Wrapping Option?	No
Delivery Area:	Worldwide	Returns Procedure:	Down to you

www.thecandlelightcompany.co.uk

Here's a very clear and easy to use candle website offering not only high quality dinner and church candles but also an interesting selection of novelties, pretty candles in boxes, scented candles and gel fish bowl candles which would be very good children's gifts. There are also some attractive candle and tea light holders. Delivery is free on orders over £50.

Site Usability:	★★★★	Based:	UK
Product Range:	★★★★	Express Delivery Option? (UK)	No
Price Range:	Medium	Gift Wrapping Option?	Yes
Delivery Area:	Worldwide	Returns Procedure:	Down to you

Garlands and Table Decorations

www.festive-dresser.co.uk

There are some really different and beautifully made decorations here including both circular and heart shaped wreaths incorporating beads, feathers, jewels and even marabou plus the more traditional autumn foliage and berries. You'll also find exquisite table decorations – beaded and feathered napkin rings, glass decorations and candle rings and garlands to decorate your home.

Site Usability:	★★★★	Based:	UK
Product Range:	★★★	Express Delivery Option? (UK)	No
Price Range:	Medium	Gift Wrapping Option?	No
Delivery Area:	UK	Returns Procedure:	Down to you

www.mithus.co.uk

This online home retailer offers mainly Scandinavian style home accessories including chic table-linens, candleholders and vases, photo frames, cushions, and rugs plus an excellent range of dinner and pillar candles in an unusual selection of colours. For Christmas there are wreaths and garlands, enchanting lights and candles and traditional decorations.

Site Usability:	★★★★	Based:	UK
Product Range:	★★★★	Express Delivery Option? (UK)	No
Price Range:	Medium	Gift Wrapping Option?	No
Delivery Area:	UK	Returns Procedure:	Down to you

www.pier.co.uk

For really gorgeous and unusual Christmas ribbon and wrap, decorations and candles, pretty tableware for Christmas day, beaded and sequinned cushions and throws you should really take a look round here, where you can not only decorate your tree, wrap your presents and create the perfect festive table for but do a lot of your Christmas shopping as well.

Site Usability:	★★★★★	Based:	UK
Product Range:	★★★★★	Express Delivery Option? (UK)	No
Price Range:	Medium	Gift Wrapping Option?	No
Delivery Area:	UK	Returns Procedure:	Down to you

Tablelinen

www.french-brand.com

This is a France based retailer offering you all those home accessories you saw on your last trip but weren't able to sneak into your suitcase. Gorgeous and colourful table linens from Les Olivades and Jaquard Francais (and lots more), quilted cushions by Souleido and toiletries and home fragrance by Manuel Canovas and Jardin Secret are just some of the things you can order online.

Site Usability:	★★★★	Based:	France
Product Range:	★★★★★	Express Delivery Option? (UK)	No
Price Range:	Luxury/Medium	Gift Wrapping Option?	No
Delivery Area:	Worldwide	Returns Procedure:	Down to you

www.purpleandfinelinen.co.uk

At Purple and Fine Linen their pure linen tablecloths, placemats, napkins and runners are designed to offer a look of timeless luxury and simple elegance. As well as traditional white and ivory you can also choose from their range in deep chilli red and damson (purple), which would be lovely for Christmas. These are investment linens rather than the throw away variety but very beautiful.

Site Usability:	★★★★★	Based:	UK
Product Range:	★★★	Express Delivery Option? (UK)	Yes
Price Range:	Luxury/Medium	Gift Wrapping Option?	No
Delivery Area:	Worldwide	Returns Procedure:	Down to you

www.thewhitecompany.com

Every year The White Company's range increases and improves and there are far too many lovely and tempting things to buy. If you're buying for your Christmas table here you'll be investing in timeless tablelinen, crockery, glassware and candles that will not only be perfect for just about any Christmas table but also last you right through the future seasons. Not only that but you'll find lots of excellent gift ideas here as well.

Site Usability:	★★★★★	Based:	UK
Product Range:	★★★★★	Express Delivery Option? (UK)	Yes
Price Range:	Medium	Gift Wrapping Option?	Yes
Delivery Area:	Worldwide	Returns Procedure:	Down to you

www.volgalinen.co.uk

Update your table linen this Christmas with the exquisite collection of Russian table linen from the Volga Linen Company. The collection consists of richly coloured paisley, white and natural double damask and bordered linen table cloths, placements and napkins, with all tablecloths available in a selection of sizes. Nothing is inexpensive but then you shouldn't expect it to be, as you're buying the very best quality.

Site Usability:	★★★★★	Based:	UK
Product Range:	★★★	Express Delivery Option? (UK)	No
Price Range:	Luxury/Medium	Gift Wrapping Option?	No
Delivery Area:	Worldwide	Returns Procedure:	Down to you

Crackers

www.christmascrackershop.co.uk

However you want your table to look this Christmas you'll almost certainly find some crackers here to match your theme. You can select from jumbo and 'fill your own' crackers to their excellently priced choices in gold, red, green, glittered sprinkled silver and Santa embellished together with their range of sizes. They ship worldwide and aim to despatch everything within 48 hours.

Site Usability:	★★★★	Based:	UK
Product Range:	★★★	Express Delivery Option? (UK)	No
Price Range:	Luxury/Medium	Gift Wrapping Option?	No
Delivery Area:	Worldwide excl US	Returns Procedure:	Down to you

www.gocrackers.co.uk

Don't wait for the last minute to order your crackers online from this excellent website. I suggest you go for it sometime during November or you may find that your chosen design has sold out. You'll find a wide selection here from the unusual (leopard print) crackers to much more traditional red and gold, burgundy and green script and holly design and there's also a wide range of high quality Christmas paper napkins to choose from.

Site Usability:	★★★★	Based:	UK
Product Range:	★★★	Express Delivery Option? (UK)	No
Price Range:	Luxury/Medium	Gift Wrapping Option?	No
Delivery Area:	UK	Returns Procedure:	Down to you

www.froufrouandthomas.co.uk

OK, so this year your crackers are going to be really special (and I mean really special). Here you'll find 'couture' crackers, totally handmade and utterly luxurious. You choose your cracker design from their selection and then whatever you want to go inside from Jasmine scented bath confetti to a mother-of-pearl caviar spoon. They also offer matching wrapping papers and ribbons and other Christmas treats.

Site Usability:	★★★★	Based:	UK
Product Range:	★★★	Express Delivery Option? (UK)	No
Price Range:	Luxury	Gift Wrapping Option?	No
Delivery Area:	UK	Returns Procedure:	Down to you

www.simplycrackers.co.uk

On this innovative website you can choose from their standard ranges which go from luxury crackers at £36 for six to mini gold and silver after dinner crackers (and in some cases you can select different types of gifts) to their 'Create your own Cracker' range where you literally choose everything from the paper colour, wording (or photo) and decoration to what goes inside.

Site Usability:	★★★★	Based:	UK
Product Range:	★★★★	Express Delivery Option? (UK)	No
Price Range:	Luxury	Gift Wrapping Option?	No
Delivery Area:	UK	Returns Procedure:	Down to you

Christmas Trees, Decorations and Lighting

www.chatsworth-dec.co.uk

If you're fed up of spending a lot of money on Christmas decorations or having to go round the heaving stores to buy them then you should take a look at this website, mainly designed to supply the leisure industry but with no minimum order value; happy to sell to you too. You'll find lots of very inexpensive Christmas decorations, baubles, tinsel and the like as well as a host of other products such as party hats, novelties and lights.

Site Usability:	★★★★	Based:	UK
Product Range:	★★★★★	Express Delivery Option? (UK)	No
Price Range:	Medium	Gift Wrapping Option?	No
Delivery Area:	UK	Returns Procedure:	Down to you

www.christmastreeland.co.uk

Christmas Tree Land have a very clear site offering trees from 3ft to 45ft and delivery to anywhere in the UK. There's a wide range of trees from Noble Firs to Norwegian Spruce and your tree will be delivered to you well in time for Christmas. They will take your order very close to Christmas but I would suggest you allow plenty of time. You can also choose from a range of artificial trees here from the pre-lit Colorado fir to fashion trees in different colours, fibre optic trees, wreaths and decorations.

Site Usability:	★★★★	Based:	UK
Product Range:	★★★★	Express Delivery Option? (UK)	No
Price Range:	Medium	Gift Wrapping Option?	No
Delivery Area:	UK	Returns Procedure:	Down to you

www.grovelands.com

You'll find a wide range of Christmas trees both real and artificial here, tree lights, pretty traditional ornaments from Germany and a good selection of gifts such as Victorinox cyber tools, gardeners tools and accessories, table football and compendium table games. So this could really be a one stop shop this Christmas.

Site Usability:	★★★★	Based:	UK
Product Range:	★★★★★	Express Delivery Option? (UK)	No
Price Range:	Medium	Gift Wrapping Option?	No
Delivery Area:	Worldwide	Returns Procedure:	Down to you

www.peeks.co.uk

Peeks is a family company established in 1946. Originally retailers of cards and toys, they have now developed their products to include themed party items (for occasions such as Halloween) games and other gift ideas and just about everything for Christmas including tree decorations, tinsel and garlands, artificial trees, crackers and balloons.

Site Usability:	★★★★★	Based:	UK
Product Range:	★★★★	Express Delivery Option? (UK)	No
Price Range:	Medium/Very Good Value	Gift Wrapping Option?	No
Delivery Area:	Worldwide	Returns Procedure:	Down to you

www.xmastreesales.com

A very clear site offering just freshly cut Christmas trees, they offer free 3 day UK mainland delivery, £4.99 for next day service and you can order right up to Christmas. The choice of trees is simple with the main varieties being Norway Spruce (the traditional tree), Nordman Fir (Non Drop Needles) and Noble Fir (Slightly Scented Tree). They also give you advice on which tree to choose.

Site Usability:	★★★★	Based:	UK
Product Range:	★★★★	Express Delivery Option? (UK)	Yes
Price Range:	Medium	Gift Wrapping Option?	No
Delivery Area:	UK	Returns Procedure:	Down to you

www.xmastreesdirect.co.uk

There's a great deal to look at on this Christmas website; from high quality real and artificial trees, tree stands, lights (including bulb testers, transformers, motors and sensors), to artificial wreaths and holly, tree baubles and a lovely selection of unusual ribbons and Christmas stockings.

Site Usability:	★★★★	Based:	UK
Product Range:	★★★★	Express Delivery Option? (UK)	Yes
Price Range:	Medium	Gift Wrapping Option?	No
Delivery Area:	UK	Returns Procedure:	Down to you

Section 10
Travel Made Easy

Travel Made Easy

This is not pretending to be a travel guide – there are plenty of other people who are expert at telling you where to go and visit, where to stay and eat out and how to get the best package deal. However, being a travel addict myself and having been asked many times about the best places online to book flights, car hire, ferry crossings and the like I decided to include this information so if you don't want to use one of the large travel companies but want to make your own arrangements, then you can just look here and find the best booking websites all together.

There are other excellent travel services websites online; from checking how many dollars you'll get for your pounds to ordering foreign currency online, from buying travel health insurance to paying the dreaded London Congestion Charge. You'll find them all here plus indispensable mapping and driving direction websites for wherever you are, or plan to visit, in the world.

Chapter 85

Essential Travel Websites

Currency Conversions

www.thomascook.com

This is a huge travel website, offering excellent deals on holidays all over the world, plus airport hotels, airport parking and other assistance. Wherever you're going and whether or not you've booked through Thomas Cook you could try out their foreign currency ordering service. Not only will you get extremely good rates but you can pay using your credit card and receive your currency at no extra charge by express courier the next day. It certainly beats standing in the queue at the bank.

www.xe.com

Don't go anywhere without using this website to check on how much you should be getting for your pounds and pence. You can convert any kind of currency into another instantly and even if you're going to order your currency elsewhere online or go down to the bank you should check the rate you're getting here as well. Just go to the home page, scroll down to the XE Quick Currency Converter and you're away.

Driving Directions

www.getamap.co.uk

This is a really speedy website containing all the Ordnance Survey maps. You just click on the area of the UK you want a map for then click again to get as close as you want. You can also search for maps anywhere in the UK simply by entering the place name, full postcode or National Grid reference – and print the maps or copy them for use on your personal or business web site. Buy maps online here too from detailed explorer maps to historical maps showing you how your town looked a hundred years ago.

www.maporama.co.uk

Here's a very easy way to find a route from one place to another with clear directions and zoom in features and this works for just about anywhere in the world. You can also see exactly where major airports are throughout the world with maps which you can zoom in on, send by email, export to your PDA or print out and use their quick links to maps of New York, Chicago, Los Angeles, London, San Francisco and Hong Kong.

www.multimap.co.uk

Multimap.com is one of Europe's most popular mapping websites, offering a range of free, useful services including street-level maps of the United Kingdom, Europe, and the US, road maps of the world, door-to-door travel directions, aerial photographs and lots of local information.

www.streetmap.co.uk

If you're looking for a particular road or street then this site will provide clear and detailed maps of exactly where you want to be. It's a simple website and although it seems to be also trying to offer you lots of other services what you really want to do here is type in the postcode, street name or even telephone dialling code and what you'll get is an excellent, clear street map without any of the frills.

www.viamichelin.com

Via Michelin will help you with all your European travel planning by giving you driving directions, across countries, to anywhere you want. You just key in your starting point and your destination and it'll tell you exactly how to get there, no matter how many borders you're crossing. It'll give you hotels and restaurants on the way and even tell you how much the tolls are going to be.

Motoring in London

www.cclondon.com

Use this site to register your car for the congestion charge and then don't, don't, don't forget to pay it when you drive into London. Although it's a complete nuisance this is by far the easiest way of paying and you can book days, weeks and months ahead. You can also get set up to use SMS text messaging so that you can pay from your mobile phone.

Traffic Information

www.rac.co.uk

Go to the main RAC website and click on Traffic News in the left hand margin. Key in the area and road your interested in and you'll get comprehensive information about what's going on (some of which you probably won't want to hear). Roadworks, delays, accidents – it's all there, giving you a chance to change your route. You can also visit the RAC main website from here.

Chapter 86

Car Hire, Ferries, Trains and Planes – Book them all online and get the best deals

Car Hire Here and Abroad

www.avis.co.uk

Avis have an extremely efficient online system for choosing your pick-up point and selecting your car just about anywhere in the world. You can also sign up for their Premium Service which means they keep all your details so you don't have to queue each time you pick up your car.

www.budget.com

If you're travelling to the USA always check the prices at www.budget.com for countrywide car hire as they often have some very good deals and special offers. With full descriptions of the types of car you can hire (number of passengers, amount of luggage) you can be certain that what will be waiting for you is what you've been expecting and in my experience their staff are some of the most helpful you'll come across.

www.hertz.co.uk

Fly to any airport in the world and pick up the car of your choice at your prearranged price. Check for locations for picking up and dropping off. With so many different destinations you need to make sure that you know whether you're going to have to pay extra taxes and insurances (and other charges) before you go (particularly for the USA) so make sure you read the small print.

Other car hire websites you may want to take a look at:

www.alamo.com
www.europcar.co.uk
www.nationalcar.co.uk

Ferries and Eurotunnel

www.brittanyferries.co.uk

If you want to take your car to Caen, St Malo, Roscoff or Santander then this is the site to use to book your journey. Book early to ensure you get the cabin of your choice and really early if you're planning to go in the holiday season. You'll find clear route guides and timetables here and you can combine your crossing with one of their holiday offers for self-catering and hotel accommodation throughout France and Spain.

www.condorferries.co.uk

Condor Ferries giant high-speed sea-cat sails from Poole and Weymouth to St Malo via Jersey or Guernsey. The company also runs a conventional five hour ferry crossing service for those who want to take a large vehicle or motor-home across. This is much the fastest way to get to St Malo but only runs during spring and summer months as the sea-cat does not suit rough seas.

www.eurotunnel.com

Eurotunnel will take you and your car from Folkestone to Calais and make the crossing in just 35 minutes. If you're slightly late for your train you can usually get onto the next one (except in peak times) as they leave every 20 minutes. A word of warning: don't forget your roofbox is on top when you drive towards the train. It's really not a good idea and no we didn't quite manage it, just very, very nearly.

www.ferries.org

Ferries.org promise to find you the cheapest current fare from a variety of major ferry operators including P & O, Stena Line, Sea France and Brittany Ferries. Sometimes this works and sometimes it doesn't because the ferry operators have special offers in very short timescales so check here and then go to the main operator's website and check there too.

www.irishferries.com

Taking you from Holyhead and Pembroke across to Dublin and Rosslare and then on down to Cherbourg and Roscoff, Irish Ferries offer you an extremely modern fleet including Ulysses, the World's largest car ferry. There's lots of information on this website about timetables and fares, on board shopping and upgrades to their Club class and (yes you guessed it) offers for holidays in Ireland.

www.wightlink.co.uk

Wightlink Isle of Wight Ferries operates a round-the-clock service between the English mainland and the Isle of Wight. They run every day of the year on three routes across the Solent and sail up to 230 times a day so if you want to cross over to the Isle of Wight, with or without your car, this is the place for you.

www.poferries.com

P&O ferries offer ferry crossings to and from the South to Calais, Le Havre, Cherbourg and Bilbao plus Zebrugge and Rotterdam from Hull and across the Irish Sea. Register your car details to make the site even quicker to use. You can book online and if you're thinking of using another website to make your booking with P & O check the price here before you do so as you'll often find excellent special offers at certain times of the year.

www.superfast.com

Superfast Ferries offer you a high quality service whether you're traveling between Italy and Greece, between Finland and Germany, or between Scotland and Belgium. You can download their Booking Request Form and fax it back to them or book online.

Flight Information

www.baa.com

The British Airports Authority website provides real time arrival and departure information for all UK airports together with excellent car parking information, travel insurance and a foreign currency ordering service. You can book Executive Lounge passes here whatever cabin you're flying in and check out the shop and restaurant listings for your airport and terminal. This is a great site to use before you fly and if you're meeting someone.

Take the Train – anywhere in Europe and the US

www.amtrak.com

Thinking of crossing the US by train? Click onto Amtrak's website, use their station list to input starting points and destinations then book your Superliner Roomette (or normal seat) for the journey. There's lots of help on the site on how to book and what type of seat or accommodation to reserve plus anything else you might need to know before making your booking.

www.eurostar.com

Eurostar will take you to Paris or Lille at high speed and will also connect you to over 100 destinations across Europe. There are special offers on the site and information about new connections plus City Guides for Brussels. Always check the Eurostar site prices before booking it through anyone else. However, there are very often good rates for upgrades to first class on websites such as www.driveline.co.uk and www.leisuredirection.co.uk.

www.nationalrail.com

There's a great deal going on this website, from train and coach ticket information for anywhere in the UK, times, fare types, luggage allowances and online booking to ferry crossings and the seemingly inevitable plane tickets, hotels and theatres. The train and coach service in particular is really excellent and easy to use.

www.raileurope.co.uk.

This is the place to book your Eurostar, TGV and high speed rail travel right across Europe. If you're a skiing or snowboarding fan you'll also be able to book the snow trains which take you from Waterloo right into the heart of the French Alps. If you want to make your journey in the summertime easier and put your car on the train all the way from Calais down to Nice or Narbonne you'll find all the information about French Motorail here as well. You can check on the interactive map at www.raileurope.com (US based) to decide on the route you want to take then use the online booking service here to get you there.

Chapter 87

General Travel Planning

www.dontforgetyourtoothbrush.com

I don't know about you, but every time I make out the holiday packing list I leave something off. Well now there's no excuse. On this clever website you'll be able to tick off every possible item for lots of different types of holiday. You just check the boxes and print off your list.

www.frommers.com

If you're planning a trip to the USA you'll need this website. US based Frommers are experts on trips within the USA (and throughout the world), helping you with hotels, flights, cars and cruises. One of the best things about this site is that you don't need to know much about the country when you start, they offer you a wealth of information. Once you've decided on a city or place to visit you can find out about nightlife, restaurants, shopping, walking tours, activities and everything else you can possibly think of.

www.viamichelin.com

Via Michelin will help you with all your European travel planning, whether you want to find a restaurant in Paris, a road map of Zurich or a hotel in Milan. This is the online version of the famous Red Guides but unlike the Red Guides, where the road maps are extremely limited (the town maps are excellent), here you just key in your starting point and your destination and it'll tell you exactly how to get there, no matter how many borders you're crossing. You can find hotels and restaurants on the way and even how much the tolls are going to be.

The All-In-One Travel Websites

www.ebookers.co.uk

www.expedia.co.uk

www.lastminute.com

www.travelocity.co.uk

On all these major travel websites you can compare flight prices for different airlines for anywhere in the World and book your hotels and car hire at the same time (sometimes making some good savings). So to get a general idea of what you're going to be looking at pricewise; check on one (or two) of these first.

You'll also find that you can book absolutely everything else for your trip, from car hire to hotels, theatre tickets, rugby matches abroad and restaurants. If you need it they'll probably already have thought of it for you.

Always check flight prices with the individual airline of your choice as well – you may find a better deal (not always, but sometimes) and you may get offered flight times that suit you better; after all, the cheapest flights here will be out of peak times and the combinations are usually fixed.

You'll find in particular that www.ebookers.co.uk can be very good for flight upgrades, www.expedia.co.uk has the best hotel guide for anywhere in the world, www.lastminute.com gives you more flexibility on flight times and more add-ons such as theatres and restaurants and www.travelocity.co.uk will let you know when your flight comes down in price.

Budget Flights

Where flights only are concerned all the airlines are competing heavily with the cut price carriers such as www.easyjet.com and www.ryanair.com.

My advice here is to think very carefully before you take advantage of the seemingly too-good-too-be-true prices you'll find from these carriers. Use them only if you don't mind queuing like a herd of cattle both to check in and to board your flight and you don't care that the airport you're flying in to may, in fact, be nowhere near your actual destination even though it bears (or they give it) the same name. Often these cheap flights are a false economy as you then have to train, bus or taxi for many miles to reach the place you probably thought you were flying to in the first place.

Be aware also (and I'm speaking from recent experience of EasyJet) that customer service really and truly may not care about you and your particular circumstance and you will have an unbelievably frustrating time trying to contact them.

Luggage and Travel Accessories

OK, I'll admit it; this is really one of my favourite areas as I love to travel. I book absolutely everything online, getting details of flights and checking out hotels down to the rooms themselves first and then going for it. I rarely book flights, hotels and car hire altogether as I prefer to be absolutely sure that I'm getting the type of room I want and the best car hire deal. That's not to say that you shouldn't book everything together, I just prefer not to (and I probably drive my family mad in the process).

For those who are also travel addicts, having the right kit (and by right I mean in terms of efficiency rather than 'of the moment') is essential, as is having the latest information, so if you know someone who's like me take a look below and get some ideas.

Sites to Visit

www.cntraveller.com

For a really excellent (and reasonably priced) gift for the travel lover just click on to the website for Condé Nast's luxury travel magazine, then go through to subscribe. You can give the gift of 3 or 12 months' subscription which (at time of writing) comes with the CN Traveller Privilege Card, enabling the recipient to save on luxury holidays worldwide. While you're on this website you'll no doubt want to have a browse too through the mouth-watering lists of wonderful places to go to next.

Site Usability:	★★★★★	Based:	UK
Product Range:	★★★★★	Express Delivery Option? (UK)	No
Price Range:	Medium	Gift Wrapping Option?	No
Delivery Area:	Worldwide		

www.goplanetgo.co.uk

If you don't find something here to give as a gift to someone who's addicted to travel it would be really surprising as the range, of both products and prices, is enormous. There's everything from Mini Compact iPod speakers and DVD players, clever chargers and gadgets, essentials from leather organisers to stylish toiletry bags and their own well edited selection of gifts such as tiny camera tripods, aluminium travel games, TVR multi function tools and spirit level cufflinks.

Site Usability:	★★★★★	Based:	UK
Product Range:	★★★★★	Express Delivery Option? (UK)	No
Price Range:	Medium/Very Good Value	Gift Wrapping Option?	No
Delivery Area:	Worldwide	Returns Procedure	Down to you

www.essentials4travel.co.uk

This is one of the best travel product and luggage websites offering everything from classic and well priced luggage by brands such as Antler, Travelpro and Skyflite to business cases and laptop bags, travel wallets, backpacks and wheeled duffles. You can also order your Michelin Red Guides and road atlases here plus electric and PDA adaptors. They do have a small Gift Ideas section but you might like also to look in Gadgets and Electronics for something for the traveller in your family.

Site Usability:	★★★★★	Based:	UK
Product Range:	★★★★★	Express Delivery Option? (UK)	No
Price Range:	Medium	Gift Wrapping Option?	No
Delivery Area:	Worldwide	Returns Procedure:	Down to you

www.nomadtravel.co.uk

If you know someone who's about to take off on safari or into the jungle firstly introduce them to this website, which offers a good, highly edited range of efficient and well priced travel clothing including lightweight trousers, zip-offs and vented shirts, base layer fleece and thermals, lots of advice on health abroad and on travelling with children. Then you could buy them a Nomad gift voucher, so they can buy anything they like, or choose for them from the wide range of travel essentials such as maps, compasses, binoculars and guides.

Site Usability:	★★★★★	Based:	UK
Product Range:	★★★★	Express Delivery Option? (UK)	Yes
Price Range:	Medium	Gift Wrapping Option?	No
Delivery Area:	Worldwide	Returns Procedure:	Down to you

www.timetospa.com

Time to Spa offers Elemis face and body products in excellent travel collections, perfect for those on the go. This is not a general retailer so much as a beauty salon, where you can register for an online consultation by one of their team of therapists for advice on your beauty regimen, find out about food and fitness for health and have your beauty questions answered. If you purchase from their online shop you'll find lots of gift ideas and can take advantage of their gift wrapping service.

Site Usability:	★★★★★	Based:	UK
Product Range:	★★★★	Express Delivery Option? (UK)	Yes
Price Range:	Medium	Gift Wrapping Option?	Yes
Delivery Area:	Worldwide	Returns Procedure:	Down to you

www.viator.com

Viator is a US-based travel company offering lots of information and advice on where to go and what to do when you arrive just about anywhere in the world. You can buy their gift certificates which can be used to purchase any of the 4,500+ suggested activities that you'll find here. A helicopter tour in Las Vegas? You bet. A hot-air balloon ride in Italy? Of course. Swimming with sharks in Australia? Absolutely. Simply choose the gift certificate you want in the recipient's local currency and let them do the rest.

Site Usability:	★★★★	Based:	UK
Product Range:	★★★★★	Express Delivery Option? (UK)	No
Price Range:	Luxury/Medium	Gift Wrapping Option?	No
Delivery Area:	Worldwide		

www.zpm.com

If you know someone who does a lot of travelling then you'll find a perfect gift here, as ZPM specialise in really pretty and useful make-up bags – everything from small cosmetic purses to hanging weekenders, all in a range of patterns. As well as these you'll find ideas for kids and babies and some attractive laundry and kitchen accessories. There's also a gift finder by occasion or personality to make life even easier.

Site Usability:	★★★★	Based:	UK
Product Range:	★★★	Express Delivery Option? (UK)	Yes
Price Range:	Medium	Gift Wrapping Option?	No
Delivery Area:	Worldwide	Returns Procedure:	Down to you

Section 11
Useful Information – The Essential Websites

Useful Information – The Essential Websites

These are the websites where you're not actually looking for things to buy but for useful information on just about everything; renewing your passport or getting a visa, having your clothes altered and converting kilos into pounds; telephone numbers and addresses and finding that final word for your crossword.

So every time you think 'I need to look up' and 'find out' just take a quick look here and you'll find some 'Little Helpers' you didn't even know existed. I know that you're used to lots of suggestions within each Chapter and Section but in most cases below you'll only find one. That's because you really don't need a choice in this case and the website has almost certainly been personally tested by yours truly more than once.

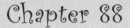

Chapter 88

Essential Services

Alterations Service

www.allalts.co.uk

Unless you're one of those lucky people who fits everything (and I certainly don't), if your trousers or skirt needs shortening, or the sleeves on a jacket turning up then just post the clothes pinned as you want them to Allalts' Leicester head office with the correct amount from the clear online price list and very reasonable return postage and they will return them to you altered to your specification within approximately seven days.

BT, Directory Enquiries and Yellow Pages

www.bt.com

Provided you have enough information this site will, through its directory enquiries link, provide you with telephone number, full addresses and postcodes for people and business anywhere in the UK. You can also get UK and international dialling codes and a great deal of other information including online billing, reporting and tracking faults and help with moving your phone number if you're changing address.

Book Search

www.bookfinder.com

The next time you see a book somewhere, decide to order it and find it's out of print, go immediately to bookfinder.com. Here you can search for all books, whether in print or not, and you'll be taken to lots of different places to buy, some of which may well be offering your (reasonably priced) book for a horrendous amount as well as somewhere you can purchase at near to the original asking price. It's an excellent website so give it a try.

China Search

www.chinasearch.co.uk

If you're looking for a particular piece of china, or want to add to a set that's no longer in production (or like me, need to replace six dessert plates that you broke in one shot), then register with ChinaSearch and they'll try to find it for you. It's incredibly easy, you just look up your pattern and then fill in their online form with all the details of what you're looking for and how they can reach you. And it works.

Citizens Advice Bureau

www.adviceguide.org.uk

This is definitely not the most exciting of websites, and one which maybe you'll never have cause to visit but if you want any information on benefits, housing and employment, plus civil and consumer issues you'll find it all here, right up to date. It also tells you who to contact if you need further help and how to make a small claim in the courts should you need to plus there are loads of fact sheets you can print off.

Conversion Tables

www.onlineconversion.com

You know that moment when you want to change miles into kilometres, inches into metres, or ounces into grams, or when you're using that marvellous cookbook you picked up in Williams Sonoma in the US and don't have a clue about the difference between a US teaspoon and the UK version? Well on this useful website you can convert just about anything including temperature, speed, volume, weight and fuel consumption plus some more unusual options such as light years to astronomical units and gram-force to micronewtons (sorry, I don't have a clue either).

Online Dictionary and Thesaurus

www.askoxford.com

You can search the *Compact Oxford Dictionary*, the *Concise Dictionary of First Names* and the *Little Oxford Dictionary of Quotations* here. Find out about and order all the books published by Oxford University Press or sign up for a free trial of the Oxford desktop One Click dictionary. It's quite a busy website to use but the search facility is excellent.

www.dictionary.com

The next time you're doing a crossword, playing Scrabble (I know, I know, you're not allowed dictionaries here, but every once in a while to check something up you'll need one) don't bother to go through the book version but go on to this fantastic website where you'll find every word and every spelling for every word plus alternatives for every word. US and UK spelling is given in each case.

Online Encyclopedias

www.britannica.com

It's no surprise that the Encyclopedia Britannica is now online and if you subscribe to the full service rather than order the volumes you'll save an enormous amount of shelf space. If you're not a member you can use their condensed service for free; however, if you are a subscriber you can access the full encyclopedia online. You can also order the books, the World Atlas and other reference products from their online shop.

www.wikipedia.org

Over the last few years Wikipedia has rapidly grown into the largest reference website on the Internet. The content is free to access, and is written collaboratively by people from all around the world. This website is a 'wiki', which means that anyone with access to an internet-connected computer can edit, correct, or improve information throughout the encyclopedia. There are over 1.15 million articles in English alone so you'll be able to obtain lots of information and I suggest that you also use Britannica.com for the full picture on any subject you're researching.

Passports, Visas and Replacement Certificates

www.passport.gov.uk

When you next need to replace your passport and provided you're not in too much of a hurry (as we were when my son left his passport in his to-be-washed sweatshirt pocket ten days before we were due to go skiing) then use this website to download the application form, fill it in and submit it to the Passport Office after which it will be completed and sent to you for final signature. If this sounds complicated, it's not. If you're in a hurry you need to call for an appointment for their fast track service, details of which, again, you'll find here.

www.ukdocuments.com

If you, like me, at some time have had a panicked moment realising that you can't find a copy of your (or one of your children's) birth certificate and you need it urgently then click to this website where you can use their two day priority service for replacement certificates. It's extremely easy to fill in their forms and your certificate will be sent by special delivery to the UK or Airsure worldwide.

www.visaservice.co.uk

Visaservice is a visa/passport processing agency based in London, UK. They will process (from online application forms) applications for UK residents, visitors to the UK and residents from other countries. With an extensive visa information database, agency facilities at most London consulates and access to all major courier and transport facilities they can process visas for most nationalities to destinations around the world, including those where representation is outside the UK.

Road Tax Disc Online Application

www.vehiclelicence.gov.uk

Here's another totally essential and often left-to-the-last-minute facility that's now online. Once you have the new form of MOT document (if you need it) plus your car insurance document you can use this website to apply for your new road tax disc, so no further need for that trek to the Post Office. If you haven't had the reminder letter you can just use the reference code and registration number from your car log book instead.

Royal Mail Services

www.royalmail.com

Go to their 'Buy Online' section and order your books of stamps here (or your Special Editions, ready stamped envelopes or personalised stamps). You do have to order quite a lot of stamps but it's the easiest way if you're going to be posting lots of mail in the near future. You can also find the package and letter weights and costs table here for the UK and overseas and look up addresses and postcodes.

Weather Reports

www.weather.co.uk

Although you can never be sure of the weather forecast (putting it mildly) and definitely don't totally rely on what you read on this site (as the situation can change so easily) you can at least get some idea of what is expected for the next ten days, hour by hour if you want and for anywhere in the world.

Chapter 89

To Buy or Not to Buy?

All the essential information you need about buying online.

Buying online can be so easy, addictive even. You can choose from products from all over the world. A range far greater than anything you could possibly find elsewhere and it's easy to get completely carried away.

Here are the important things you need to know before you buy. Just keep them in your mind before you start ordering and you should have no problems. Happy shopping.

1 Before you buy.

There are so many websites to choose from, for just about every product you can think of, not just fashion and beauty. Whether you're buying kitchen equipment, a new bed, cashmere knit or lipstick the basic rules for buying online are the same:

- *Secure Payment.* Make sure that when you go to put in your payment information the padlock appears at the foot of the screen and the top line changes from http://to https://. This means that your information will be transferred in code. To make sure you're clear about this just go to www.johnlewis.com, put something in your basket then click on 'Go to Checkout'. You'll immediately see the changes and those are what you're looking for each time. If they don't happen, don't buy.
- *Who are they?* Don't buy from a retailer unless you can access their full contact details, ideally these will be available from the 'Contact Us' button on the home page but sometimes it's hidden in Terms and Conditions. You should be able to find their email address plus location address and telephone number. This is so that you can contact them in case of a problem – I get really annoyed by websites who hide behind their email addresses – they need to be out

457

there saying to you, the prospective customer 'This is who we are and this is where we are, get in touch if you need us', sometimes they don't.

- *Privacy Policy.* If it's the first time you're buying from this retailer you should check their privacy clause telling you what they'll be doing with your information; I suggest you never allow them to pass it on to anywhere/anyone else. It's not necessarily what *they* do with it that'll cause you a problem, but if they pass it on ...

- *Returns Policy.* What happens if you want to return something? Check the retailer's policy before you order so that you're completely informed about how long you have to return goods and what the procedure is. Some retailers want you to give them notice that you're going to be sending something back (usually for more valuable items) and others make it quick and simple, the latter are definitely the best.

- *Keeping Track.* Keep a record, preferably printed, of everything you buy online, giving the contact details, product details and order reference so that if you need to you can quickly look them up. I also keep an email folder into which I drag any orders/order confirmations/ payment details just in case I forget to print something. Then if you have a problem you can just click on the link to contact them and all the references are there.

- *Statements.* Check your bank statements to make sure that all the transactions appear as you expect. Best of all keep a separate credit card just for online spending which will make it even easier to check.

- *Delivery Charges.* Check out the delivery charges. Again, some retailers are excellent and offer free delivery within certain areas and others charge a fortune. Make sure you're completely aware of the total cost before you buy. If you're buying from the US you will have to pay extra shipping and duty, which you'll either have to fork out for on delivery, or on receipt of an invoice. My advice is to pay it immediately.

- *Credit Card Security.* Take advantage of the new MasterCard SecureCode and Verified by Visa schemes when they're offered to you. Basically they offer you the extra facility of giving a password when you use your registered cards to buy online from signed up retailers – a kind of online chip and pin – they're excellent and they're going to grow. For extra security pay online with a credit, rather than a debit or any other type of card as this gives you extra security from the credit card companies on goods over £100 in value

- *Shred the Evidence.* Buy a shredder. You may think I'm daft but most online and offline card fraud is due to someone having got hold of your details offline. So don't let anyone walk off with your card where you can't see it and don't chuck out papers with your information on where they can be easily accessed by someone else. You have been warned.

- *Payment Don'ts.* Don't ever pay cash, don't pay by cheque (unless you've got the goods and you're happy with them), don't ever send your credit card details by email and don't give your pin number online to anyone EVER. I'm amazed at the stories I hear.

- *PC Security.* Make sure that your computer is protected by the latest Anti Virus software and an efficient firewall. Virus Scan your system at least once a week so that you not only check for nasties but get rid of any spyware.

- *Auction Websites.* Be very careful using an auction website. Make sure that you know absolutely what you're doing and who you're buying from. This is not to say that everyone who sells on auction websites is waiting to get you, but some of them definitely are.

- *Fakes and Replicas.* Be wary of anyone selling you 'replica' products – don't go there. If you're tempted to buy from someone selling you something that looks too cheap to be true then it probably is. If you're buying expensive products always check on the retailer's policy for warranties and guarantees.

- *Additional Information.* Don't give any information that isn't necessary to the purchase. You're buying a book, for goodness sake. Why do they need to know your age and how many children you have?
- *Take Your Time.* Don't buy in a hurry. Take the time to check the above before you click on 'Confirm Order'. If in any doubt at all: *don't buy.*

Have I managed to put you off yet? I assure you that's definitely not my intention but you really need to be aware of the above. Once you've carried out the checks just a few times you'll do them automatically. The internet really is a marvellous place but it's also a minefield full of unscrupulous people waiting to catch you out. Don't let them.

2   Deliveries and Returns – What to look for and how to make them easier

Deliveries

Deliveries from online retailers are getting increasingly better and more efficient. In many cases you can have your order tomorrow. Find a retailer you like who's stating the old 'within 28 days' policy and call them to find out if they're really that daft (being polite here). With most companies offering express delivery who on earth is willing to wait for 28 days? That is, unless something is being specially made for you – in which case it may well take longer but at least you'll be aware before you order.

Most companies offer the following:

- Standard Delivery
- 24 Hour Delivery (for a small extra charge)
- Saturday Delivery (very occasionally)
- EU Delivery and sometimes EU Express
- Worldwide Delivery and sometimes Worldwide Express.

The problem is that you very often don't find out about all these and the relevant charges until you've put something in your basket (note to online retailers: please make 'Delivery Information' a key button on your home page, it saves so much time). Yes I have researched this information for you but sometimes I had to practically place an order to discover a retailer's policies – ridiculous (are you listening out there?).

Returns

This is an area that often puts people off buying online (or from catalogues, for that matter). Well don't be put off.

You will, of course, have read up the company's Returns Policy before you buy so you know how much time you have but you might like to know the following:

- You are entitled to a 'cooling off' period (usually seven days), during which you can cancel your order without any reason and receive a full refund.

■ You're also entitled to a full refund if the goods or services are not provided by the date you agreed. If you didn't agree a date, then you are entitled to a refund if the goods or services are not provided within 28 days.

Having said that and assuming that once you've started you're going to become a regular online shopper, these things will make your life easier.

■ Buy a black marker pen, roll of packing tape and some different sized jiffy bags (I use D1, H5 and K7 which are good for most things) just in case you only want to return part of an order and the original packing is damaged or too big.
■ Keep these where the rest of the family can't get at them (and that tells you something about my family, doesn't it? Why doesn't anyone, ever put things back?).
■ Make sure that you keep the original packaging and any paperwork until you're sure that you're not sending stuff back and keep it somewhere easy to find.
■ If you want to be really clever go to www.vistaprint.co.uk and order some address labels. They're really cheap and incredibly useful for returns, Recorded and Special Delivery postings and lots of other things.
■ Don't be put off if a premium retailer wants you to call them if you're returning something valuable. It's essential that the item is insured in transit and this is something they usually arrange – for really expensive goods they may well use a courier service to collect from you.
■ Rejoice when returns are free, standard postage and packing is more and more free of charge from large online retailers, we'll be ordering far more when returns are free as well.

3   Comparison Websites and how to use them

If you've read through this book you'll already know how strongly I feel about these websites, where you can find the best prices for almost everything. However they're best for electrical equipment, computers, cameras and everything photographic plus books, DVDs, CDs and games and I would repeat that you do need to know exactly what you're looking for. You can't just type in 'camera', or 'fridge'. You need to know the exact model and have done your homework (research) first.

So go to a dedicated product website where they offer you full specifications and advice for the type of product you want. Research an offline magazine, such as *What Digital Camera* (if you're looking for a camera, of course), look at some of the excellent photographic websites for the latest models and information or subscribe to *Which?*, either online at www.which.co.uk or offline through the magazine, where thousands of products are reviewed and they'll give you their opinion of the best on the market. This is great if you know the product you want but you don't know exactly which one to buy and you need an independent assessment.

With regard to books, CDs and DVDs etc. there are websites other than Amazon (I know, it's an amazing thought, but there are). You can often find other editions, speedy delivery and very good prices on different websites so it's worth having a look just to make sure before you spend.

There are also lots of other price comparison websites. These are the ones I always use and find the best so rather than giving you a huge choice I've just selected a small number to make things easy.

General comparison websites;

www.uk.shopping.com

The next time you're looking for a new washing machine, or mobile phone, or camera, click straight through to this excellent price comparison website. If you haven't given them an exact specification of the product you want (and as I've said it's better if you can) you'll get a list of all the possible options and the relevant websites plus website reviews. Make your choice and then you can compare prices on the one you want and you'll get all the information you need to decide – from price (of course), stock availability, delivery charge and site rating. You then just have to click through to buy from their preferred retailer or wherever you choose.

www.kelkoo.co.uk

With Kelkoo you really do need to know the exact specification of what you're looking for to get the best results, as you don't get a defined product list offering you everything containing your initial search criteria but a mixture of relevant products. If you specify exactly what you want you'll get all those products at the top of the page with prices, site ratings, descriptions and delivery costs.

Food and wine price check sites

www.tesco.com/pricecheck

Believe it or not Tesco offers you the opportunity of pitching its own prices against those of Sainsbury, Morrisons and Asda although it's not always the cheapest (but of course they're doing it to show you that they usually are). You can compare the prices of most of your general groceries right down to the basics but it's most useful when you want to buy booze. For example, at time of writing I'm checking on a 75cl bottle of Talisker Malt Whisky. Tesco's price is £19.97 and Sainsbury's is £25.99. Quite a difference, I'm sure you'll agree.

www.winesearcher.com

Looking for a particular vintage of Pomerol or just Oyster Bay Chardonnay? With prices differing by as much as 40% you need this site if you're considering buying more than a single bottle of wine. Do register for the pro-version to get all the benefits and they'll search for you throughout the world if you want. Bear in mind that the prices you're given don't include VAT, nor do they take into account any special offers that retailers such as Majestic may have going at any time so you should check those as well.

Books, games, CD and DVD price check

www.bookbrain.co.uk

www.best-book-price.co.uk

These are two excellent places where you can compare book prices and see who has the book you're looking for in stock to send out immediately. They're both very easy to use – not really for buying ordinary paperbacks, although you can use them for that if you want to, but when you've found a special hardback that you want to give as a gift next week you're being quoted 4-6 weeks delivery you may be able to find another bookshop who has it ready to send out with the added benefit that you can also compare the prices from all the bookstores.

www.best-cd-price.co.uk

Know the CD you want to buy but want to make sure you get the best price? Use this price comparison website, which not only shows where you'll find the best deal but includes the postage details as well so you absolutely know where you are. This website is almost unbelievably quick to use and you can use it for DVDs and games as well. As an example, if you do a search on *The Lord of the Rings, The Return of the King*, you'll be given twelve places where you can buy it online, with prices from an amazing £7.49, up to £22.49. Quite a difference, I'm sure you'll agree.

www.dvdpricecheck.co.uk

If you're looking for a particular DVD this is the place to start and you can see what's available throughout all the world regions. With so many places to buy DVDs online it's hard to know which is the best site without spending hours; and with different sites charging different amounts things get even worse. So here it is, the website that'll compare the worldwide prices for you. Just key in your title and region (UK is Region 2) and you'll get all the answers.

Many of the websites they offer don't charge you delivery on top so you can order from as may as you want and as often as you like. Sounds tempting? It's hard to know when to stop.

www.uk.gamestracker.com

However much you may dislike those extremely noisy (and often horrifically violent) computer games, you won't want your precious ones spending more of their not-so-hard-earned pocket money than they need to. If you want to get them the latest game for Christmas or they want to choose one themselves then send them to Games Tracker, where you/they can compare the prices with all the retailers for any specific game and get the deal of the moment.

Motor and Home Insurance

www.confused.com

This is a price comparison website for car and home insurance. You just need to fill in all the forms once and then you'll receive a list of quotes in just a few minutes online. If you then want to add or change anything you can do that as well and all the information is retained in a clear and easy format. This is incredibly useful particularly for car insurance as, having young drivers in the family now and having spent hours (literally) on the phone trying to find insurance quotes, I couldn't believe how much time I saved doing it this way and yes I will give credit to Sholto for having discovered it. Well done you.

4 Internet Auctions

You may feel really tempted by some of the items you can find on auction websites, and in particular eBay. But bear in mind the following as it can be extremely risky:

- You may well be buying from a private seller and so you won't really know who you're dealing with or where they're based. Find out before you commit.
- You have fewer rights when you buy from a private seller. Although the goods must be 'by law' as stated, a seller who is not acting as a business is not covered by the rules on satisfactory quality and fitness for purchase.
- If you have a problem, it could be harder to put right than if you bought from a shop although some auction websites do offer complaints resolution processes and anti-fraud guarantees. If you're going to use an auction website, make sure that it's one of these. Ebay, whose Safety Centre (click at the foot of the page at www.ebay.co.uk), is excellent and is definitely one of the best auction sites to buy from.

Top Tips

- Check the feedback about the seller on the auction site and send an email query to the seller who should welcome your enquiry.
- Know exactly what you're buying, including the normal retail price. As I've said before, if the price seems too good to be true, it usually is. Check the authenticity of any antique or collectable.
- Use a credit card to pay through a secure website, which gives you the most protection if there's a problem.
- Don't up your bid in the last few minutes unless you know exactly what you are doing. You may well find yourself being tempted to go outside your range in the excitement of the last minute bidding (yes you guessed, that's happened to me).
- Read the small print. Make sure you know if postage and insurance are included in the price. Is the seller based in the same country as you? What action should you take if something goes wrong?
- Remember that this can be a risky way to buy so be very, very careful. That's not to say don't do it, just make sure you know what you're doing first.

5 Once you've bought

- Very quickly after you've made your purchase you should receive email confirmation about your buy including all necessary purchase details – order number, date, details of the goods you've ordered and purchase price plus in most cases a link back to the website you've ordered from.
- You are entitled to a 'cooling off' period (usually seven days), during which you can cancel your order without any reason and receive a full refund.
- You're also entitled to a full refund if the goods or services are not provided by the date you agreed. If you didn't agree a date, then you are entitled to a refund if the goods or services are not provided within 28 days.
- Keep an email and paper folder into which you can save all relevant information about your online purchases. Call it something like 'Web Orders Outstanding'. Whittle it down to just the confirmation email with the order number and purchase details once you've received your order and you're happy. There's nothing more infuriating than not having the right information if something goes wrong later.
- Note that the above entitlements do not apply to financial services such as insurance or banking, online auctions, or purchases involving the sale of land.

6   Help If Something Goes Wrong

If something goes wrong, and you've paid by credit card, you may have a claim not only against the supplier of the goods, but also the credit card issuer.

This applies to goods or services (and deposits) costing more than £100 but less than £30,000 and does not apply to debit or charge cards.

Contact the retailer with the problem initially by email and make sure you quote the order number and any other necessary details.

If you don't immediately get assistance ask to speak to the manager. Normally this will end your problem, however, if I tell you that I ordered some expensive goods from a luxury store recently which didn't arrive when I expected them to, was treated rudely by the call centre assistant and then unbelievably rudely by the manager you'll get the message that this doesn't always work.

OK, it's the company's fault for recruiting these people in the first place and not instilling in them the message that even if the customer isn't always right they should always be treated with the utmost care and politeness. What they're looking for is not your first order, believe me, it's turning you into a loyal repeat customer. Those types of customers are the most valuable of all.

Again it's not things going wrong that causes most of the trouble. It's how the company sorts things out. Do it right, make you feel really important and do that little bit extra and they've got you hooked. Handle things badly and they've not only lost this order but any future orders. Not only that but they've lost your goodwill with regards to recommending them to others. Stupid– are you listening out there?

In my case and probably because I'm more pushy than most people and didn't stop at the manager, I got what I wanted (note: push hard. Contact the company's owner if you can or press office if need be and tell them what's going on). And no I'm not going to tell you who my problem was with, sorry.

If after all of this you do not get a satisfactory result to your complaint you can contact www. consumerdirect.gov.uk (for the UK) or call them on 08454 040506 for what to do next. If your problem is with a retailer based in Australia, Canada, Denmark, Finland, Hungary, Mexico, New Zealand, Norway, South Korea, Sweden, Switzerland or the USA you can click through to www. econsumer.gov, a joint project of consumer protection agencies from 20 nations for help.

If (horrors) you find that someone has used your credit card information without your authorisation, contact your card issuer immediately. You can cancel the payment and your card company must arrange for your account to be re-credited in full.

UK, European and US Clothing Size Conversions

Here's a general guide to the clothing size conversions between the US, Europe and the UK. If you need size conversions for other specific countries, or other types of conversions go to www. onlineconversion.com/clothing.htm where you'll find them all.

To be as sure as possible that you're ordering the right size, check the actual retailer's size chart against your own measurements and note that a UK 12 is sometimes a US 8 and sometimes a 10 so it really pays to make sure.

Women's clothing size conversions

US	UK	France	Germany	Italy
6	8	36	34	40
8	10	38	36	42
10	12	40	38	44
12	14	42	40	46
14	16	44	42	48
16	18	46	44	50
18	20	50	46	52

Men's clothing size conversions

US	UK	EU
32	32	42
34	34	44
36	36	46
38	38	48
40	40	50
42	42	52
44	44	54
46	46	56
48	48	58

Women's shoe size conversions

UK	3.5	4	4.5	5	5.5	6	6.5	7	7.5	8	8.5
EU	36.5	37	37.5	38	38.5	39	40	41	42	43	43.5
US	6	6.5	7	7.5	8	8.5	9	9.5	10	10.5	11

Men's shoe size conversions

UK	7	7.5	8	8.5	9	9.5	10	10.5	11	11.5	12
EU	40.5	41	42	42.5	43	44	44.5	45	46	46.5	47
US	7.5	8	8.5	9	9.5	10	10.5	11	11.5	12	12.5

Index

1001beautysecrets.com/beauty/
    caswell 131
118golf.co.uk 350

a2z-kids.co.uk 174
abebooks.co.uk 373
abel-cole.co.uk 313
abentleycushions.co.uk 247
absolutepearls.co.uk 94
accessoriesonline.co.uk 100
accessorize.co.uk 100
activekid.co.uk 336
activitytoysdirect.co.uk 337
adidas-shop.co.uk 39
adonisgrooming.com 130
adventuretoys.co.uk 337
adviceguide.org.uk 454
ae.com 34
aehobbs.com 131
agentprovocateur.com 46
agnesb.com 8
agold.co.uk 396
agoy.com 333
airandwater.co.uk 209
airfix.com 171
albumania.com 421
alexandermiles.co.uk 232
alicecaroline.co.uk 76
alisonhenry.com 247
allalts.co.uk 453
allegrahicks.com 21
allsaintsshop.co.uk 14
allweathers.co.uk 340

aloud.com 367
amandalacey.com 216
amandawakeley.com 20
amara.co.uk 405
amazon.co.uk 373
amoralia.com 66
amtrak.com 445
ancienneambiance.com 200
andreabrierley.com 409
angeljackson.co.uk 75
anonymousclothing.com 26
antique-glass.co.uk 422
anula.co.uk 54
anusha.co.uk 4
anyahindmarch.com 72
apc.fr 8
apeainthepod.com 61
arenaflowers.com 414
armoirelinen.com 228
arranaromatics.com 183
artboxdirect.co.uk 364
artigiano.co.uk 11
artist-supplies.co.uk 364
artrepublic.com 270
ascolights.co.uk 267
ashridgetrees.co.uk 282
askoxford.com 454
aspaceuk.com 158
aspenandbrown.co.uk 410
aspinaloflondon.com 76, 104, 418
asquith.ltd.uk 40
astleyclarke.com 93
auravita.com 191

austinreed.co.uk 116
austique.co.uk 401
authenticfoodandwine.com 308,
    427
avis.co.uk 443
axminster-carpets.co.uk 273

baa.com 445
babas.uk.com 410
babeswithbabies.com 414
babiesbaskets.com 410
babycare-direct.co.uk 151
babycity.co.uk 152
babydazzlers.com 155
babygiftgallery.co.uk 410
babygurgles.co.uk 152
baby-pages.co.uk 152
baer-ingram.com 228
baileys-home-garden.co.uk 285
bakinboys.co.uk 293
baldwins.co.uk 210
ballooninabox.co.uk 381
balloonsweb.co.uk 147
ballsbrothers.co.uk 325
barbican.org.uk 368
barenecessities.co.uk 46
barkerandball.com 288
barkerandstonehouse.com 241
barneys-newsbox.co.uk 172
bartspicesdirect.co.uk 317
bathandunwind.com 184
bathroomheaven.com 237
bathroomluxury.co.uk 237

bayley-sage.co.uk 396
bbqworld.co.uk 280
bbr.com 326
beautique.com 203
beautyandtheeast.co.uk 216
beautybay.com 184
beautyexpert.co.uk 217
beautyflash.co.uk 217
beautynaturals.com 217
beauty-republic.com 210
beautysleuth.co.uk 194
beautyxposure.com 217
bedworld.net 233
belenechandia.com 76
belindarobertson.com 27
belladinotte.com 46
bellini-baby.com 411
benefitcosmetics.co.uk 204
besselink.com 267
best-book-price.co.uk 373, 461
best-cd-price.co.uk 376, 462
bettysbypost.co.uk 294, 426
beverlybeaute.com 195
beverlyhillsbakery.com 294
bexley.com 125
beyondtherainbow.co.uk 155
biju.co.uk 228
billamberg.com 76
biondicouture.com 55
birstall.co.uk 280
bitsnstuff.co.uk 419
bjornandme.com 63
black.co.uk 105
blackface.co.uk 298
blacks.co.uk 341
blackstonelewis.co.uk 117
blackwell.co.uk 373
blisslondon.co.uk 204
bloom.uk.com 392
bloomingmarvellous.co.uk 63
blossommotherandchild.com 62
boardsonline.co.uk 343
bobbibrown.co.uk 204
bobijou.com 95
bodas.co.uk 46
boden.co.uk 11
bodyshop.co.uk 210
bombayduck.co.uk 406
bonsoirdirect.com 47
boodles.co.uk 93
boogaloo.co.uk 172
bookbrain.co.uk 373, 461
bookdepository.co.uk 374
bookfinder.com 453
bookgiant.com 374
bootik.co.uk 402

boots.com 205
borderlinefabrics.com 262
borders.co.uk 374
botham.co.uk 294, 426
boutiqueenfant.com 147
boutiquetoyou.co.uk 402
boxinthepost.com 4
bradleysthetannery.co.uk 285
brainydays.co.uk 167
branded.net 79
bravida.co.uk 77
bravissimo.com 47
braybrook.com 422
brissi.co.uk 406
britannica.com 455
brittanyferries.co.uk 444
brittique.com 4
brooksbrothers.com 34
brora.co.uk 27
broughs.com 299
brownes.co.uk 387
brownsfashion.com 21
bs4health.com 191
bt.com 453
bucklesandbows.co.uk 83
budget.com 443
burberry.com 21
butlerandwilson.co.uk 100
butlerswines.co.uk 397
buyaswatch.co.uk 102
buyersandsellersonline.co.uk 257

cabane.co.uk 247
caketoppers.co.uk 294
caleyco.com 314
cambridgewine.com 326
cameraking.co.uk 360
cameras.co.uk 360
cameras2u.com 360
canapeum.com 428
candle-city.co.uk 432
candlesontheweb.co.uk 432
cannockbeds.co.uk 233
caramel-shop.co.uk 162
carluccios.com 309
carmalondon.com 47
carnmeal.co.uk 384
carterandbond.com 131
cartoonstock.com 357
casacopenhagen.com 248
cashmere.co.uk 27
caspiancaviar.co.uk 309
cathkidston.co.uk 229
caxtonlondon.com 105
cclondon.com 442
cdwow.com 377

celtic-sheepskin.co.uk 59
champagnewarehouse.co.uk 326
chandlerystore.co.uk 345
chapmansjewellery.co.uk 95
charitycards.co.uk 382
charliecrow.com 175
chatsworth-dec.co.uk 436
cheese-board.co.uk 301
cheesecake.co.uk 295
chelseatextiles.com 248
chemistdirect.co.uk 191
chessbaron.co.uk 135
chezbec.com 100
childrenssalon.co.uk 162
chinasearch.co.uk 454
chococo.co.uk 388
chocolatebuttons.co.uk 388
chocolatetradingco.com 388
christmascrackershop.co.uk 435
christmasdinnercompany.co.uk 428
christmastreeland.co.uk 437
christopher-wray.com 268
christy-towels.com 236
cinnamonfashion.co.uk 30
cityorg.co.uk 105
cku.com 48
claireid.com 27
claire-macdonald.com 397
clarissahulse.com 248
clickgolf.co.uk 351
clinique.co.uk 205
clintoncards.co.uk 382
clothes4boys.co.uk 163
cntraveller.com 448
cocoaloco.co.uk 388
cocoribbon.com 5
coffeeandcream.co.uk 406
coffeebypost.co.uk 322
colemancroft.com 352
coles-shirtmakers.com 112
collinstreet.com 295
cologneandcotton.com 184
compass24.com 345
completeoutdoors.co.uk 341
compman.co.uk 374
comptoir-sud-pacifique.com 185
condorferries.co.uk 444
confused.com 462
conran.com 253
contactsdirect.co.uk 191
contessa.org.uk 47
cooksknives.co.uk 253
cookware.co.uk 253
corioliss.co.uk 195
corneliajames.com 106

cosmeticsalacarte.com 205
costumecrazy.co.uk 175
cosyposy.co.uk 163
cotswoldoutdoor.com 341
countryattire.co.uk 121
county-golf.co.uk 351
cowshedproducts.com 402
coxandcox.co.uk 419
crabtree-evelyn.co.uk 184
cravematernity.co.uk 63
crewclothing.co.uk 345
cricketbits.co.uk 356
crocus.co.uk 283
crombie.co.uk 117
cromwellandsmith.co.uk 117
crumpetengland.com 28
ctshirts.co.uk 111
cucinadirect.co.uk 253
culinaryconcepts.co.uk 422
culpeper.co.uk 318
curtisanddyer.co.uk 112
czechandspeake.com 237

d2-clothing.co.uk 122
dabs.com 257
dalvey.com 126
dancedepot.co.uk 178
dancedirectworld.com 179
dariopaganini.it 112
darksugars.co.uk 389
darlingsofchelsea.co.uk 241
dartington.co.uk 244
davidaustin.com 283
davidclulow.com 89
davidhampton.com 141
davidlinley.com 248
davidmellordesign.com 244
dawsonsonline.com 365
deadfreshfish.co.uk 304
debenhams.com 14
deliinthenook.co.uk 309
derek-rose.com 133
designerflowers.org.uk 393
designer-lighting.com 268
designersguild.com 229
designsoncashmere.com 28
devon-house.co.uk 402
dianaforrester.co.uk 249
dibor.co.uk 249
dictionary.com 454
digitalfirst.co.uk 360
digitalframesdirect.com 361
diningstore.co.uk 254
dinnyhall.com 95
dior.com 21
discountpublications.co.uk 368

divertimenti.co.uk 254
dlux-ltd.co.uk 59
dobies.co.uk 283
dollshouse.com 167
donaldrussell.com 299, 429
dontforgetyourtoothbrush.com
    446
dorothyperkins.co.uk 14
dragonflysaddlery.co.uk 353
dreambabyuk.com 415
drhauschka.co.uk 218
drury.uk.com 323
dualit.com 254
duchyofcornwallnursery.co.uk 284
dudethatscoolmagic.co.uk 175
dukeshillham.co.uk 309, 429
dune.co.uk 84
dunhill.com 126
duoboots.com 84
dutchbydesign.com 249
dvdpricecheck.co.uk 377, 462
dvflondon.com 22

ebookers.co.uk 447
eddiebaur.com 35
edge2edge.co.uk 343
efoodies.co.uk 310
egyptiancottonstore.com 229
ejk.biz 28
elanbach.com 263
elanthy.com 310
elc.co.uk 156
electricshop.com 257
elingerie.uk.net 48
elizabethhurley.com 55
elliegray.com 40
ellis-brigham.com 343
emily-b.co.uk 67
emmabridgewater.co.uk 244
emmachapmanjewels.com 95
emmahope.com 81
emmawillis.com 112
enchanted-wood.co.uk 337
eno.org 368
eric-bompard.com 28
erinhousegifts.co.uk 419
ernestjones.co.uk 103
escada.com 22
escentual.co.uk 185
espadrillesetc.com 55
espaonline.com 218
esperya.com 310
essentials4travel.co.uk 448
esteelauder.co.uk 205
euroffice.co.uk 260
eurostar.com 445

eurostore.palm.com 137
eurotunnel.com 444
evelom.co.uk 218
eveningdresses.co.uk 8
eversfieldorganic.co.uk 299
evertrading.co.uk 255
everywine.co.uk 327
evisu.com 9
ewenique.co.uk 59
exclusivefootwear.com 82
expansys.co.uk 361
expedia.co.uk 447
extremepie.com 122

fabricsandpapers.com 263
fabulousfurs.com 59
faith.co.uk 84
farrow-ball.com 265
farscapegames.co.uk 172
fatface.com 122
faux.uk.com 60
fcukbuymail.co.uk 15
featherandblack.com 234
ferries.org 444
festive-dresser.co.uk 433
figleaves.com 48
filofax.co.uk 141
finecheese.co.uk 303
finetable.co.uk 245
fishit.com 348
fishworks.co.uk 305
fitness-superstore.co.uk 334
flamingbarbecues.co.uk 281
fleurt.com 48
florislondon.com 185
flowersdirect.co.uk 393
flowerworksoxford.co.uk 393
floydshoes.co.uk 84
fly-fishing-tackle.co.uk 349
footlux.com 85
forgoodnesscake.co.uk 397
formanandfield.com 310, 428
formes.com 64
fortnumandmason.com 323
fortyweeks.co.uk 62
forzieri.com 72
fotosense.co.uk 361
foweyfish.com 305
franceshilary.com 285
fredafashion.com 9
french-brand.com 245, 434
frenchgourmetstore.com 311, 429
frenchsole.com 85
freshfood.co.uk 314
freshsoapdeli.com 210
freyadesign.co.uk 276

fromages.com 301
fromheretomaternity.co.uk 67
frommers 446
froufrouandthomas.co.uk 436
fruit-4u.com 398
funkymoose.co.uk 416
funkyrugs.co.uk 274
fushi.co.uk 211

gaiamdirect.co.uk 236
gallowaysmokehouse.co.uk 305
game.co.uk 377
gamleys.co.uk 156, 168
garden.co.uk 206
gardenadventure.co.uk 337
gardencentredirect.co.uk 280
gardenfurnitureworld.co.uk 281
gardengames.co.uk 338
gardentrading.co.uk 286
gbbulbs.co.uk 259
georgieporgiespuddings.co.uk 430
getamap.co.uk 441
gievesandhawkes.com 113
giftinspiration.com 419
gifts4fishing.co.uk 349
gina.com 82
glamonweb.co.uk 49
glamorousamorous.com 49
gleneagles.com 351
gltc.co.uk 159
glyndebourne.co.uk 368
goclothing.com 35
gocrackers.co.uk 435
gogofruitbasket.com 398
goldshield.co.uk 192
goldsmiths.co.uk 103
goodnessdirect.co.uk 192, 314
goplanetgo.co.uk 448
gorgeous-food.co.uk 398
grahamandbrown.com 265
grahamandgreen.co.uk 406
grahamkandiah.com 35
graigfarm.co.uk 314
grandillusions.co.uk 286
grayandosbourn.co.uk 30
greatexperiencedays.co.uk 136
greatlittleparties.co.uk 175
greatoutdoortoys.co.uk 338
greenfingers.co.uk 280
green-frederick.co.uk 96
griffithsbutchers.co.uk 299
grovelands.com 281, 437
gucci.com 72
gymworld.co.uk 334

hackett.co.uk 122

haggarts.com 117
hamleys.co.uk 168
handbagcrush.co.uk 79
harriet-whinney.co.uk 96
harrods.com 185
harvieandhudson.com 113
hasbean.co.uk 323
hatchards.co.uk 375
hattiesmart.com 351
hawesandcurtis.com 118
haywoods-tapestries.com 271
healfarm.co.uk 300
heals.co.uk 237
heavenlybodice.com 49
heidiklein.com 55
helenbateman.com 85
helenbroadhead.co.uk 159
henrilloydstore.co.uk 346
heroshop.co.uk 106
herringport.co.uk 241
hertz.co.uk 443
hibiscushome.com 229
hickorydickory.co.uk 411
higgs-leathers.co.uk 60
highlandsoaps.com 211
hilditchandkey.co.uk 113
hillco.co.uk 274
hmv.co.uk 377
hobbs.co.uk 9
holloways.co.uk 242
homefayrelimited.co.uk 295
hopscotchdressingup.co.uk 176
horn-trading.co.uk 249
hotelchocolat.co.uk 389
hot-headz.com 318
hqhair.com 195
hqman.com 132
h-s.co.uk 142
hush-uk.com 50
hyde-online.net 60

iberianfoods.co.uk 311
icecool.co.uk 96
ignesbags.com 77
ilovejeans.co.uk 15
imogenstone.co.uk 393
in2decor.com 407
indian-ocean.co.uk 282
indigofurniture.co.uk 233
interiorsathome.co.uk 263
interiors-tides.co.uk 250
irishferries.com 444
isabellaoliver.com 62
isla.uk.com 29
italian-lighting-centre.co.uk 268
iwantoneofthose.co.uk 136

izziwizzikids.co.uk 156

jackwills.co.uk 40
jaeger.co.uk 9
janconstantine.com 407
jandmdavidson.com 73
jane-asher.co.uk 296
janepackerdelivered.com 394
janetreger.co.uk 50
japanesekitchen.co.uk 318
jasonshankey.co.uk 132
jaycotts.co.uk 384
jdsports.co.uk 40
jeannepetitt.com 5
jeans-direct.com 15
jeroboams.co.uk 398
jewel-garden.co.uk 101
jigsaw-puzzles-online.co.uk 416
jim-lawrence.co.uk 269
jimmychoo.com 82
jobuckler.com 106
johnlewis.com 255
johnmasters.co.uk 195
johnnorris.co.uk 349
johnnylovesrosie.co.uk 196
johnsmedley.com 29
johnsoncrafts.co.uk 179
jojomamanbebe.co.uk 64
jomalone.co.uk 186
jonkers.co.uk 375
josephturner.co.uk 113
joulesclothing.com 41
jowoodorganics.com 211
juliannebalai.com 422
julieslaterandson.co.uk 77, 106
justbeautifully.co.uk 196
justchampagne.co.uk 399
justdivine.co.uk 101
justerinis.com 327
jwflowers.com 394
jwminteriors.com 242

kabiri.co.uk 96
kanishkabags.co.uk 77
karinherzog.co.uk 220
kaven.co.uk 196
kelkoo.co.uk 461
kelly-turkeys.com 431
kennethturner.com 186
kentandcarey.co.uk 148
kew-online.com 15
kiarie.co.uk 201
kickmaternitywear.com 64
kiddicare.com 153
kiddies-kingdom.com 152
kidscavern.co.uk 163

kidsrooms.co.uk 159
kikoy.com 56
kingofcotton.co.uk 230
kinlochanderson.co.uk 118
kirstengoss.com 97
kitbag.com 357
kjbeckett.com 126
koodos.com 80
kornerskincare.com 219
kurtgeiger.com 85

laboutiquedelartisanparfumeur.
   com 186
ladress.com 10
ladybarbarella.com 50
laithwaites.co.uk 327
lakelandlimited.co.uk 255, 430
laline.co.uk 219
lambertsflowercompany.co.uk 394
lambstoys.co.uk 168
lancome.co.uk 206
landsend.co.uk 11
lanefarm.co.uk 300
laprovence.co.uk 407
laragrace.co.uk 264
lasenza.co.uk 50
lastminute.com 447
launer.com 73
lauraashley.com 12
lavenderandsage.co.uk 250
lawrence.co.uk 364
layer-up.co.uk 16
laywheeler.co.uk 327
leadingspasoftheworld.com 222
leatherglovesonline.com 107
lego.com 172
lensway.com 192
leonidasbelgianchocolates.co.uk
   389
lessenteurs.com 186
lewisandcooper.com 399
lilyandagathe.com 169, 417
lineafashion.com 22
linenstore.co.uk 159
lingerie-company.co.uk 52
linksoflondon.com 97
littlefashiongallery.com 148
littlefolk.co.uk 417
littlepresentcompany.co.uk 411
littlesky.co.uk 343
littletrekkers.co.uk 148
lizcox.com 78
lizearle.com 219
llbean.com 35
loccitane.com 212
lochfyne.com 305

locketts.co.uk 407
loddonequestrian.com 353
lolarose.co.uk 101
longmire.co.uk 114
longtallsally.co.uk 31
lookfantastic.com 196
lordswines.co.uk 399
louisesandberg.com 56
louisvuitton.com 73
lounge-about.com 274
lovelula.com 212
luella.com 73
luisaviaroma.com 22
luluguinness.com 74
lumadirect.com 230
luxuryfrenchlingerie.com 51
lyttonandlily.co.uk 250

maccosmetics.com 206
mad4ponies.com 353
magazine-group.co.uk 369
magazinesofamerica.com 369
magictricks.co.uk 176
mailorderexpress.com 169
maisoncollection.com 230
majestic.co.uk 328
mamasandpapas.co.uk 64
mandala-aroma.com 212
mango.com 16
manjoh.com 97
mankind.co.uk 132
manning-and-manning.com 114
maporama.co.uk 442
mariechantal.com 148
marinestore.co.uk 346
marksandspencer.com 16
marni.com 23
marnys.co.uk 192
marston-and-langinger.com 242
martins-seafresh.co.uk 306
martynmaxey.co.uk 197
masterandmiss.com 149
mastersgames.com 338
matchesfashion.com 23
max-oliver.co.uk 5
meats.co.uk 300
megrivers.com 296, 427
miam-miam.co.uk 187
microanvica.com 137
mikimoto-store.co.uk 93
milanclothing.com 118
millcrofttextiles.co.uk 385
millerharris.com 187
misamu.com 5
mischiefkids.co.uk 163
missselfridge.co.uk 17

mithus.co.uk 250, 433
mittyjames.com 164
mjtrim.com 385
modainpelle.com 86
modelhobbies.co.uk 173
modelrockets.co.uk 173
moltonbrown.co.uk 187
monogrammedlinenshop.co.uk
   230
monsoon.co.uk 17
montezumas.co.uk 389
montgomerycurtainsdirect.co.uk
   264
moonpig.com 382
morelloliving.co.uk 412
mortimerandbennett.co.uk 311
mossdirect.co.uk 118
mothercare.com 153
mothernaturebras.co.uk 67
moysesstevens.co.uk 394
mrpen.co.uk 142
muddypuddles.com 149
mujionline.co.uk 276
mulberry.com 74
mulberryhall.co.uk 423
multimap.co.uk 442
murdocklondon.com 132
murrayforbes.co.uk 98
musicroom.co.uk 365
musthave.co.uk 213
myakka.co.uk 242
myfirstday.co.uk 415
myla.com 51
mysanatural.com 212
mytheresa.com 23
mytights.co.uk 51
my-wardrobe.com 6

nailsbymail.co.uk 197
nailsinc.com 197
natco-online.com 318
nationalrail.com 445
nationaltrust-shop.co.uk 385, 420
naturalcollection.com 213
naturalmagicuk.com 201
naturescape.co.uk 284
nautical-living.co.uk 346
nealsyardremedies.com 213
need-a-cake.co.uk 296
neimanmarcus.com 36
nespresso.com 323
net-a-porter.com 23
nevertoobusytobebeautiful.com
   206
newandlingwood.com 119
newitts.co.uk 357

nextday-champagne.co.uk 399
nicetouch.co.uk 213
ninacampbell.com 408
nomadtravel.co.uk 41, 449
no-one.co.uk 10
norbitoncheese.co.uk 302
northerntapestries.com 271
notonthehighstreet.com 420
npg.org.uk 369
nspccshop.co.uk 385
nt-online.org 370
nurserywindow.co.uk 160, 412

oasis-stores.com 17
obadash.com 56
objects-of-design.com 408
oddbins.co.uk 328
okadirect.com 243
oki-ni.com 123
old.co.uk 143
oldeglory.co.uk 408
oliverbonus.co.uk 420
oliversweeney.com 126
ollieandnic.com 78
ollipops.com 176
onestopcandleshop.co.uk 432
onlineconversion.com 454
onlinegolf.co.uk 352
oregonscientific.co.uk 137
organics-4u.co.uk 315
originalbooks.net 277
origins.co.uk 214
orlakiely.com 78
ormondejayne.com 187
orvis.co.uk 12, 349
osprey-london.co.uk 79
otherlandtoys.co.uk 173
outdoortoystore.co.uk 338
owzat-cricket.co.uk 356

pakeman.co.uk 119
palenquejewellery.co.uk 98
panacheshoes.co.uk 86
pantalonchameleon.com 6
pantheronline.co.uk 257
paramountzone.com 137
parfumsdorsay.com 188
parkscandles.com 201, 432
parseme.com 403
partyark.co.uk 176
partydelights.co.uk 177
pascal-jewellery.com 98
passport.gov.uk 455
patagonia.com 344
paulsmith.co.uk 24
paxtonandwhitfield.co.uk 302, 428

peeks.co.uk 437
penandpaper.co.uk 142
penhaligons.co.uk 188
pennyplain.co.uk 31
penshop.co.uk 142
perilla.co.uk 107
perlui.co.uk 119
peruvianconnection.co.uk 12
petcompany.co.uk 288
peterdraper.co.uk 143
petitpatapon.com 164
petplanet.co.uk 289
petspantry.tv 288
petsparade.com 289
pharmacy2u.co.uk 193
physicalcompany.co.uk 334
piajewellery.com 101
pickett.co.uk 127
pier.co.uk 251, 434
pierotucci.com 127
pinehouse.co.uk 233
pineonline.co.uk 234
pixibeauty.com 207
pixmania.co.uk 361
planet.co.uk 10
planetgolfuk.co.uk 352
plantconnection.com 284
plantpress.com 285
plants4presents.co.uk 286
plantstuff.com 286
play.com 375, 378
pleasemum.co.uk 164
plumbworld.co.uk 238
plumo.co.uk 6
plusinboots.co.uk 86
pocket-venus.net 6
poetrycollection.co.uk 12
poferries.com 444
pollyanna.com 24
polly-online.co.uk 408
postershop.co.uk 271
potions.org.uk 214
pout.co.uk 207
powderpuff.net 207
preciouslittleone.com 153
precis.co.uk 11
premierbathrooms.co.uk 238
pretavivre.com 264
prettyballerinas.com 86
primrose-aromatherapy.co.uk 214
principles.co.uk 17
procosmetics.co.uk 207
puma.com 41
purecollection.com 29
pureskincare.co.uk 214
purpleandfinelinen.co.uk 245, 434

pushmaternity.com 62
pushposters.com 271
pwp.com 355

qed-uk.com 258
quba.com 42
queenshill.com 264

rac.co.uk 442
rachelriley.com 149
racinggreen.co.uk 120
racquetlink.com 356
raileurope.co.uk. 445
raindrops.co.uk 164
realcoffee.co.uk 324
reallylindabarker.co.uk 231
realmeat.co.uk 300, 431
redhouse.co.uk 376
redletterdays.co.uk 138
reglisse.co.uk 98
rhs.org.uk 287
rhug.co.uk 315
rickstein.com 255
rigbyandpeller.com 51
riverford.co.uk 315
riverisland.com 18
rkalliston.com 287
rocktheboatclothing.co.uk 346
rohan.co.uk 123
roho.co.uk 347
room7.co.uk 24
rose-apothecary.co.uk 215
routeone.co.uk 123
rowlandsclothing.co.uk 31
royalacademy.org.uk 370
royalmail.com 382, 456
royalopera.org 370
rubbersole.co.uk 87
rugbymegastore.com 357
rugbyrelics.com 358
rugbystore.co.uk 358
rugsdirect.co.uk 274
rupertsanderson.co.uk 82

saddler.co.uk 353
safigloves.com 107
saloneasy.com 198
salonlines.co.uk 198
salonskincare.com 219
saltpepper.co.uk 319
saltwater.net 7
sand-monkey.com 56
sandstormbags.com 127
saralouisekakes.co.uk 296
sassyandrose.co.uk 52
savagelondon.com 18